"In a new preface, Horne [...] plicit.... But many other [...] Horne's lucid, well-organiz[...] [...] to deepen our understanding of [...] war...there are numerous suggestive parallels—mainly relating to conventional Western militaries fighting primarily urban insurgencies in Arab cultures while support for their wars dwindles back home and while the insurgents hope to outlast their better-armed opponents. As such, anyone interested in Iraq should read this book immediately."

—Thomas E. Ricks, *The Washington Post*

"This thirty-year-old history, written before the Iranian revolution, the Algerian civil war, and Al Qaeda, captures a contingent moment in the conflict between the West and the Arab world, when present-day dogmas were hardly imagined by most. It provides a much needed reminder that modern history is not made by the 'clash of civilizations' but by people."

—*Harper's Magazine*

"An awesome and superlative piece of historical narrative.... Mr. Horne has a terrible and tremendous tale to tell, one full of omen for posterity."

—*The Times* (London)

"Alistair Horne is one of the best writers of history in the English-speaking world. *A Savage War of Peace* shows him at the peak of his powers."

—*The Financial Times*

"The present conflict in the Middle East is frighteningly similar, making this book a good volume to have..."

—*Library Journal*

A SAVAGE WAR OF PEACE

Algeria 1954–1962

ALISTAIR HORNE

NEW YORK REVIEW BOOKS

New York

THIS IS A NEW YORK REVIEW BOOK
PUBLISHED BY THE NEW YORK REVIEW OF BOOKS
1755 Broadway, New York, NY 10019
www.nyrb.com

Library of Congress Cataloging-in-Publication Data
Horne, Alistair.
  A savage war of peace : Algeria, 1954–1962 / by Alistair Horne ; preface by
Alistair Horne.
      p. cm. — (New York Review Books classics)
  Includes bibliographical references and index.
  ISBN 1-59017-218-3 (alk. paper)
  1. Algeria—History—Revolution, 1954–1962. I. Title: Algeria, 1954–1962. II.
Title. III. Series.
  DT295.H64 2006
  965'.046—dc22

                              2006003506

ISBN-13: 978-1-59017-218-6
ISBN-10: 1-59017-218-3

Printed in the United States of America on acid-free paper.
10 9 8 7 6 5 4

To
A. D. M. *and* C. D. H.
the only begetters

Take up the White Man's Burden
The Savage wars of peace—
Fill the mouth full of famine
And bid the sickness cease.
—Rudyard Kipling

Contents

PART THREE
The Hardest of All Victories 1958–1962

Illustrations

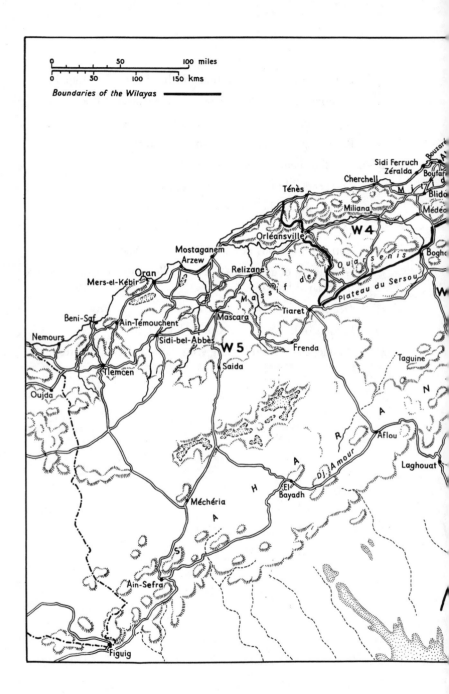

0   50   100 miles

0   50   100   150 kms

Boundaries of the Wilayas ━━━━━━

Sidi Ferruch
Zéralda
Cherchell
Ténès
Miliana
Blida
Médéo
Boufar
Boutar

Orléansville

W 4

Ouarsenis

de

Boghā

Mostaganem
Arzew

Relizane

Plateau du Sersou

W

Oran

Mers-el-Kébir

M a s s i f

Tiaret

Beni-Saf

Mascara

Ain-Témouchent

Nemours

Sidi-bel-Abbès

W 5

Frenda

Taguine

Tlemcen

Saida

N

Oujda

A

Aflou

R

Laghouat

A

Dj Amour

H   El
Bayadh

Méchéria

A

S

Ain-Sefra

Figuig

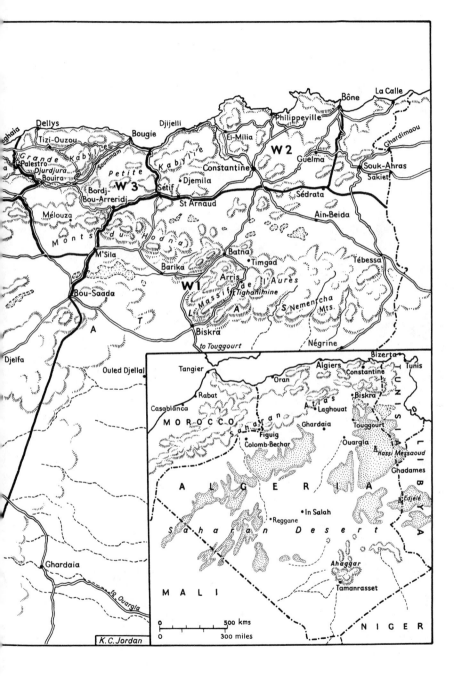

K.C. Jordan

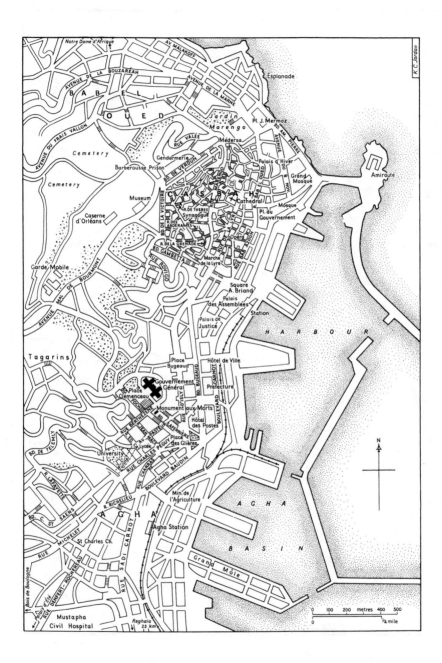

Preface to the 1977 edition

I intend to write the history of a memorable revolution which profoundly disturbed men, and which still divides them today. I do not conceal from myself the difficulties of the enterprise...whereas we have the advantage of having heard and observed these old men who, still full of their memories, and still aroused by their impressions, reveal to us the spirit and the character of the causes, and teach us to understand them. The moment when the actors are about to expire is perhaps the suitable one to write history: one can glean their evidence without sharing all their passions...I have pitied the combatants, and I have freely applauded the generous spirits.

Adolphe Thiers, preface to *Histoire de la Révolution Française*, 1838

IN January 1960 I was in Paris, researching into World War I, when "Barricades Week" broke out in Algiers. The European settlers, or *pieds noirs*, were in revolt against de Gaulle and the elite "paras" were openly siding with them. For the first time the press began using the ugly word "insurgents," menacingly evocative of Franco and the Spanish Civil War. Momentarily it looked as if the still-fragile structure of de Gaulle's Fifth Republic might crack. Then de Gaulle delivered one of his magical appeals, and the crisis dissolved like a puff of smoke. What most vividly remains in my mind of that tense week in Paris was the passionate involvement of members of the foreign press; beyond the excitement of events and professional detachment they agonised at France's dilemma and, during de Gaulle's television appearance, tears of emotion were brought to more than one otherwise steely eye. "The history of France, a permanent miracle," says André Maurois at the end of his *Histoire de la France*, "has the singular privilege of impassioning the peoples of the earth to the point where they all take part in French quarrels." This is true. Writing about the history of France has the elements of a love affair with an irresistible woman; inspiring in her beauty, often agonising and

3

maddening, but always exciting, and from whom one escapes only to return again. After nearly ten years spent on writing about Franco-German
conflicts I felt instinctively that, sooner or later, I would be lured back to
"take part" in this latest drama of French history, in one form or another,
once the dust had sufficiently settled. It took my publishers to propose the
idea.

I also happened to be in France on two other occasions when events in
Algeria threatened the very existence of the Republic—in May 1958 and
again in April 1961, the latter the most dangerous of all when ancient
Sherman tanks were rolled out on to the Concorde to guard against a possible airborne coup mounted from Algiers. Each episode seemed to me, in
retrospect, to bear a curious resemblance to the essential rhythm of other
great crises in modern French history, whether in 1789, 1870, 1916 or even
1940: a headlong rush to the brink of disaster, or even beyond it, followed
by an astounding recovery and eventually leading to a re-flowering of the
creative energies and brilliance that are France. The war in Algeria (which
lasted nearly eight years—almost twice as long as the "Great War" of
1914–18) toppled six French prime ministers and the Fourth Republic itself.
It came close to bringing down General de Gaulle and his Fifth Republic
and confronted metropolitan France with the threat of civil war. Yet, when
defeat led to the cession of this corner-stone of her empire where she had
been "*chez elle*" for 132 years, out of it arose an incomparably greater France
than the world had seen for many a generation.

What in France is called "*la guerre d'Algérie*" and in Algeria "the Revolution" was one of the last and most historically important of the grand-
style "colonial wars," in the strictest sense of the words. Many a French
leader, and especially the *pieds noirs* of Algeria, waged the war in the good
faith that they were, indeed, shouldering the "White Man's Burden."
Many a French para gave his life heroically, assured that he was defending a
bastion of Western civilisation, and the bogey slogan of "the Soviet fleet at
Mers-el-Kébir" retained its force right until the last days of the *présence
française*. It was a "war of peace" in that no declaration of hostilities was
ever made (unless one should recognise the first FLN proclamation of
1 November 1954 as such), and during most of the eight years the vast
majority of Frenchmen lived unaffected by it. Equally, it was undeniably
and horribly savage, bringing death to an estimated one million Muslim
Algerians and the expulsion from their homes of approximately the same
number of European settlers. If the one side practised unspeakable mutilations, the other tortured and, once it took hold, there seemed no halting

the pitiless spread of violence. As at a certain moment in the Battle of Verdun in 1916, it seemed as if events had escaped all human control; often, in Algeria, the essential tragedy was heightened by the feeling that—with a little more magnanimity, a little more trust, moderation and compassion—the worst might have been avoided.

Important as it was in the history of France, for Algerians the Revolution obviously meant far more. War, said General de Gaulle, "gives birth and brings death to nations." To Algeria it brought birth. But, during that war, more was involved than simply the issue of whether nine million Muslims should gain their independence or not. Not merely one but several "revolutions" were taking place on a variety of distinct levels; there was, *inter alia*, a profound social revolution going on within the framework of Algerian Muslim society; and, on the French side, "revolutions" first by the army and later by the OAS against the political authority of France. Finally, there was the tug-of-war for the soul of Algeria as fought externally on the rostrum of the United Nations and the platforms of the Third World, and in the councils of both Western and Eastern blocs. For the West as a whole the Algerian War contained the lessons of two classic failures. First, the failure either to meet, or even comprehend, the aspirations of the Third World. This is with us today not least—or so it seems to me —because Boumedienne's Algeria is very much a creature of its revolutionary experiences and, if the consequences of its powerful influence over the Third World are not always agreeable for the West, the reasons might well be sought in the years 1954–62. Secondly, the lesson of the sad, repeated failure of the moderates, or a "third force," to compete against opposing extremes is one of constant relevance to the contemporary scene; whether it be in Northern Ireland, Southern Africa or Latin America. As in 1793 or 1917, in modern revolutions it is the Montagne that triumphs over the Gironde.

The reader should not be plagued too much by the technical difficulties of the historian's trade—except, perhaps, where they may affect his comprehension or confidence. The treatment of the Algerian War or Revolution does, however, present certain peculiar problems that require mention in passing. The sheer length of it, in months and years, with a huge *dramatis personae* constantly appearing, reappearing and disappearing, and with its multiple levels of action often out of phase with each other, presents a canvas of daunting size. There is no obvious single focus, or climax, and possibly only one obvious *entr'acte*: the coming of de Gaulle in 1958. There is also the major problem of perspective; in terms of time it falls between the two stools of being neither, strictly speaking, history nor non-vintage contemporary events. I am conscious of the warnings of several participants in the story, including President Bourguiba of Tunisia, that "*un peu plus de recul*" might be necessary before any definitive account of the Algerian War could be written. On the other hand, I was flattered by one of the five ex-premiers of France kind enough to see me, who felt that no countryman of his could yet write a truly objective study, and that maybe "only an Englishman could," and I am equally encouraged by Thiers's wise and apt preface to his *Révolution Française* with which I humbly associate myself. I have been greatly aided in my research, in the cross-checking of facts and the correct gauging of moods, by the "memories" of surviving participants of the Algerian War (many of them by no means yet "old men"), and I would have been helped still more had I had recourse to those—especially on the Algerian side—who are no longer alive, or (like Ahmed Ben Bella) simply "unavailable." I have tried to emulate Thiers in pitying the combatants "without sharing all their passions."

Apart from these problems of perspective, perhaps the greatest obstacle lies in the inequality of source material. The number of books relating to the Algerian War published in France alone runs into four figures, varying widely in quality, while the periodicals and other printed sources can be more readily measured by the cubic metre. As *Le Nouvel Observateur* remarked of this profusion, "still, and despite this, the Algerian War is the little historical eczema of every Frenchman." In interviewing French participants—Gaullists and anti-Gaullists, OAS and *barbouzes*, rebel generals and serving soldiers, right-wingers and left-wingers—I expected to encounter inhibitions about discussing the war, if not total refusals. In fact I found almost an *embarras de richesses* of frankness and helpfulness, with only one downright rebuff: an eminent lady writer, who indicated that the last word on Algeria had been written in her own memoirs, and there thus remained nothing more of value to be said.

The solution on the Algerian side, however, was quite different. At an early stage in my research, a senior Algerian diplomat, who had played an important part in the Revolution, while expressing personal enthusiasm for my project, warned me that in his country I might be discouraged by the shortage of written source material and also by a reluctance, both private and official, to talk. In fact, I was received with courtesy, interest and hospitality—and was *not* discouraged; but otherwise he was right, and for reasons that demand sympathetic understanding. First of all, on the purely military level, the style of guerrilla warfare was such that, with the FLN constantly on the move, few men in the field had either the time or circumstances to keep coherent journals.* And, it must be remembered, many were illiterate. Unlike the Yugoslav partisan war of 1942–5, with its rich literature, there was no centralised command. Many of the records that would normally have found their way into the archives of the new state were (so Algerian officials claim) either destroyed, or "removed" in the last desperate days of the OAS, and in the exigencies of creating a new state the work of collating the archives that exist is also not very far advanced.

The high walls that surround the houses in Algeria, the delightful courtyards concealed in total privacy behind squalid exteriors in the Casbah, hint at an Algerian characteristic that also does not ease the path of an historian. This natural instinct for secretiveness, developed over the five generations of French suzerainty, was further heightened to the point where few inklings leaked out during the eight years of clandestine warfare of the many internal splits that repeatedly threatened to rive the FLN leadership. It is no less difficult to discover the truth of such divisions today. Compounded with secretiveness there also remains some degree of apprehension. Factionalism of the Revolution continued long after Independence in 1962, and as late as 1967 there was an abortive coup against Boumedienne. Two of the *neuf historiques* founders of the revolt against France have been mysteriously murdered in exile in Europe; Ben Bella remains in prison, who knows where? Several other former revolutionary leaders live, like Trotsky, nervously in disfavour abroad. Though Algeria is today far from being a police-state on the Soviet model, it is an authoritarian regime, and the risk of a fall from grace can be incalculable.

One of my earliest surprises in Algiers was that in the Casbah, where the highly emotive Battle of Algiers had been waged against Massu's paras, there is not the smallest plaque or commemoration to indicate where such heroes of the Revolution as Ali la Pointe fought and died; and often it is hard to find residents who can guide or inform you, even though little more than a decade has elapsed. The same applies elsewhere in Algeria, and the explanation is, in part, that the Algerian Revolution was, from the beginning, a movement of *collectivity*: of collective leadership, of collective suffering, and collective anonymity. Thus, deliberate efforts have been

---

* There is a certain parallel with the French campaign of 1940. Lasting a matter of weeks instead of seven and a half years, it granted few war diarists (especially on the French side) any opportunity to keep up their diaries or even scribble a letter home; as I discovered when researching *To Lose a Battle*.

made to veer away from anything resembling a cult of the individual hero or martyr. There is, additionally, a more general factor in that the Arab tradition holds a concept of history that is rather different from the European. It rates altogether lower priority, insofar as the essential fatalism of religious teaching suggests that man is strictly limited in his capacity to shape his destiny. Thus there is a tendency to write off the past, relegating its events—whether they occurred yesterday or in A.D. 600—to the same vast limbo.

The wounds of the war still lie deep, and it was not until April 1975 that the tricolour could fly again in Algiers, with the first state visit of a French President. Yet an expression I heard many times in Algeria was "the page is turned." On the one hand, this is a sentiment of the most admirable magnanimity; indeed, how many other peoples could—within two or three years of the close of an eight-year war that cost the lives of almost one in ten of the population—make a film, *La Battaglia di Algeri*, where a colonel of the dreaded French paras appears almost as its hero? On the other hand, it in no way helps the historian in his work. The most elementary precisions become obscure, or difficult to verify; for example, birthdates of leading revolutionary figures often differ radically, according to the source, and for the key FLN "Meeting of the Twenty-two" in the summer of 1954 no less than six different dates have been provided from the memories of those present.

Perhaps the best of much advice I received in the preparation of this book came from another of Algeria's top ambassadors abroad. "Be absolutely honest," he said, "and admit it if you have only seen part of the picture." For the very real difficulties outlined above, I cannot claim to have seen anything like the "whole picture"; but it may be open to doubt whether anyone—French, Algerian or outsider—could do so at this moment. Possibly now no one ever will.

In the course of research I made two trips to Algeria and Tunisia, where I received the maximum co-operation from the authorities. I was received with warmth and openness by President Bourguiba of Tunisia; but a similar interview kindly sponsored by my publisher, Mr Harold Macmillan, with President Boumedienne was, alas, vitiated by its coinciding with the "Ramadan War" of 1973. I made many trips to France where, as previously noted, I was almost overwhelmed by a surfeit of information and helpfulness. My researches took me on vertiginous leaps across the over-hanging roofs of the Casbah, and to third countries for shadowy appointments with anonymous "Jackal" killers still "on the run"; though, as far as personal hazard is concerned, nothing was more alarming than a drive across Paris in Jacques Soustelle's Mini, the former Governor-General reminiscing at 80 k.p.h. with both hands!

There remains the insidious problem of Arabic transliteration. When chided by his publishers for spelling inconsistencies in *The Seven Pillars of Wisdom,* in that "Jedha the she-camel was Jedhah on slip 40," T. E. Lawrence riposted dismissively: "She was a splendid beast." Later on there was this exchange: "Slip 78. Sherif Abd el Mayin of slip 68 becomes el Main, el Mayein, el Muein, el Mayim and el Muyein." T. E. L.: "Good egg. I call this really ingenious." If so distinguished an Arabist as Lawrence should admit defeat over the endless variation in the spelling of proper names in Arabic, I hope I may be allowed some indulgence. Otherwise, on the advice of Dr Albert Hourani, I have tried to adopt the European transliteration of the appropriate "colonising" power; i.e. French for Algerian and Maghreb names, and English for the occasional Egyptian or Palestinian reference.

Of the many in France, Algeria and elsewhere who helped me, a number specifically requested not to be mentioned in this book or to have information attributed directly to themselves. Regretfully, I must comply with their wishes, but thank them sincerely in my heart. For the rest, I am particularly indebted to the following who have been kind enough to give me their time and assistance:

President Habib Bourguiba; MM. les Présidents Georges Bidault, Michel Debré, Pierre Mendès-France, Antoine Pinay and the late Guy Mollet; Dr Mahieddine Aminore, Mme Lorette Ankaoua, the late General André Beaufre, S.E. M. Mohammed Bedjaoui, Mr Edward Behr, S.E. M. Abdelmalek Benhabyles, M. Ben Youssef Ben Khedda, General Maurice Challe, M. Abdelkader Chanderli, Professor Pierre Chaulet, Colonel François Coulet, the late Mr Christopher Ewart-Biggs, M. Christian Fouchet, Colonel Jean Gardes, General James Gavin, Mr Omar Haliq, Dr Albert Hourani, S.E. M. Louis Joxe, Professor Mostefa Lacheraf, Senator Robert Lacoste, M. Mohamed Lebjaoui, General Jacques Massu, M. François Mitterrand, Dr Jean-Claude Pérez, Dr Pierre Roche, General Raoul Salan, Captain Pierre Sergent, Comte Alain de Sérigny, M. Jacques Soustelle, Maître Paul Teitgen, Mme Germaine Tillion, M. Bernard Tricot, M. Gérard Viratelle, Mr Sam White, Mr Robin Wu.

I am also grateful to the French Embassy in London, the British Embassy in Algiers, and especially to H.E. M. Lakhdar Brahimi, Algerian Ambassador in London, for his constant help and kindness; to Lady

Liddell-Hart for access to her late husband's remarkable collection of personal archives; to Reggane Films, M. Jean Fontugne and *Historia* magazine; to the irreplaceable London Library, the Royal United Service Institution, the Bibliothèque de Documentation Internationale Contemporaine at Nanterre and the library of the French Senate at the Luxembourg (surely the world's most sumptuous surroundings in which to research) and its librarian, M. Jean Bécarud.

For their unfailing hospitality in Paris, as well as performing endless commissions, my warm thanks are due (once again) to Mr and Mrs Walter Goetz and to Mr Michael Edwards; for help in my travels to, and inside, Algeria and Tunisia, I am indebted to the Algerian and Tunisian governments, the Algerian National Travel Agency, Tunis Air, the Tunisian National Tourist Office, the *Evening Standard* and the *Observer*.

As frequently in the past, an occasional haven of enlightened peace was offered me by St Antony's College, Oxford—and additionally, this time, the benefits of their affiliated Middle East Centre.

In France I owe a particular debt of gratitude to my old friends Gérard Minvielle, the Socialist Senator from Les Landes, and his charming wife, Jany, who between them opened many doors to me that might otherwise have been closed—and, in addition, those of the Senate Library. I am also warmly appreciative of the patient friendliness of M. Yves Courrière who, in his four volumes on the Algerian War, carried out invaluable pioneer work in personal interviews and who responded to my endless enquiries with a goodwill not always to be found between fellow authors. More sadly, I am beholden to Sir Anthony Nutting, Bt, for graciously withdrawing from an identical project where his wide knowledge of the Arab world might have stood him in better stead than mine.

For the toilsome work of processing the manuscript I am first of all indebted to Mrs Angus Nicol for the typing and many items of research (alas, probably for the last time); to my wife for her reading and assaults on the extraneous gallicism; to Mr Alan Williams of the Viking Press, New York, for his long-range help and good sense, but especially to Mr Richard Garnett for his exacting editorial work and boundless patience. (Needless to say, all faults and errors that remain are mine alone.)

Finally, I owe a particular debt of gratitude to my publisher, the Rt Hon. Harold Macmillan for his counsel and constant encouragement to write about a part of the world that—since 1942—has held his imagination; and to Alan Maclean and Caroline Hobhouse for the actual idea which has committed their willing slave to more than three years' hard labour, without remission.

Preface to the 1996 edition

SOME fifty miles westward along the coast from Algiers lie the ancient Roman ruins of Tipasa. There are few more idyllic spots in the entire Mediterranean, and it provoked from that great French humanist, Albert Camus, one of his most eloquent and nostalgic essays. Writing in those tranquil pre-war days of colonial Algeria, Camus—in some ways the typical *pied noir*—described euphorically how he had experienced there "the happy lassitude of a wedding day with the world." Lapped by a peacock-coloured sea, Tipasa remains an absinthe-perfumed paradise of expressionist colours. "Happy is he among the living who has seen such things," exulted Camus.

Five years after he wrote these words, when Algeria was occupied by the Allies in the Second World War, General Charles de Gaulle and Harold Macmillan, then Churchill's plenipotentiary in Algiers, spent an historic afternoon together amid the joys of Camus's Tipasa. Macmillan had bathed naked, but de Gaulle—always ram-rod correct and conscious of his dignity—sat bolt upright on a rock, in full uniform under the Algerian summer sun, while ceaselessly they thrashed out the future of the post-war world. Little could de Gaulle have realised then just how closely his own future was going to be linked to the fate of Algeria.

When I first discovered Tipasa while researching *A Savage War of Peace* in 1973, it moved me almost as strongly as it did Camus. Revisiting it twelve years later, I was still able to find the small memorial to Camus that bears the now worn quotation from his works, in French: "Glory consists of the ability to love without measure." Camus loved his native Algeria, *algérie française*, without measure, and in a way the aging obelisk stands as a memorial to all the heartbreak, savagery and bitterness that now lies fading with extraordinary rapidity. Since Camus, Macmillan and de Gaulle, the glory that colonial France once created in Algeria has largely passed into limbo, and the gently peaceful beauty of Tipasa casts a deceptive cloak over a much more ferocious past. For it was on a sunny beach close to Tipasa that French women and children, as well as men, were machine-gunned as they bathed by freedom-fighters of the Algerian FLN. At Zeralda, just a few miles to the east, Algerian suspects died in a French torture camp; and it was from barracks in this same Zeralda that rebel units of the élite French paras launched a nearly successful coup against President de Gaulle's Fifth Republic in April 1961.

Four decades have gone by since the FLN declared war on the French in Algeria on that historic All Saints' Day of 1954. It is a long time in modern memory, and one tends to forget the passions stirred by this appallingly savage contest, not only in France, but the impact it also caused throughout the world. Yet it remains on the statute books as a prototype of the modern war of national liberation. It was as appropriate as it was imaginative that President Chadli Bendjedid's government should, in November 1984, mark the thirtieth anniversary celebrations of the beginning of the Algerian War of National Liberation with the first ever international conference of historians studying that war. That it should have been held at all, given the pain of memories only so recently in the past, was a remarkable—and courageous—feat on the part of the Algerians. But, in the openness of discussion and the factual revelations that emerged, the conference was also a considerable success in itself, and showed a significant break with the reticences and the repressiveness of the immediate post-war Algeria of Houari Boumedienne.

Alas, the terrible events of the 1990s—up to 50,000 killings in a new civil war every bit as horrendous as the War of Liberation—attest that the angry echoes of Algeria 1954–62 have still not yet died away.

In my preface to the first edition of *A Savage War*, I drew attention to some of the difficulties encountered when trying to study the Algerian side of events in 1973. Eleven years later an invitation to participate in the Algiers' historical conference provided me with a unique opportunity to meet some of the participants of the war who had been inaccessible to me in 1973. As Michael Holroyd once remarked, one of the privileges of writing contemporary biography—or, for that matter, contemporary history—

is that you meet, usually on friendly terms, people you have always wanted to meet...

Certainly this was true for me in Algiers in 1984. It was immensely exciting to meet for the first time men about whom I had written, but—because of circumstances—never previously been able to see.

This new edition was stimulated by that Algiers Conference; on the other hand, it also contains some factual corrections and amendments noted down over the years (for which I am deeply indebted to the help given by very many correspondents), and some new assessments and up-dating. I remain, however, painfully aware that the last words on the Algerian War are far from being written. In France the sack-loads of archives removed from the *Gouvernement-Général* in the last days of the war lie, sealed from the public gaze, in the repositories of the University of Aix-en-Provence; in Algiers, the official archives were only just beginning to be assembled in a splendid new centre in 1984. Yet, meanwhile, memories are fading and eye-witnesses dying, their recollections unrecorded. It is with that in mind that I hope this revised edition may offer at least a part view of a key episode in our times, which—like the inscription on the Camus memorial—is rapidly being eroded away by the passage of time.

Sadly, at the time of writing, overlaying all that bitter past in Algeria has come a new civil war to rend its fabric once more, overflowing yet again to plague and perplex Metropolitan France.

Preface to the 2006 edition

OVER half a century has now passed since that All Saints' Day in the Aurès Mountains, historic for Algeria, dreadful for France, when two young French schoolteachers on their honeymoon, the Monnerots, were hauled off their bus and shot down. That is a long time in modern memory. Yet this story of how a handful of Algerian guerrillas, primitively armed, but masterfully deploying the weapon of terror, outwitted and out-fought over eight years the best armies that France could provide, remains on the statute books as a prototype of the modern war of national liberation. In South Africa the ANC studied it carefully, prior to the release and apotheosis of Nelson Mandela; in their unleashing of intifada against Israel, Palestinian leaders have looked ardently towards it. So has al-Qaeda. Since the events of September 11, 2001, particularly, the West has needed to take a new, hard look at Algeria's "Savage War of Peace," and all that has flowed from it.

Four decades of independence provided little of peace, or prosperity, for the Algerians. At many times the peace has been no less savage than the war, with the ghosts of it coming back to haunt both Algeria and France. Under the gaunt and unyielding figure of Boumedienne, for a while Algeria carried an influence above its weight in world affairs—to the embarrassment of the West. The Arab-Israeli War of 1973, with its accompanying surge in oil prices, was partly orchestrated in Algiers. When Boumedienne died in 1978, the seemingly more benign Chadli Benjedid brought hopes of a more liberal Algeria. But these faded as the country wrestled with mountainous economic problems, amid murmurs of corruption estimated to have cost the impoverished country the equivalent of the entire national debt. During its brief period of liberalism in the 1980s many who had not dared speak during the Boumedienne years now appeared from the woodwork. Then, in 1984, I was able to meet many important participants who had been unapproachable in the 1970s, such as the son of Si Salah and some of the (still young) women who had risked their lives to plant bombs in French targets. I was also able to meet Ben Bella and Ait Ahmed, two of the six leaders "hijacked" by French intelligence in 1956, in exile in Switzerland. These were exciting encounters for an historian, and helped provide fresh substance to what I had written in the previous decade.

Fundamentalism and Civil War

By the 1990s, however, the harsh voice of Islamic fundamentalism was heard across the land. Those young, progressive-minded war heroines whom I met in 1984, with their bright hopes of the future, were forced back once more behind the veil, or, like Maître Marie-Claude Radziewsky, the courageous Polish-French woman lawyer who had represented them during the war, to emigrate abroad. The state continued to be run by the men who still controlled the guns, the FLN Party. In the early 1990s, revolt broke out, led by the fundamentalist and aggressively dynamic FIS (Front Islamique du Salut—"Islamic Salvation Front"). Significantly pronounced *fils*, the FIS also proclaimed itself the *fils*, or sons of the heroic and high-principled FLN of the war years. Abassi Madani, the President of the

FIS, who was one of the original volunteers from 1 November 1954, explicitly claimed that the FLN revolution had been "confiscated" by Marxist and secular forces following independence). Many of its leaders were the kind of young Algerian who joined the struggle against the French occupiers in the 1950s. Their grievances were similar—unemployment and overpopulation, and no say in the administration of the country. The FIS took advantage of the upsurge in hostility and disillusion with the regime, which had first been expressed in riots in October 1988. After the creation of a new multiparty system in 1989 the FIS successfully posed as the only viable alternative to the regime capable of ejecting the corrupt and despised existing system. In 1992 elections were cancelled, and the FIS disenfranchised. Elements of it took to the hills and the streets in much the same way as the FLN had in 1954.

Starting with the killing of local policemen and regional administrators—just as in 1954, but displaying less coordination—an appalling civil war ensued, with the Algiers government proving as incapable of crushing the revolt as the French Army had been in 1954–62. The FIS was in turn thrust aside by a far more extreme band of revolutionaries, the GIA (Armed Islamic Group), prepared to wage war with total ruthlessness. Its origins and leaders were surrounded in mystery—but its aims appeared to be projected towards a complete and anarchic destruction of the existing order. On a note that was to become pointedly ominous on September 11, 2001, some of its killers were known as the "Afghans," highly trained volunteers who had served their apprenticeship in that country. The economy was targeted, and so at one point were foreigners, businessmen and journalists, promiscuously massacred with the clear intent of driving out foreign capital. Whole villages—including women and children—would be slaughtered by unknown guerrillas, for unknown motives.

The techniques of murder equally had echoes from the grisly *égorgements*, the throat-slittings, from days of the Savage War, the "Kablyie Smile" as French servicemen dubbed it with unpleasant humour, frequently accompanied by castration. Beheading victims became common, their heads stuck on road signs as a kind of gruesome sport. Algerians themselves spoke of the "blind war," but in its prolonged, random senselessness it came almost more to resemble Europe's Thirty Years' War of the seventeenth century. Power now came to reside essentially in the hands of the military, and its role in the coming civil war remains a murky if not repugnant one. There were even ugly rumours that somehow the Army itself was involved in some of the uglier massacres. Reports seeped out via eyewitnesses and defectors suggesting that the security services and the regime, or at least elements within them, had a hand in some of the extreme violence initially attributed to Islamists. The main motivation for this was never quite clear, but there appeared to be a desire to demonise the Islamists and win over the bulk of the population—which seemed to be bewildered as to exactly who was killing whom.

All the time the economy suffered, leading to ever worse unemployment—one-third of the labour force, in a population well over three times that of 1954, produced by one of the world's highest birthrates, and concentrated (in Algiers) in some of the world's worst slums. All more incentives for bringing recruits to the revolt. By the end of 2001 at a rough estimate 100,000 Algerians had died—and 120 foreigners—with a cost to the economy running into billions of dollars. With strong US support, the Bouteflika regime has to some extent been successful in suppressing the Islamicist revolt, winning over the pious middle classes, and providing the Pentagon with a staunch ally in the war on terror—but at a questionable price in human rights.

In 1962, a popular slogan heard among exhausted Algerians was "*Seba'a snin, barakat!*" ("Seven years, that's enough!") Yet, five decades after independence, a savage war still continued in Algeria. It was a country exhausted by seven years of senseless violence, of not knowing who were the "good guys" and who the "bad." As much as any other factor, it was this exhaustion that helped bring the civil war to an end.

Though the parallels may be only partially exact, dark comparisons also offer themselves between the two former French colonies both "liberated" in the 1950s and 1960s: Vietnam, infinitely more devastated than Algeria over twenty years of war, and lacking its natural wealth of oil and gas, but now rapidly emerging as the new Taiwan of Southeast Asia; Algeria wracked by internecine fundamentalism, and economically impoverished. Students of contemporary Islam and its incompetence in the world of material progress might wish to draw their own conclusions.

Shadows in France, Too

As for France, if at every hand in Algeria one could detect the roots, and pattern, of the war of 1954–62, so too in a similar fashion did the civil war between Algerians of the 1990s soon overflow across the Mediterranean. In 1995 and 1996 feuding between rival clans of the GIA brought terrorism to the Paris Metro, killing and wounding over eighty persons. Supposedly aimed at dissuading the French from backing the repression of the Algiers government, in what could have been a hideous preview of 9/11, an Air France plane hijacked, pointedly, on Christmas Eve, 1994, was evidently programmed to be flown suicidally into the Eiffel Tower. The problem of immigration became an ever hotter issue for any French government to handle, as carnage in Algeria—on top of overpopulation—persuaded increasing numbers of Algerians to seek refuge, and employment, in France. In the winter of 2005–6, outbursts of rage in the overcrowded *banlieues*, with their substandard housing, gave the lie to the Gaullist notion that, with the end of the war in 1962, France could wash its hands of the "Algerian Problem." Now there are over five million of Algerian extraction living in France. On top of this there is the residual bitterness and strife between the "new" immigrants and the *Harkis*, the Algerians loyal to the French Army who took root in France in 1962 and have assiduously resisted integration. The Algerian War has effectively crossed the Mediterranean to France, bringing with it raw sensitivities that almost rival the legacy of collaboration in World War II. France has still not come to terms with it. Just a tip of the iceberg of Algerian émigré sensitivities in France could be detected in the extraordinary head-butting episode (as of writing still cloaked in mystery) of the Algerian-French football champion Zinedine Zidane, which may have caused France to lose the 2006 World Cup. In lieu of the decisive post-colonial divorce that was envisaged in 1962, a messy relationship continues with each country deeply, and unpredictably, involved in each other's histories. All of this is grist to the mill of Le Pen—and to al-Qaeda.

After 9/11 and Parallels with Iraq

Following September 2001, whether in Paris or London, intelligence evolving about the terror networks of al-Qaeda indicated numerous links with Algeria. In turn there were roots of jihad laid back in the Savage War —though it was not of itself a conflict rooted in Islam. It was, in effect, first and foremost, an anti-colonial war of national liberation. One cannot stress this fact too often. Nevertheless, in many ways the horrors suffered in Algeria's own civil war do read like a paradigm, a microcosm of present-day Islam's frustrated inadequacy to meet the challenges of the modern world, the anger generated thereby finding itself directed into lashing out against the rich, successful West.

Generally, the old saw about history never repeating itself holds true. Nevertheless, its bad elements may well do so if national leaders pay no attention to its lessons. A few years back the Israeli press reported that Ariel Sharon's favourite bedside reading was the Hebrew translation of *A Savage War of Peace*. Writing in *The New York Review of Books*, Amos Elon commented that "[Sharon] must have tragically misunderstood it. That book could not tell him what to do, but it could have told him what *not* to do." The lessons surely apply today. At the time of writing, one feels that Bush's Washington (and Blair's London) also went blindly into Iraq —and into collision with the Islamic world—without the kind of necessary preparation, where study of Algeria in 1954–62 might have helped. At the very least its lessons might have imposed caution before getting involved in Iraq in the first place. There are at least three areas where the echoes are particularly painful, if not deafening.

ONE: In the early days of the Algerian War, once the FLN realised it was not strong enough to take on the powerful French Army, it concentrated its attacks on the native police loyal to France. Result: a deadly loss of morale among the police, with defections to the FLN, and the French Army defensively reduced to protecting the police, instead of concentrating on active "search-and-destroy" missions. The "insurgents" in Iraq have learned from this strategy with deadly effect.

TWO: The benefit of porous frontiers. In 1954–62, the winning French Army was paralysed by its inability to pursue its FLN enemy across into its friendly bases in neighbouring Tunisia and Morocco. This is what, in effect, led to the collapse of the French government and the advent of de Gaulle in 1958. In their turn, the Iraq insurgents have been able to use Syria—and now, much more dangerously, Iran—to similar advantage.

THREE: The vile hand of torture; of abuse, and counter-abuse. In the Algerian War what led—probably more than any other single factor—to the ultimate defeat of France was the realisation, in France and the world at large, that methods of interrogation were being used that had been condemned under the Nazi Occupation. At the dawn of the new century, the ugly ghosts of torture returned to plague France. In 2001, an eighty-three-year-old former general, Paul Aussaresses, published a book in which he unashamedly, indeed proudly, admitted to having tortured—in a good cause, he claimed. After a trial which gripped France, the aging general got away with a fine of one hundred thousand francs, on a uniquely worded charge "in the name of respect for the victims."

Because of the slowness of communications in the 1950s and 1960s, it took a year or more for the message of abuses perpetrated in Algeria to sink in. Now, with the Internet and al-Jazeera, one set of photos from Abu Ghraib is enough to inflame hatred across the Islamic world against the West, providing excuse for all the beheadings and atrocities carried out by al-Qaeda. From the Inquisition to the Gestapo and the "Battle of Algiers," history teaches us that, in the production of reliable intelligence, regardless of the moral issue, torture is counter-productive. As a further footnote to my tenet, learned in Algeria, that torture should *never, never, never* be resorted to by any Western society, I draw readers once again to the testimony of Prefect Teitgen of Algiers (see pp. 203–204) which —three decades on—I still find deeply moving. Teitgen had been informed by the Algiers police that they had intelligence of a bomb which could have caused appalling casualties. Could they put a suspect to "the question"? Himself a deportee in World War II, Teitgen told me he refused:

> ... I trembled the whole afternoon. Finally the bomb did not go off. Thank God I was right. Because if you once get into the torture business, you're lost. . . . All our so-called civilisation is covered with a varnish. Scratch it, and underneath you find *fear*. . . . When you see the throats of your *copains* slit, then the varnish disappears.

How applicable this still is to the dilemmas facing the West in the war on terror!

In passing, one should also note France's painful discovery that, fifty years on, many former "torturers" in the armed services were having to resort to psychiatric "counselling." The inflicters of torture as well as their victims remain grievously impaired.

In 2005, at the suggestion of his staff, I sent a copy of *A Savage War* to US Secretary of Defense Donald Rumsfeld, underscoring the evils of torture—and, not least, the propaganda value even the least substantiated rumours of it can arouse. I received a flea in the ear—courteous, but a flea nevertheless—for my trouble.

After all the hopes generated for a free, happy and prosperous Algeria at Evian in 1962, within years of the departure of the French Army she was tearing herself apart in the most senseless and bloody civil war (between fellow Muslims) of recent times.

Does much more need to be said about the relevance of Algeria's Savage War to contemporary Iraq? History continues to take its toll.

We historians, perhaps fortunately, are not permitted to see the future. Certainly when I started writing *A Savage War* back in 1973, I had not the least thought that it might find a new relevance, or modernity, in the twenty-first century. At the time it seemed a very tragic story sufficient within its own bounds. Now, for all the lessons it may contain—not just for the conflict in Iraq, but for wider issues in the world at large, and those as yet unforeseen which may still lie ahead—it affords me great satisfaction humbly to offer this book up once again.

The preface to the first edition of *A Savage War of Peace* included an accounting of kind friends, associates and agencies to whom I expressed warm appreciation. As many have since passed on, as have twenty-nine years, I hope my grateful thanks of yesteryear may remain on the record and that I may gratefully add three new names to the list: those of Dr. Eugene Rogan and Michael Willis Ph.D., of the Middle East Centre, St. Antony's College, Oxford, and Edwin Frank, of New York Review Books, for their most helpful editorial inputs. One particular debt, I feel, needs to be reiterated, however. The very genesis of writing *A Savage War* was proposed to me by my then publisher, and former Prime Minister, the late Harold Macmillan. To him Algeria—with its lasting impact on de Gaulle— had held his imagination ever since World War II, and, though already in his eighties, he was to give me invaluable counsel and constant encouragement, actually reading the manuscript himself three times.

PART ONE

Prelude

1830—1954

*Qu'importe si cent mille coups de fusil partent en Afrique!
L'Europe ne les entend pas.*

Louis-Philippe, 1835

CHAPTER ONE

"A Town of no Great Interest"

> As long as you keep Algiers, you will be constantly at war with Africa; sometimes this war will seem to end; but these people will not hate you any the less; it will be a half-extinguished fire that will smoulder under the ash and which, at the first opportunity, will burst into a vast conflagration.
>
> Baron Lacuée, 1831

Sétif, 1945

THE market town of Sétif sits haphazardly on a high and treeless plain some eighty miles west of Constantine. Even in early summer a thin, mean wind whirls up the dust along its rectilinear streets of typical French colonial design. Passing rapidly through it in March 1943, Churchill's Minister Resident in North Africa, Harold Macmillan, noted with the eye of a classical scholar that, in comparison with the nearby ruins of Trajan's Djemila, Sétif was "a town of no great interest".

On the morning of 8 May 1945, the inhabitants of this largely Muslim town were preparing for a mass march. It was V.E. Day; for Europe, the first day of peace following the Nazi capitulation the previous night.

All across the mother country, metropolitan France, there would be fervent celebrations to mark the end of the nightmare five years of defeat, occupation and the destructive course of liberation by her own allies. But compared with the frenzied joy of Armistice Day 1918, France's jubilation was somewhat muted by the sober backdrop. The scattering of antique cars that crepitated along the *grands boulevards* of Paris, propelled by cylinders of floppy bags of coal gas, perched on the roof like great duvets, symbolised the state of France herself. Plundered by the occupiers, bombed by the liberators, deprived of fuel and every raw material and fed by a crippled railway system, industry faced a grim struggle for rehabilitation. The *épiceries* were empty – and already there were grave menaces of industrial unrest. French society was riven; the hunting down of those who had collaborated (or were said to have collaborated) went on apace; politicians were already rending one another, as in the bad old days of the Third Republic, while an aggressive Stalinist Communist Party seemed poised for takeover. Such was the scene that confronted a generation of prematurely fatigued Frenchmen: those who had fought all the way from Lake Chad with Leclerc, or had more recently come limping home from deportation and the prisoner-of-war camps of Hitler's Reich. The prevailing note was perhaps struck by one returning veteran when he remarked to an American journalist: "That great world insomnia which is war has come to an end, once again." Like a weary insomniac, France too greeted the relieving dawn chiefly longing for one thing only – repose.

If it was liberation that a haggard France was fêting that May day, that too was the magic word mobilising the Muslim community of Sétif. The difference was that the one was celebrating its return; the other, marching in quest of something it considered to be still denied it. Over the past weeks, hints of what might be to come had percolated through Algeria. There had been a mounting series of minor incidents against *colons*, as the European settlers were called; cars, and even children leaving school, had been stoned; *fatmas*, or domestic servants, told their employers that they had been warned no longer to work for them. On walls graffiti appeared overnight exhorting: "Muslims awaken!" "It's the Muslim flag that will float over North Africa!" Or, with more direct menace: "*Français*, you will be massacred by the Muslims!"

The hot-blooded *colons* riposted with aggressive scorn, laced with such epithets as *sale race*, which tripped all too readily off the tongue. Passions between the two communities had risen. Then, in mid-April, information had been received by the French authorities that a general insurrection was brewing, to be accompanied by widespread sabotage. The conspirators appeared to be a nationalist movement called the Parti du Peuple Algérien, or P.P.A., so as a precautionary measure its leader, Messali Hadj, was packed off into exile to the desert, thence to Brazzaville.

In contrast to the heavily *colon*-dominated enclaves round Oran and Algiers, Sétif was predominantly Muslim and had a long history of radical nationalism. But apart from this ground-swell of political discontent, there were more immediate economic motives for trouble. Algeria had suffered harshly from two years of crop failures, on top of severe hardships imposed by wartime shortages. Emergency rations normally stocked against the eventuality of famine had been depleted by the Vichy French for the benefit of *Festung Europa*; the black market had thrived, but was beyond the means of most Algerian peasants. Revisiting his native land that year, Albert Camus was horrified to find Kabyle children fighting with dogs for the contents of a rubbish bin. Although relatively rich compared with Kabylia, the countryside round Sétif had received no rain since January – and resentments had been fanned by the prosperous harvest reaped by the foreign-owned Compagnie Genevoise, which held nearly 15,000 hectares of the best farmlands.

If there was indeed to have been a concerted demonstration in favour of Algerian independence (although the evidence for this remains still inconclusive), there could hardly have been chosen a better day than V.E. Day; nor a better place in which to ignite the spark than Sétif. All Europe – and especially France – was rejoicing at deliverance from an occupying power; the United Nations Charter was about to be signed at San Francisco amid pious declarations of self-determination for subject peoples; while in Cairo birth had been given to the Arab League, a day of importance in the cause of Muslim independence everywhere. The French army was still largely preoccupied in Europe, and in Sétif itself there were no more than twenty gendarmes to maintain order.

There could be no question of M. Butterlin, the sub-prefect of Sétif, halting the 8 May parades. After all, were they not nominally celebrating the triumph of the mother country and her allies, and specifically processing to lay a wreath on the *monument aux morts* in memory of the Algerian troops fallen in the recent conflict? And, in any case, how could his twenty gendarmes physically contain 8,000 Muslims pouring in from the outskirts of Sétif? At least, he decided, he would impose a strict ban against the march assuming any political character; above all, no seditious banners. But as soon as the procession had formed up outside the mosque, Butterlin received a telephone call from his chief of police, Commissaire Valère, that the demonstrators had, nevertheless, deployed banners bearing such provocative slogans as: "Vive Messali!" "Free Messali!" "For the Liberation of the People, Long Live Free and Independent Algeria!" They were also flourishing, for the first time, the green-and-white flag that had once been the standard of that legendary hero of resistance against the French, Abd-el-Kader, and was later to become that of the F.L.N. liberation movement. He at once ordered Valère to intervene and seize the banners. Valère warned that that might mean a fight (*une bagarre*). "All right," replied Butterlin, "then there'll be a fight."

At this point, as so often happens with such incidents, the record is obscure as to who actually fired the first shot. According to the investigating Tubert Commission, based on French police reports, Commissaire Valère was knocked down by a stone while trying to seize one of the offending banners, and had to defend himself with his walking-stick. Some of the demonstrators then opened fire with concealed weapons. Another account has it that a police inspector in plain clothes came out of a café, was surrounded by shouting demonstrators, lost his nerve and shot in the stomach a young Muslim bearing a relatively unexceptionable banner, mortally wounding him. Whatever the truth, it seems fairly clear that there were armed men, bent on trouble, among the Muslim marchers, and these – egged on by the blood-curdling *you-you* ululations of their women – now began an indiscriminate massacre of any Europeans caught out in the streets. Valère's gendarmes returned the fire, but were soon overwhelmed. Small groups of killers, the scent of blood in their nostrils, now fanned out by taxi, bicycle or even on horseback into the surrounding countryside, spreading the word that a general *jihad*, or "holy war", had broken out. At Chevreul European small farmers found themselves – like the Kenyan settlers under Mau-Mau – attacked by faithful servants whom they had employed for thirty years, and survivors huddled for protection in the local gendarmerie. At Périgotville Muslims seized an arms magazine, slaughtered a dozen Europeans, including the administrator and his assistant, then pillaged and burned the town. At the charming small seaport of Djidjelli four forest guards were among the murdered; at Kerrata a justice of the peace and his wife. In many cases it was the *petits fonctionnaires*, symbols of the *présence française*, that the assassins seemed particularly bent on hunting down. Meanwhile, at Guelma, the other focus of revolt two hundred kilometres away to the east of Constantine, there were similar scenes of demonstrators run amok, killings, rape and pillage.

For five dreadful days the madness continued, until troops hastily rushed up by the army managed to restore order. The accumulated casualty reports made grisly reading: 103 Europeans murdered, plus another hundred wounded; a number of women brutally raped, including one aged eighty-four. Many of the corpses were appallingly mutilated: women with their breasts slashed off, men with their severed sexual organs stuffed into their mouths.

There now began the grim work of repression. The army, incorporating Senegalese units legendary for their ferocity, subjected suspect Muslim villages to systematic *ratissage* – literally a "raking-over", a time-honoured word for "pacifying" operations. This involved a number of summary executions. Of the less accessible *mechtas*, or Muslim villages, more than forty were bombed by Douglas dive-bombers; while the cruiser *Duguay-Trouin* lying off in the Gulf of Bougie bombarded the environs of Kerrata at extreme range (and, presumably, comparable inaccuracy). The casualties inflicted by the armed forces were set officially (by the Tubert Commission Report) at 500 to 600, but the numbers of Muslim villagers killed by the more indiscriminate naval and aerial bombardments may well have amounted to more. Nevertheless, the figure seems to have been but a small proportion of the dead accounted for by the vengeful backlash of an outraged and frightened European population. Spontaneously organised vigilantes seized prisoners out of country gaols and lynched them; Muslims found not wearing the white brassards as prescribed by the army were simply despatched on the spot. At one village alone, held under siege by the Muslims during the uprisings, 219 were reported to have been shot out of hand. At Guelma, where the European fury reputedly reached its highest point, the Algerian Communist Party was well to the fore in the work of reprisal – a factor of significance in the forthcoming revolution. Describing the uprising as "Hitlerian", the P.C.A. secretary-general, Amar Ouzegane, wrote in *Liberté*, the party journal: "The organisers of these troubles must be swiftly and pitilessly punished, the instigators of the revolt put in front of the firing squad".

Estimates of the toll of Muslim dead exacted in the wake of Sétif fluctuate wildly, as is so often the case. The Tubert Report placed the figure at between 1,020 and 1,300; while Cairo radio immediately claimed that 45,000 had been killed – a total which was to become accepted more or less unquestioningly by the Algerian nationalists.* Robert Aron advances a figure of 6,000 which (although the basis whereby it was derived is not entirely clear) now seems generally acceptable to moderate French historians. But even if one were to accept the *very lowest* figure proffered by the Tubert Report, it still represents a ten to one "over-kill" in relation to the numbers of Europeans massacred; especially when, as was later officially estimated, no more than five per cent of the population had been tainted anyway.

Details of the Sétif bloodbath were played down with remarkable success in metropolitan France. Simone de Beauvoir recalls: "We heard very little about what had happened at Sétif," and noted that the Communist *L'Humanité* acknowledged only a hundred or so casualties, while de Gaulle in his memoirs dismisses the bloody episode in one terse sentence: "a beginning of insurrection, occurring in the Constantinois and synchronised with the Syrian riots in the month of May, was snuffed out by Governor-General Chataigneau". Yet the army repression must have been carried out on orders from de Gaulle's coalition government, and it must equally have been fully aware of the extent of the ensuing bloodbath; on both scores it is to be noted that the Communist ministers shared responsibility without a murmur.

For all the general ignorance in metropolitan France of what happened at Sétif, the impact on Algerians was incalculable, and ineradicable. Kateb Yacine, the liberal poet, records that it was at Sétif

> that my sense of humanity was affronted for the first time by the most atrocious sights. I was sixteen years old. The shock which I felt at the pitiless butchery that caused the deaths of thousands of Muslims, I have never forgotten. From that moment my nationalism took definite form.

* In an interview with the author in October 1973, President Bourguiba of Tunisia persisted in the belief that "more than 50,000" had been killed after Sétif. Maître Teitgen, the liberal secretary-general of the Algiers prefecture in 1956-7, told the author that he reckoned the Muslim dead at "probably 15,000". The discrepancy in the figures may (according to Robert Aron) be partly accounted for by the fact that many of the inhabitants of suspect *mechtas* "disappeared" into the hills in advance of the army *ratissages*, and were thus subsequently accounted for among the presumed dead.

Of more direct significance was the disembarkation, shortly after Sétif, of the 7th Regiment of Algerian Tirailleurs, a unit that had distinguished itself in battle in Europe. Many of its men came from the Constantine area and were utterly appalled by the stories they heard. A number of these returning soldiers were subsequently to become leaders of the F.L.N. Among them was a much-decorated sergeant, Ben Bella, who wrote: "The horrors of the Constantine area in May 1945 succeeded in persuading me of the only path; Algeria for the Algerians." The Algerian liberal leader, Ferhat Abbas, had condemned the wanton slaughter of Europeans by declaring, at the beginning of the uprising, "those who have urged you to rebellion betray you". But, on his way to congratulate the Governor-General on the Allied victory, he – like 4,500 of his followers who had had nothing whatever to do with the uprising – was arrested and, later, was forced to admit that Sétif "has taken us back to the days of the crusaders". It was indeed hardly an exaggeration to describe it, as did Edward Behr while the war was still in progress, as

> an event which, in one form or another, has marked every Algerian Muslim alive at the time. . . . Every one of the "new wave" of Algerian nationalists prominent in the National Liberation Front today traces his revolutionary determination back to May 1945 . . . each of them felt after May 1945 that some sort of armed uprising would sooner or later become necessary.

The reaction of the European *colons*, a mixture of shock and fear, was to demand further draconian measures and to suspend any suggestion of new reforms. "When the house is on fire," wrote the *Écho d'Alger*, "when the ship is about to sink, one calls for neither the insurance company nor the dancing-master. For the house, it's the hour of the fireman; for the ship, the hour of the lifeboat. For North Africa, *c'est l'heure du gendarme.*" With remarkable prophetic accuracy the French divisional commander, General Duval, who had already been responsible for much of the "gendarme" action in the immediate aftermath of Sétif, reported to Paris: "I have given you peace for ten years. But don't deceive yourselves. . . ." In fact, the precarious peace was to last nine and a half years; but, in effect, the shots fired at Sétif represented the first volley of the Algerian War.

The conquest, 1830

Though immediate causes, such as hunger and the years of deprivation of the Second World War, may partly explain the fateful explosion at Sétif, for deeper motivations one needs to skim back swiftly over 115 years of the *présence française* in Algeria.

In 1830, the country lay nominally under a loose suzerainty of Turkish military rule. Successive generations of French historians have, for fairly obvious reasons, claimed that a state approximating tribal anarchy prevailed. This view is now contested by "neutral" as well as Arab historians. In 1847 de Tocqueville declared to the French National Assembly that "The Muslim society in North Africa was not uncivilised; it only had a backward and imperfect civilisation." He went on to claim "we have rendered Muslim society much more miserable and much more barbaric than it was before it became acquainted with us". Even some of the early French conquerors paid tribute to signs of Algeria's civilisation, however rudimentary, with one general noting in 1834, "nearly all the Arabs can read and write; in each village, there are two schools". What is indisputable, however, is that in 1830 Algeria was suffering from acute political instability internally and therefore presented a feeble exterior to the world outside. It was indeed quite difficult to establish a national identity for a territory that had been little more than a corridor for successive conquerors, and known little but turbulence over many previous centuries. The Carthaginians had ruled for some seven centuries; they had been followed by the Romans; who had in turn been followed by the Byzantines, the Arabs, the Spaniards and the Turks. In the early nineteenth century the troublesomeness of corsairs operating out of the rugged Algerian coast had provoked thoughts of occupation among various European powers, and even troubled the United States. Back in the sixteenth century, the first European consul to El-Djezair, as the city was then called, had been a Frenchman, and Napoleon I had himself cast covetous eyes in its direction. From then on French merchants had become progressively involved in a series of complex and tangled trade details, and it was during a row provoked by one of these that, in 1827, the reigning Dey of Algiers (half of whose twenty-eight predecessors are said to have met violent ends) lost his temper with the French consul, struck him in the face with a fly-whisk, and called him "a wicked, faithless, idol-worshipping rascal".

France waited three years before avenging the insult. It then presented a useful pretext for Charles X's regime which, increasingly unpopular, adopted the time-honoured formula of distracting minds from domestic problems by the pursuit of *la gloire* abroad. There were at once voices raised against the Algerian "adventure", arguing that it was a deviation from France's essential interests in Europe ("I would gladly", declared one deputy, "exchange Algiers for the most wretched hole on the Rhine"). And in fact the Algerian entanglement was to play an important role in bringing down the regime – not for the last time in French history. Marching to plans based on a Napoleonic project, the French expeditionary force landed at Sidi-Ferruch, a sheltered beach some twenty miles west of Algiers. The enterprise was accompanied by a touch of the *fête galante*, with elegant ladies booking accommodation aboard pleasure boats to observe the naval bombardment of Algiers. A few weeks later the city fell, taking with it Dey Hussein; but too late to save the restored Bourbons in France.

But despite initial French optimism, the fighting continued in the interior. In 1832 there arose a fierce and dedicated Algerian resistance leader, Abd-el-Kader, then aged only twenty-five. With intermittent cease-fires, Abd-el-Kader waged war against the French occupation over the next fifteen years. Though winning remarkably wide support in western and central Algeria, he was never able to unite totally the warlike Algerian tribes which, traditionally, were little more inclined to submit to his authority than they were to the French. In the context of the nineteenth century the weight of colonialist France was, in any event, altogether too great for Abd-el-Kader to have achieved anything resembling a united, modern nation. Militarily, the struggle assumed forms that were to become painfully familiar. Ill-prepared French troops would freeze to death in the harsh mountains in pursuit of an elusive foe, or fall into well-laid ambushes. Little quarter was given. The French army retaliated with scorched-earth reprisals; on one occasion French public opinion was deeply shocked to learn how fires had been lit at the mouth of a cave where 500 men, women and children had taken refuge, asphyxiating all but ten of them. "It was not a pretty war, nor an amusing war," wrote one military commander. A legendary figure in French nurseries, Père Bugeaud, pressed operations ruthlessly to a conclusion, and in 1847 Abd-el-Kader finally surrendered—to spend the rest of his life in honourable exile in Damascus. In December the following year, a time when the U.S.A. had admitted little more than half its eventual complement of states to the Union, the Second Republic declared Algeria an integral part of France, transforming its vast territories into three French departments. It was a historic, indeed unique, step, and one which thereby set up for successive French republics a deadly trap from which they would find it well nigh impossible to escape.

La présence française

Pari passu with Marshal Bugeaud's "pacification". French colonisers steadily took root in Algeria. Said Bugeaud in a renowned statement before the National Assembly in 1840: "Wherever there is fresh water and fertile land, there one must locate colons, without concerning oneself to whom these lands belong." By 1841 the numbers of such colons, or pieds noirs as they came to be called,* already totalled 37,374 – in comparison with approximately three million indigènes. There were a number of sources from which French administrations furnished the necessary land;

---

* There are at least two schools of thought on the origins of pied noir; one, on account of the black polished shoes worn by the French military; the other based on the somewhat patronising view of metropolitan Frenchmen that the colons had had their feet burned black by an excess of the African sun.

the state domains which the French government had inherited from its Turkish predecessor (some one million hectares – nearly 4,000 square miles), forestry domains (much of which was in a condition of neglect), and agricultural land simply expropriated because it lay uncultivated, or for punitive measures. One such example of the last was 500,000 hectares seized from the Kabyles in 1871 in reprisal for their revolt against the pressures of French colonisation (about a quarter of this was later handed back as being *inutilisable*). On top of this there came the land which the *colons* acquired through direct negotiation with the owners. Various laws were passed to protect Algerian property from land-greedy *colons*, but all too often they were easily circumvented.

Napoleon III, who was perhaps one of the first French leaders to concern himself seriously with the Algerian plight, in 1863 passed a law aimed at "reconciling an intelligent, proud warlike and agrarian race" in which was stipulated, *inter alia*, that "France recognises the ownership by Arab tribes of territories of which they have permanent and traditional benefit". As so often with the more liberal acts of this well-intentioned ruler, however, their execution did not match up to his ideals; while a decade earlier he had himself pushed the floodgates of immigration ajar with his own political exiles and the unemployed of the Parisian ateliers. In his constant search for fresh funds abroad, he had also sold to the Compagnie Genevoise some fifteen thousand hectares of the best land round Sétif; but in the long run this would benefit neither France (in that the substantial income off it flowed into the pockets of Swiss bankers) nor Algeria (in that, contrary to Louis-Napoleon's intentions, its intensive operations offered but little employment for land-hungry peasants), and in itself was to provide one of the contributory causes to the 1945 events. Another subsequent piece of protective legislation was the Warnier Act of 1873, which aimed at preventing the sub-division of Muslim lands, but left loopholes whereby such scandals as the following could occur: near Mostaganem a Jewish lawyer's clerk acquired 292 hectares, which was tenanted by 513 *indigènes*, for no more than 20 francs. The costs imposed on the "vendors" somehow amounted to 11,000 francs, and they now became the purchaser's labourers at starvation wages.

In France voices continued to be raised against the colonisation of Algeria; Clemenceau bitterly attacked the "colonialist" Jules Ferry on the grounds that he was serving the designs of Bismarck by helping distract France from her destiny in Europe; agronomists feared that, because of the lower wages paid the Algerian peasants, French farmers and vine-growers would be threatened. But still the European immigrants arrived in their various waves. There were the unemployed and unwanted from the revolution of 1848, who hardly formed the best material for breaking the stern soil of Algeria; after 1871 (when immigration first began on a large scale) there came industrious and efficient Alsatians, refugees from the provinces forfeited to a triumphant Prussia. There came Spaniards, Italians and Maltese in their thousands; so much so that by 1917 only one in five of the non-Muslim population was said to be of French origin. As Anatole France muttered angrily: "We have despoiled, pursued and hunted down the Arabs in order to populate Algeria with Italians and Spaniards."

Undeniably, however, much of the land colonised by the *pieds noirs* had been carved out of insalubrious wilderness, some of which may have been used as migratory grazing grounds, rather than grabbed directly from Muslim farmers. This was especially true of the mosquito-ridden marshes of the Mitidja, inland from Algiers. Its reputation in the early colonial days was so bad that anyone with a face rendered sallow by fever was said to have a "Boufarik complexion", but under French expertise it was rapidly to become Algeria's richest farming area. In 1843, Trappist monks introduced the vine to the Mitidja; thirty-five years later the coming of phylloxera to France launched the Algerian wine industry, and by the mid-twentieth century it had grown to be one of the Mediterranean's biggest producers. Thus in the all-important realm of agriculture, as indeed in that of industrial development later, the *colons* could reasonably claim that they had created the country out of virtually nothing. But it was the old, old story of the Europeans with their superior technique, resources and aggressive vigour progressively assimilating the best lands, while at the same time the more numerous *indigènes* were being pushed out on to the more peripheral lands.

During the first forty years of the *présence française* Algeria was chiefly run by the military; administration at the local level being in the hands of the Bureaux Arabes created by Marshal Bugeaud. These were adapted from the Turkish system, except that plenipotentiary powers resided with the French administrator, who combined the roles of governor, judge, inspector of taxes, technical adviser and welfare officer. Often these came to be highly expert in their field, as well as deeply dedicated to the welfare of the people under their charge. By 1870, however, the *pied noir* population had risen to over 200,000 and an uprising against the military-style administration forced Paris to grant them greater control over their affairs and something more closely resembling the forms of government enjoyed by metropolitan Frenchmen. The institutions that then evolved were to remain, with little basic change, over the next eighty and more years. At the top, Algeria – since it had been annexed as an integral part of France – was governed through the French Ministry of the Interior. This was in sharp contrast to its closely related Maghreb* neighbours, over whom

---

* Meaning, literally, the "land of the setting sun", the Maghreb embraces the western territories of the North African littoral: Tunisia, Algeria and Morocco.

France established only "protectorates" during the nineteenth century and which were consequently dealt with by the Ministry of Foreign Affairs. Thus it would always prove difficult to formulate any co-ordinated policy for the Maghreb as a whole, and in fact such disparate territories as French West Africa and Indo-China came to have more homogeneous links through both being subordinated to the same Ministry of the Colonies.

Appointed by, and responsible to, the Minister of the Interior was the governor-general, one of the most senior functionaries of the French republic. By unwritten tradition he was never a *pied noir*, any more than the prefect of Corsica was a Corsican. Directly under him came the prefects of Algiers, Oran and Constantine; which, as departments of France, were entitled to send senators and deputies to the mother parliament in Paris. Originally only the *pied noir* population enjoyed the right to vote for these representatives. Then came the creation of the double electoral college system; the first college consisting of all "French citizens", plus a modest proportion of select Muslims, the number of which was augmented over regular intervals – though at a painfully slow rate; the second embracing the whole Muslim population. Each college (in 1946) could elect eight senators and fifteen deputies to the National Assembly. In effect this meant that one million Europeans had voting rights equal to those of over eight million Muslims. Laws specifically relating to Algeria were adapted or initiated by a "regime of decrees" established in 1834, controlled by the administration and thus escaping any parliamentary control. The nearest semblance to any Algerian legislative assembly was the Délégations Financières, composed of mixed European and Muslim members, but the competence of this body was strictly limited to budgetary matters; and, in practice, for one reason or another it tended to reflect the interests of the *grands colons*.

At lower levels – although the vast, empty Saharan territories continued under military control – the administration was divided between *communes de plein exercice* and *communes mixtes*. The former were established in communities where Europeans predominated (though there were some glaring exceptions, such as Constantine, where the Muslims were in an overwhelming majority), and they were based on the French model with a ruling mayor (invariably European) and an elected municipal council, three-fifths of whose seats were reserved for Europeans. The *communes mixtes* held sway in the areas where the Muslims had clear numerical superiority, and each was headed by an appointed European administrator, governing through the medium of local *caids* – all of whom derived their office through the governor-general.

The institution of the *commune mixte* contained many of the elements of what, by the mid-twentieth century, was most unsatisfactory about French rule in Algeria. It was, in fact, an adaptation in modern dress of

33

Père Bugeaud's Bureaux Arabes, which had worked well enough in the early days, but it was simply not equipped to cope with either the advanced technical problems of the twentieth century or its vastly expanded Muslim populations. It is revealing that, whereas in 1922 there were 300 European administrators for the *communes mixtes* for three million Muslims governed by them, by 1954 the ratio had shifted to 257 for four and a half million. At Arris, for instance, the epicentre of the 1954 revolt in the Aurès, one administrator and two assistants were in charge of 60,000 dispersed over a wide and inaccessible area. The fault lay, to a large extent, with French policy which – possibly out of fear of releasing a genie from the bottle – had consistently shied away from creating an indigenous administrative corps. A passing comparison could be made with India, where, after a long participation in government, by the time of the British devolution of power in 1947 something like half of the civil service was "Indianised".* In contrast, by as late as 1956 – two years after the Algerian war had broken out – Governor-General Lacoste admitted that no more than eight out of 864 higher administrative posts were held by Muslims; and it was not until 1959, after the coming of de Gaulle, that the French army could proudly announce the appointment of the first Muslim regimental commander. Though often excellent and dedicated men in themselves, the French (or frequently *pied noir*) administrators tended to become an ingrowing race. As Professor Émile-Félix Gautier, a distinguished scholar and fervent admirer of *Algérie française*, wrote at the time of the 1930 centenary:

> The administrative career in Algeria has been a closed shop; the official enters at the beginning of his life to become later, if he succeeds, a director with grey hair; he doesn't leave it; normally no door opens on to other French or colonial administrations. The result is that the Government-General is permeated by an Algerian [i.e. *pied noir*] spirit.

The "cadi's ear"

Paradoxically, the advent of modern communications meant that the over-worked administrator became more, rather than less, out of contact with his flock; he communicated by telephone instead of riding out by horseback, as in the good old days, to stay overnight in the various *douars*. Many inhabitants in the remoter mountains of the Aurès and Kabylia never saw a European in their lives, their sole contact with France being through a *caid, bachaga*† or the hated local tax-collector. More and more the administrator came to rely on these Muslim intermediaries; some were venerable and honourable old men, laden with decorations, who had

---

* It would be unfair to extend it too far, as the British had never colonised India with a view to permanent settlement; to correspond with the *pied noir* problem there would have had to have been roughly 30 million Britons in India in 1947.
† The Algerian equivalent of pasha.

fought for France, or served her loyally and with integrity; others owed their position purely to family and tradition, and were known contemptuously by young nationalists as the *Beni-Oui-Oui*, the rubber stamps of French policy; still others were appallingly corrupt. In the Turkish tradition, the bribe was all too often an indispensable fact of life. Jean Servier, a well-known French ethnologist, describes his outrage when an elderly illiterate produced a piece of paper stating that a local Muslim judge, or cadi,* was charging him 2,000 (old) francs ($6) for obtaining a copy of his marriage certificate, plus "scribal expenses, 1,000 francs".

> "That's not the normal fee," I told him, "France does not charge so much for justice."
> "The cadi assures us nevertheless, that it is France which obliges us to pay so much money."
> He added with a knowing smile. "Among our people there is a large cake called 'the cadi's ear' – because it requires a lot of honey to sweeten it!"

The "sweetening" often descended to the level of sheer swindle; 100,000 to 200,000 francs for a Legion of Honour or a post of *caid*, which might never materialise; or a desert sheikh who would bully the government into digging at great expense artesian wells to provide poverty-stricken *fellahs* with a living – these would prove to be dry and investigation would reveal that the arid land had in fact been sold (again, at great expense) to the Government by the said sheikh. The capacity (and ingenuity) of the "cadi's ear" seemed boundless; it increased hand in hand with the gulf between the French rulers and the ruled in Algeria – and so did resentment.

There was an important additional anomaly that provoked bitterness whenever the *bona fides* of "assimilation" with the mother country were questioned. This was the issue of French citizenship. Muslims were automatically French "subjects", but not French "citizens". From the early days legislation had permitted them to be subject to Islamic, as opposed to French, law; this may have been designed as a cultural and religious protection, but it became in effect a prison, because a Muslim wishing to adopt French citizenship had to renounce these rights, thereby virtually committing an act of apostasy. Moreover, in practice many obstacles were placed in the path of the Muslim seeking French citizenship. Back in 1871 tribesmen reporting in front of a judge at Bougie to fill in naturalisation papers were, reportedly, thrown into prison – *pour encourager les autres*. As a result, by 1936, after seventy-five years of "assimilation", no more than 2,500 Muslims had actually crossed the bar to French citizenship. There were two further inconsistencies. To begin with, in having imposed upon them by the French the Arab judicial

* The offices of Turco–Arab origin, cadi=judge and *caid*=a local governor, should not be confused.

system, the Berber Kabyles had been made to accept a social structure that had been alien to them in the first place. Secondly, in 1870 the Crémieux Decrees had made the exception of conferring automatic French citizenship upon the whole Jewish community of Algeria. Here, for Muslims, was a constantly open wound: why should the Jewish minority be open to political privileges denied to the indigenous majority?

Attempts at reform

Before Sétif, various attempts had been made at political and social reform – in 1868, 1919 and 1944. By and large they had followed a dismally stereotyped pattern; initiated by metropolitan French governments, frustrated by *pied noir* pressure-groups. In 1914–1918 Algerian troops fighting alongside the French had suffered appalling casualties of 25,000 killed out of 173,000 joining the colours. By way of recognition of their courage and loyalty legislation was introduced in 1919 to facilitate Muslim access (in modest numbers) to French citizenship. It aroused the most intransigent and violent opposition from the *pieds noirs*, reluctant or fearful of change, typical of which was this expostulation by the senator from Oran. "The *indigènes* have fulfilled their duty *vis-à-vis* ourselves and deserve to be recompensed. But to do this, is it necessary to resort to imprudent measures?" The same kind of smug, myopic reliance upon Muslim "duty" and docility was abundantly evident at the lavish and self-congratulatory centenary celebrations of the conquest in 1930, which included a re-enactment of the landing at Sidi-Ferruch. At one of the many such ceremonies one *Beni-Oui-Oui bachaga* was heard to declare that if the Muslims had known the French in 1830 as they now knew them, "they would have loaded their muskets with flowers"; while another proclaimed that the legions of his countrymen who had died in the First World War in the cause of the "civilising work of France in Algeria" had atoned for the French killed in 1830.

The centenary of the conquest was indeed a glittering colonial occasion reminiscent of the British Raj in India at its peak, and showed evidence on every hand of the genuine, and remarkable, benefits that France had bestowed on Algeria in so many fields over the preceding hundred years. Summing up, a British writer, Mary Motley, wrote: "In the golden glow of the centenary there seemed no reason why the existing regime should not last indefinitely." This optimism, however, was far from being shared by Maurice Viollette, who had been one of France's most visionary governor-generals. Deeply aware of the stirrings of discontent beneath the then apparently placid surface of Algeria, he issued this prophetic warning the year after the centenary: "before twenty years are up we will know the gravest of difficulties in North Africa". Five years later, Viollette succeeded in getting a set of liberal reforms tabled by the Assembly, the Blum–

Viollette Bill. His declared ideal was that "Muslim students, while remaining Muslim, should become so French in their education, that no Frenchman, however deeply racist and religiously prejudiced he might be . . . will any longer dare to deny them French fraternity". It spelt, in one word, "assimilation". The provisions of his bill, however, were once again extremely modest, notably offering citizenship to no more than 25,000 (out of some six million) Muslims, without renouncing their statutory rights to Islamic law. It would have been one of the most impressive pieces of legislation by Leon Blum's Popular Front, then in power. But the well-oiled mechanism of *pied noir* protest began to run; the Algerian Press fulminated against the "explosive situation" provoked by Parisian ignorance; the *anciens combattants* marched through the streets; the mayors threatened to resign; the powerful lobbies in Paris burrowed away. "We will never tolerate that in even the smallest commune an Arab might be mayor" was a not untypical *pied noir* reaction. Under pressure at home and the threat of Hitler abroad, Leon Blum's Popular Front hesitated, and finally collapsed before the bill could be passed. A bitterly disillusioned Viollette said to the Assembly in an eloquent warning that has been variously quoted:

> When the Muslims protest, you are indignant; when they approve, you are suspicious; when they keep quiet you are fearful. *Messieurs*, these men have no political nation. They do not even demand their religious nation. All they ask is to be admitted into yours. If you refuse this, beware lest they do not soon create one for themselves.

The still-born Blum–Viollette Bill was the ultimate plea for "assimilation". It aroused the most glowing hopes among Muslim liberals, but when – like every other endeavour of reform between 1909 and 1954 – it was thwarted, they were replaced by black despair.

Growth of nationalism

Back in 1894 Jules Cambon, then governor-general, wrote to the Senate describing the consequences of the French policy of breaking up the great traditional families of Algeria,

> because we found them to be forces of resistance. We did not realise that in suppressing the forces of resistance in this fashion, we were also suppressing our means of action. The result is that we are today confronted by a sort of human dust on which we have no influence and in which movements take place which are to us unknown.

It was a profound and far-sighted analysis. When France, *in extremis* between 1954 and 1962, was to cast around for *interlocuteurs valables*, moderate nationalist representatives with whom compromise solutions might be negotiated, among this "human dust" she was to find virtually none. On the other hand, from earliest days the colonial structure had so functioned as to impede and obviate the emergence of any concerted Muslim opposition body, and for long years it succeeded marvellously; yet again, when the ultimate disaster did occur, France would be taken by surprise, because – for the reasons suggested by Cambon – the resistance movements would be "unknown".

Because of Algeria's unique status as an integral part of France, which cut it off from undercurrents of Arab nationalism in the outside world more than its neighbours, one cannot easily state – as with other colonial territories – at what precise point a "resistance movement" began. In broad terms, three separate strands of Algerian nationalism have been defined, each identified with a particular leader. There was the religious movement, as embodied by the Association des Ulema of Sheikh Abdulhamid Ben Badis; the revolutionaries following Messali Hadj; and finally the liberals of Ferhat Abbas. Over the past century of French rule, French education and French culture, Muslim scholars consider that it was the religious doctrine which, more than anything, had kept alight the fires of nationalism in Algeria, and – although they were not the first in the field – it was probably the Ulema (founded in 1931) that provided the nationalists with their first momentum. Certainly their philosophic influence was of primary and inestimable significance, even remaining very much of a force in present-day Algeria. A Berber from Constantine descended from a family with centuries of tradition in political and religious leadership, Ben Badis was an ascetic and deeply conservative theologian who believed that Algerian regeneration could only be achieved by a return to the first principles of Islam. He remains the only one of the early nationalists who is still regarded as something of a national hero by most Algerians today. In their puritanism of outlook, the Ulema perhaps most resembled the Wahabi sect which, under Ibn Saud, had swept through the Arabian peninsula from the early 1900s onwards. They rigorously condemned alcohol, tobacco, dancing, music and sport, and one of their principal targets was the *marabouts* – or holy men and leaders of mystic orders – whom they accused both of corrupting the faith by their espousal of mysticism and of being the "domestic animals of colonialism". The Ulema also campaigned, with patriotic motives, for the separation of church and state; their programme was cultural as well as religious; and in schools set up widely across the country the values of Arabic as a language, of Algeria as a national entity and of pan-Arabism as an ideal were pressed home with considerable effect. Stated in all simplicity, their creed was: "Islam is my religion, Arabic is my language, Algeria is my country.... Independence is a natural right for every people of the earth...." The Ulema did more than any other body to rekindle a sense of religious and national consciousness among Algerians, but, tied up in their own theological coils, they failed to find pragmatic applications of their doctrines.

Messali versus Abbas

To some extent, this gap was filled by the "revolutionaries" of Messali Hadj.* Born in 1898, the son of a shoemaker from Tlemcen near the Moroccan border, Messali received little formal education; he served in 1914–1918 in the French army, and then went to work in France. Here he married a Frenchwoman, who brought him for a short period into the ranks of the Communist Party (but the role played by the P.C.A. in the repressions at Sétif finally caused him to break with the Communists). Always studiously dressed in the traditional attire of djellaba and red fez, with his broad face and vigorous beard, Messali was an imposing figure and an inflammatory orator. A journalist of *Le Monde* visiting him in 1952 was reminded of "Rasputin of 1916, Gapon of 1905 ... a magus, a prophet, a miracle-worker". In 1927 Messali became president of a political grouping recently formed from Algerian workers in the Paris area, called the Étoile Nord-Africaine, which under his lead soon became the most radical of all the nationalist organisations. Through the working-class origins of both Messali and its founding members, the Étoile came to have a proletarian character superimposed over its nationalist and religious doctrines. It differed from the Ulema both in a more modernistic interpretation of Islamic dogma and in its social demands, which included the redistribution of land among the *fellahs*. Much of Messali's ideals of popularist socialism was later to be inherited by the F.L.N. and present-day Algeria. By 1933 Messali was already talking of "revolution", and the Étoile programme declared for universal suffrage in Algeria, "a struggle for the total independence" of all three Maghreb nations, and confiscation of all property acquired by the French government or *colons*. Messali's revolutionary zeal was to bring him several spells in prison or exile, and make him – until the outbreak of the war in 1954 – the best known of all the Algerian nationalist leaders. The Étoile was dissolved, then recreated by Messali in 1937 as the Parti Progressiste Algérien (P.P.A.), with roughly the same platform but concentrating its activities on Algeria alone; after 1945 the P.P.A. – banned again – assumed the more dramatic title of Mouvement pour le Triomphe des Libertés Démocratiques (M.T.L.D.).

The third strand of Algerian nationalism in the inter-war period, the liberal movement, is less easy to reduce to party terms than the other two, but can perhaps best be studied through the person of its central figure, Ferhat Abbas. His whole career is one of utmost relevance in this story, for it was symptomatic of how the liberal moderate – through successive disillusions – becomes superseded by the revolutionary extremist. Born in 1899, Abbas, like Ben Badis, originated from the Constantine area, but his father, unlike Messali's, had risen from being the son of a *fellah* to be a

* Hadj is a title bestowed on Muslims who have made the pilgrimage to Mecca.

39

caid and Commander of the Legion of Honour. To Abbas, his father's career exemplified how the best of the French colonial system could be exploited to the advantage of the Muslim, and he himself rose successfully through the ranks of legislative posts that were open to him. He did his secondary studies at a French lycée in Constantine, then adopted the profession of pharmacist* in Sétif. Everything about Abbas was orientated towards the West, specifically France, and a bourgeois France at that. Linguistically, he never felt as at home in Arabic as he did in French, which he spoke with great skill and charm. He divorced his Muslim wife, and then, like Messali, married a Frenchwoman – a marriage that in itself was symbolic of his divided loyalties between France and Islam, where he could not support puritanical zeal to the same extent as Sheikh Ben Badis. In the Second World War, at the age of forty, Abbas promptly enlisted in the French army, but never received a commission.

It was during his time at Algiers university, however, that Abbas was first influenced by nationalist sentiment, through contact with other young *évolués* like himself. As president of the Muslim Students Association he entered the political arena and began ardently to pursue a goal of Franco-Algerian equality. Of pacific temperament, although he was a skilful debater, he was no rabble-rouser like Messali, and he and the proletarian supporters of Messali felt mutually ill at ease. To them, remarks one French writer: "he was a little like the cousin who had gone up to the big city, educated himself, and succeeded, but having forgotten his origins". With his clipped moustache, long, cultured features and neatly sober dress, Abbas was the essence of the westernised, middle-class Arab *évolué* – and so were the majority of his followers. Until relatively late in his career he was a passionate protagonist of assimilation – in equality – with metropolitan France, and unlike Messali and Ben Badis he did not believe in an Algeria with a separate identity. In a much-quoted passage, he declared in 1936:

> Had I discovered the Algerian nation, I would be a nationalist and I would not blush as if I had committed a crime.... However, I will not die for the Algerian nation, because it does not exist. I have not found it. I have examined History, I questioned the living and the dead, I visited cemeteries; nobody spoke to me about it. I then turned to the Koran and I sought for one solitary verse forbidding a Muslim from integrating himself with a non-Muslim nation. I did not find that either. One cannot build on the wind.

Two months later Ben Badis riposted fierily that he and the Ulema sages had also "examined History", and had indeed discovered a "Muslim

---

* It will be noted that many of the nationalist intellectuals (like Ben Khedda, president of the provisional Algerian government in 1962, who was also a pharmacist) were doctors, pharmacists or lawyers – professions where Muslims generally encountered the least barriers to advancement.

Algerian nation", which "has its culture, its traditions and its characteristics, good or bad like every other nation of the earth. And, next, we state that this Algerian nation is not France, cannot be France, and does not wish to be France."

The schism within the nationalist movement was wide open, a prelude to those that were to plague the Algerian revolutionary movement throughout its existence. In June 1936 a "Muslim Congress" was convened in Algiers for the first time, but the display of unity it produced was short-lived. The Blum–Viollette proposals of the same year themselves provided the root cause of a fresh split. While Ferhat Abbas and the liberals warmly welcomed them, they were attacked by Messali in violent terms as "a new instrument of colonialism aimed at dividing the Algerian people, by the usual French methods of separating the élite from the masses".

When the Blum–Viollette Bill collapsed, however, an impossible predicament confronted the liberals: on the one hand, they saw themselves looked on as renegades by Messali and the Ulema; on the other, they were rejected by the French. It was a bitter personal disillusion for Abbas, who, from this moment, began to move away from the ideal of assimilation towards some form of autonomy for Algeria. Thus, at least ideologically, he and his supporters were brought a long step closer to the "revolutionaries" – a progression, tragic for France, that was to be repeated each time "moderate" Algerian nationalists found their overtures repulsed by the government of France, or by the *pied noir* lobbies. Modest as were the reforms it would have introduced, the abortion of the Blum–Viollette Bill undoubtedly marked a vital turning-point for the Algerian nationalist movement. At the same time it also bestowed on the *pieds noirs* a first dangerous awareness that they could call the tune on *any* reform initiated by a government in Paris.

Impact of the Second World War

The Second World War came, and with it France's crushing defeat in 1940. To Muslim minds, particularly sensitive to prestige and *baraka*,* the humiliation made a deep impression. The reaction of many was: "France has had it; so why not pay our taxes to the Germans, instead of to France?" For the *pieds noirs*, circumstances were austere but not impossible: "there were restrictions, shortage of oil, and chickens on the balconies to lay eggs. Life was tolerable, we all more or less had a photograph of the Maréchal in the dining-room, but simply because he had a fine head of an old man," recalls a Jewish resident of Algiers. But discrepancies with the Muslim population were marked; economic severance from the mother country, with its 100,000 Algerian wage-earners there, and successive famines

* *Baraka*, hard to translate, is a special grace or good fortune accorded from on high.

caused standards of living to sink acutely. As Harold Macmillan noted in his wartime memoirs:

> It is as if the Irishmen in the U.S.A. and Great Britain were to cease sending money home, and at the same time no Irish labour was going over to England for the harvest, etc., and earning money in that way.
>
> The population is therefore very poor, and the food and clothing position among the people has caused us all a lot of worry.

On top of the humiliation of defeat was compounded the confusion of not knowing what authority represented the true France. After 1940, while the French colonies in Equatorial Africa went over to de Gaulle, Algeria remained pro-Vichy; thus, within three years, Algerians found their loyalty invoked first to Pétain, then to Darlan, then Giraud and finally de Gaulle. But even after the rise to eminence of de Gaulle, it was the shadow of the Allied colossus in the background that constantly obscured the rekindled, feeble light of the *présence française* in Algeria. Landing – once again at Sidi-Ferruch – in November 1942, the Anglo-Americans with their overwhelming weight of war material and the power and riches that this implied, in contrast to the puny resources of the Vichy French, made a powerful impact on the Algerian nationalists. They were also soon aware of the anti-colonialist creed of Roosevelt's America, and Abbas had several meetings with Bob Murphy, the President's personal representative in Algiers, to explore the possibility of applying the Atlantic Charter to Algeria.

But when, early in 1943, a Muslim delegation approached the Free French leader, General Giraud, with a petition of reforms, they were headed off with "I don't care about reforms, I want soldiers first." And, indeed, Algeria did provide France with soldiers – as in the First World War: magnificient Tirailleurs and Spahis, to whom General Juin was heavily indebted for his victorious progress through the grinding Italian campaign. These Algerian soldiers at the front were either largely unaware of, or had their backs turned upon, the turmoil brewing at home – until Sétif. But the camaraderie of the battle-front, their contact with the more privileged British and American troops, as well as the training they received, were things not to be lightly forgotten.

In 12 February 1943, Abbas produced his own "Atlantic Charter" called the "Manifesto of the Algerian People". In a more virulent tone than heretofore, he claimed savagely: "The French colony only admits equality with Muslim Algeria on one level; sacrifice on the battlefields." More ambitious than his previous demands, the "Manifesto" now marked a clear turning away from assimilation, calling for an "immediate and effective participation" of Muslims in the government and the establishment of a constitution guaranteeing *inter alia*, liberty and equality for all Algerians, the suppression of feudal property – as well as various other planks borrowed from the more radical platform of Messali. At this point, Messali was under house arrest (a sentence commuted from sixteen years' hard labour imposed following an army mutiny in 1941), his P.P.A. was in dissolution and the Communist Party of Algeria (P.C.A.) banned – so, temporarily, Abbas reigned supreme. Next, in May 1943, pressed on by the followers of Messali, Abbas came out with a "Supplement" to the "Manifesto" which demanded nothing less than "an Algerian state" – though still through recourse only to legal and peaceful means.

This was too much for the French authorities, and Abbas too was consigned to house arrest. In protest against French policy the Muslim representatives on the Délégations Financières refused to take their seats that September. Perhaps realising that he had gone too far, Abbas recanted, affirming his "fidelity to France", and was released again at the end of the year. Then, in January 1944, de Gaulle gave an epoch-making declaration in Brazzaville; it was French policy, he announced, amid some typical oratorical ambiguities "to lead each of the colonial peoples to a development that will permit them to administer themselves, and, later, to govern themselves". Algerian Muslims were offered equal rights with French citizens, and an increase in the proportion of representatives in local government. To the Algerian nationalists this was little more than Blum–Viollette warmed up, and, by 1944, it was too little too late. (Nor, indeed – like other promises of reform – was the Brazzaville declaration ever to be implemented.) Abbas's reaction was to bury the hatchet with Messali, and on 14 March in the fateful town of Sétif, and in another rare moment of unity, all the principal components of nationalism joined hands in a new grouping called Amis du Manifeste et de la Liberté (A.M.L.). In the most precise terms yet, it restated its aim as being "to propagate the idea of an Algerian nation, and the desire for an Algerian constitution with an autonomous republic federated to a renewed French republic, anti-colonial and anti-imperialist". This new brief moment of unity was to perish finally amid the bloodshed and recriminations of Sétif the following year; nevertheless, the A.M.L. declaration did establish a principle of immense political and propaganda importance. Indeed, in the opinion of Albert Camus the movement was "the most original and significant that has been seen to emerge since the beginnings of the conquest".

And so France in Algeria staggered from war into peace, her prestige in Algeria gravely tainted, her power and influence in the world sorely reduced. United in despair, the Algerian nationalists saw, in the ending of the war, prospects of a return to "colonialism as usual", a powerful French army returning to police the country and aid the *pieds noirs* prevent implementation of the reforms they so ardently demanded. The scene was set for the terrible, unforeseen and unexpected explosion at Sétif – and, in its wake, *l'heure du gendarme*.

CHAPTER TWO

Ici, c'est la France

Magnanimity in politics is not seldom the truest wisdom; and a great empire
and little minds go ill together.

Edmund Burke, *On Conciliation with America*, 1775

The country

SETTING the scene for the quite irrational murder of the anonymous
Arab by his *pied noir* anti-hero, "The Outsider", that great native-born
writer of Algeria, Albert Camus, paints in words that scorch the mind:

> There was the same red glare as far as the eye could reach, and small
> waves were lapping the hot sand in little, flurried gasps. As I slowly
> walked towards the boulders at the end of the beach I could feel my
> temples swelling under the impact of the light. It pressed upon me,
> trying to check my progress. And each time I felt a hot blast strike my
> forehead, I gritted my teeth, I clenched my fists in my trouser-pockets
> and keyed up every nerve to fend off the sun and the dark befuddlement
> it was pouring into me . . . all I had to do was to turn, walk away, and
> think no more about it. But the whole beach, pulsing with heat, was
> pressing on my back.

He goes on, kills, and accepts – inarticulately and impassively – the penalty
of the guillotine.

Environment shapes men, and none more so than the vast skies of
Algeria – generally blazing down without pity or moderation, but capable
of unpredictable, fierce change. Immense, beautiful, sudden, savage and
harsh; one gropes inadequately for the right adjectives to describe the
country. Distance never ceases to amaze; from Algiers to Tamanrasset in
the barren, lunar mountains of the Hoggar is 1,300 miles, or roughly the
same as from Newcastle to Algiers; from Algiers to Oran, a flea's hop on
the map of North Africa, is little short of 300 miles by road. Four times
as big as metropolitan France, with its land area unchanged since the
colonial era, present-day Algeria is the tenth largest country in the world.
Nine-tenths of it are comprised by the endless Saharan under-belly that
sags below the Atlas mountains, the endless wasteland of blistering rock
and shifting sand. Sparsely inhabited by troops of wandering nomads, or
exotic tribes like the Ouled-Nail, whose comely dancing daughters tradi-

tionally used to offer themselves as courtesans in other regions, then returned with rich dowries to transmute themselves into honoured wives, dotted with mysterious M'zabite cities such as Ghardaia, and policed by isolated Foreign Legion forts, the Sahara once formed the average Englishman's romantic *Beau Geste* image of all Algeria. It is a world of seizing visual beauty, of shimmering whites and yellows that shift to glowing apricot, pink and violet with the sinking of the saturant sun. "A magnificently constructed Cubist painting," was how an enraptured Simone de Beauvoir saw Ghardaia: "white and ochre rectangles, brushed with blue by the bright light, were piled on each other to form a pyramid...." Few French soldiers remained impervious to its dangerous allures, yet this great backyard seemed real estate without value – until, during the Algerian war itself, discovery was made of the vast reserves of natural gas and oil that were to provide the basis of the wealth of independent Algeria.

For all its immense scale, the Algerian scene shifts with unexpected rapidity. Within a few hours' drive northward from the desert oasis of Bou-Saada, you are up in the 7,000-foot Atlas range of the Djurdjura, where (as I once discovered to my cost) even as late as mid-May roads can be blocked or swept away by avalanches and landslides. Beyond the mountains lies a totally other world. The hundreds of miles of rugged, indented coastline where the Barbary pirates had their lairs is the true Mediterranean; but a Mediterranean where secret, sandy bays are often pounded by seas of Atlantic force. Parts of it, like the aptly named Turquoise Corniche, are as breathtaking as the Amalfi peninsula but without its hordes and hoardings. There is the beguiling Roman site of Tipasa, on its gentle promontory where "the sea sucks with the noise of kissing", drenched at midday by the scent of wild absinthe, and where Camus repeatedly experienced "the happy lassitude of a wedding-day with the world". In springtime the ruins are a blaze of contrapuntal colour: wild gladioli of magenta, bright yellow inulas and spiky acanthus thrust up among sarcophagi carpeted with tiny blue saxifrage and sprawled over by convolvulus with great pink trumpets. The ochre stones and iron red soil contrast joyously with the silvery-grey of the olives and absinthe and a peacock sea. "Here the gods themselves serve as tryst-places, or beds," says Camus. "Happy is he among the living who has seen such things." And happy, indeed, were the *pieds noirs* who, in the "good days" owned summer villas – such as one might find in Brittany or Arcachon – at Tipasa or on other stretches of Algeria's unspoilt coast-line.

Pied noir Algeria

The centre of gravity of French colonisation lay close to the coast, with its big, Europeanised city ports of Algiers, Oran, Bougie, Philippeville and Bône, and the Mitidja – the rich, flat farmland which French ingenuity had created out of malarial swamps. Here, in country which might have been Languedoc, straight eucalyptus-shaded roads led through a prosperous and tidy succession of cereal and citrus farms, drenched with orange-blossom scent in May, and vast vineyards, owned by *pieds noirs* and operated by Muslim labour. The Mitidja towns – like Blida, where Oscar Wilde, Lord Alfred Douglas and André Gide once vied for the charms of "Arab boys as beautiful as bronze statues" – were unmistakably French. Their main squares, surrounded by well-pollarded plane trees (as well as containing the inevitable, graceless *monument aux morts*) would almost invariably boast a highly ornate bandstand where, of a Sunday, the band of the local garrison would endeavour to distract the *indigènes* from their lack of more worldly privileges with rousing martial music. The names of the townships founded by the *colons* were just as uncompromisingly French; Victor-Hugo, Rabelais, Orléansville, Aumale, Marengo and Inkermann.

Algiers itself, cradled in steep hills green with pine and palm that offer countless superb panoramas, was one of the pearls of French Mediterranean culture. Arriving by ship in its bay – which, next to Rio, must be one of the most beautiful in the world – one's eyes were blinded by the massed whiteness of the terraces climbing up from the sea. It deserved its sobriquet of *Alger la Blanche*. High above Algiers on one side was perched Notre Dame d'Afrique, a Catholic shrine of prime sanctity for the *pieds noirs* (and also of appalling taste, a little reminiscent of Montmartre's Sacré-Cœur), containing a black madonna with the paternalistic inscription "Pray for us and our Muslims". On another hill nestled the luxurious Hôtel Saint-George, where General Eisenhower set up his Allied Head-quarters in 1942, and through whose exotic gardens of giant contorted euphorbia and sweet-smelling moonflowers Churchill and the titans of the Second World War strolled, laying plans for a world in which Anglo-Saxon predominance seemed assured in perpetuity.* After the war it reverted to being a haven for senior French officials, high army brass and their ladies. Just down the hill from the Saint-George lay the Palais d'Été, a dazzling white mauresque mansion where the governor-general resided in full vice-regal splendour. Once the centre of Algiers was the Place du Gouvernement, close to the harbour whence creep fishy smells, and where the corsairs used to auction their slaves; but the true solar plexus (and certainly in the years after 1954) was formed by the Plateau des Glières, leading up from the sea, past the palatial Hôtel des Postes, up steep steps to the imposing *monument aux morts* and thence to the open space, or Forum, in front of the modern block that housed the offices of the Gouvernement-Général.

---

* Today a commemorative plaque is still kept attentively burnished, the Algerians counting the overthrow of Vichy by the Anglo-Americans an important milestone on the road to independence.

With its waterfront of grand prosperous arcaded buildings belonging to the banks, big mercantile companies, the Hôtel Aletti and the *Écho d'Alger*, its red-tiled bourgeois villas gazing out over the bay, this could easily have been Nice or Cannes. Yet of its total population of 900,000 only one-third was in fact European. In their different enclaves the two communities coexisted closely together – which, in time of peace, was to provide Algiers with its most fascinating contrasts, and, later, its most savagely bloody collisions. The elegant, thoroughly French boulevards of Rue Michelet and Rue d'Isly, with their expensive shops and *trottoir* cafés thronged with chattering students, terminated abruptly in the Casbah. This, the old Turkish quarter, embraced in its compressed and nigh-impenetrable confines, redolent with all the odours of spice and oil of any Arab city and resounding with its ululations, a totally Muslim population bursting at the seams. The squalid, labyrinthine alleys often concealed ancient houses built around open courtyards of great charm. Abutting the Casbah on the other side lay the tenements of the European working class of Bab-el-Oued, so heavily impregnated with Spanish blood that its inhabitants were known collectively as the "Hernandez-and-Perez". At the opposite, south-east, end of Algiers, in the seedier *pied noir* quarter of Belcourt, the boundary between the poor whites and their Muslim counterparts was still less distinct.

The summer in Algiers is long and torrid, and by the end of it the Europeans tend to feel like fruits that have ripened too long in the sun. Tempers fray, until at last the potent September rains bring liberation and new life. Through much of the year – winters that sparkle and springs that warm – the climate, like the architecture, is that of the northern Mediterranean. Then, suddenly, with the least warning, the sky yellows and the Chergui blows from the Sahara, stinging the eyes and choking with its sandy, sticky breath. Men think, and behave, differently. It is a recurrent reminder that this is indeed Africa.

Oran, the second city of Algeria, was even more European than Algiers; in fact, with 300,000 *pied noir* inhabitants to 150,000 Muslims, it was the only centre where they predominated. The scene of the Royal Navy's tragic action to sink the French fleet in 1940, rather than risk it falling into Nazi hands, Oran was to suffer but little until the last days of the Algerian war. Camus condemns it as a city of ineffable boredom, where the youth had but two essential pleasures – "getting their shoes shined and displaying those same shoes on the boulevard" – and found its streets "doomed to dust, pebbles and heat", its shops combining "all the bad taste of Europe and the Orient". To him, while Algiers had an Italian quality, Oran with its "cruel glitter" had something more Spanish about it; and Constantine reminded him of Toledo. But, he added harshly, in contrast to those of Italy or Spain, "These are cities without a past. They are cities without abandon, without tenderness. In the hours of boredom which are those of the siesta, the sadness there is implacable and without melancholy.... These cities offer nothing to reflection and everything to passion...."

Kabylia and the Aurès

In a country full of violent contrasts none could be greater than that between the Mediterranean littoral with its Europeanised cities, beaches and flat, cultivated hinterland, and the almost entirely Muslim-populated wild mountain massifs of the Aurès and Kabylia. Separating Constantine from the desert, the Aurès is a land of savage, inhospitable grandeur with Algeria's highest peaks occasionally (and surprisingly) relieved by a few fertile strips along the floors of narrow canyons, and an occasional forest dense with scrub oak and entangling ivy. Of spring in one such oasis, El-Kantara, André Gide writes lyrically:

> the apricot trees were in bloom and humming with bees; the waters were out and irrigating the fields of barley; nothing more lovely can be imagined than the white blossoms of the apricots overshadowed by the tall palm trees, and themselves, in their turn, overshadowing and sheltering the bright tender green of the young crops. We passed two heavenly days in this paradise, and they left me no memory that is not pure and smiling.

But for the most part the Aurès is a treeless wilderness where it looks as if nothing but stone will grow. Even the shallow graves of the native Chaouias are marked only with jagged splinters of rock. The square dwellings of the villages that nestle on top of unassailable mountain spurs are built of the same ochreous stone, the only material available, and thus blend with such perfect camouflage into the natural backdrop as to be all but invisible from below. Searingly hot summers are succeeded almost immediately by the cutting winds of winter, and the Aurès has long suffered perhaps the most woeful poverty of all Algeria. Equally like the north-west frontier of India, which it closely resembles, it has from time immemorial been a land of unvanquishable guerrillas and banditry.

Kabylia in springtime is surely one of the last unspoilt, bucolic paradises of this world. Cornfields are pink and azure with wild flowers spared the tidy rapacity of English herbicides; the foothills to its rugged mountain chains blaze with saffron masses of wild broom, or are shaded by groves of smoky blue cedars or dense forests of cork and Spanish chestnut reminiscent of the hinterland of the Alpes Maritimes. Clear streams burble through poplars that sing with the loving calls of doves, or tumble forcefully through rocky gorges as savage and beetling as the floor of the Grand Canyon. Above it floats the great jagged spine of the Djurdjura, mantled with winter snows till early summer. Riddled with caves, Kabylia is ideal country equally for ambushes and for guerrillas to melt away when hunted.

In many ways it could be called the Scotland of Algeria but, in contrast to most highland or alpine countries whose villages crouch for shelter in the valleys, Kabylia's white-walled and terracotta tiled *douars* perch defiantly atop razor-backed ridges. They are a reminder of a turbulent history when safety from raiders, floods or landslides often lay in the high ground – as well as providing the traveller with one breathtaking panorama after another, since the tortuous roads follow the line of the villages. But the lyrical beauty of Kabylia is deceptive. Like so much of Algeria, it has a stern ecology. The stony outcrops are often covered but thinly with arable soil; winters are bitingly cold, and rainfall scanty and unpredictable. In relation to its fertility, Kabylia had also become the most acutely over-populated region of Algeria.

Whether it was the vast *bled* (as the French army called the outback) of desert, mountains, pasture and vineyards, or the cities and beaches, on French administrators and soldiers alike the country as a whole produced a curiously intoxicating effect. As the man who was to sign the settlement finally terminating the *présence française* there, Louis Joxe, remarked to the author: "*Algérie montait à la tête.*"

Kabyles and Arabs

The Muslim native of Algeria can trace his origin back to a multiplicity of racial and tribal stocks – Kabyle, Chaouia, M'zabite, Mauretanian blacks, Turkish and pure Arab – producing some particular and some general characteristics. The oldest inhabitants are the Berbers of Kabylia and the Aurès who, like their kinsmen in the Moroccan Atlas, fell back into the mountains under pressure from first the Roman, then the Arab, invaders. Together they comprised (in 1954) the largest proportion of the Muslim population. But probably less than a third still retained their separate identities of language and culture, the rest being rated by ethnologists as Arabised Berbers. Among themselves, the Kabyles have difficulty under-standing the dialect of their kinsmen in the nearby Aurès, and have different customs. For instance, although in contrast to the Arab women with their more sombre clothing and faces concealed behind the *haik* both the Kabyles and Chaouias traditionally walk outside without the veil, in boldly coloured *foutahs* and often wearing exquisite necklaces of silver and coral, the Chaouia woman keeps possession of her dowry and plays a force-ful role in married life; privileges which were not to be found in Kabylia. The Berbers through history have been a warlike and unruly people; as far back as 950 B.C. they are chronicled as fighting the Pharaohs on the Nile; they provided two Roman Emperors, Septimus Severus and Caracalla, and were with the vanguard of the Muslim conquest of Spain. But they tended to be as unsuccessful at ruling as being ruled. Revolt, and revenge in the Corsican fashion, were honoured occupations from time immemorial.

Like the Scots they are a people imbued with intense national and regional pride; they are not great smilers, but if you tell a Kabyle waiter in Algiers that you have been to Tizi-Ouzou, his face will explode with pleasure. Jean Amrouche, the Kabyle writer, characterises his people as swinging between extreme enthusiasm, when inspired by an idea, and an apathetic withdrawal when that idea has lost its charm.

In the past, the Kabyle and the Arab had little love for each other, and – in the best colonial tradition – it was often the policy of French administrators to set one off against the other. More orthodox in religion than the Kabyles, the Arabs were at the same time perhaps more supple in their mental processes, and shrewder businessmen. As townsmen and lowlanders they had had the most contact with French culture, and had also suffered, directly, the most in that it was largely their patrimonial lands that had come within the grasp of the *colons*. Nevertheless, at the risk of generalisation one can isolate certain "Algerian" characteristics shared by Kabyle and Arab alike. ".Here everything is rock, even the men – as if, like the land on these slopes, they were lacking in some essential grace," wrote Jules Roy, a *pied noir* deeply sensitive to the Muslim predicament. He was thinking specifically of Kabylia, but it might have applied equally to other Algerians. Like the soil, they are dour, uncompromising, sometimes harsh – and capable of extreme cruelty. In contrast with the sunny volubility of the Tunisian, the subtlety and humour of the Cairene, they are the Aberdonians of North Africa. "The Algerian mentality is characterised by the right-angle. There are no contours or compromises," explained the Algerian leader, Abderrazak Chentouf, to an American professor. *Complexe et complexé*, the Algerian is allured by ceremony, military parades and decorations (a susceptibility readily exploited by the Europeans), but at the same time antipathetic to any showy, "cult of the personality" leadership (a Bourguiba would never hold sway in Algeria). He is distrustful by nature, reluctant to place himself under the authority of another – and exceptionally secretive. The Algerian male prides himself on a sense of courteous dignity and reserve – while, in praise of the essential toughness of the Algerian woman, Jules Roy remarks: "They do not betray, nor do they forgive. More easily than one supposes, the men sell their brothers.... But not the women, who are incapable of subterfuge, except in love...." All these were characteristics that were to display themselves with emphatic relevance from 1954 onwards.

The Muslim Algerian and the *pied noir* communities were separated by a wide gulf that was at once religious, cultural and economic. Solid friendships could exist between the two but seldom matured into anything more intimate because, says Jacques Soustelle, ethnologist and future governorgeneral: "the traditional status of the Muslim woman, recluse and veiled, hindered families from getting together, from households entertaining each other." There was a fundamental divergence of orientations: when the *pied noir* went on holiday he made for the beach, and instinctively he gazed out over the Mediterranean towards Europe. In contrast, the Arab or Kabyle would head for the cool verdure of the mountains or the desert oases; he looked inland, towards the land-bound heart of Africa. Yet a number of qualities united the two peoples – at least in the eyes of metropolitan Frenchmen, or other Europeans. There was, noted a dispassionate Swiss journalist, Henri Favrod: "the same energy, the same indolence, the grandiloquence, the enthusiasm, the gambling instinct, the dressiness, the sense of hospitality, the arrogance of the male, the respect for the mother". He might have added the common temperament of passion, and indeed violence.

The pieds noirs

The diverse origins of the *pieds noirs* have already been noted. By 1917 it was estimated that only one European in five was of true French descent (and these included Corsicans and Alsatians), and in the 1950s you could still hear more Spanish than French spoken in the poorer quarters of Oran. Arriving, many of them, under the Second Empire, these Spaniards had adapted themselves readily to the climate and had proved perhaps the best workers on the land. Then there were the Italians who, like most of the Spaniards, had come with empty pockets and with little more than the hope of an Eldorado where either work or land would be readily available. They were artisans, builders, miners and fishermen. There were the Maltese who, being Catholic and speaking a language akin to Arabic, had a foot in both camps and established themselves swiftly as a class of *petits commerçants*. Of the French, apart from the Alsatians of post-1870, most came from the climatically similar Midi; especially after the phylloxera had wiped out the vineyards there. If there was one single common denominator for the *pieds noirs*, they were, in the expression coined by the French army, *mediterranéens-et-demi*. It was an important factor in understanding their motives and behaviour from 1954 onwards.

The *pieds noirs* had developed some of their own peculiar customs, some borrowed from the Muslims. There was the traditional outing on Easter Monday, a picnic centred around the ceremonial "breaking of the *mouna*", a hemispheric and sickly sweet cake scented with orange-blossom. But essentially their life and pleasures were those of the true Mediterranean being: the old women knitting and gossipping on shaded park benches, the men arguing and story-telling over the long-drawn-out *pastis* outside the bistros; the protracted silence of the siesta; then the awakening in the cool of the evening, the games of *boule* in dusty squares, under trees populated with revivified and chattering birds. It was a good life, with not too many cares. For the affluent there was the Algiers Yacht Club, the Golf Club, the Club Anglais and the Club Hippique, and skiing up at Chréa in the winter; for the *petits blancs* of Algiers there was the racecourse at Hussein-Dey and football at the Belcourt stadium. The heavy red wine of Algeria was both plentiful and cheap, and above all there was the beach. "The Outsider" of Camus, who perhaps personifies the *pied noir* mentality better than any other fictional character, describes his anguish of privation while in prison, awaiting the guillotine:

> I would suddenly be seized with a desire to go down to the beach for a swim. And merely to have imagined the sound of ripples at my feet, and then the smooth feel of the water on my body as I struck out, and the wonderful sensation of relief it gave, brought home still more cruelly the narrowness of my cell.

On the beaches nearest Algiers, the young of the poorer whites would spend their entire week-end splashing joyously in the sea, then dancing under the stars to the music of a juke-box. The slang they used – *se taper un bain*, "indulge in a swim", rather than "go for a swim" – was perhaps suggestive of the sheer sensuality of their attachment to the sea.

"I learned not to separate these creatures bursting with violent energy from the sky where their desires whirl," says Camus of his fellow *pieds noirs*. The sea and sun, these were factors that were all-conditioning, responsible for their best as well as their worst characteristics. In contrast to the Cartesian rationale in which the northern Gaul so prides himself, the meridional *pied noir* was first and foremost a creature of the senses. Everything was excess: excessive exuberance, excessive hospitality, excessive affection – and excessive hate. "Stopping to think and becoming better are out of the question," claims Camus. "The notion of hell, for instance, is merely a funny joke here. Such imaginings are allowed only to the very virtuous. And I really think that virtue is a meaningless word in all Algeria...." Under the implacable sun the *pied noir* married young and was burnt out young. For as well as nurturing and stimulating life, the sun society also caresses death. It was quite customary for a murderer – whatever the rights or wrongs of his case – to be referred to, compassionately, as "the poor fellow", and the acceptance of violence and death lay never very far beneath the surface. Among his *pieds noirs*, Camus himself was mystically aware of a "merciless *tête-à-tête* with Death, this physical fear of the animal who loves the sun". The conditions of Algerian life bestowed upon the European there a sense of mortality, of transience, which, writing even before the Second World War, Camus was able to discern in some remarkably prophetic passages:

> he is born of this country where everything is given to be taken away...
> here is a race without past, without tradition...wholly cast into its
> present lives without myths, without solace. It has put all its possessions

on this earth and therefore remains without defence against death. All the gifts of physical beauty have been lavished on it. And with them, the strange avidity that always accompanies that wealth without failure. . . .

The sentiments of the *pied noir* towards metropolitan France (for so many not their mother country at all) were compounded of resentment, love, disdain and an inferiority complex with the undertones of superiority that so often accompany it. For "The Outsider", Paris was "A dingy sort of town, to my mind. Masses of pigeons and dark courtyards. And the people have washed-out white faces." The women of Bab-el-Oued found it hard to understand how, without a "true sun", the laundry would ever dry in Paris. If the *pied noir* loved France, it was with a love that sought constant reassurance: "The French of Algeria would like to be reassured that. . ." was a theme frequently to be found in Press editorials. For his part, he felt that he had well deserved France's love through his sacrifices in two world wars. "Where is our promised land?" one of the rebel generals of 1961, Edmond Jouhaud, was to demand: "I think we have paid for the right to be French, by the blood that we shed from 1914 to 1918 and from 1939 to 1945." It was an argument with which Britons were made familiar early in the Rhodesian crisis. Perhaps because so many *pieds noirs*, or their antecedents, had come to Algeria after a *vie manquée* in Europe, there was a residual misgiving that the metropolitan Frenchman regarded him as a second-class European, and this inferiority complex could manifest itself in a display of extreme sensitivity: "the least reserve about the climate is to say that their mistress is one-eyed," comments Pierre Nora sardonically; "to permit a remark about their manner of overtaking an automobile and running over pedestrians is an insult to their virility. . . ." Again, it was an attitude that some Britons may at times have encountered in countries of the old Commonwealth, and its inversion was an isolationist, separatist sense of superiority that could vest the *pied noir* with a vastly over-inflated notion of his own weight in world councils. With a feeling of just pride the *pieds noirs* recalled that, in 1914, it was Bône and Philippe-ville that had drawn the first German naval salvoes; and, once more, Camus seems to strike a chord of utmost fidelity when, at the conclusion of *The Outsider*, he reveals that the last wish of his anti-hero was to occupy the centre of the stage: "for me to feel less lonely, all that remained was to hope that on the day of my execution there should be a huge crowd of spectators and that they should greet me with howls of execration".

At the time of the projected Blum–Viollette reforms, a *pied noir* financier remarked to Viollette: "Monsieur le Gouverneur-Général, you reason in the French of France, but we reason in the French of Algeria." It was not at all the same language, as was to become tragically plain later, and in order to understand events from 1954 onwards it is necessary to accept the existence of three totally distinct peoples – the French of France, the French of Algeria, and the Muslims of Algeria.

In the outer world, the most obvious kinsmen to the *pied noir* are the whites of South Africa, Rhodesia and the "Deep South" of the United States. In terms of the numbers of generations that had come to regard Algeria as "home", and had absolutely nowhere else in the world to go, he stood somewhere between the Afrikaaner and the Rhodesian. At the opposite ends of the social scale, comparisons in their way of life and attitudes could be made between the *grands colons* and the plantation owners of the "Old South", while the least privileged elements of Bab-el-Oued or Belcourt bore a marked affinity to the "poor whites" of Faulkner, coexisting uneasily alongside the blacks in the torrid, over-crowded American cities of the same epoch. In Algeria, however, there was no form of segregation so overt as apartheid, or "Jim Crow" laws on buses; on the other hand, there was nothing resembling the miscegenation of Brazil, or even Mozambique.

An Arab, but dressed like a person. ...

If the *pied noir* attitude to the indigenous Algerian could be summed up in a word, it was, simply, indifference. He was regarded, says Pierre Nora, "as an anonymous figure of whom it sufficed to know that one provided his welfare, so that one had no need to be concerned about him". In so far as he supplied the labour essential for exploiting the country, he was simply "a part of the *patrimoine immobilier* [real estate inheritance]". At best he would be treated with paternalism, fairness and a kind of formal acceptance of his different religion and culture. But too often he was regarded with disdain, and from a vantage of superiority; which manifested itself in many different ways, and more insidiously among the poorer levels of whites where the frictional contact was closest. *Bicot, melon, figuier, sale raton** – there was a plethora of derogatory slang for an inferior race that sprang all to readily to the lips. Equally a host of preconceived inherited notions about the Algerian were accepted uncritically, without examining either their veracity or causation: he was incorrigibly idle and incompetent; he only understood force; he was an innate criminal, and an instinctive rapist. Sexually based prejudices and fears ran deep, akin to those elsewhere of white city-dwellers surrounded by preponderant and ever-growing Negro populations: "They can see our women, we can't see theirs"; the Arab had a plurality of wives, and therefore was possibly more virile (an intolerable thought to the "Mediterranean-and-a-half"); and with the

---

* Bicot, opprobrium of unknown meaning, or origin; *melon*, slang for "a simpleton"; *figuier*, "fig tree", because the Algerian peasant allegedly spent his day sitting under its shade; *sale raton*, "dirty little rat"; hence, later, the odious expression *ratonnade*, rat-hunt, or Arab-killing (not to be confused with *ratissage*).

demographic explosion spawned by his potency, he was threatening to swamp the European by sheer weight of numbers.

The *pied noir* would habitually *tutoyer* any Muslim – a form of speech reserved for intimates, domestics or animals – and was outraged were it ever suggested that this might be a manifestation of racism. Commenting on this, Pierre Nora (admittedly a Frenchman often unduly harsh in his criticism of the *pieds noirs*), adds an illustration of a judge asking in court:

"Are there any other witnesses?"

"Yes, five; two men and three Arabs."

Or again: "It was an Arab, but dressed like a person. . . . "

With shame, Jules Roy admitted:

One thing I knew because it was told me so often, was that the Arabs belonged to a different race, one inferior to my own. . . "They don't live the way we do. . . . " The sentence drew a chaste veil over their poverty. . . . Yes, their happiness was elsewhere, rather, if you please, like the happiness of cattle . . . "They don't have the same needs we do. . . ," I was always being told. I was glad to believe it, and from that moment on their condition could not disturb me. Who suffers seeing oxen sleep on straw or eating grass?

Later on, he confesses: "It came as a great surprise to realise – little by little – that the *figuiers* were men like ourselves, that they laughed, that they wept, that they were capable of such noble sentiments as hatred or love, jealousy, or gratitude. . . . "

Even great-hearted Camus, who was among the first to expose the dreadful economic plight of the Algerians, both shortly before and after the Second World War, occasionally reveals a curious blindness, almost amounting to indifference, towards them as human beings. His Oran of *La Peste* appears to be devoid of Muslims; although he writes so sensitively (albeit often censoriously) of his kindred *pieds noirs*, his vendors selling lemonade for five *sous* a glass on the Algiers streets, his Oran shoe-shine boys ("the only men still in love with their profession") seem to be accepted as part of the essential, *touristique* backdrop, without his pausing to question the penury that must inevitably accompany the "profession" he believes them to be in love with. Again, in *The Outsider* he seems oblivious to the other victim of tragedy, the Arab girl whose lover beats her up and whose brother is killed while trying to avenge her. It is as if Camus, too, cannot be bothered to understand this "anonymous figure", this portion of the *patrimoine immobilier*.

Petits blancs and grands colons

But how difficult it is to generalise about a people so diverse as the *pieds noirs!* Apart from their mixed racial origins, they represented a wide spectrum of political hues, and the span between the top and bottom of the economic scale was even wider. At one end of the political spectrum there were the diehard conservatives, both rich and poor, some of them later to become known as "ultras", who stubbornly resisted all change; at the other end, various kinds of liberals supporting reform of one sort or another. By the 1950s, these latter were reckoned to comprise twenty to twenty-five per cent of the overall population, loosely embracing the European professional classes; these figures also include the Muslim évolués and a large section of the Jewish community. But the liberals had little or no proletarian support. Many of the *petits blancs* were failed farmers who had gravitated towards the cities, and this in itself was to grant them a collective political consciousness not to be found among the more rural settlers of Morocco and Tunisia. Like the poor whites of Rhodesia, they could not afford to be liberal, but tended to be either Communist or reactionary; and, curiously enough, these two opposing forces were largely at one, at least where liberalisation for the Muslims was concerned, as has already been noted at the time of the Sétif uprising. Between the top and bottom of the economic scale, the span was even wider. On the whole, earnings were lower than in France; perhaps as many as eighty per cent of the *pieds noirs* were merchants or salaried employees, and among them a father of three might earn less than half that of his metropolitan opposite number (on the other hand, it would buy benefits inaccessible to the latter, such as the cheap domestic services of an Algerian *fatma*). Yet the prosperity gap between very rich and very poor in France was less than that between the handful of most affluent *grands colons* of Algeria and the *petit blanc*; while between the latter and his Muslim competitor, the differential was, in contrast, extremely slender.

Who in fact were the *grands colons*, the men of power, in Algeria by 1954? Three names, Borgeaud, Schiaffino, Blachette, were the big entrepreneurs of Algeria, between them controlling the greater part of the economy, and, *pari passu*, wielding immense political power. Top of the list was Henri Borgeaud, a Swiss by origin (two generations back), a big man in his mid-fifties who looked like a jolly farmer from the Auvergne and who was proud to proclaim himself a pioneer of the soil. Centre of the Borgeaud empire was the magnificent mansion of La Trappe at Staouéli, close to Algiers, which had passed to the Borgeaud family after its founders, the Trappist monks who gave it its name, were dispossessed during France's secular "war" in 1905. La Trappe embraced 1,000 hectares of the best land in Algeria, producing regularly four million litres of wine per annum. But if wine was the chief source of the Borgeauds' fortunes, it was only one of many interests; they were major food producers, and owned Bastos cigarettes (the Gauloises of Algeria); while the name of Henri Borgeaud appeared on the boards of, *inter alia*, the Crédit Foncier d'Algérie et de Tunisie bank, the granary Moulins du Chélif, the transportation Cargos

Algériens, the Lafarge cement works, the Distillerie d'Algérie, the cork industry, the timber industry, etc., etc. Hence came the popular saying: "In Algeria, one drinks Borgeaud, smokes Borgeaud, eats Borgeaud, and banks or borrows Borgeaud...." In addition he was senator for Algiers, and had powerful allies in the form of Comte Alain de Sérigny, the conservative owner of the *Écho d'Alger*, and, at the Palais-Bourbon, the deputy Réné Mayer who headed an influential pro-*pieds noirs* lobby. The archetype of a paternalist seigneur, he apparently enjoyed the affection of many of the Muslims among his 6,000 employees, who were (relatively speaking) both well-paid and well-cared-for. But politically Borgeaud was a deep-dyed conservative. At the Evian peace negotiations in 1962, one of the F.L.N. leaders, Ben Tobbal, claimed to Favrod, the Swiss journalist: "Henri Borgeaud deserves the title of national hero. Without him and those like him, there would never have been a united Algeria."

Then there was Laurent Schiaffino, who controlled probably the biggest fortune in Algeria, including most of its shipping. Although a third-generation Neapolitan, Schiaffino revealed few of the extrovert characteristics one might have expected; with a greyish complexion, he was a cold and retiring personality with a meticulous knowledge of the marine world, but seldom seen outside family or business circles. He too was a senator for Algiers, and owner of the *Dépêche Algérienne*, which held a reputation principally for being "anti", that is to say, "anti" any measure of liberalisation. (Yet, after 1962, because of the efficiency and indispensability of his marine fleet, he was the only one of the *grands colons* to be invited to stay on by the new Algerian republic.) Third among the triumvirate of *pieds noirs* tycoons was Georges Blachette, whose family, originating from the Midi, were among the earliest pioneers of Algeria. A small, rotund figure with a delicate stomach and said to live on Evian water, Blachette was known as the "king of alfalfa". In the area south of Oran his alfalfa fields reached the horizon on every side; most of his crop was earmarked for British paper mills, and it provided the source of no less than twenty per cent of all Algeria's foreign earnings. In addition, Blachette had fingers in a number of other agricultural and industrial pies; he owned the *Journal d'Alger*, was elected deputy to the Assembly in 1951, swiftly proved himself a skilled lobbyist there, and was even considered by Mendès-France for a ministry. In contrast to Borgeaud and Schiaffino, however, Blachette set out to be a liberal and progressive. Nevertheless, it could not be overlooked that the Muslim alfalfa workers were among the most poorly paid in the country.

As a liberal – and a sincere and dedicated one – Blachette's principal ally was Jacques Chevallier. In his mid-forties, Chevallier swiftly achieved a kind of La Guardia reputation as mayor of Algiers, with his slogan of "a roof for everybody" which he had put into action by the construction of impressive numbers of low-cost housing units for the city poor. But he was to be constantly torn in his liberalism between responsibility for the Muslims and for the poorer *pieds noirs*. Also a deputy, in 1954 he accepted from Mendès-France the portfolio of Secretary of State for National Defence declined by Blachette. Finally there needs to be mentioned, briefly, among the powerful conservative adversaries of Chevallier and the liberal lobby three other figures: Raymond Laquière, President of the Algerian Assembly, a shrewd political operator, with an eroded face, utterly dedicated to European supremacy and going as far as to aspire to be leader of a separatist Algeria; Amédée Froger, mayor of Boufarik and president of the Federation of Algerian Mayors; and, finally, Comte Alain de Sérigny. A tall, nervous, fast-talking aristocrat of roughly the same age as Chevallier, de Sérigny was deeply proud of his colonial ancestry; he could trace it back to Le Moyne who had colonised Hudson Bay, and other forefathers who had fought against the Spaniards in Florida, or struck roots in Louisiana. Brought up in Algiers, he became a journalist in 1941 only after escaping from a German prisoner-of-war camp. As the fire-eating editor of the ultra-conservative *Écho d'Alger*, founded in 1912, and the most influential *pied noir* paper, he was to play an important role.

The Jews

There remains, finally, one other important minority group to be identified – the Jews of Algeria. Comprising approximately one-fifth of the non-Muslim population, they – rather like the unhappy Asians of East Africa – tended to find themselves in the tragic position of being caught between two fires: between the European and the Muslim world. Many could trace back their antecedents to the expulsions from sixteenth-century Spain; some even claimed them to pre-date the invaders who had surged out of the Arabian peninsula during the eleventh century. Thus they could argue that only relatively were they later arrivals than the Muslims. However, by 1830 the Algerian Jews had become an under-privileged community, fallen into backward squalor, and the advent of the French gave them an opportunity to improve their status. The Crémieux Decrees of 1870, conferring automatic French citizenship, attracted more prosperous Jews from outside Algeria; while at the same time they provoked a sense of unfair prejudice among Muslims. However, it was not the Muslims but the Catholic Maltese, Spanish and Italian *pieds noirs* who, at the turn of the century, launched a minor pogrom against the Jews, smashing up their shops in protest against the competition of this new class of *petits commerçants*. (Analysing the various degrees of disdain in Algeria, a *pied noir* journalist, Albert-Paul Lentin, observed how "the Frenchman despises the Spaniard, who despises the Italian, who despises the Maltese, who despises the Jew; all in turn despising the Arab." In the Second World War,

Pétain's anti-Semitic regime repealed the Crémieux Decrees, and Jewish teachers and children alike were summarily flung out of European schools; the whole community was menaced with deportation to Nazi camps.* Yet during all this time (so several Algerian Jews averred to the author), there was barely a breath of anti-Semitism from any Muslim quarter. By the 1950s the Algerian Jews were tugged in several directions; the least privileged tended still to identify themselves with the Muslims rather than the *pieds noirs*, and many were members of the Communist Party, while the wealthiest had developed distinctly Parisian orientations. Perhaps typical of the latter was Marcel Belaiche, who had inherited a large property fortune from his father; politically, however, he leaned strongly towards the liberal camps of both Chevallier and Ferhat Abbas, and away from the Borgeauds and Schiaffinos. After 1954 a significant proportion of the Jewish intellectual and professional classes was to side with the F.L.N.

* Following the Anglo-American arrival in 1942 the Pétainist measures were swiftly reversed.

CHAPTER THREE

In the Middle of the Ford

In this admirable country in which a spring without equal covers it with flowers and its light, men are suffering hunger and demanding justice.

Albert Camus, 1958

France's gift to Algeria – education

THERE was never a shortage of motives for political discontent among the Algerian Muslims to explain the Sétif explosion of 1945, but close behind them always lay equally cogent economic factors (and, associated with them, those of training and education). These were to become acutely aggravated between 1945 and 1954. Before one dissects the deficiencies, however, one needs briefly to pay tribute to the truly remarkable material achievements that France had wrought in Algeria during the course of her tenancy of a century and a quarter. Even a decade after the ending of France's rule, a visitor to Algeria could not help but be impressed by the depth of the roots her civilisation left behind; an excellent network of roads often as good in quality as those of France, and over terrain as difficult as anywhere in the world; modern railways and airfields; great cities and a score of ports; electricity and gas and a (slightly less efficient) telecommunications system. She created a medical service and imposed standards of hygiene where none had existed. In agriculture, she increased the 2,000 cultivable square miles of 1830 to 27,000 in 1954; with her capital and know-how, she dug mines and set up vast industries that would not otherwise have existed; she provided jobs in France for several hundred thousand Algerian immigrant workers, and subsidised some eighty per cent of the country's budget deficit.

Perhaps the greatest of France's gifts to Algeria, however – as elsewhere in her sprawling empire, and, indeed, anywhere caressed by her culture – was education. And yet, paradoxically, both at its strongest as at its weakest points, French education tended to bolster her opponents at France's expense. At its weakest, it was simply a matter of too few schools, too few teachers, and too little money to provide them. As far back as 1892, while the budget earmarked 2½ million francs for the schooling of European children, only 450,000 francs was allocated for the vastly more numerous and illiterate – and therefore more needy – Muslims. Over the years the situation showed little change; except that the numbers of the Muslims and their educational needs expanded ever more dramatically. By 1945, the picture was as follows:

Europeans: 200,000 children of school age at 1,400 primary schools.

Muslims: 1,250,000 children of school age at 699 primary schools.

By 1954 it was estimated that, of the Muslims, only one boy in five was attending school, and one in sixteen among girls (though in some country areas the ratio could rise as high as one in seventy); illiteracy (in French) was set at ninety-four per cent for the males, ninety-eight per cent for the females. Sometimes, also, the priorities of the funds actually spent on education looked bizarre; in 1939 Camus acidly criticised the construction in Kabylia of magnificent school buildings, costing the taxpayer up to one million francs apiece, yet seemingly designed chiefly to impress "tourists and commissions of enquiry", and which, because of lack of space, had to turn away one in every five applicants.

Excellent as was the general standard of French education, its content sometimes struck Arabs and Berbers as painfully incongruous: as for instance the history text-books beginning "Our ancestors, the Gauls. . . ." And then they were sooner or later confronted by the inevitable factor of discrimination; Ahmed Ben Bella recalls that in his childhood at Marnia he "did not feel the difference between Frenchmen and Algerians as much as I later did at Tlemcen", because in the first football teams were integrated, whereas in the latter Europeans and Muslims each had their own. The little French learning was also dangerous, in that it aroused a powerful appetite for more; and it threatened (because of economic problems) to create a class of "literate unemployed". In words that could have applied to more than just education, an old Kabyle complained sadly to Germaine Tillion: "You've led us to the middle of the ford, and there you've left us. . . ."

Furthermore, with its traditional emphasis on the grandiose liberal principles of the "Great French Revolution", French education could hardly help but divert perhaps otherwise passive minds to the nobility of revolt. M'hamed Yazid, one of the more intellectual F.L.N. leaders, notes that school heroes for his generation included Mustafa Kemal, Gandhi and the Irish rebels of the First World War. At their best, the French schools provided an admirable breeding ground for revolutionary minds. In a novel by Mourad Bourboune, *Le Mont des Genêts* (1962), a French official tells a young Muslim *évolué* that he is now too French to continue to wear a burnous, and receives the devastating reply: "It's not with you but against you that we are learning your language."

The shrinking land ...

Without schools you cannot have industrialisation and, for all French endeavours to this end, agriculture remained the mainstay of Algerian life. But, successful as French technology had been at opening up new lands by drainage or irrigation, it continued to provide a precarious living of ever-diminishing returns. As the European slice of the cake grew, so, relatively speaking, the Muslim slice shrank. Since 1830 the area of cultivable land owned by Muslims had almost doubled; but the population trebled. In 1956 Germaine Tillion reckoned that the country could feed no more than "between two and three million"; and there were then almost nine million Muslims alone. By 1954 some twenty-five per cent of all the farming land was reputedly owned by only two per cent of the total agricultural population. (Of the country's total wealth at that date, ninety per cent was accounted as held in the hands of ten per cent of the inhabitants.) With growing mechanisation and efficiency, whereas before the First World War over 200,000 *pieds noirs* lived off the land, by 1954 the figure had sunk to 93,000; and, naturally, the numbers of Muslim labourers to whom they gave employment had shrunk correspondingly. At the same time, the size of the individual European holdings had increased markedly in size. In the Department of Oran alone, 750 Europeans owned between them 55,832 hectares, while on average the vineyard of Algeria was notably larger than its French counterpart. In contrast, as a result of hereditary governances, it was not unusual to find in over-populated Kabylia one fig tree owned by several families. The statistics (from reliable French sources) relating to the average Algerian farm holding in 1954 are eloquent:

	European	Muslim
Size in hectares	123.7	11.6
Annual earnings (approx)	£2,800	£100

The creation of the Algerian wine industry, following the phylloxera catastrophe in France, had only added to the agricultural imbalance. Although it had come to account for half of Algeria's exports to France and had granted considerable economic power to the wine lobby (as personified by Senator Borgeaud), it hardly helped the economic predicament of the Muslims, providing him with but little steady work, and producing a crop which did not nourish him and offended his religion. After the Second World War acute and growing over-production set in, forcing the French treasury to intervene and subsidise surplus stocks, costing annually (according to *Le Monde* of 17 August 1955) a sum "equivalent to the total value of credits voted to Youth and Sports since 1946".

The official Maspétiol Report of 1955, which deeply shocked the French government, revealed that nearly one million Muslims (or *one in nine* of the overall population) were totally or partially unemployed, and that another two million were seriously underemployed; in the country this meant that the agricultural worker worked no more than an average of *sixty-five days* a year – or *thirty-five days* if female labour were included in the reckoning. The human consequences of these bald statistics were devastating: before the war (admittedly in a time of famine) Camus had found in Kabylia families where only two out of ten children survived; he had seen children in Tizi-Ouzou fighting with dogs for the contents of a rubbish bin, and had reckoned that at least half the population was living on nothing but grass and roots. Since then, conditions had improved, but still a large proportion of the Kabyles could not support their large families on their meagre earnings, and lived themselves in grinding poverty at subsistence level. Malnutrition induces lethargy at work, which doubtless could to a large extent explain the commonly held *pied noir* notion that the Algerian worker was, by nature, indolent and idle.

When he was able to find a day's work, the Algerian agricultural worker would often earn no more than 100 (old) francs a day (about 2s. or 22¢), and in other walks of life the prospects were not much rosier. For a Muslim average earnings throughout Algeria were estimated at 16,000 francs a year – whereas the European equivalent was 450,000 francs, or nearly thirty times as high. At the same time, the taxes he paid on his meagre pittance seemed unfairly weighted. It was reckoned that the 100,000 most impoverished Algerian families might be milked of twelve per cent of their incomes; while at the other end of the scale the 14,000 best off (of whom 10,000 were European), with incomes five times higher than the average for French families, were called upon to pay only twenty-nine per cent of earnings vastly larger than those of the Muslims. But at the same level in France they would have paid thirty-three per cent. Nevertheless, to escape from a life that held little prospect on the land, as in the poorer countries of Latin America the Algerian peasantry gravitated increasingly towards the cities. Here they found that nearly half of all available jobs in industry were firmly occupied by the *pied noir* eleven per cent, while twenty-five per cent of the urban Muslims were unemployed. The results were that during the twelve years between 1936 and 1948, as an example, the population of Algiers soared by forty-two per cent and with it the mushrooming of wretched *bidonvilles* and the simmering of new kinds of urban discontent.

The next logical haven for the agrarian jobless was France herself. The largest numbers came from Kabylia, the most overcrowded region of Algeria and where land-hunger had long been most acute; in 1912, only 5,000 Kabyles left for France; by 1924 they had risen to 100,000. But after 1945 economic adversity pushed the immigrant waves to new heights, and by the outbreak of the revolt the total of Algerian workers in France was over the half-million mark. Economically they were a godsend to

Algeria; the wages they sent home equalled about a third of those of the whole agricultural labour force in Algeria, and at home they sustained some million and a half of otherwise indigent dependents. Equally, for France they provided a source of cheap labour for the work of reconstruction in the less agreeable tasks – such as road-building, ditch-digging and rail-laying – where a Frenchman might be more choosy. But usually they were forced to live in the worst city slums of Paris or Marseilles, in family-less celibacy and dispiriting isolation in overcrowded tenement houses. Their contacts with French life would often be limited to members of the Communist Party and other disgruntled proletarian militants, so that when they returned to Algeria they brought with them seeds of more coherent discontent, awaiting germination.

... and exploding birthrate

The most ineradicable cause of all Algeria's economic woes from 1945 onwards, the factor constantly nullifying any French ideal or scheme of improving things had one simple, insoluble root: the net Muslim birthrate. At the time of the conquest the indigenous population stood at somewhere less than three million; then a combination of war, disease and disastrous famine reduced it by fifty per cent. But by 1906 it had re-established itself at 4,478,000, and from then on it began to take off, as European medical prowess made its impact. Such population inhibitors as malaria, typhoid and typhus all but disappeared; infant mortality shrank to a percentage not far from that of metropolitan France; penicillin became known as "the drug that brings children", for it stamped out venereal diseases causing sterility. According to figures cited by Robert Aron, if between 1830 and 1950 the population of France had risen at the same rate as that of Algeria, it would by then have reached more than 300 million. As it was, by 1954 the Muslim Algerians numbered nearly nine million, and were increasing in a geometrical progression. Over the previous twenty years the urban population had more than doubled, and it was reckoned that it would double again over the next twenty years – which, but for the war losses, it probably would have done.* With one of the highest net birthrates in the world, the Muslims were estimated to be breeding at *ten times* the rate of the *pieds noirs* – hence the very real basis of their fears of being demographically "swamped", for they could reasonably reckon that, within the next generation, instead of representing eleven per cent of the total population they would have shrunk to a mere five per cent. Here also, by extension, lay one of the root sources of opposition in metropolitan France to a policy of "assimilation", or "integration"; for, by the end of the twentieth century, what kind of France would there be if she were wedded

---

* The estimated Algerian population today stands somewhere short of sixteen million.

inextricably to an Algeria by now of almost equal population, and increasing more rapidly, and with equal rights and representation in all her councils?

As a summing up on how Algerians viewed the material benefits bestowed on them by France in 1944, the words of Messali Hadj strike a relevant note: "The achievement of France is self-evident. It leaps to the eyes, and it would be unjust to deny it; but if the French have done a lot, they did it for themselves." Or, phrased perhaps even more succinctly by a Frenchman, Robert Aron: "France did much for Algeria, too little for the Algerians."

France distracted

But if she stands accused of doing "too little for the Algerians", it would be only fair to consider the problems – beyond the ever-present nightmare of Algeria's demographic explosion just discussed – confronting France from 1945 onwards. The world has become so accustomed to a strong, rich and politically stable France as it was under de Gaulle that it is easy to forget the prolonged malaises of the Fourth Republic (which in so many ways resembled those of Britain of the mid-1970s); equally one forgets her quite spectacular feats of reconstructing an economy gravely mauled by war, and of uniting a broken Europe. In 1945 de Gaulle warned his countrymen that it would take "a whole generation of furious work" to resuscitate the nation, and his estimate proved to be remarkably accurate. In his *Memoirs of Hope* he describes how "a few months after victory, the State was on its feet, unity re-established, hope revived, France in her place in Europe and the world". But then, "the parties had reappeared, to all intents and purposes with the same names, the same illusions, and the same hangers-on as before. While displaying towards my person the respect which public opinion demanded, they lavished criticism on my policies." Exasperated by the wheeling and dealing identical to that which had so disastrously undermined the Third Republic during the inter-war years, on 20 January 1946 he suddenly resigned the premiership with that hauteur, just tinged with the irresponsible, which characterised both his earlier and later career. He had not, he remarked with crushing causticity to one of his ministers, liberated France "to worry about the macaroni ration".

Though, like its predecessor, the Fourth Republic was born as a consequence of military defeat by the Germans, the constitution it gave itself started with what looked like a bright enough image. Its preamble led off that: "It . . . solemnly reaffirms the rights and freedoms of man and citizen as set forth in the Declaration of Rights of 1789" and went on to declare that: "France, together with the overseas peoples, forms a Union founded upon equality of rights and of duties, without distinction of race or of religion." France would, it stressed, "never employ its forces against the liberty of any people". Yet already France was fighting the nastiest of all colonial wars, which would drag on for another eight weary and debilitating years, in Indo-China. Politically, the components of the new republic were unpromising from the very start; in the words of that highly astute American observer, Janet Flanner, it was "like a woman with three hands, two Left and one Right". The former were constituted by the Socialists and the alarmingly powerful Communist Party, the latter by the Catholic, moderate conservative Mouvement Républicain Populaire (M.R.P.). In the running conflict between these elements, "whose simultaneous presence in government", said the veteran Léon Blum, "is at once indispensable and impossible", agreement on any decisive issue could seldom be reached. As de Gaulle justly complained, the old political life of the Third Republic resumed; governments came and went, twenty of them between 1945 and 1954; M. Pleven succeeded M. Queuille, who then replaced M. Pleven, who in turn pushed out M. Queuille – all in the space of thirteen months.

Strikes endlessly paralysed the economy; many were politically motivated, others sparked off by incredibly trivial causes. One such was the strike of August 1953, set off by two postmen who inadvertently did a Watergate on an incomplete draft of a government economic project which, they noticed, appeared specifically to omit postmen. They brought out all the postal workers who, twenty-four hours later, were followed in sympathy by two million other government employees. Soon four million Frenchmen were on strike, and the country was at a standstill. In a miraculous way, year after year, the farmers and the middle-classes, as well as the very rich, somehow avoided paying taxes with impunity. Inflation ran wild, resulting in a regular devaluation of the franc. In 1951 (so Edgar Faure, premier for just two months, told the Assembly), France's cost of living rose thirty-nine per cent, compared with only twelve per cent in Britain, while spiralling prices and an overvalued currency had dragged exports down twenty per cent and pushed imports up thirty-six per cent; and there was only three days' worth of reserves left in the coffers. By 1953 prices stood at *twenty-three times* their pre-war levels, and while, on a basis of comparison with 1929, United States industrial production had doubled, Britain's had risen by fifty-four per cent,* and war-shattered Germany's by fifty-three per cent, France's had expanded by a mere eight per cent. Everything conspired to lower morale: an alarming number of Frenchmen sought refuge in acute alcoholism (which sometimes caught in its sinister embrace nine-year-old Normandy schoolchildren), and this in turn slashed at productivity.

* The reversal of situations between the Fourth Republic of 1953 and Britain of 1974 onwards is, *en passant*, instructive.

And yet, and yet, beneath the surface and beyond the bickering of the politicians, favoured by the same system of excessive centralisation that proved a bugbear in other ways (not least in the administering of Algeria), France's new technocrats – supported by bountiful Marshall Aid – were laying the foundations for her astonishing economic recovery. Under the Monnet Plan, vast hydro-electric systems and oil refineries were being built to power new industrial complexes. France's railways, electrified and modernised, were already running the fastest express services in Europe; but the maximum benefits would not be reaped until the Gaullist era of the 1960s.

On the world scene, France was fearful of Stalinist Russia and, increasingly by 1953, fearful of a more traditional enemy – a resurgent Germany. She was distrustful of her more powerful friends, Britain and Eisenhower's United States, while the pusillanimity of her divided leaders over ratifying the European Defence Community (E.D.C.) and West German rearmament maddened the inflexible John Foster Dulles. In North Africa and the Middle East she felt her position seriously undermined, first by Britain's forcing her out of her Syrian and Lebanese Mandates, and secondly by Britain's own withdrawal, first from Palestine, then Egypt; followed swiftly by the arrival of the nationalist Nasser. The protectorates of Tunisia and Morocco were already clamouring for independence. But worst of all was the predicament in which France found herself endlessly trapped in Indo-China, where the war ground on year after year and where, said de Gaulle: "the determination to win the war had alternated with the desire to make peace without anyone being able to decide between the two". The war was a running sore that had consumed over the years more than France received in Marshall Aid; that cost annually ten per cent of the national budget, that swallowed up an entire class of St Cyr officers every three years, and that by the time it ended was to account for 75,000 French casualties in dead and missing alone.

Dien Bien Phu and Mendès-France

In 1953 a new and ambitious military command embarked on a calculated risk to lure the Viet-Minh forces into a pitched battle and destroy them. The field chosen was Dien Bien Phu, a camp fortified up to almost Verdun standards; but isolated far away in the interior of North Vietnam, too close for comfort to the Chinese frontier, and tactically badly sited in a hollow overlooked by dominating hills. The French generals overestimated their capacity to supply and support the garrison by air power, and underestimated the ability of an irregular colonial guerrilla force to bring heavy artillery to bear. General Giap took up the French challenge, and for fifty-six days the defenders heroically withstood a siege accompanied by a bombardment of First World War intensity. On the eve of the ninth anniversary of V.E. Day, 7 May 1954, Dien Bien Phu fell, at a cost of some 13,000 dead among the defenders. Psychologically, there was no more devastating defeat ever inflicted on a Western regular army by a colonial "resistance movement", and it was to have far-reaching repercussions in Algeria.

The immediate consequence of Dien Bien Phu was to cause the downfall of the government of Joseph Laniel, a weaver from Calvados known to his associates as "poor Joseph" – France's twentieth premier since the Liberation. In his place there now entered a new and imposing figure – new to the front benches, though long familiar on the back benches of the Assembly as a figure in the wilderness – Pierre Mendès-France. Scion of a prosperous and old-established family of Sephardic Jews, aged only forty-seven in 1954, he had already been Under-Secretary of State for Finance under Blum in 1938, at the tender age of thirty-one. Mendès-France was an unorthodox leftish radical with an austerely cold and penetrating intellect which made him the maverick of the Fourth Republic. He had had a distinguished war record, escaping from France to join the Free French air forces, and he brought the same courage into post-war politics, refusing to curry favour or peddle alliances. Minister for Economic Affairs in de Gaulle's first government, he had been, refreshingly, the only Fourth Republic politician to resign on an issue of national policy – with the exception of François Mitterrand (who was later to become his Minister of the Interior and, still later, President of France at the head of a Socialist–Communist alliance). In the world of finance Mendès-France stood for austerity, currency reform and a controlled economy; but above all he had long stood for an end to the war in Indo-China. "If you ask me to sum up in one word my policy," he told the Chamber of Deputies, turning upside-down Clemenceau's famous bellicose utterance: "*Je ferai la paix.*"

To an astounded Chamber on 17 June he promised that within thirty-three days he would not only make peace in Indo-China but also produce an economic reform programme for France, a new political deal for the protectorates of Tunisia and Morocco where riots had been steadily worsening through the summer, and an untying of the Gordian knot of the E.D.C. If he could not deliver the goods within the appointed time, then he and his new government would resign. The following month the Geneva accords brought an end to the fighting in Indo-China. For the first time since 1939 France was at peace – but only for three months and four days. On 23 July Mendès-France and his government received an un-precedentedly overwhelming vote of confidence of 471 to 14. A week later (a Henry Kissinger ahead of his time) he flew off on a whirlwind trip to Tunisia to speed the transfer of autonomy. Though his conservative opponents growled that he was selling the empire down the river, by and large Mendès-France was – briefly – fêted in France as a national hero for his ending the "dirty war" in Indo-China; while in Algeria the moderate nationalists regarded his coming with intense hope.

Because of France's long involvement in Indo-China, wrote Mitterrand, she "would miss her European rendezvous and neglect her African mission. She had fallen into the trap." And Indo-China had been but one of the numerous factors all conspiring to avert France's gaze from Algeria in the post-war years. During that cruel summer of 1954 there were many Frenchmen who, with the insouciance of the little pigs, consoled themselves with the thought, "well, at least Algeria has remained calm!" There had, after all, been nine years of tranquillity there. But what, in fact, had been happening during this time of French preoccupation elsewhere?

Algeria after Sétif

After the ruthless crushing of the Sétif revolt in 1945, and the splintering of the Algerian nationalist factions that followed it, the *pieds noirs* found themselves in a position of supreme – but temporary – power somewhat similar to that gained by the Israelis through their crushing victory of 1967. Here was the superlative opportunity to make a generous and lasting settlement from a posture of strength; but the *pieds noirs*, like the Israelis, and from not altogether dissimilar motives, were to muff it. Shaken by the events at Sétif, the French government decided it was time to draft a new "bill of rights" for Algeria, and present the country with her first *statut organique*. For the usual reasons of the opposed forces at the Palais Bourbon, and the very diverse propositions put forward by them, the statute ended as a compromise, having nearly brought down the Ramadier cabinet. Nevertheless, on 27 August 1947 it was finally voted in by 328 to 33, with 208 abstentions – including, discouragingly, those of the fifteen Muslim deputies. The 1947 statute tabled five important reforms which the Muslims had been demanding for many years:

The suppression of the *communes mixtes*, and their replacement by democratically elected local councils.

The suppression of the military government of the Saharan territories, and their replacement by civil departments.

The recognition of Arabic as an official language alongside French.

The separation of Church and State for the Muslims, as for the other religions.

The electoral enfranchisement of Muslim women.

At the same time it abolished the system of "government by decree", replacing it with an elected Assemblée Algérienne composed of 120 members (sixty from each electoral college), with powers to modify metropolitan laws applicable to Algeria, and also to vote in the budget and finance bills.

The statute, however, still retained the inequitable double college principle,* whereby, in effect, the European minority were balanced against the entire Muslim population. It met neither the demands of the Muslim parliamentary group for sovereignty to be granted to the Algerian Assembly, with the exception of reserve rights of defence and foreign affairs; nor for the according of dual citizenship rights. During the debate, among the various heated exchanges there was one that spoke volumes about the problem of national identity of the Algerian:

M. BOUKADOUM – "Don't forget that I'm an Algerian, first and foremost!"
M. LOUVEL – "That's an admission!"
From several benches, in the centre – "You are French, first and foremost!"
M. BOUKADOUM – "I am a Muslim Algerian, first and foremost!"
M. MUSMEAUX – "If you consider the Muslim Algerians as French, give them all the rights of the French!"
M. LOUVEL – "Then let them declare that they're French."

In effect, the statute satisfied few; the Algerian deputies (as already noted) abstained; the supporters of Messali's M.T.L.D. refused even to recognise the competence of the French Assembly to legislate the statute; and the *pied noir* conservatives – Borgeaud, Laquière and their supporters – declared that national security would be threatened by opening the door to a Muslim majority in the Algerian Assembly. Nevertheless, if the statute had been enacted it would at least have represented a more important reform than anything preceding it. As it was, the *pied noir* lobby managed to block it just as they had the Blum–Viollette proposals of 1936. A procedural clause was inserted into the statute whereby its five crucial reforms would be made subject to the approval of the Algerian Assembly. Thus, so long as the *pieds noirs* maintained a majority there, these – like every other attempt at major political reform since 1909 – would never see the light of day. All that remained to be ensured was that this majority would not ever be at risk – which the *pied noir* politicians set about achieving with ruthless efficiency.

Electoral swindles

In the municipal elections of 1947 sweeping victories by Messali's followers alarmed the *pied noir* leaders. This could not be permitted on a national level. Consequently, when, in 1948, elections for the new Algerian Assembly took place as required by the 1947 statute, they turned out to be a masterpiece of rigging. There was widespread evidence of

* The first electoral college comprised all French citizens, some 500,000 eligibles (in 1954), plus a number of "meritorious" Muslims; these included recipients of higher education, civil servants, *bachagas* and *caids*, holders of the Legion of Honour and distinguished *anciens combattants*, and they then numbered 60,000. The second college embraced the eligible voters of all the remaining nine million Muslims.

"stuffing" of election boxes by "loyal" *caids* or local officials; in some villages registration cards were never issued; in others heavily armed police (sometimes supported by tanks) assumed a menacing presence, and at Dechyma, where the populace refused to vote, the *gardes mobiles* opened fire, killing seven; nationalist election meetings were broken up and numerous arrests made. At Guelma and Sétif, the two centres of revolt in 1945, the results were simply never announced. Discrepancies between the first and second run-offs, too, were suggestive; at Guelma, Messali's M.T.L.D. candidates got 6,544 on the first, and only 96 on the second; at Blida, 10,647 was reduced to 2,534. Even in France voices (not only of the Left) were raised against the electoral fraud in Algeria; in a letter of 14 April 1949 to the Minister of the Interior, one M.R.P. deputy, Fonlupt-Esperaber, reported an incident where, although voting ended at ten-thirty,

> one of my M.R.P. colleagues from Algiers was invited to leave the polling centre at 10.45, but returned there a quarter of an hour later, because it was snowing, and observed that whereas at the moment of his departure the electoral list contained only some ten entries, it contained one hundred and ninety-four on his return. Having stood in the doorway of the polling centre throughout this quarter of an hour, he avouched that no one had entered. . . .
>
> None of the officials I saw disputed for a single second that the elections in Algeria were the work of the administration. . . .

Whereas the administration had been warned in advance that, if given a free rein, the M.T.L.D. might gain ninety per cent of the Second College seats, the final figures were in fact as follows:

"Independents" (i.e. government candidates, or Beni-Oui-Ouis) 55 seats

M.T.L.D. (Messali) 9 seats

U.D.M.A. (Abbas) 8 seats

Independent Socialists 2 seats

It was a result of which a Communist bloc regime could have been proud. Naegelen, the governor-general, declared smugly: "I congratulate myself that the Algerian populations have accomplished their electoral duty in tranquillity, and I thank them . . . we are marching towards liberty and fraternity, towards ever greater democracy. . . ." "Reason", Algiers radio blared forth, "has triumphed in Algeria." Neither were views that many Algerians could endorse. M'hamed Yazid, later F.L.N. Minister of Information, claimed in a letter to the *New York Times* of 1958 that when he was standing for election in 1948, "more than thirty of us were arrested during the electoral campaign and put into jail for years. A look at the list of those then jailed will give you an approximate list of the actual leadership of the Algerian revolution today." Even the most pro-French among the Algerian *évolués* was profoundly shocked by the blatancy of the electoral fraud. But the technique was to be improved upon by the next elections for the Algerian Assembly and the National Assembly, in 1951. At Djelfa neither the M.T.L.D. nor U.D.M.A. collected a single vote; while the government candidate managed to tot up 800 – out of 500 eligible voters! At Port-Gueydon 23,671 votes were cast; 23,645 registered for the government candidate. As a result, the opponents of the regime were reduced in Algiers to no more than seven or eight; in Paris the M.T.L.D. and U.D.M.A. between them were deprived of every single representative – including Ferhat Abbas.

"The rigging of the elections of the Second College has become a byword in Algeria," deplored a correspondent of Le Monde normally sympathetic to the regime: "Today, even the most évolué of Algerian nationalists will say to you: 'These elections are a farce. If you consider us incapable of voting, then why not admit it openly...?'"

Said Ahmed Boumendjel, the distinguished liberal leader from Constantine:

> It is a question of contempt, and beyond this the oppression of the mass of our people; that is what is impossible for us to tolerate. Why should we feel ourselves bound by the principles of French moral values... when France herself refuses to be subject to them and to accept the essential rules?

"The French Republic has cheated," he declared bitterly, "she has made fools of us." For liberals like Boumendjel and Abbas these were bitterly frustrating experiences. Combined with the emasculation of the 1947 statute, the electoral frauds marked an important stage in the crystallising of Muslim rage; it also meant that, after 1954, when any French leader talked about offers of "free elections" no Muslim would believe him.

The attitude of the average pied noir was one of thankfulness that the feared and disliked statute had been nullified, and that the Muslims had accepted the electoral results with such apparent passivity. "Rid of their psychosis about civil war," says Professor Charles-André Julien, they returned to their traditional concepts of colonial Algeria: "little by little the liberal achievements of Governor Chataigneau crumbled; the municipal centres stagnated;... projects in rural communes were abandoned; the rehousing of fellahs was considered to have been finished... even education ...suffered from a dearth of credits...." Not every pied noir leader, however, was quite so short-sighted at this time. Liberals like Jacques Chevallier foresaw a grave danger that French tactics would force the Muslims "to attempt to unite themselves in a kind of policy of the worst, and to push them into compromising themselves in a desperate gesture." To do something about it, to attempt to see the 1947 statute loyally and properly enacted, Chevallier himself resigned his mandate in Paris to take a seat in the Algerian Assembly in 1951. From then on, until November

1954, this body under Chevallier's influence began to assume a more hopefully liberal aspect; but it moved too slowly – and too late (though Germaine Tillion believes that even if, by 1 November 1954, genuine elections could have been held in Algeria, "they probably could have spared us a long and cruel war"). Writing in 1953, Professor Julien warned prophetically: "It is by closing the normal paths of legality to a mass of eight million people that one risks driving it back into the arms of the declared adversaries of *la présence française*, who aim to solve the Algerian problem by violence."

Nationalism after Sétif

The reasons for the apparent political torpor of the Algerian Muslims, which gave the *pieds noirs* such a false sense of complacency over the long nine years of deceptive tranquillity, can be traced back to the aftermath of Sétif. The nationalist movements were virtually decapitated by the seizure of their leaders – Messali Hadj deported to the French Congo, Ferhat Abbas under house arrest. Messali's M.T.L.D. in particular had been disrupted by French repression, and all groups were more disunited than ever before, with the liberals fiercely reproaching the M.T.L.D. for their role in the disastrous revolt of 1945. (To this day, Abbas believes that Messali, in collusion with the colonial police, instigated it with the aim of destroying the unity achieved by his Amis du Manifeste et de la Liberté created the previous year.) Released in March 1946, Abbas had launched a new, more coherent party called the Union Démocratique pour le Manifeste Algérien (U.D.M.A.), but otherwise he resumed his moderate policies very much as before: "Neither force nor base submission", he declared, addressing Muslim youth, "will bring a veritable solution." Elected to the National Assembly, he was shocked by the lack of understanding, and often sheer racial arrogance, that he and his fellow Muslim deputies encountered there. During one particularly stormy, and deplorable, session in August 1946 Abbas rose with great dignity to state: "It is a hundred and sixteen years that we have been awaiting this moment, that is to say the opportunity of being here and making ourselves heard among you.... Therefore, have patience, I ask and beg of you.... We are but a very small minority. Be generous...!"* But, as the preceding pages have shown, France could not, the *pieds noirs* would not, be sufficiently generous. As rage succeeded

---

* Early in this debate one of Abbas's fellow deputies had declared: "You showed us the way, you gave us the taste of liberty, and now when we say that we wish to be free, to be men – no more and no less – you deny us the right to take over your own formulas. You are Frenchmen, and yet you are surprised that some of us should seek independence." After this eloquent plea, he had been brought to order by the President of the Chamber in this contumelious fashion: "Monsieur Saadane, I have already reminded you that you are at the French tribune. I now invite you to speak in French there...."

frustration with the sabotaging of the 1947 statute, so the support for Abbas and his liberals began to slip away, and Abbas himself was forced to move steadily to a less moderate position. The returning war heroes who had fought so fiercely under Marshal Juin were particularly disillusioned to discover how little things had changed at home after all they had seen and learnt in the outside world. Many gravitated towards the more extreme doctrines of Messali, and began to clamour for yet more direct action than even the M.T.L.D. was proposing. A new post-war generation was emerging that had acquired some knowledge of Marxist revolutionary techniques; that was impatient with interminable political dialogues, meaningless manifestos and unfulfilled promises; that respected strength and force, and that, in short, would not flinch from violence.

Ben Bella and the O.S.

One of these new figures was a strongly-built young Arab called Ahmed Ben Bella. He was born at Marnia, west of Oran, in 1918 of a father engaged in petty commerce who also owned a small farm. His oldest brother died of wounds suffered in 1914–1918, and his two other brothers died at early ages. Although, as already noted, Ben Bella first became aware of racial discrimination at secondary school, this did not inhibit him from joining up – twice – with the French army. In the 1940 campaign he was awarded the Croix de Guerre. Demobilised after the fall of France, he rejoined a Moroccan regiment to fight at Monte Cassino and all through the Italian campaign, where, rising to the rank of warrant officer, he had the Médaille Militaire pinned on his chest personally by de Gaulle, who little knew that he was decorating the man who would become one of the initiators of revolt against France and the first president of an independent Algeria. During this campaign Ben Bella had contact with the Italian resistance, for whom he formed lasting admiration. On returning to North Africa in 1945 news of Sétif so shocked him that he refused to accept a commission, and instead entered local politics, running successfully as a municipal councillor. There now follows a confused episode, related by Ben Bella himself, in which the administration attempted to neutralise him by means of a "plot" involving another Muslim set up to confiscate the farm Ben Bella's father had left him. In protecting this property, Ben Bella got into a shooting match and wounded his adversary. This, he claims, forced him to abandon his office as municipal councillor, assume a false name and go underground with Messali's M.T.L.D. as a "clandestine militant". Disgusted with its unproductive dialectics and outraged by the administration's electoral frauds, Ben Bella soon became one of the founder members of a new splinter group inside the M.T.L.D. called the Organisation Spéciale – or O.S. Pledged to fight colonialism "by all means", legal or illegal, the O.S. was in effect the first nationalist body dedicated to preparing for an armed confrontation with France – now considered inevitable – and thereby it became the immediate predecessor of the F.L.N.

By 1949 Ben Bella had emerged as the most forceful leader of the O.S., and, together with a twenty-six-year-old Kabyle called Ait Ahmed, organised its first major coup: an armed raid on the central post office of Oran. Amateurishly mounted, the raid netted a sum of three million francs (little more than £3,000), while leaving ten times this amount scattered on the floor; nevertheless, this modest booty provided the future F.L.N. with its first operational funds. But although it was constructed on a system of watertight compartments that was to be successfully emulated later by the F.L.N., the security of the O.S. was poor and French intelligence efficient. The following year Ben Bella was arrested and sentenced to eight years' imprisonment. By this time O.S. membership numbered some 4,500, and many of those who escaped imprisonment either fled abroad or formed the nucleus of a growing maquis in the more inaccessible parts of the country. Some of the names are worth mentioning, as all were to reappear later as founder leaders of the F.L.N.:

Ahmed Ben Bella: *imprisoned, subsequently escaped.*
Ali Mahsas: *imprisoned, subsequently escaped.*
Mostefa Ben Boulaid: *imprisoned subsequently escaped.*
Belkacem Krim: *underground in Algeria.*
Omar Ouamrane: *underground in Algeria.*
Lakhdar Ben Tobbal: *underground in Algeria.*
Mohamed Boudiaf: *underground in Algeria.*
Mohamed Khider: *in refuge in Cairo.*
Hocine Ait Ahmed: *in refuge in Cairo.*

As an organisation, however, the O.S. was effectively broken up by the French police action. Ben Bella himself, together with another member of the O.S., Ali Mahsas, managed to escape from Blida prison after sawing through the bars of their cell with a blade hidden, romantically, in a loaf of bread. He made his way to Tunisia, France – and finally to Cairo. In Tunisia he confided to the then outlawed nationalist leader, Habib Bourguiba, that his Algerian counterparts had still not yet recovered from Sétif, and were in no position to embark on full-scale armed revolt.

Fresh splits among the nationalists

In reaction to the electoral frauds of 1951, all the nationalist parties – U.D.M.A., M.T.L.D., the Ulema – joined by the Algerian Communist Party, had come together to constitute a "Common Front for the Defence and Respect of Liberty". It was promptly branded by the *pieds noirs* as a threat of "Communist totalitarian fanaticism", but in fact it represented little more than yet another ephemeral papering-over of differences. For the liquidation of the O.S. was to cause the gravest split to date among the ranks of the Algerian nationalists: straight down the centre of the M.T.L.D. itself. A group of young intellectuals, headed by Hocine Lahouel and calling themselves "centralists", decided to break away from the leadership of "El-Zaim", the "unique", as Messali was then venerated. Once again Messali himself was in exile, this time in France, as a consequence of the O.S. round-up; he was beginning to show his age and was able to do little effectively to prevent the split. In the summer of 1954 the "centralists" declared their intention of creating yet another new nationalist party, to be called the National Algerian Congress, from which El-Zaim would be expressly barred; all of which was accompanied by a spate of internecine killings between the two rival groups. Meanwhile, the *pied noir* leaders rejoiced to observe this further disarray among the Muslims, resuming their habitual complacency with little heed to the warnings of Chevallier and other prophets without honour. A point of no return, however, had now been reached by the Algerian revolutionaries.

The dispersed leaders of the O.S. soon appreciated angrily that this new schism within the M.T.L.D. could only postpone still further the day of armed revolt. In March 1954 Ben Bella's fellow escapee, Ali Mahsas, met furtively at a café near the Odéon in Paris with Mohamed Boudiaf, then head of the M.T.L.D. in France, plus his deputy, a young Arab called Mourad Didouche. They agreed that it was essential to create, without delay, a new "third force" that would have armed revolt as its sole objective. That night Boudiaf and Didouche flew back to Algeria to get things under way there; Mahsas remained in France to organise the 60,000 M.T.L.D. supporters among the Algerian immigrants round Paris. Through the summer of 1954 and into the early autumn there now followed a series of frequent conspiratorial meetings, in France, Algeria and Berne. Because of its proximity to France, its removal from the vigilant eyes of the French security services (D.S.T.) and the ease with which Ben Bella and the outlaws from Cairo could fly there, Swiss territory was to play an important role in rebel preparations – as indeed it was to do in the final act of the war. One of the most historic meetings, in July 1954, was held in Berne under cover of the Germany–Hungary World Cup.

The "neuf historiques"

By the end of April the new body had given itself a name, a rather ponderous title of the Comité Révolutionnaire d'Unité et d'Action – C.R.U.A. It also appointed nine leaders – known henceforth as the *neuf historiques* – to head the C.R.U.A. They were:

Hocine Ait Ahmed
Ahmed Ben Bella
Mostefa Ben Boulaid
Larbi Ben M'hidi

IN THE MIDDLE OF THE FORD

Rabah Bitat
Mohamed Boudiaf
Mourad Didouche
Mohamed Khider
Belkacem Krim

In 1954 the average age of these *neuf historiques* was thirty-two (Didouche, the youngest, was only twenty-seven); they originated from all parts of Algeria; all were literate, though they came mostly from modestly-off artisan or middle-class families. None was an *évolué* intellectual, or liberal – let alone a supporter of Ferhat Abbas. All were dedicated revolutionaries, holding violence to be indispensable. Ben Boulaid was a miller from the Aurès with seven children who, like Ben Bella, had been a much decorated warrant officer in the Italian campaign; Ait Ahmed, aged thirty-three, was the son of a Kabyle *caid*; his brother-in-law, Khider, had been a deputy for Algiers from 1946; Boudiaf, from the south Constantine area and, at thirty-five, one of the oldest, had had his schooling cut short by chronic tuberculosis.

Krim

Though Boudiaf in the initial stages seems to have been the moving force behind the C.R.U.A. together with Ben Bella, it was Belkacem Krim who was perhaps the most outstanding figure at this time – if for no other reason than that he was the only one to bring with him an operational maquis already in being – and in the key region of Kabylia. He was the only one of the nine to survive the whole war, alive and at liberty, while always holding a high office in revolutionary councils. Born in 1922, Krim was a Kabyle from the Dra-El-Mizan area who had served in the wartime army as nothing more than a corporal-quartermaster, but had become an excellent shot. Earlier, in his school days, he already noted resentment at having to write down the names of his European colleagues in blue, Muslims in red, and later complained: "My brother returned from Europe with medals and frost-bitten feet! There everyone was equal. Why not here?" On demobilisation Krim broke with his father, who was a retired *caid* well-trusted by the authorities, and joined the M.T.L.D. After the arrest of fourteen nationalists, of whom he was to have been the fifteenth, Krim organised a sit-down strike outside the local administrator's office. He describes himself at this time as belonging "to that Algerian generation which passed from the total innocence of childhood into the maturity of the man". In March 1947 he was summoned to appear in court and, rather than face the prospects of a prison sentence, he took off, armed with an old Sten gun, into the maquis in the wild mountains of Kabylia. He was then aged twenty-five. Later that same year he "executed" a Muslim *garde-champêtre*, or village constable, and from that time on he became a much-wanted outlaw, with four separate death sentences imposed on him *in absentia.*

At an early stage Krim was joined in the maquis by Omar Ouamrane, another Kabyle three years his senior and a former sergeant who had served in the same Tirailleur regiment as Krim. Of immense physical strength and with a vast jaw, Ouamrane throughout the war was to be Krim's inseparable chief lieutenant. Starting from a small handful of men, the Krim–Ouamrane maquis could, by 1954, claim some 500 at least partially armed members, with a further 1,200 *militants* standing by. A small man with flabby features and blubbery lips, and often photographed in an impeccable city suit, Krim himself could have passed more readily as an urban mafioso than as the tough, long-seasoned maquisard that he was – indeed, the only one of the *neuf historiques* with so extensive an experience of this kind.

During the spring of 1954 Krim and Ben Boulaid, the maquis leader of the ever-turbulent Aurès, both agreed to bring their groups to participate in a general revolt. A first full meeting of the C.R.U.A., attended in Algiers by Krim with the faithful Ouamrane (and with a heavy price on his head), provoked a certain amount of acrimony. Krim, smarting some-what from the preponderance of Arabs over Kabyles within the C.R.U.A., yet knowing also that he had control over the most effective insurrectionary body already in existence, refused point-blank to submit to the orders of any commander located in Algiers. After some heated discussion it was agreed that Kabylia should be an autonomous operational zone.

The C.R.U.A. had thus managed to bridge at this first session the previously disastrous animosity between Arab and Kabyle. Yet it marked the seeds of dissension within the revolutionary camp that were to dog it incessantly through the war, and beyond. At the same time it was to have its bearing on the supreme leadership of the revolutionaries. The *neuf historiques*, deeply admiring of Ho Chi Minh at that time, would have liked initially to appoint from their ranks a similarly prestigious figure to head them; but, while there was no candidate of obviously oustanding stature, to have selected either an Arab or a Kabyle might have run the grave risk of alienating one or other race. Thus the principle of collective leadership was adopted right from the beginning, and it was to constitute a vitally important feature of the revolution all the way through to 1962.

"Arm, train and prepare!"

By historic chance, this first full meeting of the C.R.U.A. took place the day that the fall of Dien Bien Phu was announced. The impact on the Algerians, many of whose kinsmen had been fighting alongside the French in the besieged camp, was electric. Employing subtlest techniques of psychological warfare, the Viet-Minh suggestively quizzed the Algerians captured there: "Since you are such good soldiers, why do you fight for the colonialists? Why don't you fight for yourselves and get yourselves a country of your own?" Suddenly this unbelievable defeat deprived the glorious French army of its *baraka*, making it look curiously mortal for the first time. Wild rumours exaggerating the defeat began immediately to take root at home in Algeria, greatly facilitating the C.R.U.A.'s work of recruitment; the well-informed J.-R. Tournoux cites a Muslim public employee declaring shortly before the outbreak of the revolt: "We were told that there was no longer any French army; that it had been destroyed in Indo-China." With this windfall, the "Nine" decided to expedite the day of the revolt at top speed, so as to catch the French government at its moment of greatest weakness. In July* a wider plenary meeting took place at the Clos Salembier, outside Algiers, comprising the C.R.U.A. plus the leading revolutionary operatives from all over Algeria, calling themselves "The Committee of the Twenty-two". Here a crucial political decision was taken by unanimous vote: the armed revolt under preparation would *not* be one single blow aimed at drawing concessions from France, but an "unlimited revolution" *à outrance* to continue until full independence was achieved.

Orders were now despatched through the underground Algerian grapevine: "Arm, train and prepare!" In Cairo, Ben Bella and his two colleagues were instructed to apply urgent pressure upon the pan-Arabist Nasser regime for maximum support in arms and propaganda. On 10 October the new revolutionary movement received its name; Front de Libération Nationale – F.L.N. That same day a date was fixed for the simultaneous outbreak of revolt all through Algeria: "00.01 hours on 1 November" – All Saints' Day.

* The exact date of this historic meeting is curiously imprecise, with different accounts putting it variously at 10, 21, 22, 25 and 27 July – or even early June. The discrepancy of memories here is in itself one indication of the difficulties of historical accuracy that historians encounter when dealing with the war as a whole.

PART TWO

The War

1954 — 1958

We had been told, on leaving our native soil, that we were going to defend the sacred rights conferred on us by so many of our citizens settled overseas, so many years of our presence, so many benefits brought by us to populations in need of our assistance and our civilisation.

We were able to verify that all this was true, and, because it was true, we did not hesitate to shed our quota of blood, to sacrifice our youth and our hopes. We regretted nothing, but whereas we over here are inspired by this frame of mind, I am told that in Rome factions and conspiracies are rife, that treachery flourishes, and that many people in their uncertainty and confusion lend a ready ear to the dire temptations of relinquishment.... Make haste to reassure me, I beg you, and tell me that our fellow-citizens understand us, support us and protect us as we ourselves are protecting the glory of the Empire.

If it should be otherwise, if we should have to leave our bleached bones on these desert sands in vain, then beware of the anger of the Legions!

Marcus Flavinius, centurion of the Augusta Legion,
quoted by Jean Lartéguy in *The Centurions*

CHAPTER FOUR

All Saints' Day, 1954

This sad day... for Frenchmen who refuse to understand, for Kabyles who refuse to explain....

Mouloud Feraoun, *Journal 1955–62*

C.R.U.A. *finalises its plans*

THE choice of All Saints' Day for launching the revolt was by no means fortuitous. Striking on a night when the staunchly Catholic *pieds noirs* were celebrating so important a festival would, it was argued, find police vigilance at its minimum; while the choice of such a date would carry with it the maximum propaganda impact. For a people as fond of symbolism as the Algerians, and with memories of Sétif still etched in their minds, the fact that All Saints commemorated the persecution of the early Christian martyrs was also not without significance.

It was with a similar mixture of care and method that the C.R.U.A. finalised its plans, borrowing organisationally from the experiences of both the French wartime resistance and, more recently, the Viet-Minh. The country was divided into six autonomous zones or Wilayas, giving the rebellion an integral structure that it would retain over the next seven and a half years. Operation groups would be formed in watertight compartments, with no more than four or five trusted men knowing each other. On D-Day each group leader was to act in accordance with a very precise plan, and attacks were to be directed against specific public installations, private property of the *grands colons*, French military personnel and gendarmes, and Muslim collaborators. European civilians – especially women and children – were to be strictly immune; there would be no repetition of Sétif. General tactical instructions to be observed went as follows: "After a *coup de main*, if it's not possible to disengage at once, hold until the arrival of reinforcements. Popularise the movement. Keep yourself informed!" and, above all: "Never accept frontal combat!" To realise its pledge that this would be no isolated blow, but the opening of a sustained revolt, greatly exacerbated the already massive triple problems of recruitment, arms and finance that confronted the C.R.U.A. leadership. For fear of alerting the French authorities it had to pursue its recruitment propaganda with the utmost discretion, creating a climate of revolt by

83

burrowing away at such essentially negative issues as agrarian discontent. Yet somehow, with the miraculous efficacy of the *téléphone arabe*, the word ran through the cafés of the Casbah to the outer fringes of the *bled* that a revolt was afoot. Enlistment of the first F.L.N. *djounoud*,* however, proceeded slowly; the prevailing attitude being cautiously one of wait and see – would the revolt succeed, or would it be instantaneously and mercilessly crushed?

Yet another obstacle was bitter opposition equally from Lahouel's and Messali's factions of the M.T.L.D. Soon after the creation of the breakaway C.R.U.A., Bitat and Boudiaf were both beaten up by the Messalists and retaliated with a violent assault on the M.T.L.D. headquarters. Warning his members against being drawn into the C.R.U.A. "slaughterhouse", Lahouel had considerable success in Algiers – with the result that, when D-Day came, Bitat, the local leader, found himself having to rely extensively on Krim's maquisards imported from Kabylia.

The provision of arms was even more critical. A network of bomb factories was set up in the Casbah and at Souma, thirty miles outside the capital, under the supervision of Zoubir Bouadjadj, the chief of the Algiers area. Bouadjadj was a dedicated terrorist from the first, with a bitter hatred for the French; his father had died as a consequence of being gassed on the Western Front, his mother had lived in miserable poverty as a laundress, and at the age of ten he had been arrested on a trifling charge of stealing photographs. The episode, he claimed, had nearly broken his mother's heart, and from that moment he never looked back; already by 1942, when he was seventeen, he was distributing illegal tracts for the P.P.A. Bouadjadj's first factories started fabricating a series of primitive devices from black powder and sodium chlorate, encased in sections of iron piping or empty Esso oil tins. Among several early disappointments, one bright young student, introduced by Bouadjadj as an expert on nitro-glycerine, managed to distil barely a glassful of the lethal explosive, while wasting vast quantities of raw material.

Under the nose of the French police, immense risks were run daily in smuggling firearms to various assembly points in readiness for All Saints. A miscellany of weapons from the Second World War – German Mausers, pistols abandoned by the Vichy French, equipment collected from careless Americans and stored in caves round Oran since the 1942 landings – trickled in. But the largest part of the initial arsenal consisted of sporting guns of uncertain antiquity and accuracy. Ben Bella claimed that the F.L.N. started the revolt with only 350 to 400 miscellaneous firearms, and virtually nothing heavier than a machine-gun. Not a weapon, it is worth noting, at this stage or for several years to come, was provided by the Communist bloc; nor was more than a modest quantity of guns acquired

---

* The Algerian word for soldiers (singular *Djoundi*).

elsewhere abroad with the F.L.N.'s slender funds. Thus, from the very beginning the theft of French arms from depots or their recovery on the battlefield became a prime military objective.

Nasser disappoints

One of the F.L.N.'s bitterest early disappointments lay in the failure of Nasser's Egypt to come forth with material aid. As the great exponent of pan-Arabism, the man who had kicked the still powerful British out of the Suez Canal zone and whose Cairo radio beamed a constant flow of anti-colonialist propaganda at the Maghreb, Nasser had aroused the most fervent hopes among the revolutionaries. All sides alike were taken in. Jacques Soustelle, writing as late as 1957, still insisted that the original impetus for the revolt came from Cairo, that the explosion was caused by the conjunction of "two inert chemicals... Egyptian pan-Arabism and Algerian terrorism"; it was a notion that would die hard and exert a fundamental, and disastrous, influence over the Suez operation of 1956. Meanwhile, in the immediate aftermath of the revolt, many a simple Auresian hillman, having heard Egypt's "Voice of the Arabs" promise extravagantly to "offer her sons in holocaust for the Arabs of the whole world", was convinced that a legendary Egyptian army of 70,000 green-clad horsemen was imminently coming to the rescue. The truth was quite otherwise. The Algerian delegation to the "exterior" had a powerful triumvirate from the C.R.U.A. "nine" – Ben Bella, Ait Ahmed and Khider – based in Cairo, but it was dogged from the beginning by personal quarrels and disputes. Partly it was a matter of communication; Ben Bella was aggravated by having to express himself in French because the Egyptians were unable to understand his Arabic. Eternally offering money and arms, when it came to the crunch the Egyptians temporised, their line being "Start the revolution first... then aid will follow."

French suspicions

Meanwhile, as preparations for All Saints inched forward through every obstacle, the French administration was beginning to form a menacingly accurate picture. As early as April 1954, the office of the governor-general, Roger Léonard, received a tip-off from an informer about the formation of C.R.U.A.; but it appears to have been filed away in some forgotten drawer. In August, Ferhat Abbas was received in Paris by Premier Mendès-France – thereby establishing a hopeful precedent for an Algerian nationalist leader – at which time he issued a clear warning that, if the 1947 statute was not applied "without fraud, and with the minimum delay", then the Algerian liberals like himself would be "swept away" by events. In Algiers, a steady flow of disquieting intelligence was reaching the competent director of the Sûreté, Jean Vaujour, including a list of camps inside

Libya where Algerian guerrillas were being trained. During the course of the summer he too visited Paris, with the aim of obtaining a direct audience with Mendès-France or his Minister of the Interior, Mitterrand. But as it was the holiday season he was fobbed off with minor functionaries, who listened with apathetic disbelief when he warned them "if Algeria moves it will be in December". By October Vaujour knew the whereabouts of the main bomb depot in the Casbah (which already contained some two hundred complete bombs). Momentarily he toyed with the idea of getting a double agent to plant a bomb detonating the stock, but was deterred by the loss of life that this would inevitably cause in so crowded a quarter. Instead he decided to shadow the bomb manufacturers in the hopes that they might lead him to the rest of the group. By mid-October French intelligence had identified Ben Bella as "leader" of the coming revolt (an exaggeration that was to have many a distortive effect on future French policy), but Vaujour had still no clue as to the identity of the C.R.U.A. members in Algeria.

Léonard, the governor-general, who during the Vichy era had been sacked by Pétain as head of the gendarmerie for courageously refusing to take action against Georges Mandel, was essentially an administrator rather than a man of action and known for his calm (it might almost have been called placid) temperament. Neither he nor the French army command took the various warnings seriously until some ten days before the revolt broke out. At a top-level conference convened by Vaujour at Constantine on 29 October, just two days before All Saints, one French colonel, when told that a hundred armed *fellagha* had been spotted in the Aurès exclaimed contemptuously: "*Monsieur le Préfet*, I've been patrolling the roads for a very long time, and I've never yet seen a *fellagha* in front of my jeep!" It was not likely that he would have done; Ben Boulaid's men were hardly moving along the highways. Even Vaujour himself, however, did not believe until after the *dies irae* that a general revolt was in the offing. Among the highest echelons of the French government the first person to register serious disquiet seems to have been François Mitterrand, the minister directly responsible for Algeria. Soon after assumption of office that June he had given voice to premonitions: "I sense something . . . the situation is unhealthy." Several trips to Algeria, culminating in a visit on 19 October after Orléansville had been shattered by a devastating earthquake, had confirmed this nervousness. Laquière, the ultra-conservative president of the Algerian Assembly, had done his best to reassure Mitterrand that all was quiet, but a warning from Vaujour that something was going to happen "within three weeks or a month" rang in his ears. Yet, curiously enough, Mitterrand seems to have done singularly little to act on his fears when returning to Paris on the 23rd, even though this coincided with a long report to the government from Léonard, expressing for the first time grave concerns by an official hitherto distinguished by his imperturbability. Certainly nothing was done to place security forces in Algeria on an emergency footing. The only minister to act positively on Léonard's letter seems to have been Jacques Chevallier, the *pied noir* Secretary of State for Defence and former Mayor of Algiers, who telephoned Mendès-France to announce: "I'm going to take advantage of the long week-end of 1 November to go to Algeria. The news is bad, and I'm going to see on the spot what is happening."

On the brink

During these last days of October a kind a tense game of "grandmother's footsteps" was played out in Algeria, with the F.L.N. completing its last preparations and French intelligence gradually catching up on their tracks – the net closing in all the time. One last, totally unexpected, hitch came with the Orléansville earthquake which, killing 1,400 people, disrupted Ben M'hidi's organisation in Oranie, where the F.L.N. were already at their weakest. On 24 October, the Sunday before All Saints, the six leaders of the C.R.U.A. still in Algeria held a valedictory meeting together, to check through operational orders once again and to vet the wording of a proclamation to be disseminated on 1 November. On leaving they went into a Bab-el-Oued photographer, each emerging with a still-moist print of a group photo in his pocket. It was an uncharacteristic breach of their previously impeccable security, as well as being perhaps a strange display of vanity; yet no copy was ever to find its way into French hands. Inept and under-exposed as it is the photograph is an historic document. With their ill-fitting clothes and awkward poses the six – only two of whom were to survive the war and its aftermath – look somehow more like the over-earnest members of a local darts team, or parish council, than hardened revolutionaries about to plunge two peoples into seven and a half years of war and, in the course of it, bring the mighty French republic crashing. Trying to divine the thoughts of the men posing there, one wonders how many genuinely reckoned that their actions, backed by such slender means, would ultimately lead to an independent Algeria; and how many would have persisted had they been able to foresee the length and immense difficulties of the struggle, let alone the terrible sacrifices it was going to impose on their fellow countrymen.

In France, all insouciant, a spate of "flying saucers" had provoked a deputy to ask the Secretary of State for Air what he was doing about them; Dérain had died at 74, after being knocked off his bicycle by a car, and Matisse was on his death-bed. The literary salons, while they mourned the death of Colette, were still chattering about the exciting first novel called *Bonjour Tristesse* by an eighteen-year-old girl; and about the Nobel Prize awarded Ernest Hemingway. Otherwise thoughts were preoccupied with

Emperor Haile Selassie's impending visit to Paris, and Mendès-France's to Canada and the United States; with the American congressional elections, and the London–Paris agreements rearming West Germany. In Britain – an unusual state of affairs – the dockers were about to go on strike.

On the eve of All Saints, Vaujour in Algeria received from the Deuxième Bureau the first example of an F.L.N. bomb, a crude device encased in a tin of jam. All day he had toyed with it in his office at the Gouverne-ment-Géneral, wondering whether he should not, after all, have laid hands on the bomb factory pin-pointed in the Casbah, but finally procrastinating. At Teniet-el-Abd, a small village in the Aurès, Jean Servier, a thirty-six-year-old ethnologist very popular in the area, received the last of a series of warnings to get out. While he was recording the songs of a blind singer, he was warned by a friendly caid: "It's going to be tomorrow." Just in case they might be a target of attack, all French schoolteachers were also ordered out of the Aurès. Only two could not be reached, a young couple called Monnerot, who were returning from their honeymoon sightseeing in a bus somewhere between Biskra and Arris.

The Aurès, 30 October

Already the first cutting winds of winter were whistling through the bleak mountains of the Aurès, causing the shepherds to huddle deeper into their thick, dun-coloured *cachabias*, which, like their rock-built villages, afford so immaculate a camouflage against the natural backdrop. To the casual visitor it seems a region almost devoid of humanity; and yet, from the valley-bound roads, one is conscious of every movement being observed by a thousand eyes in the invisible villages above. Each one is like a watch-tower, ideal for providing advance warning of the approach of an enemy or a policeman in a country where the *bandit d'honneur* and the partisan have been honoured since before Roman times. On the plains fringing the Aurès, at Timgad and Lambesis, the Romans built splendid great cities, the glories of which still remain; their legions made frequent punitive forays into the turbulent massif but they never attempted any permanent occupation. Over the centuries the Chaouias managed to keep their own language, customs and beliefs, and to resist all attempts at assimilation. The various tribes habitually lived in a state of bloody, Corsican-style vendetta with each other, but would unite when threatened by an outside force. They would complain to the administration at its failure to protect them from banditry; yet, at the same time, they would as a matter of principle not denounce a bandit, or refuse him food and lodging. It was a system ready-made for exploitation by the F.L.N. The Aurès had revolted in 1859, 1879 and 1916 against the French, who – like their Roman predecessors – had never really succeeded in penetrating it. Instead they built a dusty and cheerless garrison town at Batna to the north, and protected the few roads, plus the one highly vulnerable railway to Biskra on the edge of the Sahara, with a series of scattered concrete guard-towers, or mini forts. Utterly isolated in the hostile landscape, they remind one of the Turkish-built structures along the Hejaz railway which Lawrence and his irregulars took such delight in blowing up during their desert revolt. Apart from Batna, the only other administrative centre was the pleasant small town of Arris, nestling in a valley in the centre of the Aurès, and dependent entirely upon the easily severed north–south road. To control the sixty-thousand Auresians of Arris and its far-flung *commune mixte*, there was precisely one French administrator, two assistants and seven gendarmes. From Arris eastwards one trackless range succeeds another, until the Aurès merge with the equally inaccessible Nementchas, and on across the Tunisian frontier. Geographically, it was ideal guerrilla country, and meanwhile, since 1951, a remarkably sophisticated political structure had been superimposed over the existing simple tribal structure. On top of the long-standing discontent with economic hardships following the fall of Dien Bien Phu, a marked waning of respect for French suzerainty had been noted in the region by well-informed residents like Jean Servier and Jean Deleplanque, the Batna sub-prefect.

All in all, it was perfectly logical that the C.R.U.A. leadership should have chosen the Aurès, under the command of its native son, Ben Boulaid, to be the focal point of operations on All Saints' Day. It was their ambitious aim to sever its tenuous communications with the rest of Algeria, spark off a general uprising there, and ultimately (according to Ben Bella) make it Algeria's "principal revolutionary stronghold".

The day of 30 October was spent by Ben Boulaid's men in cleaning and preparing their weapons. The next day, from a command post which he and his lieutenants, Bachir Chihani and Adjel Adjoul, had set up in the dense oak forest of Beni Melloul, safe from any aerial reconnaissance, Ben Boulaid issued his detailed orders. The most important objective was at Batna itself, where a group of three commandos each comprising ten men was to attack Deleplanque's sub-prefecture, the gendarmerie and two barracks; the latter with the aim of seizing arms. A second detachment under Chihani was to cut the main Biskra–Batna highway eleven miles south of Arris in the Tighanimine gorges, with orders to ambush vehicles and kill any "Beni-Oui-Oui" Muslims found in them. Also under Chihani another group was to besiege the isolated gendarmerie at T'kout sitting astride a commanding ledge five miles off the main road south of Arris; meanwhile, a further commando would also be blowing the road bridge just north of Arris. All telephone lines between Arris and the outside world were to be sabotaged, and simultaneously an all-out attack was to be made on the small garrison there. Similar blows were to be struck at the lead mine of Ichmoul, at Khenchela on the road eastward through the

Nementchas, and at the big garrison town of Biskra on the edge of the Sahara. The most precise, synchronised timing was to be observed; under strictest orders from Ben Boulaid not a shot was to be fired until 03.00 hours on the morning of 1 November.

"It's a general uprising...."

It was at Biskra that the Aurès suffered its first major setback. There trigger-happy rebels attacked the police station half an hour in advance of Ben Boulaid's H-Hour. At about the same time, Hadj Lakhdar and his group, crouched in position outside the Batna sub-prefecture, watched while a car drew up and Deleplanque and his wife got out, having just driven back from dining with his superior in Constantine, the prefect Pierre Dupuch. Sighting his carbine on Deleplanque's chest no more than thirty yards away, Lakhdar reflected on his orders: "No attacks on European civilians" – but was a sub-prefect a civilian? On the other hand, Ben Boulaid had been totally emphatic about no shooting before 03.00 hours. He lowered the carbine. Deleplanque entered the building, went into his bedroom and was taking off his shirt when the telephone rang. It was an apologetic but excited Commissaire of police at Biskra reporting that he had been attacked and had suffered two casualties. Deleplanque immediately telephoned the captain of the gendarmerie in Batna, ordering a state of alert for all units. Next he telephoned Army headquarters, but here there was an aggravating delay while a sleepy colonel (the same who had recently claimed never to have seen a *fellagha* in front of his jeep) at first insisted on receiving written orders "through the proper channels". Trying to contact Arris, Deleplanque found the lines cut, but on getting through to his host of a few hours ago in Constantine he was told: "It's a general uprising. There have been incidents both in Algiers and the surrounding region. It began at 01.00 hours...." At this point a volley of shots was fired in the street outside. "*Ça y est!*" shouted Deleplanque. "It's begun here!"

With ten minutes to go before H-Hour, Lakhdar's men outside the gendarmerie were suddenly taken by surprise as all lights flashed on inside the barracks, alarm bells started ringing and searchlights sprang into life. Cursing, they fired off a red rocket, signifying "abort", and withdrew at the double, firing as they went. Two twenty-one-year-old Chasseurs, Pierre Audat and Eugène Cochet, mounting guard at the gate of the regimental barracks, heard the shooting and saw the rebels running past. In accordance with peace-time standing orders, their rifles were unloaded and the ammunition *sewn up* in their pouches. With never a chance to get a round off, they were mown down – the first army personnel to be killed in the Algerian war. But – thanks to the premature action at Biskra – that was the end of the F.L.N. attack on Batna.

At Khenchela, Ben Boulaid's men showed similar precipitateness. Their first fusillade of shots, punctually at 03.00 hours, drew from his quarters the commander of the small garrison, Spahi Lieutenant Gérard Darneau. Still buttoning up his shirt, he was mortally wounded by sub-machine-gun fire – the first French officer to be killed by the F.L.N. In the ensuing shoot-up, however, two of the rebels were wounded and the remainder took off into the maquis – with a booty of only three pistols to show for the night's operation. At the Ichmoul lead mine, an attack aimed at seizing some 1,500 pounds of dynamite failed equally, with a commando of wildly firing rebels driven off by a Muslim night-watchman, who returned their fire from under his bed with an antique cavalry rifle. Against the isolated gendarmerie post of T'kout, with its garrison of seven gendarmes, three wives and five children, matters were pressed rather more energetically. A nearby explosion abruptly woke up one of the gendarmes, Martial Pons. His eight-month-old daughter started bawling. Pons went out on the terrace to see what was happening, while his wife tried to soothe the baby with a bottle. There was a burst of fire, and the bottle was smashed in Madame Pons's hand. For the next thirty-six hours T'kout was under siege.

The Monnerots

There now ensued the most tragic episode of this night of violence. Chihani and his group had been waiting since 3 a.m. in the rugged defile called the Tighanimine gorges, where the river tumbles through a narrow canyon. Nearby a marble plaque set in the cliff walls by the Romans commemorates the crushing of a revolt by the Legio Augusta. They knew that at approximately 7 a.m. the Biskra–Arris bus would pass their ambush, and that on board would be a loyal *caid*, Hadj Sadok, who had the previous day received a roneo copy of the F.L.N.'s proclamation – which he had thrown away in contempt. Also on the bus were the young couple of French teachers, Guy Monnerot and his wife, whom Deleplanque's office had been unable to contact the previous day. In their early twenties and recently returned from their honeymoon, the Monnerots had taken up their posts at the school in the small Aurès village of Tiffelfel only three weeks earlier, and were using the long week-end to see something of the countryside. Dedicated liberals, the Monnerots had arrived full of youthful enthusiasm for tackling the appalling problems of illiteracy in the Aurès; Guy, gangling, bespectacled and bookish, could hardly have conformed less to the image of a "colonialist oppressor".

The driver of the bus, it appears, had been warned by the F.L.N. to expect a hold-up at kilometre stone 79 and, as he rounded the bend at the appointed spot on the twisting road, saw it blocked by a makeshift barricade. Faithful to his instructions, he jammed on the brakes so violently that the passengers were thrown forward on to the floor. In the confusion Chihani leapt on to the bus and ordered Sadok and the Monnerots to get outside, where they were covered by Mohamed Sbaihi armed with a Sten gun – the only automatic weapon possessed by the group. Chihani demanded of Sadok: "You received our proclamation; now which side are you going to take?"

Sadok replied with an hauteur that apparently infuriated Chihani: "Do you think I'm going to talk to bandits!"

It then seems that the *caid* made a move to reach a pistol under his cloak. Sbaihi fired a burst with his Sten, mortally wounding Sadok and also hitting Guy Monnerot in the chest, his wife in the side. Chihani ordered the bus driver to take the dying *caid* on into Arris, *pour encourager les autres*, leaving the badly wounded Monnerots on the roadside; and then retired into the hills.

In Arris, which had awoken in panicky chaos after the confused shootings of the previous night, and in the unpleasant realisation that it was completely cut off from the outside world, Jean Servier, the ethnologist, had assumed command by default. His immediate fears had been that either the whole township would be massacred by the rebels – whose strength no one could then estimate – or that the trigger-happy Europeans, all armed and anticipating another Sétif, would launch a pre-emptive, promiscuous *ratissage* of the Muslims. He thus set about withdrawing the Europeans and their families into the local *bordj*, or fort (which seems to have been virtually unmanned), and organising it into an armed camp. Next, his training as an ethnologist enabled him to glean the vital intelligence that the local rebels belonged to a tribe called the Ouled-Abdi and that their mortal, blood-feud enemies, the Touabas, would remain loyal to France. Swiftly, and taking a considerable risk, Servier distributed arms to them and brought the Touabas into the defence of the town; it was a scene that P. C. Wren could hardly have improved upon.

When the ambushed bus reached Arris, Servier immediately set forth with an armed patrol to try to bring back the Monnerots. It was midday before he reached them. Chihani's group had either disappeared or were lying low, invisible on the mountainside. Guy Monnerot had already bled to death; miraculously his wife was still alive, by his side on the edge of the road. In view of the pattern that the war was to assume, there was something tragically symbolic in the fact that among the seven to die on that first day would be a loyal *caid* and a "liberal" French teacher.*

* Inevitably there was some dispute as to how deliberate, or accidental, had been the shooting of the Monnerots. The "execution" of Sadok had evidently been predetermined, and one early account suggests that the Monnerots were shot down getting back into the bus afterwards. In support of this, there were warnings received earlier that French teachers might be rebel targets; on the other hand, Ben Boulaid is recorded as having passed on the C.R.U.A.'s strict interdiction of attacks on civilian personnel. None of the F.L.N. principals survived the war; Sbaihi was

Servier accompanied Madame Monnerot back to the simple hospital at Arris, and settled down anxiously to await a further attack at nightfall. If it came he reckoned there would be a fair chance of the defenders – armed only with fifty rifles and thirty rounds apiece – being overwhelmed and massacred. Apart from sporadic sniping from rebel nests in the surrounding heights, nothing, in fact, occurred – partly owing to the defection of the attacking group – and after a sleepless night Servier was relieved by a column from Batna that had managed to negotiate the blown bridges. It was his thirty-sixth birthday, he suddenly recalled in some surprise at having reached it alive.

Elsewhere in Algeria

Outside the Aurès the night of All Saints had followed a similar pattern of failures and half-successes for the rebels. Because of Lahouel's counsels of prudence, the F.L.N. network in the Mitidja had virtually collapsed and had had to be fortified at the last minute by two hundred of Ouamrane's men smuggled in from Kabylia. Barely fifty of them, however, possessed a gun, and some of the rest were armed with scout knives; thus there was a particular immediacy about succeeding with their attacks on the arms depots at Blida and Boufarik. Right in the heart of *pied noir* Algeria, outside the Boufarik barracks, Ouamrane and a hundred Kabyles had waited for midnight, at which time a disaffected Moslem corporal was to effect a Trojan horse entry through the main gate for them. But with five minutes to go there was a series of violent explosions as panicky demolition commandos blew up nearby road-bridges thirty-five minutes ahead of schedule. Enraged, Ouamrane precipitated his attack before the alert could be sounded, and in the confusion was only able to seize six rifles and four sub-machine-guns before his group, too, scattered into the darkness. At Blida, Rabah Bitat had come off even worse, with three men killed and several wounded without procuring a single weapon. Both groups then fled up into the cedar mountains round Chréa; the net results of so much planning and so many risks were ten weapons, one of Blachette's alfalfa depots burnt down and a few bridges destroyed.

In Algiers itself the principal targets had been the radio station, the telephone exchange, the gasworks, a petroleum depot and a cork warehouse belonging to Senator Borgeaud. Through a combination of panic and inexperience all five operations aborted. The attack on the gasworks was probably the most risky, as none of the rebels had any idea of just what kind of blast an exploding gasometer might produce; of Bouadjadj's home-made bombs, however, those that had gone off had proved too feeble to

killed a few months later; Chihani was liquidated the following October by his fellow-lieutenant, who then changed sides; Ben Boulaid was blown up by a booby-trapped radio in the Aurès in March 1956.

breach the steel of the gasometers, and an insignificant fire they had started in the petroleum depot had been swiftly extinguished by the Algiers fire brigade. The leader entrusted with incendiarising the cork warehouse had simply "gone sick" shortly before H-Hour; while the automatic relays in the unscathed central telephone exchange continued to click out a flood of messages reporting incidents from all over Algeria. In agonised frustration Bouadjadj, watching from the superb vantage-point of the Bois de Boulogne that crowns Algiers, had awaited the great bursts of flame that never materialised. Descending the mountain he vented his rage on his lieutenants and proposed that they set off the remaining bombs promiscuously in Bab-el-Oued and the Rue Michelet, the main shopping boulevard of Algiers. But he was dissuaded with a reminder of the strict adherence to orders that had been imposed by the C.R.U.A.

In the Oran area, where, as previously noted, the F.L.N. had been particularly weak from the beginning and had, additionally, never received any of the weapons promised from Morocco, it suffered its worst setback. While moving into position, a group of Ben M'hidi's men were surprised by a tiny Renault 4 c.v. driven by a French civilian, Laurent François. They fired at him, wounding him, but he managed courageously to drive to the gendarmerie at Cassaigne and give the alarm before he died. A vigorous manhunt was launched, and by dawn eight Muslims had been killed, six of them carrying arms. Among them was Abdelmalek Ramdane, one of those who attended the "Meeting of the Twenty-Two", and the first F.L.N. leader to be killed.

The balance for All Saints' Day

Slightly more encouraging results had been achieved in Kabylia where Belkacem Krim's outlaws were both the most experienced and also familiar with the terrain. Telegraph poles were felled and communications cut in numerous areas; barracks and gendarmeries attacked, and cork and tobacco stores fired. Total damage was assessed at 200 million francs. But, all in all, for the immense effort, risks and hopes that had gone into launching the All Saints revolt, it had achieved precious little in material terms. Nowhere had it aroused anything approaching immediate popular support – with the possible exception of the Aurès. Therefore, on the face of it, the clarion terms of the F.L.N.'s initial proclamation, beamed out by Cairo radio and scattered in pamphlets across the country, seemed more than a little presumptuous:

> To the Algerian people,
> To the militants of the National Cause!
> ... After decades of struggle, the National Movement reached its final phase of fulfilment.
> ... a group of responsible young people and dedicated militants,

gathering about it the majority of wholesome and resolute elements, has judged that the moment has come to take the National Movement out of the impasse into which it has been forced by the conflicts of persons and influence, and to launch it into the true revolutionary struggle at the side of the Moroccan and Tunisian brothers. . . .

Our movement of regeneration presents itself under the label of:

FRONT DE LIBÉRATION NATIONALE

thus freeing itself from any possible compromise, and offering to all Algerian patriots of every social position and of all parties . . . the possibility of joining in the national struggle.

GOAL: National independence through:

1. restoration of the Algerian state, sovereign, democratic, and social, within the framework of the principles of Islam;

2. preservation of all fundamental freedoms, without distinction of race or religion.

INTERNAL OBJECTIVES:

1. political house-cleaning through the destruction of the last vestiges of corruption and reformism, the causes of our present decadence. . . .

EXTERNAL OBJECTIVES:

1. internationalism of the Algerian problem;

2. pursuit of North African unity in its national Arabo-Islamic context;

3. assertion, through the United Nations Charter, of our active sympathy towards all nations that may support our liberating action.

MEANS OF STRUGGLE:

. . . by every means until the realisation of our goal . . . action abroad to make the Algerian problem a reality for the entire world, with the support of- our natural allies . . . the struggle will be long, but the outcome is certain . . . in order to limit bloodshed we propose an honourable platform for discussion with the French authorities. . . .

1. recognition of Algerian nationhood by an official declaration;

2. opening of negotiations . . . on a basis of recognition of Algerian sovereignty, one and indivisible;

3. . . . liberation of all political prisoners. . . .

IN RETURN FOR WHICH:

1. French cultural and economic interests will be respected, as well as persons and families;

2. all French citizens desiring to remain in Algeria will be allowed to opt for their original nationality, in which case they will be considered as foreigners, or for Algerian nationality, in which case they will be considered as Algerians both in rights and duties;

3. the ties between France and Algeria will be defined by agreement between the two powers, on a basis of equality and mutual respect!

Algerians! We invite you to meditate on our Charter set out above. It is your duty to associate yourselves with it to save our country and to give it back its liberty. The FRONT DE LIBÉRATION NATIONALE is your front, its victory is yours. . . .

Excessively grandiloquent as it may have sounded at the time, the truly remarkable feature of the F.L.N. proclamation as a document was that its basic principles were to be adhered to with absolute fidelity during seven and a half years of war, right through to the final settlement.

Certainly on that 1 November 1954 few at the Gouvernement-Général treated it with the respect it deserved. One of the immediate consequences of the ineptness with which the previous night's operations had been executed (which paradoxically would possibly aid the F.L.N. in the long run) was to persuade the authorities that the revolt was less serious than it was, and that it could soon be crushed with recourse to swift and draconian repressive measures. At a first emergency conference summoned by Léonard early on the morning of the 1st, he, Vaujour and General Cherrière, the Army Commander-in-Chief, all agreed that, from the evidence already available, it was a question of isolated incidents rather than of any general insurrection. Equally it was agreed (thus giving roots to the fateful legend) that all must have been decreed from Cairo, and not set up within Algeria itself. The general – nicknamed "Babar" Cherrière because of an elephantine physique and manner – maintained that it was another "tribal uprising" such as France had experienced many times in her North African past, and grumbled angrily that the "loyal" Muslim leaders had been faithless in not tipping off his Deuxième Bureau. The Aurès looked by far the most dangerous area, and Cherrière was instructed to despatch all available army units there, with the particular aim of clearing the road through to beleaguered Arris. Cherrière pointed out that he had 57,000 men in Algeria but that most of these were garrison troops, or units in transit that had been sent there awaiting despatch to Indo-China; he could muster at most 3,500 fighting troops, and with great difficulty. Reporting to Paris what had happened, Léonard called for the urgent despatch of the 25th Airborne Division, then training in the Pyrenees, but otherwise described the situation as "disturbing but not dramatic". For the rest, it was a matter of police action.

French reactions

On the ground, the physical reaction – or over-reaction – was predictable. It was predictable, not specifically because of the *pied noir* mentality, but because this is the way an administration caught with its pants down habitually reacts under such circumstances; whether it be the British in Palestine, Cyprus or Northern Ireland, the Portuguese in Mozambique, or the French in Indo-China. First comes the mass indiscriminate round-up of suspects, most of them innocent but converted into ardent militants by the fact of their imprisonment;* then the setting of faces against liberal reforms designed to tackle the root of the trouble; followed, finally, when too late, by a new, progressive policy of liberalisation.

---

* One is here reminded of the line of Claude Rains, as the cynical Vichy police chief, at the end of that cinema classic, *Casablanca*: "Arrest the usual suspects!"

The first obvious police target was Messali's M.T.L.D. At dawn on 1 November its secretary general, Moulay Merbah, was arrested in his bed, totally unaware of the night's events. On first hearing of the F.L.N. revolt, Messali Hadj himself flew into a violent rage; but, astute politician that he was, promptly let the word percolate down the bush-telegraph that his men had been responsible. As a result, on 5 November the M.T.L.D. was outlawed, its files confiscated and its supporters arrested. The police net swept wide. Bouadjadj was caught at dawn on the 5th; Bitat's Algiers network was effectively broken up, and he himself tracked down the following March; while in Oran thirty-eight of the All Saints activists were rounded up. On the other hand many innocents fell into the bag. Ben Youssef Ben Khedda, a pharmacist whose hands were clean, wrote a joint letter to the *Alger Républicain* complaining about the blind arrests. Two days later he too was in prison, followed shortly by his fellow signatories; immediately he was released, five months later, he joined the F.L.N.

The reactions of the *pieds noirs* were, predictably, sharp – mixed with a strong element of "I told you so". In the *Dépêche Quotidienne*, Senator Henri Borgeaud demanded that: "The evil must be pursued where it is to be found and the ringleaders routed out where they are.... The security measures must be reinforced...." More outspokenly, the Conseil-Général for the department of Algiers, at an extraordinary session called on 2 November, voted unanimously:

(a) that order be firmly and rapidly restored
(b) that the guilty, whoever they are, be exemplarily punished
(c) that, henceforth, no weakness be tolerated
(d) and that French policy ... be founded upon the healthy elements of the population.

Clause (c) could well have been adopted from a rallying-cry at the Battle of Verdun; altogether it meant, as liberals like Jacques Chevallier at once feared, a setting back of the clocks on any suggestion of reform. There could be no question of implementing the statute of 1947 now, let alone of conceding electoral equality to a Muslim community that could murder young French teachers, and certainly not before order was fully restored.

The prevailing mood was made explicit on 26 November when Ferhat Abbas had wanted to make an eloquent but moderate statement in the Algerian Assembly, which included these words:

at no moment in the history of Algeria, has the Algerian *fellah* felt so scoffed at, so scorned.... If only the statute had been applied, if, for example, the *commune mixte* of Arris ... had been abolished and substituted by municipalities which would have permitted the inhabitants to conduct democratically their own affairs, I say that perhaps we should not have had a maquis and maquisards....

But he was prevented by Laquière, the President of the Assembly, from taking the floor. Where the conservative *pieds noirs* placed the blame for All Saints was made quite explicit by François Quilici, Deputy for Oran:

> when M. Mendès-France proclaimed Tunisia's internal sovereignty and turned the government and Tunisia itself over to the Néo-Destour [Bourguiba's party], he showed that terrorism paid off....The evil is spreading. The admirable Algerian peace, French peace in Algeria, is ruined, for...weakness always encourages new adventures.

And in France....

In France, however, the revolt in Algeria did not arouse the greatest public interest. Janet Flanner, who seldom missed an important "story", does not even mention it in her journal; recording instead the death of Matisse and the runaway sell-out of de Gaulle's first volume of war memoirs. L'*Humanité*, on 9 November, wrote condemning acts of terrorism but supporting "the Algerian people in their mass struggle against repression and for the defence of their rights". Leading off with news on the United States congressional elections, *Le Monde* devoted no more than two columns to the events (compared with three for the American elections), under the bland caption "Several Killed in Algeria in the Course of Simultaneous Attacks on Police Posts". The Mendès-France government, for whom the news could hardly have come at a worse time, was immediately unequivocal in its condemnation of the revolt, and its zeal to repress it. In a fighting speech to the Assembly on 12 November, Mendès-France declared:

> One does not compromise when it comes to defending the internal peace of the nation, the unity and the integrity of the Republic. The Algerian departments are part of the French Republic. They have been French for a long time, and they are irrevocably French.... Between them and metropolitan France there can be no conceivable secession.
>
> This must be clear once and for all, in Algeria and in metropolitan France as much as in the outside world. [Applause from left, centre, right and extreme right]. Never will France – any French government, or parliament, whatever may be their particularistic tendencies – yield on this fundamental principal.
>
> *Mesdames, Messieurs,* several deputies have made comparisons between French policy in Algeria and Tunisia. I declare that no parallel is more erroneous, that no comparison is falser, or more dangerous. *Ici, c'est la France!*

It was an uncompromisingly forthright, fatefully binding statement, and Mendès-France the radical was more than backed up by his Socialist Minister of the Interior, François Mitterrand. He had equally refuted any parallel between French policy in Morocco and Tunisia on the one hand and Algeria on the other at a session of the Assembly's Commission de l'Intérieur on 5 November, adding the challenge that here, in Algeria, "the only possible negotiation is war". On the 12th he rose in the Assembly to declare with his leader, "Algeria is France. And who among you, *Mesdames, Messieurs*, would hesitate to employ every means to preserve France?"

In a vote of confidence on the 12th, Mendès-France scraped home with 294 to 265, saved, in effect, by the score of votes controlled by René Mayer's pro-*pied noir* lobby. Such subsequent "hawks" as Bidault, Soustelle, Mollet and Lacoste all voted for the government. No ultra-conservative imperialist could have been much more forthright than Mitterrand, and in view of his subsequent career his statements may seem additionally surprising. But in November 1954 the unyielding gospel of *l'Algérie, c'est la France* very much represented French political opinion of almost all hues; on the other hand, Mendès-France also had reasons of internal politics for making quite such bellicose noises. The fate of his reforming government was at stake. The initial charisma acquired by his liquidation of the Indo-China war in the summer had waned; the Assembly was suspicious (as it had shown on 12 November) of his dealing in Tunisia and Morocco, and it disliked the way he had simply shrugged off responsibility for the torpedoing of the European Defence Community in August; the vocal bistro-owners were up in arms at his worthy but much derided campaign to replace alcohol by milk. Mendès-France was, however, profoundly a reformer and, privately, he was pledged to introduce a "new deal" for Algeria. To him it was clear that colonial rule in Algeria would have to end ultimately, as it was about to do in Morocco and Tunisia. The question was, when? And with whom to negotiate? In Indo-China, Tunisia and Morocco there had been the leaders who were present on the spot – the Ho Chi Minhs and Bourguibas. But in Algeria, because a century and a quarter of francisation had destroyed the native cadres, there existed no ready-made *interlocuteurs valables* with whom Mendès-France could negotiate, if and when he so wished. Therefore, although initially he would have to act unilaterally, with his incisive intelligence he grasped what it would take his successors another five years to realise; namely that, sooner or later, contact would have to be taken up with Algerians who were, to some extent or other, associated with the revolt. But All Saints had struck him a *mauvais coup*; if he were now to start implementing the 1947 statute and instituting honest elections (as he desired) – let alone negotiating with any Algerian nationalists – then the *pied noir* lobby would cause his government to fall overnight. Thus order had first to be restored. He found himself clad in an "iron maiden" that successive French governments after him – left, liberal and conservative – would be forced to don.

First repression, then reform

Upon the programme of repression the government now found itself forced to adopt, Mitterrand attempted to impose two immediate and important restraints. First, there were to be no promiscuous bombardments, by napalm or high explosive, of suspected rebel villages; secondly, the police forces in Algeria (which had hitherto been autonomous) were to be fused with those of metropolitan France. By this means Mitterrand hoped to be able to remove some of the more brutal and racist elements. To this day he regards it as one of his most noteworthy achievements – "a test to prove our good will to the Algerians". On both issues, however, there seems to have been a lacuna between intent and practice; the effect of police fusion proved slight (nine of the senior officers considered by Mitterrand as the most undesirable were simply re-transferred back again from France, after a decent pause); chiefly, it provoked the additional mistrust of the *pieds noirs*, which in turn led to the overthrow of the Mendès-France government. And although napalm may not have been used, there were certainly not infrequent cases where local commanders "used their own discretion" without recourse to the political authorities, and *did* carry out punitive artillery and aerial strikes on *douars*.

Deployed in the Aurès, "Babar" Cherrière's ponderous, N.A.T.O.-style forces found themselves at an impossible disadvantage. Beyond clearing the road to, and liberating, Arris and T'kout, tanks and armoured troop-carriers proved useless. As the colonel commanding an armoured regiment remarked despondently to Jean Servier, "All that I can do is to hold the road . . . and as for the rest. . . ," he shrugged his shoulders; to which Servier commented, "If in 1830 the French Expeditionary Force had had tanks, they wouldn't have got beyond the beach at Sidi-Ferruch!" There were no mules or horses available and one solitary helicopter in all Algeria, and neither Cherrière – a fifty-eight-year-old veteran of the First World War and a disciple of Weygand – nor his area commander, General Spillmann, had any experience of guerrilla warfare. The troops under their command were equally untrained. An F.L.N. ambush would surprise a road-bound mechanised patrol, burn a vehicle or two, and kill several men; the ambushers would melt into the trackless hills. There was a certain similarity with scenes from Flaubert's *Salammbô* where the wily Spendius stampeded the Carthaginian elephants by driving pigs smeared with flaming bitumen towards them.

"A whole winter on our own. . . ."

That first winter was a grim one for the French forces in the Aurès. A young regular who had signed on for three years, Pierre Leulliette, was left with enduring memories of the early operations, to which a few days hunting Krim in Kabylia in late November had provided an introduction:

all we had for pillows were our packs, and for mattresses a few large, rotting leaves; not enough to prevent us feeling the cold, hard earth against our backs. . . . A prelude to what was to torment us most over the three years; lack of sleep, and the cold, the harsh unexpected cold to which we never really got used. . . .

On arriving in Khenchela ("a dismal town swept by an Arctic wind"), his first reaction was one of shock at the undernourishment of the people and their scrawny goats "the size of small dogs", living "merely on stones and air"; followed by anger at the rich *pieds noirs* who, when told of this, would indignantly trot out that hardy perennial, "They don't have the same needs as us!" Though battle casualties were few, conditions were unpleasantly harsh for the French infantry when they did move off on sweeps into the mountains. No army bivouac could keep out the penetrating wind, and glacial rains turned the thin soil into "a revolting, yellow, gluey swamp. Everything was drenched, even our weapons." Caves that might have concealed rebels crawled with "vicious yellow and black scorpions and snakes with beady eyes". Unnerving anxiety alternated with boredom, but always physical exhaustion predominated – the fatigue of arduous marches and repeated night patrols.

Rebel intelligence always seemed to be one leap ahead of the cumbersome, weary French columns: "We had to get there by forced marches," says Leulliette. "Too late: the Arab bush-telegraph – fires which suddenly lit up from peak to peak – had moved faster than us." Another excellent "early warning system" was provided by the large yellow and white dogs of the Aurès, which the French discovered could hear a patrol of six men in sandals a mile off. It was a tense and lonely existence: "We were to spend a whole winter on our own, more isolated than conquistadors forgotten in some new world," Leulliette recalled, "if we passed through one of the *douars* by day, the *fellaghas* went there at night. If we camped there at night, they came back the next day, often only a few hours after we had left." Interrogations conducted in front of the local *caid* produced little: "you couldn't see any expression in the Arabs' eyes, except a kind of timid curiosity, but now hatred flashed there, like fire. . . ." Fear was everywhere. The bodies of loyal Muslims would be discovered, often appallingly mutilated or having been subjected to slow deaths that the adjacent army posts would be powerless to prevent. "Tongues were paralysed with terror." At T'kout Leulliette records how, almost by the camp gates, the village policeman was found with his throat slit and eyes gouged out, a scrap of paper signed "F.L.N." pinned to his skin. "In spite of our twenty-four hours a day sentry-watch a rebel could therefore come within a hundred yards of the camp and commit a crime without risk. The colonel was mad with rage." As soon as the French turned their backs, "honourable old men", their chests laden with decorations, would grab their ancient firearms and open fire. The army learnt the harsh rules of the game at an early stage: "We don't take prisoners," a sergeant instructed

Leulliette. "These men aren't soldiers. Besides they don't take any either."

Again and again such punitive expeditions despatched into the Aurès came back empty-handed, and in the face of frustration General Spillmann's instinct was to withdraw his undermanned forces and concentrate them on certain armed camps, like Arris, thus leaving the hills, temporarily anyway, to the rebels. Cherrière on the other hand was all in favour of the "fine-tooth comb", the ruthless *ratissage* with resort to exemplary bombardments of suspect areas. But this was expressly forbidden by the Minister of the Interior. Finally it was agreed to bomb the *douar* of Ichmoul – on the condition that, well in advance, warning leaflets be dropped on the populace. Local administrators pleaded that the leaflets should on no account be dropped unless the bombing were definitely to take place, because of the loss of face that this would inevitably cause. Nevertheless, thousands of melodramatic warnings were cascaded on the *douar*:

APPEAL TO THE MUSLIM POPULATION
Agitators, among them foreigners, have provoked bloody troubles in our country and have installed themselves notably in your region. They are living off your own resources. . . .
SOON A TERRIFYING CALAMITY, FIRE FROM THE SKY, WILL CRASH DOWN ON THE HEADS OF THE REBELS. After which, the *paix française* will reign once more.

But, for all the trumpeting, there was no bombardment – called off after much argument. As predicted, the army gained the worst of both worlds, bringing down on itself as much ridicule as the fruitless *ratissages* that repeatedly let Ben Boulaid and his men slip through the teeth of the "fine" comb. And with such losses of face, combined with the inevitable rigours and humiliations imposed on the Auresians in the course of *ratissages*, a steady flow of the uncommitted began to join the F.L.N. – "more impressed by their cunning and agility than by our ineffectual power", comments Leulliette.

The first paras arrive

Then the first of the vaunted French paras arrived, the 25th Parachute Division that Governor-General Léonard had called for on the day following the revolt. Leading its combat group was an already legendary colonel, Ducournau, a native of Pau who had distinguished himself as a commando during the 1944 landings in the south of France. Ducournau had recently returned from Indo-China, where he had narrowly escaped the catastrophe of Dien Bien Phu, and he had made a thorough study there of Viet-Minh tactics. With Ducournau the school of Indo-China arrived in Algeria. Setting up his headquarters in Arris, he immediately decided to pursue relentlessly the F.L.N. into the hills, living with the *indigènes* according to Mao's often quoted principle of the "fish in water", and taking with him as guides and trackers some of the loyal Chaouias that Jean Servier had recruited for the defence of Arris. On 29 November, after weeks of hard slogging and heartbreaking lack of success, a detachment of Ducournau's paras was ambushed by an important rebel band in a cave-riddled ravine just north of Arris, and suffered several casualties. The colonel (who had already earned the sobriquet of "Ducournau-le-Foudre") promptly rushed to the scene and personally took charge of operations. Pinning the rebels down with heavy fire, he encircled them in a swift and skilful turning movement. There was a fierce battle, at the end of which twenty-three dead F.L.N. were picked up, plus eighteen captives. The French lost four dead and seven wounded. Among the rebel dead – clad in an American uniform with two stars on his shoulder – was Belkacem Grine, one of the most celebrated and respected *bandits d'honneur* of the Aurès with a million francs on his head.

Hard months for the F.L.N.

The killing of Grine caused a considerable impact in the Aurès, and a serious blow to F.L.N. morale. It could be rated the first major French success of the shooting war so far; yet, in effect, it was something of a flash in the pan. The F.L.N., growing more experienced, wilier and more cautious about accepting combat with superior French forces, became like mountain sheep – always one ledge, one ridge higher up in the wintry mountains than their pursuers. The war in the Aurès began to bog down, to the deep dissatisfaction of Mendès-France and, even more, of the impatient *pied noir* leaders in Algiers.

Although this could not be perceived by the French, the situation on the rebel side during that first winter was far from encouraging. In the whole country only the Aurès had responded enthusiastically to the F.L.N.'s call to rise, and there their plight became graver week by week as Ducournau's paras harried them from one sanctuary to another. It was an exceptionally hard winter, and the civil population, itself badly short of food, was not always hospitable to Ben Boulaid's men. Constantly on the run, they froze and starved; a week after the tracking-down of Grine, Mohamed Sbaihi, the killer of Guy Monnerot, was himself killed; by February, Ben Boulaid had been captured. The revolt touched bottom, reduced to little more than 350 active maquisards. About all there was to show for it in the Aurès was the capture of six French paras, whom Bachir Chihani contemplated offering in exchange for Ben Boulaid.

In Kabylia, Krim experienced a similarly grim period; unable to descend from the icy mountains, and with the Kabyle villagers showing themselves by no means entirely sympathetic, he and his band had restricted them-selves to blowing up electric pylons and telegraph poles, and selectively liquidating Muslim "collaborators". In Algiers, Bitat's and Bouadjadj's organisation had been broken within the first ten days by police arrests, and by the spring both leaders were themselves in prison. Mourad Didouche was dead, and much of the original top and secondary leadership had disappeared; this was, admitted Ben Bella, "a terrible hindrance to our movement". If one could draw up a balance-sheet for that first winter of the war in terms of rebel manpower alone, on the debit side the "old guard" had been largely mopped-up; on the credit side there was a plentiful substitution of new recruits resulting from the indiscriminate mass arrests in the cities and overzealous *ratissages* in the *bled*. But this remained to some extent a potential, rather than actual, asset.

Most disappointingly of all perhaps for the F.L.N. was the fact that, after the initial shock of All Saints had subsided, the *pieds noirs* resumed their way of life as if absolutely nothing had happened; if anything, they had averted their gaze still further from the root causes of Algerian discontent. In metropolitan France, Mendès-France had not been deflected from carrying out his North American tour in mid-November, and it was still not yet considered necessary to decree a state of emergency in Algeria. Deadlock threatened. Says Pierre Leulliette: "Fear engenders cruelty; cruelty, fear, insanity and then paralysis. In the centre of Dante's circle, the damned remained motionless." This vicious circle now began in Algeria.

CHAPTER FIVE

The Sorcerer's Cauldron

February 1955 – February 1956

Algeria! Divided most profoundly within herself, torn between the past and the future, quartered by desires and rancours, she discharged into my face, when I leaned anxiously over her, the ardent and heavy breath of a sorcerer's cauldron. How could one not love her, especially in her ordeal. "When your son has grown up, treat him like your brother," says the Arab proverb; it was certainly painful, but the son had become a man, our equal, our brother. That was what one had to understand. . . .

Jacques Soustelle

Soustelle comes: Mendès-France goes

By the new year Mendès-France had decided that, in order to further his policy and break the deadlock in Algeria, he had to replace the incumbent governor-general, Léonard, by a more imposing figure. He needed a man who was a good liberal but at the same time tough; and not just a civil servant. He needed somebody with practical experience in the underground work of the Resistance, which would help in devising anti-terrorist strategy in Algeria; and also – when the moment came – in the highly delicate work of establishing clandestine contacts in advance of negotiations. One man seemed to fill the bill: Jacques Soustelle.

"This gifted man, this brilliant intellectual, this passionate politician," as de Gaulle termed him, was aged forty-three in 1955 and already had behind him a multiple career of academic, political thinker, administrator and man of action perhaps second only to André Malraux in his generation. After a meteoric university career he had established himself as an ethnologist of great distinction, deputy-director of the Musée de l'Homme and expert on the Aztec and Mayan civilisations. Born of working-class stock in Montpellier, Soustelle (like Malraux) had started off far to the left in his political ideology, and in 1935 he became one of the leaders of the "Vigilance Committee of Anti-Fascist Intellectuals". On a cultural mission to Mexico in 1940, he was one of the first to rally to de Gaulle, who made him chief of the Free French secret service. Here Soustelle the academic showed both considerable talent for organisation and a perhaps surprising aptitude for cloak-and-dagger work. After the Liberation he became de

Gaulle's Minister of Information, then his Minister of the Colonies; since 1951 he had been a Gaullist deputy for Lyon, though still maintaining his left-wing orientations. Tubby and owl-like, with a meridional complexion, Soustelle, for all his intellectual brilliance and affinity for the conspiratorial, was far from being the traditional cold, steely-eyed intelligence operator; he was also a man of heart, generosity, capable of the emotions of a true "southerner", and with an acute sense of humour – characteristics that were to shape his judgement over the ensuing crucial twelve months.

Ever loyal, Soustelle's first act before accepting the post was to consult his old chief. "Why not?" said de Gaulle. On reporting to Mendès-France for his first briefing, Soustelle found the premier being shaved and was shocked to see how cadaverous and careworn he looked. "You will have to make the feudal forces that reign there give way," he told Soustelle. "You will need courage to confront those big panjandrums in Algiers who, up to now, have decreed rain or shine.... Your mission will be difficult." Above all, Mendès-France instructed him, works must be got under way to remedy unemployment, "this Algerian scourge". Otherwise, noted Soustelle, the Mendès–Mitterrand so-called programme of reform comprised little more than total application of the 1947 statute – which "did not seem to differ very much from my own ideas". Soustelle's appointment was followed by long and heated discussion in the Assembly, accompanied by a vituperative whispering campaign – emanating from Algiers – in which it was suggested that he was, *inter alia*, a Soviet agent, a Jew like Mendès-France and his real name was "Ben-Soussan". On 6 February, on the point of departing for Algeria, Soustelle was dismayed to learn that the Mendès-France government had fallen, torpedoed by René Mayer's Algerian lobby and the enemies made during six brief but dynamic months in office, this time on a no-confidence vote of 319 to 273. Above the hubbub of the chamber, a defeated Mendès-France was heard to shout prophetically: "In North Africa ... either there will be a policy of reconciliation, or the policy of repression and force – with all its horrible consequences...."

Deeply bitter, Mendès-France now saw the complete collapse of his reforming radicalism. To this day he believes that, had he been enabled to continue, and backed by an Assembly of the left, he could have introduced reforms that might at least have prevented the ensuing slaughter and hatred, and have led Algeria along the evolutionary path to independence which had succeeded in Morocco and Tunisia. Who, with hindsight, can deny that he might have been vindicated? In Algeria, moderate nationalists greeted his demise with gloom; and the F.L.N. with joy, in that they regarded Mendès-France with his promises of liberal reform as the one French leader capable of achieving reconciliation and thus halting them short of their goal of total independence.

For three weeks France teetered without leadership, with various stars of the Fourth Republic failing to muster sufficient support to create a new government. Meanwhile, at a mass meeting in the "Vel d'Hiv", a new threat to parliamentary equilibrium flexed its muscles; Pierre Poujade and his U.D.C.A. movement of militant small shopkeepers. As de Gaulle remarked with acid hauteur at the time, "In my day, grocers voted for solicitors. Today, solicitors vote for the grocers!" In Algeria there was no governor-general, Léonard having already departed to assume the presidency of the Cour des Comptes, and Soustelle was still hovering unconfirmed in limbo in Paris. By 15 February, however, it seemed certain that Edgar Faure – a more conservative radical, author of detective stories notable for their evasive endings, who in 1952 (when he had lasted forty days) had been the youngest prime minister (aged forty-four) to hold that office since the eighteenth century – would form the next government. His chosen Minister of the Interior, Bourgès-Maunoury, an old friend of Soustelle's from Resistance days, told him that his appointment would be reconfirmed and that he should hasten to Algiers. Arriving inconspicuously in civilian clothes, instead of the regalia of office (the first governor-general to do so), Soustelle was greeted by an icily silent city: there was "not a cat on the streets". He was "Mendès man"; or – almost as pejorative in *pied noir* eyes – "de Gaulle's man". Only Jacques Chevallier breached an implicit boycott. It was hardly an auspicious beginning.

Soustelle's reforms

At his first meeting with the Algiers Press, Soustelle stated: "To instruct and construct, to assist to live better, to accelerate the tempo of progress already imprinted by France upon this province which is so dear to her, these are our objectives." Next, almost immediately, he set off on a tour of the crisis zone of the Aurès. Quickly he realised both that poverty was far more dire and that the revolt was far more serious than metropolitan France yet appreciated. "Terror had taken hold. No one spoke," he wrote later. "The population as a whole, without throwing in its lot with the rebels...remained frightened and noncommittal." He also saw the futility of General Cherrière's grandiose and elephantine *ratissages*, the ill-named Operations "Véronique" and "Violette" that were then under way, and agreed with the analysis Vaujour prepared for him on his return to Algiers: "To send in tank units, to destroy villages, to bombard certain zones, this is no longer the fine comb; it is using a sledgehammer to kill fleas. And what is much more serious, it is to encourage the young – and sometimes the less young – to go into the maquis." No less overweight than the military effort was the administration, with its several thousand officials concentrated in Algiers, while areas half as big as France were left in charge of one French administrator and a handful of gendarmes. Everything, Soustelle found, was in need of change.

Making his début in the Algiers Assembly on 23 February, Soustelle began by reassuring the *pieds noirs* with the firm assertion that pacification would be his first aim. "France is at home here...," he declared like Mitterrand and Mendès-France before him, "or rather, Algeria and all her inhabitants form an integral part of France, one and indivisible. All must know, here and elsewhere, that France will not leave Algeria any more than she will leave Provence and Brittany. Whatever happens, the destiny of Algeria is French." So far, so good. Then Soustelle introduced a new concept: "This means that a choice has been made, and this choice is called 'integration'. It is to make Algeria each day more completely a province, different from the others, certainly, but fully French." Elaborating, later, on the difference between his new policy of "integration" and the old Blum–Viollette ideal of "assimilation", Soustelle explained that it was much the more "realist"; that it recognised the original "personality" of Algeria; that, in economic terms, it aimed at sweeping away "obsolete legacies of an imaginary autonomy affording Algeria no other privilege than that of her misery"; and that, in political terms, it was to be based upon the "immutable equality of all its inhabitants".

After so frigid a welcome on his arrival, Soustelle was encouraged by the initial warmth with which his "integration" programme was received by the Assembly in Algiers. At top speed, and fortified by a vastly expanded budget promised by Premier Faure, he pressed ahead with his basic reforms. The administration was to be decentralised by creation of several new departments, and a dramatically increased number of Muslims was to be brought into positions of responsibility. Some of the deeply resented electoral inequities of the two-college system were to be expunged; among such reforms Muslims in the towns were to be granted parity of representation. The equally resented *communes mixtes* (which Soustelle saw as being "the heart of the political problem" in Algeria) were to be suppressed and broken up into elected rural communes; while to remedy the acute problem of under-administration whereby many an Algerian never encountered a representative of France, Soustelle created an entirely new corps, the Sections Administratives Specialisées or S.A.S. On the cultural scene, Arabic was to be made an official, obligatory language in Muslim schools, and the school-building programme was to be doubled. In agriculture, an embryo agrarian reform was to be initiated; while on the industrial scene a credit of five milliard francs ($148 million) was to be earmarked for the creation of public works, aimed at achieving Soustelle's top-priority goal – "to breach the front of misery".

Of all these measures, the most ambitious – as well as the one that was to leave the most lasting imprint of Soustelle's regime – was the formation of the S.A.S. corps. Their aim, essentially, was to take into their protective net populations in the remoter *bled* that might otherwise become subject to the rebels, or buffeted by the army – or both. Some 400 S.A.S. detachments were created, each under an army lieutenant or captain who was an expert in Arabic and Arab affairs and could deal with every conceivable aspect of administration; from agronomy, teaching and health, to building houses and administering justice. The *képis bleus*, as they were affectionately called, were a selflessly devoted and courageous band of men, who made themselves much loved by the local populace, and for that reason were often the principal targets of the F.L.N., suffering the heaviest casualties of any category of administrator. Foreign journalists who saw them at work in the remoter *bled*, isolated and in constant danger, never ceased to be impressed. Unfortunately, there were always too few *képis bleus* with all the numerous qualifications that the job required; and, inevitably, there were the bad ones who transformed the S.A.S. into "intelligence centres" where torture was not unknown.

Soustelle's "liberals"

Soustelle soon found himself instinctively with considerable sympathy for the predicament of the *petits pieds noirs*, but with little for the "feudal" bosses against whom Mendès-France had warned him. At the beginning he was influenced by two liberals who comprised the so-called "left wing" of his office – Germaine Tillion and Commandant Vincent Monteil. Madame Tillion was one of those remarkable and heroic Frenchwomen who had gone through hell for her passionate liberalism. In 1940 she had founded a Resistance group in Paris, which, among other acts, had helped British prisoners-of-war to escape after Dunkirk. Arrested by the Gestapo, she was the only one of four leaders of the group to survive torture, deportation and three years in the appalling women's concentration camp of Ravensbrück. For her wartime record she was awarded the Croix de Guerre, *avec palme*, and made Officer of the Legion of Honour. Before 1940 Germaine Tillion, an ethnologist like Soustelle, had just spent six years in the Aurès – living a fourteen-hour horseback journey from the nearest European, at Arris. There was no Frenchwoman who knew the region better. At the beginning of the revolt she had been in New York, working on an official commission on war crimes – German and Russian. Returning to France, she was asked by Mitterrand to go back to the Aurès that winter to report on conditions. Immediately she had been "deeply shocked to discover how much the level of life had sunk since I had been there fourteen years previously". It was not so much the fault of the French – "because they simply weren't there" – but the sheer harsh facts of population pressure. In that grim winter of 1954 she had observed the Aurès peasants "watch their goats dying for want of a little fodder . . . or starving workers eat their grain seed, their hope for the following year". She had been equally shocked by the heavy-handedness of the army's counter-measures.

Germaine Tillion's findings on the economic plight of the Algerians were substantially corroborated by the Maspétiol Report, published about the same time as a result of an extensive survey made by a group of senior French officials and economists. They reported that one million Muslims were totally or partially unemployed, while a further two millions were seriously under-employed. About three-quarters of the Muslim population was illiterate in Arabic, and ninety per cent in French. Although France appeared to be spending more on Algeria, in real terms – because of depreciation of the franc – the sum earmarked for 1953 had not exceeded that for 1913. On her return to Algiers, Germaine Tillion met Soustelle and recounted what she had seen. The two found themselves widely in agreement, and Soustelle immediately asked her to join his inner cabinet, charging her to set up a network of *centres sociaux*. Designed to supplement Soustelle's S.A.S. scheme, these *centres* were to bring aid to the more backward Muslim communities in the form of sanitation, elementary education and economic assistance, according to specific needs. She was also given a wider-ranging brief to study and report on the conditions of the rural populations; and, from this moment, she became in effect Soustelle's liberal conscience.

Commandant Monteil's impact on the Algerian scene was both more immediate and more controversial. A fluent speaker of several dialects of Arabic, Monteil had spent ten years in Morocco, followed by several stints served in other Near East capitals as military attaché. Under the Mendès-France regime he had been attached to Christian Fouchet, the Minister for Moroccan and Tunisian affairs, until called by Soustelle to join his staff. The day Soustelle took up his appointment, Monteil was informed that an important rebel had just been captured in the Aurès – one Mostefa Ben Boulaïd. Monteil persuaded Soustelle to allow him to make contact with him. Up to this point Ben Boulaïd had not been identified as a member of the C.R.U.A., and at first in his interview Monteil gleaned nothing more than that he was a local leader. Then, after Monteil had begun speaking in Chaouia, Ben Boulaïd revealed the whole story of the uprising and his own function. Persuasively he pointed out to Monteil how the French *ratissages* operations were "our best recruiting agent", and after this extra-ordinary first meeting between a F.L.N. leader and a French official, Monteil left with the firm impression of "a man of faith, and of good faith, pushed to the limits by a lively sentiment of the injustice that has hit his people".

Back in Algiers, Monteil was also influenced by Jacques Chevallier, who told him how he had offered his resignation as Secretary of State for

Defence to Mendès-France after the indiscriminate arrest of 2,000 suspects of Messali's M.T.L.D. in the wake of All Saints. Soustelle agreed with Monteil that Mendès-France's action had "done more harm than good", and commissioned him to follow up his interview with Ben Boulaid by seeing the imprisoned leaders in Algiers's Barberousse prison. Maître Kiouane, at twenty-nine a leading Algiers barrister and a recognised moderate, assured Monteil that he had known nothing whatever of the F.L.N. conspiracy, that he had only been arrested after publishing a letter protesting at the dissolution of the M.T.L.D. He warned Monteil "in six months' time people like me will be overtaken. It will be too late for any pacific solution." Ben Khedda, arrested on the same pretext, was then a thirty-five-year-old pharmacist who gave Monteil the impression of being rather timid and buttoned-up, speaking in similarly moderate terms to Kiouane. After this interview Monteil worked on Soustelle to expedite the release of the imprisoned suspects. But, through a combination of the slow processes of bureaucracy and *pied noir* opposition restraining Soustelle, they were not in fact liberated for another two or three months. Immediately both Kiouane and Ben Khedda, as well as a number of the lesser M.T.L.D. detainees, joined the F.L.N.

Would the detainees still have gone over to the rebels if they had been released when Monteil interviewed them at the beginning of March? Or if they had never been arrested in the first place? One may speculate, but all one can be sure of is that here Soustelle got the worst of both worlds: the Ben Kheddas were lost to the rebellion; the mistrust of the *pieds noirs* for French policy was exacerbated. Prison – as was to be relearnt by the French repeatedly in the course of the Algerian war, by the British in Northern Ireland and by every other mid-twentieth-century regime faced with a similar insurrectionary problem – is a marvellous recruiting and training centre.

The "smallpox chart"

With the arrival of spring and the F.L.N.'s survival of that first winter, battered but still intact, the inflow of new recruits – whether motivated by French mismanagement or sheer allure of the apparently inextinguishable F.L.N. – soon brought about a sharp recrudescence of "incidents". At army headquarters intelligence officers maintained what was known as the "smallpox chart", marking up the occurrence of fresh outbreaks of violence, and the blotches were beginning to spread rapidly. First they appeared in the hitherto unblemished region of North Constantine, between the city itself and Philippeville on the coast; then, in March, at Bône in the north-eastern extremity of the country, and in the Nementchas close to the Tunisian frontier. Already the rebels were showing themselves better organised, fighting in sections of ten to fifteen men or even companies fifty strong, more and more aggressive, and even sometimes better armed. On 13 April Adjoul successfully ambushed a detachment of Algerian Tirailleurs near Djellal in the Nementchas; eight were killed and a number of the survivors defected to the F.L.N. – an ominous warning of new perils that might lie ahead. On 24 May the F.L.N. inflicted on the army its most deadly blow to date, wiping out a convoy of thirty Goums on the edge of the desert between Tébessa and the remote outpost of Guentis. Six bodies were found and the remainder of the Goums – and their weapons – disappeared without trace. Among the dead, his head crushed by a rock, was the French administrator from Guentis, Maurice Dupuy, who left eight young children and whom a deeply affected Soustelle esteemed as a "lay saint".

Worse still, the F.L.N. seemed to be switching their attacks from barracks and police stations to "softer" targets. Brutal murders of Muslim "friends of France", from *caids* to humble village constables, multiplied, totalling eighty-eight in April alone, with a similar number hideously mutilated – as a terrible warning for the rest. At the same time the F.L.N. issued an edict enforcing a ban on Muslims smoking or drinking alcohol, as an economic blow against the *pied noir* tobacco- or vine-growers like Senator Borgeaud. Penalty for a first offence was the cutting off of lips or nose; for a second, *égorgement* – or what the army dubbed with black humour, "the Kabyle smile". Most nations have their favourite unpleasant way of death; to the Algerians throat-slitting is associated with the killing of sheep, and therefore the most humiliating fate an enemy can be made to suffer. On European-owned farms, more and more *pieds noirs* would wake up to discover vines ripped up, cattle poisoned, dogs with their throats slit or hanged. Although direct attacks on French civilians had hitherto been minimal, May brought the killing of four – also found *égorgés*.

With the civil authorities apparently impotent to prevent either the mutilations or the killings, the army could show no substantial success in the field since Ducournau's tracking-down of Grine the previous November, and it was becoming clear to Soustelle that it was not up to the job facing it. It was still altogether too much of a N.A.T.O.-style force, both in equipment and technique, and it was by no means clear-minded about its tasks. Did "pacification", for instance, mean trying to regain the confidence of the inhabitants; or did it mean crushing the rebellion by whatever means available? "Limited repression" did not always make the clearest sense to a patrol of young soldiers caught in a vicious ambush. What was needed were new ideas, new leaders, new weapons, and more men. As Soustelle noted, a few planes or guns were enough to destroy a *douar*: "But to defend the same *douar* day after day up to the day when it could take up its own arms, that needs people. . . ." Under strong pressure, the Faure government agreed to send another ten battalions to Algeria, bringing the total there from 74,000 up to 100,000 men – already almost double the number at All Saints 1954. It was a further escalation towards total warfare, yet still too little; and at no time during his stewardship, claims Soustelle, were there to be sufficient troops. "But where to find them?" On his arrival the army possessed one solitary Bell helicopter, rented from a private firm. Soustelle pressed the government into persuading the U.S.A.F. in Germany to turn over eight of its Sikorskys to the French Air Force. It then concluded a purchasing agreement to obtain other helicopters in the U.S.A.

By June Soustelle had achieved a thorough shake-up of the army High Command; Generals Cherrière and Spillmann had been replaced by Lorillot and Allard; and an officer who had proved himself during the recent "pacification" of Morocco, General Parlange, was put in sole charge of the Aurès, where a state of emergency had finally been decreed in April. Another newcomer was General André Beaufre, leading the élite 7th Rapid Mechanised Division into Kabylia. Beaufre was one of France's most intellectual soldiers, a precise and analytical intelligence who, as one of the legendary Marshal de Lattre de Tassigny's right-hand men in Indo-China, had made a close study of guerrilla techniques. Like Ducournau, he believed in an active policy of "living on top of" the F.L.N.; but, again, was to find after the first skirmishes that even his highly mobile units were too unwieldly for Krim's wily maquisards.

"Collective responsibility"

Pressed increasingly by the *pieds noirs* to "do something", Soustelle, reluctantly found himself forced into accepting a draconian new measure to redress the army's lack of more positive results. The dubious principle of "collective responsibility" seems to have been foisted on Soustelle by the army; certainly it was never discussed with the "left wing" of Soustelle's cabinet, the Tillions and Monteils. Soustelle had issued the following strict, and clear, instructions concerning reprisals that closely adhered to the line originally laid down by Mitterrand:

> every indiscriminate reprisal is strictly forbidden . . . all individuals arrested, whether their culpability is certain or probable, are to be handed over to the qualified authorities, police, gendarmerie . . . etc. No one must substitute himself for these authorities to re-establish order or punish the guilty. . . . Police operations . . . interrogations, etc, must be conducted without brutality . . . every offence against human dignity . . . rigorously forbidden.

This was a lapidary and admirable code of conduct that was to become a major bone of contention with the army as the years went by; however, early in Soustelle's term of office he was virtually short-circuited by "Babar" Cherrière, the military commander already under notice. On 14 May he sent this crucial signal to his subordinate in the Constantine area,

General Allard: "I delegate you powers to decide, depending circumstances, employment machine-guns, rockets and bombs, on bands in new rebellion zone. Collective responsibility to be vigorously applied. There will be *no written instruction given by the Governor* [author's italics]."

The previous day Cherrière had spelled out what was meant by "collective responsibility" by providing examples: "Destruction of ninety-nine telegraph poles near Oued-Zenati. It is known that all the males of a *douar* were involved. The *douar* must pay for the destroyed poles, replace them. Then remove all the males." To "remove all the males" meant, in effect, to herd them together into newly created internment camps, equivalents of Long Kesh in Northern Ireland and forerunners of the "regroupment centres" that were to cause so much discontent in years to come. What "collective responsibility" often actually entailed for the Auresian villagers at its lowest and least pernicious level is well depicted by Pierre Leulliette: "Cutting down tough tree-trunks at night, digging wide holes in the stony track, menaced by rebel guns. And, in the morning, the exhausting work would hardly be finished when they would have to replant the poles and fill up the potholes, once again menaced by guns, this time ours." Somewhat defensively, Soustelle claims that "collective responsibility" *was* effective, at least when applied to repairs of roads and telegraph poles; it accorded with the Arab mentality of respecting strength, despising weakness. At the same time, however, as Germaine Tillion pointed out, it gravely offended the Chaouias' deep-rooted sense of justice, and, in the eyes of Yves Courrière, based on his interviews of F.L.N. leaders, it provided the F.L.N. with one of its "principal psychological trump cards".

Moreover, "collective responsibility" did not – could not – stop at the re-erection of telegraph poles. The unsolved killing of a French soldier, or ambushing of a patrol, would lead to the evacuation of a suspect *douar*, followed by its destruction. Pierre Clostermann, the French air ace of the Second World War, records how, in 1958, the bombing of these poverty-stricken *douars* "broke my heart", while a senior officer admitted to him: "Well, the *mechta* that I can't defend, I am obliged to destroy, for above all I have the duty to protect the life of the soldiers entrusted to me." Then, as the horrible savagery of the war mounted, increasingly blind eyes would be turned on the humanitarian fiats of Mitterrand and his successor, and villages would *not* always be evacuated before the bombing started. In his novel *The Centurions* Jean Lartéguy relates how when two of "Colonel Raspeguy's" paras were found "with their throats slit, their guts ripped out and the sexual organs stuffed into their mouths", and bodies pointed towards Mecca, it was followed by a spontaneous, immediate reprisal: "Twenty-seven Muslim bodies were lined up together, their heads turned towards the West." It was a fair portrayal of how the vicious escalation of brutality established itself. News films of the epoch that were widely distributed in France would show a young French soldier, clad in shorts, kicking a trembling prisoner captured with a rifle in his hands; or there would be shots of jeering troops, with Gauloises dangling casually from the lower lip, twisting the heads of F.L.N. captives so as to make a good pose for the camera. With the increase of rebel atrocities, the time was approaching when the army would regard almost every Muslim as a potential killer.

In his book *Les Français d'Algérie*, Pierre Nora recounts an episode that was to become, depressingly enough, perhaps not so exceptional as the war dragged on: near Sidi-Bel-Abbès a Foreign Legion patrol systematically searched a *pied noir* farm where they believed *fellaghas* were hiding, and discovered two in the corner of a barn. They were interrogated, with blows of rifle butts, but appeared not to understand French. This enraged the Foreign Legion lieutenant, who accused nine agricultural workers on the farm of complicity. After further interrogation had produced nothing, the two rebels, plus the nine farmhands, were put against a wall forthwith and shot in the presence of wives and children, according to the *pied noir* proprietor (who told the story). He attacked the Legionnaires violently: "How could you shoot down workers who saw me born! Without warning me? How do you expect me to continue to work now? Even the *fellagha* respect the harvest. Assassins, vandals – is this how you pacify. . . ?"

This was the road along which "collective responsibility" inevitably led. Pierre-Henri Simon, the Catholic writer, who had spent nearly five years in Nazi prisoner-of-war camps and was to become a fierce critic of his own country's conduct in Algeria, comments that "collective responsibility" was "exactly the principle by which Hitler's men justified the massacre of Oradour". Happily, during the Algerian war nothing took place approaching the atrocity of Oradour, when in June 1944 an entire French village – totalling 643 men, women and children – was massacred in reprisals by the German S.S. But the doctrine of "collective responsibility" threatened to annul at one stroke the work of conciliation by the "left wing" of Soustelle's cabinet, Germaine Tillion and Commandant Monteil. As Madame Tillion warned General Parlange: "the cycle of repression getting ever tougher, and the rebellion ever stronger, will ruin all your efforts of pacification. . . ."

Soustelle under cross-fire

By the summer of 1955 Soustelle, always trying in Algeria to find a delicate third path between the opposing extremes of the *pied noir* lobbies and the Muslim nationalists, was being buffeted by mounting pressures from a multiplicity of directions. A second visit to the Aurès in May had left him profoundly depressed; on the one hand, the security situation was still deteriorating, the "smallpox" spreading; on the other hand, he was shocked by the human consequences of the policy of tougher measures which the hard-pressed army imposed on him. At a clinic where Soustelle was shown a child with its eyes eaten away by trachoma, his own feelings were voiced by an aide who was heard to murmur: "Do we really have to bombard such poor devils?" It was typical of the conflicting emotions that the sight of actual suffering, or inhumanity, invariably aroused in Soustelle. Meanwhile, in Paris, resistance to his "integration" concept was gathering momentum as opponents warned of the implications that parliament would eventually be "swamped" by the populous Muslims; that, in its present delicate state of balance, the Assembly might find the casting vote held steadily by a cohesive Algerian bloc. Faure, too, under the customary pressures of the Fourth Republic, was threatening to back-slide on the support promised to Soustelle's reforms. Already on 23 March Soustelle had threatened to resign when it seemed his budget was menaced; and again in June he had written protesting that his policy was constantly being impeded by "petty politics in Algiers and Paris, and by the daily harassing of the Press" – as well as by rebel activity.

Like "assimilation" before it, "integration" (once the novelty had worn off) was viewed with distrust by Europeans and Muslims alike. With the parliamentary and bureaucratic delays in Paris holding up both ratification of Soustelle's policy and the necessary cash, Algerian Muslims could still find few enough concrete examples of integration at work. There remained curious, and sometimes insulting, anomalies in the administration; as a minor example, because of the merging of the departments of Beaux Arts et Cultes, a devout marabout visiting the Gouvernement-Général on a religious mission would be gravely affronted by a print of Le Déjeuner sur l'herbe. The State of Emergency Bill, finally introduced on 1 April, had also resulted in some additional absurdities; control of press and cinema banned such films as The Bridge on the River Kwai (because it showed Europeans in humiliating circumstances) and Ill Met by Moonlight (because the kidnapping of a German general by British and Cretan partisans might have seemed altogether too suggestive!). But it also resulted in more serious irritations; there were mesures d'exception, rights of night searches and powers of arrest, that seemed to strike indiscriminately at Muslim citizens. Germaine Tillion had been particularly disturbed by the little alienating unfairnesses she observed – such as Muslims being subjected to the humiliations of personal frisking, while Europeans were tacitly exempt. Soustelle was also not helped when, playing to the pied noir gallery, Bourgès-Maunoury in a hard-line speech to the Algerian Assembly on 27 May promised that his government "will never look about for what are called interlocuteurs valables. I go still further; I claim that no national government after ours will be able to venture upon this path."

Meanwhile, by resorting to all manner of procedural devices, the adroit and ultra-conservative president of the Algerian Assembly, Laquière, had managed repeatedly to delay debate on the Soustelle programme, so that it was not ready for presentation to the government in Paris until 1 June. As a result, what chances Soustelle might have had of gaining the enthusiasm of the moderate Muslim leaders slipped by. Once again it was to be the old story of too little, too late.

As fresh incidents of terrorism succeeded each other unimpeded by the army, the frightened *pied noir* community also – and not altogether unreasonably – showed itself less and less inclined to surrender its existing privileges in the name of "integration". With the heat of summer, Soustelle noted a steady build-up of passions, and of pressure on himself for not being "tough enough"; in July, Deleplanque's sub-prefecture at Batna had been "literally besieged" after two *colons* had been horribly killed. It was becoming more and more difficult for Soustelle to manoeuvre between the opposing poles, and one of the inevitable consequences of these external stresses was a split between the "hawks" and "doves" within Soustelle's own cabinet. At the end of June Commandant Monteil resigned. The original *casus belli* had been an episode where five Kabyles from Ighil-Ilef had been arrested under "collective responsibility" and had been tortured. Soustelle, informed of this by Monteil, had been outraged and ordered the prompt release of the suspects; but all five were almost immediately rearrested by the police. Monteil considered this a breach of trust by Soustelle, and had threatened to resign then. By June he felt events were passing totally out of his control, and in his letter of resignation he explained: "arbitrary arrests are increasing; the so-called 'lodgement camps' are filling up with more and more innocents (in a proportion of 167 in 200, on the evidence of the Prefect of Constantine himself, M. Dupuch); the army destroys, bombards, summarily executes. . . ." "Integration", he concluded, was already a dead letter. Germaine Tillion, too, found herself at odds with Soustelle. When, at the end of May, she came to him with proposals for a new initiative towards the Algerian nationalists, he turned a deaf ear. From that moment until her departure the following January she was hardly to see Soustelle again. Although there was no question of her resigning, "We were no longer", she said, "on the same wavelength."

Though Soustelle himself denies it, it seems that a change of heart set in somewhere about this time. In a private visit to Mendès-France he confessed despondently "I am discouraged . . . the government is against me . . . everybody is against me." He too wanted to resign, but Mendès-France persuaded him to stay on – as "a good liberal". What is also on record, however, is that on 28 May Soustelle had shown himself to be deeply affected at the emotion-charged funeral in Tébessa of the murdered administrator from Guentis, the "saintly" and much loved Dupuy. Pinning a posthumous Legion of Honour on the oldest of Dupuy's eight children, a boy in shorts, Soustelle – himself on the verge of tears – declared with meridional vehemence: "Let us swear before these coffins to do everything, without sparing anything, to revenge those who have been taken away from us...." The use of the word "revenge" by the governor-general certainly shocked Monteil, and the funeral of Dupuy with its demonstration of what F.L.N. terrorism meant to the French families of Algeria may well have marked an important milestone in the conversion of Soustelle – a conversion that was to be completed later that summer by the most appalling events yet witnessed in the rebellion.

The Philippeville massacres

The strategy for modern terrorism was recently well defined by the Brazilian guerrilla leader, Carlos Marighela, before he was hunted down and killed:

> It is necessary to turn political crisis into armed conflict by performing violent actions that will force those in power to transform the political situation of the country into a military situation. That will alienate the masses, who, from then on, will revolt against the army and the police and blame them for this state of things.

Marighela's essential philosophy was that a resort to blind terrorism would inevitably provoke the forces of law and order into an equally blind repression, which in turn would lead to a backlash by the hitherto uncommitted, polarise the situation into two extreme camps and make impossible any dialogue of compromise by eradicating the "soft centre". "The government can only intensify its repression," wrote Marighela in a passage of transcending importance for the modern world:

> thus making the life of its citizens harder than ever; homes will be broken into, police searches organised, innocent people arrested and communications broken; police terror will become the order of the day, and there will be more and more political murders—in short a massive political persecution. The population will refuse to collaborate with the authorities, so that the latter will find the only solution to their problems lies in having recourse to the actual physical liquidation of their opponents. The political situation of the country will become a military situation....

It was along this road of war without quarter against the civil population that the F.L.N. now began to move, as other terrorist bodies have done since. The consequences would not be all that far-removed from the situation envisaged by Marighela.

Since the death in January, at the hands of Ducournau's paras, of Mourad Didouche, the F.L.N.'s Wilaya 2 covering the North Constantine region had come under the command of Youssef Zighout, a thirty-four-year-old wheelwright, and his right-hand man, Lakhdar Ben Tobbal. Both men had been veterans of the underground O.S. from the 1950s onwards, and both had been present at the "Meeting of the Twenty-two" in the summer of 1954. Ben Tobbal was the more intellectual of the two, was well-versed in guerrilla theory and was to prove himself one of the more ruthlessly efficient of the F.L.N. leaders; aged thirty-two, and of peasant background, his rather oriental features (possibly a consequence of Yemeni blood) earned him the nickname of *le Chinois*. Deeply attached to the youthful Didouche, Zighout had been anguished by his death and subsequently outraged by the mounting brutality of the *ratissages* conducted within his Wilaya by the French army, and their refusal to accord to any captured F.L.N. *djounoud* the rights of a combatant. His own forces had taken a severe hammering from the hands of Ducournau (worse than the French High Command realised), and by May had been reduced to two hundred men with only seventy weapons between them. Yet – as a direct consequence of "collective responsibility" – by August they had risen again to five hundred, each armed with at least a sporting rifle. Although cut off from contact with the other Wilayas, Zighout and Ben Tobbal were aware that these were in poor shape; Wilayas 5 (Oranie) and 4 (Algérois) were only capable of feeble efforts, and 3 (Kabylia) was little better off, while, since the capture of Ben Boulaid, the vigorous Wilaya 1 in the Aurès was partly paralysed by bitter dissensions within the leadership. Only Wilaya 2 seemed in a position to strike a major blow to keep the revolution going.

In a mood almost of desperation, Zighout and Ben Tobbal convened a council of war at the end of June to launch, for the first time, a policy of total war on all French civilians, regardless of age and sex. Justifying it, Zighout declared: "To colonialism's policy of *collective repression* [author's italics] we must reply with collective reprisals against the Europeans, military and civil, who are all united behind the crimes committed upon our people. For them, no pity, no quarter!" Simultaneously with military action by cadres of the F.L.N., a true "people's revolt" was to be unleashed in the Constantine region, in which "the largest possible number of Algerians, even hastily armed with only sticks, pitchforks, axes, sickles and knives", was to be involved. Principal targets were the harbour city of Philippeville and its surrounding neighbourhood, El-Milia and the area around Contantine itself. It would, in effect, be another Sétif – only worse – and Zighout and Ben Tobbal accepted that the losses would be severe.

20 August was a day of the kind of stifling Algerian summer heat when passions readily boil over. The killing started in Constantine, perched high above its great gorge and where, in happier days, Pierre Louÿs had completed his *Chansons de Bilitis*. Almost the first victim was Ferhat Abbas's

nephew, Allouah Abbas, a municipal councillor for Constantine, an U.D.M.A. supporter and a moderate like his uncle. His execution had been ordained by Ben Tobbal for his criticism of F.L.N. excesses, and was systematically carried out. For the rest, the mob took over, goaded on by armed F.L.N. regulars. In the port of Philippeville, with its thoroughly European, Côte d'Azur atmosphere, which Pierre Leulliette remembers from leave as a "happy, sweet-smelling town", Muslims of both sexes swarmed into the streets in a state of frenzied, fanatical euphoria. Grenades were thrown indiscriminately into cafés, passing European motorists dragged from their vehicles and slashed to death with knives or even razors. Altogether some twenty-six localities came under sudden attack.

The peak of horror was reached at Ain-Abid, twenty-four miles east of Constantine, and at El-Halia, a small pyrite mining centre close to Philippeville. El-Halia housed 130 Europeans and some 2,000 Muslims who for years had coexisted amicably enough together. Some were on friendly terms with each others' families, while in the mine labour relations had been exceptionally good, with a rare degree of equality between the two races. It appears that the whole Muslim community had been aware of what was brewing at least twenty-four hours previously, and a number of families left the village. On the morning of the 20th some fifty Muslim workers absented themselves from the mine – but not an inkling of this was passed on to any of the Europeans. Shortly before noon, when it was known that the *pied noir* women would be preparing lunch and their men would have returned home from the midday heat of the mine, four groups of fifteen to twenty men attacked the village, taking it completely by surprise. They were led by mineworkers who knew each house and its occupants. Telegraph lines were cut, the emergency radio transmitter was found to be "out of order", and the village constable who was equipped with warning rockets had "disappeared". The attackers went from house to house, mercilessly slaughtering all the occupants regardless of sex or age, and egged on by Muslim women with their eerie *you-you* chanting. According to Jacques Soustelle, in some of the attacked towns the *muezzins* even broadcast from their minarets exhortations to slit the throats of women and nurses in the cause of "the holy war".

It was not until two o'clock that a forest guard managed by a miracle to dodge ambushes and bring the news to Philippeville en foot; and still another hour and a half elapsed before a para detachment could reach the village. An appalling sight greeted them. In houses literally awash with blood, European mothers were found with their throats slit and their bellies slashed open by bill-hooks. Children had suffered the same fate, and infants in arms had had their brains dashed out against the wall. Four families had been wiped out down to the last member; only six who had barricaded themselves in a house in the centre of the village and had held out with sporting rifles and revolvers had escaped unscathed. Men returning home from the mine had been ambushed in their cars and hacked to pieces. Altogether thirty-seven Europeans had died, including ten children under fifteen, and another thirteen had been left for dead.

Among other butchery, at Ain-Abid an entire *pied noir* family called Mello perished atrociously: a seventy-three-year-old grandmother and eleven-year-old daughter, the father killed in his bed, with his arms and legs hacked off. The mother had been disembowelled, her five-day-old baby slashed to death and replaced in her opened womb. There were similar scenes of such revolting savagery in attacks elsewhere that day, and what heightened the horror (particularly at El-Halia) was the carefully pre-meditated planning which clearly lay behind them, with the wanton participation of so many deemed "friendly" Muslims or fellow-workers. The details sicken the stomach, but they need to be recounted for no other reason than to explain the potent and profound effect that the "Philippe-ville massacre" was to have on the *pieds noirs*, on Jacques Soustelle, and indeed on the whole subsequent history of the Algerian war.

The reaction of the French army units in the area was immediate. A friend in Ducournau's crack 18th Régiment de Chasseurs Parachutistes described the scene in Philippeville to Pierre Leulliette. They had been asleep in barracks after night operations when the killing began. Out in the streets they found

> bodies literally strewed the town. The Arab children, wild with enthu-siasm – to them it was a great holiday – rushed about yelling among the grown-ups. They finished off the dying. In one alley we found two of them kicking in an old woman's head. Yes, kicking it in! We had to kill them on the spot: they were crazed....

Catching up with a group of "rebels", mingled with civilians,

> We opened fire into the thick of them, at random. Then as we moved on and found more bodies, our company commanders finally gave us the order to shoot down every Arab we met. You should have seen the result.... For two hours all we heard was automatic rifles spitting fire into the crowd. Apart from a dozen *fellagha* stragglers, weapons in hand, whom we shot down, there were at least a hundred and fifty *boukaks* [another derogatory term for Muslims]....
>
> At midday, fresh orders: take prisoners. That complicated everything. It was easy when it was merely a matter of killing....
>
> At six o'clock next morning, all the l.m.g.s and machine-guns were lined up in front of the crowd of prisoners, who immediately began to yell. But we opened fire; ten minutes later, it was practically over. There were so many of them that they had to be buried with bulldozers.
>
> Now you see why there are so few people left in the town. The few European survivors are still so paralysed with fright that they stay at home, and those natives who are still alive do the same. Personally I can't wait to go on leave....

It seems unlikely that this was just one isolated incident; French newsreels at the time showed one sequence of a young para shooting down an unarmed Algerian in a road, then casually reloading his rifle as the man lay, still agonising and clutching at his belly. Meanwhile, by way of explanation for the "liquidating" of the Muslim prisoners, Leulliette's Chasseur added meaningfully: "the Europeans who had survived the massacre would never have forgiven us. . . . They'd have come and finished them off themselves." And, indeed, in many instances they did. In what seems like a mistaken over-reaction, the administration allowed European settlers to arm themselves in self-defence – which had been expressly vetoed by Soustelle a few months earlier. The result was that in Philippeville, claims Edward Behr, *pieds noirs* formed "vigilante committees, summarily executed Muslims and buried them surreptitiously while armed civilians held over-inquisitive correspondents at bay".

As always, there is a discrepancy in the casualty figures. Soustelle states that 123 were killed by the F.L.N.-led mob on 20 August, of whom seventy-one were Europeans; while 1,273 of the "insurgents" died, two-thirds during the actual attacks. He admits, however, that "our reprisals were severe", and it will always be open to suspicion that a great many more innocent Muslims were killed in the backlash than was ever admitted; the F.L.N., giving names and addresses, claim as high as 12,000.

The conversion of Soustelle

Immediately on hearing the news, Soustelle flew to the scene of the massacre. Nothing was concealed from his gaze; the mutilated men, the disembowelled mothers, and in Constantine hospital he visited women and children survivors "groaning in fever and in nightmare, their fingers severed, their throats half-slit". At the burial of the victims in Philippeville, grief and rage took over, with distraught relatives trampling on the flowers sent by the administration. "The bright gaiety of the August sun," says Soustelle of that day, "looking down with indifference on all the horrors, made them even more cruel." He returned to Algiers utterly nauseated, deeply affected and with despair in his heart. Though he has been at pains to deny it ever since, it does seem that Philippeville marked the turning-point in the conversion of Soustelle. Certainly, from this date on determination to crush the rebellion began to assume priority over any hopes of liberal compromise, while those close to him – like Mendès-France – detected an unmistakable hardening of line. And for the Algerians of both races it was a terrible Rubicon over which there was to be no return. "It was not only the sacked houses or the poor mutilated corpses that the *fellagha* left in their passage," says Soustelle "it was confidence, hope, peace. A sombre harvest of hatred sprouted in the bloodshed. Terror dominated minds. Far from being brought together by the ordeal, human beings were going to divide themselves and tear themselves to pieces."

Horrible as it was, there is no doubt that – on the principle set out by Carlos Marighela – for the F.L.N. this new Sétif was to prove a net gain. Though some Muslims may have recoiled in disgust, by October recruitment in the North Constantine area had risen to an estimated 1,400 "regulars" – almost the highest of any of the Wilayas – and from then on it was to remain throughout the war one of the most highly contaminated areas on the army "smallpox chart". As Soustelle himself admitted, in the war of subversion the Philippeville massacre was a victory; for, between the two communities, "there had been well and truly dug an abyss through which flowed a river of blood". What had hitherto been, in many respects, a "phoney war" – or *drôle de révolution* as some French called it – now became a full-blooded war to the end. August 1955 was the beginning of what Mitterrand termed the real *cercle infernale* in Algeria.

Returning in September, Soustelle recorded:

> One could not imagine anything more lugubrious than the atmosphere prevailing at Philippeville. It was a season of storms, and sombre clouds filled the sky. The streets were almost deserted, with the exception of armed patrols. The Europeans saw terrorists in every Muslim, the Muslims feared reprisals by the Europeans. . . .

The stormy skies were symptomatic of the troubles pressing in on Soustelle from almost every side as 1955 drew to a close. The first, and perhaps most disappointing, blow came on 26 September when sixty-one Muslim second college deputies signed a statement repudiating "integration". Denouncing "blind repression" and "collective responsibility" as a cause of their dissatisfaction, they declared the concept of integration to be "now out-dated", adding: "The overwhelming majority of the population now supports the Algerian national idea." The impact of Philippeville and its ensuing backlash was clear here, and moderate Muslim leaders had been left in no doubt that the assassination of Ferhat Abbas's nephew had been intended as a warning for them. Next, Jacques Chevallier, in what seemed like a real stab-in-the-back to Soustelle, published a stinging criticism of his policy in *Le Monde* of 5 October, withdrawing his support from integration as now being "practically inapplicable". In pain and anger Soustelle responded to the "Motion of the Sixty-one" by simply suspending the session of the Algerian Assembly. This in turn had its echo in the Palais Bourbon. For three days the National Assembly debated Algeria in mid-October; Premier Faure gave what looked like only a lukewarm support of integration, and there was increasing talk of a new solution – "federalism". The government scraped by with 305 to 274 votes, but the only result of the prolonged debate was indecision. Another shock came from New York where, under pressure from Third World representatives and by a majority of only one in the General Assembly, the Algerian problem was tabled for the first time on the United Nations Assembly order of the day. The French delegation promptly withdrew, but it was, says Soustelle, "worth more than a convoy of arms" to the F.L.N. In the military sphere, forces at Soustelle's disposal had now been inflated to the large total of 160,000, and towards the end of the year he claims the situation was beginning to look much brighter. A successful raid on the desert head-quarters of Bachir Chihani had produced a windfall of documents, giving the Deuxième Bureau its first clear view of the overall structure of the F.L.N. On the other hand, this had been offset by the disturbing news of the first significant desertions from Tirailleur units returned from Indo-China.

But, in Soustelle's view, it was from Paris that the coldest wind blew. On 21 October, while inspecting army units near Constantine with Bourgès-Maunoury, the latter confided that he had to return to Paris that same night as Edgar Faure, under pressure of events in Algeria, wanted to discuss bringing the date of the forthcoming general election six months earlier. Soustelle was aghast. Flying to Paris, he pleaded with Faure that to hold elections and risk a change of government at this moment would have "lethal" consequences in Algeria. Faure was adamant, and the dissolution of the Assembly was decreed for 2 December. Time was fast running out for Soustelle.

Camus and the "civil truce"

The "Motion of the Sixty-one" and the defection of Chevallier signified that the "men of good will" of both races had got sadly thinner and thinner on the ground, as their liberal ideas became more and more diffuse and divergent. But towards the end of Soustelle's term, however, a phenomenon occurred that kindled a brief flicker of hope; though, seen in retrospect, it was to be one of the last of its kind. The initiative had come from that great son of *pied noir* Algeria, and true liberal humanitarian Albert Camus. Born in 1913 of working-class *petits blancs* (his father was killed on the Marne the following year), Camus had made his name by the inspiring leaders he wrote in *Combat*, the underground newspaper he had helped found in Nazi-occupied France. After 1945 he had emerged as the intellectual conscience of the post-war generation of left-of-centre Frenchmen, had established his reputation as a major novelist, and had written a number of articles eloquently drawing attention to the plight of the indigenous Algerians. Through 1955 he had watched in anguish the escalation of atrocity and "collective responsibility" reprisal. "Everybody leans on the crime of the other to justify himself." After Philippeville he wrote to an "Algerian militant" that he was "ready to despair", adding his fear that unless there were restraints imposed by both sides "tomorrow Algeria will be a land of ruins and dead which no power in the world will be capable of resurrecting in this century". The horrors of August decided Camus to launch a "holy war" of liberals himself, and on 16 December he proclaimed in *L'Express* – amid a forceful attack on Soustelle's failure to effect "genuine reforms" – the opening of a campaign for a "civil truce". His aim was to start by placing a limitation on the murderous character of the war through a "truce" that would outlaw all attacks on civilian non-combatants.

From the beginning the odds were heavily weighted against this idealistic sortie by Camus, perhaps a more effective writer than a politician. In France, led by his old friends Sartre and Simone de Beauvoir, the Left had dismissed him as a "bourgeois" renegade because of his criticism of repression in Stalinist Russia; acidly Simone de Beauvoir remarked that his language "had never sounded hollower than when he demanded pity for the civilians. The conflict was one between two civilian communities." In Algeria the Muslims felt (not entirely without reason) that he understood their predicament less well than that of his own *petit blancs*; while to a large body of the more conservative *pieds noirs* he was totally suspect. Worst of all, the two men whom Camus selected as the Muslim lynch-pin of his campaign – Mohamed Lebjaoui, a prosperous middle-class merchant, and Amar Ouzegane, leader of the Algerian Communist Party and an old friend of Camus from his Communist days – had both become, secretly and unknown to Camus, members of the F.L.N. They decided to "penetrate" thoroughly the "civil truce" organisation and use it for their own purposes as an instrument of F.L.N. propaganda.

Arriving in Algiers, Camus was immediately shocked by the virulence of anti-liberal sentiments among the *pieds noirs*. At his first public meeting on 22 January 1956, a hostile mob congregated outside the hall and their shouts of "*Camus au poteau!*" were clearly audible inside. On the dais with Camus was Ferhat Abbas, in one of his own last appearances as a moderate nationalist. Eloquently Camus urged: "We can at least exercise some influence on the most hateful aspect of the fight; we can propose, without making any change in the present situation, that we refrain from what makes it unforgivable – the murder of the innocent." If this were to fail, the only prospect would be one of "definitive divorce, destruction of all hope, and a calamity of which we have so far only the feeblest idea". Though an F.L.N. militant present accused Camus of having spoken like "a soft sister" (*bonne soeur*), for a time he held his mixed Muslim and European audience in a unique mood of fraternal fervour that was not to be witnessed again in Algiers until, briefly, the euphoric days of May 1958. Then the mounting hubbub outside forced Camus to cut short the meeting. The inspired but perhaps hopelessly over-idealistic notion of the "civil truce" collapsed from the stresses within and without; and with it there also died the last hope of a liberal compromise in the war.

Camus, bitterly disillusioned on discovering how he and the "civil truce" movement had been traduced and "used" by the F.L.N., wrote to a close friend: "I thought myself able to speak in the name of reason, but all that is out of date, and passion carries everything before it. One has to come here to understand." From now on he withdrew into his shell. Breaking with *L'Express, Combat* and *France-Observateur*, he was to re-emerge to write only once more about Algeria, at the beginning of 1958, before his tragic death in a car accident two years later.

The failure of the "civil truce" campaign also coincided with the end of the year of Soustelle. As Soustelle had warned Edgar Faure, the febrile uncertainty generated by the French election campaign (during which Mitterrand received a bloody nose from a well-aimed pear) had produced disastrous reactions among both Muslim and *pied noir* communities. The F.L.N. had seized its opportunities, and 1956 began on a thoroughly bad note for the security forces. On 2 January twenty-seven million French went to the polls and returned an astonishing and disquieting result; Faure's governing coalition of moderates lost some hundred seats, while the Communists gained fifty-two to make them the dominant party. But the biggest shock was the phenomenon of the virtually unknown Pierre Poujade, whose faction of militant small shopkeepers collected no less than two and a half million votes and fifty-two seats, to hold a balance of power in the new Assembly. Proclaimed by his hysterical supporters as "Jeanne d'Arc and Henri IV rolled into one", the stationer from the Auvergne was also described as being "anti-Semitic, anti-Communist, anti-democratic, anti-parliamentary"; now he had hopped on the band-waggon of being pro-*pied noir*. The Bourse slumped fifteen per cent, the Eiffel Tower caught fire, Mistinguett died, and the Seine froze in the most bitterly cold winter since the war. For three weeks Faure struggled to form a new government, but on 24 January he resigned and two days later Guy Mollet, the secretary-general of the Socialist Party (S.F.I.O.) took office. One of his first moves was to announce Soustelle's replacement by the seventy-nine-year-old General Catroux, the wartime High Commissioner in Algiers. Also in Mollet's cabinet were Mendès-France and Mitterrand.

Like his patron, Mendès-France, Soustelle had been removed from office by the caprices of French politics before anything but a superficial portion of his reform programme could be enacted. In advance of his departure he addressed to the government an important and prophetic "testament", warning it of three main dangers ahead. First, he feared lest the morale of the army might break: "disquiet, discouragement and disgust among the military is at its peak, especially in the lower echelons, that is to say those who get themselves killed feeling that France has no gratitude for them". Secondly, there was the danger of announcing publicly an intention to negotiate with the rebels; this would "suffice to convince the population once and for all that the rebels are winning and to induce it, for fear of reprisals, to take refuge in the camp of the victors". Thirdly, it would be disastrous to attempt to negotiate a settlement through an *ad hoc* Algerian Assembly acting as an *interlocuteur valable* because rebel terror would swiftly reduce such a body to subservience, and it would then inevitably opt for secession from France.

On 2 February, as Soustelle made his way to the port of Algiers to embark finally for France, there took place one of those extraordinary displays of volatile and passionate emotion of which the *méditerranéen-et-demi pieds noirs* were capable. Tens of thousands thronged the streets shouting, *"Ne partez pas!"* *"Revenez!"* and *"Soustelle, Soustelle, avec nous!"* At the harbour the police lines broke and Soustelle was engulfed in a raging human sea, in which here and there a general's kepi or an admiral's white cap could be seen bobbing on the surface. Soustelle had to be rescued and transported to the ship on the front of an armoured car: "It took us nearly an hour to cover the 200 metres which separated us from access to the quay." Never before, or afterwards, had any French official had such a send-off as the despised "Ben-Soussan" whom, just a year ago, the *pieds noirs* had received in such icy silence as the figure appointed by Mendès-France to sell them down the river. With tears in his eyes, Soustelle watched "the bay and city of Algiers in its unforgettable majesty" as it receded into the wintry haze. "But it was man, that day, who held the foreground of the scene, the people of Algiers massed on the Corniche and on the quays, their voice dominating that of nature. *Ce n'est qu'un au revoir*, the crowd sang." He was deeply, passionately stirred. Never in his life before had he tasted such popularity, such a warmth of human affection. For Soustelle at this moment – and henceforth: *"Algérie montait à la tête."*

CHAPTER SIX

The F.L.N.: from Bandung to Soummam

1955–1956

It is easier to fight one's enemies than to get on with one's friends.
Cardinal de Retz

The F.L.N. consolidates

FROM the point of view of the F.L.N. leadership, the period of 1954 to
1957 has aptly been called the "heroic years". It falls roughly into three
phases; first there is that of establishment and survival, over the cruel
winter of 1954 – the truly "heroic" days. Then comes the time of
consolidation: new recruits, new leaders – and with them new policies
and new discords – were now acquired. Falling into several distinct
categories, the new recruits included a large body from previously
uncommitted Muslims; the wholesale "conversion" of Messali's rival
M.N.A.,* and the absorption of members of the Algerian Communist
Party (P.C.A.) and desertions from the Algerian units serving with the
French army; and the support of pro-Muslim individuals among the European and Jewish communities.

This expansion of the F.L.N. was by no means uniform. There were
times when the affairs of one Wilaya would prosper while another would
falter and almost collapse. Sometimes such faltering came about as a direct
consequence of French military pressure, but much more often it was
related to internal dissension among the local F.L.N. leaders, or to a combination of both. Throughout the war internal dissent and personal
animosities were the F.L.N.'s single greatest enemy; on the other hand, its
greatest strength was the secrecy which (like the mutinies in the French
army of 1917 that the Germans never learned about until too late) prevented the French from seizing an advantage.

* By way of "keeping up with the Joneses", shortly after the F.L.N. had launched
the revolution, Messali had reshaped his M.T.L.D. into the tougher sounding
Mouvement Nationaliste Algérien, or M.N.A.

Various reasons have already been suggested for the F.L.N.'s recruitment successes in 1955. There was, first of all, the anger provoked by the excessive zeal of French repressive measures, in disregard of Machiavelli's axiom, "An enemy should be destroyed or bought – and never made a martyr." Then, perhaps more important still, there was the success of success itself: the mere fact that the F.L.N. had survived through that first winter against all the might of France was in itself a most potent recruiting agent. In the eyes of a people regarding *baraka* as a heaven-sent attribute, this was also greatly increased by the sheer audacity with which the *moudjahiddine* carried out their forays, made their proclamations and struck down those earmarked for liquidation. And there was the weapon of terror, which, with the escalation of savagery, with new leaders and new policies, was to become accepted as a technique of proven efficacy.

Internationalising the struggle

It will be recalled that one of the declared top priority objectives of the C.R.U.A. in November 1954 had been the internationalisation of the conflict, and that Ben Bella and his team in Cairo had been charged with this. As far as material support was concerned, in terms of urgently required weapons and ammunition, Nasser, for all his grandiose exhortations, continued to prove a bitter disappointment to the Algerians. It was, says Abdelkader Chanderli who was in charge of arms procurement from Yugoslavia at the time, "negligible". But "because of the need for solidarity, we could not say so". Though its value as a factor of psychological warfare was undeniable, the bombast poured out from Cairo radio about Arab unity and the heroic Algerian *moudjahiddine* deceived the F.L.N. as much as it did the Mollet government whom, by the autumn of 1956, it was to lead into a misappreciation of historic dimensions. Through much of 1955 Ben Bella himself scurried from one capital to another, canvassing financial support and arms deals. The menace that he had already assumed in French eyes as Number One leader of the revolt is indicated by two mysterious assassination attempts against him behind which the long arm of French secret intelligence seemed unmistakable. The first was a bomb explosion outside Ben Bella's Cairo office at the beginning of 1956; the second, later in the year, was an attempt from which he had the narrowest of escapes in Tripoli, mounted by a *pied noir* called Jean David who belonged to a shadowy organisation called the "Main Rouge" with its own subterranean links to French intelligence. Jean David was later shot while attempting to escape over the Libyan border. One of the first efforts at gun-running to the F.L.N. came in February 1955 with the "borrowing" of the Queen of Jordan's private yacht, the *Dina*. Beached off the Spanish Moroccan coast, the *Dina* off-loaded a quantity of weapons; Rif peasants drove their sheep back and forth along the beach to cover up traces. More such operations followed – though most of them were to be apprehended by the French as interception techniques improved.

But the greatest bonus for the F.L.N. cause, both in terms immediately of arms supplies and later of troop movements, came with France's granting of independence to Morocco and Tunisia in March 1956, the paths to which had been pioneered by Mendès-France. From then on the F.L.N. had friendly and open frontiers to east and west, of which the Tunisian in particular was to provide benefits of inestimable value. In the opinion of a *New York Times* correspondent, Michael K. Clark,

> but for the aid and protection afforded it by Tunisia and Morocco, the rebellion would have been circumscribed and perhaps crushed before the end of 1957. But, as the United States learned in Korea,* it is singularly difficult to destroy an enemy enjoying the sanctuary of an inviolable frontier.

Although, in retrospect, any further delay in according independence to these two Maghreb territories seemed out of the question by 1956, to do so without also doing the same for Algeria looked like a major error, in purely strategic terms if no other. Initially, France retained certain reserve rights enabling her to keep military units on Tunisian soil, which in theory might have helped her to prevent the F.L.N. from using it as a sanctuary, but in practice it was to work out quite otherwise. President Bourguiba, always apprehensive that too overt a support for the F.L.N. could provoke a French reoccupation of his country, and in any case a dedicated exponent of maximum co-operation with France, provided Ben Bella with somewhat less than he wanted. His policy remained consistent throughout: Tunisia would grant the F.L.N. rights of sanctuary, but it would not openly join in the war, and its highest goal would be to persuade both parties that their only prospect lay in negotiation. These restraints imposed by Bourguiba would always cause a certain coolness between himself and the F.L.N. leadership; nevertheless, what he did afford it proved enough to assure its military survival.

On the diplomatic level the F.L.N.'s most outstanding feat of inter-nationalisation began in April 1955. After some energetic lobbying by Ait Ahmed, his brother-in-law Khider and M'hamed Yazid (a former principal in Lahouel's faction of the M.T.L.D.), the F.L.N. gained an invitation to attend the Bandung Conference, that landmark for the emerging Third World in which twenty-nine nations representing some 1,300 million people were to take part. Although the Algerians, with no recognised government behind them, could only attend as "unofficial"

---

* Subsequent history might have led him to add: in Vietnam also.

delegates, their presence at Bandung was sufficient to achieve a notable victory on the international scene. After condemnations of colonialism in all forms were pronounced by the conference, it adopted unanimously an Egyptian motion proclaiming Algeria's right to independence, and called upon France to implement this forthwith. Behind the scenes, in private meetings with other Arab delegates, Yazid and Ait Ahmed gained pledges of vast sums of money to support the cause, and in a long conversation with the already legendary Ho Chi Minh they were told encouragingly: "*Les français* ... that's a problem we know well!" With Bandung a vital watershed had been reached for the F.L.N., and the road to the United Nations was open. Five months later the word Algeria was formally inscribed on the agenda of the General Assembly.

New leaders – new policies

Among the new faces coming to the fore with the expansion of the F.L.N. and the steady attrition of such old-guard leaders as Bitat, Ben Boulaid and Didouche, was Mohamedi Said, who was to become the effective leader of Wilaya 3 (Kabylia) upon the promotion of Krim and his lieutenant Ouamrane. A Kabyle born in 1912, and thus one of the oldest F.L.N. leaders, he had grown up with early memories of a French officer slapping his grandparents. Fanatically religious, he claimed to have worked during the Second World War with the pro-Nazi Mufti of Jerusalem, Hajj Amin Husaini, joining the Muslim S.S. legion formed by the Mufti. In 1943 he was parachuted into Tunisia as an Abwehr agent, was caught and sentenced to life imprisonment, but was paroled in 1952. Later, when a colonel in the F.L.N., he explained to an American journalist: "I believed that Hitler would destroy French tyranny and free the world." Whether out of nostalgia for the good old days or detestation for the French, in photos he almost invariably appeared in an incongruous Wehrmacht steel helmet. Under Mohamedi Said, and frequently at odds with him, arose another new figure who was renowned and dreaded for his remorseless cruelty, Ait Hamouda, alias Amirouche. A skeletally tall *montagnard* from the Djurdjura with wide-set eyes and a heavy moustache, Amirouche had been a member of both the religious Ulema and, in Paris, of Messali's M.T.L.D. Of remarkably quick and decisive intelligence, Amirouche when still under thirty had assumed command of a group in Kabylia on his own initiative, following the death of its leader. He swiftly imposed an iron discipline and amazed a somewhat dubious Krim by his ability to exact from his men forced marches of seventy kilometres a day. Within six months he had under his command eight hundred well-trained and exceptionally mobile men, and had firmly established himself in the Soummam region of eastern Kabylia, which had not previously been pro-F.L.N., by a reign of sheer terror.

Ramdane Abane

A third new figure who shared the creed of Amirouche and Zighout that terror was the ultimate weapon, but of far greater weight than either of them, was another Kabyle called Ramdane Abane. Involved in the Sétif massacre of 1945 as an underground operator for Messali, he had been tracked down in 1950 and sentenced to five years' imprisonment. During this time he had undertaken the longest hunger strike yet seen in a French gaol, giving himself acute stomach ulcers with a resultant short temper. Although he came of poor parentage, Abane had succeeded in educating himself to gain his *baccalauréat* and become municipal clerk to a *commune mixte*, while during the war he had served as secretary to the colonel of the same unit as Sergeant Ouamrane. But his real education had come in prison where he had applied himself to the voracious reading of revolutionary studies, Marx and Lenin – and even *Mein Kampf* – and to studying minutely the political aspects of the F.L.N. revolution. Recruited by his wartime acquaintance Ouamrane, on leaving prison in the spring of 1955 (by which time he was thirty-five) Abane was put in charge of re-organising the Algiers networks that had been so badly disrupted the previous winter. Immediately he made his mark as an outstanding political intellect, something which the F.L.N. had previously lacked.

Abane has been variously described as the Robespierre, the Jean Moulin or the Bourguiba of the F.L.N.; or, by Robert Lacoste, simply as its "best brain". One revolutionary leader in exile went so far as to claim that, had Abane lived, "he would have become (although not a Marxist) the Mao of Africa; and he was the only member of the F.L.N. with the breadth to become a leader of the calibre of a Tito". To Yves Courrière Ouamrane remarked of him:

> I've known quite a few intellectuals, but Abane was remarkably intelligent. He was, moreover, a simple man of absolute sincerity. He was not interested in clothes, nor money. The only thing of importance to him was national unity, and he was determined to obtain it by any means. This is what shocked many militants. He was violent, brutal, radical and expeditious in his decisions. He knew nothing about the "velvet glove" (*mettre de gant*). Discussions with him were very violent.... He always used to say "*Messieurs*, look and judge," but that didn't deter him from then insulting anybody who opposed his ideas....

Short in stature, Abane had a smiling, chubby face with lively eyes. They belied a morose personality imbued with an unwavering belief that, just as France had conquered Algeria through violence, nothing but violence would ever shake loose her grip. The sinister dictum, "one corpse in a jacket is always worth more than twenty in uniform", was a favourite of Abane's, and representative of his basic thinking.

From the spring of 1955 Ramdane Abane's philosophy was central to the F.L.N., both in its external operations and internal dissensions, leaving its physiognomy radically altered. His first notable achievement was to draft a new proclamation, dated 1 April 1955, by way of a riposte to France's declaring a state of emergency in Algeria. Compared with the wordy initial statement of the previous November, it was a masterpiece of skilful propaganda, audacious optimism and conciseness. Beginning with an assurance to the Algerians that, over the first five months of activity, "in almost all encounters, our groups composed of ten to twenty men have defeated French army units and inflicted serious losses", it went on to cite, with some exaggeration, various specific military "triumphs". The proclamation ended with a clear menace to such "deviationist" bodies as the Algerian Communist Party and Messali's M.N.A.: "The tribunal of the A.L.N. [Armée de Libération Nationale, as the military arm of the F.L.N. had now become known] will be pitiless towards traitors and enemies of the country...." On reading it for the first time, Soustelle's chief political adviser, Colonel Eydoux, was heard to remark: "Something has changed in the management of the rebellion."

In addition to his involvement on a regional level in resuscitating the Algiers network, Abane busied himself with restructuring the revolution in its every aspect. Being himself neither a Marxist–Leninist nor a devout Muslim theologian, he wanted the F.L.N. to fill a critical void by adapting its own ideology to embrace both creeds without becoming committed to either. Politically, he was the first F.L.N. leader to begin thinking ahead to requirements beyond merely the compass of the war. Deficiencies of discipline and internal security, of finances and propaganda, all came under fire from Abane – as well as such issues less immediately connected with the war as education and cultural affairs. Under particularly his and Krim's impetus, politicisation of F.L.N. cadres moved into higher gear. In June 1956 the first copy of the F.L.N.'s own newspaper, El Moudjahid, appeared in a scruffily roneo'd format and was distributed secretly through the Casbah. By the end of the year, with the establishment of the clandestine Voix de l'Algérie, the transistor radio had become a major weapon of war, with the Algerians – not previously so addicted – buying up the country's entire available stock. At first the French authorities tried to control sales, then jammed transmissions; both had but little success, and the Voix de l'Algérie established itself as a vital factor in maintaining morale and spreading the revolt still further. By this time it could genuinely be said that the F.L.N. had become a "mass movement".

Abane: terror pays

Though Abane could hardly express satisfaction at the savage slaughter of innocents that accompanied it, his cold reasoning told him that the consequences of the Philippeville uprising would be a net gain for the

F.L.N., and they were to encourage him in the initiation of a new offensive of urban terrorism – the Battle of Algiers. Like other revolutionaries both before and since, Abane concurred with his fellow F.L.N. leaders who had reached the conclusion that terror paid. As far as the uncommitted mass of rural Muslims was concerned, Soustelle notes the extreme susceptibility to pressure and blackmail of the average poverty-stricken *fellah* to an F.L.N. band, when, "with the knife literally under his throat they make him hand over 50,000 francs, they hurt him much more than the better off farmer who has had a tractor burnt worth two million francs". It was remarkable, added Soustelle, that the F.L.N. "never sought to attach the rural populations to their cause by promising them a better life, a happier and freer future; no, it was through terror that they submitted them to their tyranny". Visiting Kabylia in 1956, Jean Servier was shocked at the "terrible silence" he found in the villages, each one of which would be held in fee by a local F.L.N. representative responsible simply for collecting "taxes" and food supplies – a kind of "alternative government" to the French system of *caïds*. One village headman to whom he tried to talk whispered, "Let another man come alongside me – so nobody will be able to say that I gave you any information. I shall have a witness. . . ." At another village, west of Algiers, Servier attended a decoration parade for men who had killed two F.L.N. representatives "with an axe and sticks", and when he asked them privately why they had done this he got the answer: "We killed them with blows of sticks and axe because the French took away our rifles." Thus, in this context, the F.L.N. through its policy of terror could claim a double advantage in increasing the vulnerability of peasants in the remoter districts.

At an early stage in the revolution it became a customary initiation ritual for a new recruit to be made to kill a designated "traitor", *mouchard* (police spy or informer), French gendarme officer or colonialist, in the company of a "shadow" who would dispatch the recruit himself should he show any sign of flinching. Admitting this policy in an interview in a Yugoslav journal, Krim stated: "An assassination marks the end of the apprenticeship of each candidate for the A.L.N." Through this "passing-out ceremony" the apprentice became both proven in reliability and bound, Faust-like, to the rebel cause by his act of outlawry. In their actual techniques of liquidation F.L.N. operatives consciously endeavoured to achieve the gruesome, *pour épater les bourgeois*, or an act of ridicule – to belittle the dead man. Mention has already been made of the Algerian predilection for throat-slitting, *le grand sourire*, and other even nastier mutilations; and a pro-F.L.N. American journalist, Herb Greer, records one deterrent execution of a renegade: "When we've shot him his head will be cut off and we'll clip a tag on his ear to show he was a traitor. Then we'll leave the head on the main road. . . ." A loyal *garde-champêtre* would be found tied to a stake, his throat cut, and right arm fixed in mockery of a French army salute; a sergeant-major of the Goums dead with a warning label pinned contemptuously to his nose beneath a jauntily tilted European slouch hat.

"Kill the *caids* . . ." instructed orders seized from Chihani's headquarters in the Nementchas in September 1955: "Take their children and kill them. Kill all those who pay taxes and those who collect them. Burn the houses of Muslim N.C.O.s away on active service. . . ." From an early stage Muslim "moderates" (like Abbas's nephew), or anyone who might play a mediatory or bridging role, were singled out. "Liquidate all personalities who want to play the role of *interlocuteur valable*", read an order sent to Chihani from Ben Bella: "Kill any person attempting to deflect the militants and inculcate in them a *bourguibien* spirit," read another. What this meant in practice, in terms of widening still further the yawning chasm between Europeans and Muslims, is revealed in some grim anecdotes about Algerian teenagers told by Frantz Fanon. In one, a thirteen- and a fourteen-year-old Muslim, who had murdered a thirteen-year-old European school friend, explained:

> "We weren't a bit cross with him. Every Thursday we used to go and play with catapults together, on the hill above the village. He was a good friend of ours. . . ."
> "But why did you pick on him?"
> "Because he used to play with us. Another boy wouldn't have gone up the hill with us."

As far as the deliberately contrived, selective killing of European settlers went, the clear-cut aim was to drive them in from the *bled*, thus further reducing existing contacts between the two communities. The anonymity of their murderers – as with the Mau-Mau in Kenya – served the same purpose by making the whole of the local Muslim population suspect in the eyes of the fearful Europeans.

Mopping up the opposition

Even after Philippeville, however, it was still their fellow Muslims who bore the brunt of F.L.N. terror. Over the first two and a half years of the war 6,352 against 1,035 Europeans were estimated, as a minimum figure, to have been killed in F.L.N. attacks against civilians. During the Yugoslav partisan war of 1941 to 1945, much of Tito's efforts was expended in combat against Mihailović's Serb Četniks, and such a simultaneous internal "civil war" is a not infrequent concomitant of revolutionary struggle against an external enemy. To the F.L.N. the Number One enemy at home was constituted by the "traitor" M.N.A. supporters of Lahouel, and the absent Messali – once again under house-arrest in France. As a result of the French over-zealous round-up of nationalist suspects in November

1954, many of the M.T.L.D.–M.N.A., like Ben Khedda, had already come over to the F.L.N. of their own volition. Those that remained became the object of ruthless attack. Warfare was particularly intense in Kabylia, which, up to 1954, had been regarded as a Messalist stronghold. The M.N.A. then tried to win it back by sending in packets of armed men to form their own maquis.

One such group five hundred strong was created, armed and uniformed in eastern Kabylia under a former M.T.L.D. municipal councillor called Bellounis. At first the F.L.N. reacted by slitting a few random throats. In Algiers, Soustelle's psychological-warfare experts began to toy with the idea of using Bellounis's dissident force as an "anti-guerrilla" along lines that had proved profitable in Indo-China. Then, with the summer of 1955, the ferocious Amirouche – in whose sector Bellounis had appeared – moved in, encircling Bellounis's camp at Guenzet and attacking it by surprise. The internecine massacre lasted forty-eight hours, watched gleefully by neighbouring French troops without intervening. Only Bellounis and a handful of his five hundred men escaped alive. Bellounis now directed his footsteps towards the French. Amirouche's operation did, however, signify the end of the M.N.A. challenge in Kabylia, and the beginning of its elimination as a serious rival to the F.L.N. throughout the country followed in the second half of 1956; an elimination that was to have meaningful echoes when, by the first Evian negotiations of 1961, Gaullist France toyed vainly with hopes of the all but extinct M.N.A. providing an *interlocuteur valable* alternative to the F.L.N.

After what the Parisian Press scathingly dismissed as this "settling of accounts between North Africans", the F.L.N. concentrated its attentions on the Algerian Communist Party (P.C.A.). All Saints' Day had placed the P.C.A. in an awkward predicament. Back in 1945 it had strongly condemned the Sétif uprising, and was actually reported to have taken part in the reprisals; in turn, it had been attacked by the rebels, who went so far as to seize the local party secretary and cut off his hands. The P.C.A. role at Sétif had never been forgotten. With Europeans comprising the large proportion of its membership (which was only 12,000), the P.C.A. tended to support the *petits blancs* rather than the Muslims, and, not without reason, Algerian nationalists had come to regard it as being tarred with the racist and anti-religious brush of Stalinism. It was closely associated with the French Communist Party and aligned to Moscow, where the acquisition of the soul of the French worker (who had only the most meagre natural sympathy for the Algerian, seen either as an immigrant worker threatening his own job, or as a rebel killing and mutilating working-class *pieds noirs*) clearly rated a higher priority than the national aspirations of a few million non-Communist Algerians. In November 1954 the P.C.F. had supported Mendès-France, offered lukewarm "solidarity" to the Algerian people, but condemned "individual acts" likely to play into the hands of the worst colonialists. When Mollet was to call for "special powers" to enable him to send conscripts to Algeria in 1956, the P.C.F. would again support the government, and as late as March 1956 it declared in words that could have come from almost any other French politician at the time: "We are for the existence and permanence of political, economic, and cultural bonds between France and Algeria.... Peace must be re-established in Algeria...."

Meanwhile, however, in Algeria individual members of the P.C.A. had become restive at the party's policy towards the rebellion. Feelers were put out to the F.L.N. about collaboration but were rebuffed on the grounds that the F.L.N. would accept members of the P.C.A. into its ranks, but only as individuals. In July 1955 the central committee of the P.C.A. decided to participate in the revolution, but under its own organisation. Stalemate. Then, in September, it found itself dissolved by the Gouvernement-Général. On 4 April 1956 a twenty-eight-year-old *pied noir* called Henri Maillot, who was a Communist and the son of a Communist, and who had been recalled to serve with the army as an officer cadet, left Miliana with a convoy of arms for Algiers, seventy-five miles to the north-east. Arriving in a wood just outside Algiers, Maillot dismissed the escort to get their breakfast, tied the driver of the arms truck to a tree, and drove off into the blue with a booty including over two hundred automatic weapons as well as a large quantity of grenades and ammunition. It was all too ridiculously easy. Two days later a body calling itself the Combattants de la Libération announced the setting up of a *maquis rouge*, which Maillot had now joined. On 5 June, in a previously unaffected region near Orléansville, militiamen under the command of a prominent "loyal" Muslim, the Bachaga Boualem, reported the presence of a new armed band. With surprising speed it was located, pinned down and wiped out. Among the dead picked up was Maillot, easily identified despite his hair and eyebrows having been bleached.

At about the same time, delicate negotiations were under way between the adroit Ben Khedda (for the F.L.N.) and P.C.A. representatives for a "takeover bid" of the party membership. In the course of them it was revealed that Maillot's arsenal lay buried in a tomb at the Clos Salembier cemetery. Disinterred, the weapons were smuggled by truck to Palestro on the western fringes of Kabylia, where, a few weeks later, they were to help Ouamrane perpetrate the bloodiest reverse to date on the French army itself. By September 1956 the remaining survivors of the short-lived *maquis rouge* had been mopped up. Then, in November, the Algiers police, evidently acting on a tip-off, caught a militant European Communist called Fernand Yveton red-handed in the act of placing a bomb in a gasworks. Yveton was tried and, though adamantly denying that his bomb was intended to inflict human casualties, guillotined a few months later.

Both he and Maillot have since been enshrined as "Heroes of the Revolution" by the F.L.N., but at the time grave suspicions existed that the *maquis rouge* might have been betrayed to Boualem's men by the F.L.N. itself. Such suspicions have never been either allayed or confirmed; while even the circumstances of Yveton's arrest strike a curious note. Whatever the truth, the F.L.N. undoubtedly viewed the rival *maquis rouge* with ill-concealed hostility, and this liquidation marked in fact the end of the P.C.A. as a separate entity. On 1 July a communiqué attributed to the Combattants de la Libération announced their dissolution and integration within the F.L.N. At the same time the important trade union, the Union Générale des Travailleurs Algériens (U.G.T.A.), now came completely under the control of the F.L.N. The Secretary-General of the P.C.A., Bachir Hadj Ali, withdrew in exile to Moscow where he spent the remainder of the war. P.C.A. members were, however, never fully trusted by the F.L.N., and were frequently detailed to undertake "suicide missions". From this background – and the prolonged Soviet reluctance to send the F.L.N. effective arms support – stems the markedly cool relations between Algeria and the U.S.S.R. that were to continue beyond the end of the war itself.

Tirailleurs desert

The reduction of the M.N.A. and P.C.A. as political rivals and the swallowing of their members constituted major successes and milestones for the F.L.N. during this period of consolidation. With less coercion, other useful allies were also flowing in to join the rebellion of their own accord. Of growing concern to the French was the effect that the more sophisticated propaganda of the F.L.N. under Abane was having on the reliability of veteran Algerian units within the army. In his novel *The Centurions* Jean Lartéguy relates how, on killing a *fellagha* leader, Si Lahcen, French paras found in his pockets a *médaille militaire* and a mention in despatches from Indo-China. "There's something wrong about this war," one para officer remarks to another. There was indeed. At night on 9 February 1956 a platoon of the 46th Tirailleurs stationed near Tlemcen was called out on an alarm – to be mown down by one of their own number, a *caporal-chef*, who wounded six soldiers before running off with the attackers. Worse followed ten days later when fifty men of the 50th Tirailleurs defected under another *caporal-chef*, a returned veteran from Indo-China, in similar circumstances. A French lieutenant and ten men were killed and twenty wounded by the mutineers, who then cleaned out the company's arms store of over a hundred weapons and joined the F.L.N. waiting ready with mules to haul off the booty. As Michael Clark of the

New York Times remarks, "The fear of betrayal now stalked every native unit, casting its pall over European and Moslem alike."

Non-Muslim recruits for the F.L.N.

Recruitment in Algeria was bringing in a growing number of non-Muslims. Among the intellectuals and doctors sympathetic to the cause, one of the earliest committed to it was a young *pied noir* surgeon, son of a prominent trade unionist, called Pierre Chaulet. In May 1955 Chaulet carried out the first secret operation on a rebel wounded painfully in the knee and brought in by Ouamrane. He was Azedine, who later emerged as an important F.L.N. leader in the last stages of the war. To Abane, who the following year became an intimate friend of both Chaulet and his attractive wife, the doctor explained: "We are not coming to the aid of the F.L.N. We are Algerians like you. Our soil, our country, is Algeria. We shall defend it with you. We are of the F.L.N."* The Chaulets were to afford immense assistance to the F.L.N. In addition to their succouring of F.L.N. wounded, Abane used their house as a kind of secret headquarters, smuggling vital documents in and out in a cake box; some of the first F.L.N. tracts were printed on a duplicator set up there, and, with great audacity, the Chaulets smuggled Krim and Ouamrane back and forth in their Citroën 2 c.v. on their frequent trips between Algiers and Kabylia.

Another doctor to come over to the F.L.N., body and soul, at this time was the impassioned Martiniquais, Frantz Fanon. During the Second World War Fanon had joined the Free French, been wounded and decorated in the liberation of France, but then made the painful discovery that a black man was not treated as an equal in the French army. In 1956 he wrote a bitter letter to the governor-general, resigning his post at the Blida psychiatric clinic, and joined the underground. He became one of the revolution's most articulate and extreme ideologues, and a violent exponent of anti-colonialism in any shape. He died of leukaemia in 1961, aged only thirty-six. Independent Algeria honoured his name with a university and a boulevard.

Among other intellectuals was André Mandouze, Professor of Literature at the University of Algiers, who formed around him an important sector of pro-F.L.N. sympathisers in the university. Mandouze had close contacts with Abane and Ben Khedda, attempting to create a bridge between them and the French government, and though he was never actually a member of the F.L.N., he was forced eventually to resign his post and return to France.

* Dr Chaulet, his cover "blown", was forced to flee to Tunisia in 1958 where he spent the rest of the war administering to the Algerian wounded and working for *El Moudjahid*. After 1962 he and his wife were among the few *pieds noirs* to remain and assume Algerian nationality.

Yet another important group to be won over to the F.L.N., by an adroit combination of carrot and stick, came from the Jewish community of Algeria, notably its intellectuals. In August 1956 a group of Constantine Jews wrote a public letter, declaring that "One of the most pernicious manoeuvres of colonialism in Algeria was, and remains, the division between Jews and Muslims . . . the Jews have been in Algeria for over 2,000 years; they are thus an integral part of the Algerian people. . . ." The Jews were to provide invaluable services as "the eyes and ears of the revolution", in the words of Frantz Fanon; often acting in the role of double agents against the French.

Abbas joins the F.L.N.

Undoubtedly the most important single acquisition to the F.L.N. during this period was the person of the arch-apostle of moderation, Ferhat Abbas himself. In the spring of 1955 Abbas had made a powerful speech at the small port of Djidjelli that had come as a shock to Soustelle. If there were any "outlaws" in Algeria today, declared Abbas, they were to be found within the "colonialist regime": "They are the prefects, they are the mayors, they are the administrators of the *communes mixtes*." He ended with the challenging words:

> U.D.M.A. addresses itself to the French government to tell it the following: as long as you continue to proclaim that Algeria is French, we shall reply that, as for us, "Algeria is Arab!" If the French government changes its line, then it and ourselves will begin to proclaim the same truths: "Algeria is Algerian!"

It marked a long march from Abbas's oft-quoted statement of 1936 – "I will not die for the Algerian nation, because it does not exist." A few weeks later, Abbas had an "exploratory" meeting with Abane, Krim and Ouamrane in Algiers. With outright frankness, Abane told him: "The revolution has been unleashed, and it is the work of neither Messali, nor the U.D.M.A. All that is out of date. Your duty is to join the Front." When Abbas asked Abane what precisely he should do, he was told: "Dissolve the U.D.M.A., and announce that you are going over to the Front."

Lest there should be any wavering by Abbas, unmistakable pressure was applied on him in the form of the "execution" of his own nephew during the Philippeville massacres of August 1955 already described. Abbas now undertook a series of final attempts to put out a tentative hand to the French government, including a trip to France where he tried, through the French delegate to the United Nations, Senator Edmond Michelet, to see de Gaulle. It was in vain, and Abbas was generally to encounter a cold shoulder.

At a further meeting with Abane on his return to Algeria, Abbas was asked: "Well, is it peace?"

He replied: "No, it's war."

In an interview with the Tunisian paper, L'Action, during January 1956, Abbas stated in tones of grim disillusion:

My party and I have thrown our entire support into the cause defended by the National Liberation Front. My role, today, is to stand aside for the chiefs of the armed resistance. The methods that I have upheld for the last fifteen years—co-operation, discussion, persuasion—have shown themselves to be ineffective; this I recognise....

In April he was in Switzerland negotiating with Ben Bella; a few days later in Cairo, declaring to the world by radio the dissolution of the U.D.M.A., and its incorporation within the F.L.N. That August, at the Soummam Conference, he was elected a member of the F.L.N.'s newly created governing body, the C.N.R.A. (Conseil National de la Révolution Algérienne).

Thus, by this time, the absorption or neutralisation of its principal political rivals, M.N.A., P.C.A. and U.D.M.A., had transformed the F.L.N. into a "mass movement" in the truest sense of the word.

Rifts within the F.L.N.: the Aurès

When Soustelle departed in early 1956 the total of F.L.N. "regulars" had already grown to between 15,000 and 20,000 from the few handfuls which had launched the revolution on All Saints' Day 1954. They had killed 550 members of the security forces, gendarmes and soldiers included, while their own losses were reckoned at three thousand, of whom a number rated as "irregulars" killed in the course of the Philippeville uprisings. By the second anniversary of the war the F.L.N. could claim to have destroyed or stolen in rural Algeria (their figures, so a margin of exaggeration for propaganda purposes should be discounted):

906 farms

38,340 head of cattle or sheep

404 agricultural machines

4,432,000 vine roots

4,583 hectares of standing crops

283 schools.

During this period of overall success and political consolidation, on the debit side the gravest threats to the F.L.N. came from within. From a largely military point of view, the worst situation had arisen in Wilaya 1, the Aurès, the very cradle of the revolt in its earliest days. Its leader, Ben Boulaid, had been captured, it will be recalled, in February 1955. Nine months later he achieved a remarkable escape from the condemned cell in

Constantine prison,* and on returning to the Aurès discovered that it had more or less reverted to its traditional state of parochial anarchy. Morale was very low, and his successor, Bachir Chihani, leader of the detachment that had ambushed the Monnerots, had aroused mounting opposition. Coming from the Nementchas, fifty miles away, he was regarded as a "foreigner"; he was accused of pederasty and other more savage excesses; and he appears to have made a series of grave tactical errors. The worst occurred at the end of September, when Chihani allowed his headquarters at Djeurf, deep in the most inaccessible wastes of the Nementchas, to be surrounded by French troops. Refusing to heed the urgings of his aides, Adjoul and Laghrour, to break out of the net, Chihani lost most of his escort and all his arms; and gravest of all, a large quantity of undestroyed documents, including directives from Ben Bella, that were to present the French Deuxième Bureau with its most valuable windfall to date. Chihani himself made a miraculous escape, having been buried for six days underground after the French had dynamited the entrance of the cave in which he was hiding, but his prestige had gone, and Adjoul and Laghrour decided on his execution. After several attempts to avoid a trap, Chihani was cornered, formally sentenced and executed – followed subsequently by eight of his "young men".

On the instructions of Adjoul, Chihani's death was kept a strict secret, and it remains uncertain whether it took place before (as Adjoul claims) or after Ben Boulaid's return. Whichever it was, the state of disintegration he found in the Aurès was extreme. Over the next few months he seems to have been partly successful in picking up the pieces. Then a French cloak-and-dagger field unit called the 11th Shock Regiment entered the scene. By carefully contriving what looked like a badly placed parachute drop, the 11th Shock floated down a booby-trapped radio close to Ben Boulaid's headquarters. As it was the latest model available to the French army, the assumption was that curiosity would induce an important rebel leader to investigate. That leader proved to be Ben Boulaid, who was blown to pieces in the ensuing explosion, together with his chief aide and two djounoud. The date was 27 March 1956; a short time later Adjoul defected to the French. For another six months the fact of Ben Boulaid's death appears to have been kept concealed even from the other F.L.N. leaders, a further testimony to the level of secrecy within the watertight compartments of the F.L.N. For the next two years the Aurès lapsed back substantially into fratricidal warfare, contributing little to the common cause.

Serious as this was for the F.L.N., more intrinsic was the widening rift

---

* This was so remarkable that *pied noir* "ultras" later suggested that Soustelle's "liberal" adviser, Commandant Monteil, who had interviewed Ben Boulaid while in prison, might have had a hand in it; in fact, however, Monteil had already left the country.

between Ben Bella in Cairo and the F.L.N. leaders of the "interior" – notably Abane. In the first instance the row was over the continued failure of the external delegation to provide the arms demanded by the "interior". An angry exchange of correspondence in April 1956 culminated with this insulting ultimatum to Ben Bella: "If you cannot do anything for us outside, come back and *die* with us. Come and fight. Otherwise consider yourselves as traitors!" It was followed by the despatch of Dr Lamine Debaghine to Cairo with full powers to supervise the activities of the external delegation. Ben Bella, who had set himself up as something of a *primus inter pares* in Cairo, seethed with resentment and refused to accept Debaghine's appointment. The differences were papered over temporarily, but beneath them also lay to some extent, dangerously latent, the mutual suspicions between Kabyles (Abane, Krim, Ouamrane) and Arabs (Ben Bella). Not a whisper of these dissensions, however, was to reach the world outside, either then or later.

"Summit" at Soummam

Already in the spring of 1956 Abane and the Algiers leaders had begun to contemplate the calling of a "summit" conference to iron out these internal differences and re-establish the basic unity of the revolution, and at the same time attempt to define its principles. The proposition was put by Ben M'hidi, then in Cairo on a liaison mission, to Ben Bella, who approved the idea and agreed that such a meeting should be held on Algerian soil. There were obvious emotive and propaganda reasons for this, but equally it cannot have escaped Abane's astute political brain that the primacy of the "interior" over the "exterior" would thereby become incontestable. The risk and sheer logistics, however, of holding such a "summit" under the very noses of the French were more than daunting. After thorough reconnaissance, choice was made of a simple forester's cottage set in idyllic but wild country of mountains and chestnut forests at Igbal, above where the Soummam valley marks the boundary between Greater and Lesser Kabylia; the date, 20 August. A hint that something was afoot seems to have reached the Deuxième Bureau, for in July there was a sharp increase of military operations in the designated area; Ouamrane himself was slightly wounded and narrowly escaped being taken in a French ambush. So, to protect the "summit", Amirouche (in whose sector it lay) concentrated several hundred men and a skilful feint was mounted to draw off security forces to another part of Kabylia.

Meanwhile, Ben Bella and his colleagues were instructed to go to San Remo in Italy and await a boat which would smuggle them into Algeria. For three weeks they sat on the Italian Riviera, kicking their heels impatiently. Various messages arrived from Abane, postponing their voyage on the grounds that French operations made it too dangerous. Finally, they received word to go to Tripoli, whence they would be "escorted" overland to the "summit". There they heard the astonishing news that the Soummam Conference had been held without them and was already over. Abane had played and won a major trick.

When the conference opened, sixteen delegates were present with the Kabyles and the Constantinois the most strongly represented. Kabylia itself sent Krim, Mohamedi Said, Amirouche and Kaci. Krim (who, following the arrest of Bitat and the break-up of his organisation, had been sent with Ouamrane to run Algiers and the neighbouring Algérois region) was doubling up as chief representative for Algiers, and Ouamrane for the Algérois. From Constantine came Zighout, the Wilaya 2 boss, his deputy, Ben Tobbal, and five others. From the stagnant Wilaya 5 of Oranie came Ben M'Hidi alone, who was also called upon to deputise for the "externals" *in absentia*, as being the delegate to have been most recently in contact with their views. The first session was presided over by Ben M'hidi, with Abane as secretary, but from the beginning it was clear that the initiative lay with Abane – and with the "interior" rather than the "exterior" – and, secondarily, with the Kabyles as opposed to the Arabs. Immediately, despite the absence of the "externals", there was dissent and mutual recrimination. Ben M'hidi criticised "uselessly bloody operations" that made a bad impression on public opinion, citing Zighout's massacre at El-Halia of exactly one year previously and a new excess by Amirouche where perhaps over a thousand dissident Muslims had been "liquidated" in a village near Bougie. (Krim, though he severely castigated his subordinate, Amirouche, in private, defended him in public at Soummam.)

As the conference progressed, bitter under-currents flowed around the personality of Abane himself. Some delegates thought him well-suited to assume the supreme leadership of the revolution, others insisted on adherence to the 1954 principle of collective leadership. Ben Tobbal made no secret of his personal antipathy to Abane; Krim, the veteran maquisard, was resentful of the way in which Abane, the politician, seemed to be acquiring more and more power; Zighout warned pointedly of the disastrous consequences that a "cult of the personality" had had for Algerian nationalism in the shape of El-Zaim, "the one and only" Messali Hadj; while Amirouche went so far as to suggest to Krim that Abane should be "despatched" before it was too late.

Soummam was, however, very much Abane's conference, and after twenty days of heated debates the lapidary conclusions which it reached strongly bore the imprint of his authority. On his urging, rigid military and political hierarchies were established with the express aim of avoiding the excesses and schisms of the past. Within the military command, ranks were ordained from private, or *djoundi*, to colonel (so as not to foster in any way the "cult of the personality", there would deliberately be no generals); units were defined from a *faoudj*, or section, of eleven men to a *failek*, or battalion, of 350 men (though, in practice this was to prove unwieldy, and operationally the biggest unit was most commonly the 110-strong *katiba*, or company). The six Wilayas, themselves subdivided into zones (*mintakas*), regions and sectors, were henceforth to be closely co-ordinated and controlled by a new supreme body, the C.C.E. or Comité de Coordination et d'Exécution. This would replace the loose, old boys' structure of the original C.R.U.A., or "Committee of the Nine", and it was designed to pre-empt situations where the Wilayas existed in a state of autonomy and out of contact with each other for months at a time. Another institution created at Soummam (and closely modelled on the French wartime Resistance) was the Conseil National de la Révolution Algérienne (C.N.R.A.), a kind of sovereign parliament composed of thirty-four elected delegates from all parts of the country, to be convened at regular intervals. To the all-powerful C.C.E., presiding in Algiers, were elected three members, Abane, Krim and Ben M'hidi, to whom another two "outsiders" acquired from the M.N.A., Ben Khedda and Saad Dahlab, were subsequently co-opted.

Triumph for Abane

The imposing document, forty pages long, that emerged after the twenty-day conference declared categorically the sole legitimacy of the C.N.R.A. in the nation; it alone had the right to make engagements concerning national sovereignty, such as ordering a cease-fire. Two important principles were established, both of them triumphs for Abane; first, the primacy of the political over the military; secondly, the primacy of the "forces of the interior" (i.e. the newly constituted C.C.E.) over the "exterior". On the other hand, as a sop to the anti-Abane lobby, the doctrine of collective leadership at all levels was emphatically reaffirmed. The Soummam platform was vastly ambitious, embracing almost every aspect remotely concerned with the revolution: relations with the P.C.A. and the Jewish minorities, the role of women and youth, of the peasants and trade unions, and social reforms to be enacted following independence. But its most remarkable feature was the terms it laid down for peace negotiations with France. *Inter alia*, there was to be no cease-fire before recognition of independence, and negotiation only on the basis of the existing Algerian territory (i.e. including the Sahara) and of no double citizenship privileges for the *pieds noirs*. Uncompromising and unrealistic as these terms may have seemed in the autumn of 1956, the F.L.N. negotiators were to stick to them, without amendment or modification, all the way through to the final act, thereby deriving an inestimable advantage over successive French governments, unable to define their war aims and negotiating from premises built on constantly shifting sands.

Still waiting in Tripoli for the invitation that never came, Ben Bella angrily received the edited "platform" as a *fait accompli*. In Algeria the consequences of Soummam were soon perceptible; returning in 1957, Germaine Tillion noted that the single most striking new factor was "the structuring of the politically clandestine organisations that had been achieved in one year". Certainly morale rose immeasurably, and a great wave of optimism pulsed through the revolution; for, as Abane pointed out, possibly the most outstanding achievement had been the mere fact of holding "for twenty days the Soummam Conference, in the heart of a Kabylia cross-gridded [*quadrillé*] and supposedly pacified by the French armed forces".

At the same time, however, over the short term the military analysis derived at Soummam was to lead the F.L.N. into its worst strategical error of the war, and to a very nearly catastrophic defeat: the Battle of Algiers.

CHAPTER SEVEN

The Second Fronts of Guy Mollet

February–December 1956

I saw the problem *durement*, but could see no solution. . . . They did not see it
durement, but saw every conceivable solution.

Robert Lacoste to the author, 1974

Mollet visits Algiers

1956, crammed with events of far-reaching import, was the year of Eden
and Mollet, of Khrushchev and the Twentieth Party Congress; of Budapest
and Suez. It was the year that Chancellor Macmillan shocked an inflation-
ary Britain by imposing the highest bank rate in a generation – all of 5½
per cent; and it was the last year that France and Britain would be able to
strut the world stage wearing morality play masks as "Great Powers". If
it was a watershed for the world as a whole, it was also a crucial year for
Algeria. Here the year opened with two manifestations of hysteria, and
closed with two far greater ones.

Barely had Algiers got over the intoxication of its adieu to Jacques
Soustelle than it had to prepare, in a very different mood, to receive Guy
Mollet, France's new Socialist prime minister and the first to visit Algeria
since the centenary celebrations of 1930. The date chosen, 6 February, had
unfortunate associations in recent French history: on that day twenty-two
years previously, bloody confrontations between Left and Right on the
Paris streets had looked almost like a prologue to civil war. Sensing that
Mollet's visit might unleash similar passions, the liberal mayor of Algiers,
Jacques Chevallier, and others urged him to reconsider. Mollet, seldom
lacking courage, stoutly refused. Much of the *pied noir* wrath generated
by his visit was directed against the unpopular appointment of General
Catroux, whom it was generally assumed Mollet would be bringing with
him in his baggage to install as Soustelle's successor. Catroux, at seventy-
nine, haggard and weighed down with medals, was of an age hardly likely

to recommend him for so arduous an office to the *machismo*-conscious *pieds noirs*. Moreover, in their eyes he was also the man who, as wartime high commissioner, had lifted the lid of Pandora's box by his proposed reforms; had then sold out France in Syria and, more recently, in Morocco. He was the quintessence of a *bradeur* (literally, a "seller-out", or capitulator), and the mere thought of his name was as a red rag to a bull in excitable Algiers. It had not been reassured even by a resolute statement by Catroux to *Le Monde* guaranteeing that the new government "does not under any circumstances intend to turn the country into a national state, inevitably marked for independence. Nor can there be any question of reducing the French to minority status...." Wild talk began to ferment in Algiers about a possible putsch to seize Mollet.

The "ultras" prepare a hot reception

In all this atmosphere of fever various organisations crystallised and personalities emerged among the *pied noir* "ultras" which were to play a persistent and decisive role on the Algiers stage over the coming six years. Well to the fore, and grouped together under a *comité d'entente*, were the *anciens combattants*; suddenly every other able-bodied male in Algiers appeared to have been a veteran of the Second World War, loudly reminding the mother country (not unlike Ian Smith's Rhodesians at the time of U.D.I.) of the debt she owed her colonial sons. Next there was the Association des Élus* d'Algérie, headed by ultra-conservatives like Laquière, Amédée Froger, and Sérigny of the *Écho d'Alger*. Among the more virulent formations was L'Action of Jo Ortiz, and the Union Française Nord-Africaine (or U.F.N.A.) founded by Robert Martel. Ortiz was a restaurateur owning the Bar du Forum, a stone's throw from the Gouvernement-Général and a leading disciple of Poujade in Algiers, a loud-mouthed demagogue with several hundred toughs at his behest who believed (especially since the pro-Soustelle demonstrations of 2 February, in which he had been a prime mover) in the power of the street. Ortiz held the black and white view that there were only two kinds of French in Algeria: "those attached to the soil...and the 'Communists'; that's to say all those who want to negotiate with the Arabs...." Robert Martel was a young farmer from the Mitidja, representing the *petits blancs* who had begun to feel painfully exposed to F.L.N. terrorism there.

Then there were recently formed counter-terrorist groups, among whom the names of René Kovacs, Philippe Castille and André Achiary figure. Achiary, a dedicated right-wing Gaullist from earliest days, had been an intelligence chief in Algiers during the war and had helped ease the way for de Gaulle's arrival there. A close associate of Achiary's from those days was a boundlessly energetic Corsican practising law in Paris, Maître Jean-

* Literally "elected office-holders".

Baptiste Biaggi. Wounded in the stomach in 1940, Biaggi had survived to found a commando in the Resistance; arrested, he had managed to saw out a plank on the train taking him to Buchenwald and escaped together with thirty-nine compatriots. Another devout Gaullist of the Right, with a considerable following among former Resistance members, he was a born revolutionary with a Corsican's instinct for passionate crowd oratory. Sought out by Achiary in Paris, he descended on Algiers like a tornado, assuming the lead in stirring up the *anciens combattants*, to whom he remarked: "We must raise the temperature and bring down the regime. The Fifth Republic must arise from the street like its most illustrious predecessors. The Fourth has had it. . . ." Biaggi was strongly influenced by what he saw in Algiers and returned to France to announce, with prescience: "The catalyst [*force vive*] is to be found on the other side of the Mediterranean. . . ."

Although differing degrees of violence were advocated by these various *pied noir* factions in Algiers, all basically agreed on one thing: a "second front" should be opened, both against F.L.N. terrorism and the government in Paris, and now. Martel was all for seizing the Palais d'Été and holding Mollet hostage; while other hotheads went so far as to suggest that Catroux should be assassinated like his wartime forerunner, Admiral Darlan. One *ancien combattant* urged that they should all go and throw their decorations in disgust at the foot of the *monument aux morts*, and finally a proposal by Ortiz was adopted that a massive protest demonstration should convene around the *monument* when Mollet came to lay the traditional wreath. Thus this sombre example of necrological architecture so dear to French hearts was to become ritualistically the focal centre of all *pied noir* protest henceforth. On 5 February a grim-faced procession of 20,000 *anciens combattants*, headed by the legless on crutches arm-in-arm with the blind in dark glasses, marched in silence through Algiers, their black-trimmed banners sodden by a glacial rain. For the following day a general strike was proclaimed.

In anticipation of trouble, Paris despatched a dozen extra companies of Compagnies Républicaines de Securité (in itself an additional irritant to the "ultras") and backed them up, for the first time, with paras commanded by a tough, newly-arrived general called Jacques Massu. Mollet arrived at Maison-Blanche airport without Catroux; which was well advised, for otherwise serious violence might have been provoked as some of Martel's demonstrators from the Mitidja appear to have come in heavily armed. It was a day of penetrating cold, and the reception was more frigid even than that accorded Soustelle just a year previously. Only the barest minimum of *pied noir* officials had turned out at the airport to greet Mollet; the road into the city was empty of all but C.R.S. and vigilant troops; Algiers itself was a silent, dead city with an occasional sign pinned to shuttered shop-windows: "Closed on account of mourning." In the European quarters the strike had been totally effective. Arriving at the Forum, Mollet found it surrounded by a vast sea of hostile *pieds noirs*. As he climbed up the steep steps to deposit his wreath solemnly on the *monument aux morts*, the chanting started:

"Throw Catroux into the sea!"

"Mollet, resign!"

"Mollet to the stake!"

Then followed the clods of earth and volleys of tomatoes supplied by the obliging restaurateur, Jo Ortiz. The impassioned mob, carried away by its own fury, broke through the C.R.S. cordon and was repelled by savage flailing of batons followed by tear gas; and correspondents present reckoned that, had it not been for the security reinforcements present, the day might well have ended with the lynching of the prime minister of France. Minutes after his departure the mob burst through the barriers to trample to pieces Mollet's wreath.

Mollet yields

With the clamour of the demonstrators close outside, a grim and white-faced Mollet withdrew to the governmental residence at the Palais d'Été, profoundly shocked by the violence and unanimity of the *pied noir* protest. The presence in the mob of such a mass of workers, small shopkeepers and petty officials – all, doubtless, steadfast Socialists – clearly made it impossible to dismiss the demonstration as a put-up job by the *grands colons*. After a brief consultation with his advisers, Mollet telephoned Paris to request that Catroux offer his resignation. Paying due homage to the general's patriotism, he then informed the Press that Catroux had offered to resign, and "anxious not to add to the drama that divides Algeria, I have accepted this resignation". The mob went wild, and shouts of "*Victoire! Victoire!*" echoed round the city. Hearing the news Ortiz promptly declared: "We've won! Mollet's yielded in face of force," and ordered his cohorts to stand down the demonstration.

Throughout the turbulent course of French history, many a vital issue has been decided by the "street", and 6 February 1956 was certainly to prove a red-letter day for the French citizens of Algeria. That night, it is recorded that Mollet – perhaps appreciating the genie that he had just unbottled – murmured miserably, "I should not have given in." But it was too late; the Ortizes of Algiers now realised that they could bend to their will – or, possibly, even bring down – any government in Paris. There was nothing that street violence could not achieve – provided it was violent enough. The Forum itself would always, henceforth, wield a strange kind of mesmeric fascination upon the mob demagogue or would-be putschist. A leader of the student faction, one Pierre Lagaillarde, remarked to a colleague that day: "Now I know that we can effect a *coup d'état* here." As far as the winning over of uncommitted Muslim hearts was concerned, 6 February sounded yet another defeat for France. A disgusted General Massu wrote: "The *indigènes* have an instinct of respect, of fear of the leader. They absolutely don't understand the behaviour of the French who insult the head of their government, bombard him with tomatoes. . . ." But beyond this, F.L.N. propaganda was to contend, successfully, that there was no point in heeding all the French promises in this world if a French government would always capitulate to the least pressure by a European mob. Said Frantz Fanon bitterly: "From 6 February onwards, we could no longer turn our eyes towards France. . . ." And a remark made by a *pied noir* demonstrator to Ferhat Abbas may well have influenced his conversion to the F.L.N. of a few months later as much as it pointed the way ominously to future trends in Algeria: "The F.L.N. has taught us that violence is profitable for the Muslims. We are going to organise violence by the Europeans and prove that that too is profitable."

Three days later – after Gaston Defferre, the Socialist leader from Marseilles, had refused categorically – Mollet announced that he was sending another good party man, his Minister of Economic Affairs, Robert Lacoste, to replace the unwanted Catroux. At the same time, in what seemed (at any rate to the F.L.N.) like another massive concession to the *pieds noirs*, he revealed his intention to increase the French forces in Algeria sharply to 500,000 by lengthening military service to twenty-seven months and recalling a whole class of reservists and despatching them and the conscripts to Algeria: *half a million men*, nearly nine times the total in Algeria on All Saints' Day, 1954. On the internal scene of French politics alone this was a devastatingly radical act. During the electoral campaign of only a few weeks past, the outgoing premier, Faure, had assured young conscripts that "military service is out of date – just a few months of it will be enough", and here now was a Socialist and pacifist by creed forced to do what previous "reactionary" French governments had never dared do in Algeria.* Mollet's action meant, in effect, that he was espousing Soustelle's "testament" and that the crushing of the rebellion would now take precedence over all else. Militarily, there were good enough reasons for it. Despite the considerable infusions of troops during Soustelle's year, which had brought the total to nearly 200,000, the situation had steadily deteriorated. The "smallpox chart" had spread to cover most of the country; the Tunisian frontier had become a running sore, and establishment of a barrier there would take a long time to be completed. An increasing number of Tirailleurs were deserting – together with their even more

* For an international parallel one is reminded of those good American Democrats, Roosevelt, Truman and Kennedy, rushing into the Second World War, Korea and Vietnam respectively, where a Republican President might have feared to tread.

valuable weapons – and now Moroccan units serving with the French had taken to refusing orders. Several senior French officers had resigned, pointedly, including one, General Zeller, Inspector-General of the ground forces, who would make his mark briefly five years later. In one of his last reports to Faure, Soustelle had stressed in January: "It would be pointless to pretend that the morale of the army is not at present at rock bottom. The general feeling is that we are going to 'do a deal' and that, consequently, present sacrifices are to no purpose." This had later been backed up by the Commander-in-Chief, General Lorillot, writing to Mollet that the military situation was "disturbing" and concluding that: "It is inconceivable that the rebels will agree to lay down their arms in the present state of their success."

Conscripts to Algeria; disaster at Palestro

The shipping of the conscripts – paid a paltry 10,080 francs (£8) a month – was not without problems. Reservists at the Gare de Lyon refused to board troop trains for Marseilles, or pulled the communication cord; 600 artillerymen near Rouen threw furniture out of the windows and staged a sit-down strike. Arriving on the quay at Algiers, the scruffy young soldiers in baggy uniforms that always looked several sizes too large gave a singularly unmilitary and unenthusiastic appearance. But, after a brief sojourn, the country worked its miraculous enchantment upon most of them: "*Algérie montait à la tête!*" Their arrival undoubtedly raised the morale of the *pieds noirs*, and it was soon having its effect within the hard-pressed army, too. Back on a *ratissage* of the Djurdjura, Pierre Leulliette records how "this time there were thousands and thousands of men with us, from every arm of the services, Parisians, Bretons and Landais. The whole of France was there that morning...." The new weight of man-power made the operation a success – marred only by a green recruit shooting his sergeant in mistake for the F.L.N.

The chances were that, sooner or later, such greenness would inevitably lead to a graver disaster. On 4 May 1956 the 9th Régiment d'Infanterie Coloniale battalion of reservists raised in the Paris region landed in Algiers. Just two weeks later one of its platoons, commanded by a thirty-year-old second lieutenant, Hervé Artur, was on patrol at Palestro, a bare fifty miles south-east from Algiers. "What a thrilling and marvellous life!" enthused Artur in an unfinished letter to his parents: "We have to protect the *douars*, and it's at night that the *fellaghas* visit them ... I am stepping up the night ambushes...." Operating in the area was Ali Khodja, an army deserter and Ouamrane's most redoubtable lieutenant. He had recently benefited by a delivery of some of the arms inherited from the cache of Aspirant Maillot's *maquis rouge*, and had successfully brought the local villagers under his sway. It was a rugged, beautiful country cut by deep gorges, prompting one of the reservists to write to his parents, in a letter that was never sent: "How good it would be to pass the holidays here!" Leaving the platoon sergeant behind at base, Second Lieutenant Artur set out for an isolated *douar*, Amal, with twenty-one men. Shortly after passing through Amal the platoon ran into an ambush well-prepared by Khodja's men; evidently with the complicity of the villagers. Lying in wait behind rocks, they caught the reservists at point-blank range. Artur was killed immediately, and within a few minutes all but six of the platoon were wiped out. The survivors were dragged off by the F.L.N., but one by one the four wounded collapsed and were left by the wayside. The remaining two, Privates Dumas and Nillet, moved from pillar to post with Khodja's band for the next five days. Meanwhile, when the patrol failed to return, the sergeant at base raised the alarm and that evening troops reached the scene of the massacre. At least two of the bodies had been atrociously mutilated; testicles cut off, disembowelled and the ventral cavities stuffed with stones. Further off one of the wounded was found, apparently despatched by the villagers, but no trace was ever found of the other three. The village itself was deserted.

From Algiers General Massu was sent with helicopters and seven battalions to mount an intensive search for Khodja and the missing reservists. On the fifth day the paras pinned down the band, killing seventeen. The unfortunate Nillet was also killed in the fight, and only Dumas survived to render account of what had happened. Another fifty dead villagers were brought in, but Ali Khodja himself escaped.

The ambush of the twenty-one roused a furore in France; these were the first reservists to die in the war, and it was the biggest single loss suffered by the army since the war began. Like all such events in war the Palestro massacre set off an immediate chain reaction. Like Soustelle after Philippeville, Lacoste was pushed into taking an even tougher stance. On 27 May 6,000 troops and 1,500 police and gendarmes surrounded the Casbah and gave it a ruthless combing through, arresting in the process nearly 5,000 people. On 19 June Lacoste went ahead with the guillotining of two condemned F.L.N., Zabane and Ferradj, whose deaths the "ultras" had been clamouring for ever since Mollet's visit. The executions were bound to cause an uproar, and the archbishop of Algiers, Monsignor Duval, was among the religious leaders pleading for clemency – particularly as Ferradj, in prison ever since November 1954, was a cripple and blinded in one eye, having been badly wounded at the time of his arrest. According to the F.L.N. version, they were the detonators to the series of terrorist outrages that were to be the preliminaries to the Battle of Algiers. In another direction, however, Palestro proved a net, long-term gain for the F.L.N.; it brought home to France for the first time, and more sharply than anything else could, the cruel realities of the Algerian war, and in doing so strengthened the hand of those few then arguing for a negotiated peace.

Lacoste: "le dernier quart d'heure"

In many ways fifty-seven-year-old Robert Lacoste was ideally suited for the post of governor-general. He had fought in the last battles of the Great War, would reminisce warmly about "old Clemenceau in 1918, when I was in Champagne, saying 'Hold on!'", and was imbued with a deep pride in the French army which he retains to this day – even to the extent of defending some of its more questionable actions and brushing aside allegations of torture. During the Second World War he distinguished himself with the Resistance, and while Lacoste was with the maquis in Savoy his father was shot as a hostage by the Nazis. From the time of de Gaulle's first post-war government up to his appointment as Mollet's Minister of Economic Affairs, he was repeatedly in and out of office, generally dealing with industrial or economic matters. A squat, stumpy figure whose ample chin seemed to grow straight from the shoulders, he came to be nicknamed *Bébé lune* (or Sputnik) – probably for his physical appearance, because he was nobody's satellite. Both he and Guy Mollet were, and looked, of the old school of French Socialists, and with their shapeless, baggy trousers both would have blended equally well into the Transport House of Ernie Bevin. In fact, there were many characteristics that Lacoste shared with Bevin; he was tough, quick-tempered, vigorous, stubborn and courageous, with an acute political nose; and though a man whose human warmth came across strongly after the briefest conversation, he did not suffer from the disadvantage of being as subject to emotion as Soustelle.

Intellectuals complained that it was easier to argue with an earthquake than with Lacoste, and indeed he consistently turned a deaf ear to any argument that France should abandon Algeria. But there was an engaging, no-nonsense forthrightness about the man that came out vividly in the earthiness of his language. His favourite expression was *Je ne me laisse pas emmerder*, and to him demonstrators were always *ces jeunes cons-là* – which he would never hesitate to point out to even the most menacing mob. To American journalists critical of conditions in Algeria he would hit back reflexively with acrid comments about Indians and Negroes. Edward Behr, who watched him in action, notes that (as Bevin did when handling foreign affairs) he "approached Moslems and Europeans alike more like an S.F.I.O. bigwig oozing bluff self-confidence among a group of Socialist party members. . . ." Sometimes it worked, sometimes it didn't. But, adds Behr, "Lacoste met only those Moslems whom his subordinates wished him to meet. . . ." If he had another fault, it was perhaps his excessive optimism. It would always be held derisively against him that he had quoted a famous wartime forebear, "We are at *le dernier quart d'heure*."

Lacoste's reforms

Immediately, Lacoste was shackled by the top priority that Mollet had prescribed and that he had himself endorsed – "First win the war". There was an unmistakable element of contradiction apparent in Mollet's policy; for, although his Socialist government was prepared to go further than any other, and at the risk of international complications, to win the war, he was at the same time dropping hints – very secretly – to the F.L.N. that a compromise might be possible. Thus on the one hand he seemed to be demanding "unconditional surrender" and on the other offering conditions; a contradiction that could only confuse, and thereby offer the F.L.N. additional excuse for intransigence.

Meanwhile, on the social scene Mollet's priorities inevitably limited Lacoste's freedom of manoeuvre, relegating vital reforms, as so often in the past, to second place. Nevertheless, with his customary energy Lacoste pushed ahead with measures that were largely the mixture as before; once again the implementation of the basic promises of the 1947 statute, now nearly ten years out of date. On the economic front Lacoste's most striking early move was to raise, by decree in March 1956, the Algerians' wretched guaranteed minimum daily wage from 340 to 440 francs (2s. 9d. to 3s. 6d.). This was followed up by a series of decrees affecting agriculture; cork and alfalfa production was nationalised (a hard blow at the monopolists Borgeaud and Blachette); credit and share-cropping terms for Muslim farmers were improved; and the redistribution of certain government-leased lands was accelerated. Optimistically, it was hoped that 10,000 landless families might be settled on 150,000 hectares, but this first timid attempt at agrarian reform, well-intentioned as it was, played disastrously into the hands of the F.L.N. Jean Servier recalls how, after a parcel of land had been handed over to a *fellah*, he "immediately found himself condemned to death. A few days later a patrol found the body of the happy proprietor with his throat slit in his own field." As a result few Muslim peasants henceforth had the courage to come forward to accept the French bounty. In Servier's view it would have been more sensible to redistribute the land to communities instead of individuals – because then the F.L.N. would be forced to kill a whole village, and the villagers might have been encouraged to protect the land collectively.

For the coming year France would contribute 80 milliard francs ($200 million) to the Algerian budget – a forty per cent increase over the previous year – to improve standards of living. Better educational opportunities were offered the Muslims through lowering school entry age by five years. Politically, however, Lacoste's most striking innovation was to decree that fifty per cent of all vacancies in public service should be reserved for Muslims. Ten years previously it would have been hailed by them as a generous and progressive move; but now it seemed tardy, introduced only under F.L.N. pressure, and a hasty improvisation that rather floated in mid-air in that it remained unsupported by what would have appeared as the essential concomitant of equal citizenship rights. Next, Lacoste completed abolition of the *communes mixtes* as a first step towards fulfilment of Mollet's somewhat vague and unspecified promise to the Muslims, in his speech of 16 February, "to hold free elections at the earliest possible moment". This also poised the axe over the entire *caid* system which, as a whole, had come to be one of the most hated features of the *présence française*. Many *caids* had been corrupt and archaic in their administration; on the other hand, perhaps equally as many had served both Algeria and France honestly and loyally, and now courageously. Since 1954 the corps of *caids* had lost twenty-seven dead, four missing and presumed dead, and nineteen wounded. The "good" *caids* were resentful of what they felt to be France's shoddy treatment of them, and one remarked pointedly: "Since France rejects us, she had better not count on us any longer." Poor France; how many of her best-intentioned reforms would end by losing as much as they gained! Another questionable measure, and disheartening to the "moderate" Muslim representatives, was Lacoste's dissolution of the Algerian Assembly on 11 April 1956. Because of the obstructionism of both European "ultras" and Muslims, there were good reasons for this move; yet it conflicted abrasively with intents expressed by Mollet and the French Socialist Party to increase, not decrease, electoral freedom in Algeria.

Administratively, Lacoste launched a sweeping reorganisation of Algeria by creating eight new departments, so that, from its original total of three, the country now possessed twelve, giving it a correspondingly greater influence in metropolitan councils. This was a wholly beneficial move, forming a preliminary to what Lacoste considered to be his (alas, never completed) masterpiece, the *loi-cadre*, or draft law. Not adopted by the French legislature until 31 January 1958, the *loi-cadre* aimed at a political solution that looked like a mixture of federalism and partition. Algeria was to be divided into several self-governing territories, with a common electoral roll, and each responsible to an elected national assembly under the sovereignty of France. The concept drew forth vigorous opposition from many, including Chevallier and Soustelle, the latter condemning it as "hastily creating an organisation that would confer upon Algeria certain characteristics of a veritable state". In contrast to Mollet, Lacoste soon showed, however, that he would not bow either to criticism or to mob pressure. On 8 May 1956 – the explosive anniversary of Sétif and V.E. Day – there was a victory parade in Algiers which right-wing European students attempted to turn into a demonstration against Lacoste's policy. But, encountering a combination of contempt and resolute force, it simply collapsed. While his forceful technique gained him respect, it also brought Lacoste – often short on diplomatic graces – a number of opponents. Perhaps the most unfortunate consequence was his poor personal relationship with Jacques Chevallier, which thereby diminished his contacts with the "third force" Europeans. As it was, however, Lacoste's cherished *loi-cadre* was to be swept away by events in France.

Secret negotiations with the F.L.N.

Early in his appointment to Algiers Lacoste remarked optimistically: "Though I promise no miracles, I have a reasonable hope that by the end of the summer law and order will reign in Algeria." But by that summer external events beyond Lacoste's control were already beginning to move towards the year's powerful climax. In March, soon after Mollet's coming to power, he had sent on a mission to Cairo, his Foreign Minister, Christian Pineau, who through Nasser had put out feelers for "conversations" with the F.L.N. These had been taken up, and the following month a first meeting took place, also in Cairo, between Mohamed Khider and a secret emissary of Mollet's, each acting with the utmost reserve and in fear of being accused of "selling-out" by their compatriots. This led, however, to a further series of talks about talks (much against the better judgement of Lacoste), five of which took place during the course of 1956, ranging from Cairo to Belgrade to Rome, and all held in the utmost secrecy. The Mollet government offered to facilitate a free entry into Algeria for Ben Bella for the purpose of negotiations, and at the final meeting in Rome in September a further rendezvous was made for the end of October; at which time a public declaration was to be drafted for signature by Mollet and the C.C.E. announcing their intent to launch full-scale peace negotiations. To this day there is disagreement as to how serious were the prospects held by the 1956 peace feelers. Ben Bella claims to have believed "that peace was within reach"; Mollet, on the other hand, remains sceptical, stating in an interview with the author "Even if Ben Bella had not been sequestrated, I doubt whether things would have turned out very differently; because the F.L.N. never accepted our basic thesis that there should be, first of all, a cease-fire."

No one will ever know.

Autumn of madness: Suez nationalised and the Athos

On 13 June the last British soldier quit the Suez Canal Zone; six weeks later Nasser shook the world by nationalising the canal. For the next months the wires between London, Paris and Washington began to hum as Western statesmen debated how to deal with the Egyptian leader and his arbitrary action. At the far end of the Mediterranean from Algeria, Ben Gurion's tiny infant state of Israel began to feel in jeopardy. Through the long summer the temperature steadily rose, with Britain and France beginning to make tentative, fumbling and long-drawn-out preparations for a military intervention over Suez. Already by 9 August, General André Beaufre at his headquarters in Constantine East had received orders to command a contingency "Force A" ready for operating against Egypt. Then, on 16 October, an event occurred that would significantly harden French policy. French naval and air interception services, which by this time had attained a high state of efficiency in picking up maritime gun-runners, had been tracking a ship called the *Athos* on its suspiciously zig-zag course round the Mediterranean. On 14 October it was reported heading for the Moroccan coast, and two days later it was stopped and boarded by a French escort vessel.

Though sailing under a Sudanese flag, with a Greek captain, the *Athos* was revealed to be carrying over seventy tons of arms and ammunition – all loaded in Alexandria and purchased with Egyptian money. The inventory read as follows:

72 mortars
40 machine-guns
74 automatic rifles
240 sub-machine-guns
2,300 rifles
2,000 mortar shells
600,000 cartridges

An insignificant cargo, perhaps, in terms of a major war, but its value to the F.L.N. can be appreciated when it is recorded that, up to that date, it possessed no more than twenty mortars and ten machine-guns throughout the country. The *Athos* cargo represented the biggest arms shipment yet to the F.L.N.; by far the greatest significance attached to it, however, was that it was the first major Egyptian arms delivery to the F.L.N. – the fruit of the months of badgering by Ben Bella and his colleagues. The weapons were believed to be intended for the opening up (on 1 November, the second anniversary of the war) of a new front in the hitherto peaceful area to the west of Oran. In the mind of the astute Nasser, this was to serve an additional tactical purpose by distracting the French, who were by now making very threatening noises about Suez.

In the heated atmosphere prevailing in Paris, the *Athos* episode caused a considerable impact. Here, at last, was conclusive evidence to confirm the long-cherished beliefs that the hub of the revolution lay in Cairo, and that Ben Bella was its lynch-pin. At the time of the seizure of the *Athos*, Ben Bella was on his way to Morocco to arrange the reception and distri-bution of its arms. Deeply chagrined by the news of the Soummam Conference and its decisions taken in his absence, he was intending to reject these (especially the primacy of the "interior" over the "exterior"), and to launch a political counter-offensive to re-establish his own personal pre-eminence. To this end he planned to fly from Morocco to Tunis, to convene there, on 22 or 23 October, his own "summit conference" of the three Maghreb powers. There they would discuss both the future conduct of the war and the furtherance of the peace initiatives then under way secretly with Mollet's representatives. With both Tunisian and Moroccan leaders disposed towards a negotiated compromise peace at this time, there seemed a reasonable prospect of success for Ben Bella's initiative. Originally Ben Bella and his party were to have flown from Rabat in the personal plane of the King of Morocco, but at the last minute the palace announced that there would be insufficient room on the King's plane and that another – a D.C.3 belonging to Air Maroc, with a French crew – would be at their disposal. According to Ben Bella subsequently, the change of plan caused him indefinable misgivings; nevertheless, he and the rest of the "external" delegation – Boudiaf, Khider, Ait Ahmed – plus an Algerian professor working for the F.L.N. called Mostefa Lacheraf, embarked on the D.C.3 for Tunis. Among other passengers aboard that 22 October was a *New York Times* correspondent, Tom Brady.

Ben Bella hijacked

From Rabat a Colonel Jean Gardes tipped off Algiers that Ben Bella would no longer be flying under the protection of the King of Morocco. Somewhere along the line between Gardes and Colonel Ducournau, the first para commander to achieve distinction in the war and currently Lacoste's chief military adviser, a spectacular coup was hatched. General Beaufre was lunching with General Lorillot when the Commander-in-Chief was called to the telephone by Ducournau and he accepted responsibility for forcing the Moroccan plane down on to Algerian soil. Lacoste was away on leave in the Dordogne, and to this day there remains some mystery as to whether the coup was in fact a first major instance of the French military acting on its own initiative, in disregard of the civil authorities, expressly with a view to torpedoing the peace negotiations; as to whether Lacoste turned a blind eye; or whether there was some degree of complicity even by the Mollet government, now deeply committed to the Suez adventure. The relevant orders are said to have been destroyed. According to Tournoux's account, Lacoste returned to Algiers just in time to countermand the interception order, but nevertheless gave his sanction to go ahead. Subsequently, however, both Lacoste and Mollet have affirmed categorically to the author their indignation at the order given.

The D.C.3 was approaching its intermediary stop at Palma de Mallorca when the French pilot, Gellier, a reservist officer, received radio orders from Oran, in the name of the French Ministry of Defence, to put down in Algeria instead of Tunis. After some argument and referring by radio back to Air Maroc headquarters in Rabat, Gellier agreed. On leaving

Palma the French air hostess, though noting with concern that Ben Bella had his revolver lodged in the seat pocket in front of him, maintained a superb poker face, chatting up the Algerians so as to distract them from detecting the plane's change of direction, and announcing coolly as it began its descent: "*Attachez vos ceintures et cessez de fumer, s'il vous plaît. Nous atterrissons à Tunis!*" The Algerians were totally deceived. One of them, noting from afar the large number of figures on the airfield, exclaimed: "Why, they've organised a very handsome reception for us!" It was not until the instant of landing and recognising the French uniforms, tanks and armoured cars that packed the runway that they realised they were in Algiers, not Tunis. With no chance to resist, the five Algerians were led out by armed gendarmes to begin five and a half years of imprisonment in the Santé in Paris, then in a series of other French gaols and strongholds. Indicted for crimes punishable by death, they were given the status of political prisoners but were never brought to trial.

On hearing the news, European Algiers erupted in unprecedented delight, while at least one French radio commentator declared: "At last France has dared!" Undoubtedly, the hijacking of Ben Bella and his companions in flagrant breach of international law was a brilliant intelligence coup; but, as so often with such coups, it was to rebound badly on the originators. Mollet, according to Mendès-France who saw him that day, was in a cold fury when he heard the news. Why, then, did he not disavow the action and release the Algerians? Because, says Mollet, "I could not liberate men who were condemned under common law; my government would have fallen overnight." And, says Lacoste, explosively: "Because Algiers would have blown up. At that moment it was like a steam-boiler.... Also, the Arabs were very sensitive to force, and – there's no doubt about it – the capture of Ben Bella did calm them for a while...." But, says Mendès-France: "It was because, like everybody else at the time, Mollet was weak." The international Press was overwhelmingly hostile to what was regarded as a flagrant breach of international law. The French ambassador in Tunis, Pierre de Leusse, and Mollet's Secretary for Moroccan and Tunisian Affairs, Alain Savary, both resigned in protest. At Meknès in Morocco forty-nine French civilians were butchered in fierce anti-French riots. The King, mortified by what he took as a personal affront, and Bourguiba, who had had triumphal arches erected in honour of the Tunis "summit", henceforth stiffened their resolve to back the Algerian war effort to the utmost. As a Tunisian spokesman told journalists at the time: "The Tunis conference, which was to have been the conference about peace in Algeria, may ... turn into a war conference."

Certainly it seems that, in the autumn of 1956, both Tunisia and Morocco had their own reasons for pressing the F.L.N. towards a negotiated peace, and now a golden opportunity of their support was sacrificed. As far as the peace negotiations, so delicately initiated by Mollet himself, were concerned, the bridges were truly down, and it would not be possible to re-erect them for many years to come. With his well-known wit, and speaking from personal experience, Bourguiba is said to have joked at the time: "Don't forget, the French have a habit of locking up their *interlocuteurs* before negotiating with them!" Mollet could still have thrown the switches. He could have released Ben Bella and his colleagues, and have dealt with them, from a position of strength, as honoured negotiators, as indeed the French dealt with Mohammed V and Bourguiba. But, as revealed, the Mollet government possessed neither the will nor the power; and, in any event, with Suez in the offing, the time would soon be quite out of joint. So the *interlocuteurs valables* (which Mendès-France had sought so anxiously for) remained in the indignity of imprisonment, becoming more embittered and intransigent, a source of constant embarrassment to successive French governments, a veritable time-bomb in their midst.

From France's point of view, in retrospect, much more might have been achieved by leaving Ben Bella well alone. For if there was any satisfaction gained from the whole episode, paradoxically it lay in the ranks of the F.L.N. leaders themselves. Overtly expressing outrage at the hijacking, privately Abane and the "interior" were delighted. The major split within the F.L.N., threatened as a consequence of Soummam, had been miraculously avoided; unity had been restored and all argument about the primacy of the "interior" resolved – because now the "exterior" had simply ceased to exist. Any flagging by potential "soft-liners" had been effectively quelled. Thus had the French army devisers of the coup really done the enemy a good turn.

Whatever else, the Ben Bella episode undoubtedly marked a major turning-point in the war. From now on the war could only proceed, savagely and irreconcilably; any other way out had been sealed off.

Suez

Almost immediately, however, other and greater events were pushing the Ben Bella episode into the background. Encouraged, briefly, by Khrushchev's "de-Stalinisation" bombshell at the Twentieth Party Congress, the captive peoples of eastern Europe had seen their hopes for a more liberal future crushed by the police apparatus. This provoked serious riots in Poland, and on the day after the seizure of Ben Bella police opened fire in Budapest. There then followed the ten days of wild, mad euphoria of the Hungarian revolt when it seemed, momentarily, as if Russia might actually allow her satellite to regain some degree of freedom. Meanwhile, America was enmeshed in the re-election of President Eisenhower, and Israel and Egypt had gone to war. Then, on 30 October, after months of huffing and puffing, of making plans and changing them, France and Britain issued – and had rejected – their ultimatum to Nasser. The next day the R.A.F.'s ponderous and protracted "psychological bombardment" of Egypt began.

The Suez "war", so well-trampled since by journalists, historians and self-justifying politicians, has a place in this story only in so far as it influenced the Algerian war and was in turn influenced by it. The lies, half-truths and fudged recollections that have overlaid Suez in the intervening twenty years have done much to confuse the prime motives of principals. None of them were identical, or even in harmony, and only Israel's seem simple and straightforward: she was fighting for what she conceived to be survival. Eden was alarmed by the threat to Britain's imperial position, and obsessed by the notion of Nasser being a new Mussolini–Hitler and Suez the Rhineland of our times; he cared little for French problems in North Africa, and probably less for Israel (which he generally referred to, revealingly, as "the Jews").

Mollet in his turn cared little about British imperial problems, but to his death insisted passionately that Israel was his first concern. He was deeply conditioned by the past betrayals of Munich and the Spanish Civil War, and, as a good Socialist, was drawn to Israel as a "pioneer country socialising itself".* He felt she had but one true friend in the world – the United States – which, in the throes of an election, would be unable to help her. He denied hotly that Suez was "done for Algeria", and yet one is entitled to pose the question: had France *not* been so embroiled in Algeria, would Mollet have been quite so open to Israeli pressure, and would he in turn have pushed Eden so hard to participate in what was to prove to be such a desperate gamble? One has seen how France, from Soustelle onwards, had persuaded herself, erroneously, that Nasser and Ben Bella were the dynamos of the Algerian revolt. This had been reconfirmed during Foreign Minister Pineau's Cairo visit of the spring, when Nasser had told him (with possibly exaggerated self-importance): "When you really have the intention of negotiating in Algeria, give me the word and it will be swiftly settled." And the *Athos* had provided a last straw. Mollet and the strong man of his government, Defence Minister Bourgès-Maunoury, as well as many lesser Frenchmen convinced themselves, intuitively, that if Nasser went the collapse of the Algerian revolt would soon follow. In the well-chosen words of Hugh Thomas: "Publicly, the *Entente Cordiale* seemed at its height. But Eden joined not Europe but the French war in Algeria."

The proclamations made to the French expeditionary force to Suez certainly had an archaic ring of the First World War about them. In words that seem unlikely to be heard ever again, General Beaufre addressed his

* Over seventeen years later he admitted: "I am now anti-Israel, because the Right is triumphant."

troops on 4 November: "Officers, N.C.O.s and men, we are going into Egypt with our British friends and allies. France and the world have their eyes on you. . . . If necessary, you will repeat the exploits of your forebears on Egyptian soil . . . [i.e. Napoleon Bonaparte]." At dawn the next morning, 5 November, 600 British and 500 French paratroops dropped near Port Said. For all the muddles and delays of the past months, the last minute changes of plan whereby élite airborne troops had been sent in on invasion barges, operations proceeded with remarkable smoothness. Brushing aside fairly feeble resistance, Massu's fast-moving paras, tempered by the war in Algeria, were well on their way to Suez when Bulganin issued his missile-rattling ultimatum to the "Allies" – just twenty-four hours after Russian tanks had rolled into Hungary to crush her short-lived liberty. The following day, 6 November, the news reached Beaufre that the British had agreed to a cease-fire and the advance was to stop. "I was in a suppressed rage, and at that moment I considered the possibility of disobeying," says Beaufre, and many French troops shared his anger. It is said that some, on their way back through Cyprus, showed their disgust with their perfide ally by selling their weapons to E.O.K.A. terrorists. In France (where, on 31 October, Mollet had received a majority of 368 to 182 – including 149 Communists – compared with Eden's 270 to 218) feelings ran high against Britain's apparent lack of moral fibre.

Thus, after just forty hours, ended the Suez "war", the shortest in history and possibly the silliest. As Hugh Thomas comments, "the grand old Duke of York" did at least get to the top of the hill! In terms of human losses it cost the French ten killed, the British twenty-two, the Israelis 200 and the Egyptians less than 3,000; in cash, instead of the figure of £5 million earmarked by Chancellor Macmillan in July, it was to cost Britain alone somewhere between £100 million and an estimated £328 million. But the unquantifiable costs were to prove far higher for both nations over the long term; even though history may not rate Suez as one of its most "decisive" battles, it may well come to be regarded as one of its most influential. "Never before", wrote Harold Macmillan, "had Western Europe proved so weak. The fact that they [Britain and France] had been met by an unnatural combination between Russia and America was almost a portent." For Britain, Suez meant that she would not henceforth be capable of a foreign policy independent of the United States; in her dealings with France it meant the end of the old Entente Cordiale and the beginning of an era of mistrust to be exemplified by the Gaullist "Non" to Britain in Europe. In France, as Roy Jenkins rightly noted, "the reaction to Suez was quite different. There was less guilt and more anger. The lesson there learnt was never to trust the Americans and probably not the British either. The 'Anglo-Saxons' became the main object of obloquy. . . ."

As far as Algeria was concerned, the impact of Suez was immense. On the one hand, F.L.N. morale soared; now they could reckon on getting *real* assistance from a victorious Nasser, and in fact a large consignment of British and French arms abandoned after the cease-fire would soon be flowing in to them. On the other hand, the French contingent returning to Algeria felt mortally discouraged. One of Lartéguy's para officers explains in *The Centurions*, "It's specially bad for our men. They thought they had escaped from prison. Now they're going to be taken back to their cells under police escort." Indeed, in the French news films of the time the contrast between the tough, confident professionals setting off for Suez and the broken men shambling from their ships at Algiers spoke volumes. Although there was a band waiting to greet them in the cold rain, Pierre Leulliette recalls feeling on his return that "the shame, ridicule and ignominy of a winner who has to run away like a pathetic loser was heaped on our backs. . . ." When the instant resentment against the British had passed, it was replaced by something far more bitter against their own civil leaders: "Even in Indo-China, said the veterans, where you were betrayed daily by everyone, they wouldn't have dared do anything like that," recorded Leulliette. Many of the seeds of revolt that were to sprout eighteen months later were sown among the paras at Suez. If acquiescing to Bulganin's threat had meant a fundamental change in the rules in the international game from 1956 onwards, it also guaranteed independence for Algeria – eventually. But, like other international realities, this was invisible to the French military in Algeria, for whom the Suez humiliation only reinforced their determination to win in Algeria.

For Guy Mollet the Suez debacle meant the torpedoing of his hopes of a military victory in Algeria, while the Ben Bella episode, at least temporarily, closed all doors to a negotiated peace. His whole policy lay in ruins; yet he was allowed to linger on in power, a lame duck, if for no other reason than that no other French politician was willing to relieve him of his burdens at this invidious time. So, after a year in which almost everything had turned out as a net gain for the F.L.N., the war ground on – with Simone de Beauvoir complaining: "My serenity was destroyed. The government was going to persist with this war. Algeria would win its independence; but not for a long time."

CHAPTER EIGHT

"Why We Must Win"

1956–1958

> We want to halt the decadence of the West and the march of Communism.
> That is our duty, the real duty of the army. That is why we must win the war
> in Algeria. Indo-China taught us to see the truth.
>
> Colonel Antoine Argoud, November 1960

France's "new revolutionary army"

OBSERVING the disembarkation in Cyprus of the French contingent
bound for Suez, a British correspondent and a former paratrooper noted a
certain embarrassment on the part of the British reception committee.
The British airborne "brass", tidily arrayed on the tarmac according to
rank and staff function, had difficulty identifying their opposite numbers
among Massu's men in their "leopard" battle kit still dusty from operations in the *bled*. In fact, the French turned out to have no "staff" as such
and paid little deference to rank and, compared with their British counterparts, seemed more closely to resemble the revolutionary forces they had
been combating. Those who saw them about their business at Suez, however, were at once impressed by their hard-hitting mobility and sheer
ruthless professionalism. As *Le Monde* was to remark: "Few armies in the
world possess a generation of officers who have fought so much."

In purely military terms at any rate, the French army had come a long
way since its first fumbling operations in 1954. At that time it had begun
by repeating the early errors of the Indo-China war, of hitting back with
tanks and heavy equipment, 1945-style, against will-o'-the-wisp guerrillas.
Now the increase in manpower ordained by Mollet, a steady flow of
American helicopters to land them swiftly where they could hurt the
rebels most, new units, new leaders, new tactics, and a whole new structure
and morale within the army itself, had radically improved its striking
power. The new commanders studied local circumstances more closely and
tailored their security actions to suit. For instance, in Kabylia General Olié
had noted the central importance in Berber life of the *djemaa*, or council
of elders, and wherever possible set about boosting the responsibility of the
reliable *djemaas* and backing up their authority by the S.A.S. detachments

so successfully fathered by Soustelle, which, in turn, could rely on speedy and massive intervention by an ubiquitous army presence.

His neighbour, General André Beaufre, promoted to command the Constantine East area in April 1956 in the wake of the bloody massacres of the previous summer, and one of the most formidable military intellects of his generation, tackled his problems quite differently.* Noting that there was no parallel *djemaa* tradition in the Arab Constantinois, and critical of the army's prevailing strategy (or lack of one) of attempting to be strong everywhere, Beaufre divided his area into different zones of varying priority. Sparsely populated regions were ordained *zones interdites*, their inhabitants resettled elsewhere and the army permitted to fire on any person observed there, thus physically denying the F.L.N. all access to food or supplies. Fertile and populous centres were dubbed *zones de pacification*, where to assure total security Beaufre concentrated the mass of his conscript and reservist forces (aiming for a minimum physical presence of one company per 100 square kilometres), accompanied by a major effort in economic advancement, education and propaganda indoctrination. Finally, there were *zones d'opérations* – "killing-grounds" where F.L.N. bands were relentlessly pursued and harried by Beaufre's élite mobile forces. It was consciously part of his "psychological warfare" technique to draw pointed comparisons between conditions there and the security of life in the *zones de pacification*. If one may disregard for a moment the psychological consequences of the more ruthless aspects of Beaufre's policy – such as in the *zones interdites* – it is undeniable that, up to his translation to Suez, he was the first senior commander in Algeria to show tangible success in beating the rebels on the purely military level.

Beaufre had been trained in the hard school of Indo-China and it was natural that this theatre, where most of the French regular army had spent nearly the whole of the first post-war decade, should become its prime conditioning factor in Algeria. The new leaders coming to Algeria had been profoundly affected by the disastrous lessons of the Indo-China campaign; particularly of Dien Bien Phu, after which a number had spent humiliating months as prisoners of the Viet-Minh. This experience had provided them with the opportunity to make an intimate study of the victors' technique. They had returned well-versed in Maoist principles and strategy, as adapted by General Giap, and persuaded of the cogency of fighting revolutionary warfare with its own weapons. If the function of the guerrilla was to move like Mao's "fish in water" among the uncommitted masses, then that must be the technique of the counter-revolutionary soldier too; if the Viet-Minh could bend the minds of the populace to their will and extract vital information by resort to subtle – or less subtle – forms

---

* Later, but for his disapproval of Gaullist policy which caused him to resign in 1961, he would have risen to the top post of Army Chief-of-Staff.

of pressure, then so must the security forces. It was no use, says Colonel Roger Trinquier, one of the leading Indo-China hands, merely destroying dispersed armed bands; one had to seek out, crush and eradicate the whole of the clandestine political organisation behind them. If Indo-China had turned its French pupils into superb warriors, it had also made them highly political animals – a fact that was to have as potent an impact upon the French republic as it did on the Algerian war.

The paras and the Legion

The Indo-China record could be played to excess; some veterans constantly referred to the F.L.N. as *les Viets*, while sceptics like Jean Servier felt that there were various headquarters where Maoist doctrines had been "poorly digested". If they had studied the lessons intimately and intensely, were the conclusions they reached always profound? Could they see the problems but not the answers? But perhaps, more than the lessons, what really counted most were the leaders produced by the Indo-China school. These were to become the legendary para colonels of Algeria; loved by their men and venerated by the *pieds noirs*, dreaded almost equally by the F.L.N. and French politicians. Ducournau, Trinquier, Bigeard, Brothier, Meyer, Jeanpierre, Fossey-François, Château-Jobert, Romain-Desfossés and Coulet: magnificent combat leaders all, their names read like a record of honour of French arms from the post-1940 resurgence onwards. Before Indo-China most had distinguished themselves in the Liberation and the final battles of the Second World War, and several had been deported to concentration camps for their work in the Resistance. They were to bestride the Algerian scene like demigods until the tragic peripeteia of 1961, and even such a pro-F.L.N. film as the remarkable Pontecorvo–Yacef production, *La Battaglia di Algeri*, comes reluctantly close to vesting its French para colonel, "Mathieu" with heroic qualities.

Ducournau, the first to arrive in Algeria, has already been mentioned, but two others, Roger Trinquier and Marcel Bigeard, emerged outstandingly at this period in the war. Born in 1908, Trinquier had served in China from 1938 to 1945, and had become perhaps *the* expert on Far Eastern subversive warfare. In 1947 he helped create the 1st Battalion of Colonial Parachutists (B.P.C.), the famous *bérets rouges*, and had spent most of the succeeding years inside Viet-Minh territory.

A rather more romantic figure was the legendary Bigeard, who, a century and a half earlier, would probably have soared to stardom as a Napoleonic marshal, and who – jointly with Ducournau – formed the model for "Colonel Raspeguy" in *The Centurions*. Born in 1916, Bigeard rose from the ranks without the benefits of either St Cyr or the École de Guerre. Rather undashingly he was captured in June 1940 as a sergeant in the Maginot Line, but escaped the following year to join a colonial infantry unit. Commissioned in 1943, he joined the paras to be dropped in France in 1944, ending the war as a captain. Like Trinquier, he spent most of the ensuing years in Indo-China, and in 1954 he was parachuted at the head of his 6th B.P.C. into the encircled fortress of Dien Bien Phu. There he had led one of the most inspired counter-attacks to regain the captured bastion of Eliane 1, for which he was promoted lieutenant-colonel. After the fall of Dien Bien Phu he spent three months as a captive of the Viet-Minh under constant brain-washing, returning to France with a bad case of the *mal jaune* and full of contempt (which he never bothered to disguise) for the defeated army commanders who had come back from Indo-China promoted and laden with medals.

For Bigeard, like the others, the "discovery" of subversive warfare had been a turning-point in his career, and he had arrived in Algeria in 1955 inculcated with the belief that Indo-China had been one battle in the Communist struggle for global domination of which this new present campaign was probably a further instalment. In Algeria Bigeard received command of the 3rd Regiment of Colonial Parachutists (R.P.C.), more than half of whose 1,200 men were reservists of very mixed quality. Immediately he weeded out a score or two of stragglers and misfits and offered any others who so desired voluntary transfers to a different unit. The remainder he led off into the *bled* for two months of back-breaking training. When they returned they were clad in bizarre-looking camouflaged caps with long visors, designed by Bigeard himself and a little reminiscent of the Chinese revolutionary army, and which caused the *pieds noirs* to nickname them, with a touch of ridicule, the "lizards". But "Bigeard's boys" were also on their way to becoming a crack force; one of the most effective in the Western world. Bigeard himself practised a Rommel style of leadership, always leading an operation from the front, jumping with the first wave, knowing exactly what kind of conditions he was taking the regiment into, carrying out his own reconnaissances. He seemed to bear a charmed life but in 1956 he was wounded, thereby missing Suez. Tall and powerful, with a beaked nose that imparted a look of a bird of prey, Bigeard had that particularly French quality of *allure* essential to an outstanding commander. He seldom did anything without panache. Instead of arriving by staff car, or even helicopter, his favourite manner of inspecting a unit was to drop by parachute, arm at the salute as he touched down.*

Bigeard's 3rd R.P.C. soon became something of a model for the other para regiments in Algeria, and altogether they were to constitute the spearhead of French offensive operations there. They exerted a powerful

---

* This nearly ended in disaster when Bigeard, by now nearing sixty and a senior general, was dropped into a shark-infested sea by mistake during a visit to troops in Madagascar. He broke an arm but was saved by his faithful staff who had parachuted into the sea with him.

attraction upon French youth, and some fifteen thousand a year were then qualifying for their *plaque à vélo*, as the para insignia was irreverently called. Next, *primus inter pares* among the élite formations, came the Foreign Legion, "La Légion", with all its romantic connotations still only somewhat dimmed by the modern age. Though it had fought everywhere the tricolour had ever waved, from the Crimea to crushing the Commune in 1871 to Dien Bien Phu in 1954, the Legion had always had a "special relationship" with Algeria. Out of necessity caused by the conquest, Louis-Philippe had created it in 1831 and the following year it established itself at Sidi-Bel-Abbès, the *Beau Geste* depot on the fringe of the desert where it remained until the loss of Algeria. Through the parade-grounds of Sidi-Bel-Abbès, dominated by a vast bronze globe bearing the motto *Honneur et Fidélité*, passed 340,000 Legionnaires, of whom one in ten would fall. Here, or wherever it found itself every 30 April – resplendent with white kepi and scarlet epaulettes, its sapper sergeants with magnificent beards – the Legion would celebrate the solemn Fête de Camerone: the battle in Louis-Napoleon's ill-starred Mexican campaign of 1863 when sixty-four Legionnaires had held out against 2,000 Mexicans, with only three survivors. Camerone had nearly been repeated at Dien Bien Phu, where the Legion alone had lost 1,500 men including 576 from its 1st Para Battalion, which had been wiped out twice over. During the Indo-China campaign a total of more than 10,000 Legionnaires had died, the majority of them Germans, who still (in 1955) provided forty-seven per cent of the Legion's complement, followed by the French themselves (renouncing their nationality) at twelve per cent and Italians at eleven per cent.

As an élite body it still enjoyed the best food in the army and was accompanied wherever it went by its own mobile brothels – "*le puff*". But discipline was rigid, and punishments – with refractories made to kneel hours long in the beating sun – almost as savage as in the days of *Beau Geste* or Ouida. On the other hand, extraordinary tolerance could be shown when a Legionnaire, suffering from a bout of the notorious *cafard*, took a shot at an officer (provided he missed). By the end of 1955 the Legion already had 20,000 men, two-thirds of its effectives, in Algeria. Supreme among its élite were perhaps the green beret paras of its 1st R.E.P. stationed at Zéralda, just west of Algiers. Since Dien Bien Phu recruitment for the Legion had fallen off; nevertheless there was still no shortage of volunteers for the glamour of its para units.

Although the discipline was tougher, in the free and easy atmosphere and relaxation of the old caste system within them the para formations as a whole exemplified post-1945 trends throughout the French army. While seventy-two per cent of all serving colonels were still St Cyriens, the percentage fell to twenty-five per cent among captains and twenty-three per cent for lieutenants. Few officers had come from the Polytechnique or any of the socially "smart" schools. The result was that the army had become a much more democratic, more representative, force than it had been for many a year. As J.-R. Tournoux remarked, "It is no longer the army of the Dreyfus Affair, of the blue line of the Vosges, of the charge in white gloves. It is an army of Valmy." In one respect, however, the development of the para regiments was to become distinctly atavistic. Tournoux adds pointedly: "certain colonels gladly regarded themselves as proprietors of their regiments, as under the monarchy". The trend towards "private armies" among the paras undoubtedly carried with it at least two pronounced disadvantages; because of this elitism, morale in the more humdrum units of the army tended to suffer correspondingly; and, when the two big challenges of military versus civil authority came, the colonels of Algeria were to prove too powerful by half.

"... anothe. quare on the map"

Through 1956 and into 1957 the overall military picture of the war did not improve for the French. It may have looked rosier in some areas (notably General Beaufre's command), but it worsened in others; while all the time those blotches on the "smallpox chart" were spreading. With the arrival of Mollet's reservists and national servicemen numbers on the ground increased, and so did the efficiency of the paras; but at the same time the numbers of the F.L.N., and their expertise and equipment, were also on the upward path. Security operations were interrupted by the withdrawal of the paras for the Suez adventure, succeeded by the serious jolt to morale caused by the debacle. From the point of view of the ordinary French combatant, if there was any change in the "war that was not a war"* it lay in its ever-increasing brutality, perhaps especially marked since the Philippeville massacres and Abane's subsequent espousal of total terror.

Continuing his tersely unromanticised account of service with the paras, Pierre Leulliette describes an episode in the Nementchas during the summer of 1956. The time had passed "since the wounding of a fellagha was considered an event. Deaths now came in dozens." A strong rebel band had been pinned down and was being strafed by French planes; but instead of attempting to slip away into the maquis, as in the past, "They went on firing back at the fighters, very confidently, at the helicopters, at ourselves, and at everything that moved or glittered." Leulliette's detachment, themselves now pinned down and unable to reach a nearby oued (river bed), began to suffer atrociously from thirst. An air-drop was made

---

* The French government assiduously refused to recognise operations in Algeria as anything more than the "maintenance of order"; it was not even a "campaign", thus the Croix de Guerre could not be awarded and a new decoration, the Médaille de la Valeur Militaire, had to be struck.

to them and they prepared to dig in for the night. Meanwhile, two hundred yards in front of them lay two wounded paras. Three men had gone out at intervals in an effort to reach them, but after each had been wounded the captain forbade any further attempts. One of them, V., returned to consciousness in the cold night air, and called ceaselessly to his comrades for succour:

> My poor friend V. lay howling on his bed of stones till morning. He suffered unimaginably, both physically and mentally, a prey to mortal terror. He only really stopped at dawn, when we could perhaps have saved him. For several hours a rebel had been slithering towards him. He could have seen him all that while. There he was. The rebel touched his body. He took away his weapons. Then he gouged out his eyes. Then he slashed his Achilles' tendons, afraid, perhaps, that he might still come back and die with us. But he didn't finish him off, merely wanting him to have to lie still and suffer. His friend T., the *sergent-chef*, also died shortly afterwards, a hundred yards away, his eyes gouged and tendons slashed; a slow death, while we were waiting for the dawn.
> ... He [V.] was crazy about war. It was just one lark as far as he was concerned. ... It was his way of enjoying life.

In the latter part of the Second World War it was customary in the French army to vaunt the ferocity of "their" Algerian Tirailleurs against the Germans, much as the British took pride in the deeds performed by the Gurkhas with their terrible kukris. But when one's own comrades became the victims ... well, that was different. In his *Lieutenant en Algérie* Servan-Schreiber notes how soldiers in Algeria accustomed themselves never to say "'Watch out, you're going to get yourself killed,' but one repeats several times a day, 'Make a mistake, and you have your balls cut off.'" It was what the French soldier expected, and he reacted accordingly. In an article entitled "Stretching a Soldier's Patience", *The Times* of 7 June 1973 described how Belfasters cheered when four British soldiers were blown up and horribly mutilated by a mine, and how other British soldiers witnessing the episode "were shocked and embittered by what they thought was a callous disregard for life". Multiply this several hundred times for the additional horrors of the fighting in Algeria (such as the experience of Leulliette's), for the far greater numbers involved, and for the altogether less phlegmatic character of the French soldier, and the occasional angry backlash or infraction of discipline becomes inevitable.

By 1956 accounts of such cases in Algeria were legion. Leulliette himself recounts relieving in the Nementchas the 1st Parachute Regiment of the Foreign Legion (1st R.E.P.), just after one of their sergeant-majors had been knifed in the street. A quarter of an hour later the entire company descended on the Arab quarter: "Sixty-four people, mostly men, were slaughtered by automatic rifle or bayonet in less than an hour. Fire did the rest." Earlier, near Philippeville, Leulliette's own unit had been involved in a massacre of civilians. The rebels had proved elusive that day. "Everything seemed to slip between our fingers. We no longer knew what we were doing." Then, suddenly, a group of women and children instead of *fellaghas* had run into the paras' fire:

> ...could the bloke thirty yards ahead of me, firing his automatic rifle at a child of ten lying astride the path, his leg broken and chest heaving, have sworn that he couldn't see? Women, old women, stiff and awkward with fear, were massacred in full view of everyone, in broad daylight, almost as if it were a game, to make our bullets "talk". Some of us would have done anything. Back at home, civilians again, they'd think: was it possible? Yes, it was with all sorts of corpses, old men's and children's mingled with those of the rebels. The sight of an old woman, with her hair down, flattened in front of you by a burst from an automatic rifle was something you never forget. "If you've no imagination," said Céline, "dying's nothing; if you have, it's too much."

Later this scene was followed by the "inevitable looting" of abandoned *mechtas*:

> We turned the village over like a field. After a while, unable to find anything, we amused ourselves by smashing the whole place, through sheer joy of destruction. Old wedding dresses, which we discovered carefully folded at the bottom of every box, were hung derisively from trees in grotesque shapes, and then dragged through the mud. Some dressed themselves up in women's clothes....The waste was so great that there was nothing left to eat amongst the rubbish. Picture of a gone age. But then war is ageless.

Conscience – a costly luxury

Describing how the eyes of a twenty-year-old French national serviceman were opened to the facts of life in Algeria, Alain Manévy relates experiences not dissimilar to those of Leulliette. After an eight-hour journey for the 200 kilometres from Algiers, during which they had passed a burnt-out train on the way, Manévy and his draft arrived in Orléansville where the first sight to greet their eyes was a group of people gathered around a large tree, with a dead F.L.N. slumped beneath it. Over the corpse was hung a black placard: "I will not kill my brothers any longer, I will throw no more grenades." It was a standing order in Orléansville, the conscripts were told, for any rebel killed to be displayed thus for a period of twenty-four hours. Their next shock was to hear, during the boring routine of barrack life, distinct murmurs about the application of torture. Then their sergeant-major gave them an introductory lecture of nanny-like matter-of-factness: "Watch out for malaria, watch out for dysentery, never less than three together for a stroll in town with at least one weapon among the three, please; curfew at 20.30 hours, no lateness, please, because otherwise the sentries have orders to shoot on sight...." Then Manévy was transferred to Constantine where he witnessed a terrorist grenade attack on a 14 July parade. Several paras were wounded. One of Manévy's age panicked, fired into the crowd, and killed a Muslim woman on a balcony. Next, a hundred of the paras, some evidently fortified with anisette, broke loose, heading towards the Casbah to avenge their wounded with shouts of "*Les melons! Les melons!*" Unable to find any Muslims, they first smashed up a Jewish shop. At the height of the *ratonnade* a large French civilian intervened angrily from a nearby billiard saloon: "I am Captain Bottier; I fought myself; I did thirty-seven jumps with the Resistance.... You band of little idiots – you're doing exactly what the F.L.N. terrorists count on you doing...." To Manévy, Captain Bottier disclosed that he was an S.A.S. officer in from the *bled*, adding, "Two months of work as an S.A.S. officer are wrecked in one evening like this."

After the paras had withdrawn, Manévy learned that twenty Muslims had been lynched in the affray. Earlier, in Orléansville, he had noted the conspicuous lack of hatred with which the F.L.N. "was presented to us as the indirect enemy"; something difficult to visualise, quite unlike "the Fritz with his swastika" of the Second World War. Now, with deep shock, he recorded: "In the Quartier Latin, certainly I had seen some fights – but never such extensive hatred of this sort...." As the war went on, what became almost worse than hatred was the indifference that grew in the army towards the hunting-down and killing of *fellaghas*; it was an indifference, experienced by troops of many another nation in similar situations, that also spread to embrace the all-too-frequent cases where innocent civilians were shot down in error by frightened, angry or trigger-happy soldiers. In a book that aroused the French conscience more than any at the time, *Lieutenant en Algérie*, one of several such episodes is described by Jean-Jacques Servan-Schreiber, the founder-editor of *L'Express*, then serving his time as a recalled reservist lieutenant. At a village near Palestro a *pied noir* postman, employed there for twenty-five years and liked by everyone, is found with his throat cut. The next day two Muslims are sitting at a café table, quite innocently. Getting up, the younger one is nearly run over by a French jeep. His friend goes to pick him up. The private in the jeep waves his automatic at the older Muslim. It goes off, "by mistake", hitting the man in the stomach. The jeep drives off rapidly, for fear of attracting trouble in the Muslim quarter, and leaving the mortally wounded man in the road. A U.T.* detachment now arrives and, in a state of nervousness because of the recent killings, assumes the victim to have been shot by the F.L.N. Next, a truck loaded with "loyal" Muslim mine-workers comes past. Terrified by a recent lynching in the nearby village, they recognise in the demeanour of the U.T. "that sort of excess of fever and physical fury which overtakes the European population of any village, when exasperated by a series of assassinations by the *fellagha*". So the driver of the Muslim

---

* Unités Territoriales, auxiliaries formed of *pieds noirs*.

truck panics, and drives off at full speed. The U.T. fire at it, inaccurately. A further army vehicle arrives on the scene and its occupants are informed by the U.T. that the Muslim truck just passed was full of F.L.N. and had been responsible for the shooting of the man lying in the road. The truck is overtaken and, refusing to halt, shot up. All its occupants are killed – but, strangely enough, not a weapon is found. Meanwhile, the culprit has reported the shooting "accident" to his commanding officer. In recording the episode, however, regimental headquarters decides that awkwardness would be avoided if it were stated that arms *had* been found in the shot-up truck. So the final communiqué reads: "Yesterday at . . . the occupants of a truck machine-gunned passers-by, miraculously only wounding one."

Discussing this episode in the officers' mess with a newly arrived captain who has expostulated that it was "a bad practice to kill possible innocents", a hardened campaigner points out that there are only two choices:

> Either you consider *a priori* that every Arab, in the country, in the street, in a passing truck is *innocent* until he's proven the contrary; and permit me to tell you that if that is your attitude . . . you will immediately be posted, because the parents of reservists one has had killed don't like it, and will write to their deputies that you're a butcher. . . . Or you will . . . consider that every Arab is a *suspect*, a possible *fellagha* . . . because that, my dear sir, is the truth. . . . But once you're here, to pose yourself problems of conscience – and treat possible assassins as presumed innocents – that's a luxury that costs dear, and costs men, dear sir, young men themselves also innocent, and our own. . . .

The choice posed was a hard one for any young soldier to have to face, and in Algeria by no means all – or even a majority – of the French army opted for the alternative of suppressing the "problems of conscience". But, as indicated by the examples above, the fierce reprisal and the cruel, indiscriminate injustice *did* take place on the French side – as indeed they take place in every similar war. What is equally sure is that, as the S.A.S. captain pointed out to Alain Manévy, such acts usually militated against French interests in the long run. Looked at from the other side of the lines, this is confirmed by Herb Greer. Reporting a particularly brutal French reprisal in which women were killed, he quotes a member of the F.L.N. as declaring: "Voilà, we've won another battle. They hate the French a little more now. The stupid bastards are winning the war for us." The conscious suppression of "conscience" also led logically to another step in the escalation of brutality, the significance of which will be seen in the following chapter. It inclines the soldier, says Pierre-Henri Simon, towards a confusion in his mind between "licit violence and culpable brutality. It is thus that one arrives at this monstrosity: the practice of torture by the military."

"Why we must win. . . ."

If there is one factor which might be found lacking in, say, British army operations in Northern Ireland but which played an important role affecting the intensity of the war in Algeria, it was a certain peculiar determination within the regular French army that it should *not be lost*. This determination did not entirely spring from a belief in the sanctity of the *présence française* – less still from any kindred feeling for the *pieds noirs* – and to understand it one needs to recall sympathetically the recent history of the French army. Generals like Beaufre were captains at the time of the 1940 debacle, regimental commanders like Bigeard either N.C.O.s or lieutenants, and all remained profoundly conditioned by it. For although, from Bir Hakeim onwards, the resurrected French army under such towering figures as de Lattre, Leclerc and Juin had covered itself with repeated distinction, there lingered a nagging complex about its inferior role alongside the vast British and American war machines perforce imposed upon it by 1940.* Intolerable to an army so steeped in legends of *la gloire*, the complex died hard. Wrote François Mitterrand in 1957: "When the war in Indo-China broke out, France was able to believe that the 1940 defeat was nothing more than a lost battle, and that the armistice of 1945 was going to restore its power at the same time as its glory."

Then followed the catastrophe of Dien Bien Phu; the most humiliating defeat suffered by any Western power since the Second World War and, in its context, as humiliating as 1940 to French army sensibilities in that the victors had been despised "colonials" and "little yellow men". Analysing the French army's determination to win the victory "which the French army desired with all its heart to put an end to the chain of humiliations" (a thesis he did not support), Raymond Aron, the historian, wrote in 1958: "The Algerian war offers one more occasion for the French to meditate on decadence. Algeria lost, and there is France on the slippery slope down which Spain and Portugal slid." Just how passionately individual officers of the wartime generation could feel is well illustrated in the remarkable career of Colonel François Coulet. Escaping to London after 1940, Coulet had become a close aide to General de Gaulle and then – as the only air force officer sporting the *plaque à vélo* – set up an airborne commando. But, missing the Normandy landings, he felt he had "not done his bit". After the war he rejoined the diplomatic corps and was Minister in Belgrade when the Algerian war began. Finding "anti-colonialist" passions in Yugoslavia intolerable, and motivated by a longing to "expunge the disgrace of Dien Bien Phu", Coulet resigned, flew back to France, equipped himself with contact lenses to look more military, and through

* The Nazi occupation following 1940 may have left other, unpleasanter, legacies to the Algerian war. John Gale, a young British war correspondent who suffered a nervous breakdown following his experiences in Algeria, records a threat made to an F.L.N. suspect by a young para: "I'll shoot your whole family like mine was shot by the Germans," and another remark passed, with perhaps a touch of grudging respect, by a para captain: "The Germans did things coldly, systematically...."

de Gaulle's influence gained permission to create and lead to Algeria France's one and only air force para commando – at the age of fifty. He also became the only reservist colonel of the paras in Algeria; trained under Bigeard, his commando of 140 men – the last of the "private armies" – acquitted itself nobly, especially when it came to close co-operation with air force strikes. For Coulet they were "the happiest years of my life" – until he was translated by de Gaulle for another mission.

On taking up the command in Algeria, General Lorillot had confided with grim emphasis to a political contact: "They made fools of us in Indo-China . . . They screwed us in Tunisia . . . We are being screwed in Morocco. But they will never screw us in Algeria, I swear to you. Let this be known in Paris." Already by 1956 there was a strong feeling in the army that the politicians were a chief source of its misfortunes, and this was to grow from Suez until May 1958. General Jacques de Bollardière, a distinguished soldier who had fought in Norway, at El Alamein, with the maquis in the Ardennes as well as at Dien Bien Phu, and who was shortly to find himself seriously at odds with army policy in Algeria, criticises the professional army after Indo-China because: "instead of coldly analysing with courageous lucidity its strategic and tactical errors, it gave itself up to a too human inclination and tried – not without reason, how-ever – to excuse its mistakes by the faults of civil authority and public opinion". He was reminded of the young Germans of post-1918 seeking to justify a notion of a "generalised treachery". The feeling ran deep; just on the eve of Suez a book was published by a young Frenchman that had a powerful impact on French opinion. Called *Les Taxis de la Marne*, by Jean Dutourd, it lambasted the middle-aged politicians of feeble will as being responsible for the collapse of 1940, praised de Gaulle as the only man of honour then alive, and demanded a recrudescence of the "Spirit of the Marne" to save France in its current dilemmas. De Gaulle himself sums up admirably the prevailing attitude of the army:

> Taking upon itself not only the burden of the fighting but also the severity, and sometimes the beastliness, of the repression, closely in touch with the anxieties of the French population of Algeria and the Muslim auxiliaries, haunted by fear of another Indo-China, another military reverse inflicted on its colours, the army, more than any other body, felt a growing resentment against a political system which was the embodiment of irresolution.

Higher ideals

At lower levels of self-interest, the continued prosecution of the war in Algeria did of course represent a last chance of gracious living and of prospects of promotion to some officers, but beyond this and even the urge to avenge past "reverses" there existed a higher, though often woolly, ideal. In *The Centurions*, Jean Lartéguy has a fanatical para officer called

"Boisfeuras", an expert on psycho-political warfare who has spent his life in the Far East. "Boisfeuras", explains Lartéguy:

> had no feeling of nationalism; he was therefore unable to invoke the defence of his country, of "Mother France". He needed a more universal cause; like many of his comrades, he believed he had found it in the struggle against Communism. Communism as he had known it in Camp One, deprived of all human substance by the Viet-Minh, could only result in a universe of sexless insects. . . .

He is compared by the author to those Roman centurions who "tried to maintain the outposts of the Empire while the people back in Rome were sinking back into Christianity, and the Caesars into debauchery". In real life "Boisfeuras" had his opposite number in Colonel Antoine Argoud, another para whose extremity in belief and deed were to bring him notoriety later on. "We want to halt the decadence of the West and the march of Communism," declared Argoud in court during the Barricades Trial of November 1960: "That is our duty, the real duty of the army. That is why we must win the war in Algeria. Indo-China taught us to see the truth. . . ." To men like "Boisfeuras" and Argoud the war against Communism was a permanent and unceasing phenomenon; while nationalism, in the Indo-Chinese and Algerian context, was largely equated with Communism. Theirs was a doctrine, says Edward Behr, "which, if carried to its logical conclusion, would have led to fascism not only in Algeria but in France as well". Certainly, in the army's contempt for the men of the Fourth Republic and the sense of its destiny to restore the *grandeur* of France, it was to be led close to destroying the nation's democratic functions.

If the Indo-China experience had succeeded in cementing the unity of the French professional army, says Behr also, it was to do so "only at the expense of turning it into a 'band of brothers' isolated from the French nation as a whole". The isolation also extended, to some extent, to the *pieds noirs* with whom the army had a prickly relationship. The dashing paras skimmed the cream of the girls on the beaches but – as usual in such circumstances – there were not enough to go round for the rest, and not every *pied noir* home was open to the army. "They made them pay for everything, and they never did anything to defend themselves," says Colonel Coulet, reflecting a popular view in the army. In one small rural settlement, Leulliette recalls the frightened *pieds noirs* angrily blaming the soldiers for the menace of the F.L.N.: "It's you who attracts them here!" As time went by the officers as well as the men became less and less sympathetic to protecting the interests, or property, of the *grands colons*. "We have not come here", declared Radio-Bigeard, the paras' own station: "to defend colonialism. We have nothing in common with the rich *colons* who exploit the Muslims. We are the defenders of liberty and of a new order. While we were fighting in Indo-China, while we were suffering in Viet-Minh prisons, men liberally paid betrayed us.... Here you will not be betrayed...." In general, the attitude towards the Muslim population tended to be one of reforming liberalism; though often, perhaps, with a distinctly paternalistic flavour. Yet, as Servan-Schreiber notes, there was a "symbiosis" gradually growing up between the regulars and the *pieds noirs*, based on accepting each other's policy – because there was no other. That policy was, simply, the waging of war à outrance against the rebels. But, in the policy of common interest, each had different objectives that, at the very end, would bring them into tragic conflict; for one, it was to survive in the order of things as before; for the other, chiefly to win a military victory.

The coming of Salan

In December 1956, the same month that Castro landed in Cuba aboard the *Granma*, the French Commander-in-Chief in Algeria, General Lorillot, left for home after seventeen months in command. A bachelor and a dedicated, monk-like soldier, Lorillot had become profoundly depressed. Although the troops at his disposal had doubled since Soustelle's day, and virtually all his demands had been satisfied, the rebellion had continued to prove uncontainable and almost nowhere in Algeria could be described as definitively "pacified". The debacle at Suez had been the last blow for Lorillot, and it was clearly time for him to be replaced by someone with a fresh outlook. On 14 December the new commander arrived, a figure who from now on would be central to the whole drama of Algeria right through to the end.

General Raoul Salan was France's most decorated soldier; it was even rumoured that he went to bed wearing his *bananes*, which included the British C.B.E. and the American Distinguished Service Cross, awarded when commanding de Lattre's old 14th Division. No Frenchman of his generation – in fact, few soldiers anywhere – had fought as much as Salan. Leaving St Cyr as an officer cadet, he had seen the last fighting on the grim field of Verdun in 1918 at the age of nineteen. After being seriously wounded in the Levant campaign of 1920-1, Salan made his debut in Indo-China as a young captain, lived in the outback, learned Laotian, fought river pirates and local warlords, and joined the Deuxième Bureau. From now on his character was shaped by the twin influences of the colonial army and clandestine intelligence work, the intrigues of which he found far from unappealing. In 1939 he was sent on an undercover mission to Italian-occupied Ethiopia, ostensibly as a correspondent of *Le Temps*, to gauge the possibility of a native uprising against the Italians. Recalled to France, he found himself commanding a battalion of Senegalese Tirailleurs thrown in to stem the German panzers on the Somme in June 1940. In

1942 he was at Dakar as head of the A.O.F. (Vichy) Deuxième Bureau, then switched to the same job with Free French Headquarters in Algiers. In 1944 he landed on the Riviera, liberated Toulon and had a street named after him by grateful citizens of a neighbouring town. Fighting his way northwards, he ended the war on Lake Constance as a general. Almost immediately afterwards he was despatched to Indo-China, becoming de Lattre's second-in-command in 1950. The marshal thought highly of Salan's capacity for detailed planning, but was perhaps critical of his excessive prudence, commenting, "He never goes on board without a lifejacket." On de Lattre's tragic death in 1952 Salan took over the command. It was remarked then that he "launched an occasional blow against the Viet-Minh 'so daring that de Lattre himself might have thought twice about undertaking it'; but then he relapsed into periods of indolence". Then, in 1954, it was Salan who had to preside over the humiliating end of the *présence française* in Indo-China.

Accompanying him on his arrival in Algiers was Madame Salan, nick-named *la biche* (the doe), the quintessence of the loyal army wife, indefatigable in welfare work with both the troops and Muslims, and inseparable from her husband in all his campaigns. In Algiers their small son was to die and be buried. Though only of medium height, physically Salan cut an impressive figure as he stepped off the plane; a chest well developed for bearing the countless rows of *bananes*; blue eyes and swept-back silver hair tinted with just a touch of blue; and a handsome profile that made journalists think of a "Roman pro-consul". But the blue eyes masked an impenetrable and complex personality. Salan was known as *le Mandarin* or *le Chinois*, but less on account of his long sojourn in the East than for the impassive mysteriousness with which he surrounded himself – and which gave rise to a multitude of rumours about him. He was, they said, a Freemason and a Protestant (in fact, he was a lapsed Catholic); he was a Socialist (in fact, though his father had been, he never was); he was an opium smoker and (according to Claude Paillat) had exploited the drug traffic in Indo-China to the benefit of French Intelligence – charges which he waves aside with a derisory gesture. During the Second World War he had managed to be "neither Pétainist, nor Gaullist; just anti-German"; a detachment which fellow-officers, who as a rule had come down heavily on one side or the other, found baffling.

What was certain about Salan was that he was highly intelligent but susceptible to flattery; ambitious; and – in contrast to his much more straightforward subordinate, Massu – an extremely well-developed political animal. Yet, at the same time, as a soldier he was a man of simple tastes, eschewing the glitter of receptions and public functions, and preferring to be at his desk or out visiting units, where he was generally to be seen in rolled-up shirtsleeves instead of the more formal attire worn by other senior "brass". There was also no doubt that, within a short time, Salan, by his energetic policy of pressing the attack home on the enemy, giving him no respite night or day, did put a new spirit into the army in Algeria.

But somehow people instinctively did not trust Salan. De Gaulle (who, when writing his memoirs, could not be regarded as quite unprejudiced) says of him: "there was something slippery and inscrutable in the character of this capable, clever and in some respects beguiling figure". In December 1956 the *pieds noirs* were certainly not "beguiled" by the new Commander-in-Chief. To them he was the left-wing general who had sold out in Indo-China and was now coming to do the same in Algeria. They reacted to his appointment with the same irrational, ill-founded rage with which they had greeted first Soustelle, then Catroux. This time, however, some of them were prepared to go much further to demonstrate their mistrust.

The Faure conspiracy, and the bazooka

Shortly after Salan's arrival two events took place that were indicative both of the neurotic atmosphere in Algeria and the mounting tensions within the army itself. Just before Christmas Paul Teitgen, secretary-general at the Algiers Prefecture and in charge of the city police, received a strange visit from a General Jacques Faure, second-in-command of the Algiers sector. Faure was a popular figure in the army, a fine soldier, champion skier and former alpine troop commander; his son was later to be killed in action in Algeria. To Teitgen's amazement, the general – whom he had never met before – promptly outlined a conspiracy to overthrow the civil government in Algeria and replace it by a military regime. After Christmas Lacoste was due to visit the oasis of Ouargla for a brief holiday; on the way his plane was to be made to land at Paul-Cazelles, where he would be arrested and conducted to a "secret destination". The conspirators would then seize Algiers radio and announce that Salan was taking over. Faure admitted that Salan was not in the plot, but it was considered that – once it was a *fait accompli* – he would accede. At the same time, Faure hinted that a number of eminent politicians in France were favourable to the *coup*, mentioning specifically Michel Debré.

Teitgen, a hero of the Resistance who had survived Dachau, was little disposed towards an army takeover in Algeria in any shape, and he could hardly believe his ears. At first he thought the bronzed and rugged general had gone slightly out of his mind. On second thoughts, however, he decided he should delve a bit deeper, and called Faure in for a further discussion, this time recording it all on a tape. Fortified with it, he then went to warn Lacoste. Distressed by this news, especially as he regarded Faure as a "stout-hearted sort" (*un coeur généreux*), the governor-general despatched Teitgen to Paris to inform the Minister of Defence, Bourgès-

Maunoury. Teitgen has told how the minister's immediate reaction was to hope that the affair would not "make it impossible for one to go ski-ing", and asked him whether he had said anything to "*ce con-là*", Mitterrand, then Minister of Justice. Shocked by Bourgès-Maunoury's apparently frivolous lack of interest, as well as his disrespect for a fellow minister, Teitgen then went on to see Mollet himself. Mollet took the matter much more seriously, but in turn used the same expression in deprecating Bourgès-Maunoury – "*ce con-là*"! Teitgen returned to Algiers, disquieted at the apparent lack of solidarity within the government. Faure was recalled and sentenced to thirty days' fortress arrest – the first senior officer to suffer such a penalty for dissidence in Algeria. Salan was enraged that Teitgen should have gone over his head and behind his back in reporting one of his subordinates; while Teitgen's action may well itself have reflected the general lack of trust inspired by Salan. Meanwhile, the nine days' wonder of the "Faure conspiracy" was submerged by news of the assassination (on the same day that Teitgen was in Paris) of Amédée Froger, mayor of Boufarik, and the prominent conservative President of the Mayors of Algeria, an act that was to unleash the "Battle of Algiers".

Hardly had the shock of Faure and the Froger killing been assimilated when there came a much more serious assassination attempt against the person of the Commander-in-Chief, Salan. At 6.40 p.m. on 16 January 1957, Salan had just left his office in the 10th Military Region G.H.Q., a large white building* on a corner of the Place Bugeaud, right in the heart of Algiers, to attend a meeting with Lacoste. From the Gouvernement-Général, some twenty minutes later, he heard a powerful explosion, shortly followed by a white-faced secretary rushing in to announce: "It's your office; Commandant Rodier is wounded!" Rushing back to the Place Bugeaud, Salan found his office blasted and in the next room his *chef-de-cabinet*, Rodier, lying dead, almost cut in two by the force of the blast. Had Salan been still at his desk he would almost certainly have shared the same fate; his ten-year-old daughter, injured by flying glass while doing her homework in the apartment above, had an even narrower escape. On investigation, Salan discovered that the explosion had been caused by two anti-tank "bazooka" projectiles, ingeniously fired from home-made tubes installed on the roof of the building opposite. One had been sighted on Salan's office, the other on Rodier's. Electric wires ran from them to the ground floor where the perpetrator had pressed the button, evidently on seeing the silhouette of Rodier, which he had mistaken for Salan's. He had then disappeared into the street.

It was immediately reckoned that the attempt was far too sophisticated for the F.L.N., and a number of suspects were rounded up among the "ultra" *pieds noirs* who had already emerged from the time of the

---

* Now, ironically, party headquarters of the F.L.N.

anti-Mollet demonstrations. They included Dr Kovacs, the ex-Hungarian doctor and hypnotist who had become passionately attached to Algeria; Philippe Castille, a former member of the 11th Shock, the para cloak-and-dagger unit that had blown up Ben Boulaid; Michel Fechoz, Dr Jean-Claude Pérez, Robert Martel, Jo Ortiz, the restaurateur, and Georges Wattin, alias "The Limp". In the motives and complicities behind it, the *affaire du bazooka* remains one of the most mysterious and shadowy episodes of the whole war. Colonel Godard, chief-of-staff to Massu in Algiers, who intensively questioned motives of the principals, himself admits: "I never understood why." According to Pierre Vidal-Naquet, supported by Maître Teitgen, many of the records were mysteriously destroyed "on orders" after May 1958; though Teitgen himself managed to keep copies and Salan himself prints Kovacs's testimony in full.

Under interrogation Castille admitted to setting up the "bazookas" and firing them; while Kovacs revealed that the object behind the plot was to replace the mistrusted *bradeur de l'Indochine*, Salan, by his former junior there, General Cogny. Following upon this, it was hoped, a "government of national unity" would then be brought to power in Paris. In his deposition Kovacs implicated the involvement behind the conspiracy of a Comité des Six of French politicians – among whom the name of Senator Michel Debré, close associate of General de Gaulle, Minister of Justice in 1958 and later prime minister, figures. After inexplicable delays the "bazooka" trial started in July 1958. Kovacs attended on a stretcher, then "disappeared" to Spain in what the *Guardian* at the time described as "preposterous circumstances". He was sentenced to death *in absentia*; Castille to ten years' hard labour, Fechoz to six years. Both were liberated by *pieds noirs* demonstrators during "Barricades Week" of January. Nobody more important was ever brought to trial; though to this day Salan, both in his *Mémoires: Fin d'un Empire* and privately, still insists on the involvement behind the scenes of Michel Debré and others, but no real evidence has ever been adduced.*

Historically, however, what is important about both the "Faure affair" and *le bazooka* is the profound malady and disaffection that they revealed in the heart of the French army, extending to the higher reaches of the Fourth Republic itself, and which were shortly to burst to the surface with revolutionary force.

* When asked by the author why he had not sued Salan for libel M. Debré replied, "I took legal advice, and was told that the charges made against me were far too vague." Debré is supported, among others, by the well-informed Brombergers in their book, *Les 13 Complots du 13 Mai* (1959), who cast doubts both on Kovacs's evidence and Salan's own conviction "that he had been shot at by other people than a small team of over-excited Algerian 'ultras'". Yes, they assessed, there was a *political* plot involving senior politicians, but Dr Kovacs had – they suggest – hypnotised himself into the false belief that the Comité had really wanted him to assassinate Salan. Such was the fervid mentality of the *pied noir* extremists.

CHAPTER NINE

The Battle of Algiers

January–March 1957

A strong dilemma in a desperate case
To act with infamy or quit the place.
Jonathan Swift

Preliminaries

IN Algeria the year of 1957 was occupied by one of the most dramatic and best-publicised episodes in the entire war. The actual date of the first salvo in the Battle of Algiers is as arguable as who actually fired it, although the assumption of civil power in the city by General Massu's paras presents a convenient one. As with the outbreak of any major confrontation it was preceded by a long chain of events, starting on 19 June the previous year. That day two members of the F.L.N., Zabane and Ferradj, who had been under sentence for many months, were guillotined in Barberousse prison after Lacoste – under heavy pressure from *pied noir* public opinion, and wanting to placate it so as to push through his own intended "bill of rights", or *loi-cadre* – had refused clemency. In the appallingly over-crowded prison where conditions were already atrocious ("It is hell," wrote Bitat, who was already imprisoned there, "men are beaten with iron bars, the heat is horrible and they are given salted water to drink."), the immediacy of the executions – the sinister preparations, the defiant shouts of the condemned, the very audible thud of the blade – provoked most violent reactions, and these were amplified outside. To the Algerian mind such judicial executions were particularly shocking, and in this instance exacerbated by the fact that Ferradj was a cripple.*

Announcing that for every guillotined member of the F.L.N. a hundred French would be killed indiscriminately, Ramdane Abane ordered immediate reprisals. Saadi Yacef (who, on the arrest of Bitat, had taken over the

---

* Zabane had killed a gamekeeper and had been in prison since the first days of the war. Ferradj, condemned for the killing in an ambush of eight civilians, including a woman and a seven-year-old girl, had lost an eye and been crippled by his wounds. Had Ferradj in particular been reprieved, the outcry among the *pieds noirs* would have been violent.

Algiers network) was told to "kill any European between the ages of eighteen and fifty-four. But no women, no children, no old people...."
Between 21 and 24 June Yacef's squads roaming Algiers shot down forty-nine civilians. It was the first time that Algiers had been hit by this kind of random terrorism, and the ineluctable escalation now began here. On 10 August an immense explosion rocked the Casbah. A house in the Rue de Thèbes had been blown up; reputedly it had housed F.L.N. terrorists involved in the June reprisals, but also destroyed with it were three neighbouring houses, and the Muslim death-roll ran to seventy, including women and children. At first it was alleged that a secret bomb factory had gone off by mistake, but soon *pied noir* counter-terrorist groups associated with Kovacs and Achiary were making no secret of their responsibility.*
The F.L.N. claim that, up to this point, no bomb directed against human life, as opposed to property, had yet been detonated in Algiers. A month later, however, under Abane's influence indiscriminate terrorism was espoused at the Soummam Conference, and orders were passed to Ben M'hidi, who had become the political leader of the Algiers Zone (Z.A.A.), and Yacef, his operational executive, to prepare for a major offensive.

Yacef was the twenty-nine-year-old son of a Casbah baker, seventh out of a family of fourteen, who had begun work for his father at the age of fourteen, a highly self-possessed young man with big, mocking brown eyes, a sensual mouth under a thick black moustache and immense confidence in himself. A keen footballer, he was daring and inventive. Arrested in France, he had managed to talk his way out of Barberousse by persuading the French gaolers of his willingness to act as double agent – to such effect that for some time he was regarded with distrust by his former colleagues. Knowing every inch of the tortuous alleys of the Casbah, so narrow that one can often jump from one roof-top to another, and where one square kilometre housed a teeming populace of 100,000 Muslims, he had persuaded Abane of the advantage of "purging" it of all doubtful elements and turning it into a fortress from which a campaign could be launched. With the aid of skilful masons Yacef had created a whole series of secret passages leading from one house to another, bomb factories, caches and virtually undiscoverable hiding-places concealed behind false walls.

By the end of 1956 Yacef had assembled in a meticulously organised hierarchy some 1,400 operators. These included a number of attractive and presentable young Muslim women. Chief among them were. Hassiba Ben Bouali, Zohra Drif, Djamila Bouhired and Samia Lakhdari. All were

---

* Acknowledging responsibility for the bombing, one of the counter-terrorist leaders who was later to become chief of the O.A.S. death squads remarked light-heartedly to the author: "They must have put a bit too much gunpowder in it!" No European, however, was ever arrested for the Rue de Thèbes bombing.

of bourgeois background. Aged eighteen, Hassiba was the daughter of a former *caid*, and, having once wanted to become a nurse, she was currently employed in a welfare office. Djamila Bouhired, who appears to have been personally devoted to Yacef, acted as his chief *procureuse* of suitable girls. Samia Lakhdari and Zohra Drif were both law students at Algiers university and the daughters of respected cadis. Aged twenty-two, Zohra Drif recalled how, as a child during the Second World War, she had heard her parents explain that Hitler's invasion of France was "God's revenge on the Frenchmen for their treatment of the Muslims". Already at the Lycée she had become aware of the Sétif massacres, and cites as her motive for joining "an essentially terrorist group" the fact that France had "consistently refused the least reform". Increasingly oppressed by the curfew, searches and daily interruptions to Muslim life in Algiers, what had shocked her most violently had been the recent executions of Zabane and Ferradj in Barberousse, which she regarded "of all the horrors of war, the most atrocious". Meanwhile, she noted angrily: "the European population, in its tranquil quarters . . . lived peacefully, went to the beach, to the cinema, to *le dancing*, and prepared for their holidays. . . ." She had studied Malraux's *La Condition Humaine* and strongly disagreed with his pre-war ideal of the terrorist as an heroic, solitary individualist; instead, she exulted in the anonymous collectivity of the group, and as such was ideal material for Yacef.*

Yacef's girls; the first bombs

On 30 September Zohra Drif, Djamila Bouhired and Samia Lakhdari, veiled, attended a meeting with Yacef in one of his Casbah hideouts. They were told that, the same afternoon, they were to place three bombs in the heart of European Algiers. They had been chosen for the job because, with their feminine allure and European looks, they could pass where a male terrorist could not. Noting the shock on their faces, Yacef treated them to a vivid description of the horrors of the Rue de Thèbes outrage, and told them that they were to avenge the Muslim children killed in it. Taking off their veils, the girls tinted their hair and put on the kind of bright, summery dresses and slacks that *pied noir* girls might wear for a day at the beach.† Each was given a small bomb of little more than a kilogramme prepared by Yacef's bomb-maker, a twenty-four-year-old chemistry student called Taleb Abderrahmane operating from a secret laboratory established, appropriately enough, in the Casbah's Impasse de la Grenade. The girls concealed the bombs, set to go off at one-minute intervals from 18.30

* In 1958 Zohra Drif was sentenced to twenty years' hard labour for her part in the Battle of Algiers; she survived the war and married Rabah Bitat, the only member of the *neuf historiques* holding power at the time of writing.
† The whole episode is re-enacted with remarkable fidelity in the Pontecorvo film, in which Yacef's role was played by himself.

hours, inside their beach bags under a feminine miscellany of bikinis, towels and sun-oil. On leaving the Casbah Zohra Drif was stopped at a check-point by a Zouave who, after examining the forged identity card provided by Yacef, said with a leer: "I'd like to give you a real going over, but it's not so easy here!"

To which she replied coquettishly: "That could be, perhaps, if you often come to Saint-Eugène beach."

Her target was the Milk-Bar, on the corner of Place Bugeaud, across from Salan's 10th Region headquarters. It was a particularly popular spot for *pieds noirs* on their way home from the beach, and on that Sunday it was filled with children and their mothers. Looking at the young faces sipping their milk shakes, Zohra Drif suffered a moment of revulsion at her task, but steeled herself by recalling Yacef's account of the Rue de Thèbes, pushed her beach-bag under the table, paid, and left at exactly 18.20 hours. Meanwhile, Samia Lakhdari, accompanied by her mother, had made for the Cafétéria on the smart Rue Michelet, a favourite haunt of European students. Several young couples were dancing to a mambo blaring from the juke-box, and on the point of departure she had to decline an invitation to dance from a good-looking young *pied noir*.

When the two bombs went off a few minutes later the carnage was particularly appalling in the Milk-Bar, where the heavy glass covering the walls was shattered into lethal splinters. Altogether there were three deaths and over fifty injured, including a dozen with amputated limbs, among them several children. Only Djamila Bouhired's bomb, placed in the hall of the Air France terminus, failed to go off, due to a faulty timer. *Pied noir* reactions were expectedly violent, and those sympathetic to the F.L.N. cause were shocked by the callous placing of the bombs. Dr Pierre Chaulet, who was sheltering Ramdane Abane, expressed his disapproval but was told coldly: "I see hardly any difference between the girl who places a bomb in the Milk-Bar and the French aviator who bombards a *mechta* or who drops napalm on a *zone interdite*."

Although the Ben Bella and Suez interludes provided a temporary distraction from what was happening in the city, by the last weeks of 1956 violence had reached an unprecedented crescendo. Yacef's organisation, now effectively and deeply rooted, and with its morale boosted by France's defeat at Suez, had both Muslim and European populations of Algiers in a grip of terror. Schools had remained closed in October; Europeans took to going out on the streets with automatics concealed on them, and when they saw a Muslim walking behind them on the pavement they would slow down to let him pass out of fear of an attack from behind. With the F.L.N. clearly winning more points in Algiers than out in the *bled*, Yacef, in agreement with his superior, Ben M'hidi, decided to exacerbate further the rift between the two communities by assassinating a prominent *pied noir* leader. The victim selected was seventy-four-year-old Amédée Froger, the "ultra" mayor of Boufarik and President of the Federation of Mayors of Algeria, a distinguished *ancien combattant* from the First World War and a figure of considerable power and influence; the assassin, Ali Amara, was better known as Ali la Pointe.

Mayor Froger assassinated by Ali la Pointe

Aged twenty-six, Ali la Pointe came of poor parents and had never been to school; instead, he had found his education in the underworld of the Casbah, selling combs and chewing-gum on the street, preyed upon as a pretty boy by pederast beggars, and joining up with gangs of shoe-shine boys reminiscent of Fagin's urchins in *Oliver Twist*. On his chest he had tattooed "Go forward or die" ("*Marche ou crève*"), and on his foot "Shut up", exhortations which he followed to the end. Growing up, he graduated to becoming a card-sharper and pimp, and was serving a two-year sentence for resisting arrest when the rebellion broke out in 1954. In Barberousse he was "got at" by F.L.N. militants, told that he was a "victim of colonialism", and urged to join the cause. On being transferred to another prison he escaped and, returning to his old haunts, made contact with Yacef, who submitted him to the accepted test of shooting down a *flic*. Ali was slipped a pistol by a veiled women, but on firing it three times at the designated victim he discovered it was unloaded. Smashing it in the man's face, he made his getaway and raged at Yacef for tricking him, but was mollified on realising that it was all part of an exacting initiation; and from that moment – with his unique knowledge of the Casbah, its petty crooks, tarts, dope-pedlars and thugs – he became Yacef's most loyal and valuable lieutenant.

As Amédée Froger left his house on the Rue Michelet on the morning of 28 December, Ali was there waiting and killed the mayor with three shots at point-blank range.* The next day, a Saturday, the whole of *pied noir* Algiers turned out, seething with anger, for the funeral procession of the murdered leader. As a last straw, a bomb was exploded inside the cemetery which would have gone off in the midst of the *cortège* had it arrived on time. The crowd ran wild. Innocent Muslims (Yacef had made a point of ordering all his operatives off the streets that day) were dragged out of their cars and lynched; young thugs smashed in the heads of veiled women with iron bars. The ugly *ratonnade* continued all day, leaving four Muslim dead and fifty injured.

"Call in Massu. . . ."

Governor-General Lacoste's patience was now at breaking-point, and

---

* It was not known until after Ali's own death that he was the assassin of Froger; meanwhile, an innocent man had already been executed for the crime.

after another series of assassinations he took a fateful decision. On 7 January he summoned to his office the newly-arrived Commander-in-Chief, General Salan, and the commander of the élite 10th Para Division who had recently led it back, frustrated, from Suez: General Jacques Massu. He explained to Massu that, since the 1,500 police in Algiers had proved unable both to prevent the F.L.N. outrages and to control the backlash of the *pied noir* mobs, he proposed reinforcing them with the 4,600 soldiers from Massu's division. More than this, Massu was to be granted full responsibility for maintenance of order in the city. On a purely tactical level, Lacoste's decision meant that, virtually for the first time in the two years of war, France was accepting the F.L.N.'s challenge, confronting it with total force and backed by the will to use it. The confrontation would have to end in a clear-cut defeat for one side or the other. But beyond this, the calling in of the paras was to signify far more than just a transient cession of power by the civil authorities to the military; for it was never fully to be restored for another five years. That good Socialist and democrat, Robert Lacoste, was in effect placing his signature on the death warrant of the Fourth Republic.

In his customary robust, military language, Massu reported to his chief-of-staff, Colonel Yves Godard, "I can tell you right away we're going to have some heaps of *emmerdements!*" It was a masterly understatement, but Lacoste could hardly have chosen an officer better equipped for coping with a really disagreeable job. Everything about the stocky, vital figure that was to become one of the best known on the world's screens and in the Press over the next few years bespoke toughness: the growling voice, the vigorous hair *en brosse* and the down-turned eyes that reminded one a little of his fierce First World War predecessor, General Charles ("The Butcher") Mangin, the square, set jaw and the aggressive, all-dominant nose, and the rugged features that altogether looked as if they had been hewn, like a Swiss bear, from a block of wood. On meeting Massu for the first time one was a little surprised to find that he was not eight feet tall – in fact, rather less than medium height. His presence commanded, and he was, as he looked, every inch a fighting soldier – and a superb fighting soldier at that, of the ilk of the campaign-hardened veterans of the Grande Armée. After leaving St Cyr he had served before, during and after the Second World War with colonial units in the vastness of French West Africa. The capitulation of 1940 caught him on a "pacification" mission in mid-Sahara as a captain; he joined up with General Leclerc on his historic march from Lake Chad and was with his 2nd Armoured Division when it entered Paris. After the war he had pioneered one of the first para units, had gained experience in maintenance of civil order when called in to "pacify" striking French miners, and had done his time in Indo-China. In 1955, at the age of 47, he had been promoted general – although, as he noted proudly, his records had contained the adverse comment: "Magnificent warrior . . . but this is not necessarily the material for a general!" On the eve of Suez he had declared, without bravado, that the 10th Para Division (which he had formed) was prepared to accept "thirty to forty per cent" casualties, and in his memoirs he states that, with it, "I would have gone to the ends of the world. Its command has been my greatest pride!"

Massu's pride in his profession, in the army itself, was quite singleminded and, a stern disciplinarian, he distrusted anything that was not of it. But if he lacked subtlety of thought, le bon Massu was also incapable of deviousness (his name itself denotes a heavy, blunt instrument). Although he had been a dedicated Gaullist since 1940 and (with one notable slip) was to remain outstandingly loyal right to the end, he abhorred all kinds of political involvement, in sharp contrast to his superior, Salan, as well as several of the para colonels under his command – notably Yves Godard, Massu's éminence grise.*

Godard

None of the "Indo-China hands" had taken the lessons of politico-subversive warfare there more closely to heart than Godard. Only three years younger than his chief, Godard was in Poland when the Second World War broke out, training with the ski troops (he was a champion skier). Returning home, he was captured in the 1940 campaign and after two attempts to escape was sent once again to Poland, whence he finally succeeded in making his way to Paris in March 1944. He then joined the maquis in Haute-Savoie. Back with the regular army, in 1948 he was given the newly formed 11th Shock, the "dirty tricks" battalion that was the joint child of the paras and the French secret intelligence organisation answerable directly to the prime minister, the S.D.E.C.E. (Service de Documentation Extérieure et de Contre-Éspionnage). For the next five years he had commanded it, taking it to Indo-China where, in the disastrous year of 1954, he had been with a column attempting to relieve Dien Bien Phu from behind the lines in Laos. Appointed to be chief-of-staff to the 10th Para Division in 1956, he was praised by Massu in his memoirs as having been "a precious right arm", though Massus added of his highly intellectual subordinate that, "reflective to the point of lacking spontaneity, he often had a tendency to miss the bus". In the coming Battle of Algiers, however, Godard was determined to miss no buses and was to make himself the expert on the underground world of the city, in all its conspiratorial complexities.

* There is the famous encounter between de Gaulle and Massu, reputed to have taken place on the former's arrival in Algeria after coming to power in 1958:
De Gaulle, teasing: "Alors, Massu, toujours con?"
Massu, respectful and straight-faced: "Oui, mon général, et toujours gaulliste!"
Hence the popular, anti-Gaullist expression of the time: "con comme un général!"

Massu's four para regiments began to move into Algiers the week after he had received his orders from Lacoste, with all the military precision of an army moving up to the front.* Under a system called *quadrillage*, Algiers was divided into squares, each one conforming to a regimental command, with the focal point of the Casbah allotted to Colonel Bigeard and his redoubtable 3rd R.P.C. They cordoned off the whole area with its teeming population, established check-points at all its exits and inaugurated a system of minute house-to-house searches. With the most recent humiliation of Suez grafted upon all the other motives that constituted for them a grim determination to prevail, the paras operated from the beginning with a swift ruthlessness that was to characterise the whole Battle of Algiers. On the eve of the takeover a major of Godard's old unit, the 11th Shock, presented himself at Sûreté headquarters with an armed escort and demanded of the flabbergasted police officials that they hand over all their dossiers on F.L.N. suspects. After an unremitting twenty-four hours' examination of the dossiers, lists of suspects for summary arrest were sent out to each regiment. A mass round-up then took place, accompanied by none of the judicial formalities of warrants or preferring of charges as required by cumbersome civil procedure, and with the suspects subjected to questionable methods of interrogation.

Breaking the general strike

The first major clash of wills facing Massu and his men was the general strike which the F.L.N. had called for Monday, 28 January 1957. The principle of the strike followed as a direct consequence of the priority of externalising the conflict, determined at Soummam the previous September, but specifically, in its timing and duration, it seems to have been the brain-child of Ben M'hidi. It was to coincide with the opening of the United Nations session in New York and was to last eight days. The reason for this protracted effort was spelled out in instructions issued by the C.C.E. in January:

> to demonstrate in the most decisive manner the total support of the whole Algerian people for the F.L.N., its unique representative. The object of this demonstration is to bestow an incontestable authority upon our delegates at the United Nations in order to convince those rare diplomats still hesitant or possessing illusions about France's liberal policy.

Ramdane Abane crossed the ts by explaining that: "Even if we take risks, our struggle must become known. We could kill hundreds of colonialist

* Just to add confusion, it was during this same week, on 16 January, that Philippe Castille fired his "bazooka" at Salan. That an attempt to assassinate the French Commander-in-Chief should be made at the very moment when he was in the process of enacting measures which, in the whole war to date, were the most favourable to the *pied noir* cause seems to exemplify better than anything else the basic unreality – indeed, sheer lunacy – of the counter-terrorist groups.

soldiers without this ever being publicly announced." The F.L.N. leaders felt that the combination of Yacef's grip of terror on Algiers and the F.L.N.'s acquired influence among the trade unions as a whole – in the shape of the recently-formed U.G.T.A. (Union Général des Travailleurs Algériens) – made them strong enough to accept the risks involved, and over so prolonged a period as eight days. In fact, it was to turn out to be perhaps the F.L.N.'s gravest tactical error of the entire war. The challenge, had it been carried out to the full, would have been only a degree or two removed from a general insurrection, and as such it was one that no French government of the time could ignore. Thus Lacoste's orders to Massu were to break the strike at all costs – and by any means.

By the evening of the 27th, Algiers was already a dead city. The next morning, Monday, the shutters of the Muslim shops remained down in their overwhelming majority; workers in the essential public services failed to turn up; schoolchildren stayed at home. Army helicopters scattered leaflets over the Casbah, and jeeps with loud-speakers roamed the streets, ordering the population back to work. At first the strike looked like being a total success. Then Massu showed his mettle, applying the full force of his division. Armoured cars arrived, attached hawsers to the closed steel shutters of the shops, and simply dragged them off their fixings. With some relish, Salan describes how the contents of the shops became exposed to the world: "oranges, bananas, honey cakes, jars of multi-coloured sweets. . . . Urchins playing in the street rushed forward, helped themselves, and took flight. . . ." Algerian sources accused the paras of joining in the pillage; whatever the truth, the unhappy shop-owners were, in any event, forced to emerge in order to protect their unguarded goods, and were then ordered to remain open under threat of imprisonment. Similar scenes took place over the rest of the country; in one provincial centre of the Mitidja, Colonel Antoine Argoud went so far as to fire a tank shell at point-blank range into a shuttered shop, wounding one of his own men but effectively cowing the strikers. At the same time, fleets of trucks were despatched round Algiers collecting strikers at their homes and physically hustling them off to work. Many of the strikers revealed themselves to be relatively lukewarm in the face of such brutal determination, as typified by one denizen of the Casbah who whispered to a para captain: "Call two gendarmes so that they can rough me up a bit, and I'll open." Meanwhile, many of Yacef's militants who might otherwise have been out stiffening resistance had either already been swept up in Massu's net, or else had their heads well down. The next day the "collection service" was repeated; this time bringing in the young Muslim truants from school. Godard claims that, whereas only seventy attended at the end of January, numbers had risen to 8,000 a fortnight later.

On the first day of the strike the postal and telegraph service reported seventy-one per cent of its Muslim personnel absent in the Algiers area, forty-one per cent in Oran and only twenty-eight per cent in Constantine; on the railways there was an almost total walkout in Algiers, fifty per cent in Oran and twenty-five per cent in Constantine. The next day, the figures had dwindled substantially and forty-eight hours after the beginning of the strike it had been effectively broken. In the opinion of Colonel Godard, Ben M'hidi had committed a cardinal error in endeavouring to keep the strike going so long; a short strike would have been hard to break, but eight days made it much more vulnerable. Unconvincingly, the F.L.N. tried to claim a victory; but even at the United Nations the strike seemed to make little impact. One American correspondent, Michael Clark (writing, admittedly, still during the war), considered that the collapse of the strike "may well have been a turning-point" in the war for the French. The main benefit for the F.L.N., however, was to be derived, unexpectedly and indirectly, rather from the methods used in breaking the strike than from anything achieved by it.

More bombings by Yacef

Two days before the strike was due to begin, Yacef launched a back-up operation with another wave of three bombings in the smart centre of Algiers. Once again his bomb-carriers were a team of girls, all the more valuable now that Massu's men were rigorously searching every Muslim leaving the Casbah, and this time one of them, Danièle Minne, was a European, the step-daughter of a militant Communist. Using more powerful explosive, the bombs provided by Taleb were far more sophisticated affairs than those of the Milk-Bar, and were little larger than a packet of cigarettes. The targets were the Otomatic, a favourite students' bar on the Rue Michelet; the Cafétéria opposite (second time over), and the nearby Coq-Hardi, a popular brasserie. It was a spring-like Saturday afternoon and all three were crowded. Placed in the ladies' lavatory, Danièle Minne's bomb in the Otomatic seriously injured a young girl and several others. Almost immediately another explosion ripped open the Cafétéria opposite. At the Coq-Hardi, diners rushing to the window to see where the bombs had gone off were scythed down by Djamila Bouazza's bomb which, exploding under a cast-iron table, turned the metal and plate-glass into lethal fragments like those of a grenade, slashing through veins and arteries. Altogether the day left sixty wounded and five killed – including an innocent young Muslim mechanic lynched in the immediate *pied noir* backlash. Fifteen days later, a Sunday, bombs were exploded in two crowded Algiers stadiums, placed by girls of sixteen and seventeen: ten dead and forty-five injured.*

* A quantitative comparison could perhaps be made here between the Battle of Algiers' bombings and those of the I.R.A. more recently in Northern Ireland and

The terrain. 1. *Above:* In Kabylia. A soldier keeps guard over a rocky pass.

2. *Below:* The Aurès. The village on the spur of the gorge is almost invisible against the parched background.

3. December 1954. Zouaves searching a Kabyle suspect.

4. In contrast to the prosperous *pied noir* farms and suburbs, over-population and under-employment in the Muslim centres.

5. *Above:* The funeral of the victims of the Philippeville massacres, August 1955.

6. *Below:* The departure of Jacques Soustelle from Algiers in February 1956.

7. *Above:* The five members of the G.P.R.A. detained at the Château d'Aulnoy. *Left to right:* Hocine Ait Ahmed, Ahmed Ben Bella, Mohamed Khider, Mohamed Boudiaf and Rabah Bitat.

8. *Below left:* Ben Bella hand-cuffed after the arrest of the five leaders in October 1956.

9. *Below right:* Belkacem Krim.

10. Pierre Mendès-France (left) and Edouard Daladier.

11. Paul Delouvrier.

12. Jacques Soustelle.

13. Guy Mollet.

14. General Maurice Challe.

15. General Jacques Massu.

16. *Above:* Bigeard's paras in their "lizard" headgear march into Algiers.
17, 18. *Below:* The Battle of Algiers, 1957. *Left:* Paras in the Rue Caton, searching for Saadi Yacef and his fellow-insurgents. *Right:* The house in the Casbah where Ali la Pointe hid, after its destruction by the French forces.

19. *Above:* 1958. The Provisional Government of the Algerian Revolution (G.P.R.A.) is proclaimed in Cairo. *Left to right:* Ben Youssef Ben Khedda, M'hamed Yazid (with arm outstretched), Ferhat Abbas, the first Prime Minister, Lakhdar Ben Tobbal.

20. *Below:* 1958. Generals Massu (left, in beret) and Salan (at microphone) with Jacques Soustelle after the formation of the Committee of Public Safety in Algiers.

21. *Above:* De Gaulle's first Algerian visit, 1958 Mobbed by euphoric Muslims, French soldiers and *pieds noirs* alike.

22. *Below:* Muslim labourers constructing the Morice Line along the Tunisian border.

Bigeard strikes: the organigramme

Because of the growing stranglehold of Bigeard's forces on the Casbah, however, such "acts of war" were becoming increasingly hard to mount and the net was closing in all the time. After the Coq-Hardi explosion a waiter stated categorically that it had been a young woman who sat at the shattered table, and he was able to give an accurate description of Djamila Bouazza. All women leaving the Casbah were now subjected to thorough searches; at first with cumbersome mine-detectors to pick out any weapons concealed under their voluminous robes, later with less chivalrous means. A patch of cloth found on the scene of one of the stadium bombs led to the arrest of the two young terrorists, Djouher Akhror and Baya Hocine. French efforts were concentrated particularly on breaking down Yacef's bomb network and its odious end-products. In October it had already suffered a setback when Kouache, the expert who had helped to set up the bombs of Zohra Drif and her comrades, blew himself up at the Villa des Roses outside Algiers. After that, bomb fabrication had been concentrated in Taleb Abderrahmane's workshop in the Casbah. But by the end of January, after three days of interrogation, a locksmith picked up by Bigeard's men with bomb blueprints on him gave its address away. Forewarned, Yacef managed to evacuate its members and hide the evidence, so that a first para raid on 8 February fell on open air. A week later, however, Bigeard made his biggest catch to date; Yacef's chief bomb transporter and the mason who had constructed the factories. From the two of them, made to talk under extreme pressure, No. 5 Impasse de la Grenade was pinpointed and the names of Mostefa Bouhired and his niece, Djamila, given away – as well as, to the shock of the French, that of a respected *bachaga*, whose house was reported to contain a substantial depot of bombs. Bigeard's troops moved with their customary speed and ruthlessness, sometimes landing by helicopter on the flat roofs of the Casbah houses to make their raids. The bomb factory in the Impasse de la Grenade was finally located, as was the *bachaga*'s hoard. On 19 February a jubilant Bigeard announced that his 3rd R.P.C. had seized eighty-seven bombs, seventy kilos of explosive, 5,120 fulminate of mercury detonators, 309 electric detonators, etc.; many of the bomb network were either identified or already under lock and key. Yacef's organisation, which had taken eighteen months to construct, had all but fallen apart. Algiers began to breathe again.

---

in England. Horrible as were the outrages in Algiers, the bombs were considerably less powerful, and consequent casualties far fewer than the twenty-one killed and 162 maimed in the Birmingham outrage of November 1974 – perpetrated evidently as retribution for an I.R.A. member who blew himself up by mistake. What *ratonnades* and lynchings would have followed a bombing in Algiers on the Birmingham scale can only be imagined, and one may ask whether the restrained British reaction could be explained by national phlegm or the torpor of a world grown blasé to horror.

Meanwhile, threads of intelligence gathered in the course of rounding up the bombers were leading back closer and closer to the really big fish. To Godard, "the man who places the bomb is but an arm that tomorrow will be replaced by another arm". It was essential to get at the brain behind the arm. Under his supervision, a complex *organigramme** began to take shape on a large blackboard, a kind of skeleton pyramid in which, as each fresh piece of information came from the interrogation centres, another name (and not always necessarily the right name) would be entered. Until the actual capture of Ben M'hidi the name at the summit of the pyramid remained blank. But Yacef had already been identified by numerous cross-references. On the opening day of the general strike he had changed hideouts no less than fifteen times; to blend more inconspicuously into the background he had even grabbed a milk churn to pretend, with total audacity, that he was one of the "good Arabs" refusing the F.L.N.'s order to stay at home. Frequently he took to circulating in the Casbah disguised as a *fatma*, a sub-machine-gun concealed under yards of linen, and nothing would budge him from his post. But the leaders of the C.C.E. in Algiers were beginning to take serious alarm. On 9 February the paras arrested Ali Boumendjel, a young F.L.N. lawyer highly valued by the leadership, and closely in touch with it. On hearing of his arrest, Ben M'hidi, dejected and increasingly aware of his error in committing the F.L.N. to the strike, and the suffering and torture that this had imposed on his followers, is said to have remarked: "We are about to lose the battle."

On the 15th there took place an anguished meeting of the five members of the C.C.E. remaining in Algiers. Abane urged that they should get out of Algiers forthwith, or be trapped like rats and have secrets of the whole movement ground out of them. Seizing the analogy, Ben M'hidi countered that they would be more like rats abandoning a sinking ship. Finally it was reluctantly agreed that, after a space of ten days in which to re-organise the Algiers command set-up, the C.C.E. would depart for safer ground. Yacef was to assume full charge of the Algiers Z.A.A.; Ben M'hidi, always loath to leave the city, decided that, as a temporary compromise, he would move from the dangerous confines of the Casbah to an F.L.N. "safe house" in the Rue Claude-Debussy. On one of his last meetings with Yacef, he is quoted as having remarked: "I would like to die in battle. Before the end."

The death of Ben M'hidi

Ben M'hidi effected his move at the worst possible moment. Acting on a tip provided by Trinquier's network of informers, the paras were, so they thought, on the track of Ben Khedda, and on 25 February the clues led them to the Rue Claude-Debussy – where, to their surprise, they found

* See page 567.

Ben M'hidi in pyjamas. In news-shots of the time the captured thirty-four-year-old ex-comedian, who had once played minor parts on Algiers radio, shows a cheerful, brave and rather distinguished face, concealing any awareness of what lay ahead. Then, on 6 March, Lacoste's Press officer announced that Ben M'hidi had "committed suicide by hanging himself in his cell with the help of strips torn from his shirt".

The exact truth about Ben M'hidi's death remains a mystery to this day. Lebjaoui, who knew him, and other Algerians insist that the devoutness of his faith ruled out any possibility of his taking his own life. Yves Courrière, generally well-informed on French undercover activities, declares categorically that M'hidi was not tortured, but that he was shot at dawn after being rendered full military honours. What seems to be fact is that Bigeard himself interrogated M'hidi after his capture; was told that the F.L.N. was bound to win eventually, but no other useful details; was impressed by the dignity and courage of the F.L.N. leader; treated him with the respect due to a captured enemy commander, and left him alive and unharmed. According to a F.L.N. spy in Algiers police headquarters, who reported to the C.C.E. on 4 March, Bigeard then "was unable to prevent Ben M'hidi being handed over to men of a 'special section' of the paratroops. These interrogated him on their own initiative, and killed him last night." Admitting that M'hidi had had to be transferred to another prison, at Maison Carrée, for administrative reasons, Massu claims that he hanged himself with an electric flex that night but was "still breathing" when taken to the Maillot hospital, while two French medical officers who examined him stated officially that M'hidi was already dead *before* reaching the hospital, but that "our attention was not attracted by apparent marks of wounds". Perhaps of all those involved, few would have been more likely to know the truth than the late Colonel Godard. In his memoirs he says, simply but revealingly, that, after first discussing M'hidi's death with Massu the following morning: "Massu made no comment. In my heart of hearts, I believe that Ben M'hidi would not have committed suicide had he remained *chez Bigeard*."

La torture

The death of Ben M'hidi left, alive and at liberty, only Belkacem Krim out of the original *neuf historiques* of the F.L.N. Like an unsightly mole-hill, it also threw up the whole ugly but hitherto largely subterranean issue of the maltreatment of rebel suspects, of torture and summary executions; or what, in another context and depending upon the point of view, might perhaps be termed "war crimes", and what in France came simply to be known as *la torture*. From the Battle of Algiers onwards this was to become a growing canker for France, leaving behind a poison that would linger in the French system long after the war itself had ended. The resort to torture poses moral problems that are just as germane to the world today as they were to the period under consideration. As Jean-Paul Sartre wrote in 1958, "Torture is neither civilian nor military, nor is it specifically French: it is a plague infecting our whole era." But what is immediately of importance here is the influence, or influences, brought to bear by it upon the subsequent course of the Algerian war. And these were very potent indeed. It is one of the most difficult things in this world to establish the truth about torture; whether it did or did not take place, and the nature and scale of it. The plaintiff is as unlikely to tell the unadorned truth as his oppressor; for it is so superlative a propaganda weapon given into his hands. All the writer can do is to state what was claimed and admitted on both sides. Here one is aided by the fact that, among others, General Massu has come forward in the aftermath of the war and declared, in his forthright way: "In answer to the question: 'Was there really torture?' I can only reply in the affirmative, although it was never either institutionalised or codified. . . . I am not frightened of the word." There was, he claimed, no other option in the circumstances then prevailing in Algiers but to apply techniques of torture.

It is essential to be clear about what one means by the word of which Massu was "not frightened". In a conventional war, so-called "war crimes" generally fall into two distinct categories; those committed in hot blood – prisoners despatched out of hand on the battlefield, shot-down bomber crews lynched by enraged civilians after an air-raid; and those perpetrated in cold blood – the concentration camps. Similarly, in an unconventional war like Northern Ireland or Algeria, there are the brutalities, the roughing-up, the *passage à tabac* that may be inflicted immediately following the arrest of a suspected terrorist; and there is the prolonged and systematic application of physical or psychological pain expressly aimed at making a suspect "talk", which constitutes torture as opposed to brutality. Though the *passage à tabac* has long existed as a police institution in France, to no people has torture been more abhorrent, morally and philosophically, especially following their own hideous experiences from 1940 to 1944. As an instrument of state, torture was expressly abolished by the French Revolution (which never practised it) on 8 October 1789, but even well before this French humanist writers had decided that it was both inhuman and inefficient. Article 303 of the French Penal Code (aiming specifically at highwaymen who had an unpleasant habit of "warming up the feet" of their victims) actually imposed the death penalty upon anyone practising torture. Nevertheless, in Algeria there appear to have been at least isolated incidents of torture even before 1954, as both Ben Khedda and François Mitterrand assured the author, and the fact of it seems confirmed by the forceful interventions made by French authorities on various occasions. In 1949, for instance, Governor-

General Naegelen in an official circular ordered: "strong-arm techniques must be absolutely prohibited as a method of investigation. I am determined to punish with the utmost severity not only those members of the public service found guilty of using violence but also their superiors." In 1955 Mendès-France declared categorically that all "excesses" "must stop everywhere and at once", and Soustelle during his stewardship issued strict instructions that "every offence against human dignity ... be rigorously forbidden", and in his memoirs he insists that any proven cases of brutality or summary executions "did not rest without punishment".

Institutionalise torture?

In March 1955, however, even more suggestive evidence came in a highly controversial proposal made in the Wuillaume Report by a senior civil servant quite unconnected with the police. Wuillaume opined that, like the legalising of a rampant black market, torture should be institutionalised *because it had become so prevalent,* as well as proving effective in neutralising many dangerous terrorists. From his researches, Wuillaume recommended:

> The water and electricity methods, provided they are carefully used, are said to produce a shock which is more psychological than physical and therefore do not constitute excessive cruelty. . . . According to certain medical opinion which I was given, the water-pipe method, if used as outlined above, involves no risk to the health of the victim. This is not the case with the electrical method which does involve some danger to anyone whose heart is in any way affected. . . . I am inclined to think that these procedures can be accepted and that, if used in the controlled manner described to me, they are no more brutal than deprivation of food, drink, and tobacco, which has always been accepted. . . .

It was a view that would not necessarily be shared by Algerians subjected to the *gégène* or having had their bellies pumped full of water during the Battle of Algiers. Noting how police morale had been affected by the "pillorying" of "such excesses as have taken place", Wuillaume concluded: "There is only one way of restoring the confidence and drive of the police – to recognise certain procedures and to cover them with authority."

Although Soustelle "categorically refused" to accept the Wuillaume conclusions, they may well have taken root already in Algeria. Citing a letter from a soldier written well before the Battle of Algiers, Pierre-Henri Simon recounts how the writer had been invited by gendarmes to attend the torture of two Arabs arrested the previous night:

> The first of the tortures consisted of suspending the two men completely naked by their feet, their hands bound behind their backs, and plunging their heads for a long time into a bucket of water to make them talk. The second torture consisted of suspending them, their hands and feet tied

behind their backs, this time with their head upwards. Underneath them was placed a trestle, and they were made to swing, by fist blows, in such a fashion that their sexual parts rubbed against the very sharp pointed bar of the trestle. The only comment made by the men, turning towards the soldiers present: "I am ashamed to find myself stark naked in front of you."

But the fact that in the army torture was by no means institutionalised yet seems to be implicit in Servan-Schreiber's *Lieutenant en Algérie* (1957), which, highly critical as it is of French army excesses, omits any specific reference to torture as such. By way of explaining the essential atmosphere in which torture could become institutionalised within the French army in Algeria, one needs to take into account all those factors touched upon in the previous chapters: horror at the atrocities of the F.L.N., a determination not to lose yet another campaign, and the generally brutalising effect of so cruel and protracted a war. Noting the growing indifference to the "enemy" as a human being, such a tough para commander as Colonel François Coulet himself admits that the army had come to regard a prisoner as "no longer an Arab peasant" but simply "a source of intelligence".

Interrogation techniques

"Intelligence", said Godard, "is capital." Massu's system of *quadrillage* and the rifling of the police dossiers was augmented by the work of a new body called the Dispositif de Protection Urbaine (D.P.U.). Created by order of Lacoste and placed under the control of that Indo-China expert on subversive warfare, Colonel Roger Trinquier, in its operation the D.P.U. carried with it sinister undertones that also could not help but recall French experiences under the Third Reich. It divided the city up into sectors, sub-sectors, blocks and buildings, each bearing a number or letter (even today the hieroglyphs can still be found painted on the fronts of houses in the Casbah). To each block was nominated a *responsable*, generally a Muslim *ancien combattant* considered trustworthy, and to this block-warden fell the duty of reporting all suspicious activities occurring within his territory. In the short term the D.P.U. – which Trinquier describes as forming "a flexible bond bond between the authorities and the populace" – undeniably produced results. It was through its information that Ben M'hidi had been caught, and, according to Trinquier, it meant that "no Muslim was able to enter the European quarters without being reported". But in the long run it was to place the "loyal" Muslim block-wardens in a thoroughly invidious position, often resulting either in their assassination or in the end of their loyalty to France.

The numbers of Muslim suspects passing through the hands of the paras as a result of the D.P.U. and the other forms of intelligence collection ran into enormous figures, with Edward Behr reckoning that between thirty and forty per cent of the entire male population of the Casbah were arrested at some point or other during the course of the Battle of Algiers. The suspects were generally, as a matter of principle, arrested at night so that any colleagues they named under interrogation could be grabbed before the lifting of the curfew, and before they would have a chance of being warned and disappearing. A directive marked "Secret" and signed by Massu (dated 4 April 1957) ordered that: "The most absolute secrecy must be ensured on anything concerning the number, identity and the nature of suspects arrested. In particular, no mention of whatever kind is to be made to any representative of the Press." This was designed as much to confuse the public as to what was going on as it was to heighten terror among the suspect's entourage at the uncertainty of his fate. He would then be handed over to a Détachement Opérationnel de Protection (D.O.P.) which Massu describes as being "specialists in the interrogation of suspects who wanted to say nothing", and would then either be released or passed on to a *centre d'hébergement*, where he might be hauled out for further and protracted interrogation.

At first his D.O.P. interrogators would attempt to trap him into admissions by displaying omniscient knowledge about the personalities and workings of his group. Often he would be confronted with a *boukkara* or *cagoulard*, a Muslim with his head covered in a sack with eye-slits who had broken under interrogation and was now acting as an informer – a particular horror for the Algerians. Then, says Trinquier:

> If the suspect makes no difficulty about giving the information required, the interrogation will be over quickly, otherwise specialists must use all means available to drag his secret out of him. Like a soldier he must then face suffering and perhaps even death which he has so far avoided.

And this is what happened. Because of the numbers of suspects involved, the D.O.P. "experts" often had to rely on outside help; "in certain cases", admits Massu, "each of the regimental interrogation teams of the 10th Paratroop Division was obliged to have recourse to violence". It was at this point, one might say, that torture became institutionalised in the army in Algeria.

"Little electrodes. . . ."

The most favoured method of torture was the *gégène*, an army signals magneto from which electrodes could be fastened to various parts of the human body – notably the penis. It was simple and left no traces. Massu states that he, as well as other members of his staff, tried it out on himself in his own office; what he failed, however, to note in his "experiment" was the cumulative effect of prolonged application of the *gégène*, as well as of all deprivation of the element of hope – the essential concomitant of any torture. Robert Lacoste also belittles the *gégène*; it was, he claims, "nothing serious. Just connecting little electrodes. And Massu's paras were, after all, *des garçons très sportifs!*" But what the *gégène* was really like is vividly described by Henri Alleg (among many others) in his book *The Question*, which caused an uproar in France in 1958 when it first revealed the systematisation of torture in Algeria. Alleg, a European Jew whose family had settled in Algeria during the Second World War, was the Communist editor of the *Alger Républicain* and had been held under interrogation by the paras for a whole month in the summer of 1957. Of his first subjection to the *gégène*, with electrodes attached merely to his ear and finger, he says: "A flash of lightning exploded next to my ear and I felt my heart racing in my breast." The second time a large magneto was used: "Instead of the sharp and rapid spasms that seemed to tear my body in two, it was now a greater pain that took possession of all my muscles and tightened them in longer spasms." Next the electrodes were placed in his mouth: "my jaws were soldered to the electrode by the current, and it was impossible for me to unlock my teeth, no matter what effort I made. My eyes, under their spasmed lids, were crossed with images of fire, and geometric luminous patterns flashed in front of them." He was left with an intolerable thirst, which his torturers refused to assuage.

Then there were the various forms of water torture: heads thrust repeatedly into water troughs until the victim was half-drowned; bellies and lungs filled with cold water from a hose placed in the mouth, with the nose stopped up. "I couldn't hold on for more than a few moments," says Alleg; "I had the impression of drowning, and a terrible agony, that of death itself, took possession of me. 'That's it! He's going to talk,' said a voice." And there were the instances (perhaps less common than publicity made them seem at the time) of the tortures still more degrading of human dignity: bottles thrust into the vaginas of young Muslim women; high pressure hoses inserted in the rectum, sometimes causing permanent damage through internal lesions.

The torturers tortured

Almost as painful as the torture inflicted on oneself was the awareness of the suffering of others nearby: "I don't believe that there was a single prisoner who did not, like myself, cry from hatred and humiliation on hearing the screams of the tortured for the first time," says Alleg, and he records the horror of the elderly Muslim hoping to appease his tormentors: "Between the terrible cries which the torture forced out of him, he said, exhausted: 'Vive la France! Vive la France!'"

But the humiliation was double-sided; as many other nations have discovered, torture ends by corrupting the torturer as much as it breaks the victim. The *centre de tri* where he was held had, says Alleg, become "a school of perversion for young Frenchmen", and his view is shared by paratrooper Pierre Leulliette of the 2nd R.P.C. who was forced, unwillingly, to take part in the torturing. Initially, says Leulliette, the paras "tackled these methods, rather new to them, first with reluctance, and then whole-heartedly". Based in an unused sweet factory, he recalls one big Alsatian sergeant who seemed particularly to relish his work: "With his fist, which could have strangled an ox, he would plunge in the heads of his clients, who were often choking with apprehension long before they touched the water. . . . He would have liked to interrogate Europeans; but they were rare. . . ." Reactions among the paras varied: "Those who flaunted their vices embroidered on it at leisure, and found it all quite normal; the 'humanists' thought they should merely be shot. Very few seemed to realise that there might have been some innocent men among them." Leulliette himself became deeply oppressed by what was going on round him in the sweet factory: "All day, through the floor-boards, we heard their hoarse cries, like those of animals being slowly put to death. Some-times I think I can still hear them. . . . All these men disappeared. . . ." Gradually, "I felt myself becoming contaminated. What was more serious, I felt that the horror of all these crimes, our everyday battle, was losing force daily in my mind." Going on a month's leave to Paris was like a deep breath of fresh air, and sufficient "to make me forget the suffering through-out poor Algeria. I felt ashamed. Ashamed of having been so happy."

"All these men disappeared. . . ."

On seeing Alleg in person at the Palais de Justice in 1970, Massu com-ments drily on his "reassuring dynamism", and questions, "Do the tor-ments which he suffered count for much alongside the cutting off of the nose or of the lips, when it was not the penis, which had become the ritual present of the *fellaghas* to their recalcitrant 'brothers'? Everyone knows that these bodily appendages don't grow again!" But, once taken away, nor does life itself "grow again", and Massu does not mention those who did not survive arrest during the Battle of Algiers. "All these men disappeared," says Leulliette, and he admits later of having "to bury one of the suspects, who had died at their hands, in the quicklime at the bottom of the garden. There were others. . . ." During the Battle of Algiers, disposal of the "inconvenient", of those who died under torture, or who refused adamantly to talk, apparently became prevalent enough to gain the slang expression "work in the woods". Courrière writes of bodies dropped out in the sea by helicopter, and of a mass grave between Koléa and Zéralda, some thirty kilometres from Algiers (though no such grave has apparently been uncovered subsequently by the Algerian government); Vidal-Naquet cites the killing by suffocation in March 1957 of forty-one out of 101 detainees locked up in wine-cellars in Oran;* Lebjaoui lists the names of a series of men to whose families either Salan or Massu stated that they had been released, but who, Lebjaoui claims, were never seen again. The number of such "disappearances" may never be verified; the distinguished secretary-general at the Algiers prefecture, Paul Teitgen, put it at just over 3,000. Though Godard disputes it vigorously and arithmetically, this was to become the figure generally accepted by the opponents of para excesses during the Battle of Algiers.

There was, inevitably, a mass covering-up within the army. As "Major Marcus" in Servan-Schreiber's *Lieutenant en Algérie* remarks: "The captains and the mayors lie to the generals and the prefects . . . when a *saloperie* is committed in my regiment by some of my men on an operation, do you think I ever hear about it? No. It's covered up 'between pals'." The cases which did, however, lift the lid to public gaze were those concerning well-known, or at least identifiable, figures. There was the ill-explained death of Ben M'hidi, and later there was the detailed account of his own tortures by Henri Alleg. Meanwhile, following closely on the revelation of Ben M'hidi's "suicide", there came the radio announcement that on 23 March the prominent young lawyer, Ali Boumendjel, had thrown himself out of a window of a building in El-Biar tenanted by the 2nd R.C.P. "to escape interrogation to which he was going to be subjected". Supporting the official statement, Salan claims that numerous incriminating documents were found in Boumendjel's possession and that he had wished "to escape from justice". Godard adds that either he "had wished to die for the cause, or was deranged in his mind". Whether or not either explanation was satisfactory, Boumendjel's death was to cause an uproar in France.

L'Affaire Audin

An even greater and more persistent outcry, however, was sparked off by the disappearance of Maurice Audin in June 1957. Audin was a twenty-five-year-old lecturer in the science faculty of Algiers University and a member of the same Communist cell as Henri Alleg. He was arrested by Colonel Mayer's 1st R.C.P. on suspicion of harbouring and aiding terrorists and – according to Salan, who cites statements made by both the sergeant and the lieutenant in charge of him – managed to escape into the night while being transported in a jeep. Shots were fired after Audin, but no body was ever found, and the sergeant was sentenced to fifteen days' arrest for his negligence. The official story was that Audin had made his way to Tunisia; but he has never been seen since. Courrière claims that he was "liquidated" by operatives of the 11th Shock in mistake for Alleg;

* An episode which Salan in his memoirs also acknowledges, though with some discrepancy in the details.

Vidal-Naquet says categorically that "It was at Fort Emperor that Maurice Audin was secretly buried after he had been murdered."

Bollardière and Teitgen protest

The French liberal conscience and instinct for humanity being what they are, however, soon powerful voices, both in Algeria and metropolitan France, were being raised against torture. One of the first was General Jacques de Bollardière – Grand Officer of the Legion of Honour, Companion of the Liberation, etc. – whose outstanding wartime career has already been noted in the previous chapter. Arriving in the latter part of 1956, he had been given command of a sector near Blida and had then been brought into the Battle of Algiers. Early on, when dressed in plain clothes, he had been shocked to overhear a young cavalry officer remark, "In Algiers, now, there is nothing but genuine chaps, paras, the Legion, fine big blond fellows, stalwarts not sentimentalists."

Bollardière intervened: "Doesn't that remind you of anything, *des grands gars blonds, pas sentimentaux?*"

The young officer replied, quite unashamedly: "If I had been in Germany at that moment, I too would have been a Nazi."

Bollardière's sense of outrage was further increased when approached by weeping Muslim women who told him that their sons or husbands had "disappeared in the night", and finally he sought an interview with Massu, telling him that the orders he had been issued were "in absolute opposition to the respect of man, which was the foundation of my life". After this Bollardière commented: "if the leadership yielded on the absolute principle of respect for human beings, enemy or not, it meant an unleashing of deplorable instincts which no longer knew any limits and which could always find means of justifying itself". He then wrote to the Commander-in-Chief requesting to be posted back to France. On returning to France he gave voice to his indignation by writing, on 27 March 1957, a letter to his friend Servan-Schreiber for publication in L'Express, in which he pointed to "the terrible danger there would be for us to lose sight, under the fallacious pretext of immediate expediency, of the moral values which alone have, up until now, created the grandeur of our civilisation and of our army". For this fundamental breach of military discipline the general was sentenced to sixty days of "fortress arrest", the most severe punishment meted out to any senior officer during the Algerian war.

Just two days after Bollardière's offence, Governor-General Lacoste received a letter of resignation from an even more influential figure: Paul Teitgen, his secretary-general at the Prefecture. Teitgen, a Catholic and hero of the Resistance, had been deported by the Gestapo to Dachau, where he was tortured on no less than nine occasions. In August 1956 he took up his post in Algiers, which carried with it special responsibilities for overseeing the police and in which he found little that was congenial. In November he was confronted with an appalling moral dilemma. Fernand Yveton, the Communist, had been caught red-handed placing a bomb in the gasworks where he was employed. But a second bomb had not been discovered, and if it exploded and set off the gasometers thousands of lives might be lost. Nothing would induce Yveton to reveal its whereabouts, and Teitgen was pressed by his Chief of Police to have Yveton *passé à la question.*

> But I refused to have him tortured. I trembled the whole afternoon. Finally the bomb did not go off. Thank God I was right. Because if you once get into the torture business, you're lost. . . . Understand this, fear was the basis of it all. All our so-called civilisation is covered with a varnish. Scratch it, and underneath you find *fear.* The French, even the Germans, are not torturers by nature. But when you see the throats of your *copains* slit, then the varnish disappears.

With Lacoste's handling over of responsibility to Massu in January, Teitgen found that his hands were tied. Thus on 29 March he wrote to Lacoste, offering his resignation on the grounds that he had failed in his duty and that "for the past three months we have been engaged . . . in irresponsibility which can only lead to war crimes". He added that, in visits to two *centres d'hébergement*, he had "recognised on certain detainees profound traces of the cruelties and tortures that I personally suffered fourteen years ago in the Gestapo cellars". He feared that "France risks losing her soul through equivocation".

Lacoste begged Teitgen to remain at his post and keep his letter secret. Feeling that it would be better for him to continue as watchdog, rather than have no watchdog at all, Teitgen assented. As a consequence of the pressures of protest, he was permitted to retain powers of detention, which meant in theory that the paras could not hold suspects; secondly, in April a "Safeguard Committee of Individual Rights and Liberties" was instituted by Paris to investigate and redress excesses. Some moderation was achieved but, says Teitgen, torture was by no means stamped out, and in September he decided he could stay no longer.* By this time, he claims, over three thousand Algerians had "disappeared".

How effective was torture?

There remains the vital question, with much relevance to today: what did torture achieve in the Battle of Algiers? Putting aside any consideration of morality, was it even effective? Massu, with a courage that demands respect, claims that the end justified the means; the battle was won and a halt was brought to the F.L.N.-imposed terror and the indiscriminate

---

* In interviews with the author, Lacoste stated that he had "punished 480 officers for brutalisation"; Teitgen, however, counters that none of the punished suffered any serious setbacks to their careers.

killing and maiming of both European and Muslim civilians. He also notes that, when critics compared them to the Nazis, his paras practised neither extermination nor the taking of hostages. And Edward Behr, who could by no stretch of the imagination be regarded as an apostle of torture, nevertheless reckons "that without torture the F.L.N.'s terrorist network would never have been overcome.... The 'Battle of Algiers' could not have been won by General Massu without the use of torture." Had the Battle of Algiers indeed been lost by the French in 1957, then the whole of Algeria would almost certainly have been swamped by the F.L.N. – leading in all probability to a peace settlement several years earlier than was otherwise the case.

This is certainly true of the short term, but in the longer term – as the Nazis in the Second World War, and as almost every other power that has ever adopted torture as an instrument of policy, have discovered – it is a double-edged weapon. In some of his last utterances even Massu's chief lieutenant, Yves Godard, expressed doubts as to the efficacy of torture; especially when weighed against the emotional weapon it presented the enemy. In what seemed like an indirect criticism of his old commander, he added:

> If I had carried a lot of brass, having first warned the enemy, I would have shot publicly any assassin caught *in flagrante*—I say advisedly *in flagrante*—if within forty-eight hours he had not voluntarily handed over his secrets....
> There is no need to torture....

From a purely intelligence point of view, experience teaches that more often than not the collating services are overwhelmed by a mountain of false information extorted from victims desperate to save themselves further agony. Also, it is bound to drive into the enemy camp the innocents who have wrongly been submitted to torture. As Camus declares: "torture has perhaps saved some at the expense of honour, by uncovering thirty bombs, but at the same time it has created fifty new terrorists who, operating in some other way and in another place, would cause the death of even more innocent people". Torture, one feels, is never warranted; one should never fight for a good cause with evil weapons. Again, says Camus, "it is better to suffer certain injustices than to commit them ... such fine deeds would inevitably lead to the demoralisation of France and the loss of Algeria". In the long run, the facile *tu quoque* arguments, such as those offered by Massu on the Alleg case, can only lead to an endless escalation of horror and degradation. In answer to the standard plaint that Muslim intellectuals were rarely heard to protest against F.L.N. atrocities, Pierre-Henri Simon counters passionately: "I would reply – 'If really we are capable of a moral reflex which our adversary has not, this is the best justification for our cause, and even for our victory.' "

One of the worst aspects of the admission of torture as an instrument is the wide train of corruption that inevitably follows in its wake. In a submission to the "Safeguard Committee" of September 1957, Teitgen wrote words that would apply equally to any latter-day authoritarian regime, whether it be Greece, Chile, Spain or the Soviet Union:

> Even a legitimate action . . . can nevertheless lead to improvisations and excesses. Very rapidly, if this is not remedied, efficacity becomes the sole justification. In default of a legal basis, it seeks to justify itself at any price, and, with a certain bad conscience, it demands the privilege of exceptional legitimacy. In the name of efficacity, illegality has become justified.

In a civilised society, torture has no more counter-productive and insidious long-term effect than the way that it tends to demoralise the inflicter even more than his victim. Frantz Fanon, the militant Martiniquais psychiatrist, cites several examples of acute, lingering neurosis induced among the tortured; a kind of anorexia suffered by the innocent who had been put to *la question* wrongfully; pins-and-needles and a lasting fear of turning on a light switch, or touching a telephone, in those who had experienced the *gégène*. But just as psychically impaired were numerous cases like that of the European police inspector found guilty of torturing his own wife and children, which he explained as resulting from what he had been required to do to Algerian suspects: "The thing that kills me most is the torture. You just don't know what it's like, do you?"

Louis Joxe, the man summoned by de Gaulle to negotiate the final peace settlement with Algeria, told the author:

> I shall never forget the young officers and soldiers whom I met who were absolutely appalled by what they had to do. One should never forget the significance of this experience in considering a settlement for Algeria; for practically every French soldier went through it. This is something that the supporters of *Algérie française* never properly understood.

Simon declares that a policeman torturing a suspect "injures in himself the essence of humanity", but for the military to resort to it was one degree worse because: "It is here that the honour of the nation becomes engaged." Certainly the pernicious effect on the French army as a whole lasted many years after the war had ended, and many officers came to agree with General Bollardière in condemning Massu for ever having allowed the army to be brought into such a police action in the first place, thereby inevitably exposing it to the practice of torture. But could Massu, in fact, have refused? Outside the army, in Algeria the rifts created by torture led to a further, decisive step in eradicating any Muslim "third force" of *interlocuteurs valables* with whom a compromise peace might have been negotiated; while in France the stunning, cumulative impact it had was materially to help persuade public opinion years later that France had to wash her hands of the *sale guerre*. As Paul Teitgen remarked: "All right, Massu won the Battle of Algiers; but that meant losing the war."

By the end of March 1957 – the first month in many when no bombs exploded in Algiers – it certainly looked as if, at any rate in the short term, the battle had been won. Sickened by what they had been forced to do, and breathing deep sighs of relief, Bigeard and his paras left the fetid city for the open air of the *bled* once more.

CHAPTER TEN

Lost Round for the F.L.N.

May–December 1957

> The common error of the one and the other is to believe that they are defending a just cause, killing for a just cause, and risking an unjust death. They become cruel like a hunted beast.... Those truly responsible keep a prudent distance.
>
> Mouloud Feraoun

Yacef's second offensive

WHILE Bigeard and the paras were returning to their old hunting-grounds, the four surviving members of the C.C.E. were making their way painfully out of Algeria, carrying with them the leadership of the revo-lution. Krim and Abane had been smuggled out of Algiers in a Citroën 2 c.v. belonging to Madame Chaulet, just an hour after her husband had been arrested. The four leaders had then parted company, with Abane and Saad Dahlab heading westward for Morocco, whence they would fly to Tunis (this time taking a safer route than Ben Bella, via Madrid and Rome). Krim and Ben Khedda, moving eastwards for Tunis overland, were to make an odyssey lasting over three months, travelling most of the time by night, and on mules. Miraculously they were not apprehended by any French patrols on the nearly 500-mile "long march", but in his native Kabylia Krim narrowly missed being swept up in a net that was closing on Mohamedi Said's headquarters. In the ensuing fight 137 F.L.N. were killed, but Krim and Ben Khedda escaped.

Meanwhile, in Algiers, though now totally isolated, Yacef remained as undisputed, supreme boss. His laboriously constructed networks lay in ruins, and all the time he himself felt the noose of Godard's Deuxième Bureau tightening around his neck. But Yacef being Yacef, he refused to accept defeat, and in a remarkable fashion began to pick up the pieces, reconstitute his organisation and prepare for a fresh offensive. Early in May, after a long period of quiet, there was an incident followed by an outrage of "overkill" by the paras. Returning from the cinema in a suburb of Algiers, two paras had been shot down in the street by terrorists. In a spontaneous reprisal, some of their comrades, led by an informer from

Trinquier's D.P.U. to a Turkish bath that was supposed to be a hideout of the F.L.N., sub-machine-gunned all and sundry in it. Nearly eighty Muslims were reported killed; a number of them were poor beggars who habitually came in to find night-time shelter in the baths. Not one of the paras involved was ever brought to justice, although their identity was said to be known at the Gouvernement-Général. At the same time it was increasingly obvious to Yacef that the F.L.N., through its mauling at the hands of the paras, was steadily losing ground in the city. So to avenge the one and arrest the other, Yacef decided upon a new round of bombings. This time he tried a new technique that was ingeniously simple but even more cruel in that it struck equally at ordinary, working-class Muslims and at Europeans.

On 3 June four of Yacef's operatives, dressed in the uniform of the E.G.A. electricity and gas corporation and equipped with special keys, opened the small inspection doors at the base of several street lamp standards by bus-stops in the centre of the city, and inserted bombs inside. One such *lampadaire* selected stood close to the Grande Poste building. Three hours later, in the midst of the rush hour, the bombs exploded, fragmenting the heavy iron bases of the lamps like shrapnel from a bursting shell. Fortunately one went off just as a trolley-bus had collected most of the crowd waiting round it, and only two people were injured. But two others claimed eight dead – including the inevitable schoolchildren – and some ninety wounded, with grievous fragmentation injuries. The casualties of the innocents were this time almost equally divided between Muslims and Europeans, which did little to improve the image of the F.L.N. among the Muslim population. So next Yacef returned to his former policy of selecting a purely *pied noir* target. His choice fell on the Casino, with gambling tables and a dance-floor, poised on a rocky promontory some half-dozen miles out on the western fringes of Algiers. Here there would be no children and no Muslims; only the pleasure- and sun-loving young *pieds noirs* from Bab-el-Oued that Camus used to write about, glowing from a day on the beach.

The Casino

It was 9 June – as usual, a Sunday – and just before seven the Casino was crowded with couples already beginning to dance. The bomb, a powerful one, had been placed underneath the orchestra platform itself by a fifteen-year-old Muslim employee. Massu, whose residence was nearby, heard the explosion and hurried to the spot, as did Salan a short time later. The scene was appalling, the carnage the worst yet. The tawdry night-club decor was splattered with blood; the whole of the orchestra platform had been ripped up, the piano smashed to pieces and the unhappy band-leader – Lucky Starway, the idol of Bab-el-Oued – disembowelled. His girl vocalist lay with both feet blown off. Altogether there were nine dead and eighty-five wounded, nearly half of them women, and many of them having lost legs as a result of the level at which the bomb had exploded. Says the hardened Massu: "I can still see that beautiful young girl of eighteen with both her legs blown off, lying unconscious, her blonde hair stained with blood."

And Salan: "There were still fragments of feet in the slippers of the young dancers.... One had to have seen such a spectacle to understand our reactions towards these assassins." On the day of the interments the following Tuesday, the *pied noir* reaction was one of greater violence than ever before. A spontaneous strike closed down all shops in the working-class European quarter of Bab-el-Oued; and then began the *ratonnade*, the most savage that riven Algiers had yet experienced.

John Gale, a young British correspondent, observed with revulsion the *pied noir* mobs sacking one Muslim shop after another. In a sheer lust of destruction, they

> hurled live chickens to one another until the birds had lost their feathers and then trampled them to death.... They broke and emptied the tanks of motor bikes over meat torn from butchers, set fire to the petrol that soaked the carcasses, and armed themselves with meat-hooks.... Streets ran with milk and broken eggs; the mob pawed and stamped the debris like animals and poured wine over one another's heads....

There seemed to be almost a curious lack of passion about it all; the young mobsters "didn't seem angry to us; they were enjoying themselves". One young girl explained cheerfully, "We're sheep. We follow." And in the background Gale noted sinister-looking men in black suits and dark glasses giving orders, one of whom, when questioned, admitted that he was a stranger to the area. Gradually, as the heat of the day built up, the *ratonnade* assumed a nastier mood. Gale saw how

> One fat old Arab in blue denims, horribly beaten, staggered off, gasping with terror; another, much younger, his skull smashed, was dragged away and flung dead into the back of an army truck. Those were Arabs, perhaps small shopkeepers, who had chosen to live in a European quarter, and must have been well known to many of the rioters.

Later he saw young Muslims gaffed by the meat-hooks looted from the butchers' shops. The old, old explanation was recited to him: "They're not like another race, the Muslims. They've really overdone it, you see. Savages. Young girls with their legs amputated from that bomb in the Casino."

What Gale found "the most frightening thing", however, was the passive complicity of the police and soldiers; of two hundred European rioters arrested that day, apparently only four were detained, and these soon released. According to Salan's rather curious account of the day, a mob now more than 10,000 strong descending on the centre of Algiers was only brought to order by Colonel Trinquier brandishing a tricolour from his jeep and shouting, "Everybody to the *monument aux morts!*" Here Salan in person called upon them to disperse which, after an impassioned singing of the *Marseillaise,* they did. The day's results were five Muslims killed, fifty injured, a hundred shops sacked and twenty cars burnt out. Enraged at the failure of the troops, Massu issued stern orders

> to avoid indulgence towards the European elements in the city. Certain individuals, men and women, have behaved themselves in a disgusting manner and should have been arrested on the spot.
> The forces of order have the absolute duty to protect all elements of the population, and therefore the Muslims, when the Europeans "run wild".

Gloomily Mouloud Feraoun recorded in his diary in the aftermath of the Casino bomb, "More and more it seems that there is no other way out than death ... for there are no more innocents, on one side or the other, are there?"

At the Gouvernement-Général Robert Lacoste recognised that there was now nothing for it but to begin once again the whole toilsome process of cleaning out the Augean stables of Algiers. Back from the *bled* were summoned a reluctant Bigeard and his paras.

The hunt for Yacef

Now all was concentrated on the hunt for Yacef and his last remaining nucleus of terrorists. All his hideouts in the European quarters had been mopped up, and European helpers like Chaulet arrested, so the net could now constrict around the Casbah alone. Already in April one of Yacef's closest and most faithful collaborators, Djamila Bouhired, had fallen into French hands. Walking out in the Casbah, with Yacef a few paces behind, disguised as a woman, with a sub-machine-gun concealed under his clothes, she had been arrested by a Zouave patrol. Yacef immediately drew his gun and fired at Djamila with intent to kill,[*] realising that she knew enough to lead to his instant betrayal, and fled. Only wounded, Bouhired on recovery was tortured but refused to give away any vital information. Yacef claims that he made more than one attempt to liberate her from the Maillot military hospital. On one occasion a message was smuggled to her, telling her to pretend that she was prepared to lead the French to Yacef. When she had arrived at the Impasse de la Grenade, he instructed "Throw yourself flat on the ground and we will open fire." But Djamila refused; she did not wish, according to Yacef, that "any brothers

---

[*] Yacef made no reference to this in his original, very sparse, reminiscences published immediately after the war. The story is told by Courrière.

should risk their lives to liberate her". A further attempt to get Djamila out of the hospital was thwarted within minutes by paras coming to take her away in a military truck. In July she was sentenced to death, and Yacef let it be known that he would blow up entire city quarters in the event of her execution. There then followed a curiously improbable romantic episode where, brutality having failed, an attempt was made to soften up Djamila through the seductive attentions of a handsome para captain, but she still refused to give away Yacef's whereabouts.

Meanwhile, the French were resorting to new and subtler techniques of penetration. Under the inspiration of Captain Léger, an Arabic expert with the 11th Shock, selected turncoats clad inconspicuously in workers' dungarees, or *bleus de chauffe*, were unleashed in the Casbah to mingle with their former terrorist associates and lead Godard's intelligence operatives to the bosses' lairs. The technique was to achieve such success that the expression *la bleuite*, or "the blues", later assumed a particularly sinister connotation in the war as a whole. Its first coup was the tracking-down of "Mourad" and "Kamel", the *noms-de-guerre* respectively of Yacef's new "bomb squad" chief and his military deputy. On 26 August the two terrorists were pinned down in a second-floor apartment in the Impasse Saint-Vincent. With helicopters whirring overhead, a massive force of Bigeard's 3rd R.P.C. closed in. In the first encounter two Zouaves had been killed and two more wounded but, for the sake of the information Mourad and Kamel might give on Yacef, the paras were prepared to take any risk to capture them alive. Through a loud-hailer a para captain offered to guarantee their lives if they surrendered. After some confabulation, the trapped men replied that they would accept, provided they could have it in writing. It was agreed that they would lower their terms of surrender to the paras in a basket. As two paras ran forward to take the basket there was a violent explosion seriously injuring the two men and wounding in the leg the battalion commander. Immediately the two terrorists tried to make a run for it through the front door of the building; but Kamel was shot down and Mourad blown to pieces by his own grenade in the act of throwing it at the paras.

Germaine Tillion's secret rendezvous

Despite this setback for the French, another *bleu* was bringing them perilously close to No. 3 Rue Caton where, in a cunningly constructed cache, Yacef now incarcerated himself most of the time. But, in the meantime, an extraordinary encounter had taken place between the Casbah leader and a French representative. Having returned to France in January 1956, Germaine Tillion had become increasingly disturbed by accounts of torture and public executions in Algeria that percolated through to her from the *centres sociaux* she had set up under Soustelle's administration. Consequently, reinforced by her own grim experiences of Ravensbrück, she had set to to organise a Commission Internationale contre le Régime Concentrationnaire en Algérie and, backed by a special dispensation from Prime Minister Mollet, she arrived with it in Algiers in June, just as Yacef's new bombing offensive was getting under way. She was at once shocked to receive confirmation of just how bad the torture had become, and to discover how many of the liberal Muslims on whom had been founded her earlier hopes for a compromise peace were now incarcerated. On 2 July a Muslim woman friend came to the Hôtel Saint-George and told Germaine Tillion, elliptically, that "they" wanted to see her. At first disquieted by her friend's involvement with the F.L.N., she expressed willingness to meet any of its leaders if they would contact her directly.

The next day Germaine Tillion received a note requesting her to be at the bus-stop opposite the hotel at two o'clock the following afternoon, from where she was to follow a young man recognisable to her "regardless of any changes of transport". With considerable courage Germaine Tillion obeyed her instructions to the letter, changed buses three times, then – at a discreet distance – followed her guide into the Casbah, to No. 3 Rue Caton. Here she was received by Madame Fathia Bouhired, aunt of Djamila and whose husband had been killed by the paras some months previously. After a brief interval the door opened and in came Yacef, Zohra Drif and Ali la Pointe, the two men armed to the teeth with submachine-guns and grenades. Without giving his name, Zohra Drif introduced Yacef as *le grand frère*. At first the conversation was strained. "We did not know what to talk about, either of us – so we discussed economics!" recalls Madame Tillion, and she pointed out to them that she was the only one in the room "to know exactly what it was like to die of hunger".

> Then our conversation shifted to the French Resistance, talking about the traitors who had betrayed us (I was betrayed by a priest, for money) —hence *our* understanding of their situation. Yacef insisted, "But we have no traitors." In fact, had they only known it, they had, and were being betrayed at that very moment—which, of course, I didn't know at the time.

She vigorously assured Yacef that the F.L.N. would never defeat the French forces; to which *le grand frère* exclaimed in a desperate tone: "Then I shall never be a free man!"

From there they began to talk about the immediate horrors in Algiers, the bombings, reprisals and torture. Yacef revealed himself to be deeply concerned both by the fate of Djamila Bouhired, then in French hands, and the human consequences of his own bombings. But he claimed:

> "We are neither criminals, nor assassins." Very sadly and very firmly, I replied: "You *are* assassins." He was so disconcerted that for a moment he remained without speaking, as if suffocated. Then his eyes filled with

tears and he said to me, in so many words: "Yes, Madame Tillion, we are assassins. . . . It's the only way in which we can express ourselves."

Yacef then claimed that he had visited the scene of the Casino bombing, as usual disguised as a woman, and had been shocked to discover that one of the dead was a *pied noir* "football friend" and that his fiancée had lost both legs. "Perhaps you won't believe me, but I cried all night." He then added, to Germaine Tillion's amazement: "I've had enough. There won't be any further attack against the civil population of Algiers!" He explained, however, that the bombings had been undertaken only in riposte to the executions of the previous summer; and that if he were to halt the bombings, then the French government would have to reciprocate by "ceasing to guillotine patriots".

The conversation lasted over four hours, and at the end of it Germaine Tillion undertook to fly at once to Paris to inform the new Bourgès-Maunoury government (Mollet having fallen in May) of Yacef's proposed deal.*

In retrospect, it seems that Yacef may well have been motivated by no more transcending intention than to save his devoted Djamila Bouhired from the imminent prospect of the guillotine. At the time, however, Germaine Tillion felt passionately that the "hysteria of the two populations constituted an almost total obstacle to any solution", and that nothing could be achieved without first lowering the temperature of hatred and terror. Now here, at last, there seemed a small glimmer of light; if only there could be a reciprocal deal, ending the bombing of European civilians in exchange for a halt to the executions. . . . It was, in effect, something like a renewal of Camus' abortive quest for a "civil truce" of a year and a half earlier. In Paris Madame Tillion immediately made contact with a close friend on Bourgès-Maunoury's staff. Yacef's "deal" was passed on to the premier, and the first indications were encouraging. She was asked to return to Algiers and resume contacts with Yacef; but "at your own risk and peril". ("Imagine!" she snorted afterwards: "to what a state French authority in Algiers had been reduced, in reality, that I had to go back at my own peril!") At the same time she had also taken the opportunity of calling upon her old wartime chief, General de Gaulle, in his private office in the Rue Solférino. He had listened to her gravely as she described the horrors of the prison executions and of the tortures she had learned about in Algiers, and then made a remark that would seem full of significance a few years later: "This proves that one must talk, negotiate, *prendre langue*. One cannot abandon a people – whoever they may be – in quarantine!" But he refused her request that he intervene

---

* Curiously enough, Yacef also makes no mention in his book of any of his meetings with Germaine Tillion, though she had first revealed them herself several years previously.

personally, adding gloomily, "If I make a declaration, it will be taken the wrong way by everybody." As she left he remarked, by way of giving comfort, but enigmatically: "Everything that we do which is human earns its reward one day . . ." (pause) "But generally after we are dead!"

No deal. . . .

Then, on the very morning of her return to Algiers on 20 July, Germaine Tillion was telephoned from the premier's office to be told that, despite everything, two executions were scheduled for the 25th. She wept tears of frustration, and considered cancelling her flight. Nevertheless, she returned to discover that Yacef had exploded a further ten bombs following the sentencing to death of Djamila Bouhired and Taleb Abderrahmane; but miraculously not a single civilian had been harmed. On the 23rd she wrote to Yacef, in thinly disguised allusion, informing him of the forthcoming executions and begging him not to retaliate – "despite the breach of faith by my old father [the French government]". She added: "My uncle [de Gaulle] deplores what is happening." Yacef replied in a similar vein:

> *Chère cousine,*
> I have received your letter which, I must admit, did not surprise me excessively. The *volte-face* of your father was not unexpected. . . .
> . . . we are totally responsible for what we do. But, alas, in your family, what is its line of conduct? One never knows. When we believe that at last reason is going to prevail, we are, alas, destined for a disappointment. . . .
> I am anxious to draw your attention to the fate of my two young sisters [the two condemned terrorists]. If they succumb to their injuries, I and my brothers and all the family and kinsmen of Algiers will be very strongly affected. Their reactions will be very violent. . . .

The next day Germaine Tillion was horrified to discover that not two but a further three terrorists had been guillotined; the third being the man wrongfully condemned for the murder of Amédée Froger. The day after that eight more bombs exploded in Algiers, one quite close to Germaine Tillion herself. In disgust she decided to return forthwith to Paris. Then she learned that, in fact, the bombs had been so placed that there had not been a single civilian victim. Changing her mind, she settled down to wait for another summons from Yacef, which she hoped would lead her to one of the C.C.E. leaders. Another two weeks elapsed before it came, and this time Germaine Tillion had to disguise herself as a Muslim woman in order to penetrate the para blockade of the Casbah without betraying Yacef's whereabouts. It was the first time that she learned the true identity of Yacef.

With Zohra Drif once again in attendance, Germaine Tillion told Yacef: "If there had been one single victim after the explosion of those bombs, I should not be here. . . . We can thank God!"

To which Yacef replied: "I had taken my precautions. It's not God that must be thanked, but me!"

She duly thanked Yacef and, after a further discussion, left. A week later, on 16 August, there were two further executions. On the point of returning to Paris, Germaine Tillion wrote a last hasty and frantic note to Yacef, on her own initiative, begging him – despite her inability "to apply brakes, on the French side, to this ferocious and stupid mechanism" – not to retaliate in kind, and to adopt unilaterally a "position of moderation". In reply, Yacef "let me know that there would not be any reprisals, and there were not any". It was the last time she was to see Yacef, or any other F.L.N. leader. She returned to Paris gravely disheartened, feeling that if the "deal" with Yacef could only have been implemented,

> then at least we could have *talked*. But I failed. That was the last moment when I felt it might be possible to talk; after the Battle of Algiers it always seemed to be too late. For that was the moment when – Lacoste having handed over responsibility to the army – the French ceased to govern Algeria. . . .

3 Rue Caton

In any event, after the hunting down of Mourad and Kamel on 26 August, time was rapidly running out for Yacef. Like Montgomery with the ever-present photograph of his adversary, Rommel, hung up in his desert caravan, Godard had come to know every feature of Yacef's face and, through intelligence received from Captain Léger's *bleus*, he had also managed to pinpoint the Rue Caton. In this dark street, so narrow that the overhanging houses almost meet on the first floor, Yacef had his final hideout – alternating between No. 3 and No. 4 opposite. But, employing his own system of "doubles", whereby the widow Bouhired – owner of No. 3 – presented herself to the paras as an informer, Yacef managed with a mixture of adroitness and extraordinary good fortune to lead them off the track a little longer, and to preserve immunity of search for the Bouhired household. Sick with flu and a minor heart condition, as well as suffering from the intense heat inside the cache, Yacef confided to Zohra Drif that in a nightmare he had repeatedly dreamt he was about to be captured. On 22 September Ali la Pointe, the former pimp and Casbah layabout, also told Yacef: "I'm going to give food to forty old paupers.* I'm going to die." Yacef ordered the headquarters to split up. Zohra Drif and he would remain in No. 3; Ali la Pointe, Hassiba Ben Bouali and Yacef's twelve-year-old nephew and courier, "Petit Omar", would move across the street to No. 4. He then wrote an urgent letter to Ben Khedda in Tunis, pointing out how desperate their situation was and requesting immediate help. His despatch carrier was a man called Hadj Smain, alias Djamal, and it so happened that he had been the principal intermediary

---

* A Muslim custom when a man feels he is about to die.

between Yacef and Germaine Tillion. The very next day, however, Djamal was picked up by Godard's men – acting, apparently, on a tip-off, but through no fault whatever of Germaine Tillion. Under extreme pressure Djamal gave away the secret of No. 3 Rue Caton; at the same time he revealed all the details he knew of the parleys that had taken place between Germaine Tillion and Yacef with the blessing of the French government. News of this association with the arch-enemy, Yacef, was regarded by the para leaders as a piece of sheer duplicity on the part of a civil government they were already growing increasingly to distrust and despise.

At 5 a.m. on the 24th, the Rue Caton was sealed off by Colonel Jeanpierre's 1st R.E.P. Warned by the widow Bouhired, Yacef and Zohra Drif, both half-undressed, managed to get into a cache, ingeniously constructed by one of Yacef's masons in a small space between the bathroom and staircase, before the paras entered the house. But, by tapping the wall, the cavity was soon discovered. A para swinging a pick-axe opened a hole in it, out of which Yacef promptly threw a grenade. Three paras were wounded, as well as the colonel himself. Meanwhile, behind the partition, Zohra Drif coolly set to burning vital documents. Godard, now arrived on the scene, took over personally and, determined to take Yacef alive, carried out a dialogue at a discreet distance, trying to persuade the Casbah leader to give himself up. Within Yacef's sight a charge of plastic fell at the bottom of the false partition, and Godard shouted to him that he was lighting a fuse to go off in exactly ten minutes. Claiming that he reckoned that, had it exploded, the charge would also have killed Hassiba, Ali la Pointe and Petit Omar across the street as well as the tenants of No. 3, Yacef capitulated. Half-naked and coughing from the smoke of the burning papers, he and Zohra Drif emerged from the cache. A jubilant Salan telephoned to Paris the news of the capture of the most wanted man in Algiers; by return he received a telegram from the prime minister ordering that on no account were Yacef and Zohra Drif to be maltreated in any way. They were not, as Yacef himself admits. Nevertheless, Yacef filled over a hundred pages in the course of his interrogation, often in a tone somewhat vaunting of his past achievements. Condemned to death three times by military tribunals the following year, he was finally reprieved by de Gaulle on his becoming president.

Ali la Pointe

Meanwhile, in the jubilation at catching Yacef the occupants of No. 4 Rue Caton were completely neglected. Creeping through a cellar exit, Ali la Pointe and his two comrades made a safe getaway to another bolthole; at 5 Rue des Abderames, near the top of the Casbah. But within two weeks Godard, acting on information provided by a *bleu* who had given himself the *nom-de-guerre* of "Safy-le-Pur" (Safy is the Arabic for "pure") and who had already helped in the tracking down of Yacef, had located this last refuge. Inside were Ali la Pointe, Hassiba Ben Bouali, and the twelve-year-old Petit Omar, who passed the painfully long hours snipping paper cut-outs. At nightfall on 8 October the house was surrounded by the 1st R.E.P. Three times Ali was called upon to surrender, but not a sound came back. Remembering what had happened at the siege of Mourad and Kamel, the paras decided to take no chances and laid three hollow charges with the aim of bringing down the partition behind which Ali la Pointe was hiding. A shattering explosion rocked the whole Casbah. The charges had apparently detonated a store of bombs hidden in the cache. Virtually nothing remained of the house, and several adjacent to it also collapsed. Beneath the ruins the bodies of Ali la Pointe (easily identified by his tattoos), Hassiba Ben Bouali and Petit Omar were dug out; but seventeen other Muslims, including four small children, died in the neighbouring houses which the paras had neglected to evacuate. Four paras were also injured in the blast.

The Battle ends

With the death of Ali la Pointe in the autumn of 1957 the grim Battle of Algiers was truly ended. The city breathed afresh. Work began again, the schools reopened, and the old agreeable life of the *pieds noirs* returned to normal with remarkable speed. The curfew was lifted, and cinemas no longer required to be searched; the Rue Michelet filled with shoppers once again, as did the cafés, *dancings* and stadiums over the beloved week-ends. The joyous picnics resumed at Pointe Pescade, where the Casino bombing was all but forgotten. Even in the Casbah fear subsided; though it was to some extent replaced by another kind of fear – that of the midnight call by Massu's all-powerful paras, and the never to be entirely absent threat of the *gégène*.

To the *pieds noirs* the glorious paras now became the toast of Algiers, enjoying a peak of popularity shared even (though briefly) by Robert Lacoste himself. As Christmas approached, the toyshops filled with red berets, "leopard" camouflage jackets, and plastic sub-machine-guns; somewhat to the chagrin of the *macho*-minded *pied noir* male, every golden-skinned beauty of Algiers had to be seen with a para boyfriend on her arm. News films showed tough but relaxed paras in shorts dancing *Il était un petit navire* with happy Muslim children. All of a sudden the army was everywhere, and everything.

No one could doubt that the paras had scored a major victory for the French army, the first clearly definable one of the war. They had faced up to a confrontation with the F.L.N. and won hands down. Some commentators went so far as speak of a "Dien Bien Phu" for the F.L.N. Says Massu in retrospect: "We had rounded up the leaders and broken up the system. There were no more assassinations or bomb attempts. And the proof of it all was the Muslim support we were to get on 16 May 1958." Certainly, if only on a strictly military level, the para commanders could be excused for considering that they had achieved success where the Lacostes, Soustelles, Mollets and Mendès-Frances – the civil leaders as a whole – had all failed miserably. The army would not now be easily persuaded to relinquish the powers which Lacoste had ceded it in January 1957. If the *pieds noirs* had shown they could sway Paris following Mollet's disastrous visit in February 1956, here now was a new factor; the army as ultimate arbiter.

For the F.L.N. the immediate consequence was to force it to face up to a serious defeat and completely review its strategy. Henceforth it realised that large-scale terrorism in the cities would have to be abandoned; and, moreover, the failure in Algiers led it to the appreciation that nowhere in Algeria was its military organisation, the A.L.N., strong enough to face any major armed confrontation with the French army. Thus, it would conclude, the war could really no longer be won inside Algeria itself. Through its defeat in Algiers the F.L.N. also lost important ground in the struggle for the souls of the uncommitted "third force" Muslims, now giving increased indication of war-weariness. Finally, as will be seen shortly, the Algiers defeat was to impose stresses on the leadership resulting in the gravest internal dissension to date. But all this was in the immediate present: in the longer term there were ways in which the Battle of Algiers was to prove a blessing in disguise (though, as Winston Churchill remarked of his electoral defeat in 1945, at the moment it may have seemed "quite effectively disguised"). First of all, by making the C.C.E. quit Algiers, the French would be assisting it to find a base of relative tranquillity in Tunis. Secondly, by pressing upon it the correct strategic conclusions it would help the C.C.E. turn a short-term defeat into a long-term victory. Thirdly, with utmost irony, the Battle of Algiers, by focusing the TV cameras, newsfilms and journalists of the world upon it, had probably done infinitely more to achieve the sought-for "internationalisation" of the war than all Ben Bella's efforts in Cairo, or Yazid's at the United Nations. Fourthly, through the reaction they produced both in France herself and elsewhere, the repugnant methods with which the paras had won in Algiers were materially to help bring victory from the outside.

Black moments for the F.L.N.

None of this, however, could be seen by the harried members of the C.C.E. as they reached sanctuary in Bourguiba's Tunis. Everything looked at its blackest. Throughout Algeria the loss of face (so important to the Muslim mentality) resulting from Massu's victory was bound to lead to a falling off of support for the cause throughout Algeria. Apart from the consequences of Massu's victory, there was a variety of additional factors acting against F.L.N. interests in 1957 and 1958. The excellent S.A.S. service, inaugurated by Jacques Soustelle, had begun to make its mark and was restoring confidence in the *présence française* in wide areas of the *bled*. The number of primary schools opened by the army had trebled, and between April 1956 and August 1957 the numbers of Muslim function-aries had been augmented from 6,847 to 9,979; not enough, but something. Reports from F.L.N. operatives in the field complained that: "Today the people of the sector no longer want to work for us; there are many others where the population has turned against us, because we do not keep our promises." Or that the *djounoud* were not receiving their pay (which in any case often amounted to no more than 10 new francs a month). Or, "We are short of everything. The colonialists are everywhere. Too many enemy posts, we cannot move. *We must have some automatic weapons, to show them to the population.*" In 1957 A.L.N. losses were double those of the previous year. Morale had slumped and desertions risen; between May 1957 and May 1958 the French claimed 928 *ralliements individuels* – or four times as many as the preceding year. Much more serious, though, were the *ralliements collectifs*, as will be seen shortly.

On the other side of the balance-sheet, however – even if little visible to F.L.N. eyes – there remained the steady and disheartening drift away from France of the middle ground, the potential "third force": liberals like Camus' friend, the writer Mouloud Feraoun, and the Kabyle poet, Jean Amrouche, who, in September 1957, wrote in anguish: "What causes me to despair . . . is to see France engaged unwittingly in a tragedy in which she may lose herself . . . my inner France, the only [nation] that every man, white, red or black can choose as the fatherland of the mind." Servan-Schreiber recalls the *pied noir* liberal who remarked angrily that there were

> a few Muslim groups who were still prepared to talk, but within one or two months it's finished. No one any longer. As a result of bullying them, arresting them, interning them, and occasionally killing them – you've won; but everybody who represents anything of importance in this country has gone over to the F.L.N. There are no more intermediaries.

One factor that was costing the French much goodwill was a new policy designed in the first instance to protect the loyal and the uncommitted from F.L.N. terrorism. This was *regroupement*, or resettlement, which – to rephrase the oft-quoted axiom – aimed at emptying the water away from the fish by isolating communities from the F.L.N. and thus denying it refuge and supplies. It involved the resettlement of over a million peasants from "exposed" communities to barbed-wire encampments, which often looked horribly like concentration camps. Through faulty organisation, privations in these camps were often excessive. Describing conditions in one such settlement, a *Figaro* correspondent wrote in 1958:

> Crammed together in unbroken wretchedness, fifteen to a tent since 1957, this human flotsam lies tangled in an indescribable state. There are 1,800 children living at Bessombourg.... At the moment, the whole population is fed entirely on semolina. Each person receives about four ounces of semolina a day.... Milk is given out twice a week: one pint per child.... No rations of fat have been distributed for eight months. No rations of chick-peas for a year.... No rations of soap for a year....

The following year a priest returning from Algeria claimed that the "re-grouped" were sometimes receiving no more than a quarter to a third of the minimum calories necessary for sustaining life, and told of children dying of hunger. "An evacuated *mechta* is not a *mechta* that has migrated ... the regrouped *mechta* is a broken, ruined *mechta*," declared Frantz Fanon, while Germaine Tillion's sense of history evoked the *grand dérangement*, the cruel displacement of the French Acadians by the British in eighteenth-century Canada.

By uprooting these Algerians from their homes and fields and placing them in camps where they led listless and largely unemployed existences, the French only created a new area of profound social discontent; while by helping "to break up an antiquated rural and tribal structure", says Dorothy Pickles, they also encouraged "a sense of national solidarity". Thousands fled over the border into Tunisia or Morocco to join the ranks of the F.L.N. there. Regroupment undeniably made life much more difficult for the A.L.N., but – as so often in the Algerian war – French policy found itself caught in the insoluble paradox of what was good militarily being bad politically, and *vice versa*. It was a pitfall into which, to some extent, the Americans were to stumble in South Vietnam. By the Battle of Algiers, Germaine Tillion concluded gloomily, "The implantation of the F.L.N. in the Algerian masses was too deep for any *détente* whatever to occur without the global agreement which it alone could give."

Mélouza and Bellounis

The F.L.N. could not entirely share her views, for it was still locked in its own struggle of intense internecine rivalry with resuscitated elements of Messali Hadj's M.N.A., a struggle which exploded in an act of appalling savagery right in the middle of the Battle of Algiers, and temporarily distracted the world's eyes from it. On 31 May the Gouvernement-Général announced that the army had stumbled upon a massacre of peasants at a *mechta* called Mélouza, down in the remote south of Kabylia. Three nights earlier, apparently, the F.L.N. had rounded up every male above the age of fifteen from the surrounding area, herded them into houses and into the mosque and slaughtered them with rifles, pick-axes and knives: a total of

301 in all, with another fourteen severely wounded survivors. Swiftly appreciating the propaganda value of this new outrage, Lacoste promptly despatched a group of French and foreign correspondents to the scene of the incident to write up and photograph what they found. At first the F.L.N. attempted to bluster that it had all been the work of the wicked paras, but the evidence – including statements later made by Yacef, and finally clinched from documents found on the dead body of Amirouche, the Wilaya 3 leader – pointed overwhelmingly to their own responsibility. Sickened by the massacre, world opinion – less hardened to atrocity in those distant days – for a brief time animadverted against the F.L.N.

The causes behind Mélouza date back to the summer of 1955 when Amirouche had encircled and wiped out at Guenzet in Kabylia an armed camp of the dissident M.N.A. under a chieftain called Bellounis. Bellounis and a handful of his men had escaped and made their way to the Mélouza area, arid and inaccessible country sloping down to the Sahara on the intersections of four Wilayas. In 1956 it had gone over to the F.L.N. after Colonel Antoine Argoud had conducted a particularly severe reprisal there, and the French had more or less abandoned the area. Around Mélouza, however, the people of the Beni-Illemane tribes constituted an important pocket of M.N.A. supporters, and it was to them that Bellounis came and assumed leadership. Soon there was friction, and after Bellounis's men had waylaid and killed several of his emissaries, the commander of Wilaya 3 gave orders to a captain and former Paris taxi-driver to "exterminate this vermin". This he had done, with deadly effect; but Bellounis himself, once again, had slipped away unscathed. In the meantime, before the Mélouza massacre, the French, who in 1955 had already toyed with notions of turning Bellounis to their own advantage, had been putting out feelers to the M.N.A. leader. Now, after Mélouza, Bellounis and the survivors of the Beni-Illemane went over lock, stock and barrel to the French. Allowed their own flag, uniforms and "programme" as a Muslim "third force" allied but not subordinate to the French, the Bellounists became the principal of several private armies. For comparisons in the Second World War, one needs to look at aspects of General Vlasov's Ukrainians, the Croat Ustaši, or the Serb Četniks. By August 1957 Bellounis already had 1,500 men under his control, operating in the marginal areas just north of the Sahara, and backed by official funds (promised, but never realised *in toto*) of 70 million old francs a month. Though in fact the whole show, under the code name of "Opération Ollivier", was "managed" by the ubiquitous 11th Shock, Bellounis took to appearing vested in the two stars of a general and a steadily inflating self-importance. As time went on he was to become an even greater thorn in the side of his Frankenstein, but for the time being his divisive activities caused the F.L.N. gravest anxiety.

More defections from the F.L.N....

At about this same time, and in the same vast marginal area which the F.L.N. had recently designated Wilaya 6, a still more menacing potential threat presented itself with the defection of Si Chérif and a whole rebel *katiba*. Aged thirty-two and an Arab, Si Chérif had spent eleven years in the French army, including two tours in Indo-China, and had been captured in an F.L.N. ambush when serving with the Spahis. After being employed for some time as a mere "coolie" by his captors, Si Chérif had risen to become military chief of the newly-formed Wilaya 6. This had been created out of a nucleus of Kabyles despatched southwards by Krim. Its political commissar was a wild and brutal figure operating under the pseudonym of "Rouget", whose apparently insatiable sexual appetites drove him to claim a kind of *droit de seigneur* whereby the prettiest girls in the villages he passed through were earmarked for his personal pleasure. As most of the villages were Arab, this fanned a violent hatred between the two races, always latently smouldering. One day, in an angry argument, Si Chérif pulled out his revolver and shot Rouget through the head in front of his men. Then, over the next six days, Si Chérif and his Arab followers killed all the Kabyles they could lay their hands on. In July 1957 he "rallied" to the French at the head of an entire *katiba* 330 strong. Turned into a *harki* – or Muslim private army fighting with the French – Si Chérif's men operated with even greater effectiveness than Bellounis, inflicting in a pitched battle the following March some seventy-two casualties on the A.L.N., as well as recovering a considerable amount of arms.

For a time the French cherished hopes that Si Chérif might bring over with him the whole of the south, but eventually the F.L.N. skilfully managed to seal off the damage. Nevertheless, in that hard-pressed summer of 1957 the Si Chérif affair opened up to the F.L.N. one of its greatest latent nightmares: the prospect of a sectarian split between Arabs and Kabyles. It was an opportunity for which French intelligence was constantly, and obviously, on the look out. At the same time, after the notable successes of Captain Léger and his *bleus* during the latter stages of the Battle of Algiers, the 11th Shock had got busy burrowing into the demoralised Wilayas outside, sowing insidious suspicions of treason at every hand.

... and rifts at the top

Although it was always less visible to the French (and in fact remained almost entirely invisible until years later), the continuing dissension in the F.L.N. leadership still posed an even greater menace to the coherence of the whole movement than any number of defections, single or collective, at lower levels. Greatly exacerbated by the defeat in Algiers and the forced withdrawal of the C.C.E. from the city, internal rifts had brought the F.L.N. leadership to the brink of disaster by the spring of 1957. Once again the basic issue lay in the contention between the "interior" and the "exterior"; and, once again, the figure of Ramdane Abane was at the storm centre. With the four surviving members of the C.C.E. themselves become, through force of circumstances, "exterior", the sniping now spilled over into Habib Bourguiba's newly independent capital of Tunis. The first shots were actually being fired while Ramdane Abane and his colleagues were on their "long march" from beleaguered Algiers. In a remarkable fashion Ben Bella, who had been under lock and key in the Santé prison since his hijacking the previous October, had managed to keep up a running correspondence with his faithful deputy, Ali Mahsas, in Tunis. Acting in harmony with Ben Bella's directives, Ali Mahsas launched a violent attack on the C.C.E. at a meeting of the like-minded held in March. He refused to recognise the motions passed at the Soummam Conference the previous September because "No representative of the 'exterior' was present. Therefore, for us the C.C.E. is nothing." The Soummam Conference, he charged, had broken the "moral contract" between the *neuf historiques*, and he accused Abane of "playing personal politics". The C.C.E.'s decision to launch the eight-day general strike in Algiers was, he said:

> the greatest folly ever committed by the Revolution. We ought to conduct a guerrilla war in the *djebel* with the support of the people. We always believed that the city ought not to intervene until the last moment.... Those of the C.C.E. have decided otherwise and now the repression is terrible. It could cut us off from the people. We have risked the dismantling of the revolutionary organisation to make a noise at the United Nations. It's stupid and ridiculous!

When it appeared that Ali Mahsas was gaining support, Ouamrane, the tough ex-sergeant with the lantern jaw and, as Krim's ever-loyal lieutenant, the most senior F.L.N. representative then in Tunis, decided to act promptly and forcefully. Sending fifty armed men into the centre of Tunis, he had Mahsas arrested at F.L.N. headquarters and placed in a guarded villa. For a moment it looked as if Mahsas was facing imminent liquidation. Then Bourguiba himself, apparently, intervened. A short time previously he had flown into a fierce rage on hearing of a series of killings between groups of rival Auresian tribesmen who had taken refuge on Tunisian soil. There were some 150,000 Algerians in Tunisia, many of them heavily armed and outnumbering the infant Tunisian army itself. Thus Bourguiba saw the whole basis of his authority undermined and reacted by arresting and disarming over a thousand of the squabbling F.L.N. He now criticised Ouamrane sharply for this new "settling of accounts"; the dissident Ali Mahsas was released and put on a plane for Rome and exile.

Abane versus the rest

Once again a breach within the top echelons of the F.L.N. seemed to have been healed over, with the C.C.E. emerging ascendant. Then, in June, Abane and Saad Dahlab arrived via Tétouan in Morocco, having been preceded shortly by Krim and Ben Khedda. Meanwhile, at various intervals, the "colonels" – as the military leaders of the Wilayas were now titled – were also congregating in Tunis. There was Mahmoud Chérif, the new chief of the troubled Wilaya 1 in the Aurès, where the revolt had first established itself; Mohamedi Said, the former S.S. man from Wilaya 3 in Kabylia; Ouamrane standing in for the absent and hard-pressed leaders of the Algérois Wilaya 4; but most noteworthy were Ben Tobbal, who had taken over the Constantine Wilaya 2 on the death of his chief, Zighout, and Boussouf, a powerful new figure who had assumed command of Wilaya 5 (Oranie) upon the elevation of Ben M'hidi.

Boussouf

Abdelhafid Boussouf was born at Milia near Constantine – like Ben Tobbal, with whom he retained a close and enduring friendship – and at thirty-one was the youngest of the Wilaya commanders. He was also the most educated, having qualified before 1954 as a teacher and taken a correspondence course in psychology. A large man with a full face, close-cropped black hair and eyes concealed behind tinted glasses, Boussouf gave an unassuming impression. Yet he was held by his subordinates in considerable awe, had imposed a strong stamp of his own personality on Wilaya 5 and would henceforth assume a central role in the F.L.N. leadership. The Wilaya had been in a state of considerable disorder when he took over, and gradually he had introduced a scrupulously co-ordinated infrastructure, intelligence and signals system that more closely resembled that of the French army itself than of the other Wilayas. Operations, though few enough to give the impression that the Wilaya was relatively inactive, were meticulously planned, and there were none of the hazard encounters that had often proved so disastrous elsewhere. Instead, Boussouf was concentrating on building up an impressive military machine. Seldom far from his side was another young man as reticent, efficient and ambitious as himself, whom Boussouf had been bringing on as his deputy: Houari Boumedienne.

On arriving in Tunis, Abane immediately singled out Boussouf for attack. He had passed through Wilaya 5 (where he had nearly been captured) on his journey from Algiers, and had not liked at all what he had seen. By his reckoning, Boussouf reigned there by sheer terror; he and Boumedienne comported themselves like "real dictators", and they controlled not only the Wilaya but also everything that went on over the border in Morocco, too. He also criticised them for their affinity with

Ben Bella, his arch-enemy. From attacking Boussouf in person Abane then spread his fire to blanket the military in general. Reminding his colleagues of the Soummam decision that the political should have primacy over the military, Abane declared that it was intolerable that the latter should presume to feudal rights, and heatedly described them as "robots". Krim, the veteran maquisard, began to bridle under these attacks and, although he had staunchly supported his fellow Kabyle in the battle against Ben Bella the previous year, now warned him to have a care in what he was saying. But for all his subtlety as a political tactician, Abane was becoming more and more intractable. It appears that his ulcers may have been at least partly to blame; and in turn his rages inflamed the ulcers. Forgetting all such good tactical principles as divide and conquer, and not fighting a war on more than one front, Abane hit out at Ouamrane, accusing him of being militarily incapable. Such an assault on his faithful lieutenant was intolerable to Krim, and he now definitively withdrew his allegiance from Abane.

In his criticism of "Wilayism" Abane was not without reason. As a consequence of the Battle of Algiers the Wilayas had become extensively isolated from the C.C.E. besieged in the capital. Thus they had had increasingly to rely upon their own day-to-day decisions, and had equally achieved freedom to develop their own distinctive styles. For instance, whereas Boussouf's Wilaya 5 was evolving into a closely-knit, disciplined military machine, with all the hierarchical formality that that implies, Wilaya 4 was evolving in quite the opposite direction – largely under the influence of the numbers of students and intellectuals that had joined it, seeking refuge from the Battle of Algiers. Equality had become the catchword, insignias of rank had been abolished, political commissars and "self-criticism" instituted, and operations initiated by communal decisions. Inevitably, the Wilayas found themselves with greater autonomy, and thus power, thrust upon them in the absence of regular directives from the C.C.E. United as never before by Abane's barbs, the Wilaya colonels now counter-attacked vigorously against the C.C.E. as a whole for its mismanagement of the war. It was criticised for its failure to maintain arms supplies, but above all for its essential strategic error in getting committed to the Battle of Algiers. Clearly the principal target was Abane, who was finding himself increasingly isolated, with only his faithful allies, Ben Khedda and Saad Dahlab, still supporting him.

On 27 July it was decided to hold, in Cairo, a second full reunion of the C.N.R.A. Abane's isolation was now final. A new, nine-man C.C.E. was elected from which Ben Khedda and Saad Dahlab were pointedly eliminated. Instead there were five colonels: Krim, Boussouf, Ben Tobbal, Ouamrane and Mahmoud Chérif, to four "politicals": Ferhat Abbas, Dr Lamine Debaghine, Abdelhamid Mehri, and Ramdane Abane. More significant still was the nomination of a permanent "inner" council within the C.C.E. consisting of the five colonels and one solitary political: Ramdane Abane. Defeated, Abane raged at the colonels: "You are creating a power based on the army. The maquis is one thing, politics is another, and it is not conducted either by illiterates or ignoramuses!" The words must have stung savagely, and Ferhat Abbas reportedly attempted to intervene and calm Abane, telling him soothingly: "We know you're very nervous, and ill. You must look after your ulcers, go and take time off to rest in Switzerland...." Abane's response was apparently to tap the butt of his pistol, declare that everybody was out to "eliminate" him, but that he was on his guard. He then threatened to return to the maquis and inform it of what was happening, a threat that the colonels could not possibly ignore because, after the death of Ben M'hidi, Abane remained incontestably still the most influential political figure in the ranks of the F.L.N. On 1 November, in the declaration commemorating the third anniversary of the war, a meaningful sentence was inserted which stated, "The cult of the personality is strictly condemned." Meanwhile, there were disturbing rumours that Abane was planning to march on Tunis at the head of an Auresian battalion and "arrest" the C.C.E. The colonels decided that Abane had to go; but how?

The liquidation of Abane

On 29 May of the following year, the front page of El Moudjahid printed a heavily black-rimmed statement bearing the block caption:

ABBANE RAMDANE*
EST MORT AU CHAMP D'HONNEUR

It announced that, in December, "brother" Abane had been charged with "an important and urgent mission of control" inside the country. After crossing the frontier defences with great difficulty, he had found himself

> surrounded by affection and admiration of all his brothers. A company of djounoud were specially charged with his protection and nothing could foresee the brutal accident that was to tear him away from the fervour of fighting Algeria.
>
> Unfortunately, in the first fortnight of April a violent encounter between our troops and those of the enemy forced the protecting company of our brother Abbane to take part in the engagement. In the course of the fighting which lasted several hours, Abbane was wounded ... hélas! A grave haemorrhage became fatal.
>
> This is the sad news which has just reached us.
>
> The fine and noble figure of Abbane Ramdane, his courage and his will, have marked essential phases of the struggle of the Algerian people....
>
> We mourn a brother in arms whose memory will help guide us.

* This is the form of the name used here, and occasionally elsewhere, but Ramdane Abane seems to be more generally used.

The lack of mention of any specific place, and vagueness about the date of the news "which has just reached us", is noteworthy; and as it is now the generally accepted view that Abane's "brutal accident" took place at the hands of his "brothers", the fulsome language of the communiqué makes cynical reading. Because of the exceptional, but habitual, secretiveness of the Algerians, it was not till several years later that rumours began to circulate that Abane might have been "liquidated". In October 1963, little more than eighteen months before he was himself deposed and hustled out of sight, President Ben Bella was quoted as declaring publicly: "Abane died, strangled by the hands of criminals of the G.P.R.A."

President Bourguiba declared to the author: "I didn't know Abane, I never saw him, and I don't know how he died." But comparing the internal dissensions of the F.L.N. leadership to the French Revolution, he added pointedly: "Robespierre himself wasn't even spared."

To this day the actual details of the death of the man who some thought might have become the Tito, or even Mao, of Algeria remain wrapped in mystery. None of those who could have thrown light on it ever talked. Various versions have appeared; those of Mohamed Lebjaoui and Yves Courrière (who, of any foreign chronicler, received probably the most complete testimony of the war from Krim before his death, and who cites a secret document of the C.C.E. dated 15 August 1958) tally most closely with each other.* According to these accounts, between 17 and 20 December Krim, Ben Tobbal and Mahmoud Chérif met lengthily in Tunis to decide the fate of Abane. Boussouf was absent, in Morocco, but his views were represented by his close ally, Ben Tobbal, who stated that there was only one choice – "death or prison". Ben Tobbal added that he was not against death "in principle", but that he would not accept the responsibility of killing Abane without trial. Krim remarked that, if prison were decided upon, it would not be possible in Bourguiba's Tunisia; whereas, in Morocco, in the charge of Boussouf, "he would not worry us again". Mahmoud Chérif protested that Boussouf favoured killing Abane; however, it was finally agreed that Abane should be imprisoned in Morocco, the ultimate responsibility for his fate in the hands of Boussouf, the hard-liner.

On the 24th Abane was lured to Morocco, ostensibly for a summit conference with King Mohammed V, accompanied from Tunis by Krim and Mahmoud Chérif. Ben Tobbal had refused to be present. Highly mistrust-

* Insofar as Krim was Courrière's source concerning the death of Abane, it should be remembered that Krim was an interested party and possibly had an axe to grind against his former colleagues. He was in fact murdered, in sinister circumstances, while in exile years after the war. On the other hand, neither his nor Lebjaoui's account – nor a similar version which appeared in the widely circulated *Historia* magazine series, "La Guerre d'Algérie", has been refuted by any Algerian source. In Algiers in 1984 a senior Algerian official told the author simply: Abane "was helped to suicide".

ful, Abane said to Krim on the plane: "I sense there's a dirty trick ahead, but you'll regret it. . . ."

Landing at Tétouan on the 26th, the three were picked up in a car by Boussouf and two unknown men. The car started off in the direction of Tangier. After a few kilometres, however, it turned off the main road, up a dirt track, and halted outside a farm. Pointing their sub-machine-guns at Abane, the two men ordered him to get out and accompany them. Krim and Mahmoud Chérif protested, with Krim declaring that Boussouf would be held responsible for anything that might happen to Abane. After driving off to a farmhouse a short distance away, Krim cautioned Boussouf at dinner that the C.C.E. had decided Abane was to be imprisoned and *not* executed. Angrily, Boussouf allegedly retorted: "I haven't got a prison here. And . . . here, in Morocco, I do what I want. Abane will 'pass on', and plenty of others will pass on too." He added that Boumedienne was also "in agreement".* After dinner the two men reappeared and the F.L.N. leaders were informed that Abane was dead. In a neighbouring room Krim saw Abane lying on a bed, strangled by a cord round his neck; a form of death that, ironically, was to be suffered by Krim himself many years later.

According to Lebjaoui, the death of Abane – "one of the most atrocious of all the tragedies marking the Algerian revolution" – could never have been accomplished without the tacit support of Krim, and it was because of Boussouf's involvement that he was given no job in the post-war Boumedienne government. After some vehement soul-searching within the C.C.E., it was agreed that the five reigning colonels – Krim, Ouamrane, Mahmoud Chérif, Ben Tobbal and Boussouf – would henceforth *jointly* accept responsibility for Abane's death. It was a decision of considerable significance for the future leadership of the F.L.N., being a triumph of the philosophy of collective leadership. As far as its unity was concerned, it represented, in effect, little more than another papering over of personal differences. Because of the equivocal position taken by Krim, so Ben Tobbal remarked to Courrière after the war, "From that moment onwards until 1962, discord between us was permanent." But that such discord should continue to exist at the top without the whole fabric of the F.L.N. being riven is a testimony to the basic solidity that the movement had achieved. As Ben Khedda told the author, "The base of the pyramid always held firm."

The colonels ascendant

With the deaths first of Ben M'hidi, then of Abane, real power in the F.L.N. devolved, for the time being, upon Krim, Ben Tobbal and Boussouf.

---

* Lebjaoui, however, who held no love for Boumedienne, denied to the author that he was in any way implicated; nor, he insists, was Abane's arch-enemy, Ben

The passing of Abane also brought with it ascendancy for the colonels over the "politicals" – a curious irony of history that this should have occurred at almost the same moment when, on the other side of the lines, the para colonels were about to impose their powerful weight on the affairs of France. The colonels now set to to reorganise the structure of the A.L.N., attacking its problems of morale and discipline, and reassessing its roles. As 1957 gave way to the new year, running weapons across the Tunisian frontier became the main effort of the A.L.N.; at one moment they totalled an average of a thousand a month. In September 1957, however, the French completed an imposing *cordon sanitaire* the length of the Tunisian border, the Morice Line, named – like its rather less successful predecessor, the Maginot Line – after the current Minister of Defence. Most of the heavy fighting now took place on the frontier rather than in the interior as A.L.N. *katibas* attempted to force their way through the barrages of electrified wire, minefields and radar alarm systems, frequently at appalling cost. By the spring of 1958 the balance of the war was, on the whole, a negative one for the F.L.N. – certainly as far as the interior was concerned. In the cities terrorism had been defeated; in the *bled* operational military successes were few and far between, and morale was down; on the frontiers there was costly stagnation. It continued to be a time of setback and failure within Algeria, but of greater success abroad – and, with historic consequences, the former was the fact most tantalisingly visible to the French army commanders on the spot. Here was the basic contrast: France was strong, militarily, in Algeria, but weak, politically, at home; the F.L.N. was weak, militarily, at home, but strong politically, abroad.

Bella. Ait Ahmed, however, claimed to the author in 1986 that, following Abane's death, Ben Bella and the other four F.L.N. leaders then in the Santé Prison signed documents supporting his "execution"; only Ait Ahmed himself had refused, on the grounds that he was fundamentally opposed to all "liquidations". To Ait Ahmed, also, "Without Abane there would have been no F.L.N. – he was *the* political head." Speaking, again, to the author in 1986, Ben Bella himself insisted that he had denounced "the style of execution; Abane should have been judged by his peers. The G.P.R.A. was not consulted; I would have refused." He had, however, always been "against Abane; because of his arrogance – his humiliation of his allies – his choice of leaders, or reformists rather than revolutionaries. He was too authoritarian; he wouldn't take criticism. Algeria is still paying the price of Abane ..."

CHAPTER ELEVEN

The World Takes Notice

1956–1958

> In war opinion is nine parts in ten.
> Jonathan Swift

France discovers the war

IT was between 1957 and 1958 that the Algerian war became well and truly "internationalised"; though not entirely through the means envisaged by the authors of the Soummam Declaration when they stated this long-term objective in the autumn of 1955. The events of May 1958 were to fix it finally and ineradicably in the forefront of world attention. In France herself Janet Flanner had recorded in her *Paris Journal* the drabness of the eleventh V.E. Day parade of May 1956: "There were no colonial troops in the parade. . . . There were no regiments in red fezzes from Tunisia. . . . There were no white-capped, bearded Foreign Legionnaires, now fighting in Algeria, where all forms of horrible death are part of the war. . . ." Hitherto the war had received only relatively minor mention in her journals, and it was virtually the first time that its impact in metropolitan France seems to have made any kind of an impression on her. Then, only ten days later, had come the shocking headline news of the massacre of the twenty-one conscripts at Palestro. The Press had spared none of the details of the dreadful mutilations and tortures that had killed the boys, most of whom came from the Paris region. The meaning of the war had been brought home to French families in the most brutal possible way and, with the return of Mollet's *rappelés* after they had served their time in Algeria, the whole country found itself increasingly involved. There were those who were against the war because they detested its horrors, or because, as next-of-kin, they lived in dread lest their young men share the same fate as those at Palestro. But there were also many who had been seduced by Algeria, who had enjoyed the adventure of their time there – or who had discovered sympathy at the predicament of the *pieds noirs*, coupled with repugnance at the F.L.N. atrocities. The *rappelés* had now made the war a topic of constant debate; one of the first of them, Jean-Jacques Servan-Schreiber, had published a controversial book about it, and was to be prosecuted for his pains as a "demoraliser" of the war effort. Various journalists, like Robert Barrat, had popped up with "scoops" of interviews from the rebel camp; Barrat had been arrested for consorting with convicted criminals, such as Ouamrane, then released; his newspaper, the Leftish intellectual *France-Observateur*, was suppressed repeatedly. All of it was good publicity, both for the paper and the war. Then there was the awareness imposed by the shattering, ever-soaring costs of the war: one billion francs (£1m.) a day in May 1958.

Torture and the French conscience

What above all else, however, most potently imprinted the war upon the French consciousness, and conscience, were the revelations of torture that multiplied as the Battle of Algiers got under way. Revisiting France towards the end of 1956, a *pied noir* psychiatrist friend of Dr Frantz Fanon and fellow sympathiser with the F.L.N., Charles Geromini, noted with disgust how

> The Parisians cared for nothing but their outings, their theatres, their vacations prepared three months in advance. I came to detest them, to despise all those French who were sending their sons to torture in Algeria and who could only be interested in their little boutiques. . . .

But this was far from being entirely accurate, or fair. From January 1955 onwards François Mauriac, in the "Bloc-Notes" which he contributed for Servan-Schreiber's *L'Express*, had been hammering away at army excesses in Algeria, and had acquired a widening measure of support. In February 1957 *Témoignage Chrétien* published the "Muller Dossier", compiled by a *rappelé* killed in Algeria in which he and fourteen of his comrades denounced "degrading practices" they had witnessed. Another organ of Catholic protest against torture was the Comité de Résistance Spirituelle, founded among others by the popular Abbé Pierre. Then appeared Captain Pierre-Henri Simon's book, *Contre la Torture*. Simon was a Catholic writer who had spent five years in prisoner-of-war camps during the Second World War; shortly after his release he had visited Belsen and, shocked by the rejection of responsibility by the local Germans, he had said to himself, "May the good people of France never fall into such a moral degradation of this order!" Though Simon was in no way an apostle of withdrawal from Algeria, his book listed malpractices witnessed there, sternly denouncing them as well as the collective culpability of the army and nation at large. Also in 1957 appeared, with considerable *éclat*, Servan-Schreiber's own book, *Lieutenant en Algérie*, followed in 1958 by Alleg's *La Question*, with its harrowing account of his torture and the disappearance of Maurice Audin. A Comité Audin, formed as a consequence, persistently attacked similar cases of malpractice throughout the rest of the Algerian war. Although members of the Left liked to claim sole proprietary rights on the anti-torture campaign – often to further political aims – the refrain was also taken up by such papers as *Le Monde* (which, later in 1957, published the critical report of the Safeguard Commission formed under pressure from Teitgen) and *Le Figaro*.

As other countries have discovered since (not least Britain), it is always easier to be coolly censorious about the excesses of the forces of order when one is happily far removed from the tragic sights of the outrages, and unaffected by the horrors of mutilated children and pretty girls. Nevertheless, in March, disclosure of the "suicide" first of Ben M'hidi then of Ali Boumendjel provoked a major outrage in France. Boumendjel, the young Algerian lawyer, had been a popular figure at the Paris Bar with many French friends, and on hearing of his death his former mentor, René Capitant, Professor of Public Law at the University of Paris, informed the Minister of Education that he was suspending his courses. Next came the Bollardière "affair", with various members of the Mollet government – including Pineau, Mitterrand and Defferre – coming forward to defend the general sentenced to sixty days' arrest for his "revolt". There was further publicity when the writer and Resistance hero, Vercors, posted his Legion of Honour back to President Coty. All these pressures led Mollet to get up in the Assembly and, by subtle implication, dissociate himself from the excesses of Massu's paras, and in May he had instituted the Safeguard Commission. It was not only public revelations that brought the "gangrene" of torture home to France; the young men who had been forced to administer it brought it back in their own persons, profoundly – and often permanently – marked by their experiences. Vidal-Naquet quotes a letter from a young soldier:

> They used to ask for volunteers to finish off the guys who had been tortured (there are no marks left that way and so no danger of a witch-hunt later). I didn't like the idea—you know how it is—shooting a chap a hundred yards off in battle—that's nothing, because the guy's some way off and you can hardly see him. And anyway he's armed and can either shoot back or buzz off. But finishing off a defenceless guy just like that—No!... [but he finally yielded] ... He looked at me. I can see his eyes looking at me now. The whole thing revolted me. I fired. The other chaps finished off the rest. After that it wasn't so bad, but the first time ... I tell you that turned me up. ...

Vidal-Naquet also notes a poll conducted in 1960 by *La Vie Catholique* in which, in answer to the question "what has been the reader's worst experience" in Algeria, 126 referred to the hardships of war as such; whereas 132 specified atrocities committed by the French, or acts of torture heard about, witnessed, or participated in; against only six who had cited their own wounds.

A distinguished member of the Safeguard Commission, Robert Delavignette, wrote prophetically at the end of 1957:

That which is true for Algeria may very soon be true for France. . . . The most serious problem is not the atrocities themselves, but that as a result of them the state is engaged in a process of self-destruction. What we are witnessing in Algeria is nothing short of the disintegration of the state; it is a gangrene which threatens France herself. . . .

Yet, against this, what was surely a most healthy sign of the moral integrity of the French nation as a whole was the unremitting breadth of protest aroused by torture. Vidal-Naquet, himself a declared opponent of the established government, admits freely that "no country involved in similar horrors has ever permitted publication of such complete documentation on the subject". The vehemence of the public outcry, however, was also to have its repercussions in other directions. Army generals like General Allard, corps commander for the Algiers area and Massu's immediate superior, themselves immaculate of any reproach of association with torture, protested bitterly to the Ministry of Defence against the anti-army attacks in the Press. Their "incessant repetition", he wrote, "places at risk the morale of the army". All through the army in Algeria, and, of course, particularly among the paras who saw themselves as the principal target of such attacks, there was an increasingly savage feeling that they had been called in to carry out the dirty work of the civil authorities and were now being carted for it. Once again the plaint, "*On nous a fait le coup*", began to be heard in the messes. It was yet another brick in the wall of resentment and contempt rapidly rising against the politicians of the Fourth Republic.

Growth of anti-war faction

"Up to 1956," says Dorothy Pickles, "the only point on which virtually the whole of France was united was that Algerian independence was unthinkable and unmentionable." From 1957 onwards the torture controversy, the forcing of issues into the limelight through the Battle of Algiers, coupled with the unsettling effect on public opinion of feeble oscillations in the Algerian policy of successive governments, and a certain degree of ennui with the whole business, led to an increasing variety of dissentient voices. In February 1957, for instance, the august *Le Monde* had intoned against the breaking of the F.L.N.-sponsored general strike, declaring: "The right to strike is an essential right in the aggregate of fundamental democratic liberties." But, much as they might disagree on the means employed, the overwhelming, not so silent majority of the metropolitan French still held – and would continue to hold – the belief that independence for Algeria was "unthinkable and unmentionable". Even the powerful Communist bloc had frequently sided in the Assembly with the extreme Right and the "Algiers lobby" to thwart reformist measures of the government of the day.

Perhaps not untypical of the growing divisions in French society were those within the Left, where Sartre and Simone de Beauvoir had split with their venerated friend and ally, Camus, whom many had taken to be the hero, "Henri", of her great post-war novel, *Les Mandarins*. Condemning even-handedly the atrocities committed by both sides, Camus (in what was a thinly-veiled criticism of the more violently militant supporters of the F.L.N.) had attacked "a section of our opinion" which "thinks obscurely that the Arabs have acquired the right somehow to slit throats and to mutilate". Still declaring himself fundamentally opposed to any policy of independence leading to "the eviction of 1,200,000 Europeans from Algeria", by the beginning of 1958 he had come out in favour of a federalist solution, as recently propounded by a liberal professor of law at Algiers University, Marc Lauriol. The Lauriol Plan envisaged a federation within the framework of the French Commonwealth similar to the Swiss cantonal system. A newly constituted French parliament would be divided into two sections, the second of which would consist, in direct proportion to the two races in Algeria, of some hundred Muslim representatives to fifteen *pieds noirs*, and would have a complete say on anything to do with strictly Muslim affairs; both "sections" together, containing a representative majority of metropolitan French, would legislate on all matters concerning France and Algeria jointly. Like most such liberal schemes for Algeria, the Lauriol Plan might well have proved acceptable to moderate Muslims four years earlier, but was totally unacceptable to the *pieds noirs*. If such a solution were not now adopted, Camus concluded sombrely and prophetically, "Algeria will be lost and the consequences terrible, for the Arabs as for the French. This is the last warning that can be formulated, before lapsing into silence once more, by a writer dedicated over the past twenty years to the service of Algeria." The impatience of the Sartre–Beauvoir team at the liberalism of Camus (and, for that matter, of Germaine Tillion too) now overflowed. Already Simone de Beauvoir had been angered by his "civil truce" initiative of 1956 and later growled, "the humanist in him had given way to the *pied noir*". The final blow had come with Camus' statement on receiving the Nobel Prize (in 1957): "I love justice; but I will fight for my mother before justice." She was "revolted".

To Simone de Beauvoir and her world, the sight of French uniforms in the streets had by early 1958 come to have

> the same effect on me that swastikas once did ... those boys in their camouflaged battle uniforms, smiling and parading with bronzed faces and clean hands; those hands.... ... Yes, I was living in an occupied city, and I loathed the occupiers even more fiercely than I had those others in the forties. ...

Those who went quite so far in their passionate opposition to the war and their support for the F.L.N. were still in a tiny minority; those who stood basically for *Algérie française* were still in the huge majority; yet, by 1958, there was absolutely no mistaking the awareness of the war that had now come to roost in France.

The F.L.N. comes to France

There was yet another factor in this awareness, and possibly the only one that had been directly fostered by the F.L.N. This was its strategy of physically extending the war to the mother country; as, indeed, the I.R.A. were to follow in its footsteps in 1972. Already, in the early months of the Revolution, Simone de Beauvoir had recorded in her diary a change in external appearances of the Algerians in her neighbourhood:

> Leather-jacketed North Africans, looking very well-groomed, began to frequent the Café des Amis; all alcohol was forbidden; through the windows I could see the customers sitting down in front of glasses of milk. No more brawls at night. This discipline had been imposed by the F.L.N. militants.

Progressively, the F.L.N. had indeed begun to impose discipline upon the some four hundred thousand Algerian workers in metropolitan France. In November 1954 Messali's M.N.A. was strongly entrenched among this Algerian proletariat, particularly in the Paris region, and if there were still "brawls at night" these were generally an extension of the vendetta from Algeria, a settling of accounts between the F.L.N. and M.N.A. At first, it seemed as if the initiative lay with the M.N.A., but swiftly the F.L.N. – with its superior organisation – assumed the upper hand. Acting under the innocent-sounding name of the Fédération de France, the F.L.N. employed methods similar to those in Algeria: the collection of funds under pressure and threats from café and hotel owners, pimps and shopkeepers, as well as down to even the poorer manual workers; and the selective elimination of informers, M.N.A. cell-leaders, and "friends of France".

Up to the beginning of the Battle of Algiers, all specifically French targets had been assiduously eschewed. Then, in January 1957, Mohamed Lebjaoui was despatched to France to hot up the war there. Lebjaoui, it will be remembered, was the bourgeois "liberal" who had infiltrated Camus' "civil truce" movement in 1956 and already the previous year he had been pressing his friend Abane to launch a campaign in France "to lead French liberals to understand our struggle". Apart from intensifying the collection of funds, recruitment and the "acquiring" of Algerian officers in the French army (where Lebjaoui says his organisation was "spectacularly" successful), his orders were to set on foot a system of eye for an eye reprisals to avenge the death of any Muslim civilians in Algeria; and, finally, to effect the speedy "liquidation" of Messali Hadj himself. Lebjaoui says that he himself objected to both these measures, and in fact he was never to have the opportunity of implementing them. Instead, he says, his aim was "to carry the war to France, so that the French should discover just how painful the war was". By destroying métros and bus stations, they would "make the Parisian people go on foot, without killing a single person. I also wanted to burn down a forest for every one destroyed by the army in Algeria. But", he added, chuckling, "I am glad that I was arrested – perhaps otherwise I might not now be able to walk in the Bois de Boulogne!" (In fact, Lebjaoui was grabbed by the Paris police at the end of February, after less than two months' activity. He then set to organising the F.L.N. within the French prisons, but in all probability much exaggerated his own importance.

His successor, however, Omar Boudaoud, who held the leading role in France through to the end of the war, maintained and improved on Lebjaoui's groundwork with considerable efficiency; between May 1957 and May 1958 the F.L.N. extended its sway to embrace something like ninety per cent of the Algerians in France. Apart from one or two ineptly handled assassination attempts on *pied noir* notables – such as Senator Henri Borgeaud – in August 1958 there was a concerted wave of sabotage as a counterblast against the initial success of de Gaulle. But on the whole the Fédération de France was never to push the war of violence in France to the limit. Its principal contribution lay in the financing of the war. Through its well-organised system of collectors, it milked every Algerian in France on a sliding scale – 500 francs a month for students, 3,000 for workers to 50,000 and upwards for shopkeepers – which were often oppressively large sums in relation to their wretched pay packets. Already by the beginning of 1958 the total thus collected reached 600 million (old) francs (£600,000) a year and was soon exceeding the two-and-a-half milliard mark. Most of it was in grubby notes of small denominations, and their safe shipment out of France to where they could be used for the purchase of arms presented a major problem. Any Algerian acting as courier would immediately attract suspicion. It was here that Lebjaoui's relations with the French intellectual Left paid off.

The Jeanson network

One of his first contacts in France had been Francis Jeanson, Marxist, professor, writer, publisher and editor. During the war Jeanson had escaped into Spain to join the Free French but had been thrown into a concentration camp, which had ruined his health. On being released he had made his way to Algeria where he acquired many nationalist friends, and in 1955 he and his wife, Colette, had published a book, *L'Algérie hors la Loi*, fiercely critical of French policy. He was a close friend of Sartre, and author of a biography of him. But, though resounding in the written and spoken word about the Algerian war, neither of the Sartre ménage was prepared to follow through with action to the same extent as Jeanson.

"I shied away," admits Simone de Beauvoir. But during Jeanson's trial three years later Sartre was to declare, with some bravado, "If Jeanson had asked me to carry dispatch cases or give shelter to militant Algerians, and I had been able to do so without risk to them, I should have agreed to do so without hesitation. . . ." Following the arrest of Lebjaoui, Jeanson had spun together a remarkable network – reminiscent of the French Resistance – of no fewer than forty like-minded French men and women. For three years he operated, without receiving any pay or direct orders from the F.L.N. Jeanson's motives, as he explains them, were the "ignoble behaviour of the forces of order" that he had witnessed in Algeria between 1945 and 1954, and he did not want to be yet another of the French "theoreticians" always giving advice to the Algerians, of which they were tired. Jeanson admits, "Yes, the arms we financed might have been used to shoot French soldiers in the back," resorting to a *tu quoque* argument on F.L.N. atrocities. In a somewhat far-flung analogy, he claims that, just as Stalinist crimes were "made almost inevitable by the hostility of the entire world", so "the Algerians do what they can, starting from the unbelievable conditions in which *you* put them – or let them be put". In addition to sheltering F.L.N. militants on the run in France, by far the most important of the Jeanson network's functions was shipping out of the country the F.L.N. funds to Switzerland in suitcases stuffed with tatty, soiled notes. For three years, until his network was broken up, in what seems like extraordinary incompetence on the part of the French security services, Jeanson carried on with this traffic undisturbed, and in one year he managed to smuggle out ten billion francs. The money was deposited in Swiss banks, where it earned a helpful interest – to the disapproval of the pure-minded Boudaoud, who considered such capitalist jugglings to be "non-revolutionary". Some, but by no means all, of this Swiss money went to the purchase of arms for the F.L.N.; the fate of the remainder was to become one of the more bizarre postscripts to the Algerian war, still unconcluded to this day.

Mollet falls: France's twenty-two days without government

On 21 May 1957 Guy Mollet fell, after a turbulent run of sixteen months – the longest in the Fourth Republic. His fall had, in fact, been on the cards since two months previously when he had faced a vote of confidence on his Algerian policy. After more than a year in office he had sadly little to show; the first and major round in the Battle of Algiers had been won, but at a considerable cost in terms of public opinion, and meanwhile the war still ground on; the basic reforms that he and Lacoste had wanted to introduce had, as usual, been diluted by the *pied noir* lobby. He had stuck faithfully to his peace time-table of (1) cease-fire; (2) elections; (3) negotiations; but the F.L.N. had assiduously ignored the fly, and there were no longer any "third force" *interlocuteurs valables* to rise to it. On 21 March Mollet had scraped by with 221 votes to 188, with 110 abstentions, but he was living on borrowed time. Since Suez the Communists had withdrawn support from Mollet's Socialist coalition, and in May they were joined by the Right in attacking the government on the acute inflation that gripped France. ("The French", commented Mollet bitterly, "have the most stupid Right in the world.") For the first four months of 1957 the national deficit had risen to three times the total for the whole of 1955, and to meet it the government was forced to introduce such unpopular measures as an increase in the price of petrol and postage, and a thirty per cent surtax on dividends. Defending his economic policy at his thirty-fourth vote of confidence on 21 May, Mollet went down with 250 votes to 213 and seventy abstentions. With him departed the last chance of stable government under the Fourth Republic.

Though the immediate cause of his defeat was the financial crisis in France, as always the dominant background factor was Algeria. "It is one of the characteristics of our regime", remarked Jacques Soustelle in his book, *Aimée et Souffrante Algérie*, published that same year, "that no issue, however vital to the nation, is ever treated fundamentally and on its own account, but as a function of other questions and above all of the parliamentary situation". He went on to predict, with some accuracy, that Algeria would be lost "not from a collapse on the military front in Algeria, but on the interior front in France". Indeed, the fall of Mollet was to bring the spotlight once more to focus on all the confusions of issues, the self-divisions, oscillations of policy and fundamental weaknesses that were intrinsic to the Fourth Republic and were rapidly making France ungovernable. In the Assembly the solid Communist bloc, representing a fairly steady fifth of the electorate, was an ever-present ingredient in the paralysis of any consistent policy. Together with the extremists of the Right, their presence meant that consensus required the support of almost all other factions combined, and there were seldom issues simple or clear enough for this. Thus, repeatedly, a tiny minority of Poujadists and the "Algiers lobby" of maybe no more than ten deputies would suffice to swing an anti-reformist vote on Algeria. As Alfred Grosser notes in his *La IVe République et sa politique extérieure*, the essential tragedy of the French liberal conscience at this time was this: "To bring liberty to overseas people, there is no majority without Communists. But to defend the liberties that Communism seeks to destroy, the only majority is with those who refuse liberty to Asians and Africans. . . ."

Bourgès-Maunoury comes and goes

After twenty-two days of comings and goings at the Elysée and no government, Maurice Bourgès-Maunoury – Mollet's former Defence

Minister, aged only 43, an energetic and distinguished Second World War combatant – managed to form a ministry. Typical of the vagaries of Fourth Republic politics, his new Minister of Finance, Félix Gaillard, succeeded in getting the Assembly to swallow a Finance Bill even tougher than that which had torpedoed Mollet. As far as Algeria was concerned, Bourgès-Maunoury pressed ahead with the old mixture as before – the twin-headed policy of pacification and reform – but with perhaps a new sense of urgency. Lacoste remained in Algiers, and a new and vigorous Minister of Defence, André Morice, rushed forward the imposing barrage system on Algeria's frontiers that was to bear his name. Its object was to "contain" the war and check the increasing supply of arms and *djounoud*, particularly from the sanctuary of Tunisia. The rotund and aggressive "Bébé-lune" Lacoste was charged with speeding through the project of a *loi-cadre* for Algeria, initiated under the Mollet regime and now to be promulgated before the new autumn session of the United Nations, which threatened to be embarrassing for France.

The first attempt to provide Algeria with a political statute since the abortive one of 1947, the *loi-cadre*, which bore some affinity to the Lauriol Plan, prescribed a degree of autonomy for Algeria, with the country divided into between eight and ten self-governing territories. Each territory would have its own separate assembly proportionately representative (by and large) of the racial majority in that territory. Eventually the territories would be united, once overall peace was restored, presumably under Muslim majority rule. Apart from introducing a multiplicity of legislators and bureaucrats, the immediate weakness of the *loi-cadre* was that, to fill these legislatory seats, it would depend essentially on men of good will of the "third force", European and Muslim, who by now had become all but nonexistent. From the Muslim point of view, whereas in 1947 the *loi-cadre* might have been acceptable to a majority of moderate nationalists, and possibly even in 1954, by 1957 it was once more the old story of too little, too late, and promptly it received an unyielding "No" from the F.L.N. The *pied noir* attitude was, as always, that it threatened the integrity of French territory and that in any case there could be no talk of a political solution until the rebellion had been finally stamped out; and, of course, a Muslim-controlled legislature would be intolerable. Lacoste's popularity, momentarily high after the winning of the Battle of Algiers, slumped to zero. On 18 September a general strike was threatened in Algiers – this time by the *pieds noirs* – but was firmly suppressed by Massu and his paras. But, as usual, the *pied noir* refrain was taken up in Paris, and on the 30th the *loi-cadre* was rejected by the Assembly on a 279 to 253 vote, with Jacques Soustelle now playing a lead role in its defeat. Viewed in retrospect, the vote might well have represented the last chance of finding an Algerian solution within a French framework.

The defeat of the *loi-cadre* brought with it the fall of the Bourgès-Maunoury government and came a step closer to the demise of the Fourth Republic. There now ensued a leaderless crisis lasting thirty-five days. First Mollet, then Pleven, followed by Pinay, Robert Schuman and finally Mollet again, tried unsuccessfully to form governments. A wave of disgust with politicians as a whole such as had not been seen since the 1930s flowed across the country. Prices escalated, and strike after strike – the railways and métros, the posts and telegraphs, and electricity – paralysed the country. Finally Félix Gaillard, Bourgès-Maunoury's successful Finance Minister, accepted the unenviable mandate on 5 November. It was his thirty-eighth birthday, which made him the youngest of all the Fourth Republic's Premiers – and the last but one. On the 29th he miraculously succeeded in getting the Assembly to pass the *loi-cadre*, but severely trimmed so as to meet *pied noir* fears of being submerged by the Muslim majority, and thus making it even less acceptable to the latter. In London, in December, Prime Minister Macmillan noted in his journal: "France was back in a self-critical and hopeless mood, which expressed itself (as I had known so well in de Gaulle's time) by being as tiresome as possible to everyone else." This was a tiresomeness with which he would very soon be reacquainted.

Oil under the Sahara

In this mood of "hopelessness", and amid the last expiring "convulsions of this absurd ballet", as de Gaulle so scathingly dubbed the gyrations of the Fourth Republic, France – just like Britain in the bleak mid-1970s, reaching out desperately for her panacea under the North Sea – saw one transcending glimmer of hope. On 7 January 1958 the stopcocks opened at Hassi-Messaoud deep in the sands of the Algerian Sahara, and its first oil flowed towards France. Already in 1945 French oil companies had begun prospecting in the Sahara, and shortly after the beginning of the Algerian war a major strike was made at Edjelé on the Libyan frontier. With the opening up of the Hassi-Messaoud field, French oilmen predicted euphorically that they had at their fingertips resources similar to those of the Middle East.* From 5 million tons in the first year, 1958, it was reckoned production would reach 14 million in 1962, and that it would suffice to satisfy all France's oil requirements by 1980. With the menace that Suez presented to Middle East oil supplies, here was a glowing prospect of securing the nation's need for the future, as well as solving her acute balance of payments problem. Quite quietly, France now found herself with a new motive for winning the Algerian war that went far beyond

---

* In fact, it later turned out that these early estimates may have been considerably exaggerated. The greater value of her energy resources probably lies in Algeria's natural gas.

any consideration for the one million *pieds noirs*. During a private visit to the Sahara in March 1957, de Gaulle declared to French oilmen: "Here is the great opportunity for our country that you have brought into the world; in our destiny, this can change everything. ..." Though, earlier, he had confided gloomily to Raymond Tournoux: "You watch, the regime will lose the Sahara. It will also lose Alsace-Lorraine. Only the Auvergne will remain to us, because nobody will want it. .. !"

Little did he foresee that it would be under his regime that the Sahara would be lost. But not everybody in France reckoned, even at that early stage, that the Algerian oil was worth fighting the war for. In a booklet, *L'Algérie et la République*, published in the summer of 1958, Raymond Aron, the distinguished writer and contributor to the conservative *Le Figaro*, pointed out that the annual cost of the war "is more or less equal to ten times the profits which would be derived from twenty million tons of crude petroleum," and that "those who insist or suggest that Algerian autonomy would entail the loss of the petroleum for France are either ignorant or liars. ..." He predicted: "The best way for France to lose the Sahara oil is to want to keep it for herself."

Certainly, if it opened bright new prospects for France, at the same time the Saharan oil also opened yet another new dimension for the "internationalising of the Algerian problem". Henceforth it would focus with sharpest clarity the covetous eyes of the all-powerful Anglo-American oil interests on Algeria. Not always without reason, France would be nagged by suspicions that shady deals were being done with the F.L.N. behind her back, with a view to ensuring that her rivals got in on the ground floor in an independent Algeria. Edward Behr, who was a correspondent in France at the time, recalls how "for a brief spell officer-cadets in French military schools were systematically taught a course in 'American imperialism', and it was stated as an incontrovertible fact that the United States had designs on the newly discovered Saharan oil deposits". In addition to the "Anglo-Saxon" villains in this shadowy oil war, there was also Italy's maverick oil operator, the unpredictable Enrico Mattei, who was openly to supply the F.L.N. with money and arms in return for future "considerations". When Mattei's private plane crashed mysteriously in October 1962, there were strong rumours that, apart from such over-exposed candidates as the C.I.A., French operatives either from the O.A.S. – or even the official secret service, S.D.E.C.E. – might be responsible for his death.

Strained relations with the "Anglo-Saxons"

In the autumn of 1957 the French Press began to find relief from their own governmental worries by knocking hard such American discomfitures as the racial disorders in Little Rock, and the humiliation in space through Russia's launching of the first sputnik. It was predominantly Algeria that gave France this low threshold of irritability in the first instance – with oil always latent in the background, but there were other factors. If Prime Minister Macmillan could growl at French "tiresomeness", they also had cause to feel that – *vice versa* – France's principal allies were being extremely tiresome to her interests.

Specifically, during the brief regime of Félix Gaillard there was an angry flare-up over American and British arms sales to Tunisia. In the wake of Suez both countries had become anxious to repair fences with the Arab world, were increasingly concerned at the incipient flood of Soviet-bloc arms into the Middle East. The United States in particular was showing sensitivity to Arab charges that equipment (notably helicopters) she had supplied France for N.A.T.O. purposes was being massively used to crush the F.L.N. Thus it was decided, by way of a counterbalance, to sell a limited quantity of small arms to the infant Tunisian army, rather than risk Bourguiba turning to the Russian market – as Nasser had done with the Aswan dam. Already there had been angry charges in the French army about British duplicity following the capture of Lee-Enfield rifles in the hands of the F.L.N., although these had in fact been obtained (at last) through the Egyptians out of the vast quantities of material left behind at Suez, and news of the Tunisian deal immediately provoked a violent storm in France. Le Figaro rated it "an odious blow by our allies", while the right-wing Aurore at once detected that *l'explication pétrolière* was only too evident; strong riot squad detachments were sent to protect the American and British embassies, and floods of letters poured in to them from parents expressing anger and shock that the Tunisian arms would inevitably end up killing their sons in Algeria. Premier Gaillard declared bitterly that, "If the Atlantic Pact should fall to dust one day, we will know the artisans of its failure"; in his memoirs Harold Macmillan admits, retrospectively, "I think we made a serious error, at a critical moment when France was already nervous and uncertain.... At the time I did not fully realise the true situation in France." And early in 1958 he was warning the obdurate Dulles "that if the over-sensitive French were upset they might well use the excuse to wreck the prospects of the European Free Trade Area". The warnings of both premiers proved all too true.

Britain and America sensitised to the war

Disheartening to France as it was encouraging to the F.L.N. in their campaign for "internationalisation" was the growing awareness of the war in both the United States and Britain. Inevitably this brought hostility to France's role in it. As in France, the Battle of Algiers had done much to publicise the war, and the French anti-torture campaign had had its echo in Anglo-Saxon liberal opinion. In London, in February 1958, Labour delegations demonstrated three days in a row in front of the French

Embassy to denounce the conduct of Djamila Bouhired's trial and demand reprieve of her death sentence. The *Observer* was ticked off privately by the French government for its critical articles by Nora Beloff and John Gale. On 1 April "Algeria Day" received unprecedented support from top Socialists. Mrs Barbara Castle explained pedantically that terrorism was the result of repression, not its cause; and Anthony Wedgwood Benn declared that the French must permit negotiations to bring an end to the war, with the right of self-determination for Algeria.

Across the ocean George Meany, the powerful boss of the American Federation of Labour, had protested to Mollet about the arrest of Algerian trade union leaders in 1956 and, it was reported, asked that Lacoste be disavowed in the name of socialism. More and more enterprising American correspondents were finding their way into the F.L.N. camp, and writing articles sympathetic to the Algerian cause, and in January 1958 two issues of the prestigious *Saturday Evening Post* were confiscated by the French police on this score. Herb Greer, an American journalist who made two clandestine visits to the F.L.N., had already had films taken by him televised across America. As well as telling harrowing tales of French brutality, he revealed to the American public disquieting instances of Algerian mistrust. One *djoundi* in the field is quoted as saying: "I don't trust America and I don't know any Arab who does.... You want to be friends with France and so you give them guns and helicopters to fight against us. But you're also afraid we might win, so just in case you express sympathy, unofficially of course...." Repeatedly Greer encountered suspicion that the Americans were after Algerian oil. Similar plaints were later recorded by Richard and Joan Brace: "on the one hand the United States helps us through the U.N. with wheat and food, and on the other furnishes her ally, France, with the finest military hardware – helicopters, napalm, everything, to kill us off. Which way do the Americans want us, dead or alive?" The essential paradox imposed an unpalatable burden upon the conscience of America which, in those days of naïve idealism as yet untarnished by Cuba or Vietnam, still sought to be beloved of all peoples in the world.

Yazid and Chanderli in New York

Through 1957 and 1958, official American policy gradually began to change under the unofficial pressures upon it. Another American correspondent, Michael Clark of the *New York Times* (who supported *Algérie française*), recalls how the "courteous briefing" handed out to itinerant journalists by American diplomats now usually took the line that their function was "to ease the French out as painlessly as possible". At home, policy had been much influenced by the vigorous campaign of the F.L.N. at the United Nations. Here the F.L.N. were fortunate in the exceptionally good choice they had made by sending in 1956 their two best-fitted talents to New York: Abdelkader Chanderli and M'hamed Yazid. Of middle-class origins, Chanderli had fought in the French campaign of 1940; escaped to Britain; joined de Gaulle; landed in Algiers in 1942; fought through Italy and ended the war in Stuttgart. From then until 1948 he had reported on Palestine for a French newspaper, and the opening of the revolution in 1954 had found him working for U.N.E.S.C.O. in Montevideo. Returning to Cairo, where he worked on Ben Bella's external delegation, he and Yazid had been sent to New York after the hijacking of Ait Ahmed, the representative-designate, in 1956, and he was to stay there for the next nine years. Yazid had been educated at university in Paris, where he became Secretary-General of the Association of Muslim Students in France. He had joined the P.P.A. at the time of Sétif in 1945, but after violent disagreement with Messali had immediately switched to the F.L.N. in November 1954, and had made his name at the Bandung Conference of April 1955 where the F.L.N. first achieved international recognition. Like Chanderli, a master at public relations, Yazid in September 1958 was to become first Minister of Information of the newly-formed Provisional Government (G.P.R.A.).

Both were extensively-travelled cosmopolitans, popular and at home in salons across the world; good talkers (Yazid often to excess) with perfect command of English, a light-handed sense of humour and easy-going manners. Both had married attractive foreign wives; Chanderli first to a Frenchwoman, then to a beautiful Italian in New York; Yazid to an American, Olive, who helped open many doors to the Algerians in the United States. Both seemed the very antithesis of the hard-eyed revolutionaries and rude men of the maquis bickering among themselves in Tunis. Chanderli exuded a mixture of humanitarian intellectualism and personal well-being, reminding one of a Roy Jenkins (to whom, indeed, he bore some passing physical resemblance), and he achieved early success on the American scene by cultivating liberal "egg-heads" like J. K. Galbraith of Harvard. And through them he became friendly with an up-and-coming young Democrat Senator, John F. Kennedy.

Operating with a tiny staff out of thoroughly bourgeois quarters on East 56th Street, Chanderli and Yazid tirelessly stomped the university campuses, toiled away at the media, lobbied opinion-makers and politicians. "I used the U.S. public relations technique to my own advantage," Chanderli claimed to the author: "I always tried to tell the truth, at least more truth than the French, and let the French get caught out in their own lies." Sagely he instructed his own staff: "The United States is the land of truth, so give it the truth. But that of others, of the French who are disgusted by the war, and we'll add no commentary." Thus the Algerians in New York accorded the maximum publicity to the anti-torture outcries in France, to the protests of General Bollardière, Professor Capitant and Maître Teitgen. The response was encouragingly favourable. Yazid played hard on America's hypersensitivity in the "cold war" to the growing Russian competition in the Arab world, and when asked in a 1957 television interview, "Is it true that the F.L.N. is Communist and that the Eastern Bloc is furnishing it with a lot of arms?" he replied: "We are far from being Communist, but when one is at war one needs arms. We prefer Western arms, and if I were to find someone who could procure us any, I can't see any reason for refusing them." Immediately a flow of offers from Western arms dealers poured in. By comparison, French public relations seemed maladroit, constrained and defensive. Repeatedly Yazid won points when Soustelle was instructed to decline his challenge to a public debate about Algeria on American television. Jacques Soustelle complained that, when sent to New York by Mollet in 1956, he had found in the French delegation offices a cupboard stuffed with unused material and photographs on F.L.N. atrocities in Algeria, sent by Lacoste for propaganda purposes at the United Nations. "But these were never used by us, for fear of offending the niceties of diplomacy. So how could you win the diplomatic war when you were fighting with your hands tied like this?"

Outrages of terrorism by the F.L.N. such as Mélouza and the Algiers bombings would indeed produce a momentary revulsion in the United States, but the eventual reaction would, perversely, somehow end up as one of irritation against France as being responsible for the war in which such horrors could take place; a psychological process not dissimilar to that in the 1970s where the spate of Palestinian hijacking and terrorism against innocent targets did nothing to make the world less hostile towards Israel. One of the F.L.N. lobbyists at the United Nations is quoted by Edward Behr as saying: "You must realise that every time a bomb explodes in Algiers we are taken more seriously here."

Support from Senator John F. Kennedy

The F.L.N. had registered its first success at the United Nations in September 1955 by getting the Algerian issue tabled, thereby administering a first rude shock to the French. In Soustelle's view, this had been "worth more than a convoy of arms" to the rebellion. Seen purely in overt terms of United Nations votes collected, however, 1957 was a disappointment for the F.L.N. despite the intense activities of their representatives there. French diplomacy had fought a hard struggle to maintain that Algeria was an "internal affair" for France, and therefore the United Nations was not competent to deal with it. Were she to be overruled, Foreign Minister Pineau warned Dulles in January, France would have no option but to walk out. Torn between increasing pressure to mollify the Arab world and back Algerian independence, and an anxiety not to hit a tottering ally too hard, the United States agreed to block a tough Afro-Asian resolution to bring the issue of independence directly into the General Assembly. At the February session, to which the F.L.N.'s abortive general strike launching the Battle of Algiers had been geared, the powerful Political Committee, by a narrow vote of 34 to 33 with 10 abstentions, threw out the Afro-Asian resolution, and it was defeated once again in December 1957. Instead, a watered-down text was introduced into the Assembly, piously expressing: "the hope that, in a spirit of co-operation, a peaceful, democratic and just solution will be found by appropriate means, in conformity with the United Nations' charter".

Below the surface, however, international victories were being chalked up by the F.L.N.; not least of all in the shifting of American policy. At the end of February 1957 an Arab "summit" composed of Syria, Jordan, Saudi Arabia and Egypt convened in Cairo and, in a first display of Middle East unity, declared its total support for the Algerian cause. All this was duly noted in Washington, and the following month Vice-President Nixon arrived in Tunis to help celebrate the first anniversary of her independence. Following his meetings with Bourguiba, Nixon proposed to President Eisenhower a referendum whereby the Algerians could choose freely between the *loi-cadre* statute being prepared by Lacoste, or total independence. Then, in July, Chanderli's influential friend in the Democratic opposition, Senator John F. Kennedy, rose to make an important pronouncement in the United States Senate. He challenged Eisenhower and Dulles "to place the influence of the United States behind efforts... to achieve a solution which will recognise the independent personality of Algeria and establish the basis for a settlement interdependent with France and the neighbouring nations". He accused United States policy of representing "a retreat from the principles of independence and anticolonialism"; and, elsewhere, that it "furnished powerful ammunition to anti-Western propagandists through Asia and the Middle East". No speech on foreign affairs by Senator Kennedy attracted more attention, both at home and abroad, and under such pressure United States official policy on Algeria now began to shift. Henceforth, instead of backing France at the United Nations, the United States would abstain. It was a serious blow for French policy, and a triumph for Chanderli, Yazid and the F.L.N. Finally, at the end of December, another success was registered by the Algerians when, at a new Afro-Asian conference hosted by Nasser in Cairo, they were accepted on an equal footing among the sovereign powers. At the same time an important first contact was made through their delegations with the U.S.S.R. and Red China.

Bourguiba

In all the F.L.N.'s aspirations for international influence over the period, there was no more important element than the dynamic figure of Habib Bourguiba. With blazing blue eyes and prognathous features that give him an appearance of determined aggressiveness, the Tunisian leader was as unashamedly unretiring and as dedicated to the "cult of the personality" as the F.L.N. was opposed to it. The world produced few more remarkable statesmen in the turbulent third quarter of the twentieth century; still in power after two unbroken decades of paternalistic though moderate rule, in terms of years at the helm Bourguiba is surpassed by few modern statesmen. But only a remarkable leader could have survived the powerful opposing pressures exerted on him: on the one hand by the French, at various times apparently poised to re-occupy his infant state;* on the other by the F.L.N., its more extreme moods backed up by the presence on Tunisian soil of seasoned, well-equipped *djounoud* that would soon be several times stronger than Tunisia's own embryo army (hence, partly, the urgency of Bourguiba's plea for Anglo-American arms). In addition, there was always the arch-enemy, Nasser, subverting from the sidelines.

Under these constant pressures Bourguiba was to remain unswervingly constant to his two principal ideals (though they were often thrown into mutual conflict); to gain independence for Algeria, while retaining a generally pro-French and pro-Western stance. Despite being imprisoned by the French during the Tunisian struggle for independence,† he seldom wavered in his francophilia, and his repeated services as a bridge between the Arabs and the Western world deserve an even greater place in history than they have achieved heretofore. Nevertheless, without Bourguiba in Tunisia, the F.L.N. would probably have been crushed – militarily – before the fall of the Fourth Republic. Though Morocco and its king, Mohammed V, were also of great importance throughout to the F.L.N. war effort, for both political and geographical reasons Bourguiba always took pride of place. To the Algerians, Bourguiba fulfilled five functions: he provided

1. The most convenient and safe route for arms supplies.
2. The most convenient and safe sanctuary for A.L.N. troops, training, resting or preparing for operations inside Algeria.
3. Military and political headquarters for the C.C.E. in exile.
4. A persuasive and articulate ally in international forums.
5. A potential bridge for negotiations with the French.

The rage of the French army in Algeria was mounting increasingly

* According to Bourguiba (in an interview with the author), there existed just such a secret contingency plan under the code-name "Charrue Longue", and Massu had once declared that he would "sleep in Bourguiba's bed".
† In his sumptuous presidential office in Carthage Palace he still leads visitors with great pride to a frame on the wall containing his prison *fiche*; while in the neighbouring Council Chamber busts of the four historic heroes of Tunis – Jugurtha, Hannibal, St Augustine and Ibn Khaldoun – are dominated by an immense portrait of the President.

against functions 1 and 2. The F.L.N. hardliners condemned as the sin of *bourguibisme* any quest for compromise peace solutions and criticised the Tunisian leader's bourgeois style of rule at home. He, in return, barred any relations between his Néo-Destour and the F.L.N. out of fear of contagion from their "revolutionary socialism". The F.L.N. leaders chafed when he intervened to bring the unruly A.L.N. camps under his control; yet both sides had to recognise the over-riding importance of Bourguiba.

Sakiet blasts Bourguiba's olive branch

Thus, armed with this vast influence, in October 1957 Bourguiba tried – once more in conjunction with King Mohammed V, their joint efforts of the previous autumn having been blighted by the hijacking of Ben Bella – to force France and the F.L.N. into negotiations. Already, at the time of the March independence celebrations in Tunis, Bourguiba had been mooting the idea of a Maghreb confederation associated with France, in which Algeria would be a self-governing and equal member; which, could it have proved workable, would have offered a generous and far-sighted solution. But it was sharply rejected by both parties. Now Bourguiba and King Mohammed returned to the theme, but this time offering themselves as mediating agents under the umbrella of the United Nations. The beleaguered Premier Gaillard replied with a brusque turn-down, repeating the formula of each of his Fourth Republic predecessors since Mendès-France: "Whatever the terms and the periphrasis, we shall never accept Algerian independence." Bourguiba responded by requesting to purchase arms from the United States and Britain, and then, on 8 February 1958, an incident took place that, in the most literal sense, blew sky-high all Bourguiba's latest hopes of a compromise peace.

Over the previous six months there had been more than eighty shooting incidents on the Tunisia–Algeria frontier. These had culminated on 11 January in the ambushing of a strong French patrol by F.L.N. bands operating in the unusual strength of a *failek* (a battalion, or three hundred men). The band had come across from Tunisia (allegedly driven to the frontier in Tunisian army trucks), laid their well-prepared ambush, in which fifteen French troops were killed, then escaped back into Tunisia, taking four French prisoners with them, before a riposte could be mounted. A few days later, in this same sector of the frontier, an investigating French plane was shot down by machine-gun fire from a Tunisian village called Sakiet, which gave every appearance of being a strong F.L.N. base. Angry warnings emanated from the French authorities, but early on the morning of 8 February another French plane was hit by machine-gun fire from Sakiet, and made a forced landing behind the Morice Line. Three hours later a squadron of American-built B.26 bombers appeared overhead and flattened the village with a massive bombing retaliation.

It happened to be a market day, and – as has occurred many times since in the course of Israeli reprisal raids against Al Fatah camps across the Lebanese frontier – the bombs and rockets hit a school and hospital (which the Tunisians claimed was well marked with a red cross visible from the air), as well as the F.L.N. base. Some eighty people, including a number of women and children, were killed. Foreign journalists were immediately ferried by the Tunisians to the still smoking scene of the raid; "We visited the wreck of a schoolroom," wrote Herb Greer. "A bomb had blown it apart in the middle of a lesson, just as the teacher had begun to sketch an airplane on the blackboard to illustrate her lecture. The blackboard was still intact and the sketch still there, pitifully crude and unfinished. . . ." The Tunisians made sure the journalists missed nothing. Hundreds of photographs were produced: "a naked child perched on a hospital bed, staring curiously at the camera, legs carefully spread out to show an obscene mutilated stump. . . ."

Angrily, Bourguiba ordered the immediate evacuation of the French garrisons still in Tunisia under treaty, in the meantime blockading them in their barracks, and accused France of "aggression" before the Security Council. Dismayed at the disarray of an ally, the United States and Britain offered to send a "good offices" mission, comprised of the veteran Robert Murphy and Harold Beeley of the Foreign Office, to heal the breach with Tunisia. The offer was accepted by Félix Gaillard but widely criticised by the French Press, who derisively dubbed the envoys *Messieurs les bons offices*. Their brief, ostensibly, was to restore relations between Paris and Tunis, regularise the presence of the French garrisons in Tunisia, and supervise the frontier. But the United States government made little secret of its hopes that the "good offices" mission might also provide a first foot in the door to direct peace negotiations between the F.L.N. and France. That France should even have accepted the principle of such foreign arbitration was, in F.L.N. eyes, something of a victory in itself. *Messieurs les bons offices* bustled back and forth between Paris and Tunis, but nothing in fact came of the mission. Bourguiba for one (under strong pressure from the F.L.N.) firmly refused any kind of international supervision of his western frontier. Its functions were in any case soon to be overtaken by events in France.

No effort of Yazid or Chanderli, or of the whole F.L.N. leadership to date, could have done more to "internationalise" the war than the French bombing of Sakiet. It also set in motion the chain of events that led directly to the final disintegration of the Fourth Republic. For what preceded this gross miscalculation, and its potent consequences, one must return to the French army in Algeria.

CHAPTER TWELVE

Le Dernier Quart d'Heure

1957–May 1958

> It is not out of any love for the Arabs or the French Algerians that I am fighting, but because it is no longer permitted to us to lose this war. Beaten, we would be the torturers of Algiers, Fascist bands in the service of the big colonialists. Victors, they will leave us alone....
>
> "Capitaine Esclavier" in Jean Lartéguy's *The Praetorians*, 1963

The Battle of Agounennda

DURING the months of 1957 that the Battle of Algiers lasted, apart from the regular interception of frontier-crossing bands and gun-runners there had been few military operations of major importance in the interior. The exception had been in Wilaya 4, or the Algérois department that surrounds the capital, embracing the rich Mitidja plains and running up into the wild Atlas ranges to the south. Security forces in this area had been substantially thinned out in order to meet the needs of Massu in the city, and in this semi-vacuum the Wilaya 4 chiefs had been urged to intensify activities so as to draw off the heat from Yacef and his besieged cadres in the Casbah. Before the Battle of Algiers the Wilaya effectives had been hard-pressed by Bigeard's crack 3rd Para Regiment, at the same time as losing political headway through the growing success of Lacoste's S.A.S. system. But the withdrawal of Bigeard had afforded them a period of relative respite in which they had reorganised to some effect.

For the time being, the Wilaya had assembled perhaps the most impressive command structure of any in Algeria, headed by an unusually cultured maquisard, Colonel Si Sadek (his real name, Slimane Dehiles), who had taken over the command from Ouamrane on his removal to Tunis and the C.C.E. Sadek's political chief was Si M'hamed (his real name Ahmed Bougarra), who, though aged only twenty-seven, was considered to be possibly the most astute political brain in the Wilayas at that time. Working with him was Omar Oussedik, in charge of intelligence, a militant Marxist and friend of Frantz Fanon, and Si Salah (real name Mohamed Zamoun), in charge of communications. The military formations were commanded by Si Lakhdar, a mason who had achieved rapid promotion through his reputation for courage and who had – together with Ali Khodja, the A.L.N. leader responsible for the Palestro "massacre" of the twenty-one French reservists in 1956 – created the A.L.N.'s hard-hitting "zonal commando" units. Under him was Si Azedine (real name Rabah Zerrari), formerly a humble coppersmith and currently commanding the commando which had taken its name from Ali Khodja. Not politically orientated, Azedine was first and foremost a guerrilla fighter of outstanding toughness and endurance. At the beginning of May 1957 his "Ali Khodja" commando had ambushed a Spahi unit, killing some sixty of them for a cost of seven dead *djounoud*. Disengaging, the commando had been strafed by French aircraft and Azedine had had his right forearm shattered by a 50 mm. calibre bullet. For two days he lay in a coma, apparently half-blinded with pain, but had refused the ministrations of even the primitive A.L.N. field hospital, dressing and removing splinters of bone from the wound himself. Exactly two years previously he had been smuggled into Algiers to have a painful knee wound treated by the pro-F.L.N. French doctor, Pierre Chaulet.

In the spring of 1957 Wilaya 4 had achieved a character all of its own by replacing the hitherto rigidly hierarchical structure by a system of "democratic equality" and political commissars, for which Si M'hamed's influence was largely responsible. Bearing a close resemblance to Marxist techniques, though none to Marxist political ideology, Si M'hamed's system was largely designed to counter the effectiveness in political warfare of Lacoste's S.A.S. teams that had become progressively entrenched in the Algérois villages. Altogether Wilaya 4 was demonstrating a new skill in revolutionary warfare, in all its aspects, that caused the French command considerable concern. With his wound still unhealed, Azedine followed up his success against the Spahis by ambushing a battalion of Tirailleurs, killing some ten – including their French captain – and causing numerous others to defect, together with their weapons. Bigeard was now rushed back to the *bled*, having won the first round of the Battle of Algiers, and with a vast sigh of relief at quitting the detested, grimy role of policeman in the city. Accurate intelligence reports revealed that two of Si Lakhdar's *katibas*, or companies, totalling 300 men, were heading westwards towards Médéa for a meeting with Azedine, following his successful ambush of the Tirailleurs. A major politico-military show of strength was then intended. Bigeard acted on this intelligence with utmost speed. During the night of 22–23 May he placed his paras astride the F.L.N.'s axis of movement near a small mountain village called Agounennda that lay south of the road from Blida to L'Arba. Employing a favourite technique, he sited his battle headquarters post on a commanding height with his companies deployed in an arc around him, his 3 Company in a rather more isolated position to the north. Close by his headquarters was a support company, ready to be helicoptered in as a stopper in the bottle to any point in the area where the main F.L.N. force might run into the net he had strung out.

The companies concealed themselves so as to be virtually undetectable among the rock and scrub of the mountainside, and settled down to one of those agonising night watches so familiar to both sides in the Algerian war. Broken up into small packets each of five groups, then a space, then another five groups, Azedine's commando ran into Bigeard's isolated 3 Company early on the morning of the 23rd. Apparently tipped off by a shepherd look-out, Azedine realised Bigeard's intentions and decided to move the main force round to the north of 3 Company in its exposed position and then take the whole ambush from the rear. For a brief period the 100-strong para company found itself dangerously outnumbered by 300 of Si Lakhdar's and Azedine's *djounoud*. Urgently the company commander radioed Bigeard "Send the *ventilos* (helicopters)." With the rapidity typical of Bigeard, the *ventilos* picked up the support company troops, dropped them without landing from six feet above the ground on a crest behind Azedine's attacking force, then flew back for another load. Within less than half an hour two whole companies had been shifted into position, in a manoeuvre that Bigeard had practised to perfection for this kind of eventuality. The stopper was well and truly in the bottle.

Meanwhile, Azedine had committed the fundamental tactical error of taking his force along the bed of the *oued*, instead of the crests of the hills, with the result that the paras were able to occupy the high ground overlooking the F.L.N. trapped below. Nevertheless, attacked by ground-strike aircraft and all the superiority of weapons in the French armoury, Azedine's men fought back with ferocious tenacity. The pitched battle raged for three days, with the F.L.N. trying to infiltrate through Bigeard's lines in small packets at night. With an area thirty kilometres square of particularly broken country covered by one solitary regiment, it proved impossible to intercept all of them. By the morning of the 26th the firing had virtually ceased. When the counts came in, the F.L.N. dead were listed at ninety-six and only nine prisoners; French losses totalled eight dead and twenty-nine wounded. But to Bigeard's disappointment only forty-five weapons had been recovered; Azedine's men had carried off most of the weapons of the fallen just as they had removed their wounded.

Militarily speaking, the encounter at Agounennda – a model of well-applied intelligence and hard-hitting mobility – looked like a triumph for the French. Yet it was an incomplete success; the well-laid ambush had not succeeded in wiping out the main body of the force trapped in it. Ideally set up for the French style of warfare, it was also the kind of opportunity that would seldom occur again. Therefore, while the French military might deduce from Agounennda as from the Battle of Algiers that the F.L.N. could never beat them in a clear confrontation, a more dispassionate observer might have questioned whether, if Bigeard's crack unit could not score a *total* victory on its own terms, there was much hope for winning more elusive engagements in a war that might be indefinitely prolonged. On the other side the conclusions drawn were that Agounennda was the kind of engagement the A.L.N. could only lose, and lose heavily, and that henceforth it must be avoided at all costs. The success of the Soustelle–Lacoste S.A.S. system in the villages (there were now nearly 600 S.A.S. administrators scattered across Algeria) and of the harsh regroupment policy also meant that the Wilayas were finding it increasingly difficult to obtain succour from the local populations for their military operations. Instead of relying on the *mechtas* and *douars* for supply depots and refuges, they were forced to use the caves that riddle the calcareous mountains of Algeria like the holes in a Gruyère cheese. As Abd-el-Kader had done before them, the A.L.N. exploited these natural caches with utmost ingenuity, but they could seldom suffice for sustaining any major operation. Thus, in the interior, the small hit-and-run actions would be resumed, while in the inviolate sanctuaries behind the Tunisian and Moroccan frontiers new *katibas* and *faileks* could be prepared, armed and trained, and then sent over into Algeria when the time was ripe.

The harkis

As the desired "killing" battles like Agounennda became the exception rather than the rule, so the minds of France's army planners turned more and more to "special" operations – of varying kinds and with mixed results. There were the *commandos noirs* of General de Bollardière, lightly equipped semi-guerrilla detachments with the role of "nomadising" with the Muslim populations in the *bled*. Contrary to the sadly accepted norm in the army, they pledged themselves to regard every Muslim "as a friend, and not as a suspect, except when proved to the contrary". With this policy of never firing first, they were often involved in situations of high risk – as well as being viewed with some suspicion by the conventional-minded authorities. Then 1957 saw the development on a serious scale of *harki* units, comprised of what the French considered "loyal" Algerians – "traitors" to the F.L.N. These were principally the brainchild of the ethnologist, Jean Servier, whose defence of Arris on the first day of the war was, it will be remembered, largely facilitated by exploiting the rivalries of two Auresian tribes. After noting instances where villagers in the Orléansville area had killed F.L.N. scouts with hatchets, Servier – despite considerable official opposition – had gained permission initially to create "light companies" from some thousand men, the able-bodied and trustworthy defectors from the F.L.N., or *anciens combattants*. Servier insisted that his *harki* units should be based near their homes, on the sensible grounds that a Muslim soldier away from his family was at the mercy of a threatening letter, and would desert – quite naturally – to save his wife and children.

Knowing every track in their neighbourhood and armed with shotguns loaded with heavy shot designed for wild boar, a terrible weapon at fifty yards' range in the forest, Servier's *harkis* soon proved a redoubtable instrument for tracking down the F.L.N. News of the good pay and conditions of the *harkis* spread like wildfire, and loyal *caids* – like the Bachaga Boualem, dedicated to the cause of *Algérie française* and in whose fiefdom the *maquis rouge* had been rounded up – came forward to form what were in effect yet more private armies. In the two years from January 1957 the numbers of *harki* "self-defence" villages rose from 18 to 385, and their total manpower was eventually to reach 60,000. Perhaps surprisingly, one American professor, stressing the equality and fairness with which the Algerians serving in the French army were treated, states categorically that "At no time from 1954 to 1962 did the numbers of Algerians fighting with the A.L.N. for independence match the number of Algerians fighting on the French side."

The value and reliability of the *harki* units varied enormously, generally in direct proportion to the quality of the S.A.S. administrator under whose jurisdiction they came. Jean Servier describes one disillusioning debacle concerning a *harki* he had created himself, where the official report stated baldly: "The treachery of elements of a *harki* facilitated an ambush against the forces of order." Servier flew in by helicopter, and what he discovered was as follows: the local S.A.S. *képi bleu* had been sacked by the military command which had disapproved of his methods. Since then a French artillery unit had gone out on patrols, quite ineffectively, using the same route every day, and employing the *harkis* as transport troops to lug munitions and radios – instead of searching the ravines and mountain crests, tasks for which they were formed and at which they excelled. Not surprisingly, in the middle of one heavy lunch hour the French gunners were taken unawares by rebels attacking from a high ridge. They panicked and scattered into the forest, while only the *harkis* held their ground. When reinforcements arrived all the *harkis* were found dead, one machine-gunner having felled fourteen rebels; in a burnt *mechta* were the remains of the French gunners who had surrendered and had had their throats slit and been thrown into the fire. Yet the *harkis* were blamed for "treachery"; in despair Servier bemoaned "the uselessness of all my efforts, all the sacrifices that I had imposed on the men that France was going to abandon".

"Oiseau Bleu" and other "special operations"

It was a regular complaint of the *harki* leaders, like the Bachaga Boualem, that the French authorities too often showed themselves less than half-hearted towards them, that they were refused automatic weapons, and that the "loyal" *caids* – always priority targets for the F.L.N. – should have had to protect themselves with pistols and shotguns. But mistrust was part of the game; and not always without reason. In one of their first "special operations", a shadowy and highly secret enterprise with the code-name *Oiseau Bleu*, the French had already had their fingers painfully burned. Exploiting the age-old hatreds between Kabyles and Arabs, an anti-F.L.N. guerrilla had been formed in Kabylia (during the Soustelle era and apparently, in the first instance, under police auspices), from Kabyle separatists. Known as "Force K", it had risen to over a thousand men clamouring for more effective arms, and responsibility for it had passed to the army. In the spring of 1956 a Captain Hentic was summoned to Army G.H.Q. in Algiers and placed in charge of "controlling" the operation. Hentic was a member of the cloak-and-dagger 11th Shock unit, which had just scored a triumph in the secret war by blowing up Ben Boulaid with a booby-trapped radio. He himself had recently arrived in Algeria, convalescent after serving in Indo-China, and from an early stage would be involved with Jean Servier in the formation of the *harkis*.* Initially, says Hentic, the impression he received of "Force K" was quite good, and an arsenal of some 300 rifles and sub-machine-guns was distributed to it. But there was immediately an element of mystery about its highly secret operations; they never seemed to be witnessed by any French units in the neighbourhood; bodies of F.L.N. rebels claimed were seldom identified; and at each receipt of a report of the elusive Krim's whereabouts he had moved on by the time "Force K" reached the spot.

Captain Hentic's suspicions grew. Jean Servier, brought in to advise, spotted with the expertise of the ethnologist that some of the "Force K" Kabyles did not come from the *douars* they claimed to; then, on the body of a dead F.L.N., Hentic found a group photograph in which one of the "Force K" operatives was clearly identifiable. The final revelation came when, at the end of October, a French unit was ambushed by what seemed unmistakably a "Force K" detachment, and the next morning Hentic was informed that the governor-general had just received the following anonymous letter:

> *Monsieur le ministre,*
> With the *Affaire K* you thought you were introducing a Trojan horse into the heart of the Algerian resistance. You were deceived. Those whom you took for traitors to the Algerian nation were pure patriots. . . . We thank you for having procured us arms that will help us to liberate our country.

* That mere captains, like Hentic, should come to acquire quite vast powers, both in military and civil operations, had – by May 1958 – become in itself a commonplace and significant feature.

Hentic now received orders to "liquidate" operation *Oiseau Bleu*, as "Force K" had now evidently gone over to the F.L.N. With the aid of a strong para force it was ruthlessly hunted down, just as it was about to be equipped with mortars. 130 of its men were killed and an equal number of weapons recovered, but a total of nearly 400 other firearms plus a similar number of sporting rifles, which the French had so lavishly distributed, were reckoned to have been lost to the F.L.N.; while some 600 "Force K" operatives survived to rejoin Krim. In the aftermath, it transpired that Krim had penetrated the leadership of "Force K" at an early stage, turned them, and even obligingly supplied them with "F.L.N. corpses" that were in fact those of slaughtered members of the dissident M.N.A. Whether all the "Force K" operatives wiped out by the French were in fact, like Tennyson's Lancelot, "falsely true", or truly false, will perhaps never be known. Nevertheless, *Oiseau Bleu* was undoubtedly a net gain in the "disinformation war" for the F.L.N. As Captain Hentic admits: "The moral prejudice was immense. The *Affaire K* had smothered and destroyed any desire of *ralliement* on the part of the local populace. . . ."

Another embarrassment for the French in the underground war of private armies was Belhadj Djillali, alias "Kobus", a corruption of the Arabic word for pistol. The son of an officer who had fought in 1914–18 and was a small property-owner, Kobus was arrested as a member of the O.S. in 1950 but released as a police informer. An expert in changing sides and treachery, he is described by Yves Courrière as an arrant liar; nevertheless, he too was encouraged (also under the aegis of the D.S.T.) to set up a counter-guerrilla in the Orléansville area, on the western fringes of the F.L.N.'s Wilaya 4. Although Kobus appears not to have betrayed the French, the Wilaya 4 leaders – the astute Si M'hamed and Omar Oussedik – cunningly created a series of incidents against the French which were made to look as if Kobus were the author. His French "controllers" reckoned that, on his past track-record, it was probable that Kobus was once more playing a double game, and began to withdraw support in April 1958. Wilaya 4 now applied extreme pressure on Kobus's immediate supporters, telling them that if they came over, bringing Kobus with them dead or alive, their lives would be spared. His second-in-command accepted the offer, had Kobus assassinated on his return from Algiers, cut off his head to take as his "pass" to the F.L.N., and left the corpse with the shaft of a tricolour thrust macabrely into its decapitated neck. The deal was not honoured, however, and all twenty-two of Kobus's defecting officers were promptly dispatched by the Wilaya 4 commanders. After *Oiseau Bleu* and Kobus, the French would be rather more cautious about doling out weapons; mistrust would linger, and even the most loyal of the *harkis* would never be quite free of it.

The end of Bellounis

Then there was, once more, Bellounis – or "Operation Ollivier". The leader of the private army of M.N.A. dissidents had, it will be remembered, twice escaped when his followers had been trapped and slaughtered by the F.L.N. Since the Mélouza massacre of May 1957, Bellounis had gone over completely to the French, had been extensively and expensively equipped by them, and at one moment his force numbered some two thousand armed men. It called itself grandly the Armée Nationale Populaire Algérienne (A.N.P.A.), and marched behind a flag of red crescent and star on a green and white field similar to the colours of independent Algeria. According himself the rank of general, Bellounis became prey to megalomania. At first he registered some notable successes against the F.L.N. in an area fringing on the north of the Sahara, coming under the newly created Wilaya 6. But then his harsh treatment of the local population, as well as of his own men, began to make the A.N.P.A. as resented as the F.L.N. Bellounis refused to hand over his prisoners to the French (it was presumed they had all been eliminated), his supporters were beginning to melt away, and it is suggested that after the events of May 1958 he was becoming disillusioned with the French cause. On 22 May he addressed a series of slightly mad letters to President Coty and General de Gaulle; three days later he refused to attend a meeting with his "controller".

Some weeks later, Simone de Beauvoir noted in her journal: "The French have killed Bellounis, who was accused of having shot four hundred of his men; the Italian newspapers say the French have killed Bellounis *and* the four hundred men." The official account is that Colonel Trinquier, who was commanding the 3rd R.P.C. after Bigeard had been repatriated and, having been despatched to wind-up "Operation Ollivier", came across the recently executed corpses of Bellounis's victims and decided to grant him no quarter. On 14 July the bullet-riddled body of Bellounis was picked up near Bou-Saada and displayed widely as a "traitor to France". With the death of Bellounis there ended disastrously yet another private army enterprise; at the same time, it also removed for the F.L.N. the last major threat of a rival military bid by the Messalists.

Léger's "bleus" turn the table

What the French lost in such debacles as *Oiseau Bleu*, Kobus and Bellounis, was probably just about balanced by the success of the reliable *harkis*, so that by the end of 1957 the score was roughly equal. It was as a by-product of the Battle of Algiers, however, and indirectly one of the rare episodes where torture did produce a net tactical gain for the victors, that the French were enabled to turn one of their most valuable tricks in the "secret" war. One of the more interesting of the shadowy, all-powerful intelligence captains thrown up by the Algerian war was a Zouave called

Christian Léger. Born in Morocco in 1922, Léger had the kind of dark, lean features with which he could pass almost equally well as a *pied noir*, an Arab or a Kabyle, and there were few subterranean episodes where he did not play a role. During the Second World War Captain Léger's father had been condemned to death by the Nazis, and he himself had volunteered to jump into occupied France in 1944. As a parachutist with de Bollardière in Indo-China, he had undertaken a number of highly risky missions in Viet-Minh territory disguised as one of General Giap's guerrillas. Returning to Algeria to perfect his Arabic and Kabyle, he then joined the S.D.E.C.E. in 1955, with whom he "disappeared" on top secret work for the next two years. During the Battle of Algiers he had been picked up by that expert on subversive warfare, Colonel Trinquier, who had known him in Indo-China and placed him in charge of a highly secret organisation called the Groupement de Renseignement et d'Exploitation (G.R.E.).

Linked to Trinquier's controversial D.P.U. with its system of block-warden informers unpleasantly reminiscent of the Third Reich, and answerable only to Colonel Godard, Léger's G.R.E. assembled a network of top-level Muslim agents, informers who, quite unbeknown to the F.L.N., had turned coat under lesser or greater degrees of coercion at the para interrogating centres. The cornering of Yacef, then of Ali la Pointe, in the final stages of the Battle of Algiers had been ultimately achieved by his *bleu* double agents. At the nucleus of the group was his right-hand man, a killer with the cover-name of "Surcouf", an Algerian who had served in Indo-China, and a young Muslim woman called "Ourhia-la-Brune" who had joined Léger out of the most basic of human motives: she had discovered that her husband, an F.L.N. militant arrested by the French, had betrayed her so as to protect his mistress. Ourhia filled a key role as a courier carrying messages for the F.L.N. in Algiers, but under Léger's control. Then there was a young man of twenty-one called Hani Mohamed, who had commanded the western zone of Algiers for Yacef until his capture in August 1957; finally, and most important, an Algiers Muslim with a string of aliases including his own cynical choice, "Safy-le-Pur". It was Safy-le-Pur, the former F.L.N. chief of east Algiers, who, by continuing to communicate with Yacef and Ali la Pointe after he had been turned, had led the paras to the hiding places of both.

No one but Yacef and his fellows, however, was aware (until after their capture) of the identity of their betrayer, and one of Yacef's last acts in freedom had been to nominate Safy-le-Pur military commander of the whole Algiers area. This appointment he communicated to the ferocious Kabyle chief of Wilaya 3, Amirouche. On learning this, with the Battle of Algiers over, Captain Léger and his superior, Godard, suddenly saw opportunities of unparalleled allure standing before them. Soon Amirouche was opening up contacts with Safy-le-Pur. With Yacef and Ali la Pointe out of the way, there appeared to remain only Safy-le-Pur among the Algiers leaders; so the C.C.E. in distant Tunis instructed Amirouche to begin reconstructing the debris there – through the medium of Safy-le-Pur. Thus Léger found himself, in effect, virtually controlling the F.L.N. apparatus that was attempting to re-establish itself in Algiers. Like any intelligence operator placed in this position, he was confronted with the difficult choice of whether to swoop and mop up the incipient network of fund-collectors and agents before the complex double-game should be "blown", or to play it to the limit, in the hopes of penetrating the whole F.L.N. structure still further back. On Godard's advice he chose the latter course, and a highly dangerous game now ensued in the last months of 1957.

To enhance credibility, Léger and Surcouf "helped" the new F.L.N. set-up to explode a few harmless bombs in Algiers, and even arranged the bombing of their own headquarters. Meanwhile, in the course of liaising with Amirouche, Hani Mohamed had succeeded in gaining access to the command of Wilaya 3's western zone, but when he was arrested by mishap by the army it was clear that the game could not last for ever, and that a big gamble must be tried without delay. At the end of January 1958 Hani Mohamed and Safy-le-Pur made a rendezvous at the zone's headquarters outside Bordj-Menaiel, on the western approaches of Kabylia. With them came Léger, disguised in a *cachabia*, Surcouf and several other members of the G.R.E. The F.L.N. leaders were completely deceived; by the following dawn the zone's entire general staff was aboard helicopters bound for French prisons; a large bomb factory and arms depot had been captured, as well as quantities of incriminating documents that would lead to the mounting of further deadly *bleu* operations.

Léger's coup was a success that more than atoned for such past debacles as *Oiseau Bleu*, Kobus and even Bellounis. The destruction of the post-Yacef network in Algiers was so complete that, in effect, the Z.A.A. was never to be usefully re-created until the last months of the war. But even more far-reaching were the consequences of the mistrust it had sown in Wilaya 3. By what was more or less a random shot, Léger had struck at the Achilles' heel of the whole F.L.N.: the mutual distrusts, hatreds and fears of betrayal that, as one now knows, seethed constantly just beneath the surface. Immediately Amirouche, like a Stalin in microcosm, launched the most savage and self-perpetuating series of purges. First of all the new leadership-designate for Algiers that had been "played" by the G.R.E. were shot or had their throats slit. Then came the wholesale liquidation of the so-called "city intellectuals", for the most part dedicated F.L.N. students who had fled Algiers during the Battle. When Léger realised what was going on, he added fuel to the flames by leaving forged documents on the bodies of killed rebels, incriminating other, loyal leaders of being traitorous *bleus.* "We must take measures to amputate all the gangrened limbs," one of his subordinates declared to Amirouche, so during 1958 and into 1959 the F.L.N. lost some of its best "limbs" through this murderous procedure. The purges were infectious and were soon spreading to the hitherto model and democratic neighbouring Wilaya 4, with consequences that were to be possibly even more far-reaching.

"Secret war" against the arms dealers

Not only inside Algeria was the "secret war" fought ruthlessly and often skilfully by the French intelligence services, or by organisations and individuals operating beneath their ample wingspan. One of the more intriguing sideshows was the campaign waged against the international arms dealers. At the beginning of 1958 an informed French army appreciation could reasonably reckon that the F.L.N. had no hope of winning a military victory – as things were. But what could upset the balance would be any new, massive infusion of weapons into Algeria. Thus the prevention of this had become a top French priority. There was the Morice Line barring movements by land; the French navy was extremely active checking shipments by sea, while any "friendly" nation endeavouring to sell arms to an Arab country that might possibly find their way to the F.L.N. met with the full force of French diplomatic wrath – as the Anglo-Americans discovered at the time of the Tunisian arms sales.

On the other hand, the funds available for arms purchases had become seductively great and were growing all the time. In addition to the money collected in Algeria, or from Algerian workers in France and funnelled out through the Jeanson network, the Arab League nations were now at last coming up with the cash, and no longer just empty promises. At the Cairo conference of December 1957 a target of ten milliard francs a year was set, but already by the last months of that year some seven milliards had flowed in. Moreover, as the watchful eye of French Intelligence noted, at that same conference an event of some historical importance had occurred when the Eastern bloc countries had, for the first time, expressed willingness to support the Algerian revolution with arms supplies. This was endorsed the following month when the French navy boarded off Oran a Yugoslav ship, the *Slovenija,* carrying 148 tons of illegal weapons, including 12,000 arms of Czech origin.

Supplying arms to the F.L.N. was now big enough business to make it irresistible to the international brotherhood of freelance arms dealers. But whereas France could do nothing to stop at source arms originating officially from the Soviet bloc, she could – and did – much to deter the private operators. The ramifications of the arms dealing world are complex, surrounded by more legend than fact, so the truth is difficult to penetrate, but some of the details that are known of the trade with the F.L.N. and the

French counter-measures read like passages from Ian Fleming or Frederick Forsyth. Respectable names from the United States and from London were involved, but the biggest traffic came through West Germany, particularly the port of Hamburg. The reason was simple to explain: since the demise of the Allied Occupation controls, the Bonn government had done nothing to replace the previous strict limitations on the arms trade. While this gap remained unplugged, the Federal Republic was a happy hunting-ground for the dealers. One shipment of German flame-throwers, for instance, came to the F.L.N. in a cargo labelled "crop-sprayers". In on the ground floor were a group of ex-Nazis who had found refuge in Cairo and had made themselves useful to Nasser; among them a former S.S. man called Ernst-Wilhelm Springer, who had helped form the pro-German Muslim Legion in the Second World War. Springer's efforts, though not always successful, illustrate the complexities involved. One of his first shipments of rifles, via Yugoslavia and Syria, was confiscated on Tito's orders, the bolts removed and the barrels bent. Enraged, the F.L.N. refused to pay Springer. He then tried to purchase 120 tons of dynamite from the Nobel plant in Troisdorf, near Bonn. When this failed, he negotiated for the same amount from Budapest, via a Finnish intermediary. After a mysterious attempt on his life, Springer faded from the scene.

At the other end of the game, in Paris, was "Bureau 24" of the French S.D.E.C.E., closely affiliated with the 11th Shock units and run by a "Colonel Lamy", which resorted freely to almost every weapon in the "007" inventory to thwart the arms dealers, though usually operating through "cut-outs" or paid killers. A consignment of plastic explosive from Sweden would turn out to have been mysteriously transformed into casein somewhere along the way. Two arms factories in Switzerland and Spain actually became "controlled" by Bureau 24 in much the same way that Léger had played the recrudescent F.L.N. network in Algiers, and busied themselves fabricating faulty firearms and instantaneous fused grenades for the arms salesmen. Finally, there were personal threats, following the dealers wherever they might go, that were by no means idle.

Dr Wilhelm Beisner, a former leader of the German Sicherheitsdienst in wartime Yugoslavia, had a miraculous escape when a shrapnel-laden bomb blew him through the roof of his car. Four separate bomb attempts, spread out over a period of two years from September 1956, were made against Otto Schlüter, an honourable third-generation Hamburg arms manufacturer. After a fourth attempt, when a remote-control automobile bomb killed his mother and injured him, Schlüter prudently abandoned his business with the F.L.N. Also in West Germany, the head of the F.L.N. organisation there, Ait Ahcène, was mysteriously shot down in Bonn in November 1957 on what were believed to be French orders. Responsible personally for many of these liquidations was a figure whose true identity still remains unknown, and who was sometimes dubbed just "The Killer". He had once worked with General Gehlen's intelligence organisation in West Germany, as well as with the French S.D.E.C.E., and the fact that he travelled with two French passports suggested that he had remained on good terms with the French government. "The Killer" and his network received considerable publicity when, in March 1957, the Swiss Federal Attorney-General committed suicide after being implicated in passing to them secret information on the gun-runners, together with telephone tappings of the Egyptian Embassy. It was the worst scandal to hit Switzerland since the war.

"The Killer" appears also to have been a specialist in style; perhaps the more to frighten off the arms dealers – *épater les bourgeois!* The most active of them all, and the top target of Bureau 24, was another German called Georges Puchert, who operated out of Tangiers, was impervious to threats and for two years led a charmed life. Dealing with Boussouf in Morocco, Puchert learned that one of the F.L.N.'s most favoured weapons was the German Mauser 7.92 mm. carbine from the Second World War. The principal stocks of these were to be found in Czechoslovakia, accumulated from the 1945 defeat, but as they were soon insufficient to meet demand the Communist Czech regime had obligingly set up plants to construct Mausers, perfect down to the last detail, including the swastika engraved in the metal, as a guarantee of top quality. Unable to tamper with this source of arms, "The Killer" was unleashed on Puchert's closest collaborators. In September 1958 one of them, a Swiss explosives expert called Marcel Léopold, was picked up dead in the corridor of one of Geneva's smartest hotels. An autopsy revealed that he had been shot in the neck by a tiny blowpipe dart, tipped with curare and fired from a contraption like a bicycle pump, which "The Killer" had thoughtfully left behind for the benefit of the world Press. Six months later, when Puchert was visiting Frankfurt, a limpet bomb was attached under the driver's seat of his Mercedes and detonated by inertia. Filled with ball-bearings, it did relatively little damage to the car, but riddled the ample arms trafficker like truffles in a Perigord pâté. With the death of Puchert, freelance gun-running more or less faded away.

France's new Maginot Line

For both sides, however, what was more important than the liquidation of gun-runners, or the "secret war" inside Algeria, or pitched battles like Agounennda, was the struggle constantly being waged on the Morice Line during this period. Completed in September 1957, this barrier was a remarkable and sinister triumph of military technology which ran along the Tunisian frontier for two hundred miles and more from the sea to the empty Sahara, where no one could hope to cross it undetected. The nucleus of the Line was an eight-foot electric fence charged with five thousand volts; on either side of this was a fifty-yard belt liberally sprinkled with anti-personnel mines and backed up with continuous barbed-wire entanglements of the style of the First World War. "An immense serpent in the style of Bernard Buffet" was how one French conscript described it. The wire was festooned with electrocuted animals – dogs, sheep, goats and even occasionally a pathetic little donkey. The German Foreign Legionnaires were particularly distressed at the sight of handsome Alsatian tracker dogs electrocuted by the Line. Immediately to the rear ran a track along which passed frequent armed patrols, equipped with powerful search-lights at night. Not only was the electric fence designed to kill but there were also electronic devices that could determine precisely where it had been cut by a raiding party. Fire from automatically sighted 105 mm. howitzers could be brought to bear on the point immediately, and mobile troops rushed to it. Defending the line was a force some 80,000 strong, the most powerful concentration of French combat troops in Algeria. There were mechanised and armoured units, four para regiments – including the crack 1st R.E.P. of Colonel Jeanpierre who had been wounded during the capture of Yacef – and plentiful helicopters to spot any crossing-points and track the crossers. In the event of a successful crossing in force, presumably made by night, it was of prime importance for the French defenders to pin down and destroy the A.L.N. unit before the end of the following day, after which time it would be able to break up into small groups and disperse into the interior.

With such an outlay in expenditure and effectives, the integrity of the Morice Line became the top military priority for the French during the winter of 1957–8. Its breaching had equally become the supreme objective for the F.L.N.; there were now some ten thousand A.L.N. troops, armed or in training, concentrated in the frontier zone, and the weapons beginning to flow into Tunisia from all over the world had totalled, over the three winter months, 17,000 rifles, 380 machine-guns, 296 automatic rifles, 190 bazookas, thirty mortars and over 100 million rounds of ammunition. Meanwhile, the Wilayas were asphyxiating for want of reinforcements.

All through the winter the two sides fenced for an advantage on the Morice Line. The F.L.N. probed, or threw itself at the barrier, constantly trying out new techniques. High-tension wire-cutters were ordered from Germany, employed with special hooks to lift up the wire; but the French electronic detectors proved capable of locating the breach all too swiftly. Groups tried burrowing under the wire, or throwing insulated ramps over it; teams specially trained with "Bangalore torpedoes" in Egypt blasted holes through it. Then they would bury delayed action mines under the lines along which ran, bristling with machine-guns, the French armoured trains; these mines were timed to explode beneath the third coach, the one usually carrying troops. But always the French mines, electrocution, or the sheer firepower of the defending patrols took a terrible toll. Diversionary tactics were tried, with a small detachment setting off the alarm system while the main body in fact attempted a breakthrough perhaps fifty kilometres further down the line. In Tunisia the breakthrough units were trained in the execution of forced marches at astonishing speeds, so as to avoid being corralled by the French once through the line. They attempted to go round the end of both the Moroccan and Tunisian lines, through the Great Erg sand deserts of the Sahara, disguised as Meharist columns. But the wretched camels would be slaughtered wholesale by strafing them from the air (and sometimes those of genuine Meharists, in error), and in one of the last operations by Bigeard before his repatriation a parachute-drop trapped and wiped out fifty of one such group of frontier runners.

In their assaults on the main line the A.L.N. at first threw in small commandos; then bigger groups; finally whole *katibas*, and even *faileks* over 300 men strong, in desperate efforts to overwhelm the defenders. But this escalation only resulted in higher and higher losses; for all the time the French were perfecting their interception techniques, speeding up mobility and increasing the firepower brought to bear on a given point. The statistics speak for themselves. One regiment in a busy part of the Line, the 9th R.C.P., recorded scores as follows for early 1958:

10 February:	39 rebels; 30 weapons
14 February:	20 rebels; 25 weapons
20 February:	78 rebels; 50 weapons
31 March:	69 rebels; 50 weapons
7 April:	86 rebels; 60 weapons

According to French estimates, the percentage of F.L.N. infiltrators "neutralised" rose as follows:

January–February:	35
February–March:	60
March–April:	65
end of April:	80

Souk-Ahras and Sakiet

The steep increase in this last figure was caused by the F.L.N.'s decision to launch an all-out offensive against the Line. The sector chosen was the so-called *bec de canard*, east of Souk-Ahras and not far from the scene of the Sakiet bombing in February. Its wooded hills provided ideal cover for *katibas* attempting to disperse once through the Line, and much of the previous barrier-crossing action had taken place in this area. Thus, also, the French forces were particularly well-prepared. But, apart from just military considerations, the F.L.N. were probably encouraged by the international uproar raised over Sakiet, as well as the accompanying political disarray in France – the Gaillard government having fallen two weeks previously, leaving the country in a vacuum. Over three nights, from 27 to 30 April, seven *katibas* totalling over 800 men, and destined to reinforce both Wilayas 2 and 3, were thrown against the Line north and south of Souk-Ahras. A large number got through the wire, but were almost immediately pinned down and encircled by a crushing superiority of airborne troops ferried in by big transport helicopters. For the best part of a week an intense and merciless battle raged. A twenty-year-old French conscript who took part, Alain Manévy, records how the entire *pied noir* population of Souk-Ahras turned out to watch, infuriating the military by blocking the highways with their cars, and accompanied by Arab street vendors plying the spectators with sticky cakes. French losses were heavy, one company of the 9th R.C.P. losing its captain and most of its effectives. But those of the A.L.N. were crippling, by far the worst that it had suffered in the war to date; out of a total of 820 men crossing the Line, no less than 620 were killed or captured, including a *failek* commander. With them were taken 416 rifles or sub-machine-guns, and forty-six machine-guns. (The disproportionate number of arms to rebels captured, however, is once again a testimony to the efficiency of the F.L.N. system of weapon recovery, which aimed at never leaving behind the previous firearm of a fallen *djoundi*.) The pile of weapons was displayed in the market-place of Souk-Ahras, though Manévy noted indifference on the part of the Muslim inhabitants: "The French have simply got out their old weapons from stores to make us believe. . . ."

Yet the Battle of Souk-Ahras undeniably marked a decisive defeat for the F.L.N. – ironically, on a line whose eponym, Morice, had recently fallen from power. In the course of the seven months since its construction, the F.L.N. was reckoned to have lost 6,000 men and 4,300 weapons (including casualties, though much less significant, on the Moroccan frontier). It signified the end of any serious attempt to breach the barrier. Henceforth the Wilayas would be virtually cut off from the exterior. It was a major military victory for the French, and clearly recognisable as such in army messes.

It was against this background of warfare on the Morice Line that the Sakiet raid of February 1958 had taken place. There were many senior French officers who agreed with Colonel Trinquier that, although the Line had served its primary purpose well, it was accompanied by all the traditional disadvantages of fixed fortifications (plus the mentality that had led, painfully, to Dien Bien Phu). The only way, they felt, to deal decisively with the F.L.N. was to strike into the foreign territories harbouring rebel forces – as indeed, noted Trinquier, had been the accepted norm in the pacification wars of the nineteenth century. In the months preceding Sakiet, French army frustration had been rising at the audacity with which the F.L.N. barrier-crossers trained in full sight of the frontier posts, mortared and machine-gunned them sporadically, and then launched full-scale raids across the Line. More and more lives were lost in this fashion, while the "neutrality" of Tunisian territory afforded the F.L.N. impunity from any riposte. After the ambushing of the French patrol on 11 January, the Gaillard government had come under strong pressure from the military of the kind that brought the Nixon government into the Cambodian adventure of 1973, or that persuades Israeli governments to hit back at P.L.O. camps in the Lebanon. Finally, at the end of January, it had acceded to this pressure and granted "right of pursuit". It did not, however, specify precisely what form this should take, nor how far it might be pressed. Too much responsibility was left with the local commanders, some of whom had evidently been thinking in terms of an armoured raid to destroy the F.L.N. camps. On 7 February Bigeard – reflecting the impatience felt by the whole army – remarked angrily to Lacoste during a visit to the frontier: "*Monsieur le ministre*, it can't go on like this! We must intervene." The very next day the provocation, followed by the reprisal bombing of Sakiet, took place. Quite clearly the action, and the excessive force of it, had been invoked by the local air force commander acting on his own initiative. Certainly Lacoste had not been consulted, and when informed of it exploded characteristically: "*Ils sont vraiment trop cons!*"

Sakiet was a revealing example of how, increasingly, the French army had become accustomed to acting without the backing of civil authority from Algiers, let alone from Paris. The first army reaction after Sakiet was one of relief; here at last was a tough line. Then, dismayed by the vehemence of international condemnation of the raid, the government had back-tracked and seemingly let the weight of calumny fall upon the local commanders responsible. Air strikes across the frontier, it was suggested, had never been envisaged. A widespread feeling of disenchantment ran through the army in Algeria that, not for the first time, it was being let down by the politicians.

The army disenchanted

Soldiers, by the very nature of their upbringing, see little more than what lies to their immediate front. The lieutenant observes what is happening to his platoon, but is little concerned with the affairs of the battalion; the colonel knows little of the overall fortunes of the division or the corps until his battalion is ordered to advance or retreat. And so on upwards. Thus, in Algeria, the senior French army commanders, under pressure from foreground events, were constantly blinkered to higher realities; to the state of the war in the international, political arena, or, later, to public opinion at home. By the spring of 1958, however, they could deduce with the most clear-cut conviction that they were winning the immediate shooting war on all fronts – and for the first time since November 1954. The Battle of Algiers, Agounennda, Souk-Ahras, the blocking of the barrier-runners on the Moroccan frontier as on the Tunisian, the new successes in the underground war; every sign vindicated this conviction. Yet, at the same time, more thoughtful senior officers felt menaced also by a mounting and harrowing sense of urgency. Was this perhaps the last moment when a military victory could be exploited? How long would it be before the flow of weapons from the Communist bloc, and possibly more direct means of support, might reverse the tide? The smell of victory was strong, but there was also, coupled with it, a nasty smell of negotiations in the air; the bons offices episode and other indications all pointed to this. And negotiations implied surrender. Were the politicians getting ready to sell the army down the river once again? The memories of the Third Republic and 1940, of Dien Bien Phu and Mendès-France, were always too close for comfort.

There were other factors, many of them of the order of minor grines, but all adding up to a massive resentment against the civil governme t in metropolitan France. The deepening economic crisis there had led it to impose a series of meanly petty privations on the army in Algeria; allocations of petrol and rations had been reduced, leave had been cut, and so on. Salan, for one, could perceive that, for all its fine military successes, the army's morale was suffering. Yet, more than ever before, the army of Algeria now realised how immense its power and influence had become, and far beyond just the realm of military matters. The process had started with Mollet's expansion of the army by recalling the reservists, and it was under that good Socialist that it had been truly introduced to politics through his encouraging it to indulge in political warfare. With Massu's takeover of civil powers during the Battle of Algiers, a point of no return had been reached. By January 1958 an estimated 1,600 army officers and 1,000 N.C.O.s – among the best in the army – were totally employed in civil affairs of one category or another. The lengths to which, from 1956 onwards, some individual officers would go to avoid losing the war, moreover, were illuminated by such episodes as the hijacking of Ben Bella and the bombing of Sakiet.

The sense of involvement in Algeria was profound. At its less idealistic level, to some of the regulars, as Colonel François Coulet noted, the war "was their raison d'être; they feared seeing it end one day". It meant professional security and promotion. On the other hand, there was a deep undercurrent of fairly noble-minded reformism, of genuinely wanting to do something about the economic plight of the Algerians, of wanting to save the country from the maw of Communism. Grafted on to it there was now a new sense of destiny that – in the face of the total debility of the civil regime in France – the army alone could influence and ordain matters in Algeria. By the spring of 1958, says General Allard, a brilliant and dedicated soldier, the military

> felt themselves neither aided, nor encouraged, nor supported. It seemed to them that those responsible had not the courage to look the situation in the face and to fight the war with a will to win, but perhaps rather to put an end to it by some kind of negotiation. . . . After Sakiet, the army felt itself betrayed, it lost confidence, not in itself, but in the effectiveness of the regime. From then on it was ready to welcome, and to take advantage of, any event announcing a change that would force Fate. . . .

The army had reached a highly explosive state; all that was needed was a detonator.

In Paris the Sakiet affair had effectually inflicted the death wound upon the Gaillard government; but, like a frog in a laboratory, the corpse had continued to twitch on for another two months. *Messieurs les bons offices* had not helped matters, the suggestion of Anglo-American interference in Algerian affairs alienating the centre from its support of Gaillard. Soustelle declared emotionally, "It's the total liquidation of the French positions in North Africa that is being prepared. That's the policy of the petroleum monopolies who want to kick us out of the Sahara." On another occasion he was heard to utter the loaded words: "A government of Public Safety must take over." Another bout of massive strikes shook the country; in March even the police demonstrated in front of the Assembly for "danger money"; on 1 April all the public services went out. On 15 April the Gaillard government fell by 321 to 255 on a vote of confidence about the *bons offices*. The Communists and the centre had improbably united forces, with Deputy Soustelle – now cast in the role of premier-slayer – putting in the boot as he had with Bourgès-Maunoury six months previously. Once more France faced a vacuum of leadership; this time, the most perilous yet.

Nevertheless, in Algiers the sturdy Lacoste soldiered on with his intention to promulgate the *loi-cadre* as soon as possible, announcing that in June he would hold the first elections for the proposed territorial assemblies. But the long-fought-for *loi-cadre* was beginning to look more and more anachronistic – both to the Muslims, who had hardly been consulted, and to the *pieds noirs*, among whom hatred for *ce traître Lacoste* was growing in violence with each successive day. Senator Borgeaud and Alain de Sérigny's *Écho d'Alger* were well to the fore in whipping up opposition to the *loi-cadre*, but among new voices joining in the noisy fugue against any legislature of moderation were now the militant *pied noir* students of Algiers University, under the lead of a recently demobbed ex-para, Pierre Lagaillarde. On the other side, the F.L.N. had launched an offensive of *égorgements spectaculaires* against the ever-shrinking numbers of "third force" Muslims upon whom Lacoste would have to rely for the success of the *loi-cadre*. In the political vacuum that succeeded the fall of Gaillard,

Lacoste was in effect a "lame-duck" governor; and, in the storm that was shortly to sweep France, his cherished *loi-cadre* would become a dead letter. Speaking to the author years afterwards, he rated its demise as "my greatest disappointment":

> I was sure that if it were put into operation, we could have continued our work towards a progressive independence. Then, when de Gaulle arrived, he swept away the *loi-cadre*. It was a *très vilain coup*, giving full satisfaction to the "ultras". If it had gone through, without sacrificing one community to the other, I do believe that all but a small fraction of the *pieds noirs* (and those would have been the *grands bourgeois*) could have stayed.... Maybe the rebellion would have continued, but with less force. Who can say what might have happened, because it was never tried? ... Metropolitan France never understood. It could never understand that the F.L.N. was not fighting to create a *bon bourgeois* government—like Abbas.... I saw the problem *durement*, but could see no solution. They did not see it *durement*, but saw every conceivable solution.

Meanwhile, Lacoste continued with his tough measures to crush the rebellion (and to sugar the pill of the *loi-cadre* for the *pieds noirs*). On 24 April, despite Germaine Tillion's endeavours of the previous year to halt the chain of executions, Yacef's bomb-manufacturer, Taleb Abderrahmane, and two other convicted terrorists were guillotined in Algiers. In advance of the execution, *El Moudjahid* had warned that henceforth "each Algerian patriot to mount the scaffold signifies one French prisoner before the firing squad". On 9 May the F.L.N. Press office in Tunis announced that three French soldiers had been sentenced to death by a special A.L.N. tribunal on charges of torture, rape and murder. The unfortunate soldiers had already been in F.L.N. hands for over eighteen months and, far from there having been any semblance of a "fair trial", it appeared, for want of other evidence, that they had simply been selected at random and killed. The French reaction, both in France and Algeria, was one of profound shock and horror. For the army, it was the missing detonator.

PART THREE

The Hardest of all Victories

1958—1962

As for myself, when General de Gaulle came to power I dreamed aloud. Drunk with wild hopes, I prophesied to my friends: "In one stride he will step over the obstacle against which every other government has come to grief. He will tell the army: 'You have won the hardest of all victories in our history, the victory over ourselves – our egoism, our stupidity, and our complacency. You have given the Algerian people a freedom and dignity it has never had, even from its own leaders. Fraternally united with it and its combatants, you will make peace....'"

The least that can be said is that I was ahead of my time....

Jules Roy, 1960

CHAPTER THIRTEEN

A Kind of Resurrection

May 1958

The Conquest, Père Bugeaud, a hundred years of French administration, slipped over the immensity of Algeria like water on granite – but here, in France, for the first time, the stone crumbles and the water penetrates.

Germaine Tillion

The "thirteen conspiracies"

IN terms of the broad canvas of French affairs, the mad May days of 1958 seem to belong to a long past era: to the storming of the Bastille, to the revolutionary scenes of 1830 and 1848, to the tragi-comic extravaganzas of the Commune of 1871, rather than to contemporary history less than two decades old. The events in Portugal since April 1974 help make the sacking of the Gouvernement-Général office in Algiers, the invasion of Corsica, the threat of paras floating down on the French homeland itself, and the overthrow of the Fourth Republic all appear not quite so improbable as they might have done a few years previously. Yet still that final fortnight of May 1958 remains one of the most extraordinary and melodramatic interludes, intoxicated and intoxicating, that the modern European mind can recall, a work of the *romancier* rather than of the historian. Out of millions of words written about it, an immense confusion of acts, motives and men emerges. One of the best works of journalistic narration published at the time calls itself *Les 13 Complots du 13 Mai*, and thirteen may well be an understatement. All one can attempt to do here is to distil from this seething cauldron the ingredients that essentially affected the course of the Algerian war, or its principal participants. The events of May 1958 seem to have burst out of the centre of the Algerian conflict to determine its subsequent course. "They changed the spirit of the struggle in one camp, and made the other hold its breath," says Philippe Tripier. For France, the coming of de Gaulle was, obviously, a critical turning-point in the war – as, indeed, it was to be on many other levels for the whole Western world. Though it was later to prove equally a turning-point for the F.L.N., its significance was not quite so clear-cut in the earliest phases; hence the ensuing pages concentrate on what was almost exclusively a French story.

The "Faure conspiracy" and the *affaire du bazooka* had already given a foretaste of the pressure of steam that the Algerian war was building up against the established authority of France. In November 1957 the thirty-five days without a government preceding Gaillard had shown the nation rising to greater heights of ungovernability at home and its prestige sinking to all-time depths abroad. From then on the plotting and counter-plotting had redoubled. The new period of parliamentary instability following the fall of Gaillard on 15 April had added a fresh fillip to the conspiracies, of which there were basically two kinds: those that were specifically for the return of General de Gaulle, and those that were not. Only the former knew precisely what, and whom, they wanted, but were disunited as to how and when. Among the many pro-Gaullists implicated to one extent or another, the following names stand to the fore: Jacques Soustelle, Michel Debré, Alexandre Sanguinetti, Maître Jean-Baptiste Biaggi, Jacques Chaban-Delmas and Léon Delbecque.

The Gaullists

Since his fervid send-off from Algiers in February 1956, Soustelle had become an impassioned protagonist of *Algérie française* and opponent of Lacoste's *loi-cadre* reforms. Returning to politics as deputy for Lyon, he had arisen as the scourge of the Assembly, bringing down both Bourgès-Maunoury and Gaillard (and frightening even de Gaulle by some of his vehemence). In the course of the 15 April debate he had declared, "I am one of those who are determined to give away nothing more."

Debré, whose name has already been mentioned in the context of the *affaire du bazooka* and who was to become de Gaulle's first prime minister, had been senator for Indre-et-Loire since 1948. Immensely hard-working and persistent, at forty-six he was described by the Brombergers as "a rather severe man, discreet, with eyes of fire, nervous, always pacing up and down". Neither the face nor the personality were particularly memorable, which made him the despair of the Parisian cartoonists. But Debré's most outstanding characteristic was his "intransigent fidelity" to de Gaulle, which never wavered all through his career. De Gaulle himself recognised this quality, and in 1956 had remarked despondently, "I have confidence only in Debré." Debré was unmistakably the *éminence grise* of all the various circles plotting the general's return, and his activities were recognised to the extent that over the past two years he had been under constant surveillance by four plain-clothes policemen at his front door. In 1957 he had published a violent attack on the leaders of the Fourth Republic, *Ces Princes qui nous Gouvernent*, which he concluded with a pointedly relevant reference to the essential "legitimacy" of de Gaulle as a saviour waiting in the wings, on the basis that "He has represented honour, national interest, popular unity and law. His legitimacy mounts

in direct proportion as that of the regime sinks. . . ." The well-named
Courrier de la Colère, which he had founded the same year, angrily drew
comparisons between Louis XV's abandonment of Canada and India and
the present-day "sell-out" of the French Empire, and hammered away with
such headlines as:

DE GAULLE
MEANS A FRENCH PEACE IN AFRICA
MEANS THE LOYAL ASSOCIATION BETWEEN
FRANCE AND ALL THE OVERSEAS PEOPLES

together with themes that were to become more familiar in later years,
such as: MUST WE GIVE UP TOULON TO N.A.T.O.?

Sanguinetti was a *pied noir* born in Cairo, where his father had been an
adviser to King Fouad; he was a rugged-looking individual who, as a
commando sergeant during the Second World War, had lost a leg on Elba
close to Napoleon's house of exile. His main contribution to the Gaullist
cause was to be secretary-general to C.A.N.A.C., the pressure group of the
all-powerful *anciens combattants* associations, which in turn was closely
linked with those in Algeria. In this context particularly, an invaluable
go-between was provided in the roly-poly shape of the Corsican lawyer
with the uncontrolled laugh, Jean-Baptiste Biaggi. Invariably described as
"a born revolutionary", Biaggi has already appeared in this story when
whipping up antagonism to Mollet and Catroux during the ill-starred
visit to Algiers in February 1956. To sympathetic ears Biaggi expounded,
with perhaps more typically Corsican passion than legal reasoning, the
view that the Fourth Republic could now claim no more legitimacy than
Pétain's Vichy in 1940. His eccentricity, his war record, but above all his
extremism made him the darling of the Right in Algiers and helped open
doors for the Gaullists to the *pied noir* veterans' organisations that were
hitherto predominantly Pétainist.

Biaggi was also responsible for winning over a key intermediary in
Algiers who would prove indispensable to the Gaullists in the critical May
days: Colonel Jean Thomazo, or "Nez-de-Cuir". The colonel gained his
nickname from an unsightly leather strap he wore across his face to hide
where the bridge of his nose had been shot away at Cassino; an irrepressible
fighter, Thomazo had refused to take time off from the battle for plastic
surgery. Of his three sons, one had been killed in Indo-China, a second in
the Aurès, and the third was to have a narrow escape in a flying accident
in Algeria. Arriving in Algeria as chief-of-staff to Ducournau's 25th Airborne Division, Thomazo had been transferred to command the Unités
Territoriales (U.T.)* of part-time *pied noir* militiamen, with whose views
he wholeheartedly identified himself. Tournoux describes him as being
"fifty years old by civil status, a thousand by right of military service, but

* It resembled in more ways than one the Ulster Defence Force.

275

eighteen years old politically". There was not an intrigue in Algiers into which he had not thrown himself with the total enthusiasm of a Dumas musketeer, and without any fear of compromising himself. He was immensely popular among all the various "ultra" circles in Algiers, and was also in close touch with the Commander-in-Chief, Raoul Salan. A true Bonapartist, his abiding belief was that the army should take over power, and he had been but lukewarm to de Gaulle until Biaggi had set to work on him.

Chaban-Delmas and the Delbecque "antenna"

In terms of the action to lead directly to de Gaulle's return, the two most important figures were probably Jacques Chaban-Delmas and Léon Delbecque. Still only forty-three, Chaban-Delmas could look back on one of the most meteoric careers under Gaullism: *général-de-brigade* at twenty-nine (something almost unheard-of since Napoleon), mayor of Bordeaux at thirty-two and leader of the Republicains Sociaux Gaullists in the Assembly since 1953. Although appointed Minister of Defence under Gaillard's government, Chaban-Delmas never made any secret of his working for the return of his old patron. He was a first-class tennis player and rugger enthusiast, with an excess of energy and enterprise. On his own initiative, and while still in the Gaillard cabinet, Chaban-Delmas had despatched Léon Delbecque to set up an "antenna" – or listening-post – in Algiers, thinly under cover of the Ministry of Defence. A self-made man from a working-class family in northern France, Delbecque was another who had made his name with the wartime Gaullist Resistance, and was now a Gaullist deputy. Between December 1957 and the early days of May 1958 he had made twenty-eight feverish trips back and forth between Paris and Algiers at the behest of Chaban-Delmas.

As indeed is the experience with most conspiracies, the moves to bring back de Gaulle were wrapped in a certain degree of amateurishness and uncertainty. There was one moment of *opéra bouffe* when the plump Biaggi and two other plotters were trapped in an antique Parisian lift between floors on their way to a top-level and secret meeting. The restless Debré, bounding up the stairs, was unable to find a mechanic to release them; so for an uncomfortable period the Gaullist *directoire* hung suspended in mid-air. As a result of telephone-tapping and normal Parisian indiscretion, the plotting seems to have gone by no means unobserved by the French authorities – such as they were in the absence of a government. At one point Delbecque toyed with the idea of some kind of army coup for the month of August 1958; because most of the Communist leaders and their cohorts would be away on holiday and it would be more difficult for them to mount a counter-coup. This seemed to show a curious insensitivity to the growing pressure of events. In February, shortly after the Sakiet incident, that outstanding African statesman and francophile, Houphouët-Boigny of the Ivory Coast, had come to de Gaulle himself to warn him that Black Africa was on the verge of revolt. Only de Gaulle could restore confidence there. The fall of Gaillard had further precipitated matters, with a deluge of letters and suppliants to the Elysée daily demanding the return of de Gaulle. By the end of April the Delbecque "antenna" had succeeded in establishing a *comité de vigilance* in Algiers. It was the aim of Chaban-Delmas that, when the day came, this should be transformed into a Committee of Public Safety – the deadly words already dropped by Soustelle in the Assembly in March – to take over in Algeria and bring back de Gaulle.

Through the helpful bridging operations of Nez-de-Cuir, a certain harmony had been created with the various militant *pied noir* organisations in Algiers; even though the words they were singing might have differed. On 26 April they had jointly mounted a successful and massive demonstration at that nerve-centre of Algiers' emotions, the *monument aux morts*. The immediate excuse was the attempt, in Paris, by the Alsatian Pierre Pflimlin to form a government in place of Gaillard, the organisers having persuaded themselves and the multitude that Pflimlin was a *bradeur* intent on "doing a deal" with the F.L.N. 30,000 people turned out, among them a number of Muslims for the first time. There were slogans of "The Army to Power" and calls for a committee of public safety, but any mention of the name de Gaulle was deliberately repressed by Delbecque. At one moment it looked menacingly as if the tide of demonstrators might swamp the nearby Gouvernement-Général, and as things were to turn out the day was to prove to be a dummy-run for 13 May. On the evening of the 26th Delbecque was able to report back to Chaban-Delmas: "I now have Algiers in my hand!"

"The Group of Seven": Lagaillarde

Apart from Alain de Sérigny, the editor of the powerful and fulminant *Écho d'Alger*, who was already in close contact with Soustelle, Delbecque's principal allies in Algiers that day had centred around a newly formed body called "The Group of Seven". Created in March, the "Seven" represented a fusion of "ultra" bodies and names – some of them with a distinctly fascist tinge – that had already been seen at the time of the anti-Mollet demonstrations of 1956, with one important addition. Among them was Robert Martel, the leader from the Mitidja and head of U.F.N.A. (Union Française Nord-Africaine) who had been arrested, and then released, on charges of involvement with a counter-terrorist group. There was Jo Ortiz, the restaurateur, Poujadist and admirer of Charles Maurras, the Fascist Action Française leader of the 1930s given a life sentence as a collaborator in 1945; and there was Dr Bernard Lefèvre, another Poujadist and admirer of Portugal's Salazar. But first and foremost there was the new and violent figure of the student leader, Pierre Lagaillarde, who would, however briefly, perform a key role on 13 May and again in the stormy January of two years later.

Aged twenty-seven and born in France, Lagaillarde had passed his childhood in Blida where both his parents had practised law. But the forebear with whom Lagaillarde liked most to identify himself was his great-grandfather, an obscure deputy and revolutionary called Baudin who had found immortality in the 1851 uprising against Louis-Napoleon. Leaping on top of a barricade and crying "I'll show you how one dies for twenty-five sous a day," he had been promptly shot.* Lagaillarde himself had returned to study law at Algiers University the previous autumn, having completed his military service as a *sous-lieutenant* with the paras. This had taken him to Suez and through the Battle of Algiers, and the redoubtable Colonel Trinquier had been sufficiently impressed to invite him to stay on, which Lagaillarde had refused with the contemptuous rebuff: "The paras have every physical courage, but no civil courage!" Nevertheless, he seldom missed an opportunity to appear (improperly) in uniform. The Brombergers describe Lagaillarde as "a character in search of an author, wanting to be a Siegfried or a d'Artagnan". But with his tall, lean figure, carpet-fringe beard and unsmiling face, Lagaillarde when wearing the shapeless and wrinkled "leopard" combat kit of the para evoked more closely the "Knight of the Sorrowful Countenance". Sometimes Ortiz, *mutatis mutandis*, played an unwittingly droll but unfunny Sancho Panza. Frequently Lagaillarde's gestures were neither less grandiloquent nor less absurd than Don Quixote's. But he was indisputably a man of action. At the university the staccato laugh and raucous, rabble-rousing oratory, as well as his sheer panache, had at once made Lagaillarde a natural leader. Taking over the Association Générale des Étudiants d'Algérie (A.G.E.A.) he had launched it fiercely into "ultra" politics.

Lagaillarde regarded the Gaullist "antenna" with detached contempt, remarking to Nez-de-Cuir at an early stage that he wanted "to have nothing to do with the Punch-and-Judy *coup d'état* of M. Chaban-Delmas". His fellow members of "The Group of Seven" went even further in their antipathy to de Gaulle. In this they were representative of the deep-seated Pétainist inclinations of the *pieds noirs*, inherited from the internal conflicts of French North Africa during the Second World War. Moreover, the immediate goals of the "Seven" and Delbecque's *comité de vigilance* differed radically both in range and breadth. The "Seven" wanted the army to take over in Algeria to preserve *Algérie française*, to give them independence from the French parliament in its present mood, but without

* On his secret insurrectionary mission to France to prepare for the para landings in May 1958, it was "Baudin" that Lagaillarde chose as his pseudonym.

any suggestion of going so far as Ian Smith in Rhodesia. There was no thought of "What then?"; and – which was typical of the inward-looking and insular mentality of the *pied noir* – no thought about France's own predicament above and beyond the problem of the Algerian war. For the Gaullists the whole "State of France" was what was at issue, of which Algeria was but part. It was admittedly a very large part, but the progressive revelation of its relativity in the mind of de Gaulle himself was to be the source of the bitterest and most dangerous disillusions in the years to come. Thus to maintain harmony between two such uneasy bedfellows was to require the utmost diplomacy and adroitness on the part of Nez-de-Cuir – greatly aided by the unexpected turn of events.

... and de Gaulle

In all this there remains one essential and enigmatic actor – the King over the Water himself. Twelve years had passed since he summarily abandoned the presidency on the mystical motivation of preserving "the spiritual national investment" from being sullied by party politics. It had been his determination to wait, and "for whatever length of time was necessary, let the party system display its noxiousness once more, determined as I was not to act as a cover or a figurehead for it. So I would depart, but intact." During these long years he had withdrawn to live in a state of genteel poverty as squire of Colombey-les-Deux-Églises with his wife and handicapped daughter, Anne. At one time in financial straits, he had been helped out with a loan arranged by a banker named Pompidou. From his lofty vantage-point he had observed with a mixture of disdain and despair "the convolutions of this absurd ballet... seventeen prime ministers, representing twenty-four ministries". In 1952 the Gaullist R.P.F., feeling abandoned by the leader, had split; as one of their number explained: "To wait in immobility for the national catastrophe, assuredly without wishing for it, so that General de Gaulle can be called to power, seems to us an insufficient plan of action." De Gaulle in turn felt "betrayed" as the faithful accepted ministries under the Fourth Republic. That same year he had renounced public life in its entirety, and settled down to write his memoirs. Publication of the first volume, coinciding with the outbreak of the Algerian war, had been a spectacular success, but most of the sixty million (old) francs of royalties he was to receive were spent on a foundation for children suffering from the same malady as the adored Anne, who had died in 1948. By May 1958 he was at work on volume three, *Le Salut*, announcing to his publishers that he expected to deliver that October.

In those years of withdrawal he had read voraciously and eclectically – Saint-Simon, Châteaubriand, Bergson and Bismarck, manuals on gardening and saddle-making, and even Françoise Sagan and Hemingway's *The Old*

Man and the Sea, with whose hero he affected to identify himself. He had travelled a little, and wherever he had stopped in the French Commonwealth warmest enthusiasm had greeted him. But above all he had thought, abstractly and with the objectivity that distance lends. For de Gaulle these were years of contemplation and spiritual regeneration, comparable to St John the Baptist in the desert, Lenin in exile, Winston Churchill in the political wilderness of the 1930s, and Konrad Adenauer at the monastery of Maria Laachs as a refugee from Nazism. It was this detachment which was to enable him to time to perfection the moment when, as he phrased it, "I would release the *deus ex machina*, in other words make my entrance."

He had also grown old, resentfully – for, as he had remarked of Pétain, "Old age is a shipwreck." As far back as 1948, ten years previously, Janet Flanner had commented unkindly: "Time, weight, and, evidently, the General's glands are giving his visage a heavy, royal outline; he looks more like a man of dynasty than of destiny". In order to preserve his deteriorating eyesight, he had given up smoking, but had still had to undergo recently an operation for cataract. This gave him a kind of agoraphobia, and made him uncertain in public without spectacles at hand. The belly had sagged, the face was greyer, the voice had lost something of its resonance. He was sixty-seven. But, as he had flatteringly been told by a youth movement delegate on the day Gaillard fell, "Stalin was older than you!" By the beginning of 1958 he may have seemed to the world at large a forgotten man, a legend but no longer a potential saviour of France; however, over all the years he himself had not abandoned the belief that France would call for him one day. He had not for a moment doubted "that the infirmity of the system would sooner or later lead to a grave national crisis". But there had been times when, after so many years in the wilderness, the flame of hope flickered low. As late as April 1958, resorting to the majestic third person singular in which he habitually referred to himself, he had remarked gloomily to Delbecque: "They will create a burnt earth, they will wait until there is nothing left before calling for de Gaulle! I shall never come back to power in my lifetime."

In response to the importuning of the Gaullist conspirators, their pressure mounting powerfully since the fall of Gaillard, he had remained characteristically aloof and enigmatic. France would have to want him very badly. Hints had been dropped; in January he told Tournoux that he considered the French government to be no longer legitimate, in that "it could no longer assure either its defence, or the security of its territory" – a clear reference to Algeria, for those who wished to find one. His price for returning, clearly implied, was the complete replacement of the system of the Fourth Republic; he would only come back if a vast majority of the French nation wanted him; he would not come back as the prisoner of any one faction, especially not on the bayonets of the army. Apart from this, all the rest was pure conjecture – and ambiguity. In despair at the state of France, pressed by the perils of the moment, his supporters permitted themselves to read into the delphic utterances what each wanted for himself. Over Algeria the ambiguity was particularly pronounced – the source of much heart-searching in the years to come. In the Second World War days in North Africa, Harold Macmillan recalls of de Gaulle that his "whole purpose" was to "sustain the spirit of France and to preserve the integrity of the French Empire". But by France's non-white subjects he was also revered as the "man of Brazzaville" in memory of his historic speech there of January 1944, when he declared that it would be French policy "to lead each of the colonial peoples to a development that will permit them to administer themselves and, later, to govern themselves. . . ." He viewed "integrity of the French Empire" as an adjunct – and therefore secondary – to the mystic *grandeur* of France, rather than something with any more practical value in itself. That elephantine memory, unforgetting and unforgiving, had unhappiest memories of the Pétainist establishment in wartime Algiers; he had little instinctive sympathy with the self-made *grands colons*, any more than he could identify himself with the aspirations and anxieties of the *petits blancs*. After an interview with him in 1958, Edmond Michelet and Maurice Schumann both came away with the impression that de Gaulle's desire for peace went as far as being prepared to "do a deal" with the F.L.N.; to an astonished Austrian journalist close to the F.L.N., Artur Rosenberg, he had declared in April, "Certainly Algeria will be independent." Meanwhile, the army, Soustelle and the rest were convincing themselves that de Gaulle would stand unfalteringly for *Algérie française*. Louis Joxe, one of de Gaulle's closer confidants, was perhaps nearer to the truth when he noted in conversation with de Gaulle shortly before his return to power that "he spoke of everything but Algeria – because he didn't want to come back for Algeria only". As Brian Crozier aptly remarks in his biography of de Gaulle: "For the army and the settlers, *Algérie française* was all; for him, it was only one element in the complex picture of his deferred ambitions. . . ."

9 May: Salan's telegram

In the midst of all the plotting, the news on 9 May of the execution of the three French soldiers hit over-excited Algiers like a whip across the face. The spontaneous *pied noir* reaction was, "So these are the kind of assassins Pflimlin wants to negotiate with. . . !" The army was enraged and outraged. It was the last blow that it could take. Already earlier that day General Salan, who had hitherto turned a prudently cold front equally to the clamour of "The Group of Seven" and to the manoeuvrings of the Gaullist "antenna", had despatched a long telegram to General Ely, the Chief of the General Staff, in Paris.

The present crisis [it began] shows that the political parties are profoundly divided over the Algerian question. The Press permits one to think that the abandonment of Algeria would be envisaged in the diplomatic processes which would begin with negotiations aiming at a "cease-fire"....

The army in Algeria is troubled by recognition of its responsibility towards the men who are fighting and risking a useless sacrifice if the representatives of the nation are not determined to maintain *Algérie française*....

The French army, in its unanimity, would feel outraged by the abandonment of this national patrimony. One cannot predict how it would react in its despair....

I request you to bring to the attention of the President of the Republic our anguish, which only a government firmly determined to maintain our flag in Algeria can efface.

It was a clear-cut ultimatum. Virtually for the first time since Napoleon's coup of the 18th Brumaire a French army was about to intervene directly in national politics.

Lacoste leaves

Salan followed up this telegram by announcing that, on 13 May, there would be a ceremony at the *monument aux morts* to render homage to the three dead soldiers, and requested that the *anciens combattants* organisations should take part. That evening, accompanied by Generals Jouhaud, Allard and Massu, as well as Admiral Auboyneau commanding the Mediterranean fleet, Salan presented himself to Lacoste to show him the telegram. That same day Lacoste had come under heavy pressure from Sérigny to publish a signed article in the *Écho* calling for a committee of public safety. At first Lacoste appeared favourably inclined; but overnight his Socialist principles asserted themselves, and on the 10th he informed Sérigny that what he asked was tantamount to requiring him to break with the Socialist party; and that was "as if you were asking me to leave my wife after thirty-two years of marriage". Instead, Lacoste promised that he would personally convey the request to the President of the Republic, "since that is just about all that's left". His last words were, "Avoid violence." Then Lacoste left Algiers, like a thief in the night, in marked contrast to the flamboyant departure of his predecessor, Soustelle, saying that he would return after his consultations with President Coty, but sensing that he never would.* Behind him he left the ruins of the

* When asked by the author why he had left Algiers before de Gaulle came to power, Lacoste explained, "I didn't want to leave in disorder, like Soustelle – so I thought it was much better to go in discretion, and not submit enflamed Algeria to another tearing-apart demonstration like that one.... So, I went quietly – no flags – no music. I left my wife behind to give the impression that I would come back; though I had decided, once and for all, to leave."

never-to-be-enacted *loi-cadre*, and all the aspirations of his twenty-seven months in office. In Algiers there was now no governor-general; in Paris, no government. A chasm gaped enticingly.

Pflimlin hopes: Lagaillarde decides

With Bidault, Pinay, Mollet and Pleven all having failed even to form a new ministry, Pflimlin was hopefully awaiting his investiture by the Assembly on the night of 13 May. Already on the 8th Sérigny had remarked to Soustelle and Delbecque that, if this were to happen, "We are lost,' and this was one factor with which all the various conspirators agreed as the temperature mounted. Disappointed by Lacoste's tergiversation on the 10th, Sérigny (always in consultation with Soustelle) was pushed into committing a desperate editorial act. On the 11th, a Sunday, he printed in the *Écho's* weekly sister, *Dimanche Matin*, an unequivocal call to de Gaulle to intervene, under the clarion headline PARLEZ, ... PARLEZ VITE, MON GÉNÉRAL. Coming from such a long-standing Pétainist, the article had – in Sérigny's own words – "the effect of a bomb in Algeria". Delbecque and the Gaullists were delighted by this powerful acquisition to their cause, but the "Seven" were thrown into a turmoil. On the evening of the 12th a meeting was held in Dr Lefèvre's villa. The Chergui, the wind from the desert that exacerbates passions and distorts reason, had been blowing for two days. Amid an atmosphere tense with febrile rumours, the *pied noir* leaders allowed themselves to be persuaded – wrongly – that Delbecque was all set to launch a coup in the name of de Gaulle the night following the morrow's demonstrations, and before Pflimlin could be sworn in. Therefore the Gaullists had to be beaten to it.

Lagaillarde, the student prince and no doubt with the image of his martyred ancestor before his eyes, now stepped forward.

> Tomorrow [he declared], I am going to seize the radio and the Gouvernement-Général, and I shall throw the files out of the windows. We shall perhaps be shot up, but Salan will be obliged to take power. As for me, I swear that I shall not leave the demonstration before getting into Lacoste's office!

A majority of the "Seven" supported Lagaillarde. Enter Nez-de-Cuir on one of his liaison rounds. When informed of Lagaillarde's intention, the colonel was horrified and told the "Seven" that they were "madmen". The next morning he repeated his warning, adding, "The army will fire on you. ... You will lose Algeria through your folly."

To which Martel retorted: "You can't fire on us. And at least *you* will have been informed."

One of the surprising aspects of the "spontaneous" events of 13 May is that so many people were informed about what was going to happen, and nothing was done to stop it. On the 12th, the correspondent of *Le Figaro* had cabled back to Paris: "It is probable that tomorrow afternoon the Gouvernement-Général will be invaded by the mob." Returning from Paris that same day, the former secretary-general of the Algiers police, Paul Teitgen, warned an impassively disbelieving Salan of the impending invasion, telling him that the paras would do nothing to stop it. He then sent a warning to Pflimlin, via the curiously circuitous route of the United States consul-general, the State Department and the Quai d'Orsay. But by the time it reached Paris it would be too late in any case.

13 May

The *monument aux morts* squats, like some hideous Aztec sacrificial altar, at the top of flights of steep steps. These, descending, lead through the gardens of the Plateau des Glières which bisect the centre of Algiers, and eventually to the sea. Just above it towers the Gouvernement-Général, a great white sepulchre of a modern building, adorned in its entrance by a bust of Marianne, a reminder of the authority of the republic. Surrounded by protective railings, it looks out on to the vast open space known officially as the Place Georges-Clemenceau, but more familiarly as the Forum, normally a parking area, and a favourite rendezvous of children on roller-skates. It was at 6 o'clock on Tuesday the 13th that General Salan was due to lay the army's wreath on the *monument* in memory of the three executed soldiers. In preparation, European Algiers had imposed on itself a total shutdown. All through the morning *pied noir* farmers from the Mitidja, whipped in by Martel, poured into the city. Cars raced through the streets, sounding out on their horns the now familiar tattoo of AL-GÉR-IE FRAN-ÇAISE. The university had been thoroughly organised by Lagaillarde, and a special "commando" detailed to stand by in readiness outside the railings of the "G-G". Shortly after midday Lagaillarde appeared at the Otomatic (now recovered from its bombing of the previous year) and announced dramatically to the students there: "From now on I consider myself an insurgent." By early afternoon the Rue Michelet and its tributaries were a solid mass of demonstrators and banners, an estimated 20,000 strong (Salan says 100,000). As passions rose, a first victim – ritualistically as in almost every civil upheaval since 1945 – was the American Cultural Centre, sacked by an angry detachment of *pieds noirs*. At about 4 o'clock the dense crowds thronging the approaches to the *monument* parted like the waters of the Red Sea as a grim-faced Lagaillarde, clad in full para regalia, strode through. Preceding him was a personal bodyguard of four tough-looking Muslim *harkis* in battle kit and carrying sub-machine-guns.

Arriving at the *monument*, Lagaillarde leaped nimbly up on to the plinth and, flanked by other leaders of the "Seven", vehemently harangued the crowd: "Are you going to let *Algérie française* be sold down the river? Will you allow traitors to govern us? Will you go to the end of the line to keep *Algérie française?*" The massed *pieds noirs* roared back their responses. It was abundantly clear that Lagaillarde had them completely under his spell by the time Salan and his party reached the scene. Accompanied by shouts of *"L'armée au pouvoir!"* *"Massu au pouvoir!"*, Salan laid his wreath; the crowd observed respectfully a minute of silence, then joined him in a frenetic singing of the *Marseillaise*. Now, immediately after Salan had departed, Lagaillarde took over with a shout of: "Let's go! Everybody to the 'G–G' against this rotten regime!" The mob surged up to the Forum, led by Lagaillarde's "commando" some five hundred strong. The C.R.S. fired a few gas canisters, then retreated behind the railings of the "G–G". Conspicuous by their absence were Trinquier's paras, who had ruled the streets of the Casbah so ruthlessly the previous year; when they did arrive they stood by apathetically, much as Teitgen had predicted the previous day, without doing anything to prevent what was impending. As stones shattered the windows of the imposing edifice, Lagaillarde's storm troops brought up a truck and rammed the iron grille gates. Lacoste's military adviser, Ducournau, tried to temporise with Lagaillarde, telling him "You're mad, you'll wreck everything!" But the mob surged on into the building, hurling down the bust of Marianne in the foyer. In a matter of moments Lagaillarde was realising his ambition of the night before. Students appeared at every window, flinging out sheaves of documents and dossiers. Standing on the roof of the central balcony that was to become the focus of world attention over the next few days, Lagaillarde was greeted in the midst of this snowstorm by wildest applause. A kind of euphoria seized the crowd, and was to hold it in its grip for many days to come.

The Gouvernement-Général seized

Meanwhile, sheltering under his desk from the flying glass and stones, Lacoste's deputy, Pierre Chaussade, telephoned the absent governor-general in Paris to ask for instructions. Lacoste ordered that under no circumstances were the insurgents to be fired upon. But beyond Lacoste no helpful authority was forthcoming; the outgoing Gaillard felt he was no longer responsible, and Pflimlin had not yet been sworn in. In an attempt to pacify the mob, Ducournau – unable to make his voice heard – appeared on the balcony with a blackboard bearing the words: "I have just telephoned Paris to call for a government of public safety." The crowd applauded, but continued with its sack of the building. Having received news of what was happening Salan, after a brief hesitation, set off for the "G–G" along a tunnel connecting it with his headquarters. It was less than an hour and a half since the ceremony at the *monument aux morts*.

He was told that there were no casualties "except Marianne, and she doesn't count". Massu had arrived at about the same time, in a violent rage at the shambles (to one eye-witness the corridors of the "G–G" resembled "a packet-boat at the moment of foundering, after the mutiny of the crew") and at the affront to good military order. Angrily he demanded, "What sort of *bordel* is this?" and, in an aggressive aside to Lagaillarde, "*Qu'est-ce-que vous foutez en uniform?*" Acclaims of "*Massu au pouvoir!*" only enraged him further, and the robust nose thrust out at a more belligerent angle than usual. Appearing on the balcony, Salan was greeted with all the long-nourished mistrust of the *pieds noirs*, dating back to the *affaire du bazooka*: "*Foutez le camp!*" "*Salan, bradeur!*" "*Indochine!*" "*Vive Massu!*" "*Vive Soustelle!*" Massu, on the other hand, the popular hero of the Battle of Algiers, received the kind of applause hitherto reserved for Lagaillarde. But when asked to say a few encouraging words to the mob about "*Algérie française*", he growled: "*Ces cons-là me font tous chier!*" Then, after a whispered conference with Salan, he turned brusquely to the nearest ringleader and asked for names for a committee of public safety.

Massu forms a committee of public safety

The invasion by the mob, the volleys of paper streaming from the "G–G" windows, all bore an extraordinary resemblance to that other bizarre episode in French history – the seizure of the Hôtel de Ville by the Paris Communards in 1870. So did the scenes that followed. A young man in glasses who pushed himself forward, when asked for his name replied: "André Baudier, clerk in council housing. . . ."

"But whom do you represent?"

"The mob!"

Massu wrote down Baudier at the top of his list. Then came Lagaillarde, followed by a series of *illustres inconnus* drawn from the crowd immediately at hand. The only senior army officers present were Colonels Trinquier (now commanding Bigeard's 3rd R.P.C.) and Ducasse (Massu's chief-of-staff), so their names too were added. Now the ubiquitous Nez-de-Cuir arrived and asked to be included on the list. Announcing the formation of the Committee of Public Safety and reading out its members from the balcony of the "G–G", Massu received a rapturous endorsement from the crowd outside, followed by another fervent singing of the *Marseillaise*. Appeased, and in a fiesta-like mood, the crowd now settled down in the Forum to await whatever further excitements this gala night would bring, with children asleep on their knees.

There now took place a telephone call between Massu and Lacoste in Paris, nervously wanting to know what had happened in Algiers. Massu was heard to say:

Yes, it's true, we have constituted a committee. . . . There is no question of a *coup d'état*. . . . It's just to confirm to parliament the will of Algeria to remain French. . . . I could not act otherwise. Or we would have had to fire on the mob. Do you give me the order to fire? No! . . .

In the meantime the Committee was drafting a telegram to President Coty, which Massu then signed and despatched. Explaining that the Committee had been formed to "maintain order" and avert bloodshed, it urged "creation in Paris of a government of public safety, alone capable of preserving Algeria as an integral part of the mother country". At about ten o'clock Delbecque arrived on the scene, having been caught out of Algiers that day and somewhat discountenanced to have been beaten to the draw by Lagaillarde, who remarked to him sardonically: "I recognise that I am a little ahead of your scenario!" Initially there were some sharp words between Delbecque and the military, with Colonel Ducournau accusing him of opening the way for a *front populaire* by his conspiracy. It was only at this point, so it seems, that an outraged Massu certainly, and Salan probably, first became aware of the various *complots*. Under the influence of Nez-de-Cuir Thomazo, however, Delbecque and several other members of the Gaullist faction were admitted to Massu's Committee of Public Safety, together with Sérigny, Martel and Lefèvre representing the "ultras". Almost as an afterthought, three Muslim worthies representing nine million Algerians were also included on the list, which would eventually reach the unwieldy total of seventy-four members.

Later that night, the Gaullists – adroitly turning the situation to their advantage – prevailed upon Salan to send a new and crucial message to President Coty, stating: "the responsible military authorities esteem it an imperative necessity to appeal to a national arbiter with a view to constituting a government of public safety. A call for calm by this high authority is alone capable of re-establishing the situation". Salan, cautious as ever, had expunged from the original draft the name of de Gaulle, but the reference to "a national arbiter" and "this high authority" was explicit enough. At the same time a direct appeal was sent to de Gaulle himself. The cat was out of the bag. The army of Algeria, though grudgingly and under pressure, had committed itself.

In Paris, Pflimlin invested

In Paris the events in Algiers had been followed by utmost confusion. There was a feeling that never since the bloody clashes of February 1934 had circumstances so favoured a seizure of power by the mob. Rumours ran round the Assembly that Chaban-Delmas was in Algiers preparing a *coup d'état*; in fact he was in his Bordeaux constituency. A number of panicky arrests were made; one major of the general staff on his way to a conspiratorial meeting was apprehended and, after lamely pretending that he was visiting his mistress, spent the next fortnight in a cell along with Algerian suspects. Soustelle, particularly, was placed under strict police surveillance. The "lame-duck" Gaillard sent a signal to Salan, granting him full powers; then regretted it and sent a further signal limiting those powers to the Algiers zone only. Under the stress of events, the Assembly hastened to invest Pflimlin, at 2.45 on the morning of the 14th – with a substantial backing of 280 to 126 votes. Pflimlin spoke critically of "factious generals", then regretted it on realising that Salan had behaved with almost complete propriety, so far, following Gaillard's act of "enablement". His new cabinet wavered between desires of keeping the bridges with Algiers open and threats of cutting off supplies and communications until the Committee of Public Safety promised loyal intent.

News of the investiture came as a severe blow to the Committee of Public Safety in the "G–G" and was greeted with howls of rage from the still attendant crowd outside. Salan, the inscrutable "Chinois", for reasons best known to himself did not immediately reveal Gaillard's "enabling" instruction to the Committee of Public Safety; on the other hand, he was also to ignore completely the second, restrictive instruction. Meanwhile, the persuasive Thomazo had got among the crowd, begging it to cry "'Vive Salan!' – because he's one of you." With all the volatility that composed the character of the *mediterranéen-et-demi pied noir*, on the next appearance of the mistrusted Commander-in-Chief whom it had booed only a few hours previously, the crowd burst forth in rapturous acclaim. As the situation grew more complex, the non-political Massu showed himself quite out of his depth, longing to get off the hook and get back to the officers' mess. To one of the journalists who saw him later on the 14th. he "resembled the cursèd Jackdaw of Rheims:

> His feathers all seemed to be turned the wrong way;
> His pinions drooped – he could hardly stand. . . ."

Salan, on the other hand, the calmest of all, instantly showed considerable political acumen, and prudence. Suddenly, overnight and for the ensuing days until de Gaulle committed himself, Salan found himself supreme arbiter of the situation

14 May

The 14th was a black day for the "factious" leaders inside the "G–G". De Gaulle had not come forward. As it was a Wednesday, he was making his weekly visit to Paris, and when his publisher expressed concern that "events" might delay completion of his memoirs he had replied absent-mindedly, "What events?" Soustelle, whose arrival Delbecque had disingenuously declared to be imminent, was more or less under house-arrest in Paris; President Coty had appealed to the army for loyalty, and units in

Germany and France showed no signs of rallying to Algiers; the Poujadists had not moved as their comrades of the "Seven" had expected. There were indications that Pflimlin would cut off supplies, and it was reckoned that petrol and money would run out within ten to fifteen days. Delbecque went through the day in fear that Salan, who showed signs of recoiling a step or two from his exposed position, might actually have him arrested. If something did not break it looked momentarily as if the "revolution" might simply collapse. Perhaps only the continuing enthusiasm of the crowd and the junior officers of the paras sustained it. Exclaimed Captain Sergent of the 1st R.E.P., who was unknowingly embarking that day on a long career of revolt: "It's a dream! It's just not possible!... So all is saved. Algeria will remain French...!" Meanwhile, in Paris that night Simone de Beauvoir recorded how, at a Brecht play attacking war and generals, a left-wing audience "nearly brought the roof down with its applause".

15 May: Salan: "Vive de Gaulle!"

15 May was a public holiday, and little effective was done by the new government in Paris that day. In bewilderment, and pushed this way and that by his ministers, Pflimlin embarked upon what looked conspicuously like a double game: on the one hand he endorsed Salan's actions and responsibility; on the other he imposed a blockade of Algeria, severing communications between it and the homeland, and entertaining the absurdity of a loyal "redoubt" in Kabylia. Encouraged by this pusillanimity and urged on by Delbecque, as well as now obviously beginning to enjoy his new position of power, Salan appeared once more on the "G–G" balcony before the ever-present crowds in the Forum below. He spoke in moving terms of his attachment to the soil of Algeria, which contained the human remains of his beloved son, and added: "What has been done here will show to the world that Algeria wants to remain French. Our sincerity will carry with us all the Muslims." He concluded his address with a vibrant "*Vive la France! Vive l'Algérie française!*", whereupon, from behind, Delbecque whispered in his ear: "Shout *Vive de Gaulle!*" Salan turned about, grasped the microphone again, and pronounced, not with the most overwhelming conviction: "*... et vive de Gaulle!*"

Though not exactly uttered fortissimo, the decisive words were nevertheless out. At lunch-time an angry Pflimlin telephoned Salan to ask what he meant by it. Salan explained that, in his view – as well as that of "the entire population of Algeria" – only de Gaulle legitimately at the head of a government could save both Algeria and France. Pflimlin hung up. Salan had stepped firmly across the Rubicon; the army in Algeria was publicly committed; the bridges with metropolitan France were down. Meanwhile, in Paris another eminent general was lobbying the Socialist leader now serving as Pflimlin's vice-premier, Guy Mollet. Maurice Challe had had close contact with Mollet dating from Suez when he had been despatched to London to co-ordinate with Eden the Franco-British plan. Now, as deputy to the Gaullist Chief of the General Staff, General Ely, he went to warn Mollet that the situation was "heading for disaster"; that the Pflimlin government was "unviable"; that if things went on as they were, the army of Algeria would be obliged to intervene, which it could effectively achieve within forty-eight hours; and that he, Challe, personally would "never fire on my brothers-in-arms". Mollet chided him for exceeding his brief, and shortly afterwards Challe too was placed under house-arrest; but not before he was able to make arrangements for a substantial portion of the air transport command to move to Algeria, to lessen the impact of the government's blockade.

Sparked by Salan's utterance, de Gaulle ("The issue which was already at the back of everyone's mind had at last been publicly raised," he explained) now came out of his hermit-crab shell for the first time. Using carefully measured words, he declared to the nation that "in the face of the trials that again are mounting toward it, it should know that I am ready to assume the powers of the republic". But there was no how or when. As Prime Minister Macmillan noted in his journal, it was "an equivocal statement, but one which has terrified the French politicians. It is cast in his usual scornful but enigmatic language."

16 May: "Here are our Muslim brothers"
In Algiers, however, de Gaulle's declaration was greeted with wildest enthusiasm. A new confidence bolstered up the leaders in the "G–G"; as exemplified by Massu, they now, said Michael Clark, "assumed the aspect of the jackdaw after plenary absolution:

> He grew sleek and fat;
> In addition to that,
> A fresh crop of feathers came thick as a mat. . . ."

More than ever, Salan was now the hero of the hour, and this sudden access of popularity and influence could not help but affect him as indeed it had Soustelle two years previously. The next day, 16 May, the euphoria of the moment occasioned one of the more remarkable and inexplicable phenomena of the whole war. Into the excited *pied noir* crowds that thronged the Forum, which had now become well-established as the centre of the daily entertainment, that evening there merged dense groups of Muslims. Waving tricolours and crosses of Lorraine, and banners that proclaimed "We demand a Government of National Unity", or even "*Vive Massu!*", they came in their thousands from the Algiers Casbah and from *douars* throughout Algeria; old men sporting wartime decorations, young students, pregnant *fatmas* in *haiks*. A voice from the "G–G" balcony shouted, "Here are our Muslim brothers! Make a place for them!" and there followed extraordinary scenes of mass emotion. *Pieds noirs* linked arms with Muslims, embraced them; European girls lifted the veils of acquiescent Muslim women; all together sang the *Marseillaise* and the military *Chant des Africains*. From the famous balcony the stentorian voice of Massu rang out, welcoming "with pride" this "spontaneously organised" assemblage of Muslims, and asserting, "Let them know that France will never abandon them." Heady new slogans of "From Dunkirk to Taman-rasset, fifty-five million French!" passed among the crowd. Suddenly the horrors of the Milk-Bar and Casino bombings, of the backlash *ratonnades*, seemed all but forgotten.

Historians still find the "fraternisation" phenomenon of 16 May hard to explain. The official line of the F.L.N., as well as that of French sceptics, is that the whole demonstration was phoney, rigged by the psychological warfare experts of the French Cinquième Bureau; that the women who had so joyfully cast away their *haiks* were simply tarts rounded up for the occasion. But this at best can only be a half-truth. It is true that on the previous day para teams organised by Godard, Trinquier and Léger, who had all become intimately acquainted with the Casbah during the Battle of Algiers, had been hard at work coaxing the Muslims to turn out and stirring them up with heady assurances of equality and integration. But, unaccountably, success snowballed beyond all their expectations; instead of a hoped-for 5,000, it was a crowd of something like 30,000 Muslims that reached the Forum that evening. Stern critics of *Algérie française* like *Le Monde* and François Mauriac agreed on the genuineness of the demonstration, acclaiming it as a basis for new optimism. What thoughts and hopes lay behind those deeply etched, inscrutable Muslim faces on the Forum that day is difficult to divine, except perhaps a mystical, irrational belief that somehow the magical figure of de Gaulle was going to solve everything. Disillusion was bound to follow on both sides as euphoria was replaced by the realisation that the fraternisers were still each worshipping different gods. It was solely the army (i.e. the paras) who were the initiators, and – though carried along by the emotion of the moment – Lagail-larde and the *pied noir* "ultras" were not prepared to pay more than lip-service to such tenets as "equality". Nevertheless, as in that other dawn celebrated by Wordsworth, it was bliss to be alive in Algiers on that day of 16 May, and for a brief spell it looked as if all might be possible – so long as de Gaulle would grasp the reins.

17 May: Soustelle arrives

On 17 May the long-awaited Jacques Soustelle arrived in Algeria; his departure from Paris had been as spectacular in its way as his send-off from

Algiers two years previously. Having failed to get away on the crucial night of the 13th, the former governor-general and arch-Gaullist had been under closest police surveillance, with some ten policemen watching his apartment in the Avenue Henri-Martin. On the 15th Soustelle let it be known that he was suffering from *la grippe* and confined to bed. Two days later friends drove a car into the courtyard, brazenly smuggled Soustelle out of Paris half-stifled under a rug reeking of moth-balls, and rushed him across the Swiss frontier where a plane ferried him to Algeria. It was a getaway worthy of his wartime operations. In Algiers news of his arrival was welcomed rapturously by the crowd, but Salan – fearing a rival in the camp – greeted him coldly. "Your presence here is not indispensable," he told him. "You are going to politicise the affair." Playing his cards skilfully, Soustelle with humility replied that he had simply come to place himself at the disposal of *Algérie française* – and therefore Salan; if he were not wanted he would fly back home again at once. Meanwhile the crowd was clamouring for their former hero; so Soustelle was duly incorporated in the Committee of Public Safety and shown off to an exultant crowd from the famous balcony.

One of Salan's anxieties about Soustelle's arrival was that it would only widen the breach between Algiers and Paris. In this he was quite right, and it was also to increase enormously the momentum for the return of de Gaulle. Another blow to Pflimlin and a point for the Gaullists at this same time was the resignation of the Chief of the General Staff, General Ely, ostensibly on the grounds of the arrest of his deputy, Challe. On 18 May Guy Mollet – for once out of harmony with his party – decided to back de Gaulle, provided he were to receive his authority from the Assembly, and not from the Algiers "rebels". The next morning a completely abortive general strike called by the Left showed just how ill-organised it would be if it came to mustering any counter-coup. But still the clear sign of assent awaited from the recluse of Colombey-les-Deux-Églises was not forthcoming.

In Paris tension was mounting; seventy American tourists refused to leave their plane at Orly for fear of being caught up in a revolution. Then, on the afternoon of the 19th, de Gaulle summoned a Press conference at the Palais d'Orsay. On his way there he noted derisively how Pflimlin's newly appointed left-wing Minister of the Interior, Jules Moch, had deployed massive police forces round the building, "as if it were conceivable that de Gaulle was about to appear at the head of a brigade of shock-troops". Inside, the hall was packed with six hundred journalists of the world Press, Graham Greene, François Mauriac, Clostermann the Second World War air ace, and all the stars of the Gaullist firmament, such as Michel Debré and Chaban-Delmas. The attentive journalists noted that the figure of the great man had thickened, the hair was whiter and the face unhealthier; the voice sounded thinner, but still he could speak without recourse to notes, and, above all, that unique tone of authority was undiminished.

Events in Algeria, he declared, had indeed led to "an extremely grave national crisis... but this could also prove to be the beginning of a kind of resurrection". Almost with modesty he added that that was why "the moment seemed to me to have come when it would be possible for me once again to be directly useful to France". Letting it be clearly known, once more, that he did not intend to come back as the instrument of any single faction, he spelled out that "when someone assumes the powers of the republic, it can be only because the republic will itself have delegated them". He was, as if it needed stating, "a solitary man... who belongs to no one, and who belongs to the entire world". In answer to questions about authoritarian intent should he return, de Gaulle retorted scathingly: "Is it credible that I am going to begin a career as a dictator at the age of sixty-seven?" Though he praised the army in Algeria, he pointedly omitted any reference to an Algerian solution as such; an omission which was only to attain full significance in later years. All that was made crystal clear was that his price for returning was, as it always had been, the sweeping away of the whole political system of the Fourth Republic as it stood. Everything else had to be inferred. He ended: "Now I shall return home to my village and there I shall hold myself at the disposition of the country." The precise formula for his return was to be left for lesser mortals to work out.

The growth of Salan: "Résurrection"

In Algiers de Gaulle's Press conference was greeted with a mixture of satisfaction and impatience. Time was clearly against the "revolt" in its increasing isolation, and the unhurried stance of de Gaulle was more than vexing. Salan now despatched similar messages of menacing urgency both to him and Pflimlin, warning that if de Gaulle did not take over power as soon as possible the high command in Algeria might be unable to prevent a "military incursion" into metropolitan France. These were indeed threatening words. Having now committed himself irrevocably to de Gaulle and broken with Pflimlin, Salan's real power was growing in leaps and bounds; his chin, remarked one of his officers, "protrudes an additional centimetre over the balcony with each day". It was patently within his capacity either to bring down the Pflimlin regime, or to provoke a military putsch in Paris. On 21st Salan made his shortest speech from the "G–G" balcony to a crowd wildly chanting "L'armée au pouvoir!", thanking them "for these complimentary words" but adding: "you must know that we are all now united and that thus we shall march together up the Champs-Elysées, and we shall be covered with flowers!" On the 23rd a new Committee of Public Safety was formed to preside over the whole of Algeria and the Sahara, and expanded to embrace a fair smattering of Muslims. Its first function was to pass a vote according a certain "statutory" legitimacy to the proceedings whereby its precursor had been formed on 13 May.

Meanwhile, plans were initiated for a physical, military intervention in France to force the hand of both the government and the slow-moving de Gaulle. Conceived by Massu, the operation originally bore the typically straightforward code-name of "Grenade" but under Delbecque's influence it was changed to the more meaningful "Résurrection", borrowed from de Gaulle's allusion at his Press conference. "Résurrection" was predicated upon the support in France of General Miquel, commanding the Toulouse area where most of the para training bases were located. A force of five thousand paras would land at Villacoublay airfield just south-west of Paris; Massu and Trinquier would arrive, naturally, with the first wave and would then speed to join Miquel at an operational headquarters set up in the Invalides. Other commando detachments would seize the Eiffel Tower so as to control communications, while the élite 3rd R.P.C. would "neutralise" such key points as the Ministry of the Interior and the central offices of the trade union C.G.T. and of the Communist Party. At the same time Colonel Gribius, commanding the Second Armoured Task Force at nearby Rambouillet, would roll his tanks into Paris in support. The impetuous ex-para lieutenant, Pierre Lagaillarde, somewhat eclipsed by developments since 13 May, hoped to regain the limelight by provoking an uprising in the Latin Quarter and then marching with the students to seize the Assembly. Once the key points of the capital had been effectively occupied, it was intended that Generals Massu and Miquel would conduct a persuaded President Coty by helicopter to Colombey, presenting de Gaulle with a *fait accompli*. The date provisionally fixed for "Résurrection" was the 27th–28th, with Massu declaring confidently in a Press interview (on 23 May): "In eight days, General de Gaulle will be in power!" It was a thoroughly makeshift plan, which depended on the assured acquiescence of the army echelons in France. Against it would stand the few sources of gendarmes and C.R.S. defending the airfields – and the unknown quantity of the Communists and their allies.

24 May: "Résurrection" in Corsica

On 24 May an astonished France learned that Massu's paras had seized power in Corsica, headed by the irrepressible Nez-de-Cuir. The coup was carried by detachments of the cloak-and-dagger 11th Shock, currently based in Corsica, without a shot being fired. When asked by journalists if there had been any casualties, Pascal Arrighi, the Gaullist deputy for Corsica who had taken part in the operation, replied: "Of course not! It was a revolution, not an election!" Only in Bastia was there a semblance of resistance by the Left, under slightly *opéra bouffe* circumstances. There the Socialist deputy mayor refused to accept Salan's nomination of Thomazo as military governor of the island, and refused to leave his office. Finally, as a face-saver, the deputy mayor announced he would depart either if formally under arrest, or arm-in-arm with the insurgents, singing the *Marseillaise*. The *Marseillaise* won.

In Paris Pflimlin was outraged by the Corsican coup and momentarily considered making an effort to reoccupy the island. But when asked where the fleet was, the Admiralty gave the unsatisfactorily evasive response that it was at sea and sailing to an unknown destination. De Gaulle, still holding back, was now moved to telephone his old banker friend at Rothschilds, Georges Pompidou, and asked him to draw up a cabinet. The main scene of the action now transferred itself from Algiers to Paris, where it became largely a matter of constitutional haggling and a race against time before Massu's paras floated down from the skies. At this point the strong man of the Pflimlin government turned out to be Jules Moch, the left-wing Minister of the Interior, who, insisting "I won't be a Kerensky", set to organising a resistance to the threat from Algiers. The C.R.S. (those that could be reckoned loyal) were mobilised, and trade union leaders briefed to halt all trains in the event of a landing (although, as one sagely pointed out, "The paras don't often go by train!"). There was dangerous talk about arming the Communists, who claimed to be able to get 10,000 militants out on the streets at a moment's notice. For several days France seemed to tremble on the brink of civil war and anarchy; although, despite the crisis, on that warm Whit Sunday of 25 May, a record number of cars headed insouciantly out of Paris for the country.

26 May: de Gaulle's secret rendezvous

That day Guy Mollet, though at first deterred by de Gaulle's refusal to disallow the use of armed force, endeavoured to act as intermediary between Pflimlin and the general. Late on the night of the 26th, the weather having turned icily cold, a clandestine meeting of the two took place at St Cloud. The choice of the place, the famous terrace of the 18th Brumaire, so steeped in associations of Napoleonic *coups d'états*, seemed a curious one. De Gaulle was embarrassed, not having thought of the historical association, while Pflimlin was frankly disturbed by it. His misgivings were not allayed by de Gaulle's continued refusal to repudiate the use of force by the Algiers leaders, and notably the takeover of Corsica. As he had insisted at every private and public meeting since 13 May, he repeated that, at his age, he had no desire to become either a Napoleon I or Napoleon III. "You know very well", he assured Pflimlin, "that I will never return to power brought in by force. I will not be the man of an insurrection. Never will I accept a military dictatorship, never, never." But he steadfastly refused Pflimlin's request to appeal to the army for restraint, as President Coty had done.

"M. Coty wasn't obeyed. I can only risk my authority. And if I am not heeded?" In view of what was to happen three years later, de Gaulle's attitude seems perhaps not entirely unreasonable. Pflimlin said he was prepared to resign to make way for de Gaulle, but there were constitutional difficulties; to begin with, he could not simply nominate his successor. The President of the Republic would have to be involved. The greatest stumbling-block, however, was de Gaulle's refusal to repudiate the army's recourse to force, and on that note the two men parted coldly. It was nearly two in the morning and, delayed by thick fog, de Gaulle did not reach home until 5 a.m.

27 May: on the brink

On the morning of the 27th the crisis reached its peak. Parisians looked up nervously at every plane passing overhead; Simone de Beauvoir had Freudian nightmares about a python dropping on her from the sky; and in the Ministry of the Interior Jules Moch received an intelligence report that "Résurrection" was now scheduled to take place on the following night. He ordered his C.R.S. force to prepare to defend government buildings. Meanwhile, young para officers were arriving in the capital in civilian clothes, carrying suspiciously heavy suitcases. Among their targets was the kidnapping of Jules Moch himself, and with them – on his own mission – came Lagaillarde. Then, early in the afternoon, de Gaulle – apparently as a result of the mounting pressures upon him – issued a communiqué announcing that he had begun the "regular process" of forming a legitimate republican government, and condemning any threat to public order. At the same time he sent a signal to Salan couched in even more categoric terms, and astutely sent via official channels, in which he called for the dropping of all thoughts of "Résurrection". In Algiers Salan was manifestly delighted to be let off the hook, and despatched his deputy, General Dulac, on a liaison mission to Colombey-les-Deux-Églises. There de Gaulle spelled out to him in the clearest terms yet:

> I want to be summoned as an arbiter coming at the demand of the whole country, to take over direction of the country so as to spare it useless rendings. I must appear as the man of reconciliation and not as the champion of one of the factions currently confronting each other.*

28 May: Pflimlin resigns: the Left reacts

In Paris there was widespread jubilation and relief. Maurice Schumann was heard to exult: "He's won. We've won. France has won." Certainly it seemed as if the menacingly close spectre of civil war had been exorcised.

---

* Soustelle, who says he was in Salan's office when Dulac returned to render an account of his meeting with de Gaulle, claims that (quoting Dulac) de Gaulle had added "If I do not succeed, *alors faites le nécessaire*." Soustelle took this to mean that de Gaulle favoured a military take-over if all else failed.

At dawn on the 28th Pflimlin – white as a candle with exhaustion – duly resigned. It was decided that it was constitutionally acceptable for a prime minister not to be an elected member of the Assembly, and feverish consultations now took place between the leaders of both Houses, the outgoing Pflimlin, de Gaulle and President Coty. Although the way now looked clear for de Gaulle, there were still formidable technical obstacles ahead, not least among them the question of whether the Assembly, with its powerful bloc of the Communists and their allies, would accept de Gaulle. On the evening of the 28th the voice of the Front Populaire briefly drowned out all others, with a mass march (500,000 according to L'Humanité; 120,000 according to Le Figaro) to the Place de la République. Apart from Jacques Duclos and the Communists, Mitterrand and Mendès-France – as well as a relic of an earlier, defunct République, Edouard Daladier – were conspicuously to the forefront, amid a sea of banners proclaiming "Down with Fascism!" and "Vive la République!" There were abusive shouts of "Hang Massu!" "Send the paras to the factories!" "De Gaulle au musée!" and "La Girafe au zoo!" though in general Simone de Beauvoir detected, regretfully, an unexpected note of respect for de Gaulle. The crowd was also surprisingly good-humoured, not at all in a fighting mood; as Michael Clark notes, they were "no revolutionary cohort; this was no lashing out of popular fury against the Bastilles of tyranny and pride. It was more in the nature of a funeral procession" – certainly an enterrement de première classe for the Fourth Republic. But, as so often in moments of crisis, the French Left was split; three days later Mollet's Socialist Party (S.F.I.O.) executive abandoned the Communists and – albeit by the slenderest of votes – decided to back de Gaulle's investiture. The theme of "rather de Gaulle than Massu" (in itself bearing echoes from the days of the pre-war Front Populaire), as expressed by Beuve-Méry, the editor of Le Monde, had become the view generally endorsed by the moderate Left of France. In purely practical terms, any physical confrontation with the paras would, said Mollet, "have been a Spanish civil war without the republican army".

Coty intervenes: de Gaulle accepts

On the night of the 28th a fresh constitutional impasse arose at a meeting convened in the Elysée by President Coty between de Gaulle and the presidents of the Senate and the Assembly. Le Troquer, President of the Assembly, raised a number of constitutional objections to de Gaulle and his terms, some of them seemingly trivial, made a few unfortunate parallels with Vichy and threatened to attempt to form a government himself. De Gaulle riposted that, if the Assembly backed Le Troquer, then "I shall have no alternative but to let you have it out with the paratroops, while I go back into retirement and shut myself up with my grief." In what seems to have been a moment of genuine despair, de Gaulle with tears in his eyes turned to Gaston Monnerville, the Antillean President of the Senate: "Is the return of de Gaulle possible? Is it not possible? After all, you know, France will bury us all. We pass. She alone is eternal. If my return is not possible, I shall go back to my village with my chagrin." The meeting broke up without conclusion. Meanwhile, a fresh ultimatum had reached President Coty from Algiers; either it was de Gaulle by 15.00 hours on the 29th, or "Résurrection" would go in at 01.00 hours the following morning. After a sleepless night and feeling the full burden of his seventy-six years, the President, "this good old Frenchman", as de Gaulle described him, took a decision of immense courage which was finally to break the log-jam. On the morning of the 29th he announced that he had himself invited de Gaulle to form a government and that if this were rejected by the Assembly he would resign. It was the first time since 1875 that a President of the Republic had threatened resignation, and the significance of it was immense. The President's announcement "tolled the knell", says de Gaulle, and it was heard in complete silence by the Assembly. On the 30th de Gaulle agreed to form a government, and – as in the final stages of a painful divorce – a long sigh of relief swept over France – or most of it. That evening, says de Gaulle, "above my house I watched the twilight descend on the last evening of a long solitude. What was this mysterious force that compelled me to tear myself away from it?"

1 June: the Assembly accepts

On Sunday 1 June de Gaulle presented himself to the National Assembly, the first time he had entered it since January 1946. The terms he announced for taking over were: full powers to rule by decree for six months, an enforced "holiday" of the Assembly for four months, and a mandate to submit a new constitution to the country. When the Coty communication was read out, pandemonium reigned; the Communists thumped their desks and shouted, "*Le fascisme ne passera pas!*" For Algeria, the prime cause of his being there that day, de Gaulle proffered no formula – any more than he had done in his previous pronouncements since 13 May. Seated in symbolic solitude on the empty front benches, he was voted into power by 329 to 224 votes. With equal symbolism, a black and violent storm broke out while the vote was in progress. De Gaulle was manifestly disappointed at being unable to obtain a greater show of unanimity from his countrymen's representatives. Also disappointed were Lagaillarde and the several hundred "volunteers" from Algiers hovering in the bistros near the government quarter, and momently awaiting orders to move in; they would be still more disappointed when the list of de Gaulle's first cabinet members was released. As de Gaulle left the Assembly and got into his car he seemed to be completely unaware of the rain that was sheeting down. The Gaullist era had begun.

CHAPTER FOURTEEN

"*Je Vous Ai Compris*"

May – December 1958

> The leader must aim high, see big, judge widely, thus setting himself apart
> from the ordinary people who debate in narrow confines.
>
> Charles de Gaulle, 1932

De Gaulle to Algeria: the "True Cross of Lorraine"

THUS ended the series of disjointed incidents, accidents and coincidences which comprised the "revolution" of May 1958. De Gaulle had let the country go to the very edge of the abyss and gaze down on the ultimate catastrophe of civil war before putting out a hand to pull it back. Yet what at the time looked like hesitation and procrastination carried to dangerous lengths must now seem like a hand played with consummate skill. By waiting, de Gaulle had come back vested, first of all, in an acceptable degree of legitimacy; and secondly, he had not come back as the army's man. If it were not for these two factors, it can be doubted whether the Algerian war could have ended without civil war in France.

Nevertheless, those May events in Algiers that led to his coming created illusions sufficient to endanger greatly the immediate path ahead for de Gaulle. On the one hand, Lagaillarde and the more excitable leaders of the *pieds noirs* were left with the dangerously heady conviction that it was their actions that had brought the Fourth Republic tumbling; just as the "ultras" had defeated Blum–Viollette in 1936, sabotaged the statute of 1947, and forced Mollet to withdraw Catroux in 1956. "We were the springboard de Gaulle used to save France," they said, "and so henceforth he will dance to our tune." On the other hand, the army leaders in Algeria had just the same feeling; as one of Lartéguy's para officers remarks in *Les Prétoriens*, it was the first time "that we have won not a battle, but a multitude. We shan't be able to forget it." They did not.

Now that the ball was over, it would be difficult for both *pieds noirs* and the army to come down to reality. The trouble was that each separate faction let itself wallow in the hopes that de Gaulle would be all things to all men. In the cynical words of Georges Bidault, everybody from Right to Left, from the army to Bourguiba and even the F.L.N., felt in the first heady weeks of June that they each possessed "a piece of the True Cross of Lorraine". In his enigmatic utterances the saviour did little to dispel such tenets, so that the eventual disillusion would be all the greater. Critics and adversaries of de Gaulle could – with reason – accuse him of every manner of volte-face in his handling of Algeria, but with their eyes blinkered by the immediacy of the war itself they were unable to see on what de Gaulle's gaze was fixed. From his great height the eyes quested far over the heads of lesser humans to the peaks of a distant promised land. If there was one thing in the pursuit of which he was unwavering all through his life, it was the grandeur de la France, dreamed of in those solitary years in the wilderness. In the long term nothing else mattered, or would be allowed to stand in its way, and this should be retained in the mind as a key to all the enigma of his subsequent actions. He would achieve his dream; even though in the course of it Algeria would be lost, had to be lost. Hand in hand with this conviction of la grandeur went a certainty that destiny had earmarked him to rediscover it for France.

Visiting de Gaulle in Paris in June shortly after his investiture, Prime Minister Macmillan recorded: "His manner is calm, affable, and rather paternal. But underneath this new exterior, I should judge that he is just as obstinate as ever." Few would suffer from this obstinacy more than Macmillan himself. And de Gaulle was sixty-seven, having already completed more than the work of one lifetime, and with such notable attributes of age as a nagging awareness of the brevity of time. Also, to the majority of his countrymen, especially those in Algeria, as Tournoux remarks: "The best known of Frenchmen remained the least known . . . a monolith of indecipherable hieroglyphs". Thus a sense of destiny, paternalism, obstinacy, courage, enigma, an inherent shortage of sympathy for the predicament of the pieds noirs, the impatience of age: these were the qualifications de Gaulle took with him on his first trip to Algeria on 4 June.

As de Gaulle arrived in his special Caravelle, the sky, recalls Lartéguy, was of "that evangelic blue depicted on certain pious faces". But in that blue there were already clouds apparent. Those on the Committee of Public Safety who had brought about the advent of de Gaulle were not happy with his first cabinet list; there seemed to be too much concession to the Left (Guy Mollet had been appointed vice-premier); there were too many little-known functionaries among the new ministers (of the activists of May only Michel Debré, made Minister of Justice, had been rewarded). The faithful Delbecque received no post, having offended by openly criticising the first choices, while even Soustelle, as too-dedicated an apostle of Algérie française, had been appointed nothing more than "Minister-Delegate" (or "Minister-Relegate", as the punsters muttered). An angry altercation took place after the hotheads of the C.S.P., Martel and Ortiz, had the temerity to imprison briefly two of de Gaulle's accompanying ministers while he spoke from the Gouvernement-Général – a barely disguised hint at the limitations of de Gaulle's power. Then, shortly after 7 p.m., wearing the uniform of a brigadier-general but bare-headed, de Gaulle appeared on the balcony where his name had been so frequently and fervently invoked during the preceding May days. Among the vast, expectant crowd were many Muslims; but behind their impassive, weatherbeaten, unsmiling faces it was as difficult to decipher what was really in their minds as it had been during those euphoric moments of fraternisation in May. Introducing de Gaulle, Salan – showing rare signs of emotion – declared, "Our great cry of joy and hope has been heard!" For a full three minutes de Gaulle was unable to make himself heard. Now followed the opening sentence that was to be repeated, interpreted and misinterpreted over the ensuing years; stretching his long arms in a vast V-sign above his head, he pronounced:

"*Je vous ai compris . . . !*"

"Vive l'Algérie française!"

The crowd went wild. Men as well as women wept; Muslims gesticulated with V-signs. In this one phrase de Gaulle had touched the hearts of the *pieds noirs* and established a remarkable harmony with the multitude in the Forum. It may also have saved his life; for there is a story that in an apartment building facing the "G-G" was an expert marksman and an unrepentant Pétainist belonging to a splinter-group of "ultras" who were convinced of de Gaulle's intention to abandon Algeria. His telescopic sights were aimed on de Gaulle in the first of some thirty assassination attempts. But when he heard the magic words, the would-be assassin leant his rifle up against the wall, listened to the rest of the speech, and finally abandoned his attempt. De Gaulle continued:

> I know what has occurred here. I see what you have sought to accomplish. I see that the road you have opened in Algeria is that of renewal and fraternity.
> I say renewal in every respect. But, very rightly, you wanted to begin at the beginning; that is, with our institutions; and that is why I am here.
> I say fraternity, for you will provide the magnificent example of men who . . . share in the same ardour and live hand in hand.
> Well then, of this I have taken cognisance in the name of France! And I declare that from this day forward, France considers that in the whole of Algeria there is only one category of inhabitants, that there are only Frenchmen in the full sense [*à part entière*], with the same rights and the same duties.

After paying tribute to the "disciplined" French army, he concluded with an appeal to "those who, through despair," had joined the F.L.N.: "I, de Gaulle, open to them the doors of reconciliation. Never more than here, nor more than this evening, have I felt how beautiful, how great, how generous is France! Long live the Republic. Long live France!"

Those looking for it noted that, despite all the oblique references to "integration", de Gaulle had specifically neglected to proclaim: "*Vive l'Algérie française!*" But the triumphal tour continued, embracing all the country's major centres. At Oran on the 6th Captain Pierre Sergent of the Foreign Legion watched with "heart-beating pride" as the Caravelle flew in, with its escort of Mistral fighters in V-formation. There de Gaulle declared, in what seemed like more explicit terms: "Yes, France is here, with her vocation. She is here forever." That same day, to a vast crowd in the nearby port of Mostaganem, and seemingly carried away by the infectious mood that fed upon itself, in his last address de Gaulle uttered the longed-for words, for the first and the last time: *Vive l'Algérie française! Vive la République!*"

That night the Caravelle flew him back to Paris, leaving behind an exultant moral triumph of almost unimaginable proportions. He had enthralled alike *pieds noirs*, Muslims and paras. At the same time, in every dealing with the representatives of the all-powerful Committee of Public Safety he had left absolutely no doubt as to who was in control. To the Europeans specifically, he had the unique advantage of never having been associated with France's post-war Algerian policy, in any aspect. His hands were clean. For the Muslim population, it was the first time that any French leader had addressed himself to them directly, and the instinctive and unreasoning confidence held in his person was immense. So, too, was the overall impact of his authority, and the opportunities open to it. At the time of the historic Liberation *promenade* down the Champs Elysées in 1944, Georges Bidault recalls how

> Practically no one shouted "Long live France!" but everyone called out "Long live de Gaulle!" In moments of great distress or great joy, the crowd has a natural tendency to turn to one man and make him the symbol of their need to admire or to be protected.

Now, in this first week of June 1958, the masses similarly turned to the magic of his person, and momentarily it seemed as if there were nothing that could not be achieved if only *he* willed it. It now only remained for the world to decipher precisely what de Gaulle had meant in the various utterances of this his first whistle-stop tour of Algeria, and how he was going to follow them up.

That he was already speaking in two voices, however – one for the elated masses, another for his own private, clairvoyant pessimism – seems to be indicated by a coldly cynical remark de Gaulle uttered to quell the jubilation of an over-eager aide immediately on his return from this peak of triumph: "*L'Afrique est foutue, et l'Algérie avec!*" Of his Mostaganem exclamation of "*Vive l'Algérie française!*" which its exponents would regard as the holy writ, he later explained dismissively that it had just "escaped" from him; it was superficial, just like talking about "French Canada". On the other hand, those even more controversial words, *Je vous ai compris*, de Gaulle states were "seemingly spontaneous but in reality carefully calculated"; their purpose was "to establish emotional contact". But just what did this mean? De Gaulle explained later that his whole message of June was "tantamount to saying that the day would come when the majority amongst them could decide the destiny of all". Certainly, however, no one who heard the words agreed on understanding exactly what de Gaulle had understood. The army for one had become "dupes", said Charles-Henri Favrod, to his "incantatory" language. At one moment army jeeps driving through the streets were heard to broadcast such wild messages to the populace as this: "Frenchmen, you have just achieved a great victory, not only over the *fellaghas*, but over the enemies of the interior, traitors, defeatists, intellectuals, Jews...." There was an equally large gulf in "understanding" among the Muslims, between those who had waved tricolours and shouted "*Vive de Gaulle!*" "*Vive l'Algérie française!*" in the Forum, and the young Algerians on the 14 July march past in Paris who (according to Simone de Beauvoir) "pulled green and white banners out from under their shirts and waved them defiantly".

It was the people to whom the enigmatic words had been principally addressed – the *pieds noirs* – however, who understood them least well. In all his speeches during that first tour de Gaulle, by constantly repeating the phrase "only Frenchmen *à part entière*", made it fairly clear that he was thinking in terms of equality between the races and thus, by extension, eventually majority rule. What de Gaulle "understood" about the *pieds noirs* was certainly by no means as flattering as they wished to believe, and as the realisation of this sank in *Je vous ai compris* became the bitterest of insults.

Such is the uncertainty of human communication.

Slow quest for a policy

Through the summer and into the autumn of 1958, as de Gaulle evolved his policy, there followed "great gusts of words", said Simone de Beauvoir caustically. The sonorous speeches on Algeria sometimes seemed "like the Seine itself, full of meandering loops followed by a long spurt forward", says Edward Behr. Five times de Gaulle flew to Algeria. But there appeared to be disappointingly little immediacy in his moves to end the war. Later de Gaulle and his apologists could offer good cause for this slow and deliberate pace; nevertheless, it was over these first months that the great momentum of May and June was to be tragically frittered away – to the immense advantage of the F.L.N. De Gaulle stated his objectives:

first, to bring Algiers completely under the authority of Paris, secondly, to show the rebels that France was aiming at peace, a peace which she would ultimately wish to conclude with them and which she counted on to preserve her ties with Algeria, and thirdly, to reinforce our military presence in such a way that nothing that happened in the field would interfere with our decisions.

Yet once the emotionalism of those "great gusts of words" had been flensed, the flesh and bones of the programme looked disappointingly like the mixture as before – even though perhaps applied with extra impetus. Still more effort and money would be expended on the Algerian economy and on education. New efforts would be made to win the war militarily. Lacoste's *loi-cadre* was swept away, but there would be a single electoral roll, with free elections, and now with a date fixed. There would be a referendum to say Yes or No to de Gaulle's remodelled constitution giving the republic a new backbone of steel; all Frenchmen would cast their vote in it, and countries of the Commonwealth would be entitled to decide whether or not they wished to be associated with it. It would be the first occasion that the Algerians were to be invited to vote on the new single electoral role. This was to be on 28 September. Then, in November, there would be elections for the National Assembly to confirm de Gaulle as Prime Minister, followed, in December, by new presidential elections.

Referendum triumph: electoral shortcomings

In the run-up to the referendum, de Gaulle with apparently inexhaustible energy stumped the French Commonwealth expounding the merits of his constitution. The alternatives were baldly stated; either continued association, with all the weighty material benefits that this would bring; or total severance. "Make no mistake," de Gaulle told the principal doubter, Sékou Touré of Guinée, "the French Republic you are dealing with is no longer the one you knew, which preferred expediency to decision. . . . She lived for a long time without Guinée. She will live for an equally long time if she is severed from her." Challenging words. For Algeria, however, the question posed was different; it was not yet one of self-determination (that would come later), but essentially one of *carte blanche* confidence in de Gaulle and his policy – whatever that might prove to be.

On 28 September all Algeria – women included – went to the polls for the first time "like Europeans", casting their votes in a single electoral college. The referendum proved to be a huge personal success for de Gaulle everywhere. In France the Communists and their allies had fought hard against it, with Sartre speaking of "this constitution of contempt" and declaring that he would "rather vote for God, He is more modest." At most both the Gaullists and their enemies reckoned on a sixty to sixty-five per cent "*oui*" vote in metropolitan France; but in the event it totalled over eighty per cent, on a record turnout of eighty-five per cent. It was the clearest possible mandate for de Gaulle (Simone de Beauvoir felt "like crying" at such "a sinister defeat...an enormous collective suicide"). Abroad, the results were even more remarkable; all Black Africa voted "*oui*" with imposing majorities, save only Sékou Touré's Guinée, which opted for outer darkness. In Algeria, despite every threat and blandishment by the F.L.N. to abstain, there was an astonishingly high turnout of 79.9 per cent and a "*oui*" majority representing 76.4 per cent of the total electorate and 96.6 per cent of those who voted. Pressure and propaganda by the Cinquième Bureau was undoubtedly strong, but there was little evidence of any fraudulent vote-rigging as had been known in Algeria in earlier times.

The Muslim turn-out in the parliamentary elections that were to follow in November fell discouragingly to sixty-five per cent, but, reflecting as this did in part vexation with having to go to the polls a second time so soon after the first, the results still showed – statistically at least – a handsome backing for de Gaulle. What was far less satisfactory about them, however, was the orientation of most of the candidates returned, who were largely drawn from the ranks of the "integrationists". There was thus a serious dearth of moderate nationalists among them, acting in defiance of the F.L.N. death-threats of those participating in this "colonialist election". The F.L.N.'s curt rebuff to de Gaulle's *paix des braves* overture, which had come in the middle of the November election campaign, also provided an additional deterrent to this eroded middle position.

Constantine plan and the "paix des braves"

Still in the full flush of his referendum triumph, on 3 October de Gaulle was in Constantine to make an important speech. In order that "this country, so vital and so courageous, but so difficult and suffering, should be profoundly transformed", an ambitious Five-Year Plan was to be launched, with the object of turning backward Algeria into an industrialised nation. 400,000 new jobs were to be created; 250,000 hectares of new land distributed to Muslim farmers; salaries and wages raised to a par with metropolitan France; and administrative posts made available to Muslims on a ratio of one to ten with those of the mother country; vast new horizons of schooling to be opened to Muslim children. In Paris Lacoste grumbled in disgruntlement that it all offered nothing new over his discarded *loi-cadre*; maybe, but the important difference was that the Constantine Plan had the name of de Gaulle, and all his newly acquired authority and weight, attached to it. In his speech de Gaulle added a reminder that in the forth-coming legislative elections Algeria would vote under the same conditions as the mother country, but that "at least two-thirds of her representatives will have to be Muslim citizens", and he concluded with a direct appeal to the F.L.N.:

Why kill? We must enable people to live. Why destroy? Our duty is to build. Why hate? We must co-operate.

Stop this absurd fighting and you will see at once a new blossoming of hope all over the land. You will see prisons emptying; you will see the opening of a future big enough for everybody, and for yourselves in particular....

To lend additional enticement to this revelation of a promised land, de Gaulle began to accelerate the number of rebels amnestied. On Armistice Day, a thousand would be released; on New Year's Day 1959, another 7,000; on de Gaulle's accession to the presidency all capital sentences would be commuted (among whom Yacef was to be a notable beneficiary); while Bastille Day 1959 would be chosen, appropriately enough, for the release of a further 5,000. Then, at his Press conference of 23 October, de Gaulle threw out his memorable soldier's offer of a *paix des braves*:

I say unequivocally that, as for most of them, the men of the insurrection have fought courageously. Let the peace of the brave come, and I am sure that all hatred will fade away and disappear. What does this mean? Simply this: wherever they are organised for combat, their leaders need only enter into contact with the French command. The old warrior's procedure, long used when one wanted to silence the guns, was to wave the white flag of truce. And I answer that, in this case, the combatants would be received and treated honourably.

The *paix des braves* utterance made an immeasurable impact. Jacques Fauvet of *Le Monde* confessed to being "arrested by the nobility of the tone, the harmony of the thought"; less romantically, Alain de Sérigny put forward in the *Écho d'Alger* the simple interpretation, "The white flag means surrender."

The overture was also to bring with it (inevitably, it seems in hindsight, because the political intent behind it remained so imprecise) the first major reversal to de Gaulle's hitherto triumphant procession. But already, soon after the initial exhilaration of June had begun to dissipate, little puffs of cloud had been appearing from a variety of directions. First of all the concept of integration, brought out of store and burnished-up by the Cinquième Bureau of the army during those heady moments of "fraternisation" in May, came swiftly under attack. In France serious intellects standing well outside the anti-Gaullist Left, such as Raymond Aron, pointed out the flaws by pragmatic arguments. On demographic calculations alone, Aron reckoned that within twenty-five years an integrated Algeria 18 million strong would swamp a metropolitan France of 48 million, politically if not numerically. Acting as a bloc, the seventy-five Muslim deputies which it would be Algeria's right to send to the Palais Bourbon could provide a balance of power to whichever side of the Assembly they wished, thus preventing it from functioning normally. Integration would also slow down, if not halt, any rise in the French standard of living, and he concluded, "An

Algerian France, if it pretends to regenerate France by governing it, will irremediably tear asunder the nation." On the other hand, as de Gaulle points out in his memoirs, in Algeria the *pieds noirs* tended to regard integration in totally false terms "as a means of warding off the evolution towards equality and Algerian autonomy, of not only avoiding being engulfed by ten million Muslims but of submerging them instead among fifty million Frenchmen". This was how they tended to interpret the idealistic slogan of the time: "Fifty-five million Frenchmen from Dunkirk to Tamanrasset."* It was a matter of mathematical juggling; the Muslims of Algeria saw the equation simply in the ratio of ten-to-one; the *pieds noirs* tried to fix it in a ratio of fifty to ten. But the basic fact was that, whereas integration, if honourably entered into, might have worked happily in 1936 and less probably in 1945, by 1958 it had become at best a romantic delusion, at worst a confidence trick.

De Gaulle seems to have seen this, and as 1958 went on his references to integration became more and more perfunctory, and he assiduously avoided any explicit commitment to it. This in turn annoyed both the army in Algeria and the *pieds noirs*, both of whom were beginning to chafe at the lack of action and the vagueness of the lofty, *ex cathedra* pronouncements. During the Constantine speech of October, members of the local Committee of Public Safety had walked off the grandstand in outrage at de Gaulle's conciliatory gestures towards the F.L.N. Closing ranks, the Left in France condemned the Constantine Plan as "neo-colonialism": an attempt at "seducing the Algerian peasants by offering to them the urban mirage" declared Francis Jeanson.

But the full storm burst, from all sides, with the *paix des braves* offer. In France, even some of the left-of-centre moderates condemned it as inexorably leading to negotiations with the F.L.N., which were far too premature. Soustelle was deeply disquieted, and a breach between him and de Gaulle began to open. Speaking for the Left, Simone de Beauvoir said the "generous offer" was tantamount to "capitulation" for the F.L.N. if they took it up. And "capitulation" was equally the word heard in army as well as in *pied noir* circles in Algeria. The whiplash blow, however, came – perhaps predictably – from the F.L.N. in Tunis. Within forty-eight hours of de Gaulle's offer of the *paix des braves*, it was rejected in summary and quite violent terms by the previously moderate Ferhat Abbas. "The problem of a ceasefire in Algeria", he said, "is not simply a military problem. It is essentially political and negotiation must cover the whole question of Algeria." He ended with a renewed appeal to the F.L.N. in Algeria for a war to the end, and his words were reinforced by a fresh campaign of terrorism.

* The slogan of "fifty-five million" was based upon obsolete figures for all the inhabitants of France and Algeria, by now nearer sixty million.

307

First disenchantments

The F.L.N. rejection came as a deep shock to de Gaulle, and it is probably no exaggeration to rate it as one of the bitterest personal blows he ever suffered. It was hardened by the fact that he had already put out feelers towards the F.L.N. in June, through the intermediary of Abderrahmane Farès, former President of the Algiers Assembly, and had hoped for a more cordial response to his overture. He seems to have nurtured a mystical belief that somehow the F.L.N. would melt before his presence; that grandeur and generosity, as guaranteed by his person, had only to be displayed for the F.L.N. to come out of its caves waving a white flag.* Both the offer and de Gaulle's ensuing discountenance betrayed a fundamental misunderstanding of the nature of the revolt as well as of the F.L.N. leadership, which could go far to explaining some of the failures of communication in the years to come. At the same time, the slap in the face to de Gaulle produced a powerful reaction among the uncommitted Muslims in Algeria who, since May, had been so enticed by the spell of his stature and authority. It was also to have its influence on the Algerian elections in November. For the French position it was a tragedy that de Gaulle could not have struck with the *paix des braves* while the iron was hot in June, when it might well have gained substantial Muslim support. By the end of October the momentum was lost.

The growth of disenchantment occurred almost simultaneously within both the Muslim and *pied noir* communities towards the end of 1958. In "ultra" circles on the Committee of Public Safety there were already rumblings about a "second 13 May" to replace de Gaulle's Neguib by a Nasser chosen among themselves. After the Constantine speech, but before the *paix des braves*, Lagaillarde, Ortiz and Martel had tried to call a general strike on 16 October in protest against de Gaulle's betrayal. The idea was squashed by some plain talk from General Massu. But the seeds of later revolt had been sown; for the "ultras" would never be able to rid themselves of the notion that, as they had brought de Gaulle to power, so they could despatch him from it. Not, however, without the army.

De Gaulle purges the army

Even if it could be said that de Gaulle had dragged his feet in formulating an Algerian policy, the same could not be held against him in his dealings with the army after May 1958. For de Gaulle, in his whole upbringing and career, the French army was everything – or almost everything – and its state of health was a far more pressing worry to him than either the F.L.N. or the *pieds noirs*. It was, however, no longer the same army that he had

---

* It was, according to his close associate, Bernard Tricot, the white flag of truce, not of capitulation, that de Gaulle had in mind – a subtle difference not appreciated by the F.L.N. any more than it had been by the *Écho d'Alger*.

known so well in 1940-5, and since February 1956 its over-riding objective had been a political one; to push the authorities into carrying out a policy of *Algérie française*. "By and large, this great body of men, by nature concerned with the short run rather than the long, clung to the idea that France should keep possession of Algeria, symbol of her ancient power." Understanding all this, he was well aware that he had to tread warily with the army in Algeria, over-sensitised and vastly powerful as it had become since 13 May. Yet at the same time he appreciated that it cried out for a firm hand and, masochistically, for a restoration of discipline. In the last analysis, he reckoned, "the army would obey". Thus "On this vast apparatus, effective in preventing the situation from worsening, but incapable of solving the insoluble, a wealth of ingenuity, conscientiousness and patience was expended." Ruthlessly, but with caution, de Gaulle embarked on a major purge of the "activists" in the army of Algiers. The loyal Gaullist General Ely was brought back as Chief of the General Staff and given the task of scattering the ringleaders of May by posting them, in twos and threes, to units in France or Germany. By the following March only two of those officers were still left in Algeria, while some 1,500 others had either been transferred, or simply retired. One of those remaining was the dependable *grognard*, General Massu, eternally faithful to de Gaulle and only too delighted to get away from the *bordel* of politics and back to his regiments.

In October Massu and the other army officers were instructed by de Gaulle to withdraw from the Committee of Public Safety (which was subsequently stood down altogether). That same day an order to Salan announced categorically: "The moment has come when the military must cease to take part in any organisation with a political character ..." Algiers seethed, and this was the *casus belli* for the "ultras" to attempt a general strike. But de Gaulle won, and for the time being the power of the army and the "ultras" was effectively separated. Next, in December, Salan, who since May had with plenipotentiary powers combined the roles of both Commander-in-Chief and *de facto* civil governor, was himself despatched into "gilded retreat" as military governor of Paris. De Gaulle had promised to recall him for "high destinies", which had made Salan hope for nothing less than General Ely's top job. Yet here, after all he had achieved in his two years in Algeria, as well as the outstanding services rendered in May – not least in the name of de Gaulle himself – was an almost insultingly sinecure appointment. On leaving Algiers shortly before Christmas, Salan received this glowing testimony from the man by whom it was painfully clear he was neither liked nor entirely trusted: "You have conducted yourself with honour ... I don't regard you just as a loyal supporter of great quality, but as my companion and my friend." But this was hardly enough to allay the deep resentment felt by Salan, chief among the many purged army officers, and in view of his subsequent career these were to become bitterly ironical words. The chagrin was increased when de Gaulle apparently lacked the thoughtfulness to inform Salan about the identity of his successor until he actually arrived in Algiers.

Exit Salan: enter Delouvrier and Challe

To replace the all-powerful Salan, de Gaulle appointed a duumvirate – Paul Delouvrier and General Maurice Challe. The civil and military powers would be divided between them but, in contrast to the past, both posts would be more subject to control from Paris. Aged only forty-four, Delouvrier had been an unknown technocrat in Luxembourg when summoned by de Gaulle that October. A practising Catholic from the Vosges, he helped a Resistance maquis near Fontainebleau where he had joined hands with General Patton during the Liberation of 1944. Considered to be one of France's outstanding financial brains, Delouvrier had been picked out by Jean Monnet to work on his team with the embryo European Community, and currently he was head of the financial division of the Coal and Steel Community in Luxembourg. Here he had demonstrated a remarkable capacity for work, and a certain high seriousness and authority in office. His tall, distinguished figure with a trim hairline moustache purveyed what the French tended to describe as a certain British elegance; but behind it lay a rather nervously sensitive personality. In no way did he resemble any of his predecessors in Algiers, and it appears that it was through his personal friendship with Michel Debré that Delouvrier first came to de Gaulle's notice. He was aghast when told in October that de Gaulle had him in mind to succeed Salan, and that he was to go forthwith on a month's "information tour" of Algeria. On his return he was received by de Gaulle at the Matignon, who asked for his impressions. Having noted how the attitude of the Muslim majority had now hardened towards independence since the initial euphoria of May, Delouvrier remarked: "*Mon général*, Algeria will be independent."

At which de Gaulle is said to have waved him aside with, "In twenty-five years, Delouvrier, in twenty-five years...." Delouvrier was unable to decipher anything more precise about de Gaulle's views on the future of Algeria. At a subsequent meeting Delouvrier remarked diffidently to de Gaulle that he felt he did not possess the "stature" for the job offered, to be told simply, "You'll grow into it, Delouvrier...." His principal, and first, task would be to get the Constantine Plan under way, for which he would be allocated funds of 100 milliard (old) francs. "You are", said de Gaulle with pointed emphasis, "France in Algeria – and *not* the representative of the Algerians in France." Apart from this, Delouvrier's instructions were extraordinarily vague – and would remain so.

Delouvrier's other half, Maurice Challe, already mentioned in the context of the events of May, was a robust fifty-three with an open face and the physique of a rugger player. The two men together gave a good impression of youth and vigour. Working for the Resistance, Challe, a regular airman, had skilfully obtained the Luftwaffe order-of-battle on the eve of D-Day and transmitted it to London, for which he was awarded the British D.S.O. and a personal citation from Winston Churchill. His next contact with Britain was during the Suez campaign, as Mollet's military envoy to Eden, and since then he had been deputy to the chief-of-staff. Well-liked by both equals and subordinates, Challe was as open as he looked: a calm, solid and tenacious pipe-smoker. There was nothing of the secretiveness of the "Mandarin" Salan about him; in fact, if anything he had a habit of speaking his mind too readily, which had slowed down his promotion on at least one occasion. He was a good Republican, an "unconditional Gaullist" but leaning marginally to the Left and maintaining close contacts with Guy Mollet. Above all, he was a highly competent airman, but also with a rare capacity for understanding land warfare; as such he was to prove the ablest of all the French commanders sent to Algeria. At their first meeting under the aegis of de Gaulle, Delouvrier and Challe took to each other instantly and were to work together throughout in the most outstanding harmony. Thus the omens could hardly have looked better. Challe's brief was to mount the most crushing military offensive yet against the F.L.N., the success of which would be intended to give de Gaulle freedom to dispose the future of Algeria as he wished. Behind there also lay the perhaps more cynical secondary motive of distracting the army from any political discontents; "Give them tasks, they will think less . . . !" de Gaulle had declared at one of his first cabinet meetings.

On 19 December the new team arrived in Algiers; Delouvrier, the "Delegate-General" (a less imposing title than "governor-general" to show a break with the past) was clad conspicuously in civilian clothes, carrying a black "Anthony Eden" hat; Challe, in uniform, walked equally conspicuously one or two paces to the rear. It was a symbolic demonstration of the civil over the military, of Paris over Algiers. De Gaulle had at least made this point forcefully and clearly. Delouvrier's first words sounded equally purposeful: "*La France reste. . . .*" But the welcome accorded by the *pieds noirs* was barely less cool and mistrustful than it had been for Lacoste and Soustelle before him.

Preoccupations in France

Less readily visible to the army and *pieds noirs* alike in Algeria was one fundamental reason for de Gaulle's dilatoriness in formulating an Algerian policy: his preoccupation with the Augean stables in France herself. The Gaullist programme called for the most thorough overhaul of France's whole political system, economy and finances – left in a critical tangle by previous governments of the Fourth Republic – and her foreign relations and alliances. In fact, there were few fronts on which de Gaulle was not attacking with vigour and dedication in his first six plenipotential months. First and foremost there was the new constitution, involving a mountainous work of drafting and consultation. "I considered it necessary", declared de Gaulle, "for the government to derive not from parliament, in other words from the parties, but, over and above them, from a leader directly mandated by the nation as a whole and empowered to choose, to decide and to act". The executive would emerge immeasurably strengthened, with many of the weaknesses that had been the undoing of the Third and Fourth Republics purged from the body politic. Well before the triumphant result of the Constitutional Referendum it was abundantly clear that henceforth France was now going to be ruled, and her voice heard abroad. Already in mid-September de Gaulle was writing to Eisenhower and Macmillan, informing them that N.A.T.O. "was no longer adapted to the needs of our defence . . . the alliance should henceforth be placed under a triple rather than a dual direction, failing which France would take no further part". In equally brutal language he was soon torpedoing Macmillan's hopes for a Free Trade Area in Europe; while to his intimates he was revealing his ambitions to create a truly modern army at the earliest opportunity: "As soon as the Algerian war is ended, I shall form five atomic divisions. . . ."

After the uncertainties of the last days of the Fourth Republic, and the real fears of May, the new authority and majesty of de Gaulle had the most immediate and galvanising effect upon the French nation at large; the full quality of which effect one tends to forget even at this short distance in time. On his first official visit to Paris in June, Macmillan noted already how the large crowds "all seemed very relaxed and in a most friendly mood . . . I have never seen a French crowd cheer in such a friendly way . . . everyone is confident that the General's policy will succeed. No one knows what it will be – all the same it commands general confidence". The coming of de Gaulle was suddenly seen to liberate one of those surges of the immense reservoir of energy that characterises the French nation, and her truly staggering moral as well as material regeneration now began. Some of the eternal aspects continued unchanged; after countless man-hours of deliberation, the Académie announced that it was changing the sex of the automobile. But as Janet Flanner observed in October, "the Western democratic peoples now eye France with real hope for the first time since November, 1945". Vast new building complexes (not always felicitous in style) began to spring up; by August 1959 Miss Flanner was recording, "This year, Paris has visibly built itself into the middle of the twentieth century at last." It was one of the tangible signs of the beginning of the Gaullist economic "miracle" – even though, admittedly, the groundwork for it had been laid much earlier. Henceforth France was on the road to recovery; maddening to her friends, destructive of the Atlantic Alliance, but on the other hand laying the foundation for the astonishing prosperity and stability of the 1970s.

In November 1958 de Gaulle followed up his referendum triumph with a major success at the elections for the Assembly; it was a grave defeat for the Left, with the Communist deputies reduced from 145 to a mere ten. In January 1959 de Gaulle took office as President, welcomed to the Elysée by the outgoing President Coty with the dignified words: "The first of Frenchmen is now the first man in France." Then, says de Gaulle, "henceforth the prisoner of my high duty, I heard all the doors of the palace closing behind me".

The first year: credit and debit
As the first anniversary of May 1958 approached, de Gaulle could look back on a number of successes, one or two half-successes, and one major setback. In the summer of 1958 Raymond Aron had predicted "The revolution of May could be the beginning of the political renovation of France on the condition that it hastens to devour its children." By purging the army in Algeria and clearing the decks there of the Committee of Public Safety which had brought him to power, de Gaulle had achieved just that. He had given France the new constitution he wanted, had established his own authority to a degree that would have seemed beyond the realms of possibility in May 1958, and had seemed to establish around his person much of the best talent in France. He had prevailed with the economic programme he wanted; though not, unfortunately, with the kind of lasting trade union support that he sought. In Algeria he had the *pieds noirs* at least temporarily under control. But as far as peace was concerned only disappointment could be recorded. His first attempt to obtain a cease-fire had been rejected with a crushing snub by the F.L.N. and the November elections had not led to the emergence of any tangible "third force" of *interlocuteurs valables*. Thus everything was at an impasse, and would remain so for the best part of the ensuing year. And, as well as that initial momentum, he had lost time that was irretrievable. Summing up on his first five months of power, Cyrus L. Sulzberger of the *New York Times* remarked, "General de Gaulle has put on the most dazzling virtuoso performance since another Frenchman, called Blondin, walked across Niagara Falls on a tight-rope just ninety-nine years ago." There was no disputing what a breathtaking feat it had been; but in the Algerian context a disquieting impression lingered that de Gaulle was left still balancing on his tight-rope above the middle of the falls.

CHAPTER FIFTEEN

The F.L.N. Holds its Breath

May 1958 – May 1959

The events of 13 May 1958 ... changed the spirit of the struggle in one camp,
and made the other hold its breath.

Philippe Tripier

The shock of de Gaulle: low ebb for the F.L.N.

Algerian leaders who survived the war do not always agree in their
analysis of the decisive moments or the turning-points, on the "ifs" or the
"might have beens". But in answer to the leading question repeatedly
asked by the author, "What was the most dangerous period in the war for
you?" they tend to show an unusual degree of unanimity. It was the time
immediately following 13 May, and the first weeks of de Gaulle. On the
fighting front the A.L.N. was already reeling from heavy casualties suffered
to little advantage on the Morice Line during the spring attacks of 1958.
The political disarray in France was looked upon at first as a heaven-sent
opportunity to relieve the military pressure. Attempting to exploit this, the
A.L.N. stepped up the tempo of operations, inflicting in the week of 13 May
alone unprecedented heavy casualties of 300 dead and wounded, among
the dead being the renowned para leader, Colonel Jeanpierre, who had
escaped with wounds during the hunting down of Yacef. But at the same
time the A.L.N.'s losses had been twice that number, and in trained
djounoud it could ill spare. Morale among the combatants in some units was
shakier than it had perhaps ever been; following the mysterious "liquidation" of Ramdane Abane, the atmosphere in the higher echelons of the
C.C.E. was far from happy; inside the country war-weariness, ever latent,
showed signs of taking a greater hold as the "exterior" proved increasingly
incapable of supplying the "interior" with the arms it so badly needed.
There was more talk about a "compromise" peace, and as morale waned
within so did enthusiasm among the Muslim "brothers" abroad upon
whom the F.L.N. relied for arms and support.

Then, suddenly, there occurred the extraordinary phenomenon of the
"fraternisation" of 16 May; rigged in part by the Cinquième Bureau but

also deeply and disturbingly symptomatic of the hope that the mere name of de Gaulle could inspire in the breast of many a simple, peace-craving Algerian. And immediately de Gaulle had begun talking about true "equality" within the French republic and the end of second-class citizenry, words that from his mouth alone sounded true and meaningful. If de Gaulle were to follow this up with a massive appeal to the battered, disillusioned but still extant "third force" of Muslims, then this could only present the F.L.N. with the gravest menace to its prestige and war aims. As François Mauriac (no disciple of Algérie française) had rejoiced after the 16 May demonstrations, they offered "a psychological and moral basis for the accords and arrangements of tomorrow, a basis infinitely better than that of battles and ambushes". But to the F.L.N. it was a basis of pure danger. There was also a second threat: that France, reunited and reinvigorated by de Gaulle, would be enabled to prosecute the war with that much greater determination and efficacy. Taken by surprise by the events of May, for the F.L.N. all was dark confusion, and momentarily it adopted the wise posture of the low profile. A counterattack, however, had to be mounted before de Gaulle could pull off single-handed a triumph in his referendum announced for September.

Countermoves: the G.P.R.A. formed

Towards the end of June the veteran Kabyle maquisard, Colonel Omar Ouamrane, addressed a secret memorandum to each member of the C.C.E. separately. "The hour is grave," he began; the military situation was worrying; the revolution was losing way: "The revolutionary spirit has disappeared among leaders, officers and militants alike, to give way to bourgeoisification, bureaucracy and opportunism." To regain the initiative that had passed to de Gaulle, and before his regime had time to consolidate itself, Ouamrane urged: the speedy proclamation of a provisional Algerian government; a new diplomatic offensive to take full advantage of East-West rivalry in the Cold War; the launching of a "second front" of terrorism inside metropolitan France itself. Ouamrane's memorandum fell upon fertile ground. Ferhat Abbas expressed strongly to Krim the view that Abane's death had left a blot on the C.C.E. which could only be expunged if it were dissolved and swallowed up in the wider framework of a properly constituted government. Certainly in recent months the C.C.E. had shown itself less and less effective in directing the revolution, while a government-in-exile could exert more authority and prestige; but, above all, on the international scene it would strike a major propaganda blow against the blandishments of de Gaulle. There was some heated discussion, notably about personalities and posts in the new regime, with Krim pressing his prerogative – as sole survivor present of the neuf historiques – to assume the leading role. But on 9 September, in Cairo, the principle and structure of a government-in-exile had been agreed. Ten days later, also in Cairo, a massive Press conference was called to announce the creation of the Provisional Government of the Republic of Algeria (G.P.R.A.). From the chair, Ferhat Abbas (speaking, significantly, in French) declared that the new government would assume its duties from 13.00 hours on that same day, "the 1,416th day of the revolution". Similar solemn ceremonies were held in both Tunis, which had been chosen as the G.P.R.A.'s capital, and Rabat.

Instead of the militant maquisard Krim, the mantle of first president of the G.P.R.A. fell upon Ferhat Abbas, the pharmacist from Sétif and former leader of the moderate U.D.M.A. nationalists, francophone and francophile, suavely courteous, the voice of sweet reason and compromise itself. It was a shrewd though somewhat cynical choice in that Abbas would soon prove to have been appointed for little more than window-dressing. Among the fourteen ministers also nominated, Krim was permitted to continue his C.C.E. function as Minister for the Armed Forces, and was also made a vice-president as a sop to his pride. Equally tactful was the appointment to vice-president of Ben Bella, while he and all his imprisoned comrades were made "ministers of state" *in absentia*. The former M.T.L.D. leader Dr Lamine Debaghine, became Foreign Minister; Ben Tobbal, Minister of the Interior; Boussouf, Minister of Communications (which also gave him the key role of running intelligence services); Yazid (who had been so successful in New York), Minister of Information; and Ben Khedda, another former member of Messali's M.T.L.D. assumed the function of Minister of Social Affairs. In effect, the key positions of power still remained in the hands of the "three Bs", Belkacem Krim, Boussouf and Ben Tobbal – the men who had brought about the downfall of Abane. The only conspicuous absentee from the new line-up was the man whose memorandum had mooted the idea of creating the G.P.R.A., Colonel Ouamrane, apparently dropped on the grounds of being a political "light-weight" and too intolerant of politicians.

The nations of the Arab world hastened to recognise the new government, though Nasser did so concealing much ill-humour at the fact of not having been consulted about the move, and at the G.P.R.A.'s choice of Tunis, rather than Cairo, for their "capital". China and other countries of the Communist bloc followed suit, but Khrushchev's U.S.S.R. remained annoyingly aloof, it being the Russian leader's evident, and excellent, calculation that by not upsetting de Gaulle more mileage could be made in the disruption of the Western Alliance than could be gained in recognising the G.P.R.A. As with past Russian snubs, it was a stance the Algerians would not forget in a hurry. The United States and Britain both played an ambivalent hand, not recognising the G.P.R.A., nor supporting French policy in Algeria, an attitude which was enough to mortify and alienate de Gaulle.

As it had done all the way from November 1954, through the Soummam Conference of 1956, and regardless of all personal conflicts and schisms, the F.L.N. kept its aims fundamentally unaltered with the creation of the G.P.R.A. With Abbas as the frontispiece, however, a new and seductive appearance of flexibility and softness of approach temporarily cloaked the G.P.R.A. In an interview with the journalist Artur Rosenberg, widely quoted in the West German Press in October, Abbas suggested that the F.L.N. might be prepared to waive its demand for instant recognition of independence as a *sine qua non* condition for any peace talks, which in the past had proved such an unbridgeable obstacle. Meanwhile, a new diplomatic offensive led to a considerable stepping-up of the already successful activities of the astute Chanderli and Yazid in New York and at the United Nations; and in December 1958 Ben Khedda led the first Algerian delegation to China. The Algerians were greeted with the greatest warmth in Peking, but with slightly less in Moscow on the return journey. The visit to China, as Ben Khedda told the author, was "of utmost importance, less because of the arms it brought than because of its psychological effect on the combatants – which was immense at that time". The threat of an outflanking entente between the F.L.N. and Moscow and Peking would also, it was calculated, alarm de Gaulle considerably. Thus, as hoped by the F.L.N., the creation of the G.P.R.A. and its accompanying diplomatic offensive made the maximum impact abroad, while helping steal some thunder from de Gaulle's referendum where a massive landslide of "*ouis*" had indeed confronted the F.L.N. with an undisguisable reverse.

Terrorist offensive in France

Hand in hand with all this went a new offensive of terrorism, launched as soon as the F.L.N. had regained its breath after the events of May. It had been presaged by El *Moudjahid* in its issue of 13 June 1958, which had singled out de Gaulle's remarks praising the French army for a particularly savage attack: "These words will remain engraved in letters of fire on the heart of each Algerian man and woman. Never before has French cynicism been displayed with such impudence... the torturers of the Algerian people have been travestied as heroes and magicians...." In another issue of the same week it published a directive ordering an intensification of terrorism throughout Algeria. In Algiers, peaceful for so many months now, a grenade thrown into a café on 20 June claimed nineteen civilian victims, of whom seventeen were Muslims. During July incidents rose to 2,024 compared with the June total of 1,585 and in one week alone there were eighty-one assassination attempts – principally against Muslims as part of the F.L.N.'s vigorous drive to deter them from voting in the forthcoming referendum and elections. A general strike invoked for 5 July, the anniversary of the French Occupation of 1830, proved a signal failure, but in

September incidents had again risen to 2,368. By January 1959 terrorist attacks were still running at a frequency of some fifty per week, and during the ensuing year no less than 148 municipal councillors were assassinated.

But it was in the mother country that the F.L.N. – similarly to the I.R.A. in times of maximum stress in the 1970s – now concentrated its terrorist activities. Between 24 August and 28 September there were 181 attacks on property and 242 against people, causing eighty-two deaths and injuring another 168. Many were Algerians belonging to the M.N.A. or other dissident groups; Janet Flanner recalled the sight of an Algerian dying in a pool of blood outside the fashionable Brasserie Lipp, while a Parisian flower-vendor looked on, quite unmoved. For the first time the networks set up by Lebjaoui and taken over by Boudaoud turned their attention to specifically French targets. The night of 24 August was like a repeat of All Saints, 1954. Across the breadth of France a miscellany of blows was struck: a train derailed near Cagnes-sur-Mer; police stations attacked at Lyon and Paris, killing four policemen; a bomb placed in a boat at Marseilles; fuel dumps blown up at a number of places in southern France which supplied the French army in Algeria. The assaults on the fuel dumps were particularly effective, and were reckoned to have sent up in flames the equivalent of one whole day's petroleum consumption in France. On 15 September Jacques Soustelle had a miraculous escape when his car was shot up by terrorists in the Avenue Friedland, right in the heart of Paris; but the would-be assassin, Ouragui, was seized by Soustelle's police bodyguard after a dramatic chase through the Étoile métro. That same night police cars were shot at in the Rue de Rivoli and other parts of Paris, while in Metz a para captain was badly wounded. A few days later an F.L.N. frogman tried unsuccessfully to place limpet charges under the battleship *Jean Bart* in Toulon harbour, while another bomb was found in the ladies' lavatory at the top of the Eiffel Tower. It was harmlessly defused.

In all this wave of terrorism it should be noted, however, that there was not one act of promiscuous bombing against civilians such as had been commonplace in Algiers and was to become so on a larger scale in Britain under the scourge of the I.R.A. a decade and a half later.

Nevertheless, the campaign provoked unexpectedly violent reactions among French workers and the Left where the F.L.N. could most expect to find friends. The Communist leader, Maurice Thorez, was particularly severe in his condemnation: "The methods employed by the F.L.N. in France have not, it must be stated categorically, served the just cause of the Algerian people. . . . If the F.L.N. is proposing to arouse public opinion, it is practising self-deception. It is arousing feelings against itself. . . ." At the same time, by taking vigorous police action of the kind familiar in Algiers, the French were soon successful in tracking down the terrorist networks, and with this went the danger that the fund-collecting organisation – considerably more important to the F.L.N. war effort – might also be caught up in the security net. Therefore on 28 September, the day of the referendum, a cease-fire was called in the terrorist offensive – an admission of failure clad under the rather thin pretext of a conciliatory gesture of goodwill.

One of the objectives of the F.L.N. offensive had also been to attempt to secure the release of Ben Bella and his colleagues, still languishing in the Santé prison after two years without trial. This too was unsuccessful, though as part of his general amnesty measures on assuming the presidency in January 1959 de Gaulle ordered the prisoners transferred to the slightly more comfortable surroundings of the Île d'Aix, the fortress isle in the Bay of Biscay where Napoleon had passed his last days on French soil in July 1815 before being transported to his ultimate exile aboard H.M.S. *Bellerophon*. The boredom and frustration there were extreme. Ben Bella devoted much of his long leisure hours to reading *Temps Modernes* and *France Football*, though he claims to have got through some seven hundred books in the course of his imprisonment. Through the remarkable "Arab telegraph" set up in the prisons of France, and frequent visits from his lawyers, he still managed to maintain regular contact with the new G.P.R.A.

The abrupt calling-off of the terrorist campaign in France also had, in all probability, a subsidiary effect of encouraging de Gaulle to make his *paix des braves* a few weeks later. From early in the summer a delicate and highly secret link had been established between, on the one hand, de Gaulle and Abderrahmane Farès, the former president of the Algerian Assembly, and, on the other, between Farès and Ferhat Abbas. At a clandestine meeting in Montreux in August, Farès informed Abbas (then not yet appointed president of the G.P.R.A.) that de Gaulle was ready to "open serious negotiations with the rebels". Abbas seemed receptive, declaring that he personally would be prepared to participate in "any kind of conversation on neutral ground". A period of nearly five weeks elapsed, during which time the F.L.N.'s terrorist campaign in France and the repressive measures it provoked had caused a distinct drop in the temperature between the two sides, as indeed was desired by the hard-liners of the F.L.N. On 17 September a message drafted by Georges Pompidou, then de Gaulle's *chef-de-cabinet*, was passed to Farès for onward transmission. It offered safe passage for an F.L.N. delegation to come to Paris to discuss conditions for a cease-fire; the discussion would centre on military matters, but "other problems" could be brought up. At the same time it suggested that the F.L.N. create "a climate of confidence" by not opposing the referendum fixed for the 28th. Abbas reacted coolly to all this, insisting that any meeting must be held on neutral territory. The G.P.R.A. followed up with a still sharper refusal, strongly attacking the referendum, and condemning the Pompidou proposal of an encounter in Paris as a "humiliating gesture".

A further rebuff for de Gaulle

Next, after its humiliation in the referendum, the G.P.R.A. issued a stinging rebuff over Cairo Radio to de Gaulle's Constantine Plan speech of 31 October: "De Gaulle offers war or fraternity. Algeria and the whole Algerian people have chosen war." At this point the F.L.N., not for the first or the last time, seem to have been speaking with two voices, for in quick succession there now followed Ferhat Abbas's much more conciliatory and widely reported interview with Artur Rosenberg. De Gaulle meanwhile was manifestly piqued by the F.L.N.'s hostility to his referendum, which he regarded in terms of the kind of "free election" which the Algerian nationalists had so persistently clamoured for in the past. In a conversation with the Moroccan politician Ben Barka, de Gaulle acidly criticised "these F.L.N. leaders who believe that the possession of sub-machine-guns and rifles gives them automatically the right to come to discuss politics with him [de Gaulle] ", On other occasions he held strongly to his view that negotiations for a cease-fire should be largely restricted to military spheres. Nevertheless, despite this evident gulf between the two sides, the G.P.R.A. was apparently prepared to announce at its session of 24 October that a "dialogue" had been opened with de Gaulle.

Then, the day before, came de Gaulle's Press conference and his bomb-shell of the *paix des braves*. The proposition had been most carefully rehearsed and could not in any way be dismissed as a "slip of the tongue" like the "*Vive l'Algérie française!*" of Mostaganem. Here was de Gaulle the soldier, believing that he was addressing himself to enemy soldiers in the language of the soldier, and offering what he genuinely considered to be preliminaries to a "peace with honour". But in fact he was addressing hardened politicians, and his phraseology betrayed the most complete failure to understand the psychology of the F.L.N. leaders. To them, however de Gaulle might construe it, the mention of the *drapeau blanc des parlementaires* could mean one thing and one thing only: capitulation. On the 25th the G.P.R.A. replied: "The declaration of General de Gaulle constitutes a refusal to negotiate . . . ." In slamming the door as brusquely as they did, the G.P.R.A. were, from their point of view, absolutely right. For, with the shaky state of morale both among the civilians and A.L.N. units inside Algeria, had they accepted the *paix des braves*, even only as preliminary parley, the revolution might well have begun to flicker out and would have been extremely difficult to rekindle if the talks assumed a course unfavourable to the F.L.N. De Gaulle would have won the war; on the other hand, by rejecting the *paix des braves* the F.L.N. were, eventually, to win it.

One of the first consequences of the F.L.N.'s intransigence towards the *paix des braves* was to confront de Gaulle with, at best, a half-defeat at the legislative elections of the following month. Out of the forty-six Muslim deputies sent to France, not one could be reckoned to constitute a potential *interlocuteur valable*. All were supporters of "integration", none represented a genuine, liberal "third force". As Michael Clark correctly observes, "the centrifugal pressure of events had driven the moderates from an untenable middle position. The chief weakness of the middle position was that it had no popular support. None but fools could expect many aspiring Muslim politicians in 1958 to risk their lives in defense of it."

The rejection of the *paix des braves* was also to mark the beginning of the decline within the G.P.R.A. of the influence of the moderates – notably, at this stage, Ferhat Abbas. Despite the collapse of his initiatives in October, over the next nine months Abbas visited no less than fifteen foreign capitals in pursuit of a new peace formula. Then, disillusioned, he withdrew increasingly from the scene. Abbas, it may be assumed, was quite genuine in his pursuit still of some kind of compromise peace solution; the same cannot be said of the increasingly powerful hard-liners behind the G.P.R.A. by whom negotiations were regarded primarily as a device for getting France involved in an endless procedure, which would provide the F.L.N. with time it so badly needed in 1958-9, and, by wearing down the patience of the enemy negotiators, eventually lead to peace on F.L.N. terms.

The A.L.N. under extreme pressure

Meanwhile, de Gaulle, thwarted in his first peace initiative, had set to prosecuting the military war with unprecedented vigour, with means that will be seen in the following chapter. As will be recalled, between its defeat in the Battle of Algiers and the spring of 1958 the A.L.N. had come under fiercest pressure, its attempts to breach the Morice Line broken with bloody losses, its valiant *moudjahiddine* isolated and hard-pressed in the Wilayas. Yet, seen in retrospect, the A.L.N. of the interior would seem to have reached its apogee of military power in 1958. At the beginning of the year French estimates had put the total strength of A.L.N. regulars, or *moudjahiddine*, at about 30,000, of whom approximately half were operating in the interior at any one time. On top of this were reckoned to be another 30,000 irregulars, or *moussebiline*, most of whom were in the interior. Of these effectives, the French claimed that 25,534 had been killed or captured during the first seven months of the year. Although (as with the notorious United States army "head counts" in Vietnam) it may be questioned just how many of these casualties were actually genuine, hardcore *moudjahiddine*, they nevertheless represented a serious drain of effectives. By the end of 1958 the G.P.R.A.'s new Ministry of Information under Yazid proclaimed triumphantly that, from 40,000 in 1957, the total of men under arms had risen to over 100,000; but, again, the proportion of *moudjahiddine* in the total could be questioned, while at the same time the ratio of effectives inside Algeria to those outside was steadily widening to the advantage of the latter.

By June 1958 the A.L.N. had been forced to reduce its basic fighting unit to the *katiba*, or company; by the following year it was to be found seldom operating on larger than a platoon level. The shortage of arms and ammunition was becoming particularly pronounced; by December 1958 Wilaya 1 (Aurès) was reporting to the G.P.R.A. that no less than 600 of its combatants were without weapons. The loss in leaders was proving equally grave; in November 1958 Wilaya 4 (Algérois) lost its military chief, Azedine, captive to the French,* and two months later one of its best field commanders, Captain Si Rachid, was also killed. In March 1959 there followed the deaths of the leaders of both Wilayas 6 and 3, Si Haouès and the ferocious Amirouche, in circumstances shortly to be described. The consequence of all this on the morale of the Wilayas could be detected in the fact that, whereas in 1956 the monthly total of *moudjahiddine* defectors to the French would barely occupy the fingers of one hand, by July–August 1958 it had risen to an average of 300. At the same time the recovery of arms by the French showed a noteworthy increase. In the new year of 1959 the Wilayas were to be found concentrating on the relatively unrisky pastime of derailing trains. It was a gross excess of optimism for the veteran *pied noir* marshal, Juin, to declare in November that "the war is virtually over", but the coming of General Challe the following month was to impose upon the A.L.N. the gravest threat it had yet faced, as well as the beginning of a decline from which it would never fully recover. On the other hand, because of timely political developments, the military potential of the A.L.N. would cease to a decisive factor in the war.

Death of Amirouche the Terrible

Under mounting French military pressure, a fresh set of rifts had been provoked in the higher echelons of the F.L.N., both between the Wilayas and the "exterior" of the G.P.R.A., and within the various Wilayas themselves. The years of 1958 and 1959 were, above all, a time when the Wilaya leaders were scourged by terrible apprehensions of treachery, or purported treachery. Genuine acts of betrayal had existed, certainly, but they had been used with extreme cunning by French intelligence operatives to demoralise the maquis through playing upon the innate suspiciousness of the Algerian. It has already been noted how teams of *bleu* double-agents controlled by Captain Christian Léger during the Battle of Algiers had subsequently succeeded in penetrating the Western Zone headquarters of Wilaya 3 (Kabylia), rounding it up in its entirety. Colonel Godard, the expert on counter-revolutionary warfare, followed up the confusion and distrust generated in the wake of this coup by adroitly "dropping" incrimi-

---

* Though he was to outwit his captors and make good his escape at a later date.

nating correspondence with French intelligence among other immaculate leaders in the Wilayas. The bait was snapped up greedily by Amirouche, the jeweller from the Beni-Yenni and the most ruthless of any Wilaya commander, entering into the "game" with unparalleled zest and instituting massive purges like a latter-day Vyshinsky. Under appalling inquisitions supervised by an F.L.N. captain nicknamed "La Torture" who had worked with the S.S. during the Second World War, admissions of treachery were extorted which led to vast chain-reactions of suspicion. Orders were given to arrest all recent Muslim deserters from the French forces, and any recruits who had come from Algiers since the beginning of the battle. A kind of madness seized Amirouche, who is said to have caused the execution of possibly as many as 3,000, women as well as men, in the course of his reign of terror. Mouloud Feraoun wrote in his diary: "Sad epoch, sad Kabylia. Sad Kabylia because every day one discovers traitors, the traitors are killed, and those who killed them end by being killed in their turn."

During this period activities against the French were all but paralysed, and, not satisfied with purging his own Wilaya, Amirouche urged similar measures upon the neighbouring Wilayas 2 (Constantine) and 4 (Algérois). Mistrust is contagious, and in rapid succession the leaders of both Wilayas followed suit. The havoc was particularly pronounced in Wilaya 4, which, with its "progressive" attitudes towards discipline and innovations of communal decision-taking, had for some time been a model sector. By the summer of 1959 all was havoc, its leader, Si M'hamed, having been encouraged – partly by the example of Amirouche, partly as a result of assiduous "moling" by Léger's teams – to carry out a murderous purge of the numerous young students and intellectuals who had joined the Wilaya on fleeing from the Battle of Algiers. The "capital" crimes of which they were found guilty often amounted to little more than asking questions, or revealing an "incorrect revolutionary stance".

By the end of 1958 Amirouche and his fellow commanders had their Wilayas in a grip of terror, while jointly the power they exerted in relation to the absentee G.P.R.A. was hardly less daunting. Hard on the heels of the purge in his own Wilaya, Amirouche was writing a fierce letter to the G.P.R.A. in Tunis, accusing it of bourgeois taints and of half-heartedness in its attempts to breach the Morice Line, and calling upon it to launch a "national purification" similar to his own. At the same time he endeavoured to canvass the support of his peers at an inter-Wilaya meeting held in December in the mountainous country round El-Milia, close to the boundary between Wilayas 2 and 3. Colonel Lotfi of Wilaya 5, who enjoyed close relations with his predecessor, Boussouf, now a powerful minister of the G.P.R.A., refused to take part, but Amirouche found degrees of support particularly from Si M'hamed (Wilaya 4) and Si Haouès (Wilaya

6). Having expressed fears (that were highly exaggerated) of the immense scale of French intelligence penetration of the entire F.L.N. movement, Amirouche persuaded the meeting to send a communiqué to the G.P.R.A. in which it was sternly criticised, summoned to "correct its errors", and exhorted to devolve greater powers upon the Wilaya leaders. It was also agreed that one or more representatives at the meeting should go to Tunis to confront the G.P.R.A. the following April.

Evidently with this ultimate objective in mind, towards the end of March 1959 Amirouche was heading south-eastwards from his Kabyle fiefdom for a rendezvous with the czar of the Sahara, Si Haouès. In the barren wastes of the Hodna that lie between Kabylia and the true Sahara, *harki* scouts attached to Colonel Georges Buis came across a fresh latrine, with signs of it having been used by a large number of men. Swiftly flying in elements of three para regiments, Buis succeeded in trapping a whole A.L.N. *katiba*. Seventy-three were killed and eight captured alive, one of them being Amirouche's private secretary on whom was found a number of helpful documents – including details of the inter-Wilaya meeting of December 1958. Amirouche himself had made his getaway only a few hours earlier. A week later, on 28 March, in a state of exhaustion he had reached Si Haouès in the desert south-east of Bou Saada. Almost immediately units under the command of Colonel Ducasse, Massu's former chief-of-staff, who (like most of those present in May 1958) had been posted away from Algiers by de Gaulle, were attacking the rebel encampment. After a brief but fierce one-sided fight between 2,500 French troops and forty *moudjahiddine*, the bodies of the two Wilaya leaders were picked up. It was a notable success for the French, by whom Amirouche was regarded as one of the deadliest enemy commanders, and Ducasse was promptly made a Commander of the Legion of Honour. But the suspicion lingered long that possibly the tip-off on the leaders' whereabouts might have been passed on by those of his colleagues to whom Amirouche, in particular, had become an embarrassment in his ruthless cruelty and lust for power. Certainly it seems a curious coincidence that, after so many years of frustration, the French should be able to lay their hands on two such important leaders of the A.L.N. at once.

The coincidence was, if anything, extenuated when, less than two months later, Amirouche's other ally, Colonel Si M'hamed of Wilaya 4 disappeared mysteriously in the course of an operation. His body was never found, but it is generally believed that he was executed by his comrades, in all probability the victim of French Intelligence *bleuite*, like so many of the young Algiers students whose deaths he had himself ordered. With the disappearance of Si M'hamed, however, the purges in Wilaya 4 by no means ceased. Shortly after being appointed, his successor, Si Salah, reported to the G.P.R.A. that he personally had interrogated, judged and sentenced to execution 312 *djounoud*, fifty-four non-commissioned officers and twenty officers.

In all this saga of upheaval in the echelons of Wilaya 4, French Intelligence suffered one notable reverse at the hands of Major Azedine, the former boiler-maker and deputy military commander to Si M'hamed. In November 1958 Massu had mounted a powerful sweep of the country round Palestro in the course of which Azedine had been captured, with a shattered forearm. Under interrogation Azedine declared convincingly that he was at odds with the conduct of the war by the G.P.R.A. He felt it should now make peace with de Gaulle, whose return to power had made the whole struggle "senseless". Azedine offered to negotiate a surrender with the leaders of Wilaya 4, and actually made several trips into the maquis to this end, on "parole". At the same time he fed his captors with quantities of false information, and exploited a local cease-fire to get a shipment of supplies through to his Wilaya. Then one day in December he vanished quietly into the mountains behind Blida and was never seen again – until he emerged as the F.L.N. commander negotiating the take-over of Algiers in the last days of the war.*

Revolt of the four colonels: enter Boumedienne

The commands of the Wilayas were in disarray; there was too much autonomous power on the part of their chiefs, verging on a "cult of the personality". All this was abhorrent to the whole philosophy of the F.L.N., opening wounds which still festered since the liquidation of Abane, and revealed anew that the military authority of the "exterior" G.P.R.A. was as frail as that of its predecessor, the C.C.E. On top of this there were, as ever, the numerous papered-over conflicts that needed only an increase of stress for them to burst through to the surface: conflicts of ideology between the veteran F.L.N. members and the former supporters of Messali and Abbas, and between the conservatives and progressives; conflicts between city intellectuals and illiterate peasant maquisards; conflicts between the thousands of refugees living, like the Palestinians, miserable and hungry in wretched camps in Tunisia and Morocco, and the growing force of comfortable bureaucrats serving the G.P.R.A. in Tunisia; conflicts between the G.P.R.A. and Bourguiba; conflicts, as always, between the "interior" and "exterior", and finally conflicts between the A.L.N. military command in Ghardimaou and the supreme leadership in Tunis. Seldom before had a strong hand seemed more necessary.

Then, in November 1958, what looked like the threat of a major revolt

* The decamping of Azedine was humiliating for French pride to swallow, but the damage may not have stopped there. A year and a half later a genuine peace offer was made by the then commander of Wilaya 4, Si Salah, perhaps one of the most important "breaks" of the whole war. But it was turned down by a mistrustful de Gaulle, no doubt in part influenced by the Azedine debacle.

appeared on the Tunisian frontier. All through the year the command of that particularly hard-pressed, key front under the former S.S. legionnaire, Mohamedi Said, with his inseparable coal-scuttle helmet, had been in a far from happy state of discord and disorder. Selecting, symbolically, the All Saints anniversary of 1 November, a full-scale offensive had been mounted to breach the Morice Line and get supplies through to the suffering Wilayas 1 and 2. It was too obvious a date for the French army to be caught napping, and – like so many of those disastrous "big pushes" on the Western Front of 1914–18 – it ended in a welter of blood and total failure in the barbed wire of the Morice Line. Morale among those involved hit rock bottom and four colonels, led by Colonel Lamouri, decided to act. With secret support, apparently, from Nasser (whose relations with the new G.P.R.A. were icy) they intended to march on Tunis, chuck out the G.P.R.A. and liquidate the "three Bs", replacing it with a completely "military" regime. Lamouri tried unsuccessfully to make contact with the disenchanted Amirouche but, before he was able to, reports of his plans reached the ears of Boussouf's intelligence network.

During the night of 16 November the four colonels were seized at a conspiratorial meeting near El-Kef, together with some twenty of their supporters. Altogether fifty-four suspects were rounded up on Krim's orders, and in March the ringleaders appeared before a court-martial on Tunisian territory. The presiding judge was an austerely efficient but little-known young colonel who first appeared as Boussouf's aide in Morocco. He had then taken over command of the Western Front where he had permitted none of the discords which had so riven its Tunisian counterpart. His name was Houari Boumedienne. The four colonels were condemned to death, and shot the following day; while the majors who had followed them, considered corrupted by their seniors, were given only two years' imprisonment.* But the sentences passed by Boumedienne were unprecedentedly harsh by (official) F.L.N. standards, and exemplary. The A.L.N.'s strong man had arrived, and from this moment on its whole character began to show a steady change.

For all his eminence in the post-war decade, Boumedienne remains one of the least known of all the war leaders of either side, and in his secretiveness and retiring modesty he is most characteristically Algerian. In 1973 one leading Western ambassador was unable to tell the author where the then President of Algeria lived, or whether he was married or not;† in three years he had met him once. There exists no official – or even unofficial – biography of Boumedienne, only the scantiest of entries in *International*

---

* It is worth noting that, while fulsome tributes were paid to Amirouche and Si Haouès by Krim and others in succeeding issues of *El Moudjahid*, no reference was made to the execution of the four A.L.N. colonels.

† He was in fact married in 1973.

Who's Who, and pen-portraits differ widely as to the date he was born, and whether it was in Oranie or Constantinois, at opposite ends of the country. There are contradictions as to where and when he received his military training; some say at a guerrilla school in Egypt, one of his closer collaborators thought it was in General Kassem's Iraq, while there were extravagant French rumours that Boumedienne had somehow found time for training in both Moscow and Peking. Yet there is, apparently, no truth in any of these speculations. Even after years of being not only President of Algeria but also one of the most influential leaders of the Third World, he has never shaken off his intense dislike of any form of publicity, and in his rare interviews with writers and journalists he steadfastly declines to discuss the war, or his role in it.

What is known with reasonable certainty of Boumedienne is that he was born in 1927 near Guelma with the name of Mohammed Ben Brahim Boukharouba, and that his father was an impoverished small wheat-farmer with seven children, an Arab and a strict Muslim speaking no French. "Houari" and "Boumedienne" were both *noms-de-guerre* he assumed while serving his first apprenticeship with the A.L.N. in Oranie; the one from a mountain range, the other from a local Muslim patron saint. Using both, for a considerable time Boumedienne deceived French intelligence as to his true identity. It was evidently at Guelma, during the Sétif revolt of 1945, that Boumedienne as a youth gained his first experience of conflict with the French. He had been sent, aged fourteen, to school in Constantine, at one of the few centres dedicated to Arab-Islamic studies, where he stayed for six years. In about 1950 he went to Cairo to study in that great fount of Muslim learning, El Azhar University. His background was thus already totally different from that of the francophone nationalist leaders of the pre-war generation, like Ferhat Abbas, and his age when the revolution started places him among the rising leaders who belonged truly to the new generation created by the war itself. In the maquis he seems first to have emerged in 1955, carrying out a beach-landing of arms west of Oran from the "borrowed" yacht of the Queen of Jordan, and was then picked out for his silent efficiency by Boussouf, currently commander of Wilaya 5, to be his adjutant. On Boussouf's promotion to the C.C.E. in July 1957, Boumedienne was himself appointed to command the Wilaya as the youngest colonel in the A.L.N. The following year he was given command of the whole Western Front, and subsequently transferred to the A.L.N. High Command at about the time of the plot of the four dissident colonels over whose judgement he was to preside.

With his curiously gaunt, high-cheekboned face, reddish hair, harshly intense green eyes and wispy moustache, to some Western journalists Boumedienne looked "more like a starving Irish poet than a guerrilla veteran". The fact that it was a face seldom seen smiling ("Why should

I smile just because a photographer is taking the trouble to photograph me?" he asked an Egyptian interviewer when President) underlined the salient characteristic of Boumedienne: his deadly seriousness. It was a seriousness that permitted him no time for the frippery of rank, uniform or decorations; no time for the foibles of personal ambition or boasting; and no time for the petty feuds with which the F.L.N. was riven. All of this made him much revered by the men under him. He was deeply serious about the study of war, particularly in its organisational aspects. Dedicated to one cause only, an independent Algeria, he had no Marxist leanings yet had closely studied the revolutionary teachings of Mao. He was an utterly unromantic revolutionary, with a coldly searching intellect, of whom it was said that he only emerged from his withdrawn taciturnity to ask a question – and his thirst for information was insatiable.* One English newspaper pen-portrait of Boumedienne (David Leitch in the *Sunday Times* of 6 August 1967) describes him as having no known vices "except chain-smoking Gauloises, and apparent total indifference to human relationships". His spartan headquarters were enlivened only by a large portrait of Abd-el-Kader, the national hero. A tremendous worker, he had the eye and memory for detail of a staff officer of genius, and his organisation left a mark on both Wilaya 5 and the Western Front that was exceptional within the A.L.N.

Following the execution of the rebel colonels, Boumedienne was given the Herculean task of restoring discipline and organisation to the army in Tunisia. Soon his efforts began to show results, one of his early tactical innovations being to halt the costly frontal assaults on the Morice Line. As 1959 progressed, it was also clear that Boumedienne had become the most influential soldier in the A.L.N.; for, having called him in to crush the insurgent colonels, the G.P.R.A. would find it difficult to check his growing influence over the "exterior" army in both Morocco and Tunisia. At the third C.N.R.A. congress held in Tripoli during January 1960, Boumedienne was confirmed in the all-powerful post of chief-of-staff of the whole A.L.N. – which he had, in effect, already been filling for some months past. Under pressure from the French army, he adopted a decisive new strategy: instead of attempting to back up the Wilayas at appalling cost across the Morice Line, the A.L.N. would be regrouped and reorganised inside the Tunisian sanctuary, and held there in readiness for future military and political opportunities. It was a strategy that would, to some extent, deceive the French Army Command into believing the military successes of the Challe Plan were greater than in fact they were – with consequences that will shortly be seen.

---

* According to one of his close entourage at the time of his flying visit to Moscow during the "Ramadan War" of 1973, Boumedienne taxed his staff to the limits by demanding almost hourly bulletins of news from home, "and you know how difficult that is to obtain in Moscow...!"

Thus a new star had been born with an import for the future which, at the time of writing, remains still incalculable. In general, however, 1958–59 had been a thoroughly bad and dangerous time for the F.L.N. Both politically and militarily it had been caught off balance by the coming of de Gaulle. If de Gaulle could have followed up the momentum of his first weeks with a concerted peace drive, or if the Challe offensive had begun in 1958 instead of 1959, the prospects would have looked incomparably bleak. But, as it happened, the long build-up to the referendum and the November legislative elections, followed by the run-down from the *paix des braves* olive-branch, had given the F.L.N. an invaluable respite in which to regain its breath. And when in 1959 the A.L.N. was confronted with the gravest military threat to its existence, it was already moving in – and under – a new direction.

CHAPTER SIXTEEN

Neither the Djebel
nor the Night

1959

We have pacified the country so well...that the *fellagha* have almost disappeared. Nowadays, almost no one joins the guerrillas....
French captain's report, quoted by Edward Behr

The Challe Plan

WITH the end of fighting in Cyprus, 1959 revealed a world with only one major active battle front: Algeria. Despite all the problems besetting it, the A.L.N. of the interior was still making its presence felt. In small packets they would descend from the *djebel*, blow up power pylons, mine a train or an army convoy, murder a pro-French *caid* or shoot up the isolated outpost of one of the heroic corps of French S.A.S. officers; and then vanish again whence they came. Existing as they did under terrible conditions of cold, hunger, and constant pursuit by the French army, that they could still act at all must of itself be a testimony to the remarkable stoicism, tenacity and dedication of the individual *moudjahid*. Revisiting his *pied noir* brother, a small farmer at Ménerville less than forty miles east of Algiers, Colonel Jules Roy found him and his wife placing flimsy metal trays ("such as you find in bakery ovens") over all the windows, like Kenya settlers in the Mau-Mau era. "We've had to do this every night for the last four years," the brother explained: "they don't kill because they have anything against you. These days they kill for the sake of killing." He added gloomily: "They'll never stop, that's for sure. We kill one whenever we manage to catch him, but the next day another starts all over again. They want us to get out." Year after year, night after night, the nervous tension among the European *colons* in the outlying *bled* must have become almost intolerable. There was virtually no corner of the country where, in the fifth year of the war, they could feel totally secure. The truth was that, for all the massive injections of men and material, the security forces were just too thinly spread to meet every possible threat everywhere.

In appointing General Maurice Challe as Commander-in-Chief, says de Gaulle, "I expected operations to take a dynamic turn which would result in our undisputed mastery of the field." Conversely, in political terms, "Nothing could have been more disastrous than some untoward incident in which we came off worst." This sense of urgency was reinforced by de Gaulle's newly appointed Prime Minister, Michel Debré, in his first visit to Algeria early in the new year. To Challe he insisted that there be swift "military successes" before the spring, and that "We must be able to put out a victory bulletin in the month of July; for France is beginning to get bored with the war." There was also a looming problem of manpower; France was entering into the "hollow classes" of the young men of military age who should have been born during the Second World War. Beyond an aim of improving security for *pied noir colons*, like the Roy family (which was never one of his highest priorities), and the more conventional one of pressing the F.L.N. into accepting a *paix des braves*, de Gaulle may have had more complex psychological motives for intensifying military operations. As Raymond Aron had noted perceptively, that deep ingrained sense of past humiliations had to be exorcised, and "If the army could achieve an incontestable success, it might be less hostile to the creation of an Algerian state."

No sooner had he arrived in his new post than Challe set to work enthusiastically to devise a new, winning strategy. He analysed carefully the shortcomings of the past. Under the established system of *quadrillage*, the army had endeavoured to be everywhere at the same time, a system that had succeeded in limiting the free movement of A.L.N. *katibas* and their infiltration into the populated centres. But it had also resulted in there not being enough troops to go round for the army to have a powerful, mobile, offensive force with which to go out and destroy the A.L.N. in its mountain strongholds. In fact, at the time of Challe's appointment this force, composed chiefly of paras and the Legion, seldom amounted to more than 15,000 men, or roughly the same strength as the total of A.L.N. *moudjahiddine* available for operations in the interior. Scattered across the four corners of Algeria, it was employed rather in fire-brigade fashion – or, indeed, like the penny-packet handling of the French armour which had brought such disaster in 1940. Algeria was divided into no less than seventy-five separate sectors – which meant there were "seventy-five ways of making war" – and offensive operations tended to be carried out haphazardly, without any co-ordinated plan. "Mounted several days in advance," noted Challe, "they often struck nothing but emptiness." The blows were too ponderous:

> They achieved success when they cornered one or two *katibas*, but this was a rare act. . . . The populace was warned not to remain in the area and would be regrouped in the plains or the plateau, then, by plane or

artillery, the area would be bombarded or fired at on sight. The results, as one could verify, were nil for a veritable orgy of ammunition.

The "stirred-up" rebels would simply slip over into the neighbouring sector, which had rarely been synchronised with the operations; then, as soon as the attacking troops withdrew, the A.L.N. would return to become "master of the mountain" once more. As Challe described it to Delouvrier, in the past the war in Algeria had been fought as "a succession of blows, sometimes spectacular, but without any political or military follow-through. In the eyes of the people, the F.L.N. remains master of the country."

In contrast to this, Challe adopted as his guiding principle the slogan "Neither the *djebel* nor the night must be left to the F.L.N." Once hit, a rebel unit must be hit again, and remain hit; the army must penetrate the *querencia* where – like a fighting bull – it was at home, and stay there, driving it out into unknown and unfriendly territory. Life must be made enduringly unendurable for the *moudjahiddine*. The hunter must become the hunted. "The *katibas* retreated into the *djebel*," Challe told the author; "so I decided to go into the *djebel* after them." The two essential components of the Challe Plan were his Commandos de Chasse, accompanied by specially trained "tracker" units of Muslim *harkis*, and a new concentrated Réserve Générale. An area for an all-out offensive having been decided upon, the Commandos de Chasse would be sent into it to identify and pin down the main A.L.N. units. In line with good rugger tactics in which Challe was well versed, each *katiba* would be "marked" by its opposite number; then the massive weight of the mobile Réserve Générale, mustered from every part of the command, would be thrown in to strike overwhelmingly at the critical point. Challe, though an airman, claims that here he was influenced by the principles of concentration developed so triumphantly in Napoleon's first Italian campaign. The attacking force would not leave, as in the past, after inflicting heavy casualties, but would continue to pursue the rebel formations until they had been so broken up that they could readily be controlled by the limited, static effectives of the local sector. Disruption, not annihilation, which he considered to be unattainable, was Challe's objective; above all, the rebel O.P.A. (Organisation Politico-Administrative) had to be so smashed that it could not re-establish itself once the offensive wave had receded.

This was all the "negative" function of the Plan; its "positive" side represented an intensification of the philosophy of past French administrators from Soustelle onwards, constructive reforms designed to make the *présence française* more palatable to the Muslim population, and to strengthen their ability to defend themselves once the immediate terror of the A.L.N. had been eradicated. Among all this was included the controversial policy of "regroupment".

Fundamental to Challe's strategy were the prerequisites that the existing military establishment in Algeria should in no way be diminished, and that the "loyal" Muslim *harkis* be increased from 26,000 to 60,000. On both these scores de Gaulle's sanction was required, and there had been a tense passage at an interview with de Gaulle when Challe had insisted, "I *must* have these effectives." De Gaulle at his iciest had reproached Challe: "One does not impose conditions on de Gaulle!" But Challe, unabashed, replied that either he got de Gaulle's approval or de Gaulle would have his resignation. Challe won, and was henceforth treated with a certain respect instead of just as the General's "man" in Algiers.* The episode was typical of Challe's uncompromising independence of mind, a characteristic which in just over two years' time would confront de Gaulle with the most dangerous challenge of his entire career.

Challe's first successes

At first the energetic, rugger-playing and pipe-smoking airman was regarded frostily by the army in Algeria. How could an aviator understand terrestrial problems, how succeed where the best army brains had failed? In a remarkably short space of time, however, Challe won over his subordinates by his straightforwardness, firmness and sheer integrity; but, above all, by his technical excellence. He soon proved himself, comments Jacques Fauvet, editor of *Le Monde*, to be "one of the rare generals in the French armed forces capable of planning and commanding in a modern war". Challe also exhibited unerring skill in sifting his commanders, bringing forward the most competent and forceful, and transferring those ageing officers who had been around too long in Algeria. Within three months he had replaced nearly half the colonels commanding sectors. While de Gaulle had permitted no ambiguity about the civilian being the boss, with Delouvrier Challe's relations were of the most harmonious from the very beginning; each month the Delegate-General would attend Challe's corps commanders' conference, while Challe took part in Delouvrier's meetings with his prefects. Thus, within a few weeks of taking over, Challe had gone far to instil a new spirit of aggressive optimism in the army in Algeria, and by February the first instalment of the Challe Plan was ready to be unleashed.

Challe decided to start operations in the western end of the Ouarsenis range round Saida, lying to the south-east of Oran. The area was the fulcrum of Wilaya 5, previously commanded by Boumedienne, and had been firmly in rebel hands for several years, although the F.L.N. had always

---

* This expansion of the *harkis*, Challe stresses with maximum emphasis to the present day, was only to be achieved if the *harkis* could be assured that France would *never* abandon Algeria and leave them to face a night-of-long-knives at the hands of a triumphant F.L.N. Challe insists that de Gaulle's *personal* guarantee was implicit.

been weaker here than in the eastern parts of Algeria. Far less rugged than Kabylia or the Aurès, the rolling country of the Ouarsenis offered French mechanisation better prospects of driving the *katibas* out into the open and rounding them up; as the "softest option" it presented an ideal starting-place while Challe was still building up his Réserve Générale. As it was, the operation was spearheaded with an unprecedented concentration of fire-power, comprising the whole of Massu's old 10th Para Division plus all the mobile troops available in the Oran zone. Challe kept up the pressure until April, when it was officially announced that the Ouarsenis had been cleaned up. Over 1,600 of the F.L.N. had been killed, 460 captured, and large quantities of arms and ammunition seized. Challe himself claimed that these losses amounted to fifty per cent of the A.L.N. manpower and forty to fifty per cent of its weaponry. Results in the Saida–Mascara sector, where the redoubtable Bigeard was once more back in action, had been particularly gratifying. The local commander, Youssef Smail, had surrendered and then broadcast an impassioned appeal to his comrades to heed de Gaulle's *paix des braves* initiative. Most important of all, however, was the fact that the O.P.A. structure had been broken up and the French garrison forces left – as Challe's strategy intended – in full command of the territory after offensive operations had moved on.

On 18 April Challe launched "Opération Courroie", shifting the whole force against the eastern end of the Ouarsenis behind Algiers, the more difficult terrain that was the heart of Wilaya 4. Once again Challe allowed himself two months. For all the internal troubles within the Wilaya, he himself admits that results were "correct, but a little less good than in Oranie because the rebels split up and ran faster". Challe also criticised the attacking forces for not having acted with quite the expected amount of vigour. Meanwhile, in March, the French had registered other successes elsewhere; Amirouche and Si Haouès had been killed, and, after suffering serious losses on the Morice Line in February, an A.L.N. line-crossing *katiba* nearly 150 strong had given itself up to the French on 22 March. By summer 1959 the Challe Plan really got into its stride, with a massive force of two first-class divisions earmarked for the key Réserve Générale. The modern, mechanised equipment backing up this force was impressive. In contrast to the early days when the French had at their behest only a handful of small helicopters, there were now enough big, American-made "Flying Bananas" to lift into action two whole battalions in a matter of five minutes. From France and Germany Super-Sabre pilots had been transferred in substantial numbers to squadrons of Harvard T.6 trainers, numbering over 300 and heavily armed with four machine-guns and two rocket pods. After the supersonic F.100s, the pilots complained that the Second World War Harvards, with their rackety top speed of little over 200 m.p.h., were like driving Citroën 2 c.v.s, but they were able to observe and pounce on the tiny target of a djounoud foxhole with far greater accuracy than their more glamorous grandchildren, and were cheap and easily patched up; and this was warfare that no one understood better than Challe the airman. (At the same time, the use of so much American military equipment supplied for the benefit of France in N.A.T.O. was the source of increasing embarrassment to the American government, and of alienation between them and the already prickly de Gaulle.)

On the ground, the expanded harki units forming the nucleus of Challe's Commandos de Chasse showed themselves contributing more effectively than ever before – or afterwards. Modelled on the katibas themselves, the Commandos would strike off into the djebel for days at a time, living off the land and at the same time severing the adversary from his sources of supply, ruthlessly hunting down the hunter. They were constantly in radio communication with Challe's command post, and immediately contact was made with a katiba the Commandos would bring down helicoptered shock troops from the Réserve Générale to hem it in from all sides. Never, says Philippe Tripier, "had the forces in Algeria been so well commanded . . . never had the military instrument been better adapted to its task, well-tuned as it was and animated by ardent and inventive leaders, under the constantly innovative drive of Challe".

Operation "Binoculars"

On 22 July Challe threw in his most ambitious effort to date against the toughest nut of all – the vast mountain fastness of Kabylia, with its eyrie-like villages and population of nearly one million. With little interruption, the F.L.N. had held sway in Kabylia ever since Krim and Ouamrane hoisted the standard of revolt in 1954; its Wilaya 3 was now in the hands of Mohand Ou El-Hadj, succeeding the slain Amirouche. "Jumelles" (or "Binoculars") involved a double-pronged assault on both Little and Great Kabylia for which Challe mustered 25,000 troops in addition to the sector forces and including marines to make amphibious landings on inaccessible parts of the coast. But on the eve of launching "Binoculars", Challe's intelligence received news of A.L.N. movements in the Hodna mountains which link Kabylia with the Aurès. Overnight Challe switched regiments due to move into Kabylia, and struck a lightning, surprise sideswipe at the Hodna which in twelve days (he claims) knocked out fifty per cent of the rebel strength there. Typical of the speed and flexibility with which Challe operated, it also, in effect, created something of a moat or *cordon sanitaire* across which it would be difficult for Mohand Ou El-Hadj's Kabyles to escape into the Aurès when fleeing from the impending pressure of "Binoculars".

On a tour of inspection at the end of August, de Gaulle found Challe at his combat post 5,500 feet up in the Djurdjura mountains in the heart of

Kabylia, personally conducting operations amid "a forest of radio aerials". His *Commandos de Chasse* were combing through the endless, dense Forest of Akfadou, hitherto always a virtually untouched paradise for Wilaya 3, and there seemed to be no inch of Kabylia that was not at Challe's fingertips. Troops seized the big crest-line villages with their marvellous panoramic fields of vision, then radiated out from them like the tentacles of an octopus. In the maquis were also operating, with extraordinary fearlessness, Captain Léger and a section of his *bleus*; their double-agent activities, as usual, were so successful that villagers refused any longer to give food supplies to the A.L.N., not knowing whether they were true *moudjahiddine* or Léger's turncoats. Conditions in the field became terrible, with men dying as often from hunger as from enemy bullets. "One could no longer move," stated one of Mohand Ou El-Hadj's lieutenants:

> One no longer ate. I was so weak that I could no longer even manage to carry my sub-machine-gun. The establishment of military posts, the multiplying of self-defence communities and intelligence agents was making life impossible, and even survival itself.... It was only by executing traitors one after the other that we did manage to survive. But one was never able to regain the initiative.

In the wake of "Binoculars", Jules Roy revisited a village called Toudja, a small demi-Eden cradled in the jumbled mountains that rise above Bougie and the Soummam valley. Its orchards of fig and olive "were as luxuriant as an oasis. There are four potato harvests a year." Before 1954, like many another Kabyle village, Toudja had no contact with the French except through the tax collector; during the war families had been divided, some with a man in the A.L.N., others with one serving in the *harkis*. Now, under Challe's operations, Roy noted: "Today life has resumed, order reigns, and it is enough to send a tank ahead of the bus that goes to Bougie three times a week." During the day the French army "ensured freedom in the commune and the nearby villages, almost all of which are in ruins. Every evening they set up ambushes to surprise the *fellagha*, who come for supplies or to see their wives." But the cost of "pacification" was high. Apart from the ruined villages, cork cultivation had had to be abandoned; 15,000 of Toudja's 17,000 fig trees no longer bore fruit for want of pruning; there was not one single head of cattle left out of the 238 that existed in 1950; out of a population of 7,230, 1,200 had died or disappeared, leaving a proportion of women to men of eight to two, which spoke volumes. And, says Roy, "compared with what I saw later on, I can affirm that the inhabitants of Toudja are well off".

The "positive" ...

For all this suffering, what were the results in Kabylia? Challe himself admits that, at first, they were "disappointing". Mohand Ou El-Hadj had reacted swiftly by splitting up his *katibas* into small packets of ten to twenty men that went to ground in caves, or escaped through the teeth of the army comb. But "little by little the regiments saw the population come to us and give us their confidence". By late October when the autumn rains brought an end to "Binoculars", the French announced that 3,746 Kabyle insurgents had been killed, captured or wounded, and their military structure fragmented, while the F.L.N. itself admitted to extremely heavy losses. And Challe had still not finished; in November, moving ever eastwards, he was "cleansing" the mountain country of Wilaya 2, north of Constantine. In the spring of 1960 he was planning "Trident" to attack in full force in the Aurès–Nementchas, the only remaining territory where A.L.N. *katibas* still remained intact and effective.

But in the meantime many things had happened on the political level, and on 23 April 1960 Challe was posted home before "Trident" could be launched.

Seen in retrospect, "Binoculars" represented the peak not only of the Challe Plan but of all French military efforts in Algeria. Should it then be compared to the victorious Haig–Foch steamroller which broke the Kaiser's army in the summer of 1918; or to the Ludendorff offensive of the preceding March, which had brought Germany to within an inch of victory, yet failed nevertheless, and not least, on account of factors far removed from the battlefield? On the balance sheet, Challe's own forces had suffered losses rarely exceeding a ratio of one to ten, a few hundred killed; while on his departure he reckoned that over half the regular *katibas* of the interior had been destroyed in the course of the past year's offensives. The proportion of prisoners to killed had, significantly, risen to forty-two per cent from twenty-seven for the previous year, and a number of those who gave themselves up switched allegiances to join the *harkis*. In arms, the French claimed to have collected five for every one lost to the rebels (also a significant change from the early months of the war; the A.L.N. were losing 300 weapons net per month, and it was estimated that by September 1959 their logistic potential had sunk more than twenty per cent over the past year). Thus, statistically, the A.L.N. looked defeated by the time of Challe's departure in 1960. This is certainly how it seemed to many French commanders on the ground. "We have pacified the country so well", Edward Behr quotes one captain as reporting to his commanding officer at about this time, "that the *fellagha* have almost disappeared. Nowadays, almost no one joins the guerrillas. It is more practical to stay put and campaign for independence in a thousand legal ways." The whole chain of command between the *katibas* and the O.P.A., and the Wilayas and the G.P.R.A., so laboriously constructed since the Soummam Conference of 1956, had been disrupted. Irregulars – *moussebiline and fidayine* – had to fill the huge holes torn in the ranks of the *moudjahiddine*. Morale had never been lower. Claimed Challe: "The rebel is no longer king of the *djebel*; he is trapped there....The military phase of the rebellion is terminated in the interior...."

There was also what Challe called the "positive" element of his campaign. Immediately a zone had been "pacified", the army engineers hastened to build roads through to its most inhospitable areas; military posts and "self-defence" communities were established and new S.A.S. centres created. More schools and clinics were constructed than at any time since 1954 – but still not enough. Deeply involved in all this, the army began to feel a renewed pride and saw itself "appointed by the nation and, almost alone, responsible for safeguarding a form of civilisation on this African soil and making possible advancement and progress there". It also felt increasingly committed to those Muslims who had accepted its shield, above all to the *harkis*, to whom it constantly repeated pledges that France would *never* now abandon Algeria.

...and the "negative"

Of all the confidence and goodwill that may have been gained here, however, as much – or more – was lost through one essential concomitant of the "negative", military element of the Challe Plan. This was the intensification of the old "regroupment" policy, aimed at draining away the "water" so that the "fish" would asphyxiate, when deprived of contact with the local population upon whom it depended for food and shelter. By July 1959 over one million Muslim villagers had been transferred to "regroupment camps", which varied from resembling the fortified villages of the Middle Ages to the concentration camps of a more recent past. In the latter conditions were nothing short of scandalous. Hunger first, and cold secondly, were the enemies. At one camp just outside Constantine, inmates were found eating grass in the field, and in the overcrowded, tented encampments for nomads of the south infants were often found dead of cold in the mornings. Tuberculosis and other ailments of malnutrition raged. Of one regrouped Kabyle village, designed for 3,000 but now holding 15,000, Jules Roy wrote: "As for leaving – at the gates of the village there is a garrison, barbed wire, an armed sentry, and trenches. And where is there to go? The land has been burned. A few onions are sprouting at the bottom of the wadis." Elsewhere he describes the terrible plight of refugees, driven out of their homes in the "pacification zones", not regrouped but living in squalid *bidonvilles* on the edge of already overcrowded towns: "without water, without sewage or sanitation of any kind, without land to cultivate and for the most part without work... what do they live on?... Returning to the city after a tour like this you feel you must wash your hands. You're ashamed of yourself." Even the hardened Massu was profoundly shocked to find at a regroupment camp less than twenty-five miles from Algiers that "the level of life, and in particular the situation of the children, was inferior to the most miserable I have known in Black Africa".

All this, however, remained concealed from the gaze of the public in France until, in July 1959, the conservative *Figaro* launched a bombshell in the form of a searing report from a correspondent who had visited a camp near Philippeville. For two years the inhabitants had been living in tents, fifteen to each, where in summer the temperature reached 110°F. Many of the children were unable to attend school because of lack of clothes, and the hunger was acute: "I shall not easily forget those arms hardly thicker than a stick, those fearful expressions, those hollow faces." The *Figaro* report provoked a major uproar, on Left and Right, and was followed by a spate of similar accounts in other newspapers. Challe was pressed to close down the regroupment camps but pleaded for their retention on grounds of military necessity; by the end of the year, however, a big effort had been made to improve living conditions within them.

At about the same time there were also murmurs that torture had raised its ugly head again, employed to extract intelligence vital for the Challe offensives. The de Gaulle government, however, had set its face resolutely against such malpractices. André Malraux, who in his own remarkable life had learned more about the full horror of torture than probably any other Western politician, had declared as Minister of Information that there would be no more of it; de Gaulle had openly criticised Delouvrier for permitting the army to resort to torture. So if it did continue it seems to have been on a basis of "private enterprise", no longer the wholesale outrage that it had been during the Battle of Algiers.

The balance

In summing up on the Challe Plan, though one may respect Challe's sincerity in claiming that "the military phase of the rebellion is terminated", one may well question just how fundamental and lasting were the consequences of this military victory; would they be decisive on the political conduct of the war; was it, on the other hand, going to prove a case of the operation succeeding and the patient succumbing nevertheless? As so often happens with the soldiers on the spot, there was a certain amount of self-deception by the "centurions" of Algeria, a self-deception that would shortly lead to the gravest of misjudgements. Even if Challe had effectively broken up the *katibas* into penny-packets of shaken guerrillas, so long as they were not all annihilated or won over there always existed the danger that at some future date they might reform themselves and recruit new replacements to fill the gaps. As Lartéguy's "Boisfeuras" remarks in *Les Prétoriens*, "In a few weeks, in a few months, the rebellion will break out

again – you know, like the algae which always comes back in aquariums."
What was not visible to the French military at the time should also be
recalled; namely, that it was already the deliberate strategy of the new
A.L.N. chief-of-staff, Boumedienne, to build up a powerful new force outside
under the safe umbrella of Tunisian neutrality, at the expense of those hard-
pressed *katibas* of the interior, but waiting for the right opportunity that
would present itself one day.

Then there was always the prospect of support from further afield. "In
its hatred for the F.L.N.," declared Jules Roy as the Challe offensives ended,
"the army refused to realise that the F.L.N. might receive outside aid that
will one day blow its barriers.... Instead of admitting that it is easier to
make peace with the F.L.N. than with the Chinese, it cherishes the illusion
that a decomposition of the rebel forces is imminent...." De Gaulle,
however, was later to claim that he for one was not deceived by the scale
of Challe's successes. During his visit to "Binoculars", after Kabyle village
children had dutifully chanted the *Marseillaise*,

> Just as I was leaving, the Muslim town clerk stopped me, bowing and
> trembling, and murmured: "*Mon général*, don't be taken in! Everyone
> here wants independence." At Saida, where the heroic Bigeard introduced
> me to a commando unit who had been won over, I caught sight of a
> young Arab doctor attached to their group. "Well, doctor, what do you
> think of it all?" "What we Arabs want, and what we need," he replied,
> his eyes filled with tears, "is to be responsible for ourselves instead of
> others being responsible for us."

Certainly de Gaulle had himself frequently stressed to the army that
military success was not an end in itself. "A request for a cease-fire by those
on the other side," writes de Gaulle's close collaborator, Bernard Tricot,
"only seems to us foreseeable if, convinced that the armed struggle had
become hopeless, they had good reasons for thinking that a return to peace
would permit them to attain their objectives by political means." All
through the hard year of 1959 there were no effective offers of a cease-fire
forthcoming from the F.L.N. – despite the relentless military pressure being
applied by Challe – and meanwhile a political formula was still wanting.

Political and economic initiatives

On the political front, Delegate-General Paul Delouvrier was continuing
to find de Gaulle's instructions discouragingly vague. The only thing that
was quite clear was the priority attached to getting the Constantine Plan
under way, to give Algeria an economic solution to its troubles even if a
political one was not immediately forthcoming. Here Delouvrier the technocrat, finding himself on his home ground, had moved energetically.
During 1959 242 milliard francs had been invested, and a further 326
milliards earmarked for 1960; 132 new industrial enterprises had been pro-

jected, 400,000 acres of arable land (still not very much in relation to demand) handed over to Muslim farmers; the number of jobs for manual workers had been increased by eight per cent in only six months, while school attendance for Muslim children had risen from 510,000 in 1958 to 840,000 at the beginning of 1960. Under the "thousand villages programme", designed to counter the miseries of regroupment, 38,000 housing units had been constructed. In November 1959 the oil pipeline from Hassi-Messaoud to Bougie entered into service; in March 1960 work was to begin on the Hassi-R'Mel–Arzew pipeline for natural gas, and plans were under way to build a major steel complex at Bône. All this represented a considerable advance over anything done, socially or economically, for Algeria in the past – as well as being a pledge and an assurance to the Muslims that France had no intention of pulling out. At the same time, de Gaulle had endeavoured to make various conciliatory gestures to the F.L.N. On the day of his inauguration as President, he had commuted all death sentences, transferred Ben Bella and his companions to more "honourable" quarters, released Messali Hadj unconditionally from his perennial house-arrest, and continued to set free Muslim internees in Algeria by the thousand.

At his first Press conference in the Elysée, on 25 March, he had told a questioner that France, "while endeavouring to achieve pacification, is working towards a transformation which will enable Algeria to find her new personality". The following month, in an interview with the liberal editor of the *Echo d'Oran*, Pierre Laffont, he had made some hard-hitting remarks aimed at the diehard *pieds noirs*. When asked why he never mentioned the word "integration" in his speeches, he had replied haughtily, "First of all, because they wanted to impose it on me"; and then he added: "What they want, is to return to 'Papa's Algeria'. But Papa's Algeria is dead, and if they don't understand that they will die with it." He had followed this up by emphasising (again chiefly for *pied noir* consumption) that it was in his name the Muslim "fraternisation" of May 1958 had taken place, and that only he and he alone could bring about a solution in Algeria.

Neither de Gaulle's clemency measures nor his other olive sprigs of 1959 produced any more flicker of a *quid pro quo* from the hard core of the F.L.N. than British governments were to obtain from the I.R.A. The principal effect they had was to anger the army and arouse mistrust among the *pieds noirs*. The first anniversary of 13 May was a sombre affair in Algiers, Lagaillarde attempting (with only modest success) to transform it into a day of mourning, and there were heard the first shouts of "*De Gaulle au poteau!*" In France, Mollet continued to support de Gaulle on Algeria, while Soustelle was becoming increasingly alienated. There also seemed to be a divergence between de Gaulle and his Prime Minister,

Debré; in August when the latter declared that "France would do anything – anything at all – to keep Algeria French," de Gaulle was saying: "Peace is a necessity. This absurd war. . . ."

Though as ever enigmatic when it came to revealing his precise intentions, de Gaulle had dropped one or two hints in the course of 1959 about the way in which his mind was working. At his inauguration on 8 January he had spoken of Algeria, "pacified and transformed, developing her own personality and closely associated with France". And on 30 January: "destiny lies essentially within the Algerians themselves". On 25 March: "a new Algeria, that is to say modern, educated and fraternal . . . will find her face and her soul". To Bernard Tricot, his newly appointed councillor on Algerian affairs who was probably as close to the General's thinking on this subject as anyone else, at that time "he gave the impression of a man who was still searching". In August de Gaulle took a relatively long vacation of three weeks, his first while in office, accompanied by a note carefully drafted by Tricot and others on the prospects for an Algerian peace settlement. Among the points studied was the pursuit of a cease-fire that could be regarded by the F.L.N. not as an act of surrender, but as a transitional period leading to definitive negotiations; also it contained the proposition that the Algerians be consulted (presumably by referendum) on the future status of their country. It was during these weeks of withdrawal from the daily pressures of the office that, one can assume, de Gaulle thoughtfully deliberated his Algeria policy.

De Gaulle visits his army

Immediately afterwards he flew to Algeria on his *tournée des popotes* (round of officers' messes), to put his intentions across to the army leaders who were fighting the war so wholeheartedly. He felt, not without reason, that communication between himself and the army in Algeria had become distinctly faulty. The military mind found the changeable nuances of de Gaulle's statements not easy to decipher; on the other hand, Tricot claims that even his clearest instructions were often deliberately misapplied by the army when they conflicted with its own philosophy. Always pointedly in uniform, de Gaulle began (on 27 August) by visiting Bigeard in the Ouarsenis, half-amused, half-irritated by the flamboyant colonel's "circus"; then on to Colonel Buis in the Hodna, followed by a lightning tour of the Morice Line in the east; ending in Kabylia (on 30 August) at Challe's battle headquarters whence he was conducting "Binoculars".

On the way de Gaulle had had an illuminating private conversation with a remarkable Muslim, Mahdi Belhaddad, a veteran who had lost his right arm at Cassino, currently sub-prefect of a one-horse town on the fringes of the Aurès, the only Muslim to hold such a post. Taking Belhaddad aside, the President had asked him for his views on the exposé of the situation that

342

the local military had just given. Belhaddad began by complaining of the limitations imposed upon his own freedom of action, and at the fact that – after all the administrative reforms of the past years – there was still no other Muslim sub-prefect apart from himself, and that there was no Muslim in Delouvrier's cabinet. He then offered the opinion that no genuine pacification could be achieved without a cease-fire. Expecting that this would provoke de Gaulle's wrath, Belhaddad was astonished to hear him reply:

> That's exactly my opinion and I am happy to hear you say it, you whose courage and loyalty are well-known. Yes, the fighting must be halted. There must be peace, it's indispensable, the people are too unhappy, peace must be brought back. Then the Algerians will freely decide their own fate. . . .

The following day, however, de Gaulle did lose his patience at the headquarters of General Faure, the sporting general carpeted for his rash involvement in the first of the Algiers plots against the Fourth Republic. After Faure had returned once too often to the theme of how greatly military operations would be helped if only de Gaulle would declare decisively for *Algérie française*, de Gaulle had exclaimed: "Ah, *écoutez, Faure, j'en ai assez!*" and broken off the discussion.

Then, at Challe's headquarters, where the Commander-in-Chief and some hundred generals and staff officers were hoping for maximum approbation on the success of the offensive, the President of the Republic made a top-secret speech, "to be used verbally for the information of officers only", charged with messages of another kind. On a note of only moderate praise, he began: "What I have heard and seen here in the course of this inspection gives me full satisfaction. I have to say that to you [*je tiens à vous le dire*]. But the problem is not solved." De Gaulle then listed its three basic ingredients: the predicament of the Algerians, which had become intolerable because France after a hundred and twenty years had not done enough for them; the progressive enfeeblement of France herself; and the present world situation, where France could no longer cock a snook at global opinion. In Algeria, "We shall not have the Algerians with us, if they do not want that themselves. . . . The era of the European administration of the indigenous peoples has run its course." In the outside world, "there is an international situation almost entirely and openly against us. This will not change if we seem to have to keep Algeria in the position where it is vis-à-vis ourselves." After paying tribute to the troops he had just seen in action, de Gaulle concluded with a solemn and direct appeal to the senior officers present:

> As for yourselves, mark my words! You are not an army for its own sake. You are the army of France. You only exist through her, for her and in her service. This is your *raison d'être*. . . .

It is I who, in view of my position, must be obeyed by the army in order that France should survive. I am confident of your obedience, and I thank you, gentlemen.

Vive la France!

In his memoirs de Gaulle declares that, "In saying this I was giving my audience an inkling of my intention to recognise Algeria's right to self-determination," and he adds that before leaving Challe that day he informed him in private "precisely what I was soon to announce publicly. Challe replied: 'It's feasible!' and assured me that I could count on him whatever happened." Challe, however, insists that he was left no wiser than any of the hundred other officers present at the earlier briefing, and never once in his whole *tournée des popotes* did de Gaulle actually mention the key-word, "self-determination", which was to create such a furore a few weeks later.

16 September 1959: "self-determination"

On 16 September, at 8 p.m., de Gaulle spoke to the nation. In Algiers there was an unusual hush as everybody clustered round radio and television sets, sensing that a major pronouncement was to be made. They were not disappointed; it was the longest and most important speech consecrated to the Algerian problem that de Gaulle was ever to make. "Our recovery is proceeding," he began, but "the difficult, blood-soaked problem of Algeria remains to be settled." Eschewing all "various over-simplifications" France would solve it "as a great nation should, choosing the only path worthy of being followed. I mean by the free choice of what the Algerians themselves want to do with their future." In a tone of the utmost solemnity of which he was capable, de Gaulle continued:

Thanks to the progress of pacification, of democracy and of social evolution, we can now look forward to the day when the men and women who live in Algeria will be in a position to decide on their destiny, once and for all, freely, in the full knowledge of what is at stake. Taking into account all these factors, those of the Algerian situation, those inherent in the national and the international situation, I deem it necessary that recourse to self-determination be here and now proclaimed.

In the name of France and of the republic, by virtue of the power granted to me by our constitution to consult its citizens, granted that God let me live and that the people lend me their ear, I commit myself to ask, on the one hand, of the Algerians in their twelve departments, what it is they finally wish to be and, on the other hand, of all Frenchmen to endorse their choice.

The fateful word was now out: "self-determination". The question, de Gaulle went on to explain,

will be put to the Algerians as individuals. For since the beginning of the world there has never been any true Algerian unity, far less any Algerian sovereignty; the Carthaginians, the Romans, the Vandals, the

Byzantines, the Syrian Arabs, the Cordoba Arabs, the Turks, the French, have one after the other penetrated the country without there being at any time in any shape or form an Algerian state.

As for the time of the election, I will decide upon it in due course, at the latest four years after the actual restoration of peace, that is to say, once a situation has been established whereby loss of life, be it in ambushes or isolated attempts, will not exceed 200 a year.

The following span of time will be devoted to resuming normal existence, to emptying the prisons and the camps, to allowing for exiles to return, to restoring the free play of individual and public freedom and to enabling the population to be fully aware of what is at stake.

I would like to invite, here and now, observers from all over the world to attend, without let or hindrance, the final culmination of this process. . . .

De Gaulle envisaged that the Algerians, thus consulted, would have but three choices for their "political destiny":

Either—secession, where some believe independence would be found. France would then leave the Algerians who had expressed their wish to become separated from her. They would organise, without her, the territory in which they live, the resources which they have at their disposal, the government which they desire.

This would, in effect, be the terrible renunciation of grace that Sékou Touré's Guinée had chosen, alone of the French Commonwealth, in 1958. Then, secondly, there was the option of "out-and-out identification with France, such as is implied in equality of rights . . . Dunkirk to Tamanrasset". i.e., the old principle of "integration". Or, finally:

the government of Algeria by the Algerians, backed up by French help and in close relationship with her, as regards the economy, education, defence, and foreign relations. In that case, the internal regime of Algeria should be of the federal type, so that the various communities— French, Arab, Kabyle, Mozabite—who live together in the country would find guarantees for their own way of life and a framework for co-operation.

De Gaulle regarded the first option, secession, as

incredible and disastrous. Algeria being what it is at the present time, and the world what we know it to be, secession would carry in its wake the most appalling poverty, frightful political chaos, widespread slaughter, and soon after the warlike dictatorship of the Communists.

By the emphasis of his words, there was little doubt that de Gaulle's own personal choice was the third, that of "association". To the F.L.N. de Gaulle renewed his year-old offer of the *paix des braves*, adding an assurance of "unhindered return" on the path towards self-determination. At the same time he let it be known that any failure to grasp this new olive branch would rest squarely upon:

the work of a group of ambitious agitators, determined to establish by brute force and terror their totalitarian dictatorship and believing that they will one day obtain from the republic the privilege of discussing with it the fate of Algeria, thus building up these agitators into an Algerian government.

This last statement, coupled to his earlier emphasis that the key question would be "put to the Algerians as individuals", seemed to convey an assurance that de Gaulle would never negotiate with the F.L.N. as a body, let alone hand over to them the future of the country. But with whom else could he, in the long run, negotiate? The bloody events of the preceding five years, as has already been seen, had gone far in destroying any viable "third force", or what used to be known as an *interlocuteur valable*. Thus, once again, as in the previous autumn, de Gaulle's future options were to some extent doomed to remain a prisoner of his own words. In a world of such rapid change it was also unreal to suggest that four whole years would have to elapse between any cease-fire and the referendum deciding on de Gaulle's three options. Given the precedent of past bad experiences with French government promises for the future, from Blum–Viollette onwards, it was asking a lot of trust and confidence from the Algerian Muslims of all political hues. Nevertheless, it is reasonable to believe (as does Edward Behr) that "Had such an offer been made in the first three years of the rebellion, it is virtually certain that it would have been immediately accepted by the rebel leaders." It is also no exaggeration to regard de Gaulle's "self-determination" speech of 16 September 1959 as one of the most decisive events of the whole war. Here was a true watershed; nothing that went before was any longer relevant, and nothing could be the same again. There could no longer be any convincing prospect of *Algérie française*. The genie was out of the bottle; once the fateful word "self-determination" was spoken, it could never be corked up again. In retrospect this was also, perhaps, the last moment in the war when there was a possibility of a compromise peace by which the *pieds noirs* could have remained in their beloved homeland, one way or another. If nothing else, certainly here was an end to *indetermination*.

First reactions

In metropolitan France de Gaulle's speech evoked general approbation. *Le Monde* intoned, "De Gaulle has given France back her old prestige as the great liberal nation." Wherever he referred to his decision, says de Gaulle, "the crowds went wild with enthusiasm". On 16 October the Assembly passed a vote of confidence by a huge majority; only the extremes of Left and Right remained unpersuaded. But a great new gap now began to open up between metropolitan France on the one hand and the army in Algeria and the *pieds noirs* on the other. Two weeks later Challe wrote a sharp letter to Debré, noting that

One does not propose to soldiers to go and get killed for an imprecise final objective.... This is the difference, moreover, between the mercenary army and the citizens' army. One can thus only ask of soldiers of the army of Algeria today that they die in order for Algeria to remain French.

At the end of October, says Challe, Delouvrier – whom he had "harassed" – returned from Paris with an assurance from Debré that "we can say both that the government wishes Algeria to remain French and that that is what the army is fighting for". Although this seems to have been curiously at odds with the message of the "self-determination" speech, Challe was appeased – at least temporarily.

Some of his subordinates, however, immediately placed a much less favourable view on de Gaulle's intent. At the 1st Para Regiment of the Foreign Legion, encamped next to Challe's headquarters in the Djurdjura, Captain Sergent told his commanding officer, Colonel Dufour: "For me, the F.L.N. flag is floating over Algiers from now on. Algeria will be independent." Dufour replied, "You're much too pessimistic." But at this moment Sergent says he asked himself, "What was the point any more? ... on 16 September 1959 I felt myself the very old citizen of a very old country." Up on the Morice Line, Jules Roy met a disgruntled captain who declared: "The French intellectuals want peace. We don't have much faith in the French intellectuals; they give up too easily." Later the captain added: "I think the army will obey. But I also think you had better not ask me to do anything more for the West." One senior officer who reacted even more passionately was forty-five-year-old Colonel Jean Gardes, now running the Cinquième Bureau (psychological and political warfare) as a successor to Colonel Godard. On his hearing de Gaulle's "self-determination" broadcast, Yves Courrière, the author (who was present at the time), records that Gardes "exploded". There and then "he had made his choice" – and it was not one of the three recommended by President de Gaulle.

For the *pied noir* population, Alain de Sérigny in the *Écho d'Alger* was, at first, surprisingly mild; in the 16 September speech, he found, "there was good and bad". Far more virulent was Robert Martel who reacted "with shame and indignation against the proposal of secession, a veritable insult to our dead and a blot upon our French dignity", and it was along these lines that the attitude of the militant *pieds noirs* was to develop. The reaction of the Muslims was also variable initially: Messali Hadj, along with what other "moderate" nationalists could still be numbered, welcomed de Gaulle's initiative. What they had striven for over the whole of a generation had been obtained, but only after five years bloody fighting by their rivals, the F.L.N. The tone of the official F.L.N. spokesmen was suspicious, critical and reserved; but the G.P.R.A. greeted the principle of "self-determination" as a step in the right direction, and announced that it was ready, under certain conditions, to begin preliminary talks. But to the most simple-minded member of the G.P.R.A. it must have been self-evident that one of the most important rounds in the war had been won, on the brink of military defeat. To his hard-pressed *djounoud* of the interior, the F.L.N. Minister of Defence, Belkacem Krim, issued a communiqué declaring: "Your struggle has obliged the enemy to talk of self-determination, thus renouncing the oft-repeated myth of *Algérie française*. His retreat is the fruit of your efforts." The principle of "self-determination" conceded, all the F.L.N. had to do now was to fight an obdurate battle to ensure that they, and no one else, would be the *interlocuteur valable* with whom de Gaulle would be forced to negotiate it.

CHAPTER SEVENTEEN

"Aux Barricades!"

September 1959 – February 1960

No, all Algeria is not fascist, all the French are not "ultras", all the army doesn't torture. But Fascism, the "ultras", and torture, they are France in Algeria.

Pierre Nora, 1961

The "ultras" inflamed: enter Susini and Pérez

ENTERING its sixth year, the Algerian war had already lasted longer than the First World War and longer than American participation in the Second. Now, as the new year of 1960 approached, it was about to bring with it events that would seal the fate of *Algérie française*. All that followed in the final two years of the struggle would be little more than a fore-ordained postscript. And the first notes of the tocsin would be sounded, not by the Muslims or the F.L.N., but by the *pieds noirs* themselves.

Since well before de Gaulle's "self-determination" speech of 16 September, passions against him had been mounting among the ranks of *pied noir* "ultras", increasingly distrustful of the policy of the man they considered they had brought back in May 1958. Already on the first anniversary of that 13 May, they had endeavoured, unsuccessfully, to turn it into a day of mourning; the "self-determination" speech, followed by another on 10 November in which de Gaulle had spelled out even more precisely his cease-fire programme, threw them into transports of rage and despair at what seemed like the certainty of his intent to sell out in Algeria. Lagaillarde, the swaggering, red-bearded ex-paratrooper, focal figure and would-be d'Artagnan of May 1958, had been elected to the Assembly that November, and had partially withdrawn from the Algiers scene. Some of Lagaillarde's more extremist colleagues regarded this as tantamount to "collaboration" with a regime of which they increasingly disapproved. Madame Ortiz went so far as to slap his face. In Lagaillarde's absence, Jo Ortiz, the noisy owner of the Bar du Forum, had moved in. Ortiz had chosen the fourth anniversary of the war, 1 November 1958, to launch a new body, the Front National Français (F.N.F.), embracing under one militant organisation "The Group of Seven" and all the other various "ultra" groupings. The political

349

orientations of the F.N.F. were left in little doubt by the symbol which Ortiz, the Poujadist and admirer of Salazar, had chosen for it; the Celtic cross of the unashamedly fascist Jeune Nation movement. In the shadows behind Ortiz there now emerged a new and more effectual figure: Jean-Jacques Susini. Aged only twenty-five in 1959, Susini, who was of Corsican origin, had missed the great moments of both February 1956 and May 1958, when Ortiz and Lagaillarde had made their names with the mob, because he was still studying medicine in France. In contrast to his father, a Communist worker on the Algerian railways with pro-F.L.N. sympathies, young Jean-Jacques was as far to the Right as his father was to the Left. Returning to continue his studies in Algiers University, Susini showed an intellectual agility, an organising ability, and above all an outstanding capacity for persuading by rhetoric, that made him a natural to assume the role of student leader left vacant by Lagaillarde.

There could hardly have been more disparate figures than the two F.N.F. leaders. Ortiz, the burly, bonhomous bar-keeper with the hooked, prize-fighter nose, whose swarthy features, bright ties and well-cut suits testified to his Spanish origins, epitomised the *pied noir* with his emotional vehemence. Born of poor parents, he had certainly shown no lack of physical courage, having fought in the French campaign of 1940, been taken prisoner but escaped, and then re-enlisted to fight again in Italy. His political philosophy, said *The Times* (of 27 January 1960), "in a woolly sort of way is authoritarian and neo-Fascist"; he was an unimpressive speaker, but a potent rabble-rouser through sheer volume of noise. On the other hand, Susini, sickly of physique and unprepossessing, with sparse fair hair and eyes of fire in a chalky face, was a frigid but brilliant political intellect and an impelling orator. The two were admirably complementary to each other. Then there was Dr Jean-Claude Pérez, also of Spanish descent, whose family had lived in Algeria ever since the Second Empire and had been driven out of the bistro they owned by F.L.N. bombing. A tall, good-looking man in his thirties, with wavy brown hair and an engaging smile, Dr Pérez was a general practitioner in Bab-el-Oued with wide contacts among the poorer Europeans there. He spoke their thick patois, and was highly sympathetic to their cause; a sympathy which he carried considerably beyond the normal prerogatives of a G.P.* Described by Yves Courrière as "made of dynamite", Pérez, having finished his national service as a medical officer in 1955, had immediately organised one of the first urban anti-terrorist units in Algiers. The way these units worked was explained to the author by a prominent member of the O.A.S. who wishes to remain anonymous.

* One of the more curious and less easily explained sidelights of the Algerian war was the presence in its more violent aspects, on both sides, of so many from a profession dedicated to the saving of human life.

Often an F.L.N. cell would be detected, and the boss known, but the police would do nothing about it. So we acted as *franc-tireurs*; we threw a grenade or bombed an apartment; then the police had to do something, so they came along and rounded up the whole F.L.N. network. Our best operation was when we placed a bomb in the Place de Lavigerie U.G.T.A. headquarters in 1956 – it blew off the legs of a couple of F.L.N. operators, and it was revealed they were making plans for seventy-three bomb attacks. Well, that was a real success; you can't tell me that the loss of two F.L.N. wasn't worth stopping what might have led to the deaths of hundreds of European women and children, in scenes like the Casino.

Like Ortiz, Pérez had been imprisoned briefly on suspicion of involvement in the "bazooka" case, and on charges of counter-terrorism, but subsequently released. Together with Susini they shared to the full one of the commoner and less attractive characteristics of the *pied noir*, that capacity for reflex violence and brutal action so penetratingly exemplified by Camus' "Outsider".

Ortiz's troops

In 1959 Pérez's principal function was to be recruiting master for the tough para-military militia Ortiz had created to give the F.N.F. teeth. These were lavishly equipped with hardware, which they kept at home, and towards the end of the year they had appeared in public for the first time, reminiscently clad in khaki shirts and brassards bearing a Celtic cross. In addition, there was the 1,200-man U.T. de Choc, an elitist offshoot of the Unités Territoriales, the *pied noir* Home Guard, created by Colonel "Nez-de-Cuir" Thomazo, which had readily put itself at the disposal of Ortiz and his F.N.F. Volunteers trained to be ready to move into action in the Algiers area at an hour's notice, the members of the U.T. de Choc also kept their weapons under the bed; meanwhile, over the preceding months there had been ominous disappearances of grenades and ammunition from the Territorial arms depots. In mid-December, when the right-wing former premier, Georges Bidault, who had formed a new grouping in France called the Rassemblement de l'Algérie française, came to Algeria to speak against de Gaulle's policy, Ortiz provided his meetings with an imposingly disciplined corps of strong-arm men 1,500 strong. All this backing of force gave the stentorian Ortiz new power and self-confidence. He raised the heat among his already fiery supporters with such incendiary exhortations as:

> We shall go right to the end of the line, even with arms in our hands, to defend *Algérie française*. . . .
> The determination of the French of Algeria will conquer the self-determination of de Gaulle. Algiers may become Budapest, but we shall remain. . . .
> For us, henceforth, it's either the suitcase or the coffin!

"The suitcase or the coffin!" – confronting the *pieds noirs* with the Hobson's choice that to yield to majority rule would inevitably mean leaving Algeria either as corpses or refugees, the slogan was to acquire a particularly sinister significance in 1962. Another orator who cried "We need a Charlotte Corday!" was also loudly applauded; while the tone of Sérigny's *Écho d'Alger* was growing daily more hostile to de Gaulle.

One of the more surprising aspects of this period was the way in which the army command permitted the creation of such a Frankenstein monster as the F.N.F., under its very nose. Harking back to an earlier period of French history, there is a curious parallel between this and the arming of the National Guard in Paris to help defend the city during the siege of 1870; the siege over, and the Prussians having withdrawn, the unruly National Guard then turned and rent the hand that had created it, setting up its own revolutionary Commune de Paris. Ultimately blame must attach to General Challe for allowing such a concentration of armed power to build up under the sway of someone like Jo Ortiz.

Meanwhile, as the F.L.N. sought to reassert itself in the wake of the military defeats imposed upon it by Challe and the political threat presented by de Gaulle's "self-determination" initiative, a new wave of bombings and terrorism was unleashed. A bomb detonated outside Algiers University during the celebration of its fiftieth anniversary killed and wounded several students; between 1 December and 10 January there were twenty-two assassinations in the Algiers vicinity, while the papers were filled with horrible details of the violation and throat-cutting of wives and children of *pied noir* farmers out in the *bled*. The F.L.N. found that such hit-and-run acts of terrorism would do more to prove to the world their continued existence than trying to mount major efforts in the Wilayas, where their forces were so sorely pressed by Challe. As a result, in response to *pied noir* pressure, forces had to be diverted from Challe's current offensive to provide new protection. In an attempt to calm *pied noir* feelings, Delegate-General Delouvrier released these figures by way of proving that terrorism was, despite appearances, decidedly on the wane:

	civilians killed	wounded	kidnapped
June 1958	259	308	242
January 1959	184	217	197
December 1959	143	142	78

Nevertheless, this recrudescence of terrorism helped reinforce in the *pieds noirs* a sense of outrage that the Paris government should even contemplate negotiating with spokesmen of those capable of such crimes. As Alain de Sérigny notes of Algiers around Christmas 1959, "The psychological climate there was detestable. I had the impression that the least spark would be enough to set off a general conflagration."

Colonels in revolt

In October 1959 the only surviving *maréchal de France*, the *pied noir* Alphonse Juin, pungently criticised de Gaulle's Algerian policy in *L'Aurore* and was reprimanded for meddling in politics. The attack, however, was symptomatic of the tense disaffection within the army which had mounted rapidly since de Gaulle's speech of 16 September, especially among the élite para units that had borne so much of the brunt of the recent fighting under the Challe offensive. 1960, says Captain Sergent of the 1st R.E.P., was to be "the year of divorce". To understand what to other Western minds may seem incomprehensible and shocking, the disaffection within the French army which was to culminate in full-scale revolt in less than eighteen months' time, one needs to consider the stresses imposed by French history beyond merely the unbroken chain of humiliation that stretched from 1940 up to the Algerian war. Since the execution of Louis XVI in 1793, the French army had been subject to the First Republic, the Directory, the Consulate, the First Empire, the First and Second Restorations, the "Bourgeois Monarchy" of Louis-Philippe, the Second Republic, the Second Empire, the Commune, the Third Republic, Pétain's Vichy and de Gaulle's Free French Committee, the Fourth Republic, and now the Fifth Republic. Each change of regime had contributed fresh divisions within the army, and added new confusion as to where loyalties were ultimately due – a compound of experience shared by no other army in the world (outside, perhaps, Latin America). By the autumn of 1959 the Brombergers likened the situation in Algiers to "Three furnaces, one within the other, a sort of Japanese cabinet – a series of boxes enclosed inside each other – but they were metallic boxes heated red hot ... three high temperatures working on each other." At the heart of the army furnace were three colonels in positions of power close to General Massu, who was one of the very few senior officers not to be transferred from Algeria in de Gaulle's 1958 "purge" but who had been promoted and placed in command of the corps controlling the whole Algiers sector. There was Antoine Argoud, Massu's chief-of-staff; Jean Gardes, who had succeeded Colonel Yves Godard as head of the Cinquième Bureau; and, more prudently keeping to the background, Godard himself, Massu's right-hand during the Battle of Algiers, and now chief of security.

Small and nervy, a superb horseman and *polytechnicien*, Argoud at forty-two had been the youngest colonel in the service when singled out to be on his staff by Marshal de Lattre, the Inspector-General of the army. He was also regarded by many as being the army's finest intellect, one of its foremost strategic thinkers, and if there was a general criticism among his peers of this secretive, ascetic and fanatical personality, it would have been that he was "too clever by half". The late General André Beaufre, with whom Argoud served on de Lattre's staff, claimed that there was a flaw in his brilliance: "He could never see things objectively. Once, when asked by de Lattre to draft a brief, he produced something quite brilliant, but totally different from what de Lattre wanted. He was just expounding his own ideas." Sometimes Argoud would set out deliberately to affront the orthodoxy of his superiors, with such a display of independence as wearing bright yellow-ochre shoes with uniform. Like the colonels from the Indo-China school (though, in fact, he was one of the few never to have been through it), Argoud was an expert on subversive warfare but perhaps prepared to go farther in ruthlessness than most. During the Battle of Algiers, Argoud had achieved notoriety by his harsh measures in pacifying L'Arba, just outside the capital. These had included public executions, and breaking the general strike by firing tank cannon at point-blank range into the shuttered shops. Sent back to France, he returned to become Massu's chief-of-staff only in the autumn of 1959. An outspoken critic of de Gaulle's policy, Argoud soon came to exert a powerful influence over his boss, Massu. Through Argoud, Gardes and Godard, Massu maintained close contact with Ortiz and his movement, feeling that he had them under his control; but perhaps the boot was on the other foot.

The slender St Cyrien, Jean Gardes, was – though he may not have looked it – every bit as dedicated as Argoud, and almost as militant as Ortiz. The only son of a Parisian heroine of the Resistance, who had run a cell through her well-known Restaurant des Ministères on the Rue du Bac, Gardes himself had won no less than twenty-four citations for bravery and been severely wounded with the Tirailleurs Marocains in Italy. From Indo-China he had derived lessons and expertise similar to that of his colleagues, as well as serving as Salan's Press officer; all of which usefully supplemented what he had learned of underground warfare through his mother's experiences. Posted to Morocco with the Deuxième Bureau, it was Gardes whose information had sparked off the hijacking of Ben Bella in 1956. Regarding himself an expert on Muslim affairs, he had a mystical attachment to the ideal of integration; he desired the Muslims to have genuine equality with the *pieds noirs*. Immediately on hearing de Gaulle's pronouncement of 16 September, Gardes made up his own mind to fight "self-determination" by every means – including open revolt. Through being in charge of the Cinquième Bureau, with its potent functions of propaganda and psychological warfare, Gardes had a powerful weapon and he now used it unhesitatingly to further the cause of *francisation* – regardless of the objurgations of Delouvrier. Already on 18 September Gardes had taken up contacts with Susini and Dr Pérez, and from then on the F.N.F. leaders became weekly visitors to army headquarters in the Quartier Rignot. Gardes impressed upon them the need to co-ordinate activities between the army and themselves, and encouraged them, exaggeratedly, to believe that they could expect full backing from the paras – if not the whole army. It was Gardes who shared considerable responsibility for uniting all the various "ultra" factions and their para-military ancillaries under the F.N.F. of Ortiz, and between them they agreed that, if there was to be a revolt, it should take place under the guise of a "spontaneous demonstration", as had happened on 13 May 1958.

It remained for de Gaulle to help them by providing a suitable *casus belli*, or detonator to explode the critical mass.

Delouvrier's isolation

By not concealing his own lack of enthusiasm for "self-determination", General Challe had more or less given tacit support for Gardes' Cinquième Bureau to put its weight behind the option of Francisation. But with his thoughts eternally concentrated on the offensive still continuing out in the *bled*, Challe seems to have been largely unaware of the extent to which his colonels were becoming committed to Ortiz and his fellow-hotheads in Algiers. Meanwhile, as the year went on the position of Delegate-General Paul Delouvrier was growing more and more unsatisfactory. When it came to advancing the Constantine Plan, the financial expertise of the technocrat was unexcelled. But there were so many other aspects of the job where Delouvrier felt frankly out of his depth; and he received distressingly little guidance or support from de Gaulle. When, under pressure from Sérigny, Delouvrier had begged de Gaulle to go slower on his clemency measures for convicted terrorists, he had received a disagreeable dressing-down for his troubles. On more than one occasion since 16 September Delouvrier had tried to press de Gaulle to reveal which of the three options he preferred, and what he expected the role of the army to be in fulfilling it. But each time de Gaulle had either changed the subject, or been maddeningly evasive. Finally, a few days before the end of the year, Delouvrier on one of his fortnightly visits to Paris had attempted to draw out de Gaulle by warning him that the army might not obey. "But they will, Delouvrier," de Gaulle replied impatiently, "the military will obey. When a soldier gets mixed up in politics he only commits stupidities [*conneries*]. Look at Dreyfus. Their job is to fight on the ground."

With the *pieds noirs*, as well as the army, Delouvrier was neither popular nor unpopular; in general he was regarded simply as a *fonctionnaire*, a mouthpiece with no real power of his own. His isolation was increasing with every day. When he tried to warn Massu of the activities of his colonels, Massu turned a deaf ear, and he concluded that the general was now virtually their prisoner. At one meeting an angry Colonel Argoud had adopted a positively insulting tone in addressing the Delegate-General:

> You are giving us a lecture worthy of a political science professor and not that of the person responsible for the government in Algeria. Your arguments referring to world opinion ... are those of a professor of history, of an intellectual. It's all very moving, but in no way does it

correspond with reality. You're not in contact with the population as we are.

By the end of 1959, as Yves Courrière remarks: "Challe had confidence in Massu, who had confidence in Argoud, who had confidence in Ortiz. Delouvrier was perhaps the only one to have confidence in no one at all!" Moreover, he was not well. An old automobile injury had left him with a badly knitted femur and Delouvrier had had to have it re-set. By the second week in January he had just returned from convalescing in the desert but was still on crutches.

Delouvrier found his relations particularly strained with General Massu. As a result of de Gaulle's clemency measures, which enraged Massu as being too dangerously liberal (he would have preferred summary military justice, including the retention of capital punishment for acts of terrorism), the two men were barely on speaking terms any longer. Massu's actual power was immense, and his potential, had he chosen to use it, even greater. He was super-prefect of Algiers city; and his command, the most important in Algeria, extended southwards to the edge of the Sahara and eastwards to Kabylia, while his role in the Battle of Algiers and, later, in May 1958, made him still the darling of the *pieds noirs*. Despite occasional growls, Massu had remained the immaculate Gaullist – which was why he alone, as one of the few generals de Gaulle knew he could trust implicitly, had kept his post in Algeria; otherwise, he was as distrustful of politics and politicians as ever. Even Massu's loyalty, however, had been sorely tested by the "self-determination" pronouncement, and he was never one to keep his feelings to himself. Massu claimed that he was "the lid on the Algiers cauldron", though, as one of his senior colleagues remarked at the time, it looked as if it might easily all blow up in his face. Massu was confident that he could contain the pressure exerted by the simmering "ultras". He even felt that Lagaillarde was sufficiently in his pocket for him to invite the fiery young deputy to join him at a Beethoven concert on 13 January, although Delouvrier had warned him, in prophetic terms: "General, you think you control these people, but watch out. The day will come when they will declare to you: 'We are at the mercy of our troops; we have to march, will you march with us?'"

The "bombe Massu"

Because of the intriguing of his colonels, Argoud and Gardes, on whom he most depended, and because of his own political naïveté, Massu was in fact being duped, and his mood of disenchantment was skilfully exploited by Ortiz and his associates. This disenchantment reached a peak in mid-January when Massu received word that one of his officers during the Battle of Algiers, Lieutenant Charbonnier, currently in hospital recovering from wounds had been summoned to appear before a civil judge on grounds of implication in the Audin affair. What he held to be an affront against military honour (and for which he held de Gaulle personally responsible) threw Massu into a violent rage lasting several days.

Just at this time Massu received in his office a West German correspondent, Hans Ulrich Kempski, of the Munich *Süddeutsche Zeitung*. The event in itself was an exception because Massu disliked and distrusted journalists hardly less than politicians. At first he had refused categorically to see Kempski, but Challe pressed him, noting that he had already himself granted an interview to Kempski, who had come fortified with a strong recommendation from the French Embassy in Bonn. Kempski, one of the most skilful of German journalists, dispelled Massu's reservations by revealing that he too had been a paratrooper, dropped in Crete in the Second World War. Speaking as one professional to another, Kempski soon had Massu letting his hair down in the most unrestrained manner. When asked what the army's principal concern was, Massu, according to Kempski, replied: "That the government should help us to see the future clearly, in order that we can succeed in maintaining *Algérie française*." From there on Massu waxed warmer and warmer in his criticism of de Gaulle: "We no longer understand the policy of President de Gaulle. The army could not have anticipated that he would adopt such a policy. . . . Our greatest disillusion has been to see General de Gaulle become a man of the Left." When the German pointed out that "It was, after all, you and your friends who brought him back to power," Massu replied bitterly: "De Gaulle was the only man available. Perhaps the army made a mistake." Finally, when asked whether the army would obey, Massu was quoted as declaring: "Myself, and the majority of officers in a position of command, will not execute unconditionally the orders of the Head of State."

Massu had plunged headlong into an elephant-trap, baited as much by the "ultras" as by Kempski. Far from being the "lid", he himself provided that extra head of steam to blow up the whole cauldron. Kempski's scoop was published with maximum prominence on 18 January. At that time the French Press was still preoccupied with news of the new "heavy" franc which had been launched on 1 January to replace the old franc at a ratio of one to 100, by the Jaccoud murder trial in Geneva, by the tragic death of Albert Camus, killed in a car accident, and by the appalling disaster on the Riviera where, on 3 December, the Fréjus dam had burst, killing over 300 people and causing milliards of francs' worth of damage. But the *bombe Massu* swept all else aside almost as devastatingly as the flood waters at Fréjus. Massu denied the words attributed to him and claimed (rather diminishing his own case) that, in any event, the interview had been off the record. But it was too late. France was staggered; it was unbelievable that such damning criticism should have come from the faithful *grognard*, Massu, of all people. According to the military aide at the Elysée, General

Grout de Beaufort, at seven o'clock that morning he was in the middle of shaving when de Gaulle, in a towering rage, telephoned to announce that he had been "insulted" by Massu and that he should be relieved of his command forthwith. De Gaulle brushed aside de Beaufort's intercession that Massu should first be allowed to offer his own explanation, and the offending general was recalled to Paris. Summoned to de Gaulle, a wrathful and stupefied Massu, who had no thought then of retirement, was told imperiously: "I'm keeping you; I ask you not to leave the army. I'm going to give you a good post!" Eventually, after a prolonged period on ice, Massu was sent to command the garrison of the dreary city of Metz – hardly a blue-chip job for a fighting soldier of his calibre, and a little reminiscent of Salan's earlier relegation as Governor of Paris. But he regained his composure, and his loyalty to de Gaulle, to remain, in essence, "*toujours con . . . et toujours Gaulliste*".

Two days after Massu's recall, Challe himself flew to Paris to learn that Massu was never going to be allowed to return to Algiers. At a meeting in the Elysée on 22 January attended by Challe and Delouvrier, Premier Debré and the Minister of Defence, Guillaumat, General Ely, Chief of General Staff, and three of the top-ranking generals from Algeria, one after another pleaded the danger that the sacking of Massu could create. Pale with cold anger, de Gaulle was obdurate. When Challe, backed by Delouvrier, prophesied, "Blood will flow in Algiers", he was told, "You exaggerate." Leaving the Elysée, Challe offered his resignation to General Ely, and then returned to Algiers to await the worst. "When thrown into a red-hot boiler," said the Brombergers, "a bucket of water does not appease the furnace. It unleashes an explosion of fire. The recall of Massu was the bucket of water thrown on to the Algiers furnace."

Green light for Ortiz

Ortiz now had his green light. The moment the news came through on the evening of 22 January that Massu was permanently banished, the F.N.F. announced that a general strike would begin on Sunday, the 24th. It would be accompanied by mass demonstrations to centre, as usual, around the *monument aux morts* and the Plateau des Glières. At the time the impression was fostered that the insurrection of 24 January was a spontaneous outburst of rage on the part of the *pieds noirs* against the removal of their beloved Massu. It was, in fact, nothing of the sort, but a deliberately and long-prepared *coup-de-main* for which the *bombe Massu* was only a pretext; in any event, as Ortiz repeatedly made plain to his associates, he had little confidence in Massu himself as being a man who would go as far as he, Ortiz, wanted. On the morning of Saturday the 23rd, Sérigny published an emotionally charged valedictory to Massu, and already the khaki-shirted storm-troops of the F.N.F., wearing their Celtic cross brassards, and the U.T. de Choc in black berets, were to be seen mustering at their local centres in Algiers, all heavily armed.

The objectives of the "ultras" were, as before, short-term and short-sighted. Ortiz aimed, immediately, for a replay of 13 May 1958, but this time ending with a total and irreversible victory for the *pieds noirs*. (Susini, characteristically, went even further, declaring to the F.N.F.: "The hour to overturn the regime has struck. The revolution will start in Algiers and move to Paris.") By taking up positions in arms in the heart of Algiers, Ortiz hoped to confront Challe with the cruel dilemma either to order the army to fire on fellow Frenchmen, or take sides with them. In this he had been powerfully encouraged by assurances from Colonels Gardes and Argoud that the paras, certainly, would never open fire. Having forced this confrontation, it was reckoned that de Gaulle would be obliged to go back on the abhorred "self-determination" principle; or, better still, to resign. Once again there was no thought in the despairing minds of the "ultras" of "what then?" Nothing revealed better the egoistic isolationism of their despair and the unreal world which it drove them to inhabit than Susini's wild declaration at this time: "The irreversible process is now under way. Between the republic and Algeria, we choose *Algérie française!*" Characteristically, the possible reaction of fifty million metropolitan Frenchmen was simply not taken into account.

As the fateful Sunday dawned, there were but two shadows cast upon what, to the *bistrotier*, Ortiz, looked like complete mastery and abundant prospects of success. One was Lagaillarde. Because of his departure for the Chamber of Deputies, and his ensuing split with Ortiz, Lagaillarde had deliberately been excluded from all preliminary councils-of-war. According to Lagaillarde himself at his subsequent trial, he knew nothing of what was afoot until rumours reached him at a café on the Saturday morning. This was not strictly true. Typically Lagaillarde, the Quixotic loner, without consulting Ortiz and unconsulted by him, had already jumped the gun the previous evening by seizing a building within the university perimeter. With a handful of armed henchmen (and, apparently, impelled by the precedent of his martyred great-grandfather) he had turned this into a first barricaded camp, bluntly informing the authorities (as well as Ortiz) that if anyone approached within thirty metres he would be fired upon, and that he would not quit the university until de Gaulle had yielded. To his intense annoyance, Ortiz now saw some of his best troops being siphoned off to join the more disciplined and military camp of the ex-paratrooper. Henceforth, right through the following week, there would not be one but two leaders, and two camps, and to the very end Lagaillarde's would prove the more orderly.

A far darker shadow, however, from Ortiz's point of view was the equivocal posture of the army. Partly egged on by the earlier assurance given by the dissident colonels, partly deluded by his own *méditerranéen-et-demi* optimism, Ortiz had persuaded both himself and his followers that, once they had moved, the army would give virtually total support. Now, at the eleventh hour, partly perhaps because they felt the movement was threatening to get out of hand, partly because of instructions from General Challe, Argoud and Gardes poured some cold water on Ortiz's expectations. (The position of Gardes was by now an anomalous one; because of over-playing his hand during the past weeks he had just been posted away from the Cinquième Bureau to replace Bigeard in the field at Saida, but had as yet avoided taking up his new duties.) Ortiz was told that the feeling of the army in general was that they would not fire on him – but, on the other hand, it would not countenance a putsch. An added dampener was provided by that prominent figure from past conspiratorial occasions, General Faure, currently commanding in Kabylia, who warned Ortiz that the time was not ripe; that opinion at home was against the "ultras", and that an insurrection now had no chance of success. Ortiz, however – pushed on by the impetus of the seething armed citizenry behind him, and driven to more precipitate action than he might perhaps otherwise have chosen by the knowledge that his rival, Lagaillarde, had stolen a march on him at the university – could not now go back. On the morning of the 24th he set up a "command post" in the elegant building of the Compagnie Algérienne, which fronted on to the main thoroughfare of the Boulevard Laferrière and Rue Charles Péguy, just across from the Hôtel des Postes. Surrounding him were 1,500 men of the F.N.F. and U.T., bristling with automatic weapons, some of them "appropriated" early that morning from an army depot.

Challe acts

Meanwhile Challe, at last appreciating the explosiveness of the situation, had taken his own precautionary measures. Realising that Lagaillarde could not now be dislodged from the university, nor Ortiz's men disarmed without risk of bloodshed, he threw roadblocks across all the routes into the city to prevent armed reinforcements from being ferried in from the Mitidja. Under command of Lieutenant-Colonel Debrosse, all available gendarmes – totalling some two thousand – were to be concentrated in and around the Gouvernement-Général to prevent any recurrence of Lagaillarde's coup of 13 May 1958. Reluctantly, he called for reinforcements from the 10th Para Division, currently fighting the F.L.N. in Kabylia, for what he scathingly called "a little local excitement". At this point Challe was evidently not aware of the extent to which, through Argoud and Gardes, the paras had become implicated with Ortiz, for the 10th (now commanded by General Gracieux) was Massu's old division, a number of its members were recruited from Algiers, and many others had sweethearts or close friends there, stemming from the days of the Battle of Algiers. Thus, ironically, both the impending insurgents and the forces of law and order were banking on the same paras as their trump card. In an attempt to calm Ortiz, at midday on the 24th Challe invited him to his headquarters and informed him of concessions that he had already "wrung" from de Gaulle; death sentences for terrorism to be resumed, "pacification" to be continued, and an assurance that there would be no political talks with the F.L.N. Ortiz found Challe munching a hasty ham sandwich at his desk, and took advantage of this to swell his esteem with his followers by boasting that he had "lunched with" the Commander-in-Chief. He also claimed that Challe had offered a "deal", whereby if the Gouvernement-Général and other public buildings were not attacked the demonstrators would be left unharassed.

By mid-afternoon the Plateau des Glières was black with demonstrators – an estimated thirty thousand. Noticeably absent were any Muslims. Gone was the spirit of fraternisation of those May days of 1958; gone also was the good-natured atmosphere of fiesta that had prevailed at that time. In its place was a tougher and altogether more dangerous mood. At Ortiz's "command post" there was chaos reminiscent of the headier days of the Paris Commune; everybody talked, gave orders and made speeches in an atmosphere dense with Bastos cigarette-smoke, the smell of sweat and beer. In the street below some young members of the F.N.F. began spontaneously to prise up paving-stones and create a barricade – again in the best tradition of the Commune. On Ortiz's balcony Gardes, though now with no official function in Algiers, was seen to appear and survey the work on the barricade with evident approbation. The sight of a full colonel in uniform beside Ortiz was about all the crowd needed to endorse its belief that the army was "marching" with it. Meanwhile, just a couple of hundred yards higher up on the Forum it could see the hated mobile gendarmes and C.R.S., helmeted and equipped for mob-bashing, forming up in a threatening black line.

The fusillade of 24 January

Confronted by the challenge of the barricades now busily under construction (those thrown up simultaneously at the university by Lagaillarde already looked even more redoubtable), Challe had to act. After an angry call from Delouvrier noting Gardes' presence with Ortiz, the dissident colonel was despatched out of Algiers to his new posting forthwith. Under Challe's seal of approval a concerted operation was ordered whereby the demonstrators were to be herded, gently but firmly, like driven game towards the west of the city and Bab-el-Oued, whence most of them had come. It depended upon a triangular, precisely co-ordinated movement in which the gendarmes under Debrosse would advance down the steps from the

Forum towards the sea (and Ortiz's "command post"), while at the same time the paras of the 1st R.C.P. and the 1st R.E.P. (Foreign Legion) were to come in from the north and east. The two regiments were commanded respectively by Colonels Broizat and Dufour, both well known to be outspokenly sympathetic to the demonstrators. Broizat, an ex-theologian, managed still to give the (quite deceptive) appearance of a mild-mannered bishop; Dufour, at forty-seven was one of the toughest officers of the Legion who had spent much of his career in conflict with the Establishment, and of whom a general once remarked: "I have seldom met an officer as hard, even brutal, as you are towards your superiors." To all three intervening forces, explicit orders were given that there should be no firing; weapons were to be carried unloaded, and those of the gendarmes were scrupulously checked by their officers. They were assured that their frontal advance would be covered by the paras moving up on their right flank.

At 18.00 hours the gendarmes began to move slowly down the steep slope from the Forum, into the Boulevard Laferrière with its lush central gardens. It was getting dark, and the F.N.F. camp seethed with intense excitement at the sight of the advancing gendarmes. Suddenly a couple of pistol shots rang out, fired in the gathering dusk by an unknown hand. As if it were a signal, volleys of automatic fire from windows and rooftops along both sides of the Boulevard Laferrière opened up on the unfortunate gendarmes caught in the middle. One particularly deadly automatic rifle was spotted firing burst after burst from the balcony of Ortiz's, "command post", where Gardes had appeared only a few hours previously; at the fifth-floor window of another elegant apartment block Colonel Debrosse observed a woman in a dressing-gown – a modern *pétroleuse* – calmly emptying her revolver into the street below. Home-made bombs were dropped on the heads of the gendarmes, and tyres stuffed with *plastique* rolled out on to the boulevard and exploded. Caught at a terrible disadvantage, the gendarmes fell like flies before they could load up and fire back. Wounded men who crept into buildings out of the line of fire were viciously attacked by the F.N.F. within. There were horrible scenes as the catchword *se payer un gendarme* ("get yourself a cop") ran round, and maddened *pied noir* youths mercilessly despatched wounded gendarmes in cold blood. One was found hanging by his feet in a stair well, while a para colonel witnessing the scene declared that he had never before seen wounded men so mercilessly machine-gunned as they crawled on the pavement. For three-quarters of an hour the massacre continued.

And where were the paras?

It was 18.45 before the advance guard of Dufour's 1st R.E.P. arrived, having taken the best part of an hour to cover six hundred yards. The shooting slowly died away; but when the casualties came to be counted there were six dead and twenty-four wounded among the civil demonstrators, and no less than fourteen dead and 123 wounded in the ranks of the gendarmes. A violent exchange now took place between Dufour and an outraged Debrosse, with the latter demanding why the paras had not turned up on time, and Dufour riposting that the gendarmes, by opening fire, had breached Challe's "pact" with Ortiz. To this day, despite the lengthy hearings of the "Barricades Trial" later in 1960, the two essential questions of who fired first, and why the luckless gendarmes were left to face the heavily armed myrmidons of Ortiz on their own, have never been satisfactorily answered. There were dubious allegations of an unknown *agent provocateur* (possibly of the F.L.N.?) firing those first fatal revolver shots, and Ortiz – not unnaturally – claimed that the gendarmes were to blame. But all the evidence, added to the disparity of the casualties, indicates that the culprits lay among the trigger-happy band of Ortiz, firing with or without orders. Challe in his memoirs admits that the manoeuvre of the gendarmes was a "gross error". The excuse offered by Colonels Broizat and Dufour (unsatisfactorily vague even in their testimonies before the "Barricades Trial") was that their two élite regiments had been held up by Lagaillarde's barricade in the university. But in fact Broizat's line of march ran through the tunnel that passes underneath the university buildings, out of reach of the barricade, while Dufour's lay well clear of the whole area. It was plain from both the preceding and subsequent events that the colonels' disastrous tardiness stemmed from a desire to avoid at all costs any clash with the insurgents.

"Barricades Week" begins

Whatever the findings of any post-mortem, however, the fact of outstanding gravity was that, for France, a catastrophic frontier in the Algerian war had been crossed. For the first time Frenchmen had fired upon, and killed, other Frenchmen; to the historically minded the dreadful spectre of the 1940s and, farther back, of 1871 presented itself. Across the breadth of France would echo the dying words of one of the Algiers gendarmerie lieutenants: "For two years I've been fighting against the *fellagha*. Now I'm dying at the hands of people who cry *Algérie française!* I don't understand . . . !"

Within an hour or two of the end of the fusillade, Challe and Delouvrier, however, were understanding all too well the full seriousness of the situation. Backed by a majority of his senior officers, General Crépin, Massu's recently arrived successor, made it plain to Challe that there could be no prospect of breaching the barricades, especially the well-organised redoubt manned by Lagaillarde. Or was Challe prepared to use tanks and risk "a new Budapest" – the still fresh memories of which held particular horror for the French army? Moreover, the para colonels upon whom all depended let it be known that their regiments would do no more than set up a ring round the perimeter of the barricades. Shattered by events and by the realisation of his own impotence, Challe that night made a stern broadcast declaring a state of siege over the city. But it had a minimal effect on either the insurgents or the sympathetic para colonels, all of whom were now convinced that the day was won, and that de Gaulle would have to give way.

In the course of that first night, the deadly fusillade soon forgotten, some extraordinary scenes of fraternisation took place on the barricades. Arriving at the university, Captain Pierre Sergent of the 1st R.E.P. strode up to shake Lagaillarde by the hand, assuring him, "I'll never have you fired upon." Women of the F.N.F. men behind the barricades were allowed to come and go as they pleased, bringing supplies of croissants, thermos flasks of coffee and wine, which were readily shared out with the passively attendant paras. On the same barricades the barmen of the Saint-George and Aletti hotels, normally bitter rivals, were found jointly dispensing hospitality. As Lagaillarde remarked at his trial, the barricades "instead of dividing, united everybody", and, for the first three days as the weird stalemate continued, a kind of picnic spirit prevailed in the unusually balmy January weather. But amid the fraternisation one important ingredient was still pointedly missing: the Muslims. With a big effort, a few pathetic handfuls of elderly veterans were drummed up, many of them maimed and of First World War vintage; but, on the other hand, large groups of Casbah urchins gathered to chant at a discreet distance: "*Algérie Arabe! À bas Massu!*"

Ortiz jubilant: but de Gaulle intransigent

On the Monday morning (25 January), Ortiz was comporting himself like a triumphant pocket Duce. There was a brief fiery exchange with Lagaillarde, who habitually referred in contempt to the restaurateur's disorderly "command post" as *le café*; after which each retired to rule his own roost, and Ortiz was heard to proclaim jubilantly: "Tomorrow, in Paris I shall be the ruling power!" Certainly, from the point of view of the authorities in Algiers, it looked perilously as though Ortiz held all the tricks. Arriving hastily in the city, de Gaulle's agitated premier, Michel Debré, found Delouvrier on crutches and Challe stricken with a bout of rheumatism, conducting operations, like Marshal Saxe at Fontenoy, from a truckle bed – both of them deeply pessimistic. At Challe's headquarters five generals and eleven field officers from General Crépin downwards told Debré flatly that the army would not fire on the barricades. It was Colonel Argoud who dotted the is by declaring that the only possible solution was for de Gaulle to renounce "self-determination"; otherwise he would be replaced by General Challe. Upon which, Debré expostulated to Delouvrier, "But you have a soviet of colonels here!" On his way out of

Algiers that evening the lesson was rubbed in as Debré observed groups of paras hobnobbing with Ortiz's men over the barricade camp-fires.

But the jubilant Ortiz reckoned without the will of one man: de Gaulle.

When the first news reached France, because of army censorship in Algiers, compounded with distraction by their own surfeit of crises at home, ordinary Frenchmen did not at first take in just how deadly was the predicament in Algeria. The country was seized by a bad bout of *la grippe*; a quarter of the population of Metz was reported stricken. In Paris the spring collections were beginning, amid much speculation about slipping waistlines and vanished sleeves. In New York General Douglas MacArthur was about to celebrate his 80th birthday in his retreat atop the Waldorf Towers, still fuming at his dismissal by Truman at the beginning of the decade. In England the Queen was about to give birth, Princess Margaret to get married, and Aneurin Bevan was dying, while fifty-six year-old Dr Barbara Moore was half-way on her walk from John O'Groats to Land's End, accompanied by a mile-and-a-half line of cars. At the other end of Africa, Prime Minister Macmillan, greeted by riots in Nyasaland, was also having his "little local difficulties".* At 1 a.m. on Monday, the 25th, the current Minister of Information, Roger Frey, told journalists in Paris, "By the end of the day there will be no more barricades", words that were soon to stick in his throat.

De Gaulle had first been alerted shortly before nine o'clock on the Sunday evening, at Colombey, and was at the Elysée by midnight, displaying, from the very first, the same Olympian calm as during the explosive days of May 1958, or, indeed, as at any time of extreme crisis. In a short, unbending broadcast to the nation, he accused the Algiers insurgents of striking "a stab in the back for France, before the world." He adjured them to return to order, adapting words that had rung out in 1940: "Nothing is lost for a Frenchman when he rejoins his mother, France." He had been brought back to lead the country, to find for Algeria "*une solution qui soit française*" (a phrasing that drew growls of rage at its ambiguity in Algiers), and he intended to carry through this responsibility. He closed with an expression of his "profound confidence" in Delouvrier and Challe (a confidence that, in fact, he was far from feeling as in private he criticised both for their "irresolution"). Like Challe's, the speech made little impact in Algiers.

The following afternoon a meeting of the cabinet was held at the Elysée in a febrile atmosphere. There were rumours of a putsch in preparation in Paris. Tempers frayed. When the old revolutionary, Malraux, declared that he could not believe "there were not four thousand men with tanks" capable of suppressing the barricades, Soustelle sneered, "Since we've got

---

* It was ten days later, on 3 February, that he made his "Winds of Change" speech in Cape Town.

an atomic bomb, why not use it? Let's drop it on Algiers, instead of at Reggane!" Less impassioned, the thirty-three-year-old Secretary for Finnance, Giscard d'Estaing, advised that any "brutal action" would simply extend the uprising all over Algeria. Over it all de Gaulle reigned aloof and unyielding. In his memoirs he wrote: "I was determined to lance the abscess, make no concessions whatever and obtain complete obedience from the army."

Stalemate in Algiers

Tuesday, 26 January, began on a note of at least negative good news for the government; the army had not crossed the Rubicon, no putsch had started in either Algiers or Paris; there had been no reaction by the Muslims in Algeria, or by the F.L.N. which remained curiously and attentively passive. But Debré reported back from Algiers, thoroughly shaken by what he had seen and heard, and warning that the least false step would lead to formation of a military junta in Algiers. During an emotion-charged *tête-à-tête* between two old soldiers, de Gaulle, who had just buried his brother, told Marshal Juin: "I am an old man. I too am going to die soon." Then, before the Marshal could wipe the tears from his eyes, in an abrupt change of tone, de Gaulle declared: "Whatever happens, I cannot give in. I will not give in to a riot. . . . If I did, I should be nothing more than a marionette and within a fortnight I would have a new uprising, a new ultimatum on my shoulders." Before the end of the day, both Debré and Guillaumat, the Minister of Defence, had joined Soustelle in offering their resignations – and had them brusquely rejected. De Gaulle also refused to accede to pressure to advance the date of a television address he was to make to the nation, already fixed for Friday, 29 January. Even the loyal courtier, Bernard Tricot, admits that at the time he felt de Gaulle's intransigence was due more to "pride than to careful calculation". The whole entourage was in despair at what seemed like de Gaulle's withdrawal from reality. Yet, in fact, events were to prove that it was de Gaulle who was instinctively, and accurately, in touch with the mood of France. With the passing of each successive day of the crisis, it became evident that public opinion – from Left to Right – was setting solidly behind de Gaulle, solidly against the Algiers insurgents and their dissident allies in the army.

By the 27th, realisation of this vital fact began to dawn upon the colonels in Algiers, with the more radical among them, such as Argoud, assessing that they had now missed the boat in not launching a full-scale putsch during the first hours of the barricades. There had been gestures of solidarity with the insurgents in other centres, such as Oran, where barricades had also been erected, largely distinguished by the entertainment of a famous clown, Achille Zavatta, who happened to be in the city at the time; but all had swiftly crumbled. Bored with the discomfort, indiscipline and empty rodomontades behind Ortiz's barricades, some of his forces had already begun to fritter away, while the civilian population was also getting fed up with the inconvenience of closed shops and uncleared garbage. Lagaillarde, always in his para's "leopard" battle-denims and red beret, continued to maintain strict military discipline in his camp; "passes" had to be applied for by "troops" wishing to sleep out in the town; "courts martial" were held, and one actually passed a mock death-sentence on a badly frightened journalist. It was also Lagaillarde who, on the 27th, pulled off a minor coup by liberating from prison Philippe Castille and three accomplices serving sentences for the *affaire du bazooka* of three years previously. Confidently he declared to the Press: "The Third Republic was born at Sedan and died at Sedan. The Fourth was born in Algiers and died in Algiers. The Fifth is born in Algiers." But still there was no news that a single senior officer, let alone unit, of the army in France or Germany had come out in support of the insurgents. Headed by Argoud, as always the most articulate, the "soviet of Colonels" now made an ultimate bid, in the presence of Delouvrier, to persuade Challe to join their cause, to force de Gaulle to conform or go.

Delouvrier and Challe withdraw

The thinly veiled threat that he and the Commander-in-Chief might soon find themselves little better than prisoners in their own headquarters helped decide Delouvrier to take a dramatic step: to leave Algiers, together with Challe. At first Challe demurred, on the grounds that it would look like desertion, but later the hitherto extraordinarily close partnership that they had enjoyed reasserted itself, and he agreed. On Wednesday 22 January, Challe broadcast a radio address aimed at the disaffected elements of the army, in which he declared emphatically that "it will continue to fight for Algeria to remain definitively French, otherwise there can be no sense in its struggle. . . . I repeat: the French army is fighting in order that Algeria shall remain definitively French." Coming from someone with Challe's reputation for integrity, the words carried considerable weight among the large majority of French officers; they were never disclaimed by de Gaulle, and the fact that Challe was permitted to utter what was later, in his eyes, revealed to be a lie would have a vital influence on his own conduct the following year.

After four gruelling days of unremitting crisis, with which he was not designed to cope either by disposition or by his training as a technocrat, Delouvrier was near the end of this tether. Late that night he sat down and drafted a highly emotional, and what afterwards seemed a faintly ridiculous, speech, which he taped and left to be broadcast after he and Challe had slipped discreetly out of Algiers the following day. He was leaving behind as hostages, he declared, his wife and son of a few weeks, Mathieu, in the hopes that he would "grow up a symbol of Algeria's indestructible attachment to France". Pointing out the folly of the insurrection, he warned the rebels: "In rejecting de Gaulle, you will sink yourselves, you will sink the army and France as well." But if they would only see sense, said Delouvrier, deferentially describing Lagaillarde's stronghold as the "Alcazar of the University", he would go there and shake Lagaillarde and Ortiz by the hand: "Then, together we shall all go to the *monument aux morts* to pray and weep for the dead of Sunday, dead in the faith that Algeria should remain French and that Algeria should obey de Gaulle...." That day, Thursday the 28th, travelling incognito in a black Citroën, he left Algiers to set up headquarters with Challe at a modest air force base in Reghaia, some twenty miles east of the city.

The turning point: de Gaulle speaks

In Paris de Gaulle was infuriated by the speech and Delouvrier's offer to shake the rebel leaders by the hand; as with those before him, it looked as if Algiers had "gone to the head" of Delouvrier. But, in fact, the speech and the news that the "authorities" had withdrawn from Algiers together produced an unexpectedly powerful effect on the insurgents, and were to mark a turning-point in "Barricades Week". The insurgents were dumbfounded by the inexplicable withdrawal, which reminded some disquietingly of the tactics of the Soviet army during the Budapest uprising, *reculant pour mieux sauter*, then returning to smash ruthlessly the surprised freedom fighters. More of the *pied noir* militiamen began to disappear from Ortiz's barricades. In Algiers the wind had changed in more ways than one; on Friday the 29th the skies darkened and rain started to patter down on the over-heated citizenry.

That night, at eight o'clock, de Gaulle made his long-awaited television appearance. With deliberate effect, he was dressed in the uniform with its two stars, familiar to so many of the army whom it had inspired two decades previously; the face was strained but determined, the fists clenched. With measured gravity he began: "If I have put on my uniform today to address you on television, it is in order to show that it is General de Gaulle who speaks, as well as the Head of State." He first of all firmly repeated his September decision: "the Algerians shall have free choice of their destiny". When peace comes,

This will not be dictated to them. For if their response were not really *their* response, then while for a time there might well be military victory, basically nothing would be settled. On the contrary, everything can be settled and, I believe, settled in France's favour, when the Algerians have had an opportunity to make known their will in all freedom, dignity and security. In short, self-determination is the only policy that is worthy of France. It is the only possible outcome.

Condemning the Algiers insurgents as "aided in the beginning by the accommodating uncertainty of various military elements, and profiting from the fears and feverish passions stirred up by agitators", he endeavoured to allay the fears of the *pied noirs*, raising his voice in passion: "Frenchmen of Algeria, how can you listen to the liars and the conspirators who tell you that in granting a free choice to the Algerians, France and de Gaulle want to abandon you, to pull out of Algeria and hand it over to the rebellion?" Nothing would bring him greater joy, he added with persuasive eloquence, than if the Muslims would choose from the three options offered them "the one that would be the most French" – but just what did he mean?

Next he turned to the army, for whose benefit he had donned his own uniform that night, speaking in the most severely paternal terms:

> What would the French army become but an anarchic and absurd conglomeration of military feudalisms, if it should happen that certain elements made their loyalty conditional? As you know, I have the supreme responsibility. It is I who bear the country's destiny. I must therefore be obeyed.... This having been said, listen to me carefully ... no soldier, under penalty of being guilty of a serious offence, may associate himself at any time, even passively, with the insurrection. In the last analysis, law and order must be re-established ... your duty is to bring this about. I have given, and am giving, this order.

After a loaded pause, de Gaulle's harsh tone gave way to a note of imploring appeal: "Finally, I speak to France. Well, my dear country, my old country, here we are together, once again, facing a harsh test." If he, de Gaulle, were to yield to "the guilty ones, who dream of being usurpers", then France "would become but a poor broken toy adrift on the sea of hazard".

It was one of de Gaulle's finest speeches, a performance of hypnotic wizardry.* The impact on Frenchmen of all walks of life throughout France was nothing short of magical. Nothing new had been said, not a single concession offered; yet it was as if, after an appallingly long week of perplexity and the nightmare of civil war, or fascism, here was the catharsis, the clear call to duty, that all Frenchmen had unknowingly been waiting for. Once again de Gaulle had got his timing superbly right. Within minutes of his ending, telegrams and messages of endorsement flowed in by the thousand to the Elysée; in Algeria, the first quarter of an hour brought Delouvrier forty declarations of loyalty from army units, including one

---

* Watching the speech on the television set of a Paris bistro, I vividly recall how tears were brought to the eyes of most of those in the room, including cynical foreign journalists, when de Gaulle uttered those words of semi-mystical communion, "Eh bien, mon cher et vieux pays, nous voici donc ensemble, encore une fois...." I do not remember any fighting, wartime broadcast of Churchill having a greater effect.

from a Dragoon colonel offering to place his tanks at the immediate disposal of the authorities to crush the insurrection. As the Chartists had been turned back from marching on the House of Commons by rain, so too the weather in Algiers now reinforced de Gaulle's cause. On the barricades his speech was heard during a thunderstorm, which, says de Gaulle, "seemed symbolic". Nothing is more miserable than Algiers under wintry rain, and now the skies opened to deluge the wretched insurgents with cataracts of icy water; huddled sodden under umbrellas or raincoats stretched out to make a tent, crouched in doorways or under trees, they listened to de Gaulle in a wet misery of defeat. "I watched men and women break down and cry with impotent rage," records Edward Behr. In the Elysée, Bernard Tricot murmured to himself: "*C'est gagné.*"

Rain and despair on the barricades

It was won, though the barricades dragged on through another forty-eight hours. Morale slumped as the rain continued to lash down. Men of the 25th Para division, in from the bled and less sympathetic towards the "ultras", began to replace Dufour's and Broizat's regiments of the 10th. The fraternisation ended, contacts were slowly cut between the insurgents and their food-bearing kindred as the new troops placed their own tight cordon round them. Grim and frightened faces peered out over the barricades, which now more than ever seemed to symbolise the isolation from the rest of the world of the "ultras", men with little henceforth left to defend. Captain Sergent of Dufour's 1st R.E.P. was implored by a distraught *pied noir* woman: "You're not going to attack them, are you? They've done nothing wrong. They want to remain French. That's all. . . . " Sergent remained one of the minority of French officers to be less moved by de Gaulle's address than by "the pathetic tone of these simple and sincere people". He told his colonel that he was ready to cross the barricade with his whole company, but Dufour dissuaded him brusquely: "You don't understand anything about revolutionary war. We've won some points. This phase is finished. . . ."

For such army dissidents as Sergent (and Colonel Dufour himself), there would be other "phases" to come. In Paris, the half-forgotten General Salan was called to Debré's office the day after de Gaulle's speech. Earlier he had offered to lead a conciliatory mission to Algiers, but without response. He was now told curtly to abstain from any intervention, receiving the hint that his own retirement from the active list was not far off.

Inside the headquarters of Ortiz and Lagaillarde an atmosphere resembling the Twilight of the Gods prevailed on 30 January. A last bitter, reproachful encounter took place between the two leaders; Ortiz, utterly exhausted and in tears, accusing the army of betrayal and Lagaillarde of being a maniac; Lagaillarde, contemptuous of Ortiz – "that dish-wipe" –

and declaring that whatever Ortiz did he himself would never surrender. The university laboratories were full of explosive chemicals, and he would blow up the whole quarter and himself with it, rather than submit in shame. The last hours of the barricades revolved around a Lagaillarde preoccupied by medieval considerations of honour; the fate of the *pied noirs* in Algeria for whom, ostensibly, the barricades had risen, was largely forgotten. Meanwhile, in Paris de Gaulle was seething at Delouvrier's apparent sloth to end matters. On the telephone that evening, he decreed: "The time for discussion is over, Delouvrier. One must not be afraid to cause bloodshed if one wants order to reign and the state to survive."

Ortiz decamps: Lagaillarde marches out

The following day, Sunday a week after the tragic fusillade, journalists observed an army chaplain dispensing Holy Communion to the insurgents from a makeshift altar made of *pavé* blocks. That same day a bomb, prematurely blowing up and killing its F.L.N. carrier, provoked an alarm that Lagaillarde was carrying out his threat. Meanwhile, Delouvrier was using Colonel Dufour – the officer most respected by Lagaillarde, the ex-para – to "negotiate terms". By that night a most remarkable "deal" had been concluded. Lagaillarde's men would be permitted to march out of their "Alcazar" as "soldiers", bearing arms, and would be accorded full honours by Dufour's 1st R.E.P. But they would not be allowed to march through the town; instead, they would be loaded into trucks and transported inconspicuously out to the R.E.P. base at Zéralda, where those who so wished could opt to join a unit attached to the Foreign Legion and fighting with them out in the *bled*.* There would be a free pardon for all – except the leaders of the insurrection. These were to surrender themselves to French justice.

By Monday morning, 1 February, Ortiz had vanished, never to be seen in Algiers again. But at midday Lagaillarde marched out of the "Alcazar", with flags flying and in full military order. In a brief farewell to his supporters he said, "*Ne regrettez rien*. You can't win them all – but a man is never vanquished when he retains deep within himself the will to fight." He embraced his father, who was in U.T. uniform, and was then flown off to the Santé prison. Alain de Sérigny, who later joined him there on account of the support his *Écho d'Alger* had given the insurgents, declares perhaps extravagantly: "If there was one man in this sinister affair, it was he, and if there was any grandeur, it was on his side."

At the very moment Lagaillarde was surrendering, a coldly furious de Gaulle was on the telephone to Delouvrier, accusing him of "showing too much indulgence. Finish it off for me, and quickly."

* Called the "Alcazar Commando", the unit, some 120 strong, operated on active service for a few weeks, then was quietly disbanded.

"*Mon général*, I have been able, up to now, to avoid bloodshed. . . . Please continue to have confidence in me. . . ."

In the middle of the conversation an aide came into Delouvrier's office with the news of Lagaillarde's surrender. After he had relayed this, de Gaulle's only comment was: "*Merci*, Delouvrier."

That evening he received the German Ambassador with the words: "We have just lived through a somewhat disturbed week. Now, let's look at the problems of Europe."

CHAPTER EIGHTEEN

"This Prince of Ambiguity"

Where will he lead us, this prince of ambiguity?
Robert Buron, 10 March 1960

The morning after

ON the day of Lagaillarde's march-out the centre of Algiers resembled an abandoned battlefield. The streets, stripped of *pavé*, were cluttered with the debris of war. Everywhere lay jettisoned weapons and cartridge belts, discarded uniforms and mess-tins. From the first cafés that opened their shutters, the cheerfully martial airs of *Colonel Bogey* seemed singularly inappropriate to the grim feeling of hangover and defeat that weighed on the European quarters of the city. For the first time the will of Algiers had been defeated by that of Paris. The future looked obscure, if not without hope. With remarkable speed army pioneers got to work, bulldozing the barricades, replacing the *pavé* and covering it with a thick, prophylactic layer of bitumen – as Paris had done after her "troubles" in the nineteenth century. The normality of life returned swiftly, but superficially; beneath remained a deep and unassuageable bitterness.

One by one the principal actors of "Barricades Week" disappeared from the Algiers scene. Lagaillarde, Ortiz, Susini, Martel, Sérigny, Dr Pérez and Dr Lefèvre were all either in hiding or under lock and key, awaiting trial.* In a second purging of the military de Gaulle sent home three generals – Faure, Mirambeau and Gracieux – and Colonels Broizat, Argoud and Godard. The last, the most experienced of the senior officers of Algiers, left angrily, protesting his loyalty to Challe and Delouvrier (though not, pointedly, to the head of state). His and Gardes' Cinquième Bureau was closed down; the Territorial Units (U.T.) disarmed and disbanded, their members made subject to military call-up. One seemingly curious omission

---

*At the long-awaited "Barricades Trial", which started in November 1960 and lasted three months, sentences were surprisingly mild; Lagaillarde, bombastic as ever in front of the court, and demanding that his "more distinguished actions" of May 1958 be taken into account, was given ten years, but placed at provisional liberty, from which he promptly absconded; Ortiz was sentenced to death *in absentia*; Susini, despite jumping bail, received no more than a two-year suspended sentence; Colonel Gardes, the only serving officer on trial, was acquitted – as were a dozen others.

from the list of *limogeages* was Colonel Dufour of the 1st R.E.P., perhaps the most effectually dissident of the "soviet of Colonels" during "Barricades Week". Dufour was no doubt "reprieved" on account of his successful arbitration with Lagaillarde; nevertheless, in the ensuing months he was twice to be found at the centre of conspiracies against de Gaulle. Meanwhile, he led his Legionnaires back to the *djebel* and the war for which they all felt better equipped than the "dirty work" in Algiers – though with little enough heart for it any more.

Finally, there was the Commander-in-Chief himself. Challe, loyal but increasingly unhappy, who had done his best under impossible circumstances both to prevent bloodshed and keep the army together during "Barricades Week" now wanted only to return to his interrupted task of smashing the A.L.N. But in de Gaulle's eyes he was the commander who had not been obeyed. The same week order was restored he despatched a rather curt letter to Challe, beginning, "Given how things went in the course of the Algiers affair," and informing Challe that he now had other plans for him: to succeed General Ely in the coveted top job of the armed forces. Unimpressed, Challe requested another five or six months to finish the job. De Gaulle said he would require him home before that.

In France, relief at the end of the crisis was reflected by the Bourse marking up share prices by ten per cent and more, while the Sorbonne departed from a century and a half of non-involvement in politics with the science faculty sending the head of state a message of confidence. From the inner entourage of the cabinet, Soustelle alone had persisted with his resignation, to become a dangerous adversary of his former idol; but his disaffection had been growing from well before "Barricades Week", and had more or less been crystallised by the "self-determination" speech of September. There were also other favourable events to distract attention. Hardly were the barricades down than France – as a kind of consolation prize – announced the successful explosion of her first atomic bomb at Reggane in the Sahara, thereby, in de Gaulle's eyes, securing for her new international regard. Khrushchev graced de Gaulle with an official visit in March; then, in April, de Gaulle was invited on a state visit to London. Orchestrated by that past master of dramatic occasion, Harold Macmillan, it was the most magnificent reception ever accorded a visiting ruler in the post-war era. Huge Crosses of Lorraine, lit by myriad fireworks, illuminated Buckingham Palace; while de Gaulle rose to the occasion with an address of moving grandeur to the Lords and Commons, jointly assembled in Westminster Hall. "What people", he asked in closing, "know better than France and Great Britain that nothing will save the world if it is not those qualities in which they excel; wisdom and firmness?" The genuine warmth of the tributes paid him in London had its appreciative echoes in the Paris Press. Later that month he was being lionised in Canada and the U.S.A., followed by rapturous welcomes in French Guiana and Martinique on his return voyage. Next, in May, de Gaulle was to host the long vaunted Summit Conference, attended by the mercurial and unpredictable Khrushchev.

When he had received Macmillan at Rambouillet in March, so soon after surmounting the terrible crisis of "the Barricades", the British leader found him serenely confident. Pointing out that Charles X had abdicated in the very room in which they were talking, and had then gone to England he added – coming as close to light-heartedness as he was ever capable – that: "Louis-Philippe went off in a fiacre – also to England. Napoleon III went to England, too. He paused – and said that he would no doubt be welcomed." At few times during his presidency, however, did de Gaulle in fact seem more secure and popular than since his unconditional victory over the Algiers insurgents, matched by goodwill flowing to him from the world at large. When, on the night of 24 January, the French army had shown that it would not suppress the barricades by arms, followed by the week of ugly stalemate, it had looked as if France – and Europe with her – stood on the brink of catastrophe. Four events broke the insurrection: the first was the withdrawal from Algiers by Delouvrier and Challe, with its implied threat that at least part of the armed forces might be prepared to face civil war; the second was the inability of Ortiz and the "ultras" to gain any palpable Muslim support; the third was the chance break in the weather and the deluging rain it brought; and the fourth was the impact of de Gaulle's speech of the 29th. But of all four it was de Gaulle's voice that proved the most effective. It had looked a dangerously fine-run thing, but once again his timing had been supreme, and when others had lost their nerve he had shown an inspiring example of dignity and leadership. Almost eagerly – with a vast majority of 441 to seventy-five – the Assembly granted him anew "special powers" for a year.

Yet, despite all this, de Gaulle looked a lonelier figure than ever before; for, if "Barricades Week" had proved anything, it was how brittle an instrument was the army – *his* army – on which to rely for the pursuit of peace in Algeria. As C. L. Sulzberger rightly remarked, "there would have been no such desperate Algerian crisis had France's professional army been truly loyal to the State. Civilian *ultras* alone were helpless and lacking in effective strength."

There was virtually no senior officer, not even the *grognard* Massu, in whom de Gaulle could have total trust as long as Algeria was at issue. Thus, if for no other reason, the war had to be finished one way or another, and as soon as possible.

If de Gaulle emerged from "Barricades Week" apparently strengthened, its initiators, the diehard *pieds noirs*, were the total net losers. As Challe wrote in 1967: "I still today consider the affair of the Barricades as an imbecile and tragic mistake by the brave people who wanted to keep

Algeria for France . . . and probably it was the critical moment marking the defeat of the policy of *Algérie française*." Even at the time, however, it was abundantly clear that the only overall beneficiary was the F.L.N., rescued at a moment when its fortunes were close to their nadir. "Barricades Week" revealed to the whole world a fundamental schism in the French camp; while, in its usual masterly fashion, the F.L.N. managed to conceal its rifts, grave as they were. Moreover, it offered the F.L.N. the hope that eventually de Gaulle would be forced to choose between making peace with them or abdicating to rebels within his own army. Meanwhile, to the Muslim admirers of de Gaulle in Algeria, the fact that for a whole week his authority had been flouted represented a grave loss of face. Delouvrier's emotional speech had been regarded as sign of total weakness: "He flatters everybody, convinces no one . . . he begs, he implores, he foresees and predicts, he preaches, he preaches . . . in the desert," wrote Mouloud Feraoun. On the whole the Muslim reaction during "Barricades Week" had been, he noted, to "remain at home out of prudence as if it were a question of dirty linen belonging to a neighbour . . . they are awaiting independence amid a disagreeable *status quo.* . . ." But there could be little doubt now that independence must lie at the end of the road, and that end looked closer than it had at the time of de Gaulle's "self-determination" promise of the previous autumn.

On his first visit to Algeria following the return of order, planned originally for the beginning of February but postponed a month by events, de Gaulle betrayed at once how weak he saw his position vis-à-vis the military, despite all the appearances of reinforced strength. Disguised with the codename of "Green Socrates", de Gaulle's three-day itinerary studiously avoided Algiers and devoted itself to the army – becoming a second *tournée des popotes*. To various units across the country he gave these categoric assurances: "There will be no Dien Bien Phu in Algeria. The insurrection will not throw us out of this country. Pacify. There is time. No need to be hustled. . . ." Then, in scathing terms, he dismissed Ferhat Abbas's call for "independence", terming it "a monstrosity", which could signify for the country nothing but "misery, a reduction to beggary [*clochardisation*], catastrophe. . . .When the Algerians will be able to choose, I do not think they will choose that. France must not leave. She has the right to be in Algeria. She will remain there. . . ." In a different key he drew the army's attention pointedly to the fact of which it seemed so often unaware, namely: "that France is a world power. . . . There is not only the Algerian affair. I must consider the whole, France in its entirety, both internally and externally. I am responsible for the whole, and the whole is not just the Algerian affair." Returning, on the last leg of his trip, to the theme of what the Algerians would choose, he said with conviction: "I believe they will say: an Algerian Algeria bound to France."

These utterances, particularly the harshness of de Gaulle's tone towards Ferhat Abbas and his stressing of France's "right" to remain in Algeria, set up a minor earthquake among his entourage at the Elysée. In Algiers, Delouvrier was equally disturbed. On the face of it, he was going back on "self-determination" and everything he had said since. Enquiring journalists were fed lame interpretations that there was no change of policy, that de Gaulle had merely been expressing himself in language tailored for army consumption. This latest set of apparent self-contradictions was well-summed up by the British cartoonist, Vicky, who depicted de Gaulle standing on his head amid a war-torn Algeria, with the caption: "As I was saying last week...."

"Prince de l'équivoque"

At this point one comes back inevitably to the riddle that was as central to the latter stages of the Algerian war as it was difficult to unravel. To one acute French observer in 1960, de Gaulle and his intentions resembled Molière's Don Juan who had "promised marriage to five or six women and absolutely had to avoid being pinned down by any one of them". But on which one had he really set his heart? Did he change his mind? If so, when? Why was he always so ambiguous in declaring his intentions? Whole books have been dedicated to the subject, and still the controversy thrives. To Massu, de Gaulle always "intended to pull out, from the beginning"; to Mendès-France, he was for *Algérie française*, from the beginning; to General Beaufre he "made a formula, then saw it didn't work"; to Louis Joxe, "he seemed always groping"; to Bernard Tricot, he never believed in integration; to Tournoux, he always hoped he could talk the Muslims out of secession; while Harold Macmillan admits, "I was rather alarmed, at one time, that de Gaulle would try to hold on to Algeria. After our experiences I was certain he couldn't do so." Who read the oracle aright?

At the heart of the matter lies the complex personality of the most impenetrable, enigmatic statesman of modern times, and much can only be surmised. In that discerning mixture of affection and antipathy which Harold Macmillan reserves for characterising de Gaulle, he recalls that during the Second World War the most popular code-name for de Gaulle was "Ramrod", a nickname recalling "the famous definition of a man who was alleged to have all the rigidity of a poker without its occasional warmth". But, unbending as he might be personally, rigidity was not de Gaulle's most outstanding defect when it came to dealing with Algeria. It will be remembered how, back in 1944, he had emerged as the "man of Brazzaville", offering liberal prospects of self-government to the Algerians; yet in 1947, the year of the ill-starred statute, he was declaring: "Whatever happens, France will not abandon Algeria... France, of which

Algeria is an integral part, is basically very determined to help all its citizens and to remain the master." By 1955, when the Algerian revolt was well under way and independence in the offing for Tunisia and Morocco, de Gaulle – at least in his statements – had already travelled some way from his 1947 position. In June he was expounding the view that "No other policy but one which aims at replacing domination by association in French North Africa can be valid or worthy of France." He later qualified this by explaining. "In the first place, I excluded from the realm of possibility all idea of the assimilation of the Muslims into the French population. . . ."

Then, in the period just before his own accession in 1958, he carefully refrained from commitment to any specific panacea for Algeria.

Of his more dramatic or delphic exegeses, some may deserve speedy recapitulation:

1957:	"Of course independence will come, but they are too stupid there to know it."
June 1958:	*"Je vous ai compris!"*
June 1958:	*"Vive l'Algérie française!"*
June 1958:	*"L'Afrique est foutue, et l'Algérie avec!"*
October 1958:	Algerian independence? "In 25 years, Delouvrier."
March 1959:	"The French army will never quit this country; and I, General de Gaulle, will never deal with those people from Cairo and Tunis."
January 1959:	"Algeria has chosen peace."
April 1959:	"I am the only person capable of bringing a solution to Algeria."
May 1959:	"a new Algeria bound forever to France. . . ."
August 1959:	"Peace is a necessity. This absurd war."
September 1959:	"I deem it necessary that recourse to self-determination be here and now proclaimed."
January 1960:	*"une solution qui soit française"*
January 1960:	"How can you listen to the liars and the conspirators who tell you that in granting free choice to the Algerians, France and de Gaulle want to abandon you, to pull out of Algeria and hand it over to the rebellion?"
March 1960	"Independence . . . a folly, a monstrosity . . . France must not leave. She has the right to be in Algeria. She will remain there. . . ."

Often de Gaulle would make a pass in the direction of the F.L.N. then immediately succeed it with a tough call to the army to step up pacification. Or his subordinates would come forth with statements, patently "cleared" by the Elysée, but sounding discordantly out of tune with what de Gaulle had just been saying himself. For instance, shortly after his "self-determination" speech, Delouvrier was telling Challe: "I've just seen the Prime Minister, and you can state that the French army will continue to fight in order for Algeria to remain forever French." Then, after de Gaulle had made his equivocal reference to *une solution qui soit française* during "Barricades Week", Challe was thrust into the breach to explain to the army: "You are the guarantors of France in Algeria. You will fight on so that Algeria remains France." Usually the lot of making the toughest *Algérie française* pronouncements fell to the devoted Debré. "France cannot abandon Algeria. France must not abandon her, and she will not abandon her," Debré declared over Canadian television in January 1959; and before the French Senate that June: "We cannot ask the army for sacrifices and at the same time pursue a policy which annihilates these sacrifices!" This propensity to permit others (often through lack of clear instructions) to stick their necks out, eventually to get them chopped off, was not one of de Gaulle's most endearing characteristics and, in the long run, it would backfire, bringing even Debré to the brink of revolt when he realised that he had uttered words that could not be honoured. Finally, there was de Gaulle's own self-confessed habit of using semantics simply "to establish emotional contact" with his audience.

What does de Gaulle himself have to say in his memoirs about his Algerian policy? Surprisingly little, but in various key passages he declares:

> Now it was too late for any form of subjection. . . . Integration, then, was in my view no more than an ingenious and empty formula. But could I, on the other hand, contemplate prolonging the status quo? No! For that would be to keep France politically, financially and militarily bogged down in a bottomless quagmire when, in fact, she needed her hands free to bring about the domestic transformation necessitated by the twentieth century and to exercise her influence abroad unencumbered. At the same time, it would condemn our forces to a futile and interminable task of colonial repression, when the future of the country demanded an army geared to the exigencies of modern power.

(For what, against whom? an innocent mind might enquire.) From the moment of taking the helm – though he admits to having "no strictly pre-determined plan", "there was in my view no longer any alternative for Algeria but self-determination". But "it must be France, eternal France, who alone, from the height of her power, in the name of her principles and in accordance with her interests, granted it to the Algerians". Christian Fouchet, de Gaulle's last representative in Algeria, who says that de Gaulle never doubted that independence of Algeria would come, adds revealingly: "But what was most important to him was that it should be done *well*, and with *honour* . . . de Gaulle always wanted to control the procedure towards independence himself." It was for this lofty purpose that Challe was called upon "to make ourselves masters of the battlefield". Finally, the ideal of *Algérie française* was dismissed as "a ruinous Utopia". On the other hand, all this was said long after the war was dead and buried. Nothing seemed by any means so cut and dried at the time.

Of all the people able to bring insight into de Gaulle's intentions, Bernard Tricot – the Elysée counsellor, distrusted alike by the *pieds noirs* and *Algérie française* army generals, but constantly at de Gaulle's elbow from 1958 onwards – should have been the best situated. Summing up de Gaulle's policy as he saw it, he says that he "undertook at first useful reforms for the future, whatever that might be, and based his long-term policy on the right of the people to dispose of themselves, ending – in default of a solution within the community – with one of independence . . . ." Admitting (which was as revealing as it was honest) that it was pure supposition on his part, Tricot goes on to speculate that, having realised it was too late for "integration", he had at least "to give a chance, if one still existed, to the idea of *francisation*". But, referring to de Gaulle's own account of his policy as rendered in his memoirs, Tricot states that when sent the manuscript he queried the passage "there was in my view no longer any alternative for Algeria but self-determination" with the rather courageous comment, "I lived through all this period at your side, and the facts then seemed to me less simple."

One is left with the question, why did de Gaulle practise such ambiguity, even to baffling Tricot and fudging up the record afterwards (a practice not unknown in the memoirs of ex-heads of state)? If he had believed in "self-determination" in 1958, why had he not then said so outright, instead of letting his supporters deceive themselves and the war drag on for over another year before coming out with it? Tricot, bravely loyal, suggests that part of the reason may have lain in the hazards of communication between de Gaulle and his subordinates. Explaining for himself why his own memoirs, covering the four crucial years of his service at the Elysée, reproduced virtually no conversations with de Gaulle in *oratio directa*, he says: "I felt there was something dishonest about coming out of his office and then immediately writing down what he had said; but then, afterwards, in a curious way one's mind became almost a blank as to what he had *actually* said." This almost mesmeric impact of de Gaulle's presence and eloquence was experienced by many others, but at best it offers no more than a fraction of the truth. Tricot recognises a more intrinsic fact: French public opinion was certainly not ready in 1958 to admit the possibility of Algerian autonomy. So many thousands of young Frenchmen had done their national service in Algeria and their emotions were still deeply committed there. Admitting his need for "tactics" whereby "to proceed cautiously from one stage to the next", de Gaulle himself explains in an eloquent metaphor:

> Were I to announce my intentions point-blank, there was no doubt that the sea of ignorant fear, of shocked surprise, of concerted malevolence through which I was navigating would cause such a tidal wave of alarms and passions in every walk of life that the ship would capsize. I must,

therefore, manoeuvre without ever changing course until such time as, unmistakably, common sense broke through the mists....

The use of the word "manoeuvre" reminds one that, above all, de Gaulle remained the eternal, quintessential soldier. The fragile "ship", in danger of capsizing, to which he referred, was not specifically public opinion. It was the army, *his* army. From his earliest days as a "prophet without glory", de Gaulle had always been a military innovator, profoundly deploring the backward mentality of the French army. "And what did he find in 1958?" asks Tricot:

> An enemy conducting a totally archaic battle, without tanks, just rifles and machine-guns, and with the French army combating them with the slowest aircraft – which were the most useful. It was all very distasteful to him. What he really desired to do was to modernise the French army, bring it into the atomic era, and this was always impeded by Algeria.

If it was for the future salvation of the army that de Gaulle wanted to be disencumbered of Algeria, then it was for the sake of preserving it intact that he could not risk telling it the whole truth of his intentions. Thus, to save it for a brilliant future that only he could see glimmering in the distance, de Gaulle had – from 1958 onwards – to speak carefully to the army in a special language; or, more crudely put, lie to it for its own good. This seems to be the most fundamental explanation for de Gaulle's "double-talk". To some extent he may have deceived himself by it. In formulating his policy for Algeria he seems throughout to have suffered from three basic misconceptions. The first was that his great personal prestige would persuade the Muslim majority to accept his terms. (Whether the *pieds noirs* would was always of secondary importance to de Gaulle.) But, as he received one snub after another from the F.L.N., his prestige waned until by the end of 1960 it was doubtful whether it could have carried an effective majority. Secondly, he fundamentally misunderstood the nature of the F.L.N., thinking, as a military man himself, that he was dealing with a conventional armed insurrection led by modern Abd-el-Kaders who would sooner or later recognise military defeat and the advantages of sensible compromise. But he could not seem to grasp that his adversaries were ruthless and adroit political revolutionaries, deeply committed to totalitarian principles of "no compromise". Finally, he somehow persuaded himself that time would wait upon him while he found the correct formula and then imposed peace with it. But time would be wrenched from him.

Challe goes: de Gaulle's new team

On 23 April General Challe left Algiers as Commander-in-Chief. At the time of his departure he had many reasons for bitterness, and better ones than his predecessor, Salan, who was already in a state of extreme disaffection. First of all, though never so ambitious as Salan for professional advancement, Challe had just cause for feeling let down personally. In February, when told of de Gaulle's intention to transfer him from Algiers, he had been promised the top job in the French armed forces. Now here he was, posted in mid-stream in April, and only to replace General Valmy as commander of N.A.T.O. forces, Central Europe, a promotion of a kind, but nothing like what had originally been proffered. But of much more serious consequence to Challe was the disruption this posting signified to the eponymous plan to which he had been so deeply committed all through his career in Algeria. The withdrawal of élite troops from the *bled* necessitated by "Barricades Week" had come as an infuriating interruption to Challe, just at a moment when Deuxième Bureau reports were giving the impression that the A.L.N. was on the verge of breaking. Immediately afterwards he had strained at the leash to get on with the Challe offensive by cleaning up the last "unpacified" area and the birthplace of the revolt: the Aurès–Nementchas. This new, final operation was due to begin on 19 April, but Challe's successor, General Crépin (promoted after replacing Massu in January), had other ideas.

Crépin was a fifty-two-year-old gunner, who during the Liberation had commanded the artillery of the famous Second Armoured Division, which had supplied France's post-war army with so many of its ranking officers. Sometimes known as "Casse-Noisette" because of a stubbornly prognathous jaw, he was a stolid personality, principally distinguished for having pioneered the S.S.-10 anti-tank missile. Crépin was unusual in the army of the time in having no political attachments, but was unconditionally loyal to de Gaulle and for this reason he had been selected to replace the fallen Massu in January 1960. The new Commander-in-Chief was a coldly scientific *polytechnicien*, totally lacking the panache of a Massu or the popularity of a Challe, and of whom para captains said "Crépin? . . . never seen him!" To Challe, on the eve of his departure, Crépin expressed reluctance to persist with the Aurès offensive, explaining: "It's a difficult operation and I wouldn't like to run up against this affair coming fresh on the job. . . ." Subsequently Crépin would, in fact, resume Challe's offensive policy – but never with quite the same thrust. Thus Challe saw himself frustrated of his final victory after such brilliant military successes over the past year. At the moment of his departure the balance sheet claimed that 26,600 rebels had been "knocked out", 11,000 captured, and nearly 21,000 arms recovered in that period, while Boumedienne's 10,000 strong "army of the exterior" showed every sign of being – at least temporarily – neutralised. The A.L.N. of the "interior" could no longer muster more than 8,000 men, in scattered and generally demoralised groups.

Painfully conscious of de Gaulle's mistrust of him, aware of the frustration of his own *chef-d'oeuvre*, as Challe left Algiers his overflowing cup of gall contained one final ingredient. During the crisis of "Barricades Week" he had been induced to give those various assurances to the men under him that they were "fighting in order that Algeria shall remain definitively French", and that de Gaulle had promised him "there will be no negotiations with the F.L.N." Over the course of the next few months he was to come to believe that he had been permitted, if not actively encouraged, by de Gaulle to perjure himself. It was therefore perhaps not surprising that Challe had refused, somewhat brusquely, the Grand Cross of the Legion of Honour which Michel Debré had come to bestow upon him on his departure.

For the other half of the ruling tandem, Paul Delouvrier, the withdrawal of Challe was also bad news. While their association had been so fruitfully close that it had been remarked "you could never slide a cigarette-paper between them", between Delouvrier and Crépin relations would never be more than stiffly formal. Like Challe, Delouvrier recognised that de Gaulle had lost confidence in him since "the Barricades", and this awareness was not helped when, in its aftermath, de Gaulle imposed on the Delegate-General "his man" to fill the re-created post of Director of Political Affairs. His choice was Colonel François Coulet, a remarkable figure. A close aide of de Gaulle's in wartime London, when the Algerian war began, Coulet had resigned a senior diplomatic post as Minister in Belgrade to rejoin the colours (at the ripe age of fifty) and form his own "private army" of air force paratroops. For the previous four years his regiment had acquitted itself with distinction; then he had been summoned to the presidential bosom, to hold himself ready for "political tasks". His new role in Algiers was clearly to act as an "observer" reporting directly to de Gaulle on the performance of the Delegate-General, and as a "stiffener" in case of a repeat of "the Barricades": – a function that was as embarrassing for Coulet as it was humiliating for Delouvrier.

Meanwhile, as de Gaulle had intimated to the army during his last *tournée des popotes* in March, consonant with his view of France's role as a great power, many things had been happening in the outside world to prove that Algeria was not his only worry. At home, de Gaulle had been confronted by the first major wave of social strife since he had assumed power: the farmers of the north had taken to the streets in revolt against his agricultural price policy; there were strikes and lock-outs in many factories; by 1 June 1,300,000 civil servants were out on strike for higher wages. But the biggest shock had come in May when, in pique at the shooting-down of Gary Powers's U.2 spy-plane over the Urals, Khrushchev had arbitrarily broken off the Paris Summit. The snub aimed at Eisenhower also rubbed off on de Gaulle, who had cherished hopes of deriving international kudos for France from the meeting. Explaining away this set-back in a broadcast at the end of May, de Gaulle declared his determination to give the lead in building up a strong, united and independent Europe. In the meantime, relations with the United States were beginning to crumble after de Gaulle (partly reacting against the Summit debacle) had banned the stocking of American nuclear war-heads on French territory. The U.S.A.A.F. riposted by transferring its bomber squadrons to Germany. De Gaulle ordered the withdrawal of French naval units from the N.A.T.O. Mediterranean fleet, and on 9 June the project of France's "go-it-alone" *force de frappe* was placed before the Assembly. Five days later, on television, de Gaulle revealed how his thoughts were now evolving. Though couched in general terms, it would also bear particular relevance to France's future in Algeria, when he told his countrymen of the urgent need "to transform our old France into a new country and make her marry her time".

The G.P.R.A. and the rough road to negotiations

Since the "self-determination" speech of September 1959, endeavours towards negotiating a cease-fire had jolted along in their usual fruitless and frustrating way, with neither side seemingly able to find a formula for beginning talks that would satisfy promises extracted for internal consumption. (And how often in the history of war does the killing of young men and civilians continue for no better reason than this failure to discover just such a face-saving formula?) The problems of each side ran curiously parallel; no sooner had a peaceful-sounding overture been made than pressure from the protagonists of "no compromise" would force the respective leader to counterpoint with harsh and intransigent noises towards the other side, which in turn would engender more mistrustful reservations. For de Gaulle the governing factor at this stage was to avoid any move that could in any way be interpreted as recognising the F.L.N. as the one competent negotiating partner, while for the G.P.R.A. recognition was their abiding objective. Already, early in 1959, an illustrative episode, one of the several mysterious *démarches* of the war, had taken place. Antoine Pinay, Foreign Minister in the dying days of the Fourth Republic and currently de Gaulle's Minister of Finance, received word through a Swiss newspaper editor that "responsible" leaders of the F.L.N. (including Ahmed Francis and Maître Ahmed Boumendjel) would be receptive to opening talks with the French government. The person of Pinay was selected on account of his previous negotiations with Morocco where he was well trusted. But de Gaulle had refused, saying: "I don't want it; because the day after you've seen them they will say that I have recognised the F.L.N. government."

Pinay: "Let me make a proposition, then: if it works, you can take the responsibility; if it fails, you can say it's just that imbecile Pinay acting on his own initiative!"

23. *Ratonnade.*

24. "Barricades Week", January 1960. Rival leaders Pierre Lagaillarde and Joseph Ortiz.

25. *Above:* "Barricades Week", Algiers. Demonstrators tear up the cobbles to make barricades while a huge crowd gathers.

26. *Below:* December 1960. Rue Michelet: scenes reminiscent of Budapest, 1956, as *pied noir* "ultras" demonstrate against de Gaulle.

27. *Above:* A paratrooper guards Algiers town hall against jeering *pieds noirs*.

28. *Below:* The Muslim reaction: a French army unit rounds up "pillagers".

33. *Above:* The "battle of the transistors". French servicemen listen to news of the putsch during the day of 23 April.

The generals' putsch, April 1961.
29-32. *Left:* The four generals who led the revolt. *Top, left to right:* General Raoul Salan, General André Zeller. *Bottom, left to right:* General Edmond Jouhoud and General Maurice Challe.

34. *Below:* Tanks guard the National Assembly, Paris.

35. *Above:* March 1962. As French and Muslim leaders prepared to meet in Evian, attacks—both F.L.N. and O.A.S. inspired—increased in Algiers.

36. *Below:* February 1962. Demonstration against O.A.S. outrages in Paris.

37. *Above:* "A solution of good sense". De Gaulle announces the cease-fire on 18 March 1962, following the Evian peace talks.

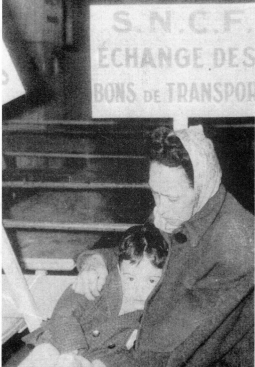

38. *Right:* Exodus: nearly a half million *pieds noirs* abandon their homes and livelihoods and pour back destitute into metropolitan France.

39. *Above:* 1962. The victorious A.L.N. welcomes the members of Wilayas 1 and 6 in the Stade Ruisseau. Centre, Ben Bella, on his left, Colonel Boumedienne, Colonel Mendjli; on his right, Saadi Yacef, Colonel Slimane.

40. *Below:* 1975. The page is turned. President Boumedienne of Algeria greets President Giscard d'Estaing as he arrives on the first visit by a French head of state since independence.

De Gaulle: "But who are they, who nominated them?"

Pinay: "In 1940 people were asking exactly the same about you."

To the chagrin of Pinay, de Gaulle remained adamant. No talks.

Then, some six months later, de Gaulle had made his "self-determination" bid, and the G.P.R.A., after carefully digesting what its attitude should be, had countered with, yet again, a discouragingly negative reply. Yes, they would discuss "self-determination" with de Gaulle, but their delegates to any talks would have to be Ben Bella and the other four hijacked leaders, still languishing under lock and key in France. It was an adroitly calculated move, designed to provoke rejection by de Gaulle. For the G.P.R.A. recognised that the "self-determination" gambit had won for France more points both in Washington and at the United Nations than anything previously attempted; therefore, de Gaulle's initiative could not be allowed to prosper, and he himself must be made to appear culpable for torpedoing it. Thrown into a state of angry pessimism, de Gaulle reacted as predicted, declaring haughtily that his olive branch was intended for "those who are fighting, not those who are *hors de combat*".

Thus, by the end of the year and the beginning of "the Barricades" crisis, the chasm between de Gaulle and the G.P.R.A. yawned unhopefully as wide as ever. On 13 December, behind the closed doors of the Legislative Palace in Tripoli and surrounded by the usual strict secrecy, the F.L.N. began its Third National Council of the Algerian Revolution (C.N.R.A.). It was immediately apparent that the revolutionary camp was confronted with its most serious crisis since the "liquidation" of Ramdane Abane, whose shadow still cast its pall over the conference table. There was, once again, the rift between the combatant leaders of the "interior" and the "ministers" of the "exterior", a rift now made more bitter than ever by the savage pressures of the Challe offensive. This time the attack was directed against the veteran maquisard, long held to be the strong man of the F.L.N., Belkacem Krim, in his capacity as Minister of War, and against the President of the G.P.R.A., Ferhat Abbas, and his fellow "moderates". In a defensive statement Krim admitted that the previous month's fighting had been "the hardest of the war", and that the A.L.N. of the "interior" had suffered heavy losses. He then came under fierce attack for failing to supply it with arms and reinforcements, and was criticised for being, though an excellent commander in the field, no chief-of-staff. The fact that his attackers included those who previously had been his loyal supporters made Krim seem increasingly isolated. At the centre of the attack appeared Boussouf, described by Claude Paillat as become "the Fouché of the rebellion, but a revolutionary Fouché like Saint-Just, and provided with troops like Napoleon". Behind Boussouf, and strongly backed by his powerful patron, stood the silent and reflective figure of Boumedienne; a new force to be reckoned with, he emerged as the focal point of what were henceforth to be recognised as the hard-liners, the *guerre à outrance* faction of the F.L.N. Boumedienne now suggested that Krim and his "Ministry of War" be replaced by an army chief-of-staff and an inter-ministerial war committee. There was little doubt whom Boumedienne had in mind for the supreme military post, and – according to Krim in the aftermath of war – he, Krim, muttered angrily under his breath, "You are just awaiting your moment!" Amid mounting passions and antagonisms, Krim found himself over a whole month fighting a fierce rearguard action for his own survival.

At the same time the hard-liners were pressing vigorously for a new policy of sharpened revolutionary zeal within Algeria, involving imposition of a tighter control over the population. Supported by the moderate Saad Dahlab, Ferhat Abbas resisted this on the grounds that it would only make the F.L.N. look more extremist to the outside world, and thus render the prospects of negotiations with de Gaulle even more precarious. But it was plain that Abbas was in a minority position, and his own future increasingly uncomfortable. After thirty-three days of heated discussion, the Third C.N.R.A. closed. On 19 January (the day after the *bombe Massu* exploded) it was announced that a new constitution for the G.P.R.A. had been evolved – as well as a new ministerial structure. Krim finally, and no doubt fortified by recollections of the fate of Abane in his isolation, had given in. Abbas would remain president – though more than ever in a "window-dressing" capacity; Krim, still vice-president, would become Minister of Foreign Affairs and one of a "troika" (the others being Boussouf and Ben Tobbal) on the new "inter-ministerial war committee" proposed by Boumedienne. And, in the new post of chief-of-staff of the army, responsible for the whole military conduct of the war in the "interior" and "exterior" – Boumedienne. It would soon be plain that this was where the real focus of power in the F.L.N. now lay; at the same time, the Third C.N.R.A. marked the beginning of the eclipse both of Abbas and the "moderates", and of Krim himself. Between Boumedienne and Krim – resentful and jealous of leaving the army in the hands of the former – the antagonism would continue.

Among the articles of the new constitution established by the Third C.N.R.A. was one which pointedly described the F.L.N. as a unique party, pursuing independence by revolution; a reassertion of primacy that was to have far-reaching consequences when the first serious negotiations took place between the French and the Algerians. Then, hardly had the F.L.N. delegates packed their bags in Tripoli than "Barricades Week" broke out in Algiers. At its end, with the will of the European "ultras" broken for the first time and de Gaulle triumphant, it would have seemed that, for the F.L.N. moderates, the omens for meaningful peace talks were never better. But with the hard-liners now well in the ascendant the interpretation the F.L.N. placed on the events of January 1960 was one of the overall weakness of the French position, presaging a total surrender to the maximum F.L.N. terms. With justification the hard-liners could point out that the first four years of fighting had overthrown the Fourth Republic and brought in de Gaulle and electoral franchise for Algerian Muslims; the next year had achieved "self-determination" and, now, the sixth year of the war had begun with Frenchmen firing on Frenchmen – altogether a not unsatisfactory balance. All that was required was to fight on for a few more months, a year or two at most, and de Gaulle would be forced to negotiate – on F.L.N. terms. Thus in their first public statements following the levelling of the Algiers barricades both Abbas and de Gaulle spoke with the same voice: that of harsh intransigence. Abbas would speak in aggressive tones of persisting with "a long and murderous war"; de Gaulle to the army in March would call independence for Algeria "a monstrosity"; Abbas would riposte by terming this "a declaration of war on the Algerian people". The language was motivated by identical stimuli: necessity to placate the hard-liners, who now, in each camp, were the army leaders. Tragically, as so often is the case in modern times, it would be the hard-liners, the apostles of "no compromise", who would triumph in the long run.

Si Salah: "Operation Tilsit"

In the midst of these unpromising auguries for peace talks, there suddenly occurred one of the more extraordinary episodes of the Algerian war. Had a stray visitor been able to penetrate the unusually rigid security guard at the Elysée on the night of 10 June 1960, he would have been amazed to see the President of the French Republic seated at his desk in conversation with three F.L.N. leaders.

The Algerians comprised the entire command of Wilaya 4, the key sector adjacent to Algiers, and they were headed by the Wilaya chief, Si Salah. The changeable fortunes of Wilaya 4 have already been recounted, from the time when, during the Battle of Algiers, it had presented a model command to the period when its infection by *la bleuite* (caught from Amirouche's Wilaya 3) had almost brought it to its knees in a welter of debilitating purges. The one bright spot for the Wilaya 4 command then had been the adroit fooling of French intelligence by that redoubtable fighting commander, Major Azedine, who, when captured, had persuaded them of his intention to negotiate a surrender on behalf of the Wilaya leaders, and had then decamped, leaving his inquisitors humiliated – and extremely suspicious.

This had been at the end of 1958. Then, on 17 March 1960, the cadi of Médéa, a small town nestling in the Atlas some fifty miles south-west of Algiers, received three clandestine visitors. They were Si Lakhdar, a former mason with a reputation for aggressive courage who had succeeded Si Salah as intelligence chief of Wilaya 4, Halim, the political boss of the Wilaya, and Abdellatif, commander of the Médéa zone. The message they brought the astonished cadi was that Colonel Si Salah and themselves were desirous of negotiating de Gaulle's formula of a *paix des braves* – so brusquely rejected by the G.P.R.A. – for Wilaya 4 and any others that might follow suit. But they would not negotiate with local military or civil representatives, of whom they were distrustful; it had to be a high authority in Paris. On receiving news of the *démarche* from the cadi of Médéa, French intelligence in Algiers immediately attached the utmost importance to it. Si Salah was respected as a highly serious and influential leader; a thirty-one-year-old Kabyle whose real name was Mohamed Zamoun, his father a teacher with Communist sympathies, he had been in the revolt from the very first day, was a close friend of Krim and Ouamrane, and had been a member of the C.N.R.A. since September 1958. His military deputy, Major Si Mohamed (alias Bounaama Djillali*), was also held to be perhaps the most dynamic of all the current A.L.N. leaders of the "interior".

There were encouraging precedents for believing that Si Salah might be on the level; under the first pressures of the Challe offensive, had not one area commander, Youssef Smail, come over and then broadcast an appeal to his comrades to accept de Gaulle's *paix des braves*? Moreover, secret radio intercepts by the French Bureau d'Études et de Liaisons (or B.E.L. – the innocent-sounding Gaullist inheritor of the intelligence functions of the somewhat discredited S.D.E.C.E.) fully confirmed how grave was the state of disaffection inside Wilaya 4. Already in the summer of 1959 Si Salah was warning A.L.N. headquarters of the serious slump in morale following the heavy casualties inflicted by the Challe offensive, and at the beginning of December he was demanding arms and ammunition from the G.P.R.A. in unusually pressing and aggressive terms. In January a message from Si Salah to Boumedienne accused the "exterior" of neglectful arrogance, and cautioned it that "the maquis is tired and disheartened. De Gaulle proposed the *paix des braves*, and complete equality for all. That's what we ourselves want. . . . If you don't provide us with the means for waging war we shall accept that proposition. You can't expect otherwise. . . ." Agitated signals flashed back from A.L.N. headquarters requesting verification and clearly suspecting the hand of French intelligence. A few weeks later Si Salah despatched a more deadly communication to Tunis.

> Is it true [he asked] that de Gaulle has addressed a peace plan to the G.P.R.A.? Why do they not take the advice of the "interior"? The struggle cannot continue: the people are tired, the combatants discouraged. If the G.P.R.A. does nothing, Wilaya 4 will make contact with the French to negotiate an end to the fighting. We shall hide a portion of the arms that remain. . . .

* Not to be confused with the "disappeared" Wilaya 4 chief, Colonel Si M'hamed, alias Ahmed Bougarra.

On 7 March a terse signal from Si Salah was intercepted by the B.E.L.: "Failing a response to our plan, we shall move to execute it on 15 March." A frantic, but stalling, reply came by return from the G.P.R.A.: "Think of the revolution. Wait. Instructions follow." On 17 March Si Salah's emissaries made their entry at Médéa.

In a very short space of time the information had passed from Colonel Jacquin, director of the B.E.L. in Algiers, upwards to de Gaulle. To all those privy to it, it looked like a first break in the monolithic façade of the F.L.N. Challe, about to relinquish his command, was especially enthusiastic. Here, it seemed, lay within reach the goal to which his whole strategy had been directed; a chance to administer the *coup-de-grâce* to the A.L.N. of the "interior", and perhaps a last chance to retain some form of *Algérie française*. De Gaulle's first reaction, rebuffed as he had been repeatedly in his overtures to the G.P.R.A., was also favourable, and from that moment was born "Operation Tilsit" – named (not without prescience) after that 1807 truce of unreality between Emperors Napoleon and Alexander aboard their raft in the middle of Niemen. For a whole year "Tilsit" was to remain a deadly secret to all but the handful entrusted with its execution.

To treat with the Wilaya 4 leaders, de Gaulle sent his own aide, Bernard Tricot, supported by Colonel Mathon from Premier Debré's staff, and in the later meetings they were also accompanied by Jacquin of the B.E.L. The first, historic encounter took place on 28 March, a grey and cold night, in the Médéa prefecture, which, for once, stood unguarded. At the appointed hour, Bernard Tricot inside nervously lifted a corner of the curtain, peering out into the garden to see if anything was going to happen. After a few minutes three figures approached, walking unconcernedly down the street, and entered the building: "three young men with brown faces, correctly dressed in civilian clothes". They introduced themselves: Lakhdar, Halim and Abdellatif. The contrast between the Algerians out of the maquis and the urban, courteous Parisian intellectual, Tricot, must have seemed extreme, and there was a moment of awkward stiffness. The most at ease, noted Tricot, was Lakhdar, and the ice visibly thawed when Tricot explained that he was there as personal representative of President de Gaulle. The Algerians stated that they wanted a cease-fire, and beyond that an end to "European domination". Soon they were spilling out their animosity against the G.P.R.A.; the people had suffered too much and "We ourselves now have hardly any regular contact with the exterior." Tricot received the impression

of men who had wanted independence but who, perhaps, would be satisfied with an autonomy where their country would enjoy both liberty and the aid of France. But they had reflected little on the shape of the future. "Maquisards don't see any further than the end of their sub-machine-guns," said Lakhdar. What was certain was that the men we had in front of us thought that their struggle no longer had a *raison d'être.*

Three days later a second meeting took place, after which Tricot verified to de Gaulle that the Wilaya spokesmen were genuine.

A long series of talks now began at highly discreet rendezvous, some-times in deserted corners of the *bled*, sometimes with the Algerians appear-ing in the guise Yacef had once favoured – with feminine garments envelop-ing their combat denims. Their first concern was that honour should remain intact; that acceptance of a *paix des braves* should in no way be allowed to look like capitulation. Accordingly, Bernard Tricot worked out a formula whereby the maquisards would "deposit for safe-keeping" their weapons in local gendarmeries (specifically *not* turning them over into army hands); they would then file away to their villages; only those guilty of "murder" would be placed under surveillance until the definitive end of hostilities; on reaching this point, France was to be trusted to institute a massive amnesty. The next hesitation of the F.L.N. leaders stemmed from an anxiety not to "desolidarise" themselves from their fellow combatants. They wanted to see Ben Bella to canvass his support; they wanted to go to Tunis to press their case there. Both propositions were refused by de Gaulle, and were indeed quite unrealistic; Ben Bella would have been unpersuadable; once in Tunis the F.L.N. would never have permitted them to return. They wanted more time to bring with them the maximum number of their ad-herents and, further, to spread the doctrine of what they called *degaullisme* to neighbouring disaffected Wilayas, notably Kabylia. They proposed an extended interregnum of eight weeks, during which time the French would cease all operations in the Wilaya.

There was consternation in the French camp at this delay, and – with memories of how they had been duped by Azedine – suspicions were aroused that Si Salah might yet be playing a double game. But Colonel Jacquin, now himself taking part in some of the clandestine meetings, was able to provide fresh assurance through intercepts of radio messages from Si Salah which disclosed a final break with the G.P.R.A.* Moreover, the

---

* In operations involving signals intelligence, the B.E.L. seems to have reached a peak of excellence at about this time. According to Jacquin, almost simultaneously with "Tilsit" a successful coup had also been mounted against the command of Wilaya 5 (Oranie). Intercepts revealed that Boumedienne's successor, Colonel Lotfi, was on his way back from Morocco to his headquarters in western Algeria. His precise route determined, he and his escort were ambushed and wiped out. Before A.L.N. headquarters in Morocco could learn of the Wilaya commander's fate, the B.E.L. had a "false Colonel Lotfi" reporting on the air over the captured transmitter. For several months the "playback" continued, with "Colonel Lotfi" calling re-peatedly for reinforcements, arms and money, all of which fell into French ambushes, until finally the ruse was tumbled to. The operation only increased the general sense of insecurity suffered by the Wilayas of the "interior", and distrust between them and the high command of the "exterior".

inducement that Si Salah might spread the spores of *degaullisme* even beyond the confines of Wilaya 4 was highly alluring. The interregnum was agreed – though not (according to Jacquin) the cessation of anti-guerrilla activities, on the ground that this would imperil the secrecy on which all were agreed.

As May arrived the F.L.N. leaders (Si Salah had not yet presented himself) still seemed haunted by fears of being accused of treachery by those of their colleagues who still harboured misgivings; among them being, apparently, that tough soldier Si Mohamed, military deputy to Si Salah. Then, on either his fourth or fifth flight between Paris and Algiers, with the inspiration that altitude sometimes brings, "an unprecedented idea" occurred to Bernard Tricot; why not confound the doubters by whisking Si Salah to Paris for a meeting with the president himself? Surprisingly, de Gaulle immediately said "Yes". Returning to Algeria, Tricot asked the F.L.N. leaders whether Si Salah would be prepared to talk to a "high political personage" in Paris, without mentioning the name of de Gaulle. On 9 June Tricot and Colonel Jacquin flew to Paris, taking with them Si Salah and Si Mohamed – both presenting themselves for the first time – and Lakhdar. Just in case the Algerians should be contemplating a Ben Bella operation in reverse, two plainclothes gendarmes were also abroad the aircraft. They were not needed; Si Salah – who turned out to be a good-looking man nearly six feet tall with intelligent features and a well-groomed moustache – suffered from air-sickness. Si Mohamed, a rugged individual with the roughness of the simple peasant, and Lakhdar – neither of whom had flown before – were preoccupied with the marvels of the flight, while Lakhdar ravenously consumed an entire camembert.

The following morning Tricot informed the astonished Algerians that, at ten o'clock that evening, the "personage" they were to see was no less than the President himself. To give them extra assurance that they came as trusted dignitaries, Tricot made a point that they should not be searched for weapons before entering the Elysée; he and Mathon would be the only others present at the interview in the room, and they would be unarmed. De Gaulle's military aide, Colonel de Bonneval, was appalled at the security hazard, and – as a single precaution – a lone marksman was installed hidden behind a tapestry. The risks remained considerable, but de Gaulle – as always entirely fearless for his own physical safety – accepted them unhesitatingly. The Wilaya 4 leaders were obviously impressed by the simple dignity of de Gaulle's reception. To Colonel Jacquin afterwards, Si Salah confided, "I had prepared a little speech, but was so moved that I let my heart speak." De Gaulle opened by recalling his "self-determination" proposals; Si Salah repeated his aims that had been thrashed out with Tricot over the past months. Nothing new on either side. Then de Gaulle revealed to the Algerians that he was about to make, in four days precisely, a new appeal to the G.P.R.A. to discuss a cease-fire. In the event of their reply being unfavourable, he would proceed with Si Salah's plan. Si Salah declared that he would go ahead and establish contact with the neighbouring Wilayas, but added that if the G.P.R.A. responded to de Gaulle's overture, "then you will hear nothing more from us". The interview over, de Gaulle rose to his feet and with proper formality declared: "Because we are fighting each other, I will not shake your hand, but I salute you."

Thus ended the first, and only, direct conversation that de Gaulle was ever to have with any leaders of the Algerian revolt by which he had been brought to power.

Already on the flight back to Algeria Si Salah was expressing misgivings about de Gaulle's projected appeal to the G.P.R.A.; if the latter were to accept, it would be nothing but a feint, he assured his French companions. On 14 June de Gaulle made his television broadcast, beginning somewhat patronisingly about the backwardness of his "old country", which he said, must be made to "marry her time". He spoke of a glowing future when "the Sahara natural gas, the reserves of which are inexhaustible, would be capable of transforming the existence of Algeria and influencing that of Europe". Finally, he addressed himself, "in the name of France, to the leaders of the insurrection. I declare to them that we await them here in order to find with them an honourable end to the fighting that drags on".

The army in Algiers was outraged by the directness of de Gaulle's appeal to the G.P.R.A.; to them it seemed to be wholly at odds with all that he had promised he would not do during his March *tournée des popotes*. Even more outraged were those leaders, like Colonel Jacquin, privy to "Operation Tilsit", who had understood from Si Salah that he would only go to Paris to deal with de Gaulle on the implicit understanding that the latter would not resume dealings with the G.P.R.A. On 18 June, though feeling that de Gaulle's speech had pulled the carpet out from under Si Salah, Colonel Jacquin met him again and agreed to escort him to Kabylia en route for his voyage of persuasion to Wilaya 3 and its leader, Mohand Ou El-Hadj. On the 20th the G.P.R.A. in Tunis announced that, under certain conditions, it accepted de Gaulle's invitation and would send a delegation to France. On the 21st Jacquin deposited Si Salah and his colleagues at the appointed meeting place in Kabylia.

It was the last time that any of them were seen alive by Jacquin or any other French official.

The final act of "Operation Tilsit" remains clad in a grim mystery. According to General Jacquin, as he is today, a "killer" despatched from Tunis from the G.P.R.A. forced Si Mohamed – always the most reluctant of the Wilaya 4 leaders – to return to the fold, and imposed upon him the execution of his guilty peers. Lakhdar, Halim and Abdellatif were summarily put to death, while Si Salah – on account of his seniority and distinction as a maquisard – was ordered to make his way to Tunis and stand trial there. Many months elapsed, unaccountably, with Si Salah apparently still under arrest in Algeria. Jacquin's B.E.L. attempted a cloak-and-dagger operation to liberate him, but without success. Then, in July the following year, Si Salah, evidently on his way to Tunisia at last, was killed in an ambush by a French patrol; little more than two weeks later, but in another corner of Algeria, Si Mohamed was also tracked down and killed in an *opération ponctuelle* mounted by the 11th Shock. The coincidence, and curious circumstances, of the deaths of the two leaders have encouraged anti-Gaullists in the French army to speculate, even today, that there may have been more to it all than met the eye. Undeniable it was that, following their deaths, no one was left on the Algerian side able to give evidence about the whole sad story of "Operation Tilsit".

De Gaulle in his memoirs remains taciturn. Yet, from what has become known since, it seems that he was always in two minds about the whole operation. Why then, despite the lengths to which he was prepared to go to receive Si Salah in Paris, did he let him drop in favour of pursuing, in the words of Jacquin, "the bird in the bush, rather than the one in the hand"? As ever, the motives are complex. Perhaps one explanation can be found in de Gaulle's remark to Pinay at the time of the secret F.L.N. initiative of 1959: "But who are they, who nominated them?" The sense of hierarchy, of order and degree was always strong in de Gaulle. Though for public consumption he could state that he would not negotiate with the G.P.R.A. as such, by the summer of 1960 he seems increasingly to have accepted it in his own mind as an "establishment" body. It was also his character to find distasteful anything that smacked of the turncoat, of double-agentry, of *la bleuite*. As Tricot remarked to the author, there was a curious, and revealing, fact that de Gaulle could never bring himself to congratulate the *harkis*, the Algerians fighting for France against their own kindred, at terrible risk to themselves. This was not, in his lights, a strictly honourable function. Suspicious by nature ("One must be suspicious when one is surrounded by troubles," he said to Harold Macmillan as far back as 1942), he instinctively mistrusted the claims of French secret intelligence; and here the story of Azedine could only lend further substance to de Gaulle's mistrust.

According to Bernard Tricot, de Gaulle's wider strategy was as follows: "If Tunis replied in a negative or dilatory fashion to the 14 June speech, the negotiations for a partial cease-fire would be resumed. If, on the contrary, the G.P.R.A. appeared to commit itself genuinely along the road to peace, the leaders of Wilaya 4 would suspend negotiations." This seems curiously naïve, and totally insensitive to the intolerable danger to which Si Salah and his fellow "renegades" would thus be submitted. But the whole truth may not have been quite so guileless. On the basis of information provided by Krim after the war, General Jacquin insists that on 26 March – only a few days after the first contacts had been taken up with Si Salah, under a veil of total secrecy – Krim received a "leak" from the French government revealing that Wilaya 4 was proposing a separate cease-fire. Thus it seems that de Gaulle may throughout have regarded "Operation Tilsit" chiefly as a powerful lever with which to prise the G.P.R.A. into negotiations on his terms – the glistening goal which had eluded him all along.* The implied menace was clear; either deal with me for a cease-fire, or I will conclude a separate peace with your subordinates.

On the other hand, de Gaulle himself was under strong counter-pressures at approximately this time. In May 1960 Krim and Boussouf were on their way back from the most high-powered and successful visit that the F.L.N. had yet made to Peking and Moscow, accompanied by well-publicised promises of greatly augmented support from the Communist bloc. As always, there was nothing which made de Gaulle more nervous than the fear of being caught in a Communist pincer in Algeria. Thus, here was a Machiavellian political game, with both de Gaulle and the G.P.R.A. playing for higher stakes than Si Salah; and with success almost bound to make inevitable the sacrifice of the pawns who had put their trust in de Gaulle. Who would win? And would the ends justify the means?

Melun

The G.P.R.A.'s response to de Gaulle's broadcast of 14 June was significantly swift. Within the week had come their acceptance; on the 25th the first F.L.N. delegation ever to fly openly to France to discuss peace arrived at Orly, enveloped in massive security precautions. Leading them were the youthful and quick-witted Ben Yahia and Maître Ahmed Boumendjel, a gallicised lawyer well-known to the Paris Bar, who had joined the F.L.N. following the "suicide" of his brother, Ali, during the Battle of Algiers. Boumendjel, a portly figure exuding bonhomie, epitomised the cheerful self-confidence the Algerians displayed on arrival. At the head of the receiving delegation was Roger Moris, de Gaulle's Secretary-General for Algerian Affairs, supported by Colonel Mathon, who had been so closely involved in "Operation Tilsit". Moris was not perhaps the happiest of choices, in that he was generally regarded as an apostle of Algérie française. The Algerians were conducted to the Louis XIII prefecture in the nearby town of Melun, where, in the words of Boumendjel, they were kept as in a "golden cage". Sleeping, eating and conferring in the prefecture, over the

---

* This was reinforced by Abdelkader Chanderli, who declared categorically to the author (in 1973) that the Si Salah episode was "just an aberration. De Gaulle had absolutely no intention of dealing with Si Salah; though Si Salah was an honest man and thought he was acting for the best."

ensuing five days they were not permitted to leave its grounds, or have any contact with the journalists clustered outside the iron railings – de Gaulle having decreed a total Press silence. The only link allowed with the outer world was a direct telephone line to the G.P.R.A. in Tunis; there was absolutely no question of any communication with Ben Bella in his "golden cage". The Algerians felt they were treated throughout with a certain arrogance by de Gaulle, to whom their French opposite numbers reported back each evening.

Under these auspices the conference opened unhopefully with each side repeating its own well-worn and mutually irreconcilable formulas for peace. The one was a step-by-step approach, with the French insisting that a cease-fire must precede negotiations; the other global, declaring with equal rigidity that a cease-fire could not be regarded separately from an overall political settlement. De Gaulle was swiftly disabused of any hopes that the emissaries had come prepared for a speedy acceptance of his *drapeau blanc* when Boumendjel demanded that there should now be direct talks between de Gaulle himself and Ferhat Abbas – or, preferably, a liberated Ben Bella. Apart from offending the niceties of French diplomatic custom, which required elaborate preparations in advance of such a "summit", it was clear to de Gaulle that this was but a skilful move to gain *de facto* recognition for the G.P.R.A. A frosty refusal was passed down from Olympus: how could there be such concessions while murders and ambushes continued in Algeria? Next, the Algerians requested that at least a member of the French government of ministerial rank should take part in the talks. After four days of the deaf speaking to the deaf, de Gaulle unilaterally broke off the talks. On the 29th the Algerians departed in a cold but courteously correct atmosphere. The following week Ferhat Abbas was declaring in the language of the hard-liners: "Independence is not offered, it is seized.... The war may still continue a long time." As the logical diplomatic follow-up, fresh threats of the F.L.N. turning its face further towards the Eastern bloc were soon in the air, with Abbas explaining: "We would rather defend ourselves with Chinese arms than allow ourselves to be killed by the arms of the West...."

Whichever way one may look at it, Melun was a total defeat for de Gaulle, while it gave the F.L.N. their second political victory of the year – if "Barricades Week" may be reckoned the first. As seen by the uncommitted Muslims of Algeria, the G.P.R.A. had been *invited* by de Gaulle, but it was on *their* initiative that they had returned home – both sure signs of strength. From this moment, claims Philippe Tripier, they "adopted an equivocal attitude" towards de Gaulle, attributing to him "the posture of the defeated". To the French investors on whom Delouvrier counted for the realisation of the Constantine Plan, the mere fact that de Gaulle had begun negotiations at all was a major deterrent, while, to the "silent majority" in France as a whole the fact that they had failed came as an unmistakable disappointment. Despite de Gaulle's clamp-down on Press coverage, the F.L.N. – consonant with its untiring pursuit of "externalising the war" – had gained another valuable world platform and much beneficial publicity. Though de Gaulle might continue to protest that he would not recognise the G.P.R.A. as a negotiating partner, by the mere presence of its emissaries at Melun it had got a first foot in the door which de Gaulle would never be able to dislodge. This was what, from his prison cell, Ait Ahmed had perceptively predicted, and urged upon the G.P.R.A., some six months earlier (and it was a lesson that was certainly not lost upon the negotiators of North Vietnam in their tediously protracted appearances in Paris over a decade later). Seen in the perspective of time, it seems clear that – although Ferhat Abbas might still have desired purposeful negotiations in that summer of 1960 – the G.P.R.A. had come to Paris with no other intention than to place its foot in the door, and then withdraw leaving it there.

No, there had been one other intention – to recoup from the Si Salah affair.

In both respects this strategy of the G.P.R.A. "hard-liners" succeeded admirably, drawing de Gaulle into a cunningly laid trap. De Gaulle seems to have totally miscalculated the hand he felt had been dealt him by "Operation Tilsit", and it may well have been one of the most disastrous miscalculations of the whole war – on a number of levels. Certainly, as far as any aim of using Si Salah as a lever to bring the G.P.R.A. to the conference table was concerned, de Gaulle fell dismally between two stools – losing Si Salah and gaining nothing from the other. Just how much might have been achieved by "Operation Tilsit" remains a matter of bitter controversy between the senior army officers concerned in it and those close to de Gaulle, like Bernard Tricot. The former claim it to be one of the capital events of the war, a full vindication of the Challe strategy. If carried through, they say, it could at its lowest have resulted in creating a "hole" right in the geographical centre of the revolt, covering a third of the area of Algeria and splitting the east from the west. At its highest, it would have deprived the F.L.N. of any claim to be the sole representative of nationalist Algeria, and have led eventually to a separate peace on terms permitting the continued existence of the *présence française*.* And once the fighting war had died away in the "interior", it would be extremely difficult to rekindle. Algeria might have been spared more than a year of war.

Whether these arguments are realistic or not is almost less important

* It should be noted here, however, that the Wilaya 4 leaders in their remarks about ending "European domination" were clearly envisaging the attainment of majority rule, and not any return to the *status quo ante* of 1954.

than the fact that General Challe, in particular, believed them and they were to play a decisive role in his own future actions. As Yves Courrière remarks, the Si Salah fiasco "was the point of departure for what, less than a year later, was to be called the Revolt of the Generals. For them, following his meeting with Si Salah, de Gaulle committed an act of betrayal on 14 June 1960."

Though the whole Si Salah* and Melun episode was far from being de Gaulle's finest hour, coming so soon after his precarious recovery from "the Barricades", it goes some way to illustrate both the complexities of the pressures upon him, as well as the essential loneliness of his position. There was one final point: whatever the potential of Si Salah, by renouncing him in favour of talks with the G.P.R.A. emissaries, de Gaulle was in effect dealing, on behalf of the G.P.R.A., yet another blow at the evanescent "third force" in Algeria. Even if he had just intended to use Si Salah as the lever to make the G.P.R.A. negotiate, the fact of their accepting it meant that de Gaulle – regardless of his protests to the contrary – would eventually be forced to negotiate solely with the F.L.N., because there would be no one else, no other *interlocuteur valable*. Thus, from "Tilsit" and Melun onwards the battle between France and the F.L.N. now began to depart from the blood-stained *bled* of Algeria for higher realms of politics and diplomacy.

---

* In November 1984, to mark the 30th anniversary of the opening of the "Algerian War of National Liberation", President Chadli Bendjedid decreed an act of amnesty embracing posthumously some fifty F.L.N. leaders who had fallen prey to internal dispute, both during and after the war. Prominent among these was Si Salah. At the time of the 1984 amnesty, among Algerian veterans knowledgeable about the episode, the author was also able to meet the son of Si Salah (alias Zamoun) himself. He was eight at the time of his father's death and anxious to ascertain the precise facts surrounding it. It is now accepted that, in the first place, the grievances of Si Salah and Wilaya 4 against Boumedienne's "exterior" were real indeed. Secondly, Si Salah on his return from Paris was *not* (as surmised on p. 393) killed by a French patrol. Instead it appears that, after spending nearly a whole year in semi-captivity, Si Salah was executed on the orders of Boumedienne and the G.P.R.A. As of 1984, the official view of Si Salah seems to be an essentially tragic one; he had breached discipline in treating with the French, but was no traitor – simply a victim of the wiles of de Gaulle at his most Machiavellian. Such revelations about the inner workings of the F.L.N. could certainly not have been made in 1973, while Boumedienne was still alive.

CHAPTER NINETEEN

Revolution in the Revolution

There are only two powers in the world ... the sword and the spirit. In the long run, the sword is always defeated by the spirit. ...

Napoleon Bonaparte

In the maquis: a grim struggle for survival

ALTHOUGH the two consecutive halves of the Vietnam war may have continued longer, in the post-1945 world no "war of liberation" has combined so long a duration with such a disproportion of logistics as the Algerian war. Because of the natural taciturnity and stoicism of the Algerian, all too little is known in the Western world of the suffering endured in the maquis by the forces of the interior. But it is reasonable to surmise that not many other peoples could have withstood better six such grim years of unrelenting hardship. It was also no accident that the end of the winter of 1960 had brought with it the Si Salah offer of a separate peace; for in more than one region of the interior the Challe offensive had reduced the maquisards to the limits of endurance. In the rugged Atlas highlands of Algeria winter can be as bitter as anywhere on earth; and it is made all the more penetrating by the extremes of heat that precede it and the lack of acclimatisation of those subjected to it. And the winter of 1960 was a particularly harsh one. Some of the rare films of the period show grim scenes reminiscent of the worst moments of the Yugoslav partisan war of 1941–5. Haggard remnants of broken *katibas* huddled over meagre fires in their mountain hideouts, while young children attempted to melt snow in steel helmets. Often the proximity of Challe's Commandos de Chasse prowling only a few hundred yards distant made it impossible to light any fire at all for days on end. There was always a shortage of warm clothing and, worse still, of food. Cut off from contact with Muslim villagers, sometimes the maquisards would endeavour to track the trackers themselves in the desperate hope of gleaning a few crusts of bread or other rations abandoned by the French. Under these circumstances nourishment would consist of nothing more than a cold gruel of wheat kernels and grass. Under the strain of being constantly pursued, and of being forced to speak in whispers perhaps for weeks on end for fear of betraying themselves to the enemy, seasoned fighters not infrequently broke down and became demented.

Possibly even worse than the tribulations of cold and hunger was the appalling suffering of the F.L.N. wounded. Unlike their well-equipped adversary, the maquisards had no helicopters with which to whisk casualties from the battlefield to a modern operating theatre in a matter of minutes. There were times when the F.L.N. wounded had to wait ten days or more before their wounds, by then probably gangrenous, could be tended. On one occasion in 1960 a young lieutenant of Si Salah's, Boualem Oussedik, despatched on an urgent liaison mission to Tunisia, was caught up in a *ratissage* on the way and had his knee shattered by a bullet. An F.L.N. doctor told him that, without proper surgery, he would lose the leg, but Boualem refused, taking with him a supply of antibiotics to tend his own wound. Bouncing about in agony astride a donkey and finally dragging his useless leg behind him under shellfire through the Morice Line, Boualem with extraordinary stoicism took six weeks to complete his journey. He survived, kept his leg, and together with another *grand mutilé*, Azedine, was to lead the last battles in Algiers. But many another wounded *moudjahid* succumbed to his wounds before he could receive treatment.

That any medical services could be organised at all under the conditions of the war was a miracle in itself. "Hospitals" would generally be sited deep in the interior of dense forests, well camouflaged from the air, near a clean stream. The wounded would be scattered about in rough shelters, lying on straw matting on the ground, with the rare mattresses reserved for only the most serious cases. Drugs and medicaments, more precious than gold, would be concealed in safe caches some distance from the "hospital", so as not to fall into enemy hands in the event of the whole encampment being forced to strike camp and move, dragging the wounded with them. Well-organised networks throughout the Wilaya were responsible for the collection of drugs, smuggled out from F.L.N. pharmacists in the cities, run at great risk through the Morice Line, or stolen from French hospitals – despite elaborate controls to prevent their reaching the F.L.N. Even so there was always a tragic shortage, with amputations all too frequently performed, without anaesthetic, by an ordinary hack-saw sterilised in a flame. Qualified doctors and nurses were equally short. Sometimes the deficit was made up by *pied noir* sympathisers with the F.L.N. like Dr Pierre Chaulet who, on being forced to flee from Algeria, continued his practice in Tunisia, tending the F.L.N. sick and wounded at the frontier posts. A number of doctors were Muslim women – like Dr Nefissa Hamoud, a petite Algiers pediatrician in her early thirties. The first woman to join the F.L.N. medical service in the field early in the war, captured by the French and released again, apparently because of her influential connections, she immediately rejoined the A.L.N. With considerable ingenuity medical and nursing "schools" were established inside each Wilaya, and more and more young Algerian women began to appear in the khaki uniform of *sanitaires* – sometimes, initially, to the shocked disapproval of the more conservative Muslim *moudjahiddine*. Nevertheless, despite the F.L.N.'s efforts and enterprise, their rudimentary field hospitals of the interior could all too seldom cope with the terrible injuries inflicted by modern warfare, above all the massive burns caused by napalm. Thus the percentage of fatalities among the wounded remained depressingly high throughout the war.

... but the political revolution thrives

As hardship and casualties compounded took an increasing toll of the battle-trained *moudjahiddine*, their replacements – often drafted direct from the *fidayine*, or village militia, because nothing but a trickle of re-inforcements was getting through the Morice Line – showed a distinct drop in combat value. By the time of the Melun negotiations in the middle of 1960, war-weariness and a defensive mentality had made their greatest impact on the interior and, from the A.L.N.'s point of view, the war was definitely running down. Therefore, on this tangible and readily discern-ible evidence Challe could well claim to have been proved right in all his calculations. Yet, paradoxically, while the armed rebellion might be seen to be "withering away", at the same time the political imprint of the revolution was imposing itself more and more indelibly on the population. As the *katibas* disintegrated under Challe's pressure, their members would filter back to their own villages and often, far from abandoning the cause, they would there reinforce the political struggle by establishing new clandestine cells under the Organisation Politico-Administrative. There was, indeed, a growing resemblance to "that algae which always comes back in the acquariums", as Lartéguy's "Boisfeuras" had seen it. Gradually, also, in a number of ways the long years of war had fundamentally infected the lives of the vast majority of Algerian Muslims, despite all the earnest and real efforts of psychological and political warfare made by successive French administrations and their S.A.S. detachments. That simple, cheap and ubiquitous miracle of the modern age, the transistor radio, had brought the war into the most remote Algerian homestead. To possess a transistor, says Frantz Fanon, "was solemnly to enter into the war". Already by 1959 more than five separate stations, located safely abroad, were beaming their transmissions to Algeria, so that millions of families could hardly avoid following the course of the revolution, discussing it and arguing over it among themselves.

The family and Muslim women at war

It was at that tight-bound, highly conservative and sacrosanct unit of Muslim life, the family, that the revolution had perhaps struck hardest.

Obviously first-hand contact with the atrocities of war had the most direct effect. Fanon relates a case of a father beaten up in the street by troops in front of his children, then interned, his wife forced to take over and fend for the headless family; and of the young taxi driver who, after his wife had been raped, became impotent and suffered from repeated obsessive nightmares about his one-year-old baby transmuted into a dead and rotting cat. But the strictly hierarchical structure of the family was also affected in less dramatic ways. A father might, naturally, take the more traditionalist line that the French were stronger, and would always win, to dissuade a son from joining the F.L.N.; but when the son disobeyed nevertheless, the father eventually "discovered that the only way of remaining upright was to rejoin his son"; or, says Fanon, there were the grievous occasions, shattering to family unity, when a son might have to be present at the trial of a father guilty of renouncing, or "betraying", the revolution. Then there were the cases of a militant wife castigating, or even breaking with, a husband condemned of cowardice in her eyes through not going off into the maquis.

"The Mediterranean woman", says Germaine Tillion, "is one of the serfs of the contemporary world." In the register of this serfdom the Algerian female stood very low down the scale, and it would be hard to find any other aspect of life more profoundly affected by the coming of the Algerian revolution. Because of her traditional seclusion inside her house and behind her *haik*, hitherto the Algerian woman had always remained more immune to French culture and social penetration than her menfolk; thus, when the revolt began, in many a household it was the woman who provided a hard nucleus of anti-colonial militancy. According to Fanon, she would use her *haik* as a weapon of war, wearing it as a symbol of resistance against the infidel "occupier"; then dropping it when called upon to mingle among *pied noir* crowds and carry bombs for Yacef and his terrorists; next resuming it when (following that brief day of fraternisation in May 1958) French psychological warfare experts had endeavoured to exploit unveiling and emancipation as a means of weaning the women away from the F.L.N. (or, says Fanon, of striking "at the culture of the male Algerian"). As far as emancipation was concerned, the Algerian woman had much to gain from the war – from both sides.

Even though, by the beginning of the war, polygamy was becoming rare in Algeria, in general women's rights remained deplorably medieval. For the young Algerian girl life tended to hold but two stages; childhood – and puberty, which meant marriage (usually in her early teens). The espousal would be arranged by the families, and it was not unusual for the couple to meet each other only on the day of the wedding. It was hard for a young girl to find any employment outside marriage, so that the longer she remained unmarried the more of an economic embarrassment she was to her family.

Divorce, or "repudiation", was easy, brutal and total – for the male. Matters were worst in Kabylia, where conditions for women were the most inequitable in all the Maghreb. Although permitted the superficial privilege of freedom to walk about unveiled, with inheritance limited strictly to the male a repudiated Kabyle wife could be turned out of her husband's house, deprived of her children and the dowry which her father had put up at the time of marriage, and forbidden by her divorcing husband to marry again – or allowed to do so only upon payment of a certain sum.

Hesitantly, because fearful of offending the "chauvinist" sensibilities of the Muslim male, French administrators made groping moves towards emancipation; at the referendum of September 1958 a major success was registered when something like eighty per cent of Muslim women turned up at the polls. On the other hand, the women left behind by their menfolk in "rebel" *douars* all too often had the French "pacifiers" to reproach for their excessive suffering. Mouloud Feraoun writes angrily of the women of his native Kabylia carrying the cross of villages emptied of men: dying at the hands of the rebels if they betrayed them to the French, or arrested and perhaps tortured by the French for helping the rebels. Rape, if one is to believe Algerian sources, assumed appalling proportions and left permanent psychological scars among the female population. All in all, the F.L.N. seemed to have far more to offer Muslim womanhood by way of an escape from thraldom than the French.

Fanon speaks of the "intense drama" of the sudden coming to maturity of the Algerian woman when drafted into the revolt. They were carefully vetted: first, married women whose husbands were militants; then widows and divorcees; single girls were rejected initially, because of the difficulty they encountered in leaving the home, but they too eventually became involved. "For months on end", writes Fanon, "parents would be without news of a young girl of eighteen who was sleeping in the forest or in caves, roaming the *djebel* dressed as a man, a gun in her hands." Here, for the first time, she met and coexisted with unmarried men on equal terms, and with equal rights. She adapted herself to guerrilla activities with remarkable speed and effectiveness. It was a heady experience: "The woman ceased to be a mere complement for the man. Indeed it might be said that she had pulled up her roots through her own exertions," says Fanon. The female recruits for the A.L.N. were not just limited to the *évoluées*, young intellectuals used by Yacef to place bombs during the Battle of Algiers, but they came from many walks of life. On occasions the role of the female in the egalitarianism of the maquis was viewed with mistrust by the more traditionalist *moudjahiddine*. "The Angel and the Man work for unity; Satan and the Woman for division," an Algerian proverb declares contemptuously. Sometimes she would be allotted little more than a propaganda function; nevertheless, on the whole the F.L.N. woman was treated with a respect never experienced before – either from her own menfolk or from even the most liberal French emancipators. Discipline was strict; as in many guerrilla movements, illicit sexual relations were ruthlessly punishable by death. For the women, perhaps even more than for the F.L.N. men, revolution and the pursuit of independence – with the promise of personal liberation at the end of the road – became an irrecusable way of life. (Alas, the promissory notes issued then in the heat of battle have yet to be fully honoured.)

Revolutionary schooling

The capture of the minds of the young, and indeed the very young, has to be one of the primary objectives of any revolution. As Mouloud Feraoun illustrates in his moving novel, *Le Fils du Pauvre*, the Algerian schools were always of capital importance in the breeding of national consciousness. The burning of new schoolhouses, proudly built by the French as part of their "cultural offensive" against the F.L.N., the terrorising of "loyal" school-teachers – these were seldom random acts of savagery. Gloomily Soustelle records a conversation during his tenure of office between an F.L.N. leader and a teacher: "We shall not cease, even after we have thrown all the French into the sea. We shall destroy all the schools because they represent the French culture, which we want nothing of." Somehow, as with their "hospitals" in the maquis, the F.L.N. managed to establish and maintain their own schools, fighting illiteracy, providing "evening courses" for adults, and keeping up the pressure of indoctrination on Muslim children. Whole new interpretations of history were introduced, sometimes going to excess in their zeal to revise the French version of the colonial past. For example, in 1830, "the Mitidja was not a barren pestiferous swamp, but a cultivated region"; "literacy was higher in Algeria [because of the many religious schools] than in France of the same period [!]", and so on. To what extent the F.L.N. was winning the battle for young minds was graphically revealed in essays shown the author by Germaine Tillion, written by ten-year-old Algerian children in answer to the question: "What would you do if you were invisible?" – a topic brightly suggested to the 22-year-old French teacher on a recent "psychological education course". Composed (with illustrations) spontaneously in the classroom, and not as homework under parental influence, the pupils wrote:

"I'd rob a French bank. . . ."

"I'd kill French soldiers; even the Zouaves. . . ."

"I'd steal my mother's sugar to make a bomb. . . ."

And so on.*

* The French army's well-intentioned efforts at psychological counter-propaganda had its absurd aspects, especially in the early days. Jean Servier recalls that when he revisited Kabylia in 1956, "Donald Duck" was being shown in English to utterly dumbfounded villagers.

This was in 1957. Four years later Richard and Joan Brace, two Americans invited by the F.L.N. to inspect refugee camps in Tunisia, noted in the boys' dormitories:

> faded and cherished newspaper clippings tacked to his wall telling the fate of one or another Algerian hero . . . the closed, tough little face of Krim, looking like a gangster from a George Raft movie, more often than not it was the prisoners of Aulnoy – Ben Bella, Boudiaf, Ait Ahmed, Khider, and Rabah Bitat – dressed in casual clothes and holding hunting guns, snapped during some happier time.

Many of the children were orphans; one ten-year-old, Mustapha from Tébessa, had seen his parents shot down in front of him, one after the other, by French soldiers when he was seven. He claimed that they had then tortured him, burning his arm on a stove, and added fiercely:

> I will burn them as they burned me. I will not burn a child, however, because the children haven't done anything wrong. Those who burned me, however, I will make suffer, and I will kill them. And I will not ever forget those who burned me; even if they come and ask my pardon, I won't pardon them.

Since 1954, alleges Frantz Fanon, common crime among Algerians had almost disappeared, for "the national conflict seems to have canalised all anger". Certainly, after six years of war, hatred and violence and their habit had become etched deep into souls, deeper than could be excoriated by any amount of purely military successes.

F.L.N. ideology: Marxist or home-grown?

"I will not die for the Algerian nation, because it does not exist." So an anguished young Ferhat Abbas had cried in the 1930s on being unable to discover an Algerian fatherland. In place of a nation a whole ethos had had to be created from 1954 onwards. When furnishing itself with a provisional constitution at the Third C.N.R.A. of January 1960, the G.P.R.A. had declared: "At the same time that it is conducting the war of liberation, the F.L.N. is also directing a revolution. . . ." Thereby "revolution" had been made statutory. But what now were its ideological well-springs? Was it Marxist–Communist, as the French colonels of the Cinquième Bureau so often proclaimed in their endeavours to frighten successive regimes in Paris with the bogey of "the Soviet Navy at Mers-el-Kébir"?

It will be recalled that the F.L.N. had sent its first team to Peking and Moscow in December 1958, gained a warm reception from the Chinese and promises of two milliard francs' worth of arms, but coolness and no firm promises from the Russians. The initiative had been proposed by Ben Khedda, who led both the first delegation and its successor in September 1959. Ben Khedda, the convert from Messali's M.N.A., was generally regarded to be ideologically the most Marxist-orientated of the F.L.N. leaders, but he never belonged to their inner circle. China was among the first countries to recognise the G.P.R.A. in September 1958, while a somewhat grudging recognition was not forthcoming from Moscow until more than two years later. A more powerful delegation to Peking and Moscow had been led by Krim (in his new capacity of Foreign Minister), Boussouf and Ahmed Francis at the end of April 1960, which had included side-trips to North Vietnam and North Korea. Again, a rapturous welcome from tens of thousands of cheering Chinese (plus offers to supply more arms than all the Arab world put together) contrasted with a coolly, diplomatically correct reception in Moscow. Five months later Ferhat Abbas was being received officially, as president of the G.P.R.A., in both Communist capitals; in Peking his visit happened to coincide with the celebrations of the tenth anniversary of the Chinese Revolution, and Abbas was placed ostentatiously as guest-of-honour at Mao's right; in Moscow he managed to extract *de facto* recognition but little else – except for a promise to supply arms once the G.P.R.A. was in control of a piece of "liberated" Algerian territory – a highly unlikely prospect in the prevailing military state of the war.

On his return from the Communist bloc, and following the deadlock at Melun, Krim warned the West – with considerable diplomatic skill – that Algeria was appealing for military assistance from the East, "including rockets", and after his visits in the autumn of 1960 Abbas was telling the *New York Times* how he expected Chinese and Soviet arms deliveries to be substantially increased. Privately, in all their dealings the Algerian delegates had insisted that there should be no political strings attached, and it was clear that – even more than the actual arms supplies themselves (which never lived up to promises made) – the F.L.N. primarily valued their relationship with Peking and Moscow for the pressure it applied upon France, both directly and through the medium of her nervous Western allies.

The coolness of the U.S.S.R. towards the Algerian revolution had several motives. In the first place they were committed to support the French Communist Party and its sister in Algeria, the P.C.A., both of whom had ambivalent attitudes in that they in turn were committed to support the *petit pied noir* workers, as well as the largely anti-Algerian workers of metropolitan France. Secondly, the advent of de Gaulle and his threats to break up the Atlantic Alliance persuaded the Kremlin that its longer-term interests lay better in doing nothing that might seriously upset de Gaulle. Thirdly, in its espousal of the new Khrushchev doctrine of "peaceful coexistence", the Kremlin was compelled to pay lip-service to condemning violent revolution as "infantile disorders"; and, fourthly, it was increasingly clear that the F.L.N. was throughout a nationalist and not a Marxist liberation movement, and showed few signs of becoming one. In turn, the coolness of the Soviets was to freeze any inclination the F.L.N. might otherwise have nurtured for Soviet Communism, leaving it with a mistrust and an aversion that would linger significantly into the post-war Algerian world.

Quoting Fidel Castro, Régis Debray says: "that there is no revolution without a vanguard; that this vanguard is not necessarily the Marxist–Leninist party". This was certainly true of the Algerian revolution; but it was not even to succumb to Marxism–Leninism in the aftermath of war – in contrast to Cuba, and despite Boumedienne's close friendship and admiration for Castro. Perhaps because of the language and proximity, the F.L.N. was always strongly influenced by the French Resistance, but if there was one Communist country – apart from Maoist China – with whose revolutionary struggle they felt a particularly warm identity, it was Tito's Yugoslavia. From the earliest days, the Yugoslavs had given the F.L.N. staunch support both in arms and on international platforms; they were of the approved "third world", not representing the massive, monolithic menace of the Soviet system; they did not thrust their ideology at the F.L.N.; and their brand of decentralised Socialism was not unappealing to the Algerians. In the style of the war of liberation there was also some kinship with the partisans' experiences of 1941–5; the F.L.N. had been waging simultaneously a "war within a war" against the M.N.A., just as Tito had had his parallel struggle against the Četniks of Mihailović; but, above all, both sets of revolutionaries were to emerge proclaiming in victory that they had won through their own courage and largely on their own resources, without "foreign" intervention. The mere fact of the Algerians' proud insistence that their war of liberation was an act of pure nationalism, borrowed from no one else's, is of itself a further point of comparison (though where it ends, of course, is that the F.L.N. never had – and as a matter of principle refused to have – a Tito).

The fact is that, despite contemporary French claims to the contrary, Communism exerted but little influence on the F.L.N. war effort. As Abbas told a French Marxist towards the end of the war, "these Communists give people bread to eat, and that's good; but man does not live by bread alone. We're Muslims, you see, we believe in God, we want to elevate their minds; the mind must be nourished too." Marxist materialism was at least as alien to the F.L.N. ethos as were other external Arab ideologies such as Moroccan monarchism, Tunisian Bourguibism, or Egyptian Nasserism. The F.L.N. had always been quite unyielding in never accepting Communists into their ranks as a "block membership"; if they came, they came as individuals, forswearing all former allegiances. The Communist world was, if anything, more exploited than exploiting; as Edgar O'Ballance aptly remarks: "The F.L.N. outsmarted the Communists all along the line by taking all it could from them, and then playing them off at their own game."

Although, because of the all-smothering blanket of secretiveness, it is hard to be categoric, the impression one has is that in general the wartime debates and dissents within the F.L.N. were far more a matter of personalities than of ideologies. Most of the leaders were men of simple learning. There was a paucity of well-read intelligentsia; few, like Boumedienne, had university educations, and they tended to be indoctrinated in Islamic rather than Marxist thought. Essentially inward-looking, the F.L.N. leaders as a whole do not impress one as having been well-read on revolutionary practice and theory; if they had absorbed the techniques of the Viet-Minh, it was through the direct experiences some had had as members of the ill-fated French forces in Indo-China. In reading *El Moudjahid*, once one has scraped away the thick gravy layers of propaganda, one finds little serious discussion of social aims of the future Algerian society, and this was especially so from the death of the super-political Abane onwards. The frustration of Abane's hopes for a "dynamic" revolution on the Viet-Minh pattern was also exacerbated by the ever-increasing isolation of the "interior" from "exterior". Communication between the two, constantly preoccupied with matters of sheer military survival, gave but little time for ideological speculation. But as the years rolled by the revolution did develop pragmatically it own social face. It was an austere one, materialistically and religiously, and borrowed more from the theological teachings of the interwar Ulema than from Karl Marx. Characteristically, the F.L.N. never offered prosperity, liberty or the pursuit of happiness as planks in its programme. Its leaders profoundly disapproved of Bourguibism, not just on account of its "cult of the personality" but also for its emphasis on the merits of bourgeois free enterprise. When one declared to the Braces, "We are not Communists, but we are *not* fighting and dying for a bourgeois capitalist state which will only benefit a few people," he could hardly have taken a more representative line.

On certain projected and far-reaching social reforms the F.L.N. had remained steadfastly consistent from the Soummam Declaration onwards; one of these was agrarian reform and land redistribution, which – combined with the high promises and sadly inadequate achievements of successive French programmes – made a progressively powerful impact on rural Algeria. With the revolt beginning in the country rather than in the cities, with educated urban rebels flowing to the *bled* in refuge from Algiers, a profound revolution had taken place in the traditionally conservative consciousness of agrarian Algeria, lying deeper than the devoted French S.A.S. administrators could gauge, let alone reverse. After only two years of war, in 1957 Germaine Tillion had noted pessimistically how almost the whole of Muslim society in Algeria was "to be found solidly, and efficaciously enclosed within a clandestine framework". Though this "framework" had only come into being with the insurrection, it almost gave the impression "that these invisible cadres, a powerful weapon of war, had been prepared for a long time". She had criticised then the failure of French politicians "not to comprehend the irreversible character of the movement which was accomplishing itself in the silent depths of the people who had neither newspapers nor representatives". On returning to her beloved Algeria some four years later, Germaine Tillion observed how, out of those "silent depths", had arisen a "national unitary, Algerian consciousness" through six years of war, which reminded her of the German unity achieved as a result of the Napoleonic wars. It was, she reckoned, "a trump card for the Algeria of tomorrow".

Proof that this kind of national consciousness existed, and of the control which the geographically absent G.P.R.A. exerted now over the Algerian people, was detectable in the local elections held in May 1960 where, though still mainly supporting de Gaulle, only fifty-six per cent of the electorate voted; while in the Casbah of Algiers the turn-out was down to thirty per cent, and in Sétif (the home town of Ferhat Abbas) to only fourteen per cent. Then, at the end of that year, further evidence was to be forthcoming in a manner even more dramatic – and discountenancing to de Gaulle.

Neutralising the "Bao-Dais"

The more one studies the Algerian revolution, the more one comes to realise how well the F.L.N. leadership succeeded in spinning an impenetrable cocoon of secrecy around the incessant rifts and dissents at the top (and it may well contain a lesson for the West in its present-day fits of political self-destruction). Much as the maquisards of the "interior" may have railed and raged at the "exterior" in its failure to furnish military replenishment, to the Muslim masses of Algeria the mere appearance of this seemingly unruffled, undivided and unrelenting façade was immeasurably heartening and encouraging, and probably did more to keep the flame of the revolution alight than a steady flow of dozens of fresh katibas across the Morice Line would have done. The moral effect of the Melun talks and their skilful exploitation by the G.P.R.A. has already been indicated, and this in turn was more grist to the mill of the hard-liners. Their line of argument was that "self-determination" had been wrested from de Gaulle simply by five years of remorseless violence initiated by the F.L.N. – not by the softer methods of Abbas or Messali. The direct consequence of "self-determination" had been the negotiating table at Melun. And who had sat at it with the representatives of the French government? Not the men of Messali or Abbas, but delegates selected by the F.L.N.

Early in November 1960 three leaders of French Black Africa had an interview with de Gaulle to discuss Algerian solutions. A few days later they were in Tunis, relaying to ministers of the G.P.R.A. de Gaulle's current preoccupation with finding "acceptable" leaders that might head an

"Algerian Algeria" of the future. This had at once thrown the Algerians into the normal state of agitation provoked whenever suspicions were aroused that de Gaulle was still looking around for that elusive "third force" to cut out the F.L.N. Ahmed Francis, the G.P.R.A. Minister of Finance and one of the older and more experienced members present, recalled how at the close of the Indo-China war the French had "produced out of a hat" the Annamite ex-Emperor Bao-Dai, whom they had then sought to impose as the "nationalist interlocutor" in preference to Ho Chi Minh. De Gaulle, warned Ahmed Francis, "would like to play the same trick on us again today.... And that's why our task is clear. We must, above all, neutralise the little Algerian Bao-Dais."

In fact, from the earliest days the F.L.N. had never let up on their ruthless campaign to "neutralise" the Bao-Dais that might have challenged their supremacy. There were the various Muslim "liberal" apostles of "association" returned in the elections since de Gaulle had come to power: courageous men whose heads, however, had been progressively kept down by selective outrages of terrorism. But still the principal foes, the modern counterparts of Tito's Četniks, were the brother nationalists of the M.N.A. With the demise of the last private army under Bellounis, the M.N.A. had all but lost its last claim to bring revolution sprouting out of its gun muzzles, and inside Algeria it no longer carried much weight as a coherent political force. Yet always there existed the fear that de Gaulle would produce it "out of a hat", like Bao-Dai.

It was inside France, though – and particularly in the Paris area, where Messali had exerted a traditionally potent influence from the days of the antediluvian Étoile – that the M.N.A. remained strongest. Starting in 1957, a savage internecine war had raged between the two factions, which by 1960 had already claimed hundreds of dead among the 250,000 Algerian workers in the Paris region alone. In 1960 the killings reached a crescendo as the F.L.N. stepped up its campaign to achieve total ascendancy. Barely a day went by without a corpse fished out of the Seine, or found hanging in the Bois de Boulogne. A favourite place of reckoning was the quiet Canal Saint-Martin, flowing towards the Bastille in the east of Paris, which with hideous regularity yielded up its crop of sacks containing the disfigured bodies of Algerians. As during the Battle of Algiers, women were often employed as executioners' "liaisons"; they would take a pistol concealed in a handbag to the appointed place, slip it to the killer, then take it back immediately the deed was done, to disappear silently into the crowd. Under the blanket of terror successfully imposed by the F.L.N., the French police received a minimum of information – even from the relatives of victims – with which to track down the terrorists. Meanwhile, the perfected system of fund-raising was bringing in from the Paris region alone something like three hundred million francs a month.

As the F.L.N. campaign hit a peak in 1960, the Paris authorities launched a counter-offensive, adopting methods that had proved so successful in Algeria. A small group of "loyal" *harkis* was created in the capital who infiltrated among the Algerian *quartiers* to track down the F.L.N. operatives. Some spectacular shoot-ups ensued in the streets and alleys of Paris; on one occasion two terrorists who made their getaway in the *métro* were pursued from station to station by *harkis* commandeering the next train, and finally catching them. Within less than a year the *harkis* suffered twenty-four dead and sixty-seven wounded, but the results seemed to pay off. In the 13th Arrondissement alone fund collections dropped by a half after the first month, while from spring 1960 to the end of the war nearly 1,200 terrorists were rounded up, including four leaders of the F.L.N.'s metropolitan network.

Yet, even inside prison walls, these militants were far from being safely neutralised. Like the detention centres of Northern Ireland where I.R.A. members blatantly drilled and trained before the eyes of British troops, the French prisons were transformed into recruiting grounds and veritable staff-colleges for the F.L.N. At Fresnes prison, for example, holding 1,500 F.L.N. suspects, discipline was exerted not by the prison administration but by a committee under the direction of Bachir Boumaza, subsequently a minister in both the Ben Bella and Boumedienne governments. As F.L.N. spokesmen were fond of boasting to journalists at the time, "We have three O.P.A.s: one in action, a second in reserve and a third in prison". Prison – so revolutionaries from the early Bolsheviks onwards have discovered – provides the best of schools.

Jewish dilemmas

Finally, as the F.L.N. raised the pressure against the "non-conformists" ever more relentlessly, there was one particular community in Algeria which found itself most cruelly caught between the fires: the Algerian Jews. Over the long years of the colonial era anti-semitism had seldom raised its head among the Muslim population, but soon after the revolt began the F.L.N. was applying the screw upon the Jewish community to force it to declare itself. As with the other uncommitted groupings, the Jews found themselves subjected to the persuasion of terrorism and economic sanctions. Typical was this threatening letter to a Jewish shopkeeper in Algiers:

> Sir,
> If on Wednesday you do not hand us a sum of two million francs, which must be deposited in the hall of the building situated at 1 Rue d'Isly, Wednesday 7th before 16.45 hours, near the staircase at the end near the cupboard, your daughter will be abducted and will serve as a mattress for the army of liberation. Useless to put her in safety, we have our eyes on her.

If you do not follow our instructions, your shop will be blown up and we shall have your skins, yours and your wife's.

In the spring of 1956 a terrorist grenade attack in the Constantine ghetto had been followed by a nasty outbreak of inter-racial killings, which showed just how precarious the war had rendered coexistence between the two peoples. In March the following year Jacob Chekroun, the rabbi of Médéa, was assassinated on the steps of his synagogue, while the following month a boycott was imposed on the Jewish merchants of Tlemcen. And so the stick-and-carrot coercion had gone on, with the Jews being made to realise with brutal clarity as the prospects of an "Algerian Algeria" came ever closer that, if they were to have any future in it, they would have to throw in their lot decisively with the F.L.N. During the latter months of the war such proclamations as this were addressed to the "Israelites of Algeria":

> Your silence must cease and you must condemn such demonstrations organised in your quarters by the O.A.S.... many Israelites are militants in our ranks...the independence of Algeria is close, independent Algeria will have need of you, and tomorrow you will also have need of her as it is your country. Your Muslim brothers stretch out the hand frankly and loyally to you for solidarity coming from your side. IT IS YOUR DUTY TO REPLY TO THIS.

The menace was thinly veiled, with pressures leading to uncharacteristic divisions among the Jewish community. Members of the intelligentsia and of the left-wing parties joined forces with the F.L.N., while the commercial bourgeoisie either strove for neutrality or supported Algérie française. Even families were tragically riven; in the Lévy family of Algiers, the father would later be assassinated by the O.A.S. as a F.L.N. sympathiser, while his son was killed by the F.L.N. on suspicion of belonging to the O.A.S. Thus there was never any such thing as a united front, or collective policy, established by the Jews of Algeria; nevertheless, when the day of reckoning came, they were all to be lumped into the same boat – a boat that was never to return to Algeria.

Boumedienne consolidates

By the latter part of 1960 the F.L.N. looked supreme and politically unbeatable on the internal Algerian scene, and it could claim that un-compromising determination had made it so. With its two cardinal events of the *pied noir* revolt in "Barricades Week" and Melun (combined with the destruction of the dangerous separatist threat of Si Salah), 1960 was the year which saw the ascendance of the hard-liners within the F.L.N. It was also the year of Boumedienne's decisive consolidation of power within, and around, the army. The Comité Interministereal de Guerre, created at the Third C.N.R.A. in January largely to placate Krim's ruffled feelings, had remained a dead letter, with the newly-appointed army chief-of-staff swiftly taking over the reins. Although the C.N.R.A. had passed a solemn motion declaring that the war would be lost if no reinforcements could be got through to the "interior" in the course of the year, it was not Boumedienne's intention to follow in the footsteps of those French generals of the First World War. He was not going to let his army of the "exterior" be "bled white" in repeated vain attacks against an almost impregnable Line, against this ideal of a Maginot system which French ingenuity had at last perfected. Boumedienne's was a calculated risk which external political developments, notably de Gaulle's peace initiatives, were to vindicate.

With the same kind of ruthless efficiency that had brought him to note in his lower echelons of command, Boumedienne devoted himself to a rapid reorganisation of the A.L.N. The 12,000 men in Tunisia under control of Mohamedi Said, the old Abwehr agent with his inseparable coal-scuttle helmet, had degenerated into a state bordering on anarchy. In the boredom of inactivity some elements had taken to "mugging" local Tunisians, and one of Boumedienne's first acts was to have twenty of these, officers and men, shot in front of the troops. (According to Ben Bella after the war, blaming Boussouf, "thousands of men" had been killed in the course of these purges.) There was also trouble in the Moroccan-based A.L.N. where a Captain Zoubir had launched an insurrection a hundred strong; with the help of the Moroccan army it too had been crushed, but not before Boumedienne's forces had been more or less neutralised there for the best part of three months. To eradicate permanently this kind of indiscipline, Boumedienne introduced his own tough deputies – Azedine (the same much-wounded hero who had deceived his French captors in Wilaya 4), Slimane (alias Kaïd Ahmed) and Ali Mendjli – to weld the whole army closely under his personal control. Mendjli was a thirty-eight-year-old former café-owner, who had enlisted on the first day of the war, served as an officer in Wilaya 2, then left for Tunisia in 1958. He was as taciturn as his chief, Boumedienne, in contrast to the volubility and noisy rages of Slimane – a farmer and local dignitary from Tiaret who had commanded one of the zones of Wilaya 5 on the Moroccan frontier.

The General Staff itself was remodelled around four bureaux integrally copied from the French system, and these were placed in the charge of officers who had defected recently from the French army, bringing with them specialist know-how. Energetic training programmes were launched as the new and heavier weapons promised from the Communist bloc began to reach it. At the same time, clearly with an eye to the future, Boumedienne subjected the A.L.N. to intensive political education.

To staff officers in Tunisia Boumedienne disclosed his new military tactics a month after his assumption of office: the previous policy of periodic, massive breaching attempts on the Morice Line with their "decimating" losses was to be abandoned; liaison agents would still have to run the gauntlet through the Line to keep up contact with the "interior", but they would only go in small, highly trained packets, taking advantage of electric storms which fused the high-tension barrier. Using its increasing firepower, the A.L.N. would harass the French army with repeated, painful "pin-pricks", shelling and mortaring units from the safety of their Tunisian and Moroccan sanctuaries. This, Boumedienne reckoned with reason, would "freeze" on the frontiers substantial numbers of French troops – thereby granting the hard-pressed "interior" as much relief as the reinforcements that could be run through to them at appalling and unacceptable cost. Meanwhile, the "interior" was instructed to maintain a low profile; to refuse combat in the face of continuing French *ratissages*; to break up and dissipate in small groups and, if necessary, take refuge in another Wilaya far from the current offensive. Without in any way launching a new wave of terrorism that would inevitably bring massive counter-measures, the *fidayine* were just to keep the pot simmering with an occasional grenade thrown into a café here, a burst of machine-gun fire against bathers on a beach there. The aim was to continue to terrorise Muslims away from lending support to any possible "third force", and also constantly to remind the outside world that the F.L.N. remained in existence.

More significant was the cautious but steady rebuilding of the Algiers network after more than two years of complete inactivity. It had started chiefly, it seems, as a defensive measure against the excesses of the "ultras" during "Barricades Week", but by the spring of 1960 the new organisation had already mustered some 250 adherents. Its leader, Larbi Alilat, son of a Kabyle *caid* from the Soummam valley and a veteran of the 1957 Battle of Algiers, renounced the old rigid pyramidal structure of Yacef's Z.A.A. which had become so disastrously susceptible to *bleuite* penetration. Instead, each trusted member of the network was instructed to recruit one lifelong friend. Co-ordinated under the aegis of a newly reconstructed Wilaya 4, a minimum of carefully chosen operations was attempted in the course of the year. Thus the growth of Alilat's force went on largely undisturbed by the French security forces. By the end of 1960 a useful and well-disciplined contingent about 400 strong had grown up in the capital in such secrecy that it would provide the French with a shock as unpleasant as it was unexpected.

During this first year of Boumedienne's command there still occurred the occasional military disaster in the "interior", or the bloody setback provoked by an over-zealous local commander on the Morice Line. But by and large the serious military war was beginning slowly to peter out as de Gaulle showed increasing signs of being bent upon a course of negotiation. As Professor Quandt remarks, henceforth to the F.L.N. "Military victory was not only widely regarded as a chimera, but also it seemed increasingly unnecessary." The top priority was to keep the military apparatus intact, and Boumedienne saw it as his longer-term function to create a well-equipped, disciplined and trustworthy army with which any future Algerian government of the F.L.N. could rule an independent Algeria, against all rivals, in the difficult days that might lie ahead.

CHAPTER TWENTY

De Gaulle Caught
in the Draught

September 1960 – January 1961

If you open a window to the right, and another to the left, don't be surprised if you get caught in the draught.

Arab proverb

Anti-war sentiments mount in France

As 1960 went on it had increasingly little of comfort to offer de Gaulle. It was the year of polarisation, with opposing extremes becoming more extreme, and more powerful, and progressively crushing the life out of the moderates in the centre. "I saw better than ever what had to be done," de Gaulle wrote in his memoirs of his sentiments in the aftermath of "Barricades Week": "I doubted less than ever that it was my duty to accomplish it. But I needed as much as ever the support of the French people."

It was a year, though, that brought de Gaulle less support and fresh enemies, as it brought the F.L.N. new allies, both in the outside world and within France itself. There the failure at Melun had provoked an unmistakable, and general, sense of discouragement, which served to side-light the war-weariness increasingly afflicting the nation as a whole. In a remarkable summer *entente*, the Communist and non-Communist trade unions had joined together to plead for successful peace negotiations, with threats of a general strike "as an answer to any insurrection or *coup d'état* that might tend to impede the Algerian peace", and the government had actually had to ban all demonstrations in favour of peace. Among the youth of France the Algerian war was coming to be known as "The Hundred Years' War". The discovery of Jean-Paul Belmondo, the impact of the *nouvelle vague* French cinema – especially of *Les Liaisons Dangereuses*, which seemed then as dangerously daring as it was embarrassing to the puritanical Gaullists – all suggested which way domestic interests were turning. More and more articles were appearing in the Press by young national servicemen returning from Algeria shocked by the "immoral" acts they had participated in, seen, or heard about there. A large sector of liberal French public opinion, barely recovered from the shocks administered during the Battle of Algiers, was now outraged anew by the resumption of executions of terrorists (agreed to by de Gaulle as a sop to the *pieds noirs* in January), and by the torture case of a young Algerian girl called Djamila Boupacha. Arrested in February for throwing a bomb into a café, she had allegedly been submitted to the most revolting tortures, which included being brutally deflowered with the neck of a bottle. Her case had received the widest publicity in France, with a portrait of her drawn by Picasso appearing in many magazines, and a highly vocal "Djamila Boupacha Committee" founded by eminent French liberals such as François Mauriac, Simone de Beauvoir and Germaine Tillion.

Out of all this inflammation of liberal feelings there emerged on 5 September the "Manifesto of the 121". Sub-titled a "Declaration on the Right of Insubordination in the Algerian War", it incited French conscripts there to desert. The 121 signatories were all celebrities, including Sartre, de Beauvoir, Françoise Sagan and Simone Signoret. Most were of the Left and many identified as committed "fellow-travellers" (but, it was worth noting, no Communist Party members); nevertheless, the presence among them of such heroes of the Resistance as "Vercors" ensured that the document was taken seriously in wider circles. "In the course of a few weeks," says Vidal-Naquet, "the political climate changed fundamentally," and at the end of October there were demonstrations in support of the "121" bringing several hundred thousand out on to the streets throughout France. The launching of the "Manifesto" also coincided with another event that afforded the anti-war lobby with the maximum publicity: the "Jeanson Network" trial.

From its early nucleus of Christian–Marxist humanists (not unlike the *tercio mundo* Catholics operating against the Chilean Junta of the 1970s), Francis Jeanson's network, created to run funds for the F.L.N. and help deserters and F.L.N. terrorists in hiding, had by the beginning of 1960 come to embrace some 4,000 members in all walks of life. Having been astonishingly tardy in tracking down its activities, the French D.S.T. then swooped on the organisation. It missed the leader, Jeanson himself, who with equally astonishing impunity continued about his work, published a book on it, and openly held a Press conference in Paris. At the trial six Algerians and eighteen French were defended by twenty-six lawyers, who skilfully used the occasion as a platform for anti-war speeches. A long statement from Sartre, absent in Brazil, was read out to the court. There was loud applause at Sartre's words: "The independence of Algeria has in fact been won. Whether it will occur in a year's time or in five years' time ... I do not know, but it is already a fact." One former French infantryman who had served in Algeria explained to his judges that it was the "misery that one encountered there at every step" which had decided him to join the "Jeanson Network" and actively aid the F.L.N. Called to the witness box, "Vercors" also declared that he, too, wholeheartedly approved of the activities of the accused. After a month of hearings, fifteen received the maximum sentence of ten years' imprisonment, with a further three sentenced to lesser penalties. The country had been shaken to discover that Frenchmen had been actively working for the "enemy" when the arrests were first announced, and now it buzzed with controversy as to the morality of their alleged treason.

In a backlash against the "Manifesto of the 121" and the Jeanson trial, and all the publicity both had attracted, in October a counter-manifesto appeared, signed by some 300 spokesmen of the Right, including the *pied noir* first soldier of France, Marshal Juin. A few days later the Assembly of French Cardinals and Bishops issued a statement condemning desertion and subversive activities, but disapproving of torture and stressing that orders to implement it should be disobeyed. In November another trial opened, this time providing a platform for the supporters of *Algérie française* and continuing for four months, when Lagaillarde and his colleagues of "the Barricades" appeared before their judges. Among other things, the defence made much of a statement uttered by Premier Debré at the time of the May "events" of 1958: "When the government violates the people's rights, insurrection becomes the most imperious duty. . . ." Meanwhile, in June 1960 the most vehement political opponents of de Gaulle over Algeria, now numbering in their ranks former premier Georges Bidault and Jacques Soustelle, had come together to form the Comité de Vincennes, uncompromisingly dedicated to the cause of *Algérie française*. Never before had the debate on Algeria become so strident. By November it was almost a positive relief to turn aside to watch the struggle of young Senator Kennedy for the presidency of the United States; though even he had launched his campaign with some pointed remarks about the necessity for France to withdraw from Algeria.

In Algiers: new "ultra" manoeuvrings

Making a fresh visit to Algiers in October, his first since "Operation Tilsit", Bernard Tricot noted a "rapid deterioration" in the atmosphere: "Among the Muslims: extreme lassitude, profound disappointment now that they had assessed better the breakdown at Melun, interest increasing for the international activities of the F.L.N. and for the U.N. debates. On the European side: profound disquiet, a lively hostility towards the government, and no real rapprochement with the Muslims."* Delouvrier's office

---

* Feraoun, on the other hand, was noting at the end of November that it was the French who were "seized with lassitude. The Muslims are regaining hope and appreciate that deliverance is close. A deliverance that will stem from this lassitude. . . . Yes, I believe it will be victory."

voiced fears that a new clandestine organisation had been set up by the "ultras", which, on a given day, might attempt to "neutralise" the authorities in Algeria. But details that Algiers security had of it were embarrassingly scant.

In the weeks that followed their defeat on the barricades, the "ultras" had seemed effectively decapitated, with most of their leaders – Lagaillarde, Ortiz, Susini, Pérez, Lefèvre, de Sérigny and Colonel Gardes – either imprisoned or in refuge. Gradually, however, the F.N.F. slogans on the Algiers walls became replaced by new graffiti: F.A.F. or Front d'Algérie Française, with its aggressively virile symbol of a ram, which made its first appearance in the wake of de Gaulle's appeal to the F.L.N. of 14 June. Initially, this time the centre of gravity of the new Front lay in France itself, where weekly meetings took place with such militant fallen angels of the Vincennes group as Soustelle and Bidault, and extreme right-wing politicians like Jean-Marie le Pen. The leaders in Algeria were unknown to Delouvrier's security branch; in any case, they were of little significance, and it was apparent that they were but a "caretaker government" pending the return of absentee big guns. On the other hand, the F.A.F. could mark up one very useful acquisition: the Bachaga Boualem, the dedicated ally of France and leader of the "loyal" harkis, who came bringing with him the declared allegiance of 120,000 Algérie française Muslims. Thus, by the time of Tricot's autumn visit the F.A.F. claimed a million supporters in Algeria alone. Though keeping Paris informed of its activities, Delouvrier refrained from taking action against the F.A.F., on the grounds that it had not yet strayed across the frontier of legality.

The return of Salan and Jouhaud

Of much more immediate concern to Delouvrier was the unexpected reappearance in Algiers of two retired military tycoons, whose committal to Algérie française had been abundantly well publicised: Generals Salan and Jouhaud. Since his abrupt recall from Algeria at the end of 1958, Salan had mouldered away in his office as military governor of Paris, smarting at the cavalier way in which de Gaulle had treated him and disastrously cherishing the conviction that without his help de Gaulle could never have succeeded in May 1958. Having reached the statutory age of sixty, Salan retired from the army on 9 June; the previous day, at the customary luncheon given in his honour in the Elysée, de Gaulle is said to have warned the five-star general: "Don't get mixed up in politics. It's a dirty business." Salan made no comment.

According to a curious, but not unwise, tradition in the French army, for a stipulated period retiring generals continue to remain subject to military discipline and all its restrictions, receiving in exchange certain privileges, such as a grace and favour office and sometimes a skeleton staff. In early

September Salan broke the rules by announcing his intention to return to Algiers to live out his retirement in the villa he had purchased there for that purpose – without obtaining permission from Messmer, the Minister of Defence. Delouvrier signalled Messmer to forbid Salan right of entry, but in vain. Thus, quietly one morning the "Mandarin", his wife and daughter, disembarked from the steamer *Kairouan* to be greeted by only one former colleague at the port of the city where he had once exerted such immense authority. That same afternoon Delouvrier grasped the nettle by going to see Salan at his villa, requesting that, as his predecessor, he should appreciate the difficulties that his return could cause him, Delouvrier. Salan, impassive as ever, replied calmly that Algeria was, after all, France; that his son lay buried there; and, thirdly, that his wife liked the climate. "*J'y suis, j'y reste!*" declared Salan, but assured Delouvrier that he would undertake no political activities in Algeria. It very soon reached the ears of the Delegate-General, however, that as well as receiving visits from army officers suspected of disaffection, Salan was also in contact with leaders of the F.A.F., by whom he was clearly regarded as a chieftain providentially sent. On 14 September, using as a pretext the current "Jeanson trial" and the incitements to military disobedience by the "121", Salan committed a second breach of discipline. Without obtaining clearance from Messmer he sent a message to a congress of the *anciens combattants* of Indo-China, in his capacity as their president, declaring sweepingly that: "It is not within the power of any authority to decide upon the relinquishment of a part of the territory where France exercises her sovereignty."

This was clearly an intolerable challenge, both to Delouvrier and to de Gaulle himself. A week later Salan received the humiliating order to report back to the Ministry of Defence in Paris. Banned also from any further access to Algeria, the former Commander-in-Chief, once covered in every glory, could now only return to his old fiefdom as an outlaw. With hindsight, one might ask whether this was not perhaps a tactical error on the part of de Gaulle; would a Salan out in the open, in Algiers and under Delouvrier's eye, have proved the lesser liability than the "Mandarin" henceforth taking to the shadows? But meanwhile, hardly had Salan departed than his fellow *Algérie française* general, Edmond Jouhaud, was arriving in Algiers to exacerbate Delouvrier's problems.

Born in 1905 in humble surroundings near Oran and educated there, Jouhaud was the only one of the dissident generals to be actually a *pied noir*; as such he could not be denied entry to his home. An air force general like Challe, Jouhaud had fought in the French campaign of 1940, had joined the Free French and then commanded the air force in Indo-China in the final months of defeat. Disgusted at the sad spectacle of the Tonkinese refugees forced out of their homes in North Vietnam, in April 1957 he had arrived in Algeria to take command of the 5th Air Region. The following May he had been one of the activist officers pushing his senior, Salan, forward and had been nominated vice-president of the Algiers Committee of Public Safety. Little trusted by de Gaulle, Jouhaud had been among the first batch of purged officers, transferred home to become chief-of-staff to the air force, from which he had retired in October 1960. A burly man whose face bespoke ill-temper, Jouhaud had neither the intelligence of Salan nor the popularity of Challe. But he was probably more violently *Algérie française* than either. One of his favourite quotations was from John Dos Passos: "You can wrench a man away from his country, but you can never wrench the country away from the heart of the man." On bidding farewell to de Gaulle, Jouhaud had delivered a forty-five minute homily on the need for it to be made clear that France had decided to "maintain the peace of France and its flag in Algeria". Thanking him perfunctorily, de Gaulle had said he hoped Jouhaud would not "lose contact" with him.* Arrived back in Algiers, Jouhaud, like Salan, assured Delouvrier that he would cause no trouble: – then immediately set to taking up relations with the F.A.F.

Back in Paris and out of grace, Salan showed himself more than ever to be a thoroughly embittered man. He was acid about the *pieds noirs* – with whom "one can never do anything serious" – and deeply distrustful of Soustelle, who had come to him to propose a *regroupement nationale* to defend the cause of *Algérie française*. Above all, he ranted at the name of de Gaulle. On 25 October he held a Press conference, declaring total war on de Gaulle, and officially placing himself at the head of the *Algérie française* movement. But it was clear that little could be achieved in France; everywhere Salan turned he met the eye of vigilant men in raincoats detailed to keep him under twenty-four-hour surveillance. One day Salan ostentatiously ordered from the concierge of his hotel tickets for Bordeaux; then doubled round to Cook's to switch them for a night-sleeper to Nîmes. Arriving there, Salan – accompanied by Captain Ferrandi, a sharp-tongued Corsican deserter who followed him devotedly into exile – after several other ruses to throw the watchers off his track, hopped into a taxi and drove over the Pyrenees. Once safely in Spain, Salan set up court, first in Barcelona, then in Madrid. The news of his flight shook France – except for de Gaulle, who dismissed it with the laconic observation, "I'm not surprised about *him*."

Delouvrier: point of no return

For the harassed Delegate-General in Algiers, the hejira of Salan came as a distinct relief. But the reappearance of the two generals represented no more than the clearly visible iceberg tip of Delouvrier's ever-mounting

---

* In fact, the next "contact" the two were to have would be at Jouhaud's court martial.

problems that were now rapidly reaching an intolerable peak. With the F.L.N.'s new programme of hit-and-run terrorist pinpricks, the security situation round Algiers, and inside the city itself, seemed to be deteriorating again. *Pied noir* opinion had been particularly outraged by an incident on 31 July, when a uniformed detachment of the F.L.N. had attacked unarmed bathers – men and women – on a beach at Chénoua, west of Algiers, killing a dozen. The incident had provided fresh grist to the mill of the F.A.F. extremists. This selective terrorism, plus the new assertiveness of the G.P.R.A. in the world at large since Melun, also made it harder than ever to find those "third force" Muslims, not just to stand as candidates in national or local elections, but simply to fill the various administrative posts which it had so long been a French priority to create in order to appease Muslim demands. Over the previous two years, no more than a hundred Muslims had actually been inducted into senior administrative posts.

It was, however, the Constantine Plan – the prime purpose for Delouvrier's appointment in the first place – which continued to be his major source of concern. The visit of Premier Debré on 3 October, to celebrate the second anniversary of the Plan, furnished an occasion to survey its achievements. The agricultural programme of constructing "a thousand villages" had been virtually completed, and arable production had been augmented from 270,000 tonnes to 390,000 in one year. Over the same period industrial output had risen by ten per cent; the 400th new enterprise had just been launched; 100 milliard francs had already been invested, while a further 400 milliard were budgeted for 1961. As far as education was concerned, the number of pupils in primary schools had increased from 650,000 in 1958 to nearly a million in 1960, an improvement of well over fifty per cent. So much for the credit side of the balance. But more than half of all Algerian children still did not attend school, and technical education was paralysed for want of skilled personnel. Technicians in the new industries were equally lacking and, for all the vast efforts made, only 28,000 new jobs had actually been created – compared with the target of 400,000. In land redistribution the original target of 250,000 hectares to be shared out among 15,000 families (there were in fact an estimated 600,000 needing land) had been revised drastically downwards to 41,000 hectares to be shared among a paltry 1,800 families. Although forty-five per cent of the investment funds for 1961 would come from government sources, little more than a quarter of the remainder was forthcoming from *pied noir* enterprises – justly apprehensive about the future. With each new advance Gaullist policy took towards Algerian independence, Delouvrier began to question more and more the honesty of a programme of enticing firms in metropolitan France to take a stake in Algeria.

Finally, by the time of Debré's October visit, Delouvrier's relations with the Commander-in-Chief, "Casse-Noisette" Crépin, had reached a nadir Despite the stresses "the Barricades" had imposed, Delouvrier deeply missed his harmonious relationship with Challe. Always rather aggressively cold towards Delouvrier, Crépin had become progressively more partisan to the Algérie française factions in his command, and he enraged the Delegate-General by criticising him openly to Debré. The Europeans were "in a state of permanent fear", complained Crépin, implying that Delouvrier was at fault for never making the least encouraging noise about "francisation". Delouvrier's protests gained little redress from Debré; meanwhile, his communication with the Elysée continued to offer minimal satisfaction.

By the beginning of November Delouvrier's isolation became absolute. On the 4th de Gaulle made a new broadcast to the nation. It was, he explains, designed to appear "full of resolution and assurance", because recent bitterness marking the budget discussions for the first time since 1958 had been taken by him to be "an indication of the intense impatience and anxiety of the French people". But what he said about Algeria was to take developments one vital stage further, showing that he was determined to execute his ideas at a faster pace. Having assumed the leadership of France, he had embarked upon "a new course" leading, he explained "from government of Algeria by metropolitan France to an Algerian Algeria. That means an emancipated Algeria . . . an Algeria which, if the Algerians so wish – and I believe this to be the case – will have its own government, its own institutions, its own laws". Later he slipped in a reference to "an Algerian Republic, which will one day exist, but has never yet existed". As so often with de Gaulle's more controversial and decisive utterances, there was an element of the impromptu about this first pronouncing of the fateful words, "an Algerian Republic". They had not figured in the typescript; de Gaulle, as was his wont had added them in as he went along. Tricot – in common with the other Elysée advisors – thought the words "bad and dangerous". Pressed by them, de Gaulle enquired whether – since the broadcast was pre-taped – it would be possible to delete the offending phrase. The technicians replied that the radio broadcast could be doctored, yes, but there would be no time to re-record the television programme. De Gaulle supposedly then shrugged his shoulders, saying: "Well, in that case, let it stand."

Since the step taken at Melun it was perhaps only logical that what de Gaulle now said about an "Algerian Algeria" with its right to secede (which, by extension, could surely lead to nothing but "an Algerian Republic") had to be said sooner or later. But, as Tricot noted, it meant the disappearance of "one of the elements of the triptych, francisation". Reactions were tempestuous. Debré, says de Gaulle, "could not hide his chagrin" – which was an understatement. After all he had been required to say in the name of *francisation*, Debré in fact felt compelled to offer his resignation that day. De Gaulle who privately called Debré his "Saint Sebastian" – "every time he receives an arrow, he suffers, but that gives him pleasure!" – waved it aside, saying, "No, Debré; remain I still have need of you." Debré remained. The next day de Gaulle's comrade-in-arms and friend of fifty years standing, Marshal Juin, broke with him publicly, accusing de Gaulle of "deserting our Algerian brothers". In Madrid, Claude Paillat recalls watching the "Mandarin", Salan, perform a curious *pas seul* in an attempt to tune a minute transistor radio he was clutching in the palm of his hand. As de Gaulle's speech came feebly through, he grunted "Oh! Oh!" on deciphering the words "Algerian Republic". Afterwards he declared to the Press, "from now on, every man must face up to his responsibilities . . . the time for evasions is over".

In Algiers Delouvrier's secretary-general and closest collaborator, André Jacomet, resigned in a manner Delouvrier construed as pulling the rug out from underneath him. "I consider it regrettable", said Jacomet, "that, before any cease-fire, the G.P.R.A. should receive satisfaction on its principal war aim – the Republic of Algeria". With other resignations in the wind, it looked to Delouvrier as if the whole structure of the Délégation-Général was tottering. At the Armistice Day ceremony of 11 November he found himself surrounded by a ragingly angry crowd at the *monument aux morts*. His car was spat upon, and a young woman thrusting her face forward shouted: "Delouvrier – Assassin!" It was too much. Never before had he been called this. Delouvrier was now at the end of his resources, exhausted after twenty-four thankless months in a hopeless task. To his cabinet he admitted: "This time I no longer feel I am master of the situation." As a final blow, de Gaulle – quite unsympathetic – had chided him when warned that it would not be safe to make the visit to Algeria he intended the following month. Delouvrier decided to resign. Speaking to de Gaulle he explained that he no longer possessed any moral authority: "All my words of hope, my contacts, the Constantine Plan, have been swept away by 'Algerian Algeria' and above all by 'the Algerian Republic'."

Another new team: Joxe, Morin, Gambiez

On 23 November Delouvrier's resignation was made public. His "loyalty had never for one moment faltered" was de Gaulle's handsome epitaph to the lieutenant whom he had never once made privy to his full intentions. The post was to be divided in two, with a new Minister of State for Algeria, Louis Joxe, answerable directly to de Gaulle and residing in Paris but in contant contact with Algiers; under him Jean Morin, the Government-Delegate (a subtle reduction in nomenclature from Delouvrier's title Delegate-General) in Algiers but with diminished responsibilities. Joxe, a sagacious, donnish figure with prematurely white hair, had been a career diplomat, Ambassador to Moscow from 1952 to 1956, then made de Gaulle's Minister of Education. The choice of such a skilled diplomatist for the new post seemed to indicate just how much de Gaulle's thoughts were now turning on the prospects of future negotiations.

Jean Morin, super-prefect of the Haute-Garonne, was another *fonctionnaire* and as unknown to the public eye as Delouvrier had been. Short, bald and with the rather sharp looks of the Meridional (though none of the warmth), at the Liberation he had been charged with the awkward responsibility of purging the *corps préféctoral*. This he had executed honestly, but with some ruthlessness; he was then France's youngest prefect, aged only twenty-six. De Gaulle despatched his new Government-Delegate with the ringing words: "Morin, if the task is arduous, the mission is noble!" Otherwise Morin left with no more precise instructions than his predecessor had had as to de Gaulle's future policy. His first task, however, was to prepare the ground for de Gaulle's visit on 9 December. Among his last communications with the General, Delouvrier had strongly advised him against coming with the mood as it was currently among the *pieds noirs*. But de Gaulle was adamant; he wanted to launch the campaign for his second referendum, announced on 16 November and to be held in early January, to gain both French and Algerian endorsement for "self-determination". Morin's second duty was to prepare, in the utmost secrecy, a new headquarters outside the dangerous cauldron of Algiers, at Rocher-Noir, a few miles along the coast. The purpose was to avoid a possible repeat of the embarrassing predicament of January, where the representative of France might find himself confronted with the choice of either beating an undignified retreat, or being made a prisoner of an "ultra" mob. The principle was a wise one; only its execution would be too late.

De Gaulle's next change in Algeria, scheduled for early in the new year, was to replace the Commander-in-Chief, General Crépin, by General Gambiez, commander of the Oran sector. Apart from the unqestionable Gaullist fidelity shared by both, there could hardly have been a greater contrast between two men. Gambiez, at fifty-seven, was diminutive with a gentle and slightly lisping voice; bald, bespectacled and studious-looking, his face bore a constantly amiable expression that reminded one more of a country curate than a fighting general. In fact, this rather timorous and unmilitary-looking exterior belied a warrior of utmost distinction who had been one of the first to set foot on French soil in 1944, Gambiez had also lost both a son and a nephew in the hell of Indo-China. But his appearance did symbolise a major change in the conduct of the war; with the departure of Crépin, military "pacification" was to reach its end. Says de Gaulle, "The war was all but over. Military success was achieved. Operations had been reduced to next to nothing. Instead, politics dominated the scene, and in this respect the two communities were further apart than they had ever been. . . ."

Mobilising for de Gaulle's visit

Regarding de Gaulle's new referendum as a major threat to their interests for different reasons, both the opposing extremes now mobilised to counter his Algerian visit of 9 December. For the F.L.N. it was of top priority that every obstacle should be put in the way of de Gaulle holding this new referendum on *his* terms. For, as always, it could not countenance any "free choice" for the Algerians which might threaten the F.L.N.'s mastery of the situation. Synchronous with de Gaulle's visit was the opening, in New York, of the crucial "Algerian debate" in the Political Committee of the United Nations. This key Fifteenth Session of the United Nations was attended by the most weighty F.L.N. delegation yet assembled. Its principal object was to fight tooth-and-nail for acceptance of the extant Afro-Asian resolution, which envisaged the holding of an Algerian referendum under control of the United Nations, which de Gaulle, backed by his Western allies, adamantly opposed, insisting as always that Algeria was an "internal" French problem. Counting heads, those veterans of United Nations infighting, Yazid and Chanderli, reckoned that the F.L.N. prospects were considerably at risk. Therefore, it was essential that the maximum display of "Algerian solidarity" be arranged to coincide both with de Gaulle's visit to Algeria and the United Nations debate. With the pressure of the Challe offensive removed, the F.L.N. was able to launch a new terrorist campaign; whereas in November 710 incidents were recorded (the lowest number since 1955), in December they rose to 1,258. This resurgence of terrorism was enough to be heard in New York, and enough to enrage the *pieds noirs*, but not enough to provoke a reluctant de Gaulle into massive counter-measures. Pre-eminent was the new F.L.N. network in Algiers, patiently and surreptitiously rebuilt by Larbi Alilat, out of sight of French Intelligence and unhindered by it. With a nucleus now some 400 strong it received orders to prepare to get the largest number of Muslim demonstrators out on the Algiers streets during the presidential visit.

At the other end of the spectrum, the reception planned for de Gaulle had a far more dangerous – and desperate – look about it. Not for nothing had Delouvrier tried to head de Gaulle off. Nearer the time he had also been warned that an assassination attempt was probable; in fact, no less than four separate plots were in the offing – though each one was more inept than the last. Delouvrier's newly-arrived successor, Morin, was aware that the F.A.F. were mobilising to the limit for the visit. But they were still, in essence, leaderless. What was far more disquieting were fresh rumbles of disaffection from the army. From now on and for the next six months, it was the army – not the *pieds noirs* – which was to call the tune. At the epicentre was the elitist 1st R.E.P., which had played such a prominent but equivocal role in the "Barricades Week" of nearly a year ago. Its fiercely outspoken colonel, Dufour, had – curiously enough – been one of the few to remain unpurged. During the Quatorze Juillet march past he had shocked Delouvrier's political adviser, Francois Coulet, a distinguished para colonel himself, by leading his much-decorated regiment without wearing a single medal. This was a clearly stated gesture of public disrespect towards the head of state, and after another outburst of the same order in November Dufour was finally posted home. But to an astonished Morin it was reported that the illustrious colonel had "gone absent", removing with him the regimental colours! Thus his successor could not take over ceremonially in front of the regiment; in theory, Dufour remained regimental colonel.

The 1st R.E.P.

The full extent of what was afoot in the Foreign Legion's First Parachute Regiment was far graver than was apparent, and it was symptomatic of the mood now prevailing in a majority of the best fighting units in Algeria. After "Barricades Week" the 1st R.E.P. had returned to active service in the *bled* – though with markedly little enthusiasm. Spearheading the continued Challe offensive against the A.L.N. in Wilaya 2, the regiment during the spring had trapped a significant enemy force just on the Tunisian side of the Morice Line. All set to pursue and destroy it with his company, Captain Pierre Sergent found his orders countermanded by the sector commander. Consequently when detailed a short time later to comb out a difficult wooded area, Sergent refused. It was, he said, the first time he had ever disobeyed a superior order. At the beginning of July Colonel Dufour had made contact in Paris with a General Marie-André Zeller, the sixty-two-year-old former chief-of-staff to the armed forces, currently in retirement in Paris, and well-known to be an out-and-out supporter of *Algérie francaise*. To Zeller Dufour made a proposition of almost *Beau Sabreur* naïveté; as his regiment marched past the tribune in full battle order at the forthcoming Quatorze Juillet celebrations, it would swoop and capture Delouvrier, Crépin and the whole Algiers administration, while Zeller was to organise an identical scenario in Paris, to grab de Gaulle and his ministers. But on the 13th word came back from Zeller: "Do nothing. It's not ready here."

Dufour had to satisfy himself with his decoration-less protest. Next he took up contact with General Jouhaud in Algiers, but from now on he was kept under close surveillance. Then, in November, shortly after de Gaulle's "Algerian Republic" speech, there was an emotional scene at the 1st R.E.P.'s depot in Zéralda during the burial of ten men from Sergent's No. 1 Company, killed in an F.L.N. ambush. With the full backing of Dufour the divisional padre, Père Delarue, declared in his benediction words then widely felt in the army: "You died at a time when, if we believe in the speeches we hear, we no longer know why we die. . . ."

This was the last straw which led to Dufour's posting. He disappeared and entered into active plotting with General Jouhaud. In his absence Pierre Sergent, the veteran Legionnaire with the small and wiry figure of a jockey, became temporarily the communications centre of the dissident military. Sergent states that, while on leave in Paris, he received instructions from Maître Tixier-Vignancour, the lawyer who for many years had been a rallying-point of the extreme Right in France. Flying back to Algiers that night, he was instructed to relay urgently to Jouhaud the message: "Salan gives the green light." To this day Sergent does not know whether this message actually originated from Salan, or through what channels. In fact, it seems improbable that it did, in that the "Mandarin" and his court in Madrid were still largely isolated from events in both Algiers and Paris. On receiving this message, which was, in effect, to mark the beginning of the army revolt, the choleric Jouhaud grumbled, "Why doesn't Salan come himself?" Nevertheless, carried along by Sergent's enthusiasm, he then set to organising a coup at forty-eight hours' notice. What regiments could be counted on? There was the 1st R.E.P., based at Zéralda just twenty miles out of Algiers, and whose allegiance to the coup was unquestionable. Then there was the 18th R.C.P. which had been fighting in Algeria intermittently since the earliest days of the war, commanded by a tough *pied noir* from Bougie, Colonel Georges Masselot; along with it could be reckoned its sister regiment of Chasseurs Parachutistes, the 14th, commanded by Masselot's friend, Colonel Lecomte. All had been finally pushed over the brink by de Gaulle's speech of 4 November.

Co-ordinated by Jouhaud and Sergent, the strategy was as follows: on 9 December, the day of de Gaulle's arrival, the F.A.F. was to impose a total strike over Algiers. F.A.F. leaflets ordered: "All life must stop. Civilian vehicles are forbidden to move. Shops are not to open on pain of being ransacked." The population as a whole was called upon to "show its indignation and disgust at the visit which General de Gaulle has the temerity to make to Algeria". Instead of one mass demonstration, as in "Barricades Week", which the reinforced gendarmes and C.R.S. would be able to isolate and crush, there would be scattered but violent attacks. As soon as action was engaged, the F.A.F. "shock troops" – armed with weapons hidden since the January fiasco – would then break ott to strike elsewhere. Thus it was intended that the forces of order, worn down, would be compelled to call in the army. Jouhaud's three para regiments, the closest at hand, would appear on the scene. They would seize the vital centres of Algiers, and lay hands on de Gaulle – one way or another. It looked like a heaven-sent opportunity one unlikely ever to recur. But the army conspirators seem to have had only

the woolliest idea of what they would do next – beyond a vague notion that
somehow the revolt would spread through Algeria, and across the Mediterranean to metropolitan France, in a manner similar to the events of May
1958. There also seems to have been little thought that de Gaulle, in his
five-day trip, might actually by-pass Algiers. What then?

Meanwhile, among the civilian F.A.F. conspirators there were those who
were bent on nothing less than the death of de Gaulle, with four separate
"freelance" operators set up for the purpose – apparently unbeknown to
the military faction.

9 December: de Gaulle's reception

Landing in Oranie on the morning of the 9th in pouring rain, de Gaulle
had an immediate shock in his first stop at the small town of Ain-Témouchent. Some 5,000 *pieds noirs* were mustered, waving hostile placards and
sounding out on whistles and car hooters the familiar "dit-dit-dit, dah-dah"
of *Algérie française*. De Gaulle betrayed only a gesture of annoyance at the
loud chants of "À bas de Gaulle!"; then, to the horror of Government-
Delegate Morin and his escort, he strode off into the crowd to shake hands
with a minority group of Muslims who, in antithesis, were shouting:
"*Algérie algérienne . . . Vive de Gaulle!*" Already the previous month word
had reached French security of a crazy plot to kidnap de Gaulle from the
Elysée, hatched by a highly decorated sergeant-major of the Indo-China
war who headed a group called the National Revolutionary Committee.
Now there were recurrent warnings of an assassination attempt, and not
least one from the ubiquitous and well-informed Israeli Intelligence Service.
based, no doubt, on information supplied by Algeria's divided Jewish community. Sent to accompany de Gaulle were four hand-picked *gorilles*, each
secreting two weapons in case the first should be wrested from him by an
out-of-hand mob. De Gaulle plunging off among the demonstrators was a
contingency for which they were least equipped. But at that precise
moment – so the story has it – the threat of death to de Gaulle came from a
totally different direction, and it was never to be closer. One of de Gaulle's
C.R.S. motor-cycle escort, moving almost within touching distance of the
President, was a *pied noir* who – revolted by the 4 November speech – had
volunteered to shoot him down, then ride off to safety. It would have been
too easy. While de Gaulle was on his walkabout, the C.R.S. telephoned his
F.A.F. bosses for confirmation; but – for reasons that remain obscure,
possibly a veto by the military – the answer he got was: "No". Serenely unaware, de Gaulle and his cavalcade moved on to Tlemcen, where, despite a
violent hailstorm, another crowd turned out to boo de Gaulle, interspersed
with Muslim applause. Right from the beginning the two communities
showed themselves divided as at no time since the coming of de Gaulle; the
Muslims displaying more audacity than ever before to proclaim *Algérie*

algérienne. At the end of that first day de Gaulle's expression was as bleak as the weather outside.

The next day, Saturday the 10th, de Gaulle was due to visit Orléansville, a city of 40,000 midway between Oran and Algiers. On the way Morin, however, received an urgent call from his office; the Intelligence now fully corroborated the Israeli tip-off, and a team of "ultra" killers had left Algiers to ambush the President on his entry into Orléansville. Nervously, knowing de Gaulle's antipathy to having his plans altered, Morin warned him and requested a change of itinerary. Quite unperturbed, de Gaulle replied: "It's you who are responsible for the maintenance of order. You decide. . . ."

At top speed the cavalcade roared up a mountain detour and swept into Orléansville by a different route. On the outskirts of the town five "ultras" had been waiting under the orders of an operative known as "Nani", who had been arrested several times for counter-terrorist acts against the F.L.N. and would later become a leading killer for the O.A.S. They were equipped with a small arsenal of weapons – machine-guns, dynamite and hand grenades – but on realising that they had been outwitted they turned tail dejectedly back to Algiers. At Blida a more bizarre, free-enterprise attempt was apparently in the offing. A handsome young *pied noir* playboy, tired of life, decided to ram de Gaulle's helicopter with his private plane. But on arriving over Blida airfield he was appalled to see a veritable cloud of helicopters take off. It was impossible to tell which one was de Gaulle's. He, too, abandoned the exercise. De Gaulle's only comment about the two visits was that he had "found the atmosphere oppressive"; while he remarked acidly to Morin on the undue "tolerance" of the local military authorities.

On the Sunday (11 December) there was yet a fourth abortive plot against his life, at the Reghaia air base on the other side of Algiers where Delouvrier and Challe had taken refuge the previous January. A second lieutenant, a much-decorated *pied noir* veteran of Indo-China who had married a Vietnamese and remained obsessed by France's "betrayal" of her empire, was waiting "to shoot down the head of this police state" when he inspected his unit of airborne commandos. But on the way from his quarters in Algiers the would-be assassin became entangled with rioting Muslims and missed the boat.

F.A.F. riots in Algiers

Meanwhile, all hell had been let loose in Algiers (and Oran, too). F.A.F. bombs exploded, wrecking cars in the centre of Algiers. Six thousand gendarmes and C.R.S. moved in, this time backed with armoured machine-gun-carriers, and even tanks. As Jouhaud had planned, gangs of F.A.F. youths attacked them, hurling stones, bottles, cast-iron bolts and every projectile that came to hand. The C.R.S. replied with tear-gas, percussion grenades and baton charges. The chic Rue Michelet became a writhing mass of demonstrators intermingled with blue-clad security forces, covered by a grey pall of tear-gas. Cars were overturned and burnt. The violence now switched to the university where, in a familiar manner, students began to tear down hoardings for barricades. But these were swiftly broken up when two gendarmerie tanks appeared. Young *pieds noirs* waved their fists at the tanks like the anti-Soviet demonstrators in Budapest or Prague. By night-fall on the first day there were 400 arrested and 100 injured. Shaken by the ferocity of the screaming mobs, British correspondents reported back: "The long-awaited fury by Frenchmen who say they will die to keep Algeria French has started – and now anything can happen...," while in Témouchent de Gaulle was declaring: "The shouts and the clamour... they signify nothing!"

The next day, Saturday, the battle resumed with even greater fury. F.A.F. action groups poured oil on steep hillside tram tracks, and parked cars athwart intersections. An attack was made in the direction of the Palais d'Été, where a helicopter pad had been built, and it was rumoured that de Gaulle was going to fly in. Although, as far as bloodshed was concerned, nothing comparable to 24 January had yet occurred, the forces of order were, as Jouhaud had hoped, tiring; there were cases of detachments being submerged, or even being disarmed. But the F.A.F. "shock troops" were also feeling discouraged. There was still no sign of the promised para intervention, and that night – as it had done at the crisis point of "Barricades Week" – a drenching, cold rain fell to dampen their spirits further. Of the F.A.F. demonstrations, Mouloud Feraoun wrote contemptuously, "they resemble senile beggars who masturbate in a corner to make people believe that they are virile. No one wants to take them seriously." Meanwhile, fighting had broken out in the mixed poor suburb of Belcourt, to the east of Algiers. It appears that confused over-zealous (and now preposterously out of touch) Europeans had approached Muslims with the purpose of getting them on to the streets to declaim against de Gaulle, and against *Algérie algérienne*. Force had been used, and the Muslims retaliated by stabbing Europeans and setting fire to a large store.

11 December: the Muslim backlash

Sunday, 11 December, was the day for which Larbi Alilat and the re-constituted F.L.N. organisation in Algiers had been so carefully preparing. It was to turn out to be one of the key days of the Algerian war for the Muslim cause. Thousands of green-and-white F.L.N. flags had been sewn together by the women of the Casbah, and distributed – together with banners and placards – clandestinely throughout the Muslim quarters. But the resultant chain reaction far exceeded anything anticipated by the organisers. Partly it may have been sparked by the *pieds noirs'* demonstrations of the two preceding days; partly by word on the swift "Arab tele-graph" of the racial violence in Belcourt the previous night. At heart, however, it seems to have been one of those inexplicable explosions caused by long-pent-up forces. Early that morning European residents of Algiers were astonished to see a green-and-white flag fluttering from the top of the Kouba mosque. Gendarmes were sent to take it down. Then more appeared from other mosques. From windows of Muslim homes first one flag was unfurled, rather tentatively – then a score along the length of the street. Out into the mean alleys of the Casbah and Belcourt Muslim youths poured – not the expected hundreds, but thousands – chanting: "*Yahia* * *Ferhat Abbas! Yahia F.L.N.! Yahia de Gaulle!*" while others took up the refrain of, "*Algérie algérienne! Algérie musulmane!*" In Belcourt Edward Behr observed a scene

> which summed up the situation . . . a Moslem came careering round a corner on a motorcycle, tied to which was an enormous F.L.N. flag. A gendarmerie captain told him to put it away. "*Pourquoi? On ne fait pas de mal,*" he replied. "*Le Général de Gaulle a dit: Algérie algérienne. On est Algérien, non?*"

Soon the tide of chanting, flag-waving Muslims began to debouch from their own quarters, sweeping aside the thin cover of local gendarmes whose main force was occupied elsewhere in the turbulent city. Behind this ever-growing mass of Muslims there arose the blood-curdling you-you-you ululations from a myriad of invisible women. A terrible atavistic fear ran through the adjacent *pied noir* quarters with a passing of the word: "*They are coming!*" As the crowd surged into the narrow streets of Belcourt, shots cracked out from tenements inhabited by poor whites, and one or two marchers fell. The word ran through the Muslim ranks, and a blind mob-madness took over. A *pied noir* caught up in the street had his throat slit; another was burnt to death in his car. Armed with iron bars and wooden staves the Muslim mob smashed up and pillaged European shops and villas, devastating everything in their path like a horde of soldier ants.

Confronted with this new and utterly unforeseen factor, the F.A.F. leaders performed a swift turnabout. Their "shock troops" were now ordered to cease attacking the C.R.S. and the gendarmes – so that these could protect *pied noir* lives and property from the Muslim terror! This all-too-human display of fickle capriciousness disgusted Sergent and the military purists. In any event, the jaded security forces rapidly proved themselves inadequate to the task. Colonel Masselot's 18th R.C.P. was rushed up in haste. The situation hoped for by Jouhaud had arrived, but not in the way he had expected it. As the picture darkened in the course of the day, with Alilat's F.L.N. members now firing back on the *pieds noirs* with their own weapons, Morin left de Gaulle's entourage in Kabylia for

* "Long live!"

Algiers and gave the army an uncompromising order to shoot at the mob, whether European or Muslim, if the necessity arose. In the shabby quarter of Belcourt, where for the past six years of war the two working-class communities had coexisted in a state of uneasy peace, scenes of unprecedented savagery now took place. A shocked young reporter of the London *Daily Express*, Ian Aitken, wrote how:

> I saw the Frenchwomen lean from the windows and balconies and yell "Kill them, kill them" as the paratroops fired on the Algerians with rifles and machine-guns . . . I saw a mob of hysterical French youths try to tear one prisoner to pieces – and then embrace the paratroops and plant kisses on their stubbly chins.

Old ladies joined in by hurling their precious potted geraniums down on the heads of the Muslims in the street below.

On the 12th the F.L.N.-impelled mobs extended the scope of their operations to sack the Great Synagogue in the heart of the Casbah which had been built during the reign of Napoleon III and was one of the most important houses of Jewish worship in Algeria. The beautiful building was gutted, the Torah scrolls ripped and desecrated, the walls inscribed with swastikas and slogans of "Death to the Jews". Several Jewish officials were kidnapped and assassinated in a series of acts of violence which fell on the Jewish community like a thunderbolt.

Sixty miles away in Tizi-Ouzou, the capital of Kabylia, de Gaulle was again risking his life by walking into the middle of a Muslim crowd. "A Franco-Algerian fraternity will take shape once the blood has stopped flowing . . .," he told them. But the blood flowing in Algiers was to mark the beginning of true civil war, and the end of any Gaullist dream of a multi-racial "*Algérie algérienne*, associated with France".

Collapse of the Jouhaud coup

Meanwhile, grotesquely enough, in Algiers Jouhaud was still cherishing hopes of a military coup. On the 10th, already appearing disguised in cloth cap and spectacles, the general had made up his mind to act, and Masselot had positively committed himself – the first of the para leaders to do so. But Sergent was shocked by the "brief briefing" given by Jouhaud, presupposing that all was ready to go – which it was not. By the 12th Masselot had changed his mind. As always when the paras were confronted with having to make a direct choice between the *pieds noirs* and the Muslims, especially when it involved shooting demonstrators, ambivalence set in. The colonel was disgusted by an F.A.F. leader who warned him that he could hold his men back no longer, and that there would be a *ratonnade*. He reminded him that "I too am a *pied noir*, and get it into your head that there cannot be any *Algérie française* without the Arabs!" And then, the principal booty of the coup, the President himself, was heading ever farther away from Algiers and showing no sign of visiting the turbulent city for which he had always nursed a particular distaste, harking back to 1942. On Monday the 12th Sergent, acting once again the role of messenger, was told by a thoroughly fatigued Masselot:

> The general situation is not favourable; we don't think that France is *dans le coup*, and Paris will react badly. We don't think we've got either the air force or the navy with us, and altogether it's only an adventure that can lead to nothing. Go and give this negative response to General Jouhaud.

On relaying the message to the general, who took it with his head bowed, looking utterly crushed, Sergent remarks, "I felt as if I had my father in front of me, to whom I had just caused an immense pain."

So ended the first projected military plot against de Gaulle. Though the full details of it were not known to the government until much later, enough suspicions were aroused for all the company officers of the 1st R.E.P. to be sent home to France. Posted "in penitence" to Chartres, Captain Sergent contemplated resigning. One thing was clear to all involved; as a leader of revolt Jouhaud had revealed himself to be as ineffective as he was lacking in allure. Somebody altogether more impressive had to be found.

Disaster for de Gaulle: triumph for the F.L.N.

Showing signs of exhaustion, de Gaulle cut short his visit by twenty-four hours, flying home from Bône. It was his last glimpse of Algeria. He appeared almost unaware of just how disastrous his visit had been, remarking that "everything seems quiet", and congratulating Morin and Crépin for having been "strong enough to prevent a drama and human enough to limit it". Returning to Paris, he found that police leave had been cancelled and tough Marine Commando units sent to stand-by in barracks round the city, in case of a revolt of which there had been unspecified rumours. As the rioting died away in Algiers and Oran, 120 dead were counted and nearly 500 injured. Revealingly, all but eight of the dead turned out to be Muslims, some of whom had been killed in an internecine settling of accounts by F.L.N. hatchet-men – including a well-known, pro-French trade unionist, Said Madani. Overnight the Casbah reverted, for the first time since the Battle of Algiers, to being a hostile enclave all but impenetrable to the forces of order. In the European quarters numerous arrests were made; all civil servants implicated in the riots were dismissed, and the F.A.F. was declared dissolved. Walking down the Rue Michelet in the wake of the riots, Bernard Tricot found a "sinister" atmosphere: little groups of men "hardly talking, arms dangling loose, with the air of people who have just received a terrible blow and no longer know where they are".

In Tunis the G.P.R.A. were manifestly staggered by the snowball spontaneity and success of the demonstrations. A jubilant Ferhat Abbas broadcast telling the Algerians that they had achieved their object. Indeed, as far as scoring points at the United Nations was concerned, they had more than achieved it. To Ben Khedda, speaking many years afterwards, the Muslim demonstration of December 1960 represented the "decisive turning-point of the war", and it is a view with which many French historians concur. To Albert-Paul Lentin it represented a "Dien Bien Phu of official propaganda". At the time, Janet Flanner jotted down in her journal:

> In Paris, it is considered that three myths died in Algeria over the weekend, these being the selfish myth of the white ultras that Algeria is French; the mendacious myth of the French army that only a fistful of fighting rebels in Algeria wanted independence in all those years of war; and the major, miracle myth that de Gaulle could make peace – though no one here, or probably anywhere, thinks that anyone else could make it.

De Gaulle's second referendum

De Gaulle was as aware of these myths as anyone, and, once the lesson of December sank in, it was to exert a profound influence on his future policy for Algeria. But meanwhile he pressed on undeterred with his second referendum, scheduled to be held on 8 January. Once again the actual wording of the referendum was adroitly chosen: "Do you approve the Bill submitted to the French people by the President of the Republic concerning the self-determination of the Algerian population and the organisation of the public powers in Algeria prior to self-determination?" It amounted, in effect, to a *carte blanche* vote of confidence in de Gaulle, for him to negotiate as he might see fit with the F.L.N. Or, as some correspondents interpreted it at the time, there were two votes of confidence – one in France for de Gaulle, and one in Algeria for the F.L.N. The referendum campaign produced some forcefully opposing views in both territories. Soustelle and his colleagues of the Vincennes Committee declared the referendum to be unconstitutional, on the grounds that no one had the right to dispose of an integral part of France. From Madrid there came an impassioned plea to vote *non* signed by Salan, Lagaillarde, Susini and Ronda (another newly-arrived fugitive from the "Barricades Trial"). Two days later sixteen distinguished generals who had all served in Algeria addressed a "letter to the French" urging them to halt "the extension of Soviet influence in the Mediterranean". Under the lead of Thorez, the Communists instructed their cohorts to vote similarly – explaining with some sophistry that they would not be supporting the "ultras", but "voting against the war". From Tunis Ferhat Abbas, broadcasting for the G.P.R.A. and, as ever, anxious that the initiative should in no way pass to de Gaulle, appealed to all Algerians to boycott the polling booths. Prominent among those campaigning for de Gaulle was a new body called the Mouvement pour la Communauté (M.P.C.) – its symbol of a figure with arms outstretched in the shape of a V, superimposed upon the Cross of Lorraine, suddenly appeared plastered on walls throughout Algeria, accompanied by a large *oui*. The M.P.C. was a last attempt to rally the liberal "men of good-will" of both races

In the event, the referendum in Algiers was held in a thick fog, symptomatic, some observers thought, of the obscurity of the political issues surrounding it. When the ballot was counted the result was another overwhelming *oui* for de Gaulle of seventy-five per cent. But four in ten voters had abstained, particularly in Algeria where Muslims had been faithful in obeying the G.P.R.A.'s appeal this time. Thus the true majority there was just over fifty-five per cent while Algiers with its preponderance of *pieds noirs* had registered a resounding seventy-two per cent of "*nons*". De Gaulle, however, took the results as a convincing endorsement for "self-determination". To his Minister of Information, Louis Terrenoire, he confided:

> Up till now I have made numerous speeches. *It was a question of progressively preparing opinion for what must come* [Terrenoire's italics]. Now it's becoming serious, one will have to keep quiet, for there will be contacts with the F.L.N. . . . Let's not recommence the misunderstanding of Melun. All we know about them [the F.L.N. leaders] is that they are divided.

Towards the end of January the Swiss government was relaying to de Gaulle fresh overtures from the G.P.R.A. for peace negotiations. De Gaulle promptly detailed his old friend, Georges Pompidou, director of Rothschild's Bank, to take up the thread with the utmost discretion.

Then, on 25 January, the French Armed Forces were shocked to hear of General Maurice Challe's resignation at the tender age of only fifty-six, the announcement of which had been held over from before the referendum at de Gaulle's express request.

CHAPTER TWENTY-ONE

The Generals' Putsch

April 1961

L'ambition dont on n'a pas les talents est un crime.
Talleyrand

It's a very strange characteristic of my life that I have always been obliged to fight against those who have been my friends.
Charles de Gaulle

Rebels in search of a leader

All but one of the familiar smells are back in autumnal Paris [wrote C. L. Sulzberger in December 1960]. There is the fragrance of dead leaves, of dank seaweed in the oyster stalls, and of sweet nougat and sugared nuts in the booths of itinerant vendors. And there is that oddly agreeable odor of mist and coal smoke. The only missing smell is the smell of danger. Now this is curious because, normally, when there is danger in the air of Paris you can almost sniff it.

But the absence of this particular smell was deceptive. The new year of 1961 certainly offered no brighter horizon for de Gaulle than 1960 had done. At home social unrest was growing; February came in with a strike by French teachers, followed up by railway workers and postmen; March brought a general strike of civil servants. An attempt by Debré to halt inflation through pegging wages provoked an angry clamour from the unions. There were ugly murmurs of corruption in high places concerning the building industry. In a winter of discontent one of the few bright reliefs was the triumphant and rather pathetic resurrection of Edith Piaf, with a new song which touched the heartstrings of all France: "*Je ne regrette rien*".

Momentarily, Algeria seemed to recede from the limelight, but meanwhile, all the time, unseen pressure from the *syndicalistes* and the "respectable" Left was mounting for de Gaulle to initiate peace negotiations in earnest with the F.L.N. The growth of war-weariness in France was becoming particularly apparent; that is, apparent to all but those army leaders now bent upon eliminating de Gaulle so as to continue the struggle to "save" Algeria. For, inept and ineffectual as it had been, the would-be coup in December 1960 had marked a crossing of the Rubicon. Sections of the French army were now irretrievably committed to revolt against the head of state in all his authority, and to all that so grave a commitment signified. It but remained to splice together the various disparate, often discordant and geographically distant strands of conspiracy, and – above all – to find a leader capable of getting them all to pull in the same direction. Finally, a D-Day had to be appointed.

In this period that prefaced open rebellion an intense subterranean activity was seething within the depths of the army. Among the élite formations that had borne the brunt of the fighting in Algeria, the lieutenants were to be found working upon the captains, and captains upon the majors and colonels – though the colonels needed little enough pressurising. As in May 1958 and January 1960, it was they, not the generals, who provided the true dynamos of revolt. Insouciantly little emphasis was placed on the views of the rank and file. There were good enough reasons of security for this omission; it was later to prove, however, the Achilles' heel of the whole movement. Among the junior officer "activists", just to mention a few names, there was Captain Sergent of the 1st R.E.P., sent to Chartres in "penitence" after the December troubles, but remaining in close contact with his kindred spirits in metropolitan France; and there was Lieutenant Roger Degueldre of the same regiment. A sombre giant of a man who had risen from the ranks, Degueldre like Sergent had acted as "liaison officer" with the F.A.F. in December, but afterwards he had simply deserted rather than be transferred out of the way to the Sahara. It was a fairly comfortable desertion, however, with Degueldre continuing to be fed and housed by officers of the 1st R.E.P. – all of which was suggestive of just how far disaffection in that regiment had gone – and apparently encountering no difficulties in his frequent travels back and forth. Degueldre is described by all who knew him as having a quite exceptional influence over all who entered his sphere, whether junior or senior. As a twenty-year-old sergeant-major in Indo-China, by 1950 he had already won three citations and a recommendation, and that same year saved from almost certain death a wounded captain, Hervé de Blignières. An aristocratic Saumur cavalryman who had escaped from the Germans (and been recaptured) no less than seven times during the Second World War, de Blignières re-encountered Degueldre eight years later in Algeria – he now a colonel and regimental commander, the latter a lieutenant. Falling under his junior's spell, de Blignières in the winter of 1961 became a leading co-ordinator and recruiter of senior militants in France.

Linked by de Blignières, many old familiar faces reappeared, meeting in such places as the office of Colonel Lacheroy in the École Militaire or provincial garrisons to which they had been banished. There was that expert on political in-fighting sometimes called the Fouché of Algiers,

Colonel Yves Godard, who – under a cloud after "Barricades Week" – had applied with extraordinary lack of realism for the post of military attaché to Poland. Although he had served there in 1939, it was hardly probable that he, with his well-known detestation of Communism, would have been acceptable in the Warsaw of 1961; so Godard had been sent to moulder in Nevers. Then, tucked away in Metz, there was his successor as chief-of-staff to General Massu, Colonel Antoine Argoud, who had organised France's first atomic age brigade and was considered to be "the ardent and secret soul" of the "Colonels' soviet", a man of extraordinary physical energy, often walking twenty-five miles a day for relaxation into the Algerian *djebel*, and of exceptional toughness when dealing with captured rebels. There was Colonel Dufour, the absconder with the 1st R.E.P.'s colours, currently exiled to the Black Forest; Colonel Broizat, the monk-crusader whose paras, together with Dufour's, had occupied the centre of the stage in "Barricades Week"; their fellow para colonels, Masselot and Lecomte, recruited during de Gaulle's December visit; and General Jacques Faure, the rugged mountaineer who had been the first to conspire against the political establishment back in 1957. A new acquisition was the acting regimental commander of Dufour's old 1st R.E.P., Major Élie Denoix de Saint-Marc. A member of an old Bordeaux family, at nineteen he had been deported to Buchenwald for his involvement in the Resistance, and had later fought in Indo-China, at Suez and in the Battle of Algiers – where he had voiced the strongest opposition to torture. With the face of a tormented ascetic, Saint-Marc was literally worshipped by his tough, pragmatic Legionnaires, who recognised and accepted the purity of his idealism. One day he was heard to exclaim, after a number of whiskies: "I've had enough, enough, enough! One day I shall commit a *connerie*, an enormous *connerie, une connerie grande comme ça!*" And he did.

A late-comer, but none the less zealous, was Colonel Jean Gardes, only acquitted at the "Barricades Trial" in March. He awaited a new posting but was still under watchful surveillance. Notable abstainers among the legendary colonels of yore were Trinquier and Bigeard, who had both had their fill of Algeria and had moved on to other things – Trinquier to organise mercenaries in Tshombe's Katanga. But the biggest (though predictable) disappointment to the army rebels was General Massu; chastised by de Gaulle after his historic indiscretion of January 1960, disgruntled, but still *toujours con, toujours gaulliste,* the true reincarnation of the Napoleonic *grognard*. When approached by "ultras" shortly after his disgrace, he had said forthrightly of de Gaulle: "*He* is a leader. I have also seen Bidault. He is small and sick, and his overcoat has a fur edging. You cannot replace de Gaulle by Bidault. Well then, *who have you got?*" In the course of the summer of 1960 Massu – still more or less unemployed – had gone canoeing with his old lieutenant, Argoud, but had carefully eschewed all political talk. Later, one by one the dissident colonels had worked on Massu to lead the revolt they were planning. De Blignières reckoned that, but for the strong-minded Madame Massu, the general might have "gone along". But he was wrong: Massu would never default on de Gaulle, would never take any step that might divide the army he so venerated.* At a last visit from Argoud and Broizat on 8 March 1961, Massu growled acridly that he had already reached the conclusion that "the *pieds noirs* would have to decide to wear the fez".

At the court of the "Mandarin"

While this quest for a leader was restlessly in train, there in the wings one was waiting – but few wanted him. One of the inherent problems of conspiracy against the established authority is always that of communication. Stuck away in Madrid, Salan since December was feeling both cut off and bored. Madrid, where the "Mandarin" had set up court at the Hotel Princesa, was a veritable colony for exiled right-wingers – Belgian Rexists, Argentinian Peronists, French Pétainists and former *collabos* – all living locked up in their pasts. One of Salan's first contacts had been Otto Skorzeny, the S.S. colonel who had spirited Mussolini out of Allied hands; he did not hold out very high hopes for Salan's enterprise. Another more encouraging, and useful, ally proved to be Señor Serrano Suñer, Franco's brother-in-law and former Foreign Minister, who showed every enthusiasm for Salan's cause. News from France and Algiers (largely through the medium of Madame (*la biche*) Salan) was sparse. These days were spent at the Tiro de Pichón, or visiting such monuments of the Spanish Civil War as the Alcazar of Toledo (which interested Salan but little), while nights were spent increasingly at the Flamenco (which interested him rather more). Gradually the *dolce far niente* of Madrileño life seemed to be taking a grip on the "Mandarin". Among the few former colleagues to come to throw in their lot with him was the diminutive General Gardy, retired Inspector-General of the Foreign Legion. The "Mandarin" was not greatly impressed by the general's "rumpled clothes ... soggy cigarette butt hanging from the corner of his lips which he tries in vain to keep going, but which refuses to light". He was even more mistrustful of Soustelle who – he claimed – came to see him, refusing to accept any initiative from the former governor-general.

Then suddenly the bail-jumpers from the "Barricades Trial", Lagaillarde

---

* When asked by the author (in 1973) what he would have done had he actually been in Algeria in April 1961, Massu sighed and admitted after a pause: "It would indeed have been a very difficult problem for me. But I would certainly not have marched with the putsch, even if I had been there. Because I would have had no intention of creating divisions within the army, and also because I have always been with de Gaulle, whatever." If nothing else, his record in the critical days of 1968 corroborates this.

and Susini, arrived in Madrid. The "Mandarin" was immediately alienated by the extravaganzas of Lagaillarde, striking poses in front of the Press, and promptly placing himself – the ex-lieutenant and former student leader – on a par with the five-star general and former Commander-in-Chief. "I would indeed like to be shot," declared Lagaillarde at an early stage, "but I want a general at my side!" Lagaillarde's horizons were widening rapidly. He produced ideas for a full-scale reform of the army, gave a large cocktail party for the France–Spain football match, and expressed positive disappointment on hearing that he had been sentenced to only ten years imprisonment (in absentia) at the "Barricades Trial" – which, commented, Salan's loyal adjutant, Captain Ferrandi, "is really very little for a future head-of-state!" By March Salan was hardly on speaking terms with Lagaillarde, and determined to exclude him at all costs from any military coup. Susini, however, the pale and deadly earnest young "ultra" who had been the éminence grise of Ortiz during "Barricades Week", was a different kettle of fish – even though his political antecedents had hardly predisposed the "Mandarin" towards him. Says Ferrandi:

> We discovered in this young man an intense intellectual agility, at the same time as a very real sense of mesure and nuances. His judgements are lively, rapid, admittedly peremptory, but finally always sharp and rarely unreasonable. This young man is made for politics. . . . It's a loss for the Gaullists that they were unable to keep him.

Salan, noted Ferrandi, seemed "literally conquered" by Susini and admitted that "with young men of this class we could finally achieve something". It was under Susini's pressure that Salan, in February, agreed to an extraordinary meeting between himself and two "ultras" currently also in refuge in Spain: Castille and Fechoz, two of the principal instigators of the nearly fatal bazooka attack on him just four years previously. Susini now became Salan's "political director", thereby beginning an association fraught with most baneful consequences for Algeria, and most especially its pieds noirs.

Birth of the O.A.S.

On 25 January a distinguished young pied noir lawyer, Maître Pierre Popie, was stabbed to death in his Algiers office by two young Europeans. The son of a magistrate, Popie was an outspoken liberal – almost the last of them – who had recently aroused indignation by a widely broadcast speech in which he had declared "L'Algérie française ets morte!" and by placards he had distributed depicting pieds noirs shaking hands with the F.L.N. The assassins, who were soon picked up by the Algiers police, turned out to be a recently demobilised para, Claude Peintre, and a former Legionnaire, Léon Dauvergne. Both were sentenced to life imprisonment. But behind them was a newly-created "ultra" terrorist organisation. The killing was apparently intended to mark the anniversary of the beginning of "Barricades Week" but had had to be postponed twenty-four hours.

Sparked no doubt by it, two weeks later in Madrid Susini and Lagaillarde sat down to devise a new body which, composed of civilians and military deserters, would continue to fight for *Algérie française* by underground techniques of terrorism. After some discussion they decided upon the title of Organisation Armée Secrète: O.A.S. When the details were reported to the "Mandarin" at the Princesa two days later, he sighed contemptuously: "Poor *pieds noirs*! They've already had the U.S.R.A.F., the F.A.F. and the F.N.F.! Now with this O.A.S. they'll never manage to recognise it! Nevertheless, if it amuses them and helps them pass the time waiting for better things, then let them get on with it."

At the beginning of March the walls of Algiers suddenly erupted with posters bearing this new set of initials; but the early operations ordered by the O.A.S. were hardly noteworthy for their success. The first, involving the "elimination" of a Gaullist leader and personal friend of the General's in Algiers, Dr Merrot, resulted only in wounding the victim, while his assailant was subsequently executed. On 2 April a bomb exploded near François Mitterrand's apartment, causing little damage; two days later another exploded in the Bourse, injuring fourteen. Then it was decided to tackle de Gaulle himself.* Susini moved in, backing an ex-Legionnaire who proposed in early April to kill de Gaulle with a telescopic rifle for the modest fee of forty million francs. But the would-be killer, having received fifty per cent on account, apparently tipped off the police, and then disappeared. Nevertheless, the O.A.S. had started its rein of terror.

"Challe marche...!"

Towards the end of March General Faure arrived in Madrid with the news that three senior generals were planning a putsch for the following month. The "Mandarin"'s role in it had not yet been defined. The generals were Jouhaud, Zeller – and Challe. The first two names (although, ironically, they had both been selected by de Gaulle as being reliably loyal to himself to replace officers purged from Algeria in the wake of May 1958) were a foregone conclusion; but Challe! Salan asked himself the same question that would perplex Frenchmen from de Gaulle down when the putsch broke on them: "*Mais, pourquoi Challe?*" The news was in fact somewhat premature; although Challe was on the brink, he did not take the final plunge until 12 April.

---

* On 24 December there had already been another abortive attempt to assassinate de Gaulle; led once again by the sergeant-major who had deserted from his para unit during "Barricades Week". This time a vast landmine of ninety pounds of explosive had been placed by the side of the route de Gaulle normally took from Colombey-les-Deux-Églises to Paris. But the look-out – a man who had served with de Gaulle in London – lost his nerve at the critical moment.

When he did take his grave decision to revolt, sudden though it was, it came at the end of a long odyssey incorporating various steps and moti- vations. Back in 1958, at the time of confusion preceding de Gaulle's takeover, Challe had seemed the embodiment of the ideal republican general, leaning if anything towards the Socialists. To his friend Guy Mollet he had remarked, "If this business goes on any longer, only de Gaulle will be capable of putting things back into order," concluding emphatically: "For my part, I will never fire on my comrades in arms." The series of disillusions that he had suffered as de Gaulle's Commander-in- Chief in Algeria have already been amply traced; then had come the President's "*Algérie algérienne*" speech of 4 November 1960, while Challe was commanding N.A.T.O.'s Central Europe theatre at Fontainebleau. Switching off the television, he confided to his diary: "From this moment I shall begin to think deeply about the sense of my remaining in the army." Feeling increasingly a sense of futility at Fontainebleau, on 30 December Challe had offered his resignation. In giving his reasons to Debré, Challe had condemned the prospect of any Algerian government being formed by the G.P.R.A. – which was where he felt de Gaulle's policy was leading. This would inevitably result in a "blood bath" and his conscience would not permit him to remain in the army. The announcement of the popular Challe's retirement caused a far greater stir within the armed forces than had Salan's departure.

From now on Challe came under steadily mounting pressure from dissidents like Argoud, Broizat and de Blignières to join their ranks. He continued to refuse. Then, some time in March after Massu's sturdy *non*, possibly on the suggestion of Gardes, the idea was mooted that Challe should be approached actually to lead the putsch. Jouhaud, Challe's fellow airman, assumed the task and tackled Challe at a wedding service in Lyon on 25 March. Enumerating the officers and units who were "ready to go", Jouhaud assured Challe that, with his great prestige and popularity, he had but to raise his hand and the whole army would follow. (It would never, hinted Jouhaud, follow "Chinese" Salan.) Three days later in Paris, with Georges Bidault and General Faure present, Jouhaud resumed the attack. Two of Challe's former subordinates, aware of the pressure he was under, offered cautionary advice; no more than ten per cent of the army would, in the event, follow him, said one; metropolitan France, "hypnotised by de Gaulle, would oppose any civil or military uprising", said the other. Challe, already a thoroughly tortured man, hesitated. Then fresh events occurred in quick succession. At the end of March simultaneous com- muniqués were published from both Paris and Tunis announcing forth- coming bilateral peace talks at Evian between the French government and the F.L.N. – just what, a year ago, de Gaulle had promised Delouvrier and Challe he would never entertain. Next, in Algeria, the new French

Commander-in-Chief, the pacific and clerical-looking General Gambiez, was relaying orders for a "unilateral truce". To persuade the F.L.N. of France's good intentions, all aggressive combat operations were to cease henceforth on the French side. A sense of fresh outrage ran through the units which had born the lion's share of the murderous fighting in Algeria, and which, in the Challe offensive, had felt they had come within an inch of crushing the life out of the A.L.N. Ominously, there were mass desertions from the *harkis*, those "loyal" Muslim units whose expansion had been one of the chief ingredients of the Challe Plan. Then, twenty-four hours after the first communiqué, the G.P.R.A. (for reasons that will be seen shortly) announced that it was opting out of the negotiations. To the plotters there was now a particular urgency to act while anger was still at red-heat in the army and before the fateful talks could be rescheduled. Challe now said, yes, in principle; the final proviso was that he should just wait to see what de Gaulle had to say at his forthcoming Press conference on 11 April.

The fall of Challe, than whom no more estimable and honourable officer could be found in any army, remains one of the great human tragedies of the Algerian war. It is also a tragedy that should perhaps be pondered by the leaders of other modern democratic armies should they ever come to impose too great a burden upon the consciences of their generals. Among Challe's several motives, it was first and foremost the call of honour that drove him to an act that in his heart he half felt was doomed from the start. Unlike the Algerian-born Jouhaud, Challe was in no way dedicated to the *pieds noirs*. Unlike Salan, he had not been at the centre of the 1958 coup, and therefore did not suffer Salan's sentiments of betrayal of purpose there – namely the safeguarding of *Algérie française* – nor did he share to the same extent Salan's sense of personal aggrievement against de Gaulle. Professionally he had deplored the premature suspension of his offensive against the A.L.N.; as General Étienne Valluy said of Challe, he was "like a craftsman who does the best work he can; it is almost done . . . then it is taken away from him and given to another". That had been a factor and, ideologically, like so many of the French military brotherhood, he too shared to the full the "reds under the bed" obsession that an independent Algeria would bring the "Soviet fleet to Mers-el-Kébir". What he considered to be the disastrously missed opportunity of Si Salah, and de Gaulle's double-dealing with the breakaway leaders of Wilaya 4, had deeply influenced him on his road to revolt. But most of all he was haunted by what he felt to be his crushing moral responsibility to the *harkis* he had levied, and to the other thousands of pro-French Muslims to whom – on de Gaulle's instructions – he had given the repeated assurance: "France will never abandon you." This was what, to Challe, really pushed him over the edge. "We were committed," he told the author. "We had given our promises to the Arabs who had worked for us, and we simply could not let them down.... We would have acted, even if I had thought there had been no chance of success – but I did think we had a chance of success." Massu corroborates that Challe "had a feeling of having betrayed his Algerian compatriots. He had, very sincerely, an ideal of honour." In view of the terrible fate that was to befall the *harkis* after Algerian independence, who can judge that this "ideal of honour" was misplaced?

On 12 April General Faure brought to his fellow conspirators, gathered in a darkened room, the simple message: "*Challe marche!*"* The previous day Challe in disgust had heard de Gaulle deliver an "inhuman homily" to the Press, declaring, "Decolonisation is our interest and, therefore, our policy. Why should we remain caught up in colonisations that are costly, bloody and without end, when our own country needs to be renewed from top to bottom?" Algeria, he was now convinced, "will be sovereign, both within and without", and France would place no obstacle in its way. That was it! Without even informing his wife, Challe decided to act. Planning for the putsch now moved into top gear with Challe at the helm. D-Day was to be the night of 20 April – only eight days away.

Over-hasty planning

As Clemenceau once remarked, for anyone about to revolt "the first day is the best day". But, as unsuccessful putschists – such as Germany's Stauffenberg – have also discovered through the ages, the twin necessities of secrecy and speed, hampered by the inevitability of faulty communication, make precipitate planning the greatest and least escapable enemy of conspiracy. The first move was for the four leaders – Challe, Jouhaud, Salan and Zeller – to reach Algeria by various means and set up the standard of revolt there. Key units, such as the 1st R.E.P., would act simultaneously to seize vital centres and officials in authority; then, by snowball effect, the rest of the army in Algeria would follow suit. But, says Challe sadly in his memoirs, though all but one sector commander had declared himself "for us ... unhappily this was only true in theory, while nothing had been fixed in practice. We were going to have a sad experience here." With typically careless improvidence, for instance, the plotters had neglected to consider that, in Oranie, where General Pouilly was hostile, his deputy, General Lhermitte, on whose support they vitally counted, would be away on leave.

There was also, as usual, inadequate thought (and considerable unresolved disagreement owing to the problem of communication) as to what to do next once the military act had been consummated in Algeria. Challe's programme was to declare solemnly that the French army's unshakable

* By the most bizarre of coincidences, the day on which the putsch was decided – 12 April 1961 – was also the centenary of the day on which South Carolina batteries opened fire on Fort Sumter, thereby sparking off the American Civil War.

intention was to remain in Algeria, and then re-launch a new flat-out "Challe Offensive" against the A.L.N., mobilising eight classes of Algerians of both races for this purpose. In three months he would present France a pacified Algeria, *sur le plateau*. He hoped, in effect (comments Jacques Fauvet): "to finish what two regimes, four commanders-in-chief and seven governments were unable to finish in seven years". During this period of three months, a breakaway Algeria could exist economically off the fat of its oil resources, an embargo being placed on their export to France. For the long-term political future of Algeria, Challe basically supported a return to the principles of Lacoste's abandoned *loi-cadre*. As regards allies, though known to be more left-wing than either of the other two services, the air force was reckoned to be in the bag – largely on account of the presence in the putsch of both Challe and Jouhaud; as for the navy, Challe relied on an out-of-context remark made by Admiral Querville some months previously: "With the navy you have no problem. Whatever happens, it's always one government behind!" On the eve of the putsch, Jouhaud seemed even to have half-deluded himself that Premier Debré might prove sympathetic.

The putsch and the C.I.A.?

In few ways did the generals' self-deception, their interpretation of desires as realities, reach a higher peak than in their almost total lack of thought as to how the outside world might react. To this day Challe insists most emphatically that he "had no contact personally with any foreign countries", and that in fact he had deliberately avoided all such contacts so as not to incur any possible charge of having been brought in on foreign bayonets. Nevertheless, some of his subordinates appear to have made informal, and highly tentative, soundings with representatives of various countries that might be considered sympathetic, among them Portugal, Spain, Israel and South Africa. But nothing more encouraging or positive had been received than offers of "hang on as long as you can, and then we'll see" – beyond a commitment allegedly made by a South African contact promising material aid after eight days. The promise was never to be invoked.

One of the more curious illusions of the putschists (especially in the light of subsequent revelations of the far-ranging activities of the C.I.A.) concerns the possibilty of an American role. At the time, rumours of clandestine United States involvement ran extremely strong in France. Undeniably, during his time at N.A.T.O. headquarters the popular Challe did make firm friends of a number of high-ranking United States generals, who made no secret of their aversion to what de Gaulle was doing to N.A.T.O., going so far – over a plethora of Scotch – as to express enthusiasm for anyone who might rid France of her turbulent president, or, at least, force him to change his tune. If Challe and his colleagues can be excused for taking these utterances at more than face value, one needs to recall the prevailing atmosphere at the time; just four days before the unleashing of the Algiers revolt, the untried and unproved new Kennedy regime had itself launched its own putsch – the "Bay of Pigs" adventure against Castro's Cuba. Writing in 1967 and noting how "only belatedly did President Kennedy declare for de Gaulle and openly condemn the rebel generals", Major Edgar O'Ballance claimed that it was then firmly believed,

> that the American Central Intelligence was actually involved in, and had knowledge of some aspects of the planning and preparation, and perhaps also of the revolt itself, but nowadays this is firmly discounted. This is mentioned to show that there might have been sound reasons for Challe expecting American aid that was not forthcoming.

The Senate C.I.A. hearings of 1975, thorough as they were in every other respect, produced no evidence, however, of any collusion with the French putschists of 1961, and Challe too is categoric on the subject, stressing how strongly antipathetic to Algérie française United States foreign policy had always been, "right from the very earliest days". Any contacts made with the C.I.A. were "not on my orders", and it seems that, if an attempt at a démarche was made at all, Colonel Godard was the intermediary.

Nevertheless, once the putsch started, strong rumours that Challe was seen accompanied by senior United States officers in uniform were lent tendentious support by the fact that the United States Military Attaché in Paris happened, quite fortuitously, to be in Algiers on that critical day of 22 April. As far afield as Tunis there were also rumours that the C.I.A. had promised Challe United States recognition if they succeeded – in order to keep the Communists out of North Africa. Any hopes, however, that all this may have engendered in the bosom of the conspiracy were to be swiftly dashed when the United States Ambassador to Paris, General James M. Gavin (himself a former para of utmost distinction), firmly assured de Gaulle that if any rebels attempted to land on French bases where there were American troops, these would at once open fire. In retrospect, the notion of C.I.A. involvement in the putsch seems to have been largely a canard launched by the Communist Press in France and Italy.*

Disagreements and leaks

Challe continues to insist that it was *not* his design to bring down the de Gaulle government, but merely "to change its policy". Under no circumstances would he, the good republican, back anything that smacked of a

---

* C. L. Sulzberger, then representing the *New York Times* in France, maintains that the C.I.A. knew no more about the timing of the putsch than did the French security services, and that the whole story was launched in Moscow's *Izvestia* of 25 April and later taken up by anti-American circles in Paris.

fascist regime. This moderation, however, was certainly not shared by his fellow plotters, for the majority of whom Captain Sergent probably speaks:

> The absolute key to the whole business was de Gaulle – it was essential that de Gaulle should be removed.... If I had known Challe's thoughts, I would not have gone with him in April 1961 ... I fought to win the war – not like those generals who fought for the sake of their good consciences.

Challe was also at odds with his fellow conspirators as to whether the army should move simultaneously in France too; Challe argued for Algeria only, on the grounds (rightly) that there would be insufficient sympathy among the home-based forces, and secondly that any division of effort would interfere with his pet hobby-horse – continuation of war against the A.L.N.

There was no dearth of latent divisions within the ranks of the putschists. Despising and distrusting the *pied noir* "ultras", Challe was adamant about having nothing to do with Susini; he was supported by para leaders like Masselot and Saint-Marc. In his whole-hearted zeal, Saint-Marc had but one reservation: "Don't let the activists interfere in this affair!" There were also those who, given a free choice, would have kept the inscrutable "Mandarin" out of the action. But that was clearly impossible; nevertheless, it was not till late in the day that a fretting Salan, still isolated in Madrid, was brought fully into the picture. Meanwhile, he in his turn was doing everything he could to conceal the putsch from his *bête noire*, Lagaillarde; it was only on the 18th that Salan, persuaded by Susini of Lagaillarde's mob-appeal, finally agreed to take him along.

With all these comings and goings it was inevitable that word of the pending putsch should reach the ears of the government in Paris. In army circles in Algeria, what was afoot had been discussed fairly widely; on the night of the putsch a notable conversation took place on the open telephone between Madame de Saint-Hillier, wife of the commander of Massu's old 10th Division, and Madame de Saint-Marc:

> "*Dîtes-moi, Madame,* is your husband up to some dirty trick tonight?"
> "Yes, I fear so...!"

Early in March Louis Joxe had heard disquieting rumours in Paris and had passed these on to Jean Morin in Algiers. Snippets of information had flowed into French Intelligence from a variety of sources. These included François Coulet, Morin's political adviser and de Gaulle's private listening-post in Algiers; Herr Blankenhorn, the West German Ambassador in Paris; and Lucien Bitterlin, leader of the Mouvement pour la Communauté in Algeria (whose informant was found floating in a river a few days later). The G.P.R.A. itself allegedly filtered back to the French Ministry of the Interior the names of the four generals as well as the precise date of the expected putsch. But, as so often happens, virtually nothing seems to have been done to act on the information received.

The putsch begins

At 19.15 hours on Thursday, 20 April, Challe accompanied by his fellow five-star general, André Zeller, and Colonel Broizat, took off for Algiers in an air force plane. The aircraft had been "purloined" by General Bigot, a *pied noir* who had had a brilliant war career flying Marauder bombers with Challe, and who now commanded the Fifth Air Region in Algeria. His superior, General Nicot, Commander-in-Chief of the Air Force, turned a blind eye, but sent Challe off with the caution: "I am convinced that you are committing a stupidity...." Lying on their stomachs under packages marked *service cinématographique de l'armée*, and flying at 150 feet to evade the French radar screen, the former Commander-in-Chief was smuggled indecorously out of France. On landing at Algiers there was a first hitch; no reception committee. The plane had been expected at Blida, not Algiers. Once again it took off. This time all was well; the anxiously waiting para officers now had their leader. Salan was still in Madrid, but Jouhaud – free to move without let or hindrance as a resident – was already in Algiers, ostentatiously lunching at the Algiers Yacht Club with his wife so as to mislead the detectives constantly shadowing him. There were immediately other hitches; Challe found an order, bearing his own signature but apparently put out by the 1st R.E.P., postponing the operation twenty-four hours for no very good reason, while Godard, the master intelligence operator, in the excitement of arriving had mislaid in a public corridor his briefcase containing all details of the putsch.

Concealed "underground" at a para headquarters in the Villa des Tagarins, Challe spent the day of Friday the 21st setting up his command network, checking Godard's tactical plan for the coup – which he apostrophised as "perfect" – drafting his first proclamation for the next day, and making numerous covert telephone calls to confirm the "loyalty" of unit leaders who had declared for the putsch. At Zéralda Captain Sergent, returned from his exile in Chartres to the 1st R.E.P., got his orders to "go" from Major de Saint-Marc. His company, the spearhead of the whole operation, was to head for Algiers, twenty miles distant, shortly after midnight. Inevitably more precise leaks now percolated through to those unsympathetic to the putschists. From Tizi-Ouzou General Simon, in command of Kabylia, one of the senior officers who was to remain rock-firm in support of de Gaulle, telephoned to warn Morin at the Palais d'Été that evening that "something was afoot". Morin telephoned the Commander-in-Chief, Gambiez, who rang back with some irritation, around midnight, assuring the Government-Delegate that all was well: "I've spoken to Saint-Marc at Zéralda. He's just returned from dining with General Saint-Hillier. When I mentioned the movement of troops of the general reserve, why, that made him laugh. Everything at his end is perfectly quiet." Next, a telephone call from the Ministry of the Interior in Paris gave Morin quite different intelligence. After Gambiez had had two more conversations, in increasing ill-humour, with the Government-Delegate, the deceived but courageous little general set off himself by staff-car towards Zéralda to find out what was happening.

On the outskirts of Algiers Gambiez ran into the 1st R.E.P., heading at fifty miles per hour for the city. Sergent's jeep, driven like Jehu by a German Legionnaire, had already crashed through several unsuspecting gendarme barricades. Almost apoplectic with rage Gambiez dauntlessly attempted to bar the way with his own car, and a singular roadside dialogue ensued between the general and a young para liutenant:

"You recognise me . . . I'm the Commander-in-Chief."

"You are nothing any longer. Challe and Zeller have arrived. It's them we obey."

"In my day, lieutenants didn't answer generals like that."

"In my day, generals didn't sell out *Algérie française!*"

Still endeavouring to "arrest" the rebels, Gambiez suffered what, for a French general, must have been the unsurpassable humiliation of watching his car heaved into a ditch and of being marched off himself by German Legionnaires, most of them understanding little of what he had to say. The column continued on to Algiers.

At the Palais d'Été de Gaulle's Minister of Public Works, Robert Buron, was asleep in his bed, having come to Algiers on a twenty-four-hour visit to attend a Chamber of Commerce banquet in the Hôtel Saint-George. There was an agitated knock on his door, and a polite voice said: "Excuse me, *Monsieur le Ministre*, and please don't laugh. The palace has been seized by parachutists. Monsieur Morin thinks that you would prefer to receive them dressed, rather than in your bed. I assure you, it's not a joke. . . ." Hastily dressing, Buron thought to himself: "What a mess! . . . I was only with Frey and Messmer [Ministers of the Interior and Defence respectively] yesterday afternoon; why didn't they know something was being prepared?" Buron found Morin and his staff under arrest, also by German-speaking Legionnaires who had "no precise orders and seemed not to know what to do with us". With remarkable incompetence, the putschists had also neglected to cut all the telephone lines from the Palais d'Été, so that Morin had managed to call Paris and many of the key command centres.* Oran and Constantine remained untroubled, with their respective generals-commanding declaring loyalty to de Gaulle. Admiral Querville, tipped off by a young naval officer, had escaped from his villa in plain clothes and locked himself up in the Admiralty, where he too declared himself "loyal". His air force opposite number, Bigot, reported – somewhat

---

* Again there is a parallel with Stauffenberg's plot of 20 July 1944, which aborted to a large extent through the failure of General Fellgiebel to destroy communications between Hitler's Wolfsschanze headquarters in East Prussia and Berlin.

disingenuously – that he had only just woken up and knew nothing of what was going on.

The first day: Challe satisfied

By dawn on the 22nd, Challe at Les Tagarins was well satisfied with the way things had gone. All the vital centres of Algiers were safely under his control; Morin and Gambiez and their staffs were under lock and key. The one black spot had been the death of a sergeant-major, shot down when trying to defend the Algiers radio transmitter; but, apart from a senior general punched by a beefy German Legionnaire (of course, the Germans got all the blame that day!), this had been the only casualty in an otherwise bloodless operation. (Meanwhile, Sergent, off his own bat, had gone and liberated various "ultra" activists, like Dr Pérez, who had been in the cells since "Barricades Week", thereby letting a considerable genie out of the bottle.) The first thing the *pieds noirs* knew of the revolt was at 7 a.m. when an anonymous voice interrupted the early morning news to announce: "The army has assumed control of Algeria and the Sahara.... *Algérie française* is not dead.... There is not, and never will be, an independent Algeria. Long live *Algérie française*, so that France may live!" A military march followed, and it was announced, with pointed symbolism, that "Radio Alger" was henceforth changing its name to "Radio France". That Saturday was one of those magical days of clear, exhilarating skies and spring warmth that makes the pulse of Algiers beat again – and rapidly. The city streets began to fill with cars beating out on their horns the notes of "*Al-gé-rie fran-çaise!*". Festoons of red, white and blue appeared on balconies, and passers-by cheered wildly as truck-loads of paras drove past.

Challe now prepared to move back to his old headquarters in the Quartier Rignot, which he had occupied the previous year. In the meantime, he had edited with his fellow generals his proclamation for broadcasting over "Radio France". "I am in Algiers, together with generals Zeller and Jouhaud, in order to keep our solemn promise, the promise of the army to hold Algeria, so that our dead shall not have died for nothing," it began. There was at first conspicuously no mention of the absent Salan until, under pressure, Challe added, after the names of the three generals, the words, "in liaison with General Salan". There then followed a diatribe against "a government of capitulation", condemning it for intending to deliver Algeria to "the external organisation of the rebellion", and making specific reference to its failure to deal with Si Salah (an episode which, up to that moment, remained still unknown to all but the inner circle).*

---

* Challe told the author that when mention of Si Salah's name was made at Challe's trial, the Public Prosecutor immediately attempted to have the session held *in camera*.

Algeria was also placed, once again, firmly in the context of the international struggle against Communism.

After a few brief instants of euphoria, Challe's troubles began. At every turn there was evidence of the lack of forethought in the planning of the coup. The generals had divided responsibilities among themselves as follows:

Challe: military matters.
Jouhaud: information and propaganda.
Salan (when he arrived): civil affairs.
Zeller: economics and administration.

The least imposing of the quartet, Zeller, was an irascible sixty-three-year-old Alsatian (described by one writer as perpetually bearing "the ruffled look of an angry hen") who had huffily resigned from the army twice in the space of four years. Finally retired as Chief-of-Staff to the Ground Forces, he was regarded as an expert on logistics, but the report he now gave Challe was unexpectedly depressing: there was only three weeks' stock of medical supplies, milk and olive oil, while the vaults of the Banque de France were found to contain no more than twelve million dollars and less than a million dollars in gold and foreign currency. Zeller now reckoned that an Algeria boycotted by France could last little more than a fortnight – a considerable reduction on the three months bandied around before the generals left France – added to which, none of the potential foreign "allies" looked like coming forward with any kind of material aid.

Of greater and more immediate concern to Challe was the allegiance of those military leaders in Algeria on whom he had counted. Admiral Querville had escaped to a warship and steamed off to the impregnable naval base of Mers-el-Kébir (though, in fact, the navy was to play little part on one side or the other during the putsch; as one officer remarked acidly, "It's always missed the boat, ever since Trafalgar!"). In Kabylia General Simon had made it clear from the beginning that he would not go along. In Oranie General Pouilly proved a disappointment, while his deputy whom Challe had hoped would activate the general had, as previously noted, gone on leave; so had a number of other army leaders when the moment for action came. General Gardy, the retired Inspector-General of the Foreign Legion whose appearance had so little impressed Salan, was sent off with Colonel Argoud to stiffen support in Oranie. Gardy was at once distressed to discover his old comrades at Sidi-Bel-Abbès refusing to collaborate. As one after another senior officer faltered when confronted by the terrible dilemma of loyalty imposed on him by the rebels, a swift chain-reaction set in until all the generals in the Oranie command had pronounced against the putsch – or, at best, offered their inert neutrality. In a rage, Argoud ordered Colonel Masselot to arrest General Pouilly, but –

typical of the interlocking relations – the two were bound by personal tragedies in that Masselot's son had been killed while serving under Pouilly, and Pouilly's son killed under Masselot. Though committed to the putsch, privately Masselot told Pouilly that he would not lift a finger against him.

Even more symptomatic of the agonies of conscience within the French army in those days was the anguish of the commander of the Constantine area, General Gouraud, scion of a renowned military family and whose uncle had been the famous one-armed hero-general of the First World War. Gouraud found himself appalled by de Gaulle's "policy of abandon", but equally appalled by commitment to revolt and all that it implied. Of his waverings, some may say he was riven by opposing vectors of honour, others that he was simply irresolute. During de Gaulle's visit of December Gouraud had (according to de Gaulle) declared solemnly: "I can answer for myself and my subordinates!" Late on the night of 21 April, when pressed by Challe he had pledged "Bien sûr, je marche"; only a few hours later, however, after Morin had got on to him over the uncut line from the Palais d'Été, Gouraud was back on the telephone to Challe telling him that he had "reconsidered". All through that first day he had wavered back and forth; meanwhile, the units under him had stood still, to the great discomfort of Challe. Gouraud's command was considered to hold the balance of the revolt. An attempt was made to replace him by another general, Maisonrouge, who had previously promised support but whose response now was "I can't, I'm ill . . . I'm spitting blood. . . ." The peppery Zeller was despatched on Sunday the 23rd to talk Gouraud round, and after an angry shouting match the Constantine commander finally committed himself publicly, too late to render much assistance to the putsch but in time to shatter in fragments a lifetime's career of honour and distinction.

Sunday, 23 April: the clouds build up; Salan arrives

As the counting of heads was completed by the morning of Sunday, Day Two of the putsch, it was painfully clear to Challe that only Algiers and its surrounding region was totally reliable; while the units committed wholeheartedly to the revolt numbered chiefly the elitist para regiments. Even among them the primus inter pares of Bigeard's and Trinquier's famous 3rd, with its "lizard's beak" headgear, had opted out under its resolutely pro-government new commander, Colonel Le Borgne.

On Sunday the halcyon blue skies of the previous day were replaced, symbolically enough, by the Chergui – that unpleasant wind from the Sahara which frays tempers and distorts thought – blowing violently and covering the city with a gritty film of sand. The paras on guard at the vital city centres lounged about, sleeping in the streets or looking bored, with little apparent discipline or direction. In the empty corridors of the

Délégation-Générale a few clerks strolled about with a lost and lugubrious air. Then, around midday, there arrived an eminent accretion to Challe's ranks – also, however, accompanied by its own additional headaches.

Since 20 April, in Madrid the "Mandarin" 's court had lived in a state of anxiety, waiting from minute to minute for the putsch to begin – all except the "Mandarin" himself, who, according to his adjutant, Ferrandi, "always impassive, returns from his cabaret at 4 o'clock each morning". At 6 a.m. on the 22nd a breathless Susini had telephoned to announce the beginning of the putsch. Dodging the half-hearted Spanish police surveillance which had been placed on him at French request, the next morning Salan and his entourage secretly boarded a plane provided by his friend and supporter, Serrano Suñer. To Salan's manifest relief, Lagaillarde was prevented by the Spanish police from joining the party. The putsch would have to manage without its "d'Artagnan". The "Mandarin" comported himself, says Ferrandi, as if "he were accomplishing the most banal of voyages on a regular line. Not a grain of dust on his clothes, his shoes glittered as always in the old *coquetterie* of the colonial soldier." Suñer had accompanied them to Barajas airport, but his send-off was hardly inspiriting. "Your affair is lost. The generals in Algiers lack energy. They have had neither Morin nor Gambiez shot. Franco would never have hesitated." At Algiers Salan was received coolly by Challe; nevertheless, the quartet presented themselves to their adherents in public as an imposing array of solidarity and five-star brass, to sing the *Marseillaise* in unison together at the Forum. But behind the scenes there was soon friction and dissent. Susini plunged into contact with the inchoate O.A.S. headquarters, who began preparing sinister round-up lists of "enemies of the nation". On hearing of this, Colonel Godard immediately announced that he would "shoot the first to touch a single hair of a civilian", and Saint-Marc reiterated that he would have nothing whatever to do with "assassins". On the other hand, the "activists" were critical of Challe's irresolution in declining to make any move that he considered might precipitate civil war. Meanwhile, to add a note of farce to events, the *bistrotier* leader of "Barricades Week", Jo Ortiz, from the distance of his Spanish retreat pronounced himself "Head of the Provisional Government of Algeria".

. . . and in France

And how, meanwhile, were de Gaulle and his government in Paris reacting to all this? On the night of the 21st de Gaulle and his new Minister for Algerian Affairs, Louis Joxe, had attended a performance of *Britannicus*, Racine's play about treason at court during the early rule of Nero. Later, well after the General had retired to bed, Joxe heard the first news of the putsch and – breaching a strict standing order – telephoned the Élysée to rouse him. With immediate *sangfroid*, as usual, de Gaulle simply enquired:

"What are you going to do, then, Joxe?"

"I suppose go to Algeria, somehow."

"*Bien*...."

Joxe says that de Gaulle then summoned him to the Élysée, "but only to shake me by the hand, say *au revoir*, and tell me, 'You have all powers.'" There were no more detailed instructions. Accompanied by the new Chief-of-Staff to the Armed Forces, General Jean Olié, Joxe flew off courageously into the unknown.

To his first meeting of cabinet ministers on the 22nd de Gaulle is recorded as declaring contemptuously, "*Ce qui est grave dans cette affaire, Messieurs, c'est qu'elle n'est pas sérieuse...!*" It was "a matter of three days", he reckoned, grumbling acrid asides about "this army which, politically, always deludes itself". To Tricot he remarked a short time later, with a gesture of weary cynicism, "If they want to land in France, they will land. That's up to them. There won't be much to stop them. What will happen? Oh, it's not difficult to guess: these are men of narrow vision; they will very soon be faced with problems that will be beyond them...."

Possibly the true hero of that first stupefying day in France was Roger Frey, de Gaulle's Minister of the Interior. Acting with speed and vigour, he swooped to arrest the sporting General Faure and several other conspirators *in flagrante*, thereby nipping in the bud an attempt to march on the capital. For this purpose, on the evening of the 22nd some 1,800 lightly equipped paras were waiting in the Forest of Orléans, and another four hundred in the Forest of Rambouillet. Joining up with tank units from Rambouillet, they were to move in three columns on Paris, seizing the Élysée and other key points of the administration. But, organised by Godard, the whole venture had a strongly amateurish note about it, with some of the waiting putschists apparently unaware even of the codeword *Arnat* (a simple elision of *Armée* and *Nationale*). Once they were rendered leaderless by Faure's arrest, no orders came through until a detachment of gendarmes appeared in the forest and gave a brusque order to disperse, with which the powerful body of paras sheepishly complied. Meanwhile, from Germany General Crépin had signalled the wholehearted loyalty of the troops under him, and similar messages of fidelity were reaching de Gaulle from all over France. A state of emergency was declared, and with it was invoked Article 16 of the Constitution enabling the authorities to hold without charge any suspect for fifteen days.

The Caravelle bearing Joxe and Olié had meanwhile touched down in Oranie unintercepted. General Pouilly asserted his loyalty but could not be sure how long he would remain at liberty, and urged de Gaulle's delegates not to tarry. Hedge-hopping at a dangerously low altitude, they then flew on to Telergma near Constantine, which Joxe reckoned would be the key to the situation. There they temporarily won over the wavering Gouraud, but as the Caravelle took off in darkness for Bône and home it narrowly escaped capture by a para column converging on the airfield. Late the following night Morin, the Government-Delegate, and the other captives in the Palais d'Été were flown for "safe-keeping" to the desert outpost of In-Salah. It gave Colonel François Coulet a queasy sensation that perhaps they were all going to end by being shot.

That Sunday, 23 April, Paris began to present an extraordinary spectacle under the warming spring sunshine. Elderly Sherman tanks of Second World War vintage rumbled out from retirement to take up positions outside the Assembly and other government buildings. Discouragingly, some broke down and had to be towed across the Concorde. Compared with the modernity of equipment in Algeria, it was painfully plain that – as de Gaulle had remarked to Tricot – there was not "much to stop them" should Challe's paras make a determined bid to land in France. All air movement round Paris was halted; buses and trains stopped running, and even the cinemas closed down; only the cafés remained open for business, and they were crammed with Parisians discussing the latest turn in the crisis. At eight o'clock that night all France clustered round the television as de Gaulle addressed the shaken, anxious nation. Once again, as during his broadcast at the time of "the Barricades", he was dressed in his brigadier's uniform. There were dark circles round the eyes which visibly filled with pain as he spoke of his beloved army in revolt. Scathingly he dismissed the rebel leaders as a "*quarteron*** of generals in retirement". But here was "the nation defied, our strength shaken, our international prestige debased, our position and our role in Africa compromised. And by whom? *Hélas! Hélas! Hélas!* By men whose duty, honour and *raison d'être* it was to serve and to obey...." With utmost forceful emphasis, striking the table with his fist to reinforce his words, he then enjoined: "In the name of France, I order that all means, I repeat *all means*, be employed to block the road everywhere to those men ... I forbid every Frenchman, and above all every soldier, to execute any of their orders...." No excuses or extenuating circumstances whatever for disobeying this order would be accepted. Finally, he ended with one of his impassioned, personal appeals: "*Françaises, Français!* Look where France risks going, in contrast to what she was about to become. *Françaises, Français! Aidez-moi!*" Among many thousand others, Janet Flanner rated the speech de Gaulle's "greatest speaking performance of his career": "When he cried three times '*Hélas! Hélas! Hélas!*' it was the male voice of French tragedy, more moving, because anguished by reality, than any stage voice in *Britannicus*...."

---

* *Quarteron*, the word de Gaulle used in a dismissive sense here, is virtually untranslatable. Literally it denotes a quarter (of a pound or of 100), but it is occasionally used to mean a handful or small group (of people).

Three hours later, as an acute anti-climax, there appeared on the screens the haggard, ill-shaven face of Premier Debré, speaking in jerky sentences and as nervous as de Gaulle had seemed sternly composed. Rebel paras were poised to drop from the skies, he warned: "As soon as the sirens sound, go on foot or by car and convince these deluded soldiers of their grave error. Good sense must come from the soul of the people and let everyone feel himself a part of the nation." Once the danger was past, Debré's melodramatic appeal was long the subject of a barrage of ridicule. However, all through that night "volunteers" flooded the Ministry of the Interior to offer assistance. Like Henry V before Agincourt, André Malraux stalked through their ranks, rekindling in his own mind Teruel, Guadalajara and other epic moments of the Spanish Civil War. Uniforms and helmets were issued – but no weapons. The next day (Monday, the 24th) a highly successful general strike of an hour's duration was promoted by the Left in protest against the putsch; the trade unions called in unison for "arms for the people"; while the Communists, reinforcing this call, claimed they could mount some 15,000 combat-worthy militiamen to meet the crisis. It was all much more impressive than the demonstrations mounted in May 1958, and suddenly the government found itself facing not merely the threat posed by a "*quarteron* of generals in retirement", but the ugly spectre of civil war at home.

Monday, 24 April

In fact, an invasion of metropolitan France was never on the hard-pressed Challe's programme, while events of the 24th were to render it physically impossible anyway. On Sunday morning Challe – full of self-assurance – had proclaimed, "Yesterday we were nothing. . . . Today we are the greater part of Algeria . . . General Olié is in flight." But twenty-four hours later the situation looked radically different. Challe had not slept for three nights, keeping himself alive on tobacco. The whole head-quarters reeked with the sour odour of stale smoke. Deepening troubles were crowding in on him. Perhaps the most humiliating blow to his pres-tige as an air force general was that – like the "god Hercules" deserting Mark Antony before Alexandria – Nicot and the air force had started defecting from the rebel cause. At the beginning of the putsch there had been forty-five big Noratlases and various other transports capable of ferrying two regiments, but one by one these now slipped off to France. Mystère fighters were sent up to patrol the Rhône valley, with orders to force down any rebel aircraft attempting to head for Paris. By Tuesday the 25th Algeria was virtually denuded of troop-carrying aircraft, even down to the hospital transports. Meanwhile, more and more ground units were denying their support. In the Constantine sector it was clear that the vacillating Gouraud, though braced up temporarily by Zeller's petulant visit on the Sunday, was being less than wholeheartedly obeyed. The situation in Oranie was worse, and at General Gardy's request Challe had despatched Colonel Masselot's and Colonel Lecomte's para regiments to seize power there. But disquietingly enough even two of Lecomte's three companies refused to move against the fortress of Mers-el-Kébir. To avert a tragic situation where it looked as if French troops were within an ace of firing on each other, General Pouilly, the loyal commander of Oranie, flew to Algiers for a remarkable confrontation with Challe. Knowing how Challe (who had been in his term at St Cyr) would shrink from any such danger, Pouilly put to him squarely just how close was civil war within the armed forces. For his pains, Pouilly was sent off to join the other government prisoners in the desert at In-Salah. But Challe took the hint, pulling back his flying columns of paras and deciding to concentrate all on the region round Algiers. At the same time he announced that any conscripts who wished to opt out would be freely repatriated back to France – but how? There would be no naval ships available, and soon no air transports.

More than any other single factor, however, what really decided the issue on that Monday, 24 April, was the remarkable impact that de Gaulle's speech of the previous night had had upon the conscripts and reservists in Algeria. In their tens of thousands they huddled round their transistor radios (the rebel generals having failed, as with so much else, to jam broadcasts from France), listening to the President's uncompromising call for obedience and loyalty to the state. It was, says one expert on the French army, Paul-Marie de la Gorce, "the first time in French military history that a chief of state appealed to troops over the heads of their rebellious superiors". Unconsulted by their officers, many of the rank-and-file had felt at least apathetic towards the putsch in the first place; there were also many, in inverted snobbery, who bore a resentment against the braggadocio of the paras – who got all the girls, the decorations and the fame, and tended to treat the "line" regiments with all the arrogance of elitism. Now de Gaulle's clearcut orders to use "all means" to stop the rebels, with their underlying threat of civil war, gave them essential moral reinforcement in their opposition. The President had absolved them of all disciplinary requirements to obey their seniors. To the waverers, here was an excuse now to be firm, and they in turn carried along those of their officers who had hitherto vacillated. Like wild-fire a kind of passive resistance spread. All over Algeria slogans appeared painted on the walls and roofs of army barracks, warning: "Don't count on the rank-and-file!" Signal units refused to pass on messages between the rebels; in Constantine arms depots were seized; in one rebel regiment a grenade was actually thrown into the colonel's command post. By the afternoon, as the exhausted and unhappy Challe noted, "failure was developing with a chain reaction".

It was no exaggeration to call this turning-point of the putsch the "victory of the transistors". Once again de Gaulle, with his uncanny sense of timing and feel for the nation's pulse, had wrought a miracle.

Challe gives in

Meanwhile, in Challe's immediate circle there were bitter grumblings at the way things were going, at the former Commander-in-Chief's apparent irresolution and absolutely steadfast refusal to undertake any measure that might lead to bloodletting between French soldiers. There were serious thoughts among the *à outrance* faction – Susini, Pérez, Degueldre and Sergent – to stage a putsch within a putsch; to seize Challe and replace him with Salan at the head of a new Committee of Public Safety. Susini proposed setting up "tribunals" to impose summary justice on all "officials guilty of sabotage". Another prominent member of the O.A.S. claimed afterwards that he wanted to kill de Gaulle and added: "If Salan had been in command, there would have been killing, because Salan – in contrast to Challe – would not have hesitated to reduce by force any units hostile to the putsch; there would have been a much more revolutionary approach." But events were moving altogether too fast. After snatching a few hours' sleep for the first time on Monday night, Challe awoke on Tuesday morning to the conclusion that all was lost. He would give himself up – but alone. Godard angrily protested, interjecting an invidious comparison that the previous year Lagaillarde with less than a thousand men had "held the government in check for a whole week, and we with two divisions, are we going to give up after four days? I can't accept it!" Zeller, as usual, flew into a rage. But, temporarily, it was the all-persuasive Susini who managed to argue Challe round, on the grounds that it would be an unspeakable crime now to abandon the civil population. Bravely, in the face of worsening news flowing in from all quarters, Challe struggled to keep the revolt going the rest of the day. Then, at midnight, he and his three colleagues in rebellion appeared for the last time on the historic balcony of the Gouvernement-Général. Almost symbolically, the microphone failed to work, and for a moment Challe wrestled with the connection. Then, says Captain Sergent, watching from the crowd, "the shadow lifted its arms in a great sign of impotence". Sergent heard an old *pied noir* woman close to him sob, "*Ce n'est pas vrai! Ce n'est pas vrai!*" Like four Chinese silhouettes, without voice or substance, the generals disappeared, for the last time.

Challe now set off to Zéralda with the 1st R.E.P., the last of the faithful. There he told Major Saint-Marc of his intention to give himself up and face the music, but exhorting him not to do the same: "the retribution is going to be tough. Get out and let me pay the bill alone. You're young, happier times will come for you." Saint-Marc refused. He had brought his regiment into the revolt, and would remain at its head until "they come for me". Challe then took leave of Salan and Jouhaud (Zeller having already put on civilian clothes and melted into the Algiers crowd), embracing both of them and handing them most of the money he had on his person. Jouhaud told Challe he understood his reasons for giving himself up, but as for himself, "I want to die on my native ground rather than in the ditches of Vincennes."* He and Salan then took off their uniforms and disappeared to "continue the fight by other means". They were followed by several other of the rebel leaders: Sergent, who had briefly toyed with the thought of committing suicide; Godard, hidden in the apartment of a pretty *pied noir* journalist; and Gardes, smuggled out of Algiers in the boot of a car.

At ten o'clock the following morning, Challe – dressed in civilian clothes and parka, a pipe clenched as usual between his teeth, his face lined with fatigue and tragedy – set off for Maison-Blanche airport, where a plane was to fly him to Paris and prison. He was convinced that he was also flying to the firing squad. At the airport one colonel who had opposed Challe throughout came up to him: "You know that I disapprove of what you have done, but your attitude has been and remains noble. I ask you for permission to embrace you." Disembarking at Villacoublay, the exhausted Challe tripped and fell, and sensationalist papers suggested he had been endeavouring to commit suicide. "I do not, however," remarks Challe drily in his memoirs, "recommend this procedure."

Down at In-Salah in the Sahara, on the Tuesday Robert Buron had been awakened by a heavy rumble in the distance. It was France's latest atomic bomb test at Reggane – an extraordinary demonstration of the realities of Gaullist power, in spite of the fact that in Algiers to the north the rebel generals were still in power. The next morning the government prisoners were flown back to Algiers, preceded by a somewhat farcical scene where the *maître d'hôtel* had questioned anxiously as to who now was going to assume responsibility for the bill for their keep, and General Gambiez had asked Buron whether he would like the Foreign Legion – their former gaolers – to render full military honours. Back in his deserted office in Algiers, François Coulet, who at one time had felt sure that he and his colleagues would be shot, found that the safe had been broken into and all the money contained in it stolen. Apart from that, a signed photograph of de Gaulle had been demonstratively ripped in pieces.

On Thursday the 27th twelve hundred "green berets" of the 1st R.E.P. pulled out forever from their base at Zéralda, *en route* for disgrace and disbandment. Before they went they had dynamited their barracks and fired off in the air all their remaining ammunition. Little was left behind but the gravestones – many of them bearing German-sounding names – of

* In 1804 the Duc d'Enghien was shot as a traitor in the castle moat at Vincennes.

the more than 300 men the regiment had lost in the six years of campaigning against the F.L.N. As the Legionnaires drove off in their transports they bellowed out in a full-bodied roar the plaintive but brave words of Edith Piaf's "*Je ne regrette rien*". Watching them go, *pieds noirs* lining the route wept hopelessly. The revolt of the Centurions against de Gaulle was well and truly finished. It had lasted just four days and five nights.

CHAPTER TWENTY-TWO

Overtures for Peace

October 1960 – December 1961

France must understand now that a negotiation can no longer be entered into today on what Ferhat Abbas demanded with moderation in 1943. Our people have not eaten grass and roots in order to obtain a new statute given as a concession.

Saad Dahlab, 20 July 1960

Purge and punishment

"THERE is one fact which *they* refuse to take into account; a fact which is nevertheless essential and which brings failure to all their calculations," de Gaulle confided to Robert Buron the day after his return from sequestration by the rebels at In-Salah: "That fact is de Gaulle. I don't always understand it very well myself . . . but I am a prisoner of it." Once again *they*, his multifarious enemies, had been routed by that old, sure touch of magic. It is just conceivable that, if faced by one of the weak governments of the Fourth Republic, the rebels might have succeeded. But there were a number of good reasons why the generals' putsch had collapsed as swiftly as it did: it was planned with undue haste; its leaders gravely over-estimated the appeal and influence that retired officers (even those as popular as Challe) can wield over ambitious serving officers; they refused to co-ordinate their plans with the *pieds noirs* "ultras"; they had no co-herent long-range strategy; they miscalculated the encouragement they might expect abroad, and the mood of French civilians at home; and – above all – they failed to consider what might be the reactions of the rank-and-file of the army in Algeria. All these were contributory factors, yet undoubtedly none carried so powerful an impact as de Gaulle's stern commands for obedience to the rank-and-file over the heads of their leaders – the "Victory of the Transistors". So the old magic had triumphed once again – but at what a terrible cost, this time!

The magnificent French army was torn in pieces. It would be many years before the wounds would heal; in some ways, perhaps they would never heal. Reading in May the long lists of the senior officers disgraced, Janet Flanner remarks that the front page of *France-Soir* "looked like a

bankruptcy report". Approximately 14,000 officers and men were estimated to have been implicated in the revolt in one degree or another, and
by the end of April five generals and 200 other officers had been arrested.
Each and every one was required to give an hour-by-hour account of his
activities during the putsch, and for months afterwards the most disagreeable form of witch-hunt ensued. Conscripts denounced regular officers,
seniors their juniors, and *vice versa*. Those who had perched unadmirably
on the fence were now praised for their "abstention", while those who
had declared themselves forthrightly were condemned. It was all a
thoroughly nasty episode, bringing out much of the worst in human
nature, and for many months its poison lingered in the body of the French
army. On 1 May there began the trial of the rebel leaders – causing
surprisingly few ripples of interest in France. Those who had "gone underground" – Generals Salan, Jouhaud and Gardy, and Colonels Argoud,
Broizat, Gardes, Godard and Lacheroy – were all sentenced to death *in
absentia*. Meanwhile, after ten days in hiding, a dilapidated, elderly figure
in civilian clothes gave himself up in a park in Algiers. It was General
André Zeller. After spending one night in a chicken coop and several
concealed by a brother-in-law, Zeller had been decided by the news that
Constantine's General Gouraud, for whose ultimate and fatal decision
Zeller felt personally responsible, had been arrested. Insisting that he
should not be arrested by the police like a common felon, but should have
a proper officer escort, Zeller surrendered to face trial with Challe.

Fully expecting the death sentence, Challe received the maximum
sentence of fifteen years' imprisonment, suffering the loss of his rank,
decorations and pension. Ruined by a participation that had been pressed
upon him, that he had never wholeheartedly wanted, he felt satisfied that
at least he had "saved the honour of the army". Zeller and Bigot, the
commander of the Fifth Air Region who had enabled Challe to make his
flight to Algiers, both shared Challe's sentence. Nicot, chief-of-staff to the
air force, received twelve years; Major Denoix de Saint-Marc of the 1st
R.E.P., ten years; Colonels Masselot and Lecomte eight years; and the
unhappy General Gouraud, seven years. Several hundred other officers
received lesser punishments.* Amid much grief, fine regiments like the
1st R.E.P., the 14th and 18th R.C.P., were disbanded and their officers
posted away to France. Units that had blotted their copy-books to a lesser
extent were sent to the frontiers of Algeria, but with their fuel so strictly
rationed as to make it difficult for any of them to make their way to the
Algiers or Oran areas. Shattered by the sentences, Massu conspicuously

* All those still serving sentences were freed following de Gaulle's massive amnesty
of 1968. It has often been alleged that, in the wake of the devastating riots that
shook Paris in the May of that year, the loyalty promised by Massu (then commanding the army in Germany) was made conditional upon an amnesty for all his fellow-
officers still atoning for sins committed during the Algerian war.

absented himself from the twentieth anniversary commemoration of de Gaulle's famous Free French address of 18 June 1940. Distinguished soldiers like General de Bollardière resigned from the army they loved; General André Beaufre, in line to become Chief-of-Staff to the Armed Forces, decided to retire that September rather than preside over an army "torn in two". Torn in two and sorely demoralised it was. In the aftermath of the putsch a public opinion poll indicated that now only twenty-four per cent of Frenchmen were confident they could "trust" their army. In Algeria the sense of let-down among the *pieds noirs* who had tacitly hoped for Challe's success was naturally enough immense. A gaping vacuum was left, which, in their despair, something grim and terrifying would have to fill.

Strong negotiating position of the F.L.N.

In practicable terms, the failed putsch meant that de Gaulle now had to abandon all hope of imposing on Algeria the kind of peace "by association with France" for which he had been hoping over the past months. The breaking of the army in Algeria and its ensuing demoralisation deprived de Gaulle of any tool for "enforcement". The April 1961 putsch, says Bernard Tricot, "made even more inevitable the result which it had wanted to prevent, at the same time reducing the chances of attaining it under acceptable conditions". It was abundantly clear that de Gaulle had now no option but to negotiate purposefully to end the war, but as the next round of negotiations approached it was equally clear just how weak his own bargaining hand had become – how strong that of the F.L.N. Over the best part of the ensuing year the talks were to drag wearily on, with the jaded French being forced to yield one bastion after another in the quest for peace.

From the moment of the Muslim riots in December 1960, which had so shaken de Gaulle in his hopes and which had occasioned a real turning-point in the war, everything seemed to be going for the F.L.N. Both at home and abroad the pressures had been mounting on de Gaulle to make peace. In the United States John F. Kennedy, the avowed friend of Algerian independence, had become president and was soon leaning heavily on de Gaulle. If the pressure needed any adumbration, in 1961 United States military aid for France was to be reduced to a tiny fraction of its 1953 total. Since the Melun debacle of June 1960, the various travels by G.P.R.A. leaders in pursuit of Communist bloc support had begun to arouse increasingly substantial echoes – none of which was missed by de Gaulle, his ears especially sensitive to this particular threat. At the end of October, on the eve of the sixth year of the war, Ferhat Abbas had rejoiced: "We had need of allies, and now we have found them in Peking and Moscow." As if to prove the point, the U.S.S.R. had followed up with a propaganda campaign of unprecedented virulence against de Gaulle's Algerian policy. Present himself for that crucial Fifteenth Session of the United Nations, the G.P.R.A.'s Foreign Secretary, Belkacem Krim, had for the first time met Khrushchev in person. The unpredictable Ukrainian had stood holding both Krim's hands for a long pause, then had posed for the photographers in almost affectionate postures. At a reception forty-eight hours later, Khrushchev informed Krim quite casually that the U.S.S.R. was about to accord the G.P.R.A. *de facto* recognition. In New York Krim, the veteran maquisard, admitted that for the very first time in his life he felt an over-powering sense of personal liberty. The strong F.L.N. delegation found itself veritably basking in an aura of warmth and goodwill among the Third World representatives at the United Nations – a token of the years of beavering which the F.L.N. had put in from 1955 onwards in its endeavours to "internationalise" the war.

But there were still some arduous battles to be fought in New York. As usual, France was boycotting the debates concerning Algeria, but Jacques Soustelle was there in a semi-private capacity representing the *Algérie française* lobby. Resorting to the American media in a way that no French representative before him had ever done, with his brilliant intellect and mordant wit the former governor-general had won some telling points. But all arguments had been swept away by the totally unexpected force of the Muslim riots during de Gaulle's December visit, which appeared to make a nonsense of Soustelle's prime contention that the F.L.N. represented nothing more than a minority clique terrorising the Algerian majority.

The Algiers riots organised by the F.L.N. during de Gaulle's visit could hardly have been better co-ordinated or more effective. On 6 December the Political Committee began its debate on the "Algerian Question"; on the 11th Belcourt and the Casbah had exploded. Of the thirteen new "franco-phone" African nations who had recently gained their sovereignty from de Gaulle, and on whom in return de Gaulle had counted for assistance at the United Nations, a critical number wavered under the impact of the December events, whipped on by the eloquence of M'hamed Yazid. After more than a dozen sessions and innumerable speeches, the F.L.N. carried the day, with the Political Committee accepting its principle that any referendum on Algeria should be supervised by the United Nations. It was a slap in the face for de Gaulle's ideal of a purely French supervised referendum; however, a last-minute face-saving compromise granted "France and her Algerian interlocutors" the right to define the supervisory body – a typical United Nations formula requiring untold further ergs of discussion before anything watertight would emerge.

On 20 December the General Assembly voted paragraph by paragraph on the motion framed by its Political Committee. By a massive vote of sixty-three to eight, with twenty-seven abstentions, it recognised:

The right of the Algerian people to self-determination and independence.

The imperative necessity for adequate and effective guarantees to assure successfully the just application of the principle of free determination, on the basis of the territorial unity and integrity of Algeria.

The responsibility of the United Nations to contribute to the success of implementing this principle.

The fourth paragraph, dealing with the referendum technicalities, failed to pass through the Assembly by one solitary vote, meaning that it would have to carry over to the next session. In effect, for de Gaulle this signified that a "suspended sentence" had been pronounced upon his policy by the United Nations. What really counted, however, was the sheer weight of support which the G.P.R.A. was now able to muster to its side, and in almost total compliance to its will. The United Nations having played its role to the full, the antagonists in the Algerian war were now virtually to leave its floor forever for the arena of a single combat between "champions" of each side.

To de Gaulle's 4 November speech which, with its first mention of *Algérie algérienne*, pushed the rebel French generals over the brink, the G.P.R.A. had reacted with its customary blend of reservation and mistrust. It had, declared Yazid, "been presented with a tricolour bouquet, with at least five cacti inside it!" All signs pointed then to de Gaulle being in utmost earnest about ending the war on any reasonable terms, but once again it sounded to the hypersensitive Algerians as if the enigmatic and lofty French leader might still be endeavouring to impose "his" peace.

As the peace wranglings drag on from one stage to another, one needs to bear sympathetically in mind the various deep-seated neuroses and inhibitions besetting the Algerian negotiators; an underprivileged people who for over six years had fought the grimmest of wars against a nation gifted to the full with every advantage of civilisation; a people aware that several times in the past their birthright had been stolen by guile, whether by fraudulent elections or unfulfilled promises (and how easily, on the very edge of success, might they be cheated yet again by French wiles or a foot placed incautiously!). On the other hand – as time passes on, moving ever to the disadvantage of the French – one must not ignore that all too human instinct of mankind to ask for more as soon as it realises that its adversary is floundering.

Because of their basic mistrust there were a number of principles on which the F.L.N. negotiators could never yield. Chief among these was their intransigent refusal to permit any cease-fire in advance of a full political settlement. Against this, from Mendès-France onwards, successive French governments had insisted on a cease-fire first. This had been the impassable stumbling-block. The F.L.N.'s motivation here was basically quite simple; once the military revolt in the "interior" was stood down, if for whatever reason the emergent solution proved unacceptable, it would be extremely hard to get it going again. A second principle for which the F.L.N. had fought with equal persistence was that it, and it alone, represented the sole Algerian *interlocuteur valable* with whom France could discuss peace. There could be no other partner, no "third force", whatever.

In the new year of 1961, as soon as memories of the bitter December days in Algiers had begun to fade, the complex spider's web of pre-negotiations was spinning again. The ever-ready, helpful and hopeful Bourguiba was at Rambouillet in February, and a Swiss journalist close to the G.P.R.A. brought encouraging noises from Tunis. In great secrecy de Gaulle despatched his trusted banker friend, Georges Pompidou (whom he had called upon to help draw up his first cabinet back in 1958) to the quiet and *bürgerlich* Swiss cuckoo-clock city of Lucerne. It was not quite Pompidou's scene, nevertheless it provided an inconspicuous backdrop against which he could meet the jovial Algerian lawyer, Ahmed Boumendjel, who had led the unsuccessful talks at Melun the previous year. The two men got on well enough together, and the mere fact of Pompidou's presence was accepted by the main body of the G.P.R.A. as a measure of de Gaulle's seriousness. He then followed it up by making an immense concession. He would abandon the *sine qua non* of a prior cease-fire. He would go further; he would – at the risk of serious trouble with his army – order it to assume a unilateral truce, not shooting at the A.L.N. and carrying out only defensive patrolling operations, even if the A.L.N. would not respond in kind. He would also release several thousand more F.L.N. militants from French prisons. And what would his Algerian *interlocuteurs valables* offer by way of concession in exchange? They would simply agree to talk.

Yet, as a G.P.R.A. minister was quoted as saying by L'Express after the conference: "We are not in agreement on any subject. We don't even know what we are going to talk about. We are going to Evian purely so that international opinion can be the judge." There was still a vast no-man's-land of disagreement to be explored and charted at the conference table. There was the role of Ben Bella and his fellow prisoners, always a sore subject for the F.L.N.; there was the question of "guarantees" for the European minority in an Algérie algérienne; there was the fate of Algeria's vast Saharan under-belly, which de Gaulle – who liked to compare it to "an interior sea, with its archipelagos and its treasures" – insisted should be held separate from the rest of Algeria; there was the question of defence interests construed vital by the French, such as the great base of Mers-el-Kébir; and finally there was the quest for a formula of "association" rather than of "abandoning Algeria to her own devices", in de Gaulle's words. Nevertheless, after the second "information" meeting between Pompidou and Boumendjel in the first week of March, it seemed that enough had been agreed for talks to begin. By the end of the month a place and a date had been appointed; Evian and 7 April. It was not to de Gaulle the most inspiriting ambience ("*Ce n'est pas très gai,*" he had once remarked to Macmillan in another diplomatic context. "*Le lac. Et puis toute cette histoire de ce Monsieur Calvin. Non. Ce n'est pas très gai. Tout de même....*") He had few illusions of speedy success. But even before the conference could sit a series of shipwrecking squalls was being whipped up on the surface of the wintry, grey and cheerless lake.

Evian: Round One

On the day of the publication of simultaneous communiqués announcing the Evian talks, Louis Joxe, de Gaulle's Minister for Algeria, committed what looked like a major gaffe. He announced that he would "be meeting the M.N.A. in parallel with the F.L.N.". It was a last final attempt by France to resurrect the idea of a "third force" – and a thoroughly unsuccessful one. The G.P.R.A. exploded; here at the eleventh hour was France trying to turn the peace talks into a round-table affair; trying to do just what Ahmed Francis had always warned they would do – "produce a Bao-Dai out of a hat". Within twenty-four hours of their own acceptance, on 31 March the G.P.R.A. proclaimed that the conference was off. Meanwhile, the infant O.A.S. marked the same day by murdering the innocent mayor of Evian, describing it as an act of "national salubrity" – a deed that was as senseless and brutal as any of their subsequent actions. Next, taking advantage of the Evian adjournment, the generals' putsch had broken out in Algiers. As soon as order had been restored, de Gaulle informed the G.P.R.A. coolly: "The Algiers parenthesis is now closed. Let us resume our affairs." On 20 May the negotiations began in Evian. But, in their post-putsch debility, the French had had to concede to the F.L.N. all notion of there being any other negotiating partner but themselves. Yet another major trick had been lost to the F.L.N. It was going to be like the peeling of an onion, layer after layer.

A sleepy spa on the French side of Lake Geneva, opposite Lausanne, Evian had been chosen carefully out of deference to F.L.N. susceptibilities, so that the Algerians should not feel themselves "prisoners in a golden cage" as they had within the confines of the prefecture at Melun the previous summer. In fact, if anything (it was indicative of trends) the Algerian delegates were accommodated in rather greater luxury than their French opposite numbers. Guests of the opulent Emir of Qatar at his charming and sumptuous Swiss chateau of Bois d'Avault, surrounded by lush meadows, the F.L.N. representatives were ferried each day across the lake to Evian by Swiss army helicopters. After the murder of the unhappy mayor by the O.A.S., the utmost security precautions had been taken, both by the Swiss and the French; the air space over Lake Geneva was forbidden to all outside aircraft, while frogmen patrolled round the helicopter landing-pad; the grounds of the Edwardian Hôtel du Parc, the actual site of the conference, had been turned into a virtual armed camp. Powerfully supported by experts, each team mounted about thirty members. Leading the French was Louis Joxe, suave historian and diplomat, wearing that hall-mark of the *carrière*, an Anthony Eden hat, and backed by Bernard Tricot from the Élysée. The Algerians were even more strongly represented, headed by Krim himself and seconded by the Minister of Finance and Economic Affairs, Ahmed Francis, with the negotiators of Melun, Boumendjel and Ben Yahia, standing behind them. Also in attendance was a figure recently emerged on the international scene, Saad Dahlab, Krim's second-in-command in Foreign Affairs and a converted Messalist. Significantly, two senior officers from the A.L.N. General Staff, Boumedienne's closest deputies, Major Slimane and Major Mendjli, were constantly hovering in the background as well. Physically absent, but very much present in spirit, were Ben Bella and his imprisoned colleagues; they had been transferred to more luxurious internment at the Châteaux de Turquant as an additional *douceur* to the F.L.N. by de Gaulle, but still not permitted to join in the negotiations.

There was a moment of tense anticipation as Krim made his début at Evian; Krim, the last of the *neuf historiques* who had launched the revolt in 1954 still alive and at liberty; founder-member of the Kabyle maquis and former French army corporal, now with the eyes of the world upon him. Nattily dressed and his normally flaccid features rendered even less taut by a recent gall-bladder operation and four years of city life following his flight from Algeria during the Battle of Algiers, Krim could have passed more readily as a Corsican mafioso than a veteran maquisard. He did not look like a hard-liner, and from the dossier compiled on Krim over the years the French negotiators regarded his presence as a hopeful sign. After the formal introductions were over, Joxe with utmost deference to Krim proposed that the Algerian should have the first word; Krim, meeting courtesy with courtesy, refused, insisting that the privilege belonged to the French host. Resorting to an Arab aphorism, Joxe declared, "the page must be turned" and stressed de Gaulle's determination to reach a peace settlement. But once these initial *politesses* had been exchanged, the French were swiftly disabused of any hopes of a smooth passage for the talks. Whatever might have been expected of Krim, rightly or wrongly, it was at once apparent that over his one shoulder there stared the uncompromising gaze of Boumedienne and the General Staff; over the other, that of Ben Bella and his colleagues, unforgiving and implacably militant after their four and a half years of sequestration.

If ever there was a moment when the birds of that French folly, the hijacking of 1956, were coming home to roost it was now, when prospects of peace seemed closest. The imprisoned leaders of the "exterior" had spent the long hours of confinement following football results, playing ping-pong among themselves (at which Boudiaf emerged the steady champion), listening to records, and endlessly reading. As well as numerous books on Algeria published by the pro-F.L.N. Paris house of Maspéro, they were plentifully provided with works by such diverse writers as Lenin, Sartre, Malraux and Ibn Khaldoun. In the latter months Ben Bella dedicated himself to perfecting his Spanish and classical Arabic, while Ait Ahmed concentrated on English literature. Maintaining from the very earliest days a remarkable constancy of communication with the leadership of the "new exterior" in Tunis, the detainees had only been helped to improve these contacts by de Gaulle's successive concessions. As 1961 went on they were holding regular telephone conversations with their families abroad, and even with Nasser in Cairo as well as with members of the G.P.R.A. Yet, inevitably, their isolation from many of the true facts of life – particularly the state of war-weariness within the Wilayas – was profound. Boredom and bitterness against the French proliferated as the months of imprisonment spun out, regardless of all efforts by de Gaulle to improve their circumstances. Many hours were spent in argument on the present, and future, of Algeria, and there were rifts (notably between Ait Ahmed and Ben Bella) reflecting those that had perpetually plagued the free F.L.N. leadership.

In one aspect, however, all were quite united; they were the hardest of hard-liners when it came to contemplating any dilution of future Algerian sovereignty, or the continuance of French influence in Algeria in any form whatsoever. Aware of their intransigence, de Gaulle was determined that this albatross which Guy Mollet's France had hung around its neck should continue to be excluded from the peace talks at all costs. But, though absent, Ben Bella and his colleagues would throughout constitute the mummy at the feast. They would exert a stiffening influence whenever there might be suggestions of flexibility, moderation or compromise in the air. Within the G.P.R.A. the prisoners of Turquant were also finding an increasingly sympathetic, and powerful, ally in the form of Colonel Boumedienne who, already in the pre-negotiation period, had sharply criticised Krim for risking peace talks at all. If these were to fall short of total satisfaction for the F.L.N., argued Boumedienne, grave damage might be inflicted to the morale of the army – which he himself had so successfully reconstituted.

The F.L.N. hardens its line

The first practical disappointment for the French negotiators came with the resolute refusal of the F.L.N. to meet de Gaulle's "unilateral truce" with anything resembling a reciprocal gesture. On the contrary. The period of May–June showed a fifty per cent increase in the rate of "incidents"; the wounded numbering 121, the dead eighty-five – which included sixty-two "third force" Muslims and twenty French soldiers. From Tunis Yazid declared: "An effective interruption of the fighting can only be the result of a bilateral accord bearing on the overall political problem." As always, the F.L.N. was remaining rigidly faithful to the line laid down at Soummam in 1956, regardless of whatever concessions de Gaulle might feel impelled to offer; there could be no cease-fire of any sort before a political solution. Worse (from the French point of view), orders captured in the Wilayas revealed the A.L.N. of the "interior" deliberately exploiting the French "unilateral truce" to replenish arms supplies and regain ascendancy over the "floating voter". Unashamedly and effectively, F.L.N. propaganda took the line: "Victory is at hand! The enemy is on the point of calling for mercy!" Desertions multiplied from the demoralised *harkis*. At Evian, says Bernard Tricot, Krim actually "reproached us for this unilateral decision, as if we had broken some unspoken law of the war". Angered at being rebuffed once again, de Gaulle used the F.L.N.'s response to the truce as an excuse for slamming the door even more firmly on any suggestion of Ben Bella and Co. playing a part at Evian. Meanwhile, just to make the role of the negotiators even more difficult, the O.A.S. had celebrated the eve of Evian with a *festival de plastique*, exploding a score of bombs in Algiers, and keeping up their offensive over the ensuing days.

As the actual negotiations at Evian got under way, a fundamental difference of approach was at once discernible between the opposing teams, with Joxe endeavouring to get down to specific details – such as the length of the "transitory phase" from French administration to Algerian sovereignty, and the "guarantees" to be provided for the Europeans – and Krim seeking refuge behind declarations of general principles. On the vital issue of "guarantees" for the *pieds noirs*, Tricot found it "intolerable" that Krim would not, or could not, "speak with precision of the future". Immediately, said Tricot, there gaped "an abyss between the global guarantees of which we were thinking and the various protestations of goodwill which our representatives had heard".

Basically the guarantees requested by the French were:

Double nationality, so that the *pieds noirs* could become Algerian citizens while still retaining their French nationality.

Assurance against discrimination, particularly regarding private property.

The normal minority rights of freedom of religion and education, and of a fair share in public life.

After Krim had rejected these demands as infringements of the sovereignty of the "Algerian people", Joxe attempted to pin him down into giving a definition of what he meant by the "Algerian people". It was, said Krim in an impassioned speech which evoked all the long pent-up resentments and chagrins of his race:

> constituted by the *indigènes* who had resisted over a long time the French conquest. They are united by language, religion, customs, a common history which contains much fighting and suffering. The war which has lasted for seven years has demonstrated the force of their national conscience, but this people has had to submit, since 1830, to the fact of colonialism. A European population has been created, heterogeneous in its origins, but soldered together by its integration within French nationality.... It has benefited from exorbitant privileges.... Independence is going to pose the problem of these Europeans. We wish to settle this in all equity, and we do not refuse to these people the right to unite themselves to the Algerian people and even to be merged into them.

Not unreasonably, Joxe and his colleagues found little for comfort here. Nor was Krim any more encouraging on the subject of European property. "Here is a people", he declared, "of whom several millions live in misery, and who after independence must not feel themselves still colonised." Land and property which had been "legitimately" acquired, said Krim, would be respected; but – coupled to the repeated F.L.N. declarations over the preceding seven years that all colonial-held assets would be expropriated and redistributed – the French negotiators found all this "rather disquieting". The burden of Krim's assurances to the *pieds noirs* was that, just as for the agreement on articles of Franco–Algerian "association and co-operation", the details must be left for the French and the future Algerian government to work out. But in what possible way could an as yet unborn Algerian government be bound to honour whatever vaguely worded undertakings might be agreed at Evian? Here it was abundantly evident to the French team that there existed a fundamental dichotomy between the "old guard" Algerian revolutionaries, such as Krim and Abbas, prepared to accept the continued existence of a *pied noir* "presence", and the hard-liners already bent upon a future Algeria from which they would eventually be excluded: Boumedienne and Ben Bella. Though, for the time being, it might seem that Krim represented the majority view, who could predict what hand would hold the reins of power in three, five or ten years' time? Moreover, with de Gaulle formally and rigidly committed to non-recognition of the G.P.R.A., Joxe the professional diplomatist was, as Tricot notes, "embarrassed" throughout the talks by not knowing precisely with whom, or what, he was negotiating. What indeed was "this revolutionary organism which had created itself into a government without ever having exercised any territorial authority, and pretended to represent a state which had never existed"?

Here, willy-nilly, the French found their heads led into a noose which, eventually, was to prove fatal for the *pieds noirs*. All right, said the Algerians, if you cannot recognise the G.P.R.A. as a legitimate government, then it cannot accept any responsibility for the future. With the G.P.R.A. black-balled, pacts could only be concluded with the F.L.N. – which, as a mere political party, would have no powers to make commitments binding upon any future Algerian government.

The Sahara, and breakdown

With the "Statute for the Europeans" threatening to reach an impasse, Joxe switched to the question of the Sahara. But here the lines of disagreement were even more sharply etched. In simplest terms, the French view was that the Algerians had no more right to the vast desert under-belly than the Indians had to Texas. Pedantically, Joxe explained how the frontiers of the Sahara were purely artificial, created arbitrarily by French cartographers. Historically, geographically and racially it had never had any connection with Algeria, and what was understood by Algeria was that narrow strip bounded by the Atlas mountains and the Mediterranean; traditionally the Algerians, claimed Joxe, had always been drawn northwards rather than southwards. Meanwhile, France had consistently accorded the Sahara special status. It required only the minimum of cynicism to comment that, ten years previously, the fate of all those millions of hectares of barren sand would not have occupied the conference table for five minutes, but now what was at stake was the untold wealth of the oil and gas beneath the surface. Vast sums of French capital had already been poured into its exploitation; the future prosperity of the Gaullist economy was predicated upon it. Altruistically, the French delegates at Evian expounded the intention of developing the Sahara resources for the benefit of *all* former French colonies adjacent. De Gaulle was adamant. "The petroleum, that's France and uniquely France," he told Joxe, adding: "The Algerian Sahara is a juridical and nationalist fiction devoid of any historical foundation." Equally immovable, the Algerian delegates declared: "The Sahara is an integral part of Algeria: there can be no discussion about the integrity of Algerian territory." It was the formula unaltered since the Soummam Conference of 1956.

By the thirteenth session on 13 June Louis Joxe was faced with a complete breakdown of the talks. The only progress made had been some modicum of agreement over the transitory period to precede full independence; but this was daily being eroded by new developments in Algeria itself – the O.A.S. and its savage onslaughts against the Muslim population. After returning to Paris for consultations with de Gaulle, Joxe informed Krim: "I am disappointed. Not discouraged, but disappointed. Your propositions are too far removed from ours." A suspension of the talks was agreed, but – because of the evident will on both sides for peace, and a desire not to repeat the unhappy atmosphere left by Melun – it was decided not to break off negotiations. Instead there would be left behind in Evian two skeleton teams to maintain contact. On 20 July a fresh attempt was made to recommence negotiations, at the ancient Château de Lugrin which dominates Evian. It lasted only six sessions, at the second of which Tricot noted gloomily, "The word '*impasse*' was pronounced." At its close on 28 July the breakdown looked even more irreparable than it had at Evian; though Saad Dahlab endeavoured to put a brave face on things by declaring: "It's not a rupture, but a new suspension; the beginnings of agreement have been reached; that which has been gained must not be lost; we shall keep in contact." Meanwhile, the war continued – with renewed beastliness.

Thoughts of partition

This fresh failure at Evian, followed by Lugrin, threw de Gaulle into an unprecedented state of gloom and pessimism. As Harold Macmillan, commenting on the increasing signs of Soviet and Chinese intervention in Algeria, noted sympathetically: "Total disorder now threatened. There seemed little or no hope of any moderate or conciliatory policy being effective." Growing ever more vocal, de Gaulle's critics in France – like Jacques Soustelle – accused him of negotiating with indecent haste, thereby throwing away vital bargaining points to the F.L.N. and encouraging their intransigence; while on the other hand the anti-war faction – such as the "121" signatories – constantly castigated him for his dilatoriness in reaching a settlement. From July onwards de Gaulle seemed to be under fire from almost every quarter, with his political prestige at home reaching its lowest watermark to date. Abroad there was the Berlin crisis hotted up by Khrushchev, deepening stresses within the Atlantic Alliance, and – quite unexpectedly – far worse trouble with Bourguiba's Tunisia. In frustration, de Gaulle displayed alternately pique, resentment, impatience, and – most uncharacteristically for him – uncertainty. At a cabinet meeting he was heard to remark that, if the F.L.N. would not permit him to "get out with honour", he would "regroup and let them all go to the devil". What he meant by "regrouping" was that hardy British favourite for de-colonising – partition. His first reaction in the aftermath of Evian was to threaten that, in the face of F.L.N. intransigence, if all else failed he would re-concentrate the *pied noir* population around Algiers and Oran and partition the country. The threat threw into despair France's now sadly depleted friends among the Muslim community, with the first Muslim prefect, the courageous Mahdi Belhaddad, condemning it bitterly and declaring that partition would "require a million men to guard the frontier between the two states".

In Algeria the F.L.N. called a general strike against the proposal of partition, beginning on 1 July and reaching a climax of violence on the 5th. Although Algiers and Constantine were the centres of rioting, the tide swept even such *pied noir* strongholds as Blida in the Mitidja. Accompanied by openly armed *fellaghas*, the Muslim mobs surged right into the European quarters. Some 35,000 French troops had to be called out, and by the time order had been restored eighty Muslims were dead and over 400 injured. This was almost immediately succeeded by a new offensive of F.L.N. terrorism, claiming eighteen dead and ninety-six wounded over one period of twenty-four hours. The discouraging revelation was also made that almost all of the 6,000 detainees released by de Gaulle as a *douceur* to the Evian talks had promptly rejoined the ranks of the revolt. Even more than the Algiers demonstrations of the previous December, the riots showed just how firmly in the F.L.N.'s hands the bulk of the Algerian population was now held. In the face of this, de Gaulle seemed to backtrack. On 12 July, in the speech beginning with the stirring words "France has wedded her century",* he returned to declaring emphatically once more that France was ready to accept "an entirely independent" Algerian state.

Bizerta; France loses a friend

Amidst all this, France found herself embroiled in a totally unwanted and profitless sideshow not of her own seeking, the net result of which was only to diminish sympathy for her abroad and to jeopardise a unique and useful friendship. On 6 July de Gaulle received, out of the blue, what he describes as "a threatening letter" from President Bourguiba, demanding that France should forthwith withdraw her forces from the key naval base leased her at Bizerta, and at the same time agree to an important frontier rectification in the Sahara adjacent to the Algerian oil discoveries. For some time past Bourguiba had been pressing for a French withdrawal from Bizerta, but what took de Gaulle by surprise was the sudden peremptoriness of the note and its sequel. Having received no answer from Paris, a fortnight later – the eve of the resumption of the Franco–Algerian talks at Lugrin – the Tunisians fiercely attacked the French base. At first it took the form of a "spontaneous" demonstration, with women and children intermingled among Tunisian militiamen and troops; then Tunisian troops brought up from the interior opened fire on the French base with mortars and artillery, blockading it by land and sea.

Bourguiba's motives remain somewhat obscure, but personal prestige

---

* As it was little more than a year since de Gaulle had said that France must be made to "marry her time", and little had happened in that period of setbacks and disasters to consummate the union, this still looked more like a statement of intent than of fact.

seems to have played its part. After a series of poor harvests and economic misfortunes, his reputation at home was badly in need of a boost, while in the Arab world he may well have felt pressed to react to the outpourings over Nasser's Radio Cairo, endlessly accusing him of having sold out to the West and of being a bad Arab. At the same time he was under pressure from his uncomfortable guests, the F.L.N., to do something more spectacular to force de Gaulle to make peace. Fed up with the way Evian had collapsed, he may also have wanted to prove to the Algerians that he too was a good radical nationalist. Whatever his motives, he seems to have believed that he could go right to the brink and de Gaulle – in his present state of debility – would yield. It was a tragic miscalculation, because – for that very reason – an obvious military challenge was something de Gaulle could not possibly countenance. "I could not permit France to be flouted," he declared, adding in a notable understatement: "Our military rejoinder was short and sharp."

In what looked a little like "overkill", 7,000 French paras were dropped to reinforce the Bizerta base, planes from the aircraft carrier *Arromanches* hammered the attacking Tunisians, while three other French warships forced the harbour entrance. For three days the battle raged, at the end of which over 700 dead and 1,200 wounded were counted among the Tunisians, at the cost of twenty-four French dead and 100 wounded. By riposting with such crushing force, de Gaulle may well also have had at the back of his mind one final display of military might to impress the F.L.N. all the way to the peace table – much as President Nixon was to launch his all-out bombing of Hanoi on the eve of peace over a decade later. But, if this was his aim, it was equally counter-productive. In disillusion Bourguiba remarked: "I had wanted little Tunisia to become the West's postage stamp on the African continent. Now all that is over." After Bizerta, it would take France a year even to re-establish diplomatic relations with Bourguiba; meanwhile, de Gaulle lost his one ally capable of exerting a moderating influence on the G.P.R.A. and of encouraging it to accept peace terms in any way beneficial to France. It was also Bourguiba who had done more than any other to persuade the F.L.N. to "play it cool" to offers of Eastern bloc aid. At the same time the alienation of Bourguiba now meant the abrupt end to de Gaulle's notions of "internationalising" the Sahara as a means of keeping it out of exclusively Algerian hands. In New York, the carnage at Bizerta brought fresh condemnations of France within the United Nations, with N.A.T.O. countries like Denmark, Norway and Turkey joining in with the Afro-Asian bloc to vote against France on 26 August.

For de Gaulle, the net effect of world opinion in the aftermath of Bizerta was simply to crystallise a growing determination to get out of Algeria at any price.

The F.L.N.: a new leadership crisis

Hard on the heels of this show of international disfavour in New York came fresh news from Tunis bearing little comfort to de Gaulle. Analysing the collapse of the Lugrin second round of talks, Bernard Tricot noted how "out of phase" the negotiators had been, with one of them going "farther than ever before", but the other executing a steady withdrawal. This latter, Tricot suggested, was chiefly motivated by "internal reasons". He was absolutely correct; for – despite the usual tight cloak of secrecy that enveloped rifts within the bosom of the F.L.N. – word had reached the outside world of a major upheaval in Tunis. What was perhaps the F.L.N.'s most serious leadership crisis of the war now boiled down to a straightforward challenge by the army hard-liners – headed by Boumedienne and backed by the absentee Ben Bella – to the political leadership of the F.L.N. Boumedienne had achieved in very few months a remarkable restructuring of the army (now 35,000 strong), which accorded him its unconditional loyalty, and, further reinforced by the flow of heavy weapons from the Communist bloc, his power and authority had reached imposing heights and continued to rise. Throughout Evian and Lugrin he had kept up a harassing fire on Krim for being "soft" on the French; which, indeed, went far to account for Krim's bouts of unanticipated intransigence. In addition, Boumedienne and the new young chiefs he had appointed under him were showing thoughts that extended beyond the *métier*, about the political future of independent Algeria. They considered that it should be markedly more Socialist-orientated and authoritarian than intended by Krim and the "old-guard" F.L.N. politicians. Here they were staunchly supported by the Ben Bella faction, but ardently opposed by Krim who had always been sensitive to any threat of doctrinaire left-wing bias at work in the Algerian revolution. For the first time Boumedienne also found himself at odds with Boussouf, his old patron, and Ben Tobbal, the other key political leaders with Krim on the Comité Interministérielle de Guerre who had in the past generally backed Boumedienne in disputes with the moderates.

In July, during the Lugrin conference, the crisis broke. Boumedienne, followed by Azedine and his two general staff "watchdogs" at Evian, Majors Mendjli and Slimane, sent in their resignations. The nominal pretext was over the fate of a French pilot, who had come down in Tunisia and whom the G.P.R.A. had removed from the hands of the A.L.N. and handed over to Bourguiba. But the violently critical tone of Boumedienne's letter accompanying the resignations revealed that much more was at issue. Condemning the "corrupted who sit at the head of the revolution", it spoke of "permanent abdication and the absence of authority . . . in one word, the most scandalous anarchy". In conclusion, Boumedienne pointedly threw out a bouquet to Ben Bella: "the glimmers of hope and confidence which remain to us go directly towards those who are in prison and who for us continue to be the arbiters". Boumedienne pledged to keep the resignations secret, but requested that the whole dispute be thoroughly aired at the forthcoming congress of the Conseil National de la Révolution Algérienne.

The Fourth C.N.R.A.: Abbas replaced by Ben Khedda

Opening at Tripoli on 5 August, and running for three weeks, the Fourth C.N.R.A. was immediately accompanied by a strong smell of sulphur in the air. Mendjli and Slimane jointly launched the attack on Krim, declaring that he and his team had gone to Evian to "liquidate" Algeria. With skill and dignity Krim defended himself, producing the minutes of the talks and proving with what resolute firmness he had stood up to the French. When a vote was taken, the C.N.R.A. showed itself almost unanimously in favour of the veteran maquisard – with the exception of Boumedienne and his army supporters. Next, however, came the elections for the supreme leadership of the G.P.R.A., which would, presumably, conduct Algeria along the last stretch of the corridor towards independence. The incumbent president, that venerable moderate nationalist of such long standing who had then turned revolutionary, Ferhat Abbas, though fatigued after all his globe-trotting and his constant repairing of fences within the G.P.R.A., was still a world figure commanding much respect. Nonetheless, he was now cast aside in terms of almost humiliating disregard for his past distinction. Once again Krim was the logical candidate for the succession; but Boussouf and Ben Tobbal begged him not to accept the presidency on the grounds that it would inevitably bring conflict with Boumedienne and Ben Bella, possibly leading to internecine bloodshed once the war with France was terminated. Under pressure, Krim acceded.

Instead of Krim, Ben Youssef Ben Khedda, the forty-one-year-old former secretary-general of Messali's M.T.L.D. who had come over to the F.L.N. after being jailed by the French in November 1954, received the nomination. An ex-pharmacist like his predecessor, Abbas, Ben Khedda had been Minister for Social Affairs in the first G.P.R.A. of September 1958, had gone on the first expedition to China, but had been dropped in January 1960. After this he had travelled on various F.L.N. delegations to the Third World, had written a series of thoughtful articles for El Moudjahid, but had never done anything to give the impression that here might be a new focus of power. With cold eyes constantly protected by dark glasses, Ben Khedda was a reserved, quiet-spoken and rather austere personality. A doctrinaire with Marxist leanings, he had none of the popular appeal of an Abbas, a Krim or a Ben Bella. Physically he was far from strong, suffering from chronic amoebic dysentery, but was respected for his firmness of character. Together with Ramdane Abane and Saad Dahlab he had drafted the famous Soummam Platform of 1956, but he had never committed himself to any of the warring factions within the F.L.N., and was not now in conflict with Boumedienne and the General Staff. For these reasons particularly there was merit in his selection for the presidency. He was also regarded as a hard-liner, certainly when compared with the outgoing friend of moderation and compromise, Ferhat Abbas.

As for the rest of the reshuffle of the G.P.R.A., Krim found himself replaced as Minister for Foreign Affairs by Saad Dahlab, his former secretary-general and Ben Khedda's close associate, and whose appointment was one of Ben Khedda's principal conditions for accepting the presidency. Krim was relegated to the lesser function of Minister of the Interior; he remained a vice-president but, instead of just sharing the dignity with Ben Bella, he was forced to accept the addition of a third in the form of another of Ben Bella's imprisoned colleagues – Mohamed Boudiaf. Meanwhile, with Abbas there also fell from grace his old comrade from U.D.M.A. days and fellow moderate, Ahmed Francis. Boumedienne and his supporters, having won most of the tricks at the Fourth C.N.R.A., withdrew their resignations – "in the name of the higher interests of the party".

Thus, as the Council closed at the end of August, the net results were: the eradication of the remaining moderates; the beginning of the total eclipse of Krim, the last of the *neuf historiques*; the influence of Boumedienne and the General Staff in no way diminished; the influence of Ben Bella increased; the hard-liners ascendant. It was also abundantly clear that the struggle for power within the F.L.N. was still by no means resolved; that the internal conflicts were more acute than they had been at any time since 1954, with the moderates deeply disenchanted by the summary eviction of Abbas and Francis, and with the Wilayas of the "interior" continuing to feel abandoned by both the General Staff of the "exterior" and the G.P.R.A. Indeed, the closer the prospects of peace came, so the G.P.R.A. found itself clutched in the ever tighter throes of internal dissent and self-division. At the same time, the battle-lines were now beginning to be drawn for the power struggle that would inevitably follow independence.

Further discouragement for de Gaulle

The communiqué of 28 August, announcing to the world the G.P.R.A. reshuffle, was couched in words which reinforced the discouragement the French peace-seekers already felt at the disappearance of Abbas and his replacement by Ben Khedda. It stressed the F.L.N.'s determination to continue the struggle, and was adamant about preserving the total integrity of Algerian territory – specifically the Sahara. For de Gaulle this seemed to mean the vanishing of any last hope of a meaningful solution of "association" with an independent Algeria, which he had always felt – dating back to his wartime acquaintance – might be possible with Abbas in charge. With Ben Khedda and the new F.L.N. direction appearing to represent the continuance of revolution, of agrarian reform, expropriation and left-wing Socialism, the prospect of any valid "guarantees" for the *pieds noirs* also looked increasingly bleak. What was the alternative? To continue a war to which the majority of metropolitan Frenchmen, not to mention the outside world, was now becoming resolutely hostile, and which was increasingly profitless to France in every sense?

By the autumn of 1961 de Gaulle's pessimism, nay, despair, over Algeria had reached a peak, and was bringing about in him a fundamental change of heart. Everything seemed to conspire to make impossible his policy of withdrawal from Algeria "with honour". The F.L.N. appeared bent on leaving him with nothing, not even honour; while the news from Algeria itself was utterly depressing. Revisiting the country in August and September, Bernard Tricot noted with disquiet the rise of terrorism by both F.L.N. and O.A.S., and the resultant, ever-widening chasm between the two communities.

As if this were not enough, Tricot found a new threat to the European community in the form of economic competition; which, no doubt unintentionally and with the best of motives, French aid schemes bracketed under the Constantine Plan may have played their part in fomenting. As an example of what was happening, Tricot recalls being struck by the fate of two old French spinsters in the rural centre of Lafayette (in Kabylia) whose small general store had long held a monopoly; now Muslims had set up an identical one (probably financed by French Constantine Plan funds), which was solidly patronised by other Muslims, leaving the two old ladies deprived of custom and confronted with bankruptcy. Robert Buron, revisiting an Algiers that had left him few agreeable memories that April, confirmed Tricot's pessimism; the Europeans could "see nothing in the immediate future for themselves but the worst", while the mass of Muslims were displaying "a tendency to 'melt into the background', waiting for their future to become definite". Back in Paris in December, Buron found de Gaulle sunk in deeper gloom than ever. The Russians were being particularly "ominous"; the log-jam of the Algerian peace-talks looked as hopelessly solid as it ever had; de Gaulle's own life seemed grimly at risk; finally, there was a fresh factor which had manifested itself with increasing menace towards the end of 1961 – the O.A.S.

CHAPTER TWENTY-THREE

The Suitcase or the Coffin

April 1961 – February 1962

The moment despair is alone, pure, sure of itself, pitiless in its consequences, it has a merciless power.

Albert Camus

The O.A.S. takes over

ON the night of Challe's surrender in April 1961, Captain Pierre Sergent of the 1st R.E.P. – in common with many of his contemporaries at that time – felt that his world had collapsed about him. A St Cyrien, he had betrayed the sacred "order". There could be no going back. He asked himself the question "Where do we go from here...?" And – in common with many of his fellow putschists in the same predicament – the ineluctable answer that came back was: join the Organisation Armée Secrète.

Though its title had been invented by Lagaillarde and Susini while in exile in Madrid, the O.A.S. was actually the direct successor of those *pied noir* counter-terrorist organisations that had flourished ever since 1956. It had started its ugly new career with the assassination, in January 1961, of the young liberal Algiers lawyer, Maître Popie, following it up with the even more irrelevant killing of the mayor of Evian on the eve of the first peace talks there. Its first leaders came from the ranks of the "ultras" whom most of the para leaders – for all that they might share the same ideals of *Algérie française* – heartily despised. Now, however, born of despair, the O.A.S. attracted – in their despair – those regular officers, like Sergent, whom the failed putsch had turned into "fallen angels". They, in effect, took it over, giving it a military organisation and structure. Since Challe (who would have been most unlikely to have had anything to do with the O.A.S., anyway) was in prison, the logical and obvious leader of the O.A.S. was Salan. The much-decorated former Commander-in-Chief, always the "Mandarin", now assumed the grandiose code-name of "Soleil".

Courageously accompanied by his inseparable wife, *la biche*, Salan after the collapse of the putsch had gone into hiding with Robert Martel, the "ultra" leader from the Mitidja, an expert at concealment. According to

Susini, Martel had installed a large barrel in his barn which he would enter on the approach of security forces, pulling a string to release an avalanche of hay totally covering the barrel.

With the foppishly blue-rinsed white hair now dyed black in disguise, Salan was to switch bolt-holes some sixty times over the next months. Yet, even as a fugitive, he remained ever the "Mandarin". "Decidedly a strange person, this Salan, who may well singularly disconcert future historians," wrote his "Boswell", Captain Ferrandi, to whom Salan seemed just as elegant and impassive as when living in luxury in Madrid; possibly "even gayer, less systematically sceptical, more confident, more resolved. The cautious dilettante found himself once again leader of a band." As leader of the band Salan also found himself now in alliance with curious bed-fellows: the "ultras" who had attempted to murder him with the bazooka just four years previously. But he was never, in fact, to be much more than titular "leader" of the O.A.S. Procrastinating, sometimes maddeningly indecisive, and removed from day-to-day control as a result of the frequent changes of domicile imposed on him by the non-stop police hunt, for much of the time Salan was completely out of touch with the O.A.S.'s activities. Frequently he would evince indignation and shock to Ferrandi at O.A.S. outrages of which he had no forewarning. Nevertheless – though vanity may have persuaded him to remain titular Commander-in-Chief – it must be to Salan's credit that, when the chips were down, he insisted on bearing full responsibility for all the bestialities perpetrated in his name, never "passing the buck" to his more ruthless subordinates.

Under the rather transparent code-name of "Soleil bis", General Jouhaud took over as Salan's deputy. Having had the modest sum of 2,000 (old) francs pressed in his hand by Challe, on the night of the surrender Jouhaud had gone into hiding first near Zéralda, then moved steadily westwards. He equipped himself with false papers as "Louis Gerbert, born in Algiers, married in Bône and a widower", shaved his head, grew a bushy moustache, dyed it black, and donned spectacles. Says Jouhaud proudly, it all gave him the air of "an austere professor, whom candidates would dread at exam time", though, in fact, photographs reveal something resembling more the coarse features of a meridional peasant. After the inevitable conflict with Salan and his juniors, the choleric ex-air force general took himself off in August to assume command of the O.A.S. in his native Oran, where he remained until the end. Among the other "fallen angels" to throw in their lot with the O.A.S. after April 1961 were General Gardy, the former Inspector-General of the Legion, and the more familiar names from the past of Colonels Godard, Gardes, Argoud, Broizat and Lacheroy. While Captain Sergent returned to France to organise the O.A.S. there, Argoud – after a nerve-racking flight from Algeria and accompanied by Lacheroy – had made his way to Madrid to join Lagaillarde (who had been frustrated from joining the putsch)* and constitute the Spanish branch of the O.A.S. As a natural choice, the complex work of setting up the infra-structure of the O.A.S. fell to Godard; Gardes, always more the ideologue than the successful man of action, was appointed to his old role of respon-sibility for propaganda and psychological warfare under the rather optimistic title: Organisation of the Masses. But apart from Godard, to whom the O.A.S. owed its organisation, the effective leaders were not the renowned colonels or generals but Susini, Dr Pérez, and Roger Degueldre.

Susini, Pérez – and Degueldre

Jean-Jacques Susini, the dedicated young right-winger who had first entered the limelight as Ortiz's *éminence grise* at the time of "the Barri-cades" provided the political brains of the O.A.S. To Pierre Sergent, ever since their first encounter that January of 1960, with his pale fanatic's eyes, his "rigid comportment and incisive speech, Jean-Jacques Susini evoked in me ... the image of St Just". Already, in Madrid, Ferrandi had noted Susini's "impressive authority", and an initially reluctant Salan had been "literally conquered" by him. With full confidence in Susini's ability, Salan became increasingly content to leave the overall management of the O.A.S. in the hands of this twenty-seven-year-old ex-medical student. Under Susini the key executive role was filled by Dr Jean-Claude Pérez as head of the O.R.O. ("Organisation–Intelligence–Operations") branch. Pérez, the tall, voluble doctor with the engaging smile from the poor district of Bab-el-Oued, regarded himself as the champion of his "parishioners" there. Compared to Susini, Pérez physically reminded Sergent of a St Bernard against "an intelligent greyhound". But Pérez "was a man of action, as well as of ideas. In his mouth the word revolution assumed the colour of blood. Hatred of injustice turned this man of heart and charity into a violent being."

Unlike Susini, Pérez claimed no political orientations: "I couldn't be called a Fascist any more than a Communist." Back in 1955 it was Pérez who had organised one of the first urban anti-terrorist units in Algiers. It was he who from his office in Algiers signed all "operational" orders for the O.A.S.

If there is one thing on which virtually all the surviving leaders of the O.A.S. are agreed, however, it is that by far the most effectual and impos-ing operative of them all was Roger Degueldre, the thirty-six-year-old ex-lieutenant who had lied about his nationality so as to join the Foreign Legion, risen through its ranks after outstanding bravery in Indo-China, and deserted from it in disgust after the abortive coup of December 1960.

* Lagaillarde continued to remain in Spain, but – according to Susini – declared his readiness to return to Algeria and join the O.A.S. provided its senior leaders would "write him personally an invitation in good and correct form".

A tough and virile figure bearing wounds from Dien Bien Phu, with vigorous black hair *en brosse* and a long horse-face, Degueldre had what his senior in the same regiment, Captain Sergent, describes as "the indispensable presence of the leader". He was "carved out of rock that doesn't crumble", says Sergent: "He was the real chief of action in the O.A.S. . . . All talked, like Susini, but Degueldre acted. Degueldre killed." Nor did he shrink from killing his own men; he once threatened his O.A.S. subordinates: "If I see one of your men in a bar, I will shoot you unless you yourselves have shot the man before I next see him." He meant what he said, executing at least two of his own killers when they were found guilty of embezzling O.A.S. funds.

Yet even those who most hated what he represented and did expressed a certain reluctant admiration for Degueldre, ruthless but utterly fearless as he was. Yves Courrière says of him: "Roger Degueldre was without doubt the strangest and the most attractive personality to traverse this tragic period. Hero for some, assassin for others." Exerting a powerful attraction over women, Degueldre was currently involved in a violent and tragic passion with a fellow officer's wife who was prepared to follow him to the bitter end. Degueldre's motive for joining the O.A.S. (according to Pérez) was contained in the simple explanation: "I've never lost a battle." Since being involved in the May days of 1958 with the 1st R.E.P., he was determined that Algeria should remain French, whatever the cost. He seems to have been obsessed by the heroic but disastrous Hungarian revolution of 1956, and in his first meeting with Sergent after Challe's surrender he declared:

We must do a Budapest! It's the only solution. The F.L.N. has imposed itself by violence, and thanks to that it's become an *interlocuteur valable* for the French government. Only violence will make us heard at present. The generals and the colonels didn't want it. . . . They failed. That proves they were wrong. Now, one must strike. Blow for blow. Unleash war on the authorities. Kill the traitors. It's the only solution remaining to us.

Sergent realised that Degueldre was in deadly earnest. After deserting, he had made contact with some of the toughest and least gun-shy elements among the "ultras", and after the "generals' putsch" he had gathered up a number of other Legionnaires who had chosen to desert rather than face purge and punishment. They included a young sergeant of Yugoslav origin, Bobby Dovecar, who was devoted to Degueldre and became his right-hand man. Within two months of the collapse of the putsch Degueldre had at his disposal some 500 armed and resolute killers, formed into "Delta Commandos" ("Delta" was the code-name he adopted).

Organisation, finances and aims

Working at top speed, and despite all the adversities of operating clandestinely, already by the beginning of May Susini and that efficient staff officer, Yves Godard, had completed the organisation of the O.A.S. At the top of the pyramid stood the *Commandement* (Salan–Jouhaud) and the General Staff (Godard); below came the three sections, each with its separate sub-divisions:

"Organisation of the Masses" (O.M.) – Gardes.

"Organisation–Intelligence–Operations (O.R.O.) – Pérez.

"Political Action and Propaganda" (A.P.P.) – Susini.

The infrastructure was modelled on a combination of the F.L.N. (which none had studied more closely than Godard) and the D.P.U.s (Dispositifs de Protection Urbaine) established by Trinquier and Godard during the Battle of Algiers to divide the city up into a grid. With comparable speed Godard managed to assemble and weld together within his organisation all the numerous "ultra" splinter-groups from the past – such as the F.A.F. and the F.N.F. – various freelance operators as well as the army deserters left stranded after the April putsch. Or, as de Gaulle less charitably described them:

> thugs consumed by totalitarian passion, such as Jean-Jacques Susini ... deserters and fanatics who were the scum of the army, particularly of the Foreign Legion units, and the underworld elements who are always brought to the surface by latent political turmoil ... finally, it was linked with all kinds of political thieves' kitchens, networks of conspiracy and scourings of ex-"militias" which, in metropolitan France, were bent on bringing down the republic at any price and in many cases on paying off old scores which they had been harbouring against de Gaulle since 1940.

Inevitably, because of the disparate strands woven into it, the structuring of the O.A.S. was accompanied by many internal wrangles through the summer of 1961; the military were at odds notably with the civilian revolutionaries (on one occasion Godard threw his lighter across the table in rage when Pérez suggested that the role of the army leaders should be confined to that of "counsellors" only).

For its finances the O.A.S. initially relied on the substantial sums of money which had been raided from government safes during the April putsch; then it supplemented these by means of levying "contributions" from the *pieds noirs* in much the same way as the F.L.N. had cajoled and bullied the Muslims. As the F.L.N. had "banned" smoking, so the O.A.S. forbade the *pieds noirs* to go abroad on holiday. Those who defied the order might return to find the following note awaiting them at home:

> *Monsieur,*
> The O.A.S. sees everything, knows everything. We know, therefore, that you went on holiday to France. . . .
> As a consequence, the O.A.S. condemns you to pay 2,000 francs to

help our organisation. This sum must be paid within twenty-four hours. If your response is negative, we shall know it and will act accordingly. . . .

The O.A.S.

Later windfalls from astutely executed bank robberies helped swell the O.A.S. "treasury", which at one point allegedly reached the staggering figure of two and a half milliard (old) francs (or neary three million pounds) for the three main cities of Algeria alone. This was also despite the considerable siphoning off of funds, diverted into the bistros or boutiques of the "collectors".*

What, then, was the overall aim of the O.A.S., in embarking upon what, by the summer of 1961, already looked like a lost cause? In simplest terms, it was to make it impossible for de Gaulle's representatives to govern in Algeria; beyond that, there was little coherent, or unified, thought. Though studiously vague at the time, Salan told the author in 1973: "I thought that we could somehow orient opinion in France towards some kind of solution like South Africa – a kind of Apartheid for Algeria." He expressed admiration for Ian Smith: "a man of spirit – and, look, Britain still has Rhodesia"! For many of the *pieds noirs* the ideal of *Algérie française* was now but a fantasy – though had it ever genuinely been much more? – and thoughts did gravitate towards a fascist kind of South Africa, with the Muslims "kept in their places". But the O.A.S. was, as one of its chroniclers, Paul Henissart, remarks: "a very odd organisation, an uncooked pudding of conflicting freakish ideas and aspirations and principles". The idealist Gardes, for instance, who still claims to have joined the O.A.S. because he "could not abandon the Muslims", continued to aim for a utopian Algeria in which the Muslims would be fully integrated. Susini, who admired the "fanaticism of the Jews of Palestine" and their passionate attachment to the soil (though he thought the *pieds noirs* too soft by comparison with the Israelis), wanted a kind of ". . . Algerian Haganah, a civil army powerful and with conviction, which would regain Muslim confidence from the F.L.N., and carry along the Europeans . . . to seize power in Algeria, in order to assume it one day in France." At the end of the road he desired a true revolution introducing reforms and a kind of socialist corporate state, but retaining French rule. Pérez, on the other hand, considered the struggle for *Algérie française* as "the last battle for White Christian civilisation in the northern part of Africa". If a common denominator in O.A.S. policy could be arrived at, it was to render peace talks impossible by killing off

---

* After the collapse of the O.A.S. with Algerian independence in 1962, the "treasury" – then still totalling several hundred million (old) francs – "disappeared". Though various allegations have been made since, the fate of it remains a mystery to this day, and (as will be seen) provides a curiously parallel story to the fate of the F.L.N. funds left over from the war – which have also never been recovered by the Algerian government.

the remaining "men of good will", the moderates of both sides, and by random outrages against the Muslim population which would create an atmosphere in which neither negotiation nor compromise could exist. In this they would be eminently successful – but it would produce quite the opposite results from those desired.

First O.A.S. successes

On 3 May a tract was circulated round Algeria, signed by the O.A.S. and making the resounding announcement: "A great army of the maquis is organising itself. . . . Listen to us and all can be saved. Don't give up your arms. Regroup in small sections. Kill those who try to arrest you. Burn the government offices. Kill all the traitors, little and big." At the same time a flood of posters and graffiti appeared on walls across the country. The first to appear showed a crude dagger striking from a map of France and simultaneously stabbing to pieces both the F.L.N.'s crescent and star and the Cross of Lorraine; others bore the bold caption, "La France Reste", or declared menacingly, "The O.A.S. strikes where it wants, when it wants"; a pair of glaring eyes daubed on walls was surmounted by the words "The O.A.S. sees everything"; and there was one produced by the ever-optimistic Gardes showing a Muslim and an European head sandwiched between the two words "Frères . . . O.A.S.". War had been declared.

On 19 May, the eve of the "scandalous" negotiations at Evian, the O.A.S. set off nineteen of the plastique explosions in Algiers, known as la strounga in pied noir parlance, and striking at European or Muslim liberals. As the conference went on, the stroungas occurred daily with the Algiers gendarmerie showing themselves helpless to intervene. On 13 June the O.A.S. celebrated the breakdown of the talks with a particularly powerful strounga right in the centre of Algiers. Up to the end of May, however, only property had been attacked, but on 31 May the O.A.S. under its new management carried out the first opération ponctuelle – the sinister euphemism used by Degueldre when issuing orders to kill. The target was Commissaire Gavoury, the senior police officer charged with tracking down the O.A.S. It was reckoned by Degueldre that the "execution" of so prominent a figure would both act as a deterrent to other "traitors", and at the same time show that the O.A.S. really meant business. Two Delta Commandos were sent out, one under Bobby Dovecar tracking the Commissioner down to his apartment. Spotting the ambush, he tried to escape, shouting in vain for help, but was stabbed to death by repeated blows of a para dagger.

At this time the Deltas were quartered in a sumptuous villa loaned them by pieds noirs in the garden suburb of Bouzaréah. Right opposite them lived a senior official of Morin's Délégation-Générale staff, with known liberal sympathies, Maurice Perrin. After the Gavoury killing Perrin reported to the police his suspicions about the neigbouring villa; but – lending substance to their boast, "The O.A.S. knows everything" – the Deltas received an immediate tip-off. Evacuating the villa, they returned a few days later to riddle Perrin with bullets in front of his horror-stricken wife. Then, between 9 and 10 June, the F.L.N. terrorist squads responded by killing four and wounding thirty-seven in Algiers. A similar picture prevailed in Oran, where the police proved both inadequate and unreliable; the prefect, freshly arrived from France, soon discovered that he could trust perhaps no more than half-a-dozen of his officers. In July the dwellings of no less than thirty-three Oran *pieds noirs* received a *strounga* after their owners had ignored the O.A.S. warning not to leave the country, even on holiday. With the onset of the summer heat tempers were rising violently, and a deadly pattern established itself, with the F.L.N. generally killing between 5 a.m. and 9 a.m., so as to catch victims on their way to work, the O.A.S. Deltas carrying out their *opérations ponctuelles* in the evening when their victims were returning from work.

On 5 August, the O.A.S. scored its first major propaganda success. Minister Joxe was in Algiers to discuss the current situation with Morin; in Tripoli, the Fourth C.N.R.A. was convening. It was a Saturday, and at 1 p.m. most *pieds noirs* were clustered around their television sets for the lunch-time news bulletin. Suddenly the screens flickered, and went blank. Then out of the pictureless sets came the voice of General Gardy, speaking for the O.A.S. as Salan's delegate. There followed an unhurried speech by Gardy, inciting the army to revolt and calling on both Europeans and Muslims to rise up and join the O.A.S. against the "Gaullist dictatorship". The coup had been achieved by Degueldre's Deltas blowing up the television cables and then using O.A.S.-recruited technicians to play a tape of Gardy's speech over the transmitter. The broadcast had a powerful effect on the *pieds noirs* of Algiers, who persuaded themselves that it meant that the O.A.S. might be about to seize power. Crowds thronged the streets, and cars beat out on their horns the old familiar refrain of *"Al-gé-rie fran-çaise"*. On 21 September a second pirate transmission by Salan himself summoned the people of Algiers to join in a three-day demonstration to attest to their unity of thought and action behind the O.A.S. Two days later, for five solid hours thousands of *pieds noirs*, seemingly from every window and balcony in the city, hammered out the *Algérie française* rhythm on pots and pans. The din was deafening. Black-and-white O.A.S. banners fluttered from public buildings, or hung from cranes in the harbour – or were paraded quite openly throughout the city.

At about the same time the Deltas grabbed eighty million francs in a first daring raid in the port; Jean Morin and his staff moved out of Algiers to the new government complex at Rocher Noir, and General Ailleret (the new army commander replacing General Gambiez, humiliated during the putsch) to Reghaia. Although both moves had been scheduled many months previously, the timing now made it look as if Algiers had been abandoned to the O.A.S. It was a situation of which the O.A.S. was not tardy in taking advantage, proclaiming itself boss of whole areas of the city. Coupled with the apparent inability of the authorities to check the O.A.S., this new self-confidence in turn caused a pronounced rise in the morale of the *pieds noirs*, shaken as it had been by so many shocks and reverses since "Barricades Week" of January 1960.

How much support, then, could the O.A.S. count upon from the *pied noir* population at large? Harassed constantly by the French security forces, scattered and often out of communication with each other, continually wrangling among themselves, the O.A.S. would have been unlikely to have got off the ground – let alone have survived as long as it did – without the utmost civil co-operation. By and large the *pieds noirs* were led to believe and trust in the O.A.S. as an organisation protecting their interests, just as the F.L.N. had fought so successfully for Muslim interests over the past seven years. In their growing despair, and with principles distorted by the isolation in which they had so long existed, perfectly decent citizens turned to the O.A.S. to reverse the trend of history. Much as the German working classes had flocked to the Nazi party in the 1930s out of fear of the Bolshevik bogey, so the poor whites – the *petits blancs* – in particular now rallied strongly to the O.A.S.

Degueldre's killers

By the autumn of 1961, it could be said that the O.A.S. had well and truly established itself, at least in the cities of Algiers and Oran. In September Degueldre's Deltas killed fifteen and wounded 144, and the volume of their operations continued to increase – with apparent impunity. A car would slow down alongside a group of Muslims and promiscuously mow them down with machine-pistol fire; a Jewish and Socialist police inspector would be shot dead at the wheel of his car on his way home through the Tunnel des Facultés. Often there was a certain carelessness about the identity of the victims; for instance, two Deltas on a motor scooter shot down the Socialist Party's secretary-general for Algiers, William Lévy,* then found that the *opération ponctuelle* had been scrubbed by O.A.S. headquarters a week earlier. Likewise, a man taken to be de Gaulle's hated "listening post", Colonel François Coulet, was "executed" – then it was revealed that the victim was just a small baker from the suburbs of Algiers. Grisly rumours (probably manufactured by the O.A.S.) circulated about young *pieds noirs* being bled to death in Muslim clinics to

---

* His son was murdered by the F.L.N.

provide blood transfusions for wounded *fellaghas*; groups of whites would then take their own reprisals, cornering a passing Muslim motor-cyclist at random and setting him alight with petrol. Sometimes the *pieds noirs'* patronal instincts would lead them into grotesquely contradictory acts; A.-P. Lentin, a *pied noir* journalist, tells of one Bab-el-Oued *bistrotier* who, at the beginning of a *ratonnade*, helped his own Muslim "boy" to escape to safety, and then "went to despatch a little street vendor fifty yards away". Almost inevitably, it seemed, when the killings took place the *gendarmerie* would not arrive until it was all safely over, giving the populace a further assurance that they too were on the side of the O.A.S.

By the end of November Jouhaud in Oran was expressing disgust at the promiscuous killings, while Salan was increasingly aggravated by his lack of control over what was going on, or of any prior consultation on the acts of the Deltas. On 31 August he was surprised to read of the assassination of the Socialist mayor of Fort de l'Eau (another "third force" moderate, but condemned by Susini as "one of the most disquieting and the most contemptible personalities of Algeria, one of those old corrupters who had hoped to found their political fortune on the success of the rebellion"). The following week Salan was even more taken aback by the attempt in France to blow up de Gaulle at Pont-sur-Seine.* On 3 November the Muslim garage opposite Salan's current hiding-place was blasted by an O.A.S. *strounga*, shattering the general's window and covering him with fragments of glass. The "Mandarin" "remained passive about it", says Ferrandi, but "asked me to inform him on the exact targets pursued by the *plastiqueurs*". A few days later, as Degueldre stepped up his *opérations ponctuelles* another notch, Ferrandi noted: "It is difficult to know the feelings of Salan on this subject. He contents himself by showing astonishment not to have known until after the incident of each enterprise." Then, on 10 November, the Muslim garage opposite was blown up a second time, once again smashing the general's windows. This was too much for him and (according to Ferrandi), losing his temper, he declared: "The order must be given to stop at once this kind of stupidity." After the killing of Lévy, Salan in anger wrote a personal letter to Guy Mollet disowning it, and blaming "extremist splinter groups". Nevertheless, the bombing and killing went on, gathering momentum all the time.

Counter-measures: effectual and ineffectual

For many months the Algiers authorities displayed a disturbing impotence to cope with the O.A.S., despite the more than 25,000 gendarmes

---

* In fact, the Pont-sur-Seine attempt turned out to be the work of an autonomous group, affiliated to the O.A.S., and calling itself "The Old General Staff", under the orders of Lieutenant-Colonel Bastien-Thiry – the only senior officer actually to be executed for his activities.

and C.R.S. available to them. The problems facing them were, admittedly, immense. In the larger part of Algiers and Oran the O.A.S. enjoyed the same advantages of being the "fish in water" among a sympathetic population that helped make the F.L.N. so elusive over the country as a whole. As with Yacef's network in the Casbah before the Battle of Algiers, the adjacent poor white district of Bab-el-Oued now became a virtually impenetrable citadel for the O.A.S. There was also a worrisome question of loyalties. Following the collapse of the April putsch, General Ailleret estimated that – while ten per cent of his officers were prepared to fight against the O.A.S. – ten per cent were actively favourable to it, and the remaining eighty per cent neutral and unlikely to obey orders to fire upon the army deserters with the O.A.S. (Despite this, in September Ailleret issued an uncompromising "Order of the Day No. 5" which was tantamount to an army declaration of war on the O.A.S.; several days later his Paris apartment was blown apart, his wife narrowly escaping with her life. From then on the Commander-in-Chief took to carrying two revolvers and travelling in a bullet-proof Citroën – passed down from Salan – filled like a mobile armoury with grenades and sub-machine-guns.)

The situation was even worse with the force most closely concerned with combating the O.A.S.; of the *gendarmerie mobile* of the city of Algiers, it was reckoned that between sixty and eighty per cent were O.A.S. sympathisers. When Morin appealed to the Minister of the Interior, Roger Frey, for reinforcements of "reliable" police from France, he was met with cool lack of interest; Algeria was lost anyway, and Paris wasn't going to bust itself to maintain order there. Morin warned of the danger that the establishment of Salan in real power in Algiers could have for metropolitan France, but this too fell on deaf ears. Morin then addressed himself directly to de Gaulle, who – having recently survived the Pont-sur-Seine attempt on his life – promised to send him a high-grade counter-terrorist team. But a further three months were to elapse before this was to become effective.

Meanwhile, Morin's chief card was Commissaire Louis Grassien, sent from the Rheims police, who had formed a tiny anti-O.A.S. squad of ten trustworthy men. After weeks of patient work Grassien managed to sketch out an *organnigramme* of the O.A.S. – similar to that which Godard had composed of Yacef's networks during the Battle of Algiers. He had managed to identify most of the O.A.S. leaders, but had proved incapable of tracking down a single one. Then, in September, a break came. An Italian ex-Legionnaire, "Pino", turned informer and led Grassien to Godard's hideout. That expert on underground techniques proved (as he always would) too elusive, but notes found in the raid revealed the name of one Maurice Gingembre, an important O.A.S. courier plying between Madrid, Paris and Algiers. Aged forty, Gingembre was a wealthy, flamboyant and indiscreet *pied noir* with a childish passion for "007" work – for which, according to Susini, he could scarcely have been less suited. On 7 September Gingembre – his briefcase stuffed with incriminating documents – flew from Paris to Algiers. With him on the plane was Colonel Debrosse himself, the head of the Algiers gendarmerie, whose men had suffered so appallingly at the hands of "ultra" sharpshooters on that "bloody Sunday" of 24 January 1960. Debrosse settled an old score by arresting Gingembre, who, says Susini, "immediately began to talk at the top of his voice". On the resultant information, police in France swooped to arrest a number of senior French army officers. These included Colonel de Blignières, one of those involved in setting up the April putsch, and General Paul Vanuxem, former deputy commander-in-chief in Germany, on the charge of being "Verdun", Salan's designate to be O.A.S. military commander in France – a charge of which he was acquitted two years later. The O.A.S. network in metropolitan France probably never recovered from Gingembre's revelations, while in Algeria networks throughout the western region were smashed; Godard's secretary was captured, but he himself once again escaped. As Susini later admitted: "The O.A.S. general staff as a whole was almost arrested. Liaison was broken off; some of our agents abruptly disappeared; for two weeks the wheels of the Resistance stopped turning. We barely escaped total disaster."

It was the closest of shaves. Next, a renegade police inspector working with Degueldre was picked up in a bar by former colleagues; tortured, he revealed the address of the Deltas' lair. On 12 October a net thrown around the house caught Bobby Dovecar, Degueldre's deputy who had led the Delta commando that killed Commissaire Gavoury, and five other Deltas. The net missed Degueldre by a matter of minutes; Dovecar died in front of the firing squad the following June.

Little time elapsed before the Deltas were hitting back. Early in November word reached Degueldre that Grassien, recalled to France, was holding a farewell party for some of his inspectors at the l'Universel bar. A car drew up outside, the occupants got out and calmly raked the bar with sub-machine-gun fire; Grassien survived, but his assistant, Commissaire Joubert, was killed. Godard and his fellow colonels expressed strong objection to the murdering of men "who wear French uniforms"; nevertheless, a few days later a "Z-Commando" – less disciplined O.A.S. rivals of the Deltas – ambushed a gendarmerie half-track on the Rue Michelet. Attacked by "Molotov cocktails", four French gendarmes were burnt to death in the very heart of Algiers. The episodes marked the beginning of what was in effect a kind of civil war, and another of those "secret wars" fought behind the scenes of the main battle-front – savage, mean and without quarter – of which the first round had been won by the O.A.S. For the time being they appeared once again masters of Algiers.

"Civil war" against the "barbouzes"

After the killing of Commissaire Joubert, over a period of forty-eight hours in mid-November six well-known Algiers cafés frequented by "ultras" were blown up. They included the "Otomatic", scene of one of the first F.L.N. bombing outrages during the Battle of Algiers. It was clear that some new counter-terrorist body was at work in the tormented city. A clue to its identity might have been gained from a rash of anti-O.A.S. posters that had appeared overnight throughout Algiers, to the surprise of its inhabitants, and bearing the initials M.P.C. The Mouvement pour la Communauté had been launched earlier in the year to boost de Gaulle's Algerian policy, receiving substantial funds from Morin's Délégation-Générale for its activities. Though its function was essentially political, with the growing ascendance of the O.A.S. its secretary-general in Algiers, a former radio producer called Lucien Bitterlin, decided that something more than words was now called for. He began gathering around him a group of strong-arm men. Bitterlin claims he did not demur when a colonel in Military Security branch supplied him with weapons, explosives and permits to move about during the curfew, and asked him to *"plastiquer* several activist cafés in Algiers" – in itself an extraordinary revelation of the state of anarchy and lawlessness already prevailing in the cities of Algeria. Short on security, the M.P.C. and its new activities were not long in reaching the ears of the French Press. Before the end of the month *France-Soir* was publishing a sensational scoop, under the banner headline: *"Carte blanche* for 'Barbouzes'* to liquidate the O.A.S." The new "anti-O.A.S. shock force", it proclaimed, was to be composed entirely of "new men":

> all the aces of espionage, counter-espionage and subversive warfare available in France are being sent to Algeria. They are trustworthy men, from the most diverse origins.... The new anti-O.A.S. formations will not belong to any classical hierarchy. They will be autonomous organisms, not subject to normal authority.... They will act largely outside the army and the police.
>
> Above all, this new force will be secret. An absolute secrecy will cover the activities and above all the identity of the members of the anti-O.A.S. formations.

Both in respect to secrecy and its members being "aces", the M.P.C. was excessively flattered by *France-Soir*. By comparison with Degueldre's highly trained and ruthless army deserters and the veteran *pied noir* counter-terrorists of Pérez, Bitterlin's *barbouzes* were a motley and amateurish crew. Their nucleus consisted of Jim Alcheik, a Jewish-Tunisian karate champion, and eight judo black belts he had brought with him; four Vietnamese expert in torture (which they not infrequently used), but who stood out like sore thumbs in the Algiers scene; and a mixture of

* Slang for "false beards".

pieds noirs of Jewish origin, Gaullist party "bouncers" and untrained muscle-men. None of them was a match for Degueldre's Deltas, by whom they were almost immediately identified before even going into action. On the other hand, the *France-Soir* report had muddled Bitterlin's amateurs with a much more professional body arriving in Algiers at the same time – that which de Gaulle had promised Morin three months previously. Called "Force C" and under the command of Michel Hacq, Director of the French Criminal Police and hero of the Resistance, it consisted of no less than 200 hand-picked police inspectors. These would be posted in quick rotation (to avoid corruption by the O.A.S.) so that none would spend more than two months in Algeria. "Force C" would work hand-in-hand with Bitterlin's team, getting it out of scrapes, deploring its fiascos, but also benefiting from the intelligence provided. Both bodies would become bracketed in the public eye as *barbouzes*; the name that would stick henceforth where any "irregular" action against the O.A.S. was concerned.

Degueldre slaughters the "barbouzes"

For Hacq, installed in an office inside the Algiers Police School under the name of "Professor Ermelin", there now began a five-months' methodical and relentless hunt, ending only when the O.A.S. had been tracked down. For Bitterlin and his *barbouzes* it almost immediately opened with disaster. Within three days of his having established Jim Alcheik's team in a rented villa in the Chemin Raynaud, Bitterlin was ambushed by four Deltas. His driver was badly wounded in the abdomen, while Bitterlin received superficial shoulder wounds; but for the heavy steel of the old Mercedes in which they were driving they would both probably have been riddled with bullets. The wounded driver was removed to the Maillot Hospital in Bab-el-Oued, and when visiting him a few days later Bitterlin nearly fell into another well-informed ambush. While he was inside the hospital with Jim Alcheik, a Delta Peugeot swept up and sprayed his two cars with automatic weapons. The Deltas obviously intended to get the *barbouzes* in the hospital. This time, however, Bitterlin had two of his Vietnamese on guard outside, who returned the fire and drove off the Deltas. No one was hit on either side, but the shooting drew a crowd from Bab-el-Oued which, recognising the Vietnamese as belonging to the hated *barbouzes*, took on an ugly aspect. With his tyres shot to shreds, Bitterlin was trapped and forced to telephone "Force C" for help; the rescuing inspector sent by "Professor Ermelin" advised him coldly to try to keep out of trouble in future. Meanwhile, in France the *barbouzes* were soon under cross-fire from the Press, with the Right criticising them as "parallel police" and the Left deriding de Gaulle's regime as "The *barbouze* Republic".

On 29 December Bitterlin received orders from Paris to cease operations but he, with some courage, turned a blind eye. Two nights later Degueldre himself, driven by his inamorata, led an all-out assault to wipe out the *barbouzes* in the Chemin Raynaud. Shortly before midnight no less than twenty-four Deltas ringed the villa with home-made bazookas and machine-guns; inside they could see lights and hear sounds of the *barbouzes* cele-brating New Year's eve. When one of the *barbouze* sentinels in the garden momentarily turned his back, Degueldre opened up with a deadly concen-tration of firepower. Seven rockets hit the villa at point-blank range, one of them exploding a cache of grenades in Alcheik's office. The fusillade con-tinued for some twenty minutes, reducing the villa to a shambles. Miraculously enough, though Susini's propaganda *apparat* claimed fourteen dead, only one Vietnamese was wounded, and a policeman of the relieving force was killed. But it marked the beginning of the end of Bitterlin's *barbouzes*, who were becoming an increasing embarrassment to the Algiers authorities – despite the flow of useful information they kept passing to Hacq's "Force C".

The *coup de grâce* was administered by Degueldre a month later. Bitterlin had returned to Paris for consultations, and had then found him-self banned by Premier Debré from returning to Algeria. But Jim Alcheik was still there, had found new hideouts for the remaining *barbouzes* and was awaiting the imminent delivery of a new printing press to step up the production of anti-O.A.S. posters. On 29 January de Gaulle's minister, Robert Buron, was dining with Morin in his new quarters at Rocher Noir when there was a series of powerful explosions and all the lights went out. The party finished dining by candlelight. The next day Buron learnt that the O.A.S. had blown up six transformers, and that a further explosion had been inside the *barbouzes'* new villa.

The previous day Jim Alcheik's printing press had arrived in a heavy crate; instead of a press, however, it contained a devastating booby-trap which Degueldre had devised himself, consisting of ninety kilos of assorted explosive, with detonators secured to the planks of the packing case by parachute silk thread. Alcheik hastened to prise open the crate; there was an earth-shaking explosion, and the three-storey building disintegrated in dust. Alcheik, the karate champion, was blown to pieces and another eighteen *barbouzes* died in the blast; two survived by a miracle. Hanging in tatters from one of the few standing walls was one of Alcheik's M.P.C. posters, proclaiming: "Neither suitcase, nor coffin, but co-operation!"

Hacq now decided that the remaining *barbouzes* had to be got out of the country, but once again Degueldre struck first. The last *barbouze* detach-ment of twenty-five men was trapped in a seedy hotel and submitted to a siege continuing forty-eight hours without the Algiers police making any effort to intervene. Four survivors tried to break out by car to get a wounded comrade to hospital, but were shot up on the way. Out of control, their car ran into a wall, and a terrible scene now took place. *Pied noir* occupants of the neighbouring apartment blocks rushed up, prevented the injured men from getting out of the car, then set fire to it and danced jubilant round the flaming pyre.

Thus died the last of Bitterlin's *barbouzes*. The operation had been a disastrous failure; on the other hand, information provided by it had enabled Hacq's professionals to arrest some 600 members of the O.A.S., including sixty-nine killers. Later, Pérez himself admitted that attacking the *barbouzes* had been a big tactical error: "They were too easy. They were sent to Algiers specifically to be killed – to distract the O.A.S. from getting on with its main job.... We fell into the trap ... Godard in fact warned us against it. He was right."

Algiers: the Muslims riposte

It was a "distraction" that did but little, however, to impede O.A.S. outrages against the civil population at large from escalating. The sheer savagery with which the last of the *barbouzes* had been wiped out exemplified the degradation of the atmosphere in Algiers and Oran by the new year of 1962. Uncannily, the two cities had acquired many of the siege aspects so brilliantly described by Camus in his grim novel, *La Peste* (first published in 1947), based upon a plague-ridden Oran. The fictitious plague, writes Camus, "had swallowed up everything and everyone. No longer were there individual destinies; only a collective destiny, made of plague and the emotions shared by all." As in Camus' Oran, in Algiers alone more than 200 check-points were set up to examine papers and control movements within the city. Trolley-bus windows bore heavy metal grilles to protect against the random grenade; a curfew emptied the streets of vehicles from 9 p.m. onwards, and at 1 a.m. the public lighting was extinguished, plunging the city into darkness. Then, in this twilight world, the O.A.S. graffiti squads took over, and as fast as they worked so officially-backed volunteers (euphemistically dubbed "Rembrandts") busied themselves scrubbing out their handiwork or amending the "À bas de Gaulle!" slogans into "Vive de Gaulle!" Trapped by Degueldre's prowling Deltas, the "Rembrandts" often paid with their lives for this infantile role in the propaganda war. But even without the curfew, Algiers had become a dead city at night. There were no longer any public distractions, and little social life. Cinemas were empty or closed down; cafés had become dispirited and iron-shuttered bunkers. Instead of lingering in them, or promenading in the leafy, cool boulevards, people were driven by fear to hurry home and stay indoors, for death seemed to lurk at every street corner. At home, families were gripped by anxiety wondering whether the menfolk would return safely from work, while bitter mistrust grew between neighbour and neighbour. Cities that had once enjoyed the flashy late-night existence of an Alicante now became East Berlins – but East Berlins ruled by the mores of Chicago of the "Roaring Twenties". (Indeed, the parallel of Chicago fixed itself on the minds of the French security forces so that an *alerte Chicago* become the standard code-name flashed between patrol cars to designate a *strounga* or a killing. But, as C. L. Sulzberger pointed out at the time, "more people in Algiers die violently each day than in the Midwestern city's gaudiest era".)

The killings continued to mount; from six killed and 430 *stroungas* in August, the O.A.S. score rose to nine and 763 in October. In December the number of deaths attributed to the O.A.S. was 98, but by February of 1962 they had risen to 553 in one month. Partly to revenge the O.A.S. outrages against their fellow countrymen on an eye for an eye basis, partly to prove their growing ascendancy over the Muslim population, the F.L.N. now staged a recrudescence of terrorism. Already in September President Ben Khedda, speaking over Radio Tunis, had issued a warning for the future to

> those European fanatics who, with the toleration of the colonialists' army and police force, indulge in lynchings, massacres and pillage.... All they do is to compromise their future in the independent Algeria ... these acts cannot but create obstacles to their coexistence with the Algerian people.

This had been followed up, even more specifically, by Yazid declaring: "If the French authorities do not take the necessary measures to put an end to murders and lynchings, the anger of our people will swoop down implacably."

In November the F.L.N. began its counter-offensive, with acts made explicit in a new *Bulletin d'Information*, published for the first time by Colonel Boumedienne's General Staff. Written in its own peculiar style that referred contemptuously to *la soldatesque française*, "traitors" and "colonialists", as opposed to "glorious *moudjahiddine* fallen on the field of honour", its first issue announced that "sixty traitors to the country or colonialists, including one major (in Kilea), one doctor (Barika) and one peace officer (Birmandreis), have been executed after being condemned for their crimes by revolutionary tribunals. Ninety-eight others have been wounded." On the one day of 1 November, it claimed that two hundred Algerians had been killed. Reporting a further "intensification" of activities in its December issue, the *Bulletin* listed:

> thirty-five colonialists, of whom nine were military, have been shot down; thirty-eight were wounded. Forty-four traitors who had been condemned to capital punishment by our revolutionary tribunals, were executed by bullets ... parallel to these executions by shootings, our *fidayine* have thrown into brasseries belonging to the colonialists more than twenty grenades which resulted in, as well as serious material damages, the death of eight soldiers of the army of occupation and twelve civil colonialists ... eighteen farms belonging to the colonialists were burnt.

Spurred on by the atrocities of the O.A.S., individual F.L.N. killings reached a new level of horror; a Jewish Algerian, sympathising with the F.L.N., told the author how "they killed a shop inspector in his car, a man who had never done anything to anyone. They sliced open his skull, took out his brains and carefully placed them on the ground – like a milestone on the roadside." The twenty-year-old son of her friend was kidnapped and found the next day in their rubbish bin: "bled white, because the F.L.N. needed the blood for their own wounded". Gruesomely improbable as this story sounded, it received some supporting evidence in the last month of the war when forty-one European bodies were discovered in an Oran abattoir, drained of blood. Meanwhile the grim year of 1961 ended with Boumedienne's *Bulletin* reporting the execution of another 101 "traitors", some of them *harkis*; at the same time claiming that in Oran terrible *ratonnades* by the O.A.S. on the one day of 3 January had left 127 Muslim dead and many hundreds wounded.

As the new year began, the O.A.S. were well on the way to succeeding in both its self-immolatory aims of bringing about a state of ungovernability in Algiers and Oran, and of creating a gulf of hatred between Muslim and European. After his trip to Algeria the previous autumn, Bernard Tricot had already observed how the O.A.S. violence and the F.L.N. riposte had resulted in "an alienation between the two communities which I had never previously detected"; and it existed "precisely where the European population was strongest, and where a possible partition could have created a French enclave". Meanwhile, the poisons of fratricidal hatred had seeped across the Mediterranean to metropolitan France itself.

The O.A.S. and the C.I.A.?

Outside Algeria the O.A.S. had various networks of its own, allies and affiliated bodies, as well as terrorist splinter-groups that seemed more often competing than co-operating. First of all, there was the much-bruited connection between the O.A.S. and the C.I.A., which remains only partially explained to this day. According to the story which seems to have originated with Susini, though he does not mention it in his memoirs, Salan in November 1961 had a personal approach from a senior C.I.A. official based in France, offering arms and material to equip a force of 50,000 men. In exchange, Salan was to cede military bases and preferential economic treatment (i.e. access to Saharan oil) in the event of his success in creating an independent, *pied noir*-dominated state along the lines of Rhodesia. Today such a notion may seem fanciful beyond the realms of credibility; but it is worth remembering that in November 1961 the O.A.S. looked very much as if they were winning the battle, while a peace agreement between de Gaulle and the F.L.N. seemed further away than ever, and his own life a poor insurance risk. Unlike Challe previously, Salan certainly showed no inhibitions about courting "external" assistance. The story continues that Salan, accepting the C.I.A. offer, followed this up with a long letter (dated 12 December) addressed personally to President Kennedy, appealing for his support, which was then flown to Washington by special U.S.A.F. plane. Salan strongly denies that he ever wrote such a letter, while those of the Kennedy entourage at the time who should have been in a position to know equally deny its receipt. At the same time, the intensive Senate hearings of 1975 investigated C.I.A. involvement with the O.A.S. and were satisfied that there had been none.

But Salan himself insisted, to the author, on the following account:

> During the anniversary celebrations of North African landings at the Arc de Triomphe on 8 November 1961, two men purporting to be agents of the C.I.A. made contact with our people who were present, saying that they wanted to come to Algiers to see me. They turned up in Algiers the following week – one of them under the conventional cover of 'Vice-Consul'. I saw them, then passed the whole affair over to Degueldre. I was sure they were serious, because they knew all the right people, and their credentials were perfect. No, they were not *agents provocateurs*. Why? Because they actually began delivering the goods; a shipment of some fifty machine-guns arrived from Spain, via a small port near Cherchell. . . . I know nothing more. . . .

In view of the incompetence being shown by the *barbouzes* during this same period, and the fact that nothing relevant has ever been revealed by any French source, it seems highly improbable that the "C.I.A. agents" were part of a cunningly laid Gaullist "double" operation to penetrate the O.A.S. The mystery remains.

Friends and rivals

Among its active allies in France the O.A.S. would have liked to number the Vincennes Committee. Formed in 1960 by de Gaulle's disenchanted one-time aide, Jacques Soustelle, the Committee embraced such disparate figures as Georges Bidault; Bachaga Boualem; Bourgès-Maunoury; André Morice; Cornut-Gentille (Gaullist ex-minister); Léon Delbecque (Gaullist "antenna" in Algiers, pre-1958); and Robert Lacoste. All were bound by a common dedication to *Algérie française*. Soustelle, who had been under constant threat of arrest ever since the April putsch, had gone into self-imposed exile in August, declaring that it was the second time since 1940 that a "dictatorship" had forced him to leave his country; then he had returned in November, briefly, to give comfort to the O.A.S. at two Press conferences. Though he condemned the "barbarous methods" it employed, the O.A.S. was, he declared, now "the real 'third force' in Algeria" with whom the French government would have to negotiate. (Why, he asked provocatively and with some exaggeration, had not the F.L.N. been opposed with one-tenth the energy currently being deployed against the

O.A.S.?) Four hours after his last Press conference an arrest order went out, and Soustelle – one jump ahead as usual – fled to Belgium. But, though he was to be accused of it by de Gaulle, Soustelle still insists he never had any direct relations with the O.A.S.

At the height of the O.A.S. offensive in Algiers in mid-November, the Vincennes Committee met in Paris and there were some provocative anti-Gaullist and pro-O.A.S. remarks from the floor. "The only effective power in Algeria is the O.A.S.," declared Léon Delbecque. "A *coup d'état* cannot be excluded," warned Bidault; while a deputy of the extreme Right, Jean Dides, exclaimed: "Glory to General Salan, who will restore France's grandeur!" On 22 November de Gaulle ordered the dissolution of the Vincennes Committee. As far as the O.A.S. was concerned, however, none of the Committee ever actively worked for it, any more than Soustelle – even Bidault, though designated Salan's heir, denies he ever gave any orders in the name of the O.A.S.

Meanwhile, in Madrid what threatened to be a rival command to the O.A.S. had set itself up, calling itself the "Direction Centrale de l'O.A.S." and centred around Colonels Argoud and Lacheroy, and Pierre Lagaillarde. In a letter to Salan in August, Argoud extravagantly declared that the Algerian problem could not be resolved in Algeria; its solution was "global and governmental". Salan replied by calling for Argoud to rejoin him in Algiers; Argoud's answer was that Salan's place was behind a safe frontier – he should come to Spain. On 2 September Salan tried to bring an end to all these divisions within the O.A.S. by issuing an "Instruction Particulière No. 1". For the first time it recognised the existence of the "O.A.S./ Métropole" organisation which Captain Sergent had left Algiers to set up in June.

At the same time, Salan designated under the code-name of "Verdun" a much more senior officer to be military leader of the O.A.S. in France. Then, almost immediately, there had followed the arrest of courier Gingembre, with all his incriminating despatches. "Verdun" – the code-name which Salan gave General Vanuxem, although in fact he had declined the O.A.S.'s tap on the shoulder – was arrested, together with most of the potential and actual network of "O.A.S./Métropole". Sergent himself was identified and forced to go into deep cover, thereby severely curtailing his activities. On top of this, there were the various independent terrorist groupings affiliated with the O.A.S., but who neither informed Sergent of their operations nor took orders from him.* Predominant among these was the "Old General Staff" gang headed by the youthful renegade colonel, Bastien-Thiry, dedicated to the assassination of de Gaulle. On

---

* In conversations with the author, Salan claimed that he had no control over O.A.S./Métropole; "There was no real chief in France, but I was prepared to accept all responsibility for what happened."

8 September, the day after Gingembre's arrest, Bastien-Thiry executed the most spectacular attempt to date, exploding a huge mine of plastic explosive and napalm at Pont-sur-Seine as de Gaulle's Citroën passed on his way home to Colombey. Supplied from old Resistance stock, the explosive had deteriorated and evidently failed to detonate properly; de Gaulle's chauffeur, handling the slewing car with exceptional skill, drove through the sheet of flame somehow managing to keep on the road. Though Sergent was totally ignorant of the plan, the O.A.S. was naturally held responsible for the outrage – lending an additional impetus to the mass arrest of suspects.*

In sum, none of these factors in any way helped Sergent in his work. There were two further disadvantages; he himself, as a mere captain, was of insufficient stature to provide effective leadership; secondly, France – in sharp contrast to the cities of Algeria with their sympathetic *pieds noirs* – was a basically hostile territory in which to operate, becoming progressively more hostile as O.A.S. activities proliferated.

The O.A.S. in France

Accepting that from the beginning the dice were loaded against him, Sergent reckoned that "our only chance to swing in our favour a significant section of metropolitan opinion is to create a situation obliging the regime to react violently and discredit itself". It was the traditional formula of the modern revolutionary terrorist, whether Tupamaros or Baader-Meinhof, and – as so often happens – it was to produce quite the opposite results from those desired by Sergent. Over the six months, culminating in February, that the main O.A.S. offensive in France lasted, it was to do as much as anything else to tilt French sympathies *towards* de Gaulle's acceptance of a precipitate withdrawal from Algeria. Even without the O.A.S., an atmosphere of violence had been mounting in France, created between the police (now reinforced by *harkis*) and the Algerian community, which in itself had been progressively alienating liberal opinion. During 1961, in this savage little war no less than sixteen police were killed and forty-five wounded, most of them during the months of August and September. The police reacted with parallel brutality; according to Vidal-Naquet, "dozens of Algerians were thrown into the Seine and others were found hanged in the woods round Paris". The *gégène* made its ugly appearance on the Parisian scene, and by January 1962 *France-Soir* was lamenting that there was "something wrong with justice" as indicted torturers repeatedly escaped sentence. In mid-October

* Salan in fact sent a letter to *Le Monde*, published on 15 September, in which he dissociated himself from the attempt, declaring melodramatically: "I would not besmirch my military past or my military honour by ordering an assassination attempt against a person whose past belongs to our nation's history." Quoted at his trial the following year, it may well have tipped the balance in saving him from execution.

1961 some 25,000 Algerian workers from the *bidonvilles* (undoubtedly activated by the F.L.N.) had launched a mass demonstration against the harsh curfew and repressive measures imposed on them by the government. Though unarmed and reasonably pacific, the demonstrators were broken up by the police with a disproportionate violence that was shocking to Parisians. It was these already muddy waters that Sergent and his O.A.S. cells had now begun to stir.

With their limited resources, the first operations of the O.A.S./Métropole had a somewhat boy scout flavour about them – especially compared with the handiwork of Degueldre's Deltas in Algiers. Walls were covered with graffiti by night; fairly ineffectual bombs were placed to damage property while scrupulously avoiding any possible injury to life or limb; menacing letters were despatched to extort funds. But these last backfired more often than not, as when a letter demanding five million (old) francs from Brigitte Bardot simply ended up in *L'Express* accompanied by an indignant declaration: "for me, I'm not going along, because I don't want to live in a Nazi country". Already in September, says Sergent, he had given orders to cease all *plastiques*, because their "psychological effect could turn against us". He dreaded "the accident which was going to cost the life of an innocent, a woman or a child". But, rather pathetically, he claims: "We were not obeyed." The bombings continued, and from here on it is extremely unclear as to who was actually responsible for each incident. In November the biggest bomb to date wrecked the "Drugstore" on the Champs Elysées, the aroma of scent from its smashed stocks lingering fragrantly on the pavement for some time afterwards. In December it was the turn of the newspapers; *France-Soir* was bombed, provoking little more than an editorial demanding "the French population has a right to be protected"; the editor-in-chief of *Le Figaro* was *plastiqué* twice. The black-and-white flag of the O.A.S. was impudently hoisted three times in a single day from the Gothic pinnacles of the Hôtel de Ville; but meanwhile, undeterred by the occasional blasting of masonry, de Gaulle all contemptuous went ahead with the meticulous cleaning of the façade of the Place de la Concorde, stage-managed by André Malraux.

"Le Monocle" steps up the bombings

At the beginning of December Sergent received an unexpected visit from an individual introducing himself under the pseudonym of "Le Monocle" (which Sergent regarded as absurdly melodramatic – and which also happened to be the name of the leading lesbian night-club of Paris in vogue at the time). His real name was André Canal, and it was his associates who had been responsible for the killing of Maître Popie before the O.A.S. had received its definitive form. Canal was a compact and muscular Frenchman in his mid-forties who had settled in Algiers in 1940 and made a fortune out of sanitary equipment. A car accident had caused the loss of his left eye, where he now wore a black monocle. To Sergent's rage, "Le Monocle" presented his credentials in the form of a "Decision No. 14", signed by Salan, in which the bearer was placed in charge of "France III" with the mission to "co-ordinate all the networks currently existing under the title of the O.A.S." "Decision No. 14" ended: "All those who will not wish to place themselves under his authority, i.e. under mine, place themselves as a result outside the O.A.S." Specifically, "Le Monocle" was to step up the tempo of the war in France. Sergent at once challenged his authority; nevertheless, under the impetus of "Le Monocle", the bombings forthwith attained a new peak. From now on a state of rivalry bordering on open warfare would exist between Sergent's and Canal's groups, with each going its own way. Yet another division had opened up in the ranks of the O.A.S., and as far as the movement in France was concerned it spelled total anarchy.

Stung into greater activity by the challenge of "Le Monocle", Sergent at the beginning of January launched into a fresh offensive; this time against the Communists. Sergent's reasoning, echoing the self-deception that had haunted the French army all the way through the Algerian war, was that ever since 1954 the Communists had never ceased to be the principal ally of the F.L.N., and now "to live in peace with French Communism while carrying on the war with the Algerian rebels was and remains a nonsense or a treason". A second, and perhaps even more naïve aim, was to force the Gaullists into an impossible position of either choosing to tolerate the angry reactions of the French Communist Party when attacked by the O.A.S., thus appearing as its accomplice, or to confront it and risk a breach with the Left. On 3 January a former leader of the Communist Party of Algeria was shot down at Alençon; the following day, one of Sergent's commandos – profiting from a recent windfall of arms gained when a defecting army lieutenant had brought with him all his platoon's weapons – machined-gunned French Communist Party headquarters in the Place Kossuth. Simultaneously, bombings were carried out on the private residences of party functionaries; but Sergent was disappointed because, for the time being, the Communists refused to react.

The fatal error: Delphine Renard

Later in January there was another sharp confrontation between Sergent and "Le Monocle", at which Sergent claims he warned his rival that his operations were going to bring disaster upon the whole organisation, "because you will end by killing a woman or a child". "Le Monocle" left, promising to exercise more moderation. But the very next night Sergent was enraged to learn that the rival gang had indulged in a "festival of plastique", setting off no less than eighteen bombs. Dubbed *la nuit bleue* by the Paris Press, though no one was killed, it was the worst outbreak of bombings to date. The following week saw another thirteen bombings, in celebration of the second anniversary of "the Barricades". Among them, on 22 January, was a bomb set off in the Quai d'Orsay, which killed one employee and wounded twelve others, the most lethal incident in the O.A.S. campaign in France so far. Plans captured by the Paris police enabled them to forestall, just in time, attempts to dynamite the Eiffel Tower and to explode another series of forty-eight bombs. But otherwise, as in Algiers, the metropolitan police showed an extraordinary lethargy in arresting any of the terrorist leaders. A savage cartoon in *Le Canard Enchaîné* depicted de Gaulle sleepwalking over the roofs of Paris while, to a crowd below waving banners of "Stop the O.A.S.!" and "O.A.S. Assassins!", Premier Debré whispers, "Quiet! You will wake him." By now the French public was becoming thoroughly fed up with the O.A.S., and it would require but one more outrage for something to snap. There now occurred what Sergent claims he had repeatedly warned against.

The bombings had continued against writers and leaders of the Left – in fact, all those considered to be anti-*Algérie française* – with increasing tempo and increasing incompetence. A bomb destined for Jean-Paul Sartre's apartment on the Rue Bonaparte was placed on the wrong floor; Sartre's front door was torn off its hinges, but the apartments on the floor above were totally wrecked. On the morning of 7 February, among ten other bombings that day, an O.A.S. commando set out to bomb the Boulogne-sur-Seine home of André Malraux, de Gaulle's Minister of Culture. Malraux lived upstairs, and anyway was absent that day. The *plastique* was detonated on the ground floor, close to where a four-year-old child, Delphine Renard, was playing with her dolls. It drove splinters of glass from the windows into her face, blinding her in one eye and threatening the sight of the other, and painfully disfiguring her. Although the atrocity against Delphine would have been regarded as little more than an everyday event in contemporary Algiers, and would probably have soon been forgotten even in London of the 1970s under the far more brutal bombing outrages of the I.R.A., in the less hardened Paris of 1962 it provoked a wave of horror and condemnation of the O.A.S. Even the normally pro-*Algérie française* French newspapers ran huge blow-ups of little Delphine's bloodied face and her shattered nursery. "France Wants No More of This", intoned one editorial headline. It was the last straw; as Pierre Sergent admits: "I felt that something had definitely broken between public opinion in France and the Organisation."*

* Sergent points out that the commando was not acting on his orders. Three months later André Canal, identified as the leader of "France III", was arrested by the French police and charged with the Delphine Renard bombing. He was sentenced to death, but his sentence was commuted to life imprisonment at the same time as General Jouhaud's, and he was later amnestied.

Massacre in the Métro

The next day the Parisian Left exploded in rage. A demonstration was hastily organised to take place at the Bastille. Perhaps mistakenly, the Minister of the Interior, Roger Frey, refused to lift the ban currently in force on all political gatherings, but some 10,000 demonstrators gathered nevertheless. Chanting "O.-A.-S. As-sas-sins!" the crowd was in an angry mood – as much against the authorities for allowing such outrages as the bombing of Delphine to occur unpunished as against the O.A.S. The police were nervous; and, as often occurs in France, when nervous they over-react. For two or three hours there were skirmishes of clubbing as the police tried to herd the demonstrators away from the Bastille. Then, without warning, they charged. In panic, some of the demonstrators tried to seek refuge down the stairs to the Charonne Métro station, but found the gates locked. The police now appeared to go quite berserk, hurling demonstrators bodily over the railing on top of the trapped mob below, and then followed this up by heaving heavy iron tree-guards and marble-topped café tables down on to the terror-struck melée. When it was all over eight dead were picked up – including three women and a sixteen-year-old boy employed by *L'Humanité*. Over 100 were injured; but the police also suffered 140 casualties. On the following Tuesday, 13 February, a silent and solemn procession bearing wreaths and estimated at half a million strong marched behind the eight coffins to Père Lachaise cemetery, the sanctum of the martyrs of the French Left from the Commune of 1871 onwards. Nothing like it had been seen in Paris since the bloody days of civil revolt of February 1934; some reckoned the funeral procession to be the biggest street turnout since the Liberation. In a surfeit of emotion, Simone de Beauvoir remarked to herself, "My God! How I hated the French!" But the sense of outrage and wearied disgust at the Delphine Renard and Charonne incidents, and at the ever-escalating O.A.S. horrors in Algiers, was no longer limited to just the French Left. The crisis in the Algerian war had been reached in metropolitan France. *Algérie française* was all but dead – killed by the O.A.S. Almost universally there was a feeling: "*Il faut en finir!*"

CHAPTER TWENTY-FOUR

Exodus

January – July 1962

The whole coast is ready for departure; a shiver of adventure ripples through it. Tomorrow, perhaps, we shall leave together.

Albert Camus, 1939

De Gaulle's "right-about turn"

"*Il faut en finir!*" Already, well before the O.A.S. campaign and its ugly climax, the outlook towards Algeria of the French majority had passed through phases of disenchantment and cynicism to reach one of pure apathy. By the latter part of 1961 it was approaching that of the "don't-want-to-know" British over Northern Ireland in the mid-1970s. Algeria had been in the headlines just too long; the country was fed up with rebellious generals, raucous *pieds noirs*, murderous *fellaghas*, anti-French diatribes at the United Nations and fruitless peace talks. Once again there were many more immediate problems at home demanding attention. There was more discontent on the social scene. Because of the rate of inflation, the *syndicats* were angered by a wage increase limited to only 2.25 per cent, and December saw a new spate of strikes in the public sector. Manifesting that political restlessness so characteristic of it, the nation was becoming bored with its government, bored with the pudgy, vehement features of Michel Debré. Though only sixteen out of twenty-seven of his original team of ministers still remained, he had survived more than a thousand days – out-distancing the previous record set up by Waldeck-Rousseau at the turn of the century. The nation was also becoming a little bored by de Gaulle; his new year address of 29 December (though, in fact, it contained some quite dramatic clues to the way ahead) was dismissed by the Partie Socialiste Unifié as his "hollowest speech" and – more cruelly – by *Le Monde* as "self-satisfaction". The O.A.S. outrages now transformed indifference into an angry impatience.

De Gaulle was, as usual, well-attuned to the country's mood. His own gloom following the collapse of the Evian-Lugrin peace talks had been reinforced by the Pont-sur-Seine attempt on his life – potentially the most lethal of a dozen previous endeavours to assassinate him. Though shaken by the fiery blast, de Gaulle showed his customary composure at the time, but the incident undoubtedly provided one more straw to his already intolerable burden.

"I have seen many brave men in the course of two wars," wrote Harold Macmillan in retrospect, "but I have seen few who had such outstanding physical and moral courage as Charles de Gaulle". Nevertheless, by the end of 1961, believes Macmillan, "it had begun to get him down". More than by any sense of personal fear, de Gaulle was probably most affected by the conviction (and not without reason) that he was indispensable to France. As ever, only he could cut the Gordian knot of Algeria, and ahead there still lay the daunting programme he had set himself for the *renouvellement* of his beloved France. None of this could be got on with so long as her gaze was distracted and her resources drained by the presence of 600,000 troops on the wrong side of the Mediterranean. And he was now seventy-one.

In the autumn of 1961 de Gaulle performed what his fellow statesman and friend, Macmillan, described as a "right-about turn". At the time of Evian he had still believed that the Sahara could be retained for France. Since then the Bizerta debacle had taken place; with it was forfeited Bourguiba's goodwill and any support which de Gaulle hoped for among the "riparian" states for his notion to share out the Sahara on a "community" basis. All the neighbours had become apprehensive of falling out with an independent Algeria. Now, brusquely, de Gaulle wrote off the Sahara. During his Élysée Press conference of 5 September he declared that in Algeria "it was now a matter of disengagement", going on to declare blandly that at Evian "the question of the sovereignty of the Sahara has not been considered, as indeed it must not be by France". For Debré, committed publicly as well as privately to retention of the Sahara, the carpet had been given a brutal tug beneath his feet. To his distressed protests de Gaulle simply replied: "This separate Sahara was an artificial construction. One must give it up." At about this same time de Gaulle received a memorandum from a counsellor whose advice he seldom disregarded, Bernard Tricot, recently returned from his latest visit to Algeria. Shocked by the animosities he had found, Tricot wrote:

> The Europeans I met there are so hardened in opposition to everything that is being prepared, and their relations with the majority of the Muslims are so bad, that I do not imagine that they will desire, or be able, to remain quietly in an independent Algeria. The essential thing, now, is to organise their return.

This was a boldly prophetic opinion of quite outstanding significance; although Tricot admits that, when writing it, he had no conception "that the exodus would be so massive, and above all so rapid".

De Gaulle was now determined to get rid of the "Algerian problem" at the earliest possible date. Like Henry Kissinger with Vietnam in 1973, he was a man in a hurry. Nothing else mattered. "Francisation", "association", all such idealistic formulae had long since been abandoned; now any claim to the Sahara must be sacrificed, and the best deal possible accepted for the *pieds noirs*. De Gaulle's haste was manifest in his new year's broadcast for 1962; in the briefest of references to Algeria he declared that France intended to terminate "one way or another" her involvement there. Then, "come what may, the year ahead will be one of regroupment in Europe and the modernisation of the major part of the French army". In Algeria, a lifelong liberal and francophile like the writer Mouloud Feraoun felt that the Algerians were being dismissed, rather scornfully, to "manage as best they can". At the same time, in Tunis the hard-eyed men of the G.P.R.A. could not escape noticing that de Gaulle, in his haste, was giving them a good look at his hand – or lack of one. When it came to the negotiating table again, de Gaulle's revelation that he intended disengaging, "one way or another", in the new year would mean placing them in a position of being able to exact the most advantageous terms.

The machinery was already in gear before de Gaulle's new year address. In mid-December French and F.L.N. representatives had agreed on an exchange of documents, stating the positions delineated at Lugrin in the summer, and defining the areas of disagreement. Narrowing down these areas, the exchange continued over the next month. Meanwhile, for de Gaulle, the omens looked good. At its December session the United Nations, accepting that peace was in the air, had been unwontedly mild, merely inviting the interested parties to resume negotiations. After his inaugural tough-talking, Ben Khedda too had shown himself equally moderate in his public utterances.

Peace pressures on the G.P.R.A., too

In fact, the G.P.R.A. had good reasons of its own for accepting de Gaulle's new offer to negotiate with an alacrity comparable to de Gaulle's in issuing it. These were not, however, apparent to the impatient French at the time. To begin with, the O.A.S. was now considered by the G.P.R.A. to represent as great a potential threat to its aims as it was to those of France. "1962 was perhaps the most dangerous time of the whole war for us," Ben Khedda told the author,

> because the union between the O.A.S. and dissident French army units was creating so much provocation, in its murders and indiscriminate massacres of Muslims, and was attempting to get the Muslims to demonstrate, out of control, in Algiers. Had they succeeded there would have been an appalling massacre.

In the minds of the G.P.R.A. at that time there always existed the mistrustful fear that de Gaulle might use the excuse of such a state of anarchy to re-establish military dominion; or, alternatively, says Ben Khedda, "there was also the possibility of the French army intervening, once again, to try to impose its own solution on de Gaulle, by removing him".

So it was imperative to reach a settlement before a complete breakdown of civil order occurred in Algeria. Just such an aim had indeed become a priority of the O.A.S.: to provoke a Muslim backlash by their ferocious outrages, which would in turn force French army riposte, thereby wrecking negotiations with the F.L.N. But it was a strategy that totally defeated its own ends; far from preventing negotiations, the O.A.S. terror was precipitating them and making both sides more disposed to concluding a final settlement.

As usual, the G.P.R.A. also had its own complex, internal motives for speeding negotiations. Though characteristically reticent on the subject of rifts within the Algerian camp – and, especially, the role played by Boumedienne – Ben Khedda himself admits the significance of the tensions existing at the time: "Our greatest danger was that, because of the O.A.S., anybody treating with the French might be regarded as a traitor by his own side." As the final negotiations approached, the line-up seemed to be Boumedienne and the General Staff versus the "politicos", as represented by Krim, with Ben Khedda generally siding with the latter. In his posture of dissent, Boumedienne and his supporters mirrored all the innate mistrustfulness of the Algerian character, exacerbated by the seven years of ferocious warfare to which his *moudjahiddine* had been subjected; mistrustful that somehow the hard fought for fruits of victory might be wrested from them by French guile. Beyond that, Boumedienne as always was resolutely determined that no concessions should be made that would permit any French influence in an independent Algeria. In opposition to Krim, Boumedienne was quite clear in his own mind that his Algeria held no future for a *pied noir* minority; therefore no guarantees should be offered them in the peace settlement. Meanwhile, as the O.A.S. killings of Muslims continued to mount remorselessly, so anger and impatience grew in the army – conscious of its new power with the influx of Soviet and Chinese arms reaching it – to the point where Boumedienne was constantly pressing the G.P.R.A. to toughen its line with the French negotiators. By the end of 1961 the General Staff was accusing the G.P.R.A. of "going too fast and too far" in its exchanges with the French. Rather than compromise, they left no doubts that the army would prefer to continue the war. Thus, to Krim and his camp, every day lost in bringing the French to the conference table presented an advantage to Boumedienne and the General Staff, and a weakening of the G.P.R.A.'s position.

On 4 January Ben Khedda, Krim and the other political heads of the

G.P.R.A. conferred in Morocco, under the guise of a courtesy visit to King Hassan. Producing a dossier of specific charges against the General Staff, Krim proposed angrily that Boumedienne and his two lieutenants, Mendjli and Slimane, should be replaced. Boussouf, Boumedienne's former patron, came to his rescue and a heated exchange ensued, lasting several days and ending with the break-up of the triumvirate of Krim, Boussouf and Ben Tobbal, which had wielded so great an influence over the F.L.N. leadership ever since the liquidation of Ramdane Abane four years previously. At the end of the session a vote was held on Krim's motion, which was lost by Krim in a minority of two. On the other hand, it was agreed unanimously that negotiations with France should be resumed at the earliest. There was one proviso: full approval must be obtained from Ben Bella and his fellow detainees.

By special arrangement with de Gaulle and travelling in utmost secrecy, Krim, accompanied by Ben Tobbal, was enabled expeditiously to visit Ben Bella and his colleagues. They were now interned in luxurious new quarters at the Château d'Aulnoy, close to Melun where the first abortive peace talks had been held eighteen months previously. It was a dramatic meeting: the first time that the former members of the "exterior" had had physical contact with any F.L.N. leader in the more than five years since their sequestration.* It was also the first time Krim had seen them since the beginning of the war, and – moved to find on the wall of Bitat's room a copy of the historic photograph of the six founding fathers of the revolt, taken a week before it began – he insisted in posing all those present for a similar photograph in the snowy grounds of the château. Krim was impressed by the high standard of life of the five, though only a few weeks previously they had emerged from a prolonged hunger strike aimed at improving the conditions of their fellow F.L.N. prisoners. Ben Bella seemed particularly bitter at his long imprisonment; he wanted to see de Gaulle personally humiliated, and be made to *bouffer son képi*. Among them there existed parallel rifts to those within the G.P.R.A., with Ben Bella and Khider tending to support Boumedienne and the hard-liners. Analysing the latest exchanges between Paris and the G.P.R.A., Ben Bella insisted on the stiffening of certain terms and the exaction of more concessions from the French. He was particularly outraged by the proposal that the naval base of Mers-el-Kébir should remain in French hands for another fifty years. But all agreed unanimously that negotiations should now proceed; for them, at least, the successful conclusion of a peace settlement would mean liberation. After offering a toast (in orangeade) to "negotiation, victory

* They consisted of Ben Bella, Boudiaf, Khider and Ait Ahmed; joined by Rabah Bitat, who had been the first of the *neuf historiques* to be captured back in November 1954. Professor Lacheraf, the fifth member of the ill-fated group on the plane hijacked in October 1956, had at last been released by the French as being not politically involved.

and your liberty", Krim returned to Tunis. The G.P.R.A. now had the green light to go ahead.

The "Yéti" preliminaries

The lengthy, wearisome, uphill climb to the final settlement now began. It would last two and a half months. Already in November the Quai d'Orsay had begun reconnoitring for a suitable site in which to hold the preliminary negotiations, which could be protracted. The choice was not an easy one; it had to be somewhere within easy reach of the Swiss frontier, so that the Algerians could sleep and lodge on neutral territory and yet attend the talks each day on French soil – as at Evian the previous year. But, unlike Evian, it also had to be somewhere well-removed from the sight of inquisitive journalists. Above all, it had to be safely beyond the reach of the O.A.S. Finally, three thousand feet up in the bleak Jura, a hideout was found which fitted remarkably all the requirements: the "Chalet du Yéti" at the hamlet of Les Rousses, half a mile from the Swiss border and connected to Geneva (twenty-two miles away) by the winding Col de la Faucille pass. To call it a "chalet" was sheer euphemism; in fact it was a bunker-like building of singularly unappealing appearance that housed the heavy snow-clearing equipment of the Ponts-et-Chaussées. Above the garages was some rather spartan accommodation used by the snow-plough teams, or by workers in the department desirous of a cheap ski holiday. Sited in a cul-de-sac well away from the public road, there could hardly have been a less likely place for high-ranking ministers to meet.

During December three pre-preliminary meetings took place at the "Yéti" between Louis Joxe and Bruno de Leusse (from the Quai d'Orsay) on one side, Saad Dahlab and Ben Yahia on the other. Progress was slow and painful (though Joxe declared stoically that it was less fatiguing than the Chamber of Deputies!). After the G.P.R.A. had given its green light, there was a further exchange at the end of January at which Joxe revealed himself unusually irritable and impatient; at one time it seemed, apparently, as if this dapper and sophisticated French intellectual might hurl himself across the table at the Algerian delegates. He requested de Gaulle to send him reinforcements. The next session in early February looked more promising, with Joxe admitting that "a hundred times as much had been achieved at a few meetings in the Jura than during weeks at Evian". More remarkable, however, was the fact that the French Press – though giving play to rumours that high-level talks were going on somewhere – were still in the dark as to their whereabouts. By Sunday, 11 February, both sides were ready to launch into full-scale preliminaries.

Leading the French team Joxe returned, a pair of skis on his car and disguised as a winter sports amateur, and now reinforced by Robert Buron, de Gaulle's fifty-two-year-old Minister of Works, and Jean de Broglie,

Secretary of State for Saharan Affairs. In 1954 Buron had defied his party, the M.R.P., to join the Mendès-France government in order to end the war in Indo-China, and he had subsequently thrown in his lot with de Gaulle because of his belief that he alone could resolve the "Algerian dilemma". Buron had made several visits to Algeria, his assassination had been ordered by the F.L.N., and he had been incarcerated by the rebel generals in April 1961; with his whimsical expression and jokey sense of humour, he was to help lighten the tenseness of the "Yéti" talks and later publish an outspoken diary on the proceedings. Like Joxe, Buron took elaborate precautions to fool the Press on leaving Paris for Les Rousses. Hiding his unmistakable carpet-fringe beard under a scarf, he was driven by his wife towards Orly, then was picked up on the roadside by a black Peugeot. Before leaving, a "sombre and physically exhausted" Debré had instructed Buron to be

> particularly firm on the military clauses . . . watch out for Mers-el-Kébir and the Sahara. The Armed Forces would not understand why we were abandoning our finest and most modern naval base in the Mediterranean. And also don't agree to our troops being pulled out too fast. Their presence is the only guarantee on which our compatriots can rely.

Throughout the coming negotiations it would seem that de Gaulle was at least as much concerned about what the military might think of real estate dispositions affecting it as about the fate of the *pieds noirs*.

The F.L.N. obdurate, once again

Led once more by Krim, the Algerian delegation consisted of Ben Tobbal, Saad Dahlab, Yazid, Ben Yahia, Reda Malek and Dr Mostefai. In giving his first impressions of the opposing team, Buron was rather surprised by the "Kalmuck" appearance of the silent Ben Tobbal, noting immediately that he was a hard-liner; Krim also tended to be silent, playing "with his chubby hands which were astonishingly young", and resembling "a Corsican dignitary from the interior"; Yazid, the F.L.N.'s propaganda ace in New York, irritated Buron by his first interventions, reminding him of a "phoney Harpo Marx". But the one who aroused the most universal respect was Saad Dahlab, Ben Khedda's new Minister for Foreign Affairs, who, "of medium height, black hair and dark skin, is the most temperate of them all", says Buron. To Joxe, who came greatly to admire Dahlab's skill as a negotiator and statesmanlike qualities, he was "very direct, very sincere. A man of the south, with links to Black Africa. Completely in Krim's confidence."

The first day looked as unpromising as the previous summer's talks at Evian had been. After the first quarter of an hour of discussions, on the Sahara, Buron realised it was going to be "long and painful", and by the end of the first day he was noting: "Our interlocutors appear to be determined to discuss indefinitely the smallest details. We must absolutely oblige them to show their cards. Up till now they haven't made one single practical proposition, and satisfy themselves by discussing rigorously our own projects word by word. This can only lead nowhere." Yet de Gaulle's final instructions on the eve of the conference had been, "Succeed or fail, but above all don't allow the negotiations to prolong themselves indefinitely . . . moreover, don't get stuck on detail. . . ." For a whole week, in a stiflingly smoke-ridden room, the delegates marched back and forth over the whole well-trampled ground: the Sahara and French petroleum rights there; the problems of co-operation – financial, economic, administrative and cultural; the question of French military bases and the duration of a military presence; the length of the transitional period, and the shape of the "caretaker government"; and guarantees for the Europeans wishing to remain in Algeria.

Working conditions could hardly have been more uncomfortable; certainly the circumstances of Ben Bella and the "prisoners" of Aulnoy were considerably more sumptuous than those of the French dignitaries confined at the "Yéti". Joxe was the only one to have a room to himself, or even a telephone; Buron slept in quarters used by day as a "withdrawing room" by the Algerians; while the unfortunate de Broglie slept in the conference room itself, in a hideous atmosphere of stale tobacco smoke, fearful of opening a window because of the arctic cold outside. To add to the overcrowding, both the French and Algerian bodyguards were positioned inside the "Yéti", peering out through steamed-up windows for a possible O.A.S. attack, rather than around the exterior where their presence might have betrayed the location of the talks. Conditions were not much pleasanter for the Algerians, forced each day to make the round trip over the Col de Faucille in one of the most wintry Februarys of recent years. One evening their return to Switzerland was blocked by a snowdrift and they had to be dug out by a snow-plough from the "Yéti" garages. On another occasion the Algerian delegation was tracked by zealous journalists, but the driver of a following escort car, using the icy road as a pretext, resourcefully threw himself into a skid, blocking off the newsmen while the delegates escaped. But the inauspicious environment had one unintended bonus in that the informality of life in the "Yéti", compared with the spacious atmosphere at Evian's Hôtel du Parc, helped break the ice and create a human contact between those who had been fighting each other so viciously over the past seven years.

Algiers: the killing escalates

Nevertheless, by Saturday, 17 February it looked as if the negotiations were drifting on to the rocks. The French delegates were under daily pressure from de Gaulle to speed things up, not to get bogged down;

"*Démerdez-vous!*" was his repeated injunction. At the same time, each day brought fresh news from Algiers tending to push things in the opposite direction, to harden the attitude of the Algerian delegates. January and February produced a new escalation of O.A.S. outrages.

> The crimes are multiplying [wrote Mouloud Feraoun in his journal for 19 January]; every day one learns of the death of a friend, of an acquaintance, of a brave man, of an innocent....
> A strike of public transport for the past few days. Naively people wait for a trolley-bus to arrive which never comes; instead, a car arrives, slows down, from it some fanatic gets out, aims, fires, fells a man, gets back behind the wheel, and drives off courageously at full speed....

Often it was boys between the ages of sixteen and twenty who were the gunmen. To step up the offensive, Salan had ordered the "general mobilisation" of the whole French population of Algeria. Special "courts" were set up to "sanction" those refusing to co-operate; a "sanction" generally meant being turned over to Degueldre's Deltas. By the end of February the death toll had risen to 553 for the one month. A grim pall of fear had settled over all Algiers, European and Muslim alike.

But as the O.A.S. bombed Communists and hostile editors in France, fought the *barbouzes* and liquidated dissidents within its own ranks, and slaughtered innocent and insignificant Muslims in Algiers, so it seemed increasingly to lose sight of its primary objectives (impossible though they might be) while all the time setting the world against it and those objectives. The provocation against the F.L.N. in their endeavours to reach a peace settlement were indeed great. After the O.A.S. killings of December, the General Staff's *Bulletin d'Information* repeated earlier threats by declaring even more pointedly: "We solemnly warn those Algerian Europeans who blindly follow the Fascists of the O.A.S. against the incalculable consequences which this unleashing of racist fury could have, which risks compromising forever the future of the Algerian Europeans."

Then, on the very last day of the "Yéti" talks, two French T.6 planes made a rocket and machine-gun attack on the F.L.N. "Ben M'hidi" base at Oujda, just inside Moroccan territory. The O.A.S. immediately claimed responsibility for the raid, though it appears that it was in fact a "free enterprise" affair by two aero-club flyers, one of whom was avenging a brother killed by the F.L.N. In itself it was indicative of the growing anarchy in Algeria. The "Ben M'hidi" base contained some ten thousand people, including refugees and a hospital centre equipped by Yugoslavia and East Germany and well marked by a red cross. With unfortunately directed aim, bullets from the T.6s killed a wounded man actually on the operating table and a nurse tending him. Three others in the base were slain and several wounded. The raid bore a close resemblance to the Sakiet raid of 1958, which had had so profound an influence on the course of the war. This time, however, the F.L.N. gritted its teeth and with remarkable restraint said nothing – at least for the time being. But the net effect of the Oujda incident, and all the other O.A.S. outrages compounded, was to play into the hands of Boumedienne and the hard-liners and make it progressively more difficult for the negotiators of both sides to arrive at satisfactory guarantees for the *pieds noirs*. Cooped up in the "Yéti" Robert Buron wondered gloomily to himself who would win: "De Gaulle or Salan? ... De Gaulle no doubt, but the loser will not be his adversary.... The poor *pieds noirs* for whom, with all our hearts, we are building a possible future, possible on paper, but which the multiplying violations are striving to make unrealisable, risk paying the bill...."

De Gaulle cuts the knot

Whether as a result of the O.A.S.'s activities or whatever other factors, by midday on Saturday, 17 February Louis Joxe felt that the talks had reached an impasse. There was a whole list of fundamental points on which, according to their brief, the French delegates could yield no further concession, and the Algerians would make no concessions:

The acquisition of Algerian nationality for the European minority; their rights during the transitory period; and the guarantees to be accorded them afterwards.

The length of the lease on Mers-el-Kébir naval base.

The length of the leases on the Saharan rocket and atomic bases.

That afternoon Joxe proposed a suspension of the talks while he telephoned de Gaulle for fresh instructions. On the Sunday de Gaulle came back with a statement of vital importance to the whole peace talks. This time he was not speaking in the sibylline manner as he had so often in the past when issuing guidance to his subordinates on Algeria.

The essential thing [said de Gaulle], is to reach an agreement composed of a cease-fire followed by self-determination.... It is this result, I repeat, this result that must be realised today....

Having said this, there is obviously an interest in then obtaining the longest lease possible for Mers-el-Kébir as well as for our military presence for experimental purposes. But since our presence at Mers-el-Kébir would be of the order of some ten, fifteen or twenty years and in the Sahara of several years only, we must concede these details rather than reject an agreement; for there is no comparison between the primary interest, which consists of reaching an agreement, and the secondary interest, which consists of holding a little longer certain things which, anyway, we do not reckon to hold forever.*

* At this point, the French had been holding out for a lease of twenty-five years while Krim was offering only ten – to which Joxe had countered that this would not make it worth while. (In the event, the French were to evauate Mers-el-Kébir in five years.) Krim was demanding that French troops in Algeria be reduced to 80,000 men (from 600,000) within six months, and withdraw completely within two years at the latest; Joxe was proposing eighteen months and three years.

Although de Gaulle was here specifically referring to the tenure of Mers-el-Kébir and the Sahara bases, in the context of the rest of his instructions it was clear that – by the "things we do not reckon to hold forever" – he also had in mind the whole *présence française* in Algeria, i.e. the future of the *pieds noirs*. Who can tell what will happen in ten or twenty years, speculated the seventy-one-year-old President? "Let us not exaggerate too much the importance of the wording of what we agree today.... If a sincerity of will is not there, the very finest agreements would be of no avail...."

Joxe returned from the telephone, notes Buron, equipped with a wide margin of manoeuvre. After an all-night session, by 5 a.m. the following morning, in an atmosphere of exhaustion all round, Krim and Joxe "exchanged two brief declarations, grey in tone, but which allow a certain relief on both sides. For the first time we all shook hands." Buron, for one, felt only limited satisfaction at what had been achieved. Remarking on the strength of the "orientals" in negotiation because of their imperviousness to the passage of time, he noted regretfully: "They guessed our own haste to get things finished, while moderating their own; but they are convinced that he who can dissimulate his impatience the best will obtain at the eleventh hour the profit of some final concessions." On his return to Paris Buron was asked by one of his colleagues in the M.R.P. whether he felt that results would not "either condemn the Algeria of tomorrow, or the validity of the agreements?" "*Hélas*, it's a little like that," he replied. Michel Debré he found already "profoundly unhappy", fearing the reaction of the *pieds noirs*, apprehensive for the future of the Muslims "compromised with ourselves", and with doubts about the practical functioning of the agreements the day after tomorrow. Nevertheless, an agreement of sorts had been reached – as instructed by de Gaulle. It now remained for the experts and lawyers to turn it into a viable document – and for the last outstanding details to be ironed out. The final phase of the negotiations was fixed to begin on 7 March. Leaving the homely confines of the "Yéti" (the location of which had succeeded in baffling the world Press right up to the very last), the delegates agreed to meet once again amid the pomp and circumstance of the Hôtel du Parc at Evian.

Salan declares total war

The reaction feared by Premier Debré in Algeria was not slow in coming once both sides announced that the makings of an agreement had been reached at the "Yéti". On 23 February the O.A.S. published a six-page *Instruction No. 29*, bearing the signature of Salan, and possibly the most important document of its whole career. "The irreversible is about to happen," it began: "I want us, wherever possible, to control the situation.

I want to bring events about: in short, at the outset, I reject any idea of defence in favour of a generalised offensive," continued Salan. For the moment the anticipated cease-fire was proclaimed, he ordered: "The systematic opening of fire against C.R.S. and gendarmerie units. 'Molotov cocktails' will be thrown against their armoured vehicles...night and day." On another front, the objective was "to destroy the best Muslim elements in the liberal professions so as to oblige the Muslim population to have recourse to ourselves". It seemed characteristically twisted thinking. The overall target was

> to paralyse the powers that be and make it impossible for them to exercise authority. Brutal actions will be generalised over the whole territory. They will aim at influential personalities of the Communist Party, at works of art and all that represents the exercise of authority, in a manner to lead towards the maximum of general insecurity and the total paralysis of the country.

It was nothing less than a formal declaration of war against the authority of France, and as such was bound to lead to a direct confrontation between the O.A.S. and the army.

As far as the general paralysis of the country was concerned, Salan was to prove as good as his word; the previous week he had congratulated the O.A.S. on its achievements – a week during which "brutal actions" had resulted in the "execution" of more than fifty people. On 22 February five postmen were shot down with careful selectivity: two Europeans, two Muslims, one Jew. Henceforth the mail was no longer delivered. Next the O.A.S. singled out the pharmacists, Muslim and European, on suspicion that some of them were aiding the F.L.N. Then came the tram-workers and railwaymen, employees of Algiers Electricity and Gas, the coiffeuses and the doctors; finally the wretched flower vendors, shot down at street corners among the pathetic debris of their carnations and roses. On 24 February, following the killing by the F.L.N. of a Bab-el-Oued taxi-driver, a *pied noir* mob trapped a score of Muslim workers in a cul-de-sac and stabbed and beat them to death. Increasingly a kind of apartheid, which had never previously existed, was growing up in the cities as Muslim workers declined to enter the European quarters – and vice versa.

Algiers alone was now averaging a rate of thirty to forty killings a day – not to mention the wounded. On 27 February, in the space of one hour at midday, right in the centre of Algiers thirteen people were killed within a radius of five hundred yards, in totally unrelated incidents. In Oran, the situation was hardly better; on 1 March, during Ramadan, two 105 mm. shells exploded in booby-trapped cars parked in the Oran Casbah, killing twenty-three Muslims and wounding another thirty-two. When the gendarmes arrived, they were in turn set upon by enraged Muslims, resulting in a further fifteen victims. Like the citizens scourged by the bubonic plague in *La Peste*, the residents of both cities began to acquire a growing familiarity with death.

> If the victim was dead [wrote Paul Henissart] a sheet of newspaper was placed over his face. If he was not, he lay on the pavement. Some passers-by detoured around him, very few would stop to assist him. An ambulance eventually arrived and he was removed. Firemen hosed off the bloodstains on the pavement.

Nor was the foreign community entirely immune. With the approach of a settlement, scores of foreign correspondents had been drawn to Algiers. The Japanese among them had already displayed nervousness at being mistaken for the *barbouze* Vietnamese and had taken to wearing little national emblems on their lapels. Then, on 3 March, two Italian journalists who had written unflattering accounts of the O.A.S. were kidnapped at gun-point from the Aletti bar, driven to an O.A.S. hideout, and given twenty-four hours to leave the country. The next day nine of the ten Italian newsmen in Algiers scurried back home. That same day the O.A.S. murdered Maître Pierre Garrigues, successor to their first victim, Maître Popie. The following day joint communiqués from Paris and Tunis announced the talks due to begin at Evian in three days' time, and the O.A.S. offensive slipped into a higher gear still. Between 120 and 130 *plastiques* went off in Algiers alone that night. On the 10th the residents of Bab-el-Oued were treated to the *grand-guignol* spectacle of a naked corpse strung from a complicated system of pulleys stretched across the street, and dancing above their heads in broad daylight. "It's a *barbouze!*" acclaimed the crowd, far from revolted, as the unknown man hung there for half an hour before being cut down. Then, on 15 March, the day after the stickiest session at Evian, the O.A.S. performed perhaps the most wantonly savage of its "brutal actions" to date. At 11 a.m. three young men drove up to a building in El Biar housing one of the *centres sociaux* which had been created by Germaine Tillion, under the aegis of Soustelle back in 1955, to improve Franco–Muslim relations. Inside a conference was under way, discussing vocational training for homeless Algerian children. The leader of the O.A.S. Delta squad took a piece of paper from his pocket and read out a roll-call of seven names. One was absent, but two school principals and four French and Muslim inspectors were led outside. Among the latter was Mouloud Feraoun, the prize-winning Kabyle author, liberal humanitarian and personal friend of the late Albert Camus. The six men were lined up against a wall; the Deltas opened fire, shooting first at the legs, then finishing off the educators where they lay on the ground.*

---

* According to Salan's aide, Captain Ferrandi, the shooting of Feraoun was a mistake; the main target was the missing man, "a certain Petitbon, a senior official of the national education services", who had decided not to attend the meeting at the last moment – so the O.A.S. squad just killed whoever was there. In view of the singling out of "the best Muslim elements in the liberal professions" in Salan's *Instruction No. 29*, the excuse – such as it is – hardly convinces.

Feraoun: last of the moderates

The last to die was Mouloud Feraoun, hit by twelve bullets in the chest. The previous month he had entered in his *Journal* on a rare note of joy: "The war in Algeria is ending. Peace to those who are dead. Peace to those who are going to survive. Let the terror cease. *Vive la liberté!*" Then, on the night before his death, he had written in a different vein:

> In Algiers, *c'est la terreur*. . . . One can no longer distinguish the brave from the cowards. Unless, as a result of living in fear, we have all become insensitive and unaware. Certainly, I don't want to die and I absolutely do not want my children to die, but I am taking no particular precaution beyond those which have become habit over the past fortnight; limitation of going outside, expeditions to buy "in bulk", an end to the visits of friends. But each time one of us goes out, on his return he describes an incident or reports a victim.

These were the last words Feraoun ever wrote. His death caused a ripple of shock passing beyond the frontiers of Algeria and France. Only forty-nine years old and born of impoverished Kabyle *fellahs* living in a one-room hut, Feraoun had established himself by his prize-winning novel *La Terre et le Sang* as one of Algeria's most distinguished writers. A Kabyle patriot, but whose humanist scholarship reflected the best of French educational influence, he was never ashamed to proclaim his dual allegiances: "There is French in me, there is Kabyle in me. But I have a horror of those who kill. . . . *Vive la France*, such as I have always loved! *Vive l'Algérie*, such as I hope for! Shame on the criminals! Shame on the cheaters! . . . When Algeria lives and raises its head (again) . . . it will remember France and all it owes to France," he had declared at various times during the war. Bespectacled and mild-mannered, his uncompromising courage belied his appearance, and he had never ceased to condemn the excesses of either side. As a French reviewer of his posthumously published *Journal* wrote, "In killing Feraoun, Frenchmen had attacked the very best of their Algerian achievement."

The death of the writer meant more than that; it symbolised the final snuffing out of the light of hope of a "third force", of moderation and liberalism, that had flickered up occasionally during the war. Attacked by such members of the Left in France as Francis Jeanson for being but an opiate of the masses and of knowing only how to spend vast sums of money on "neo-colonial" schemes, besieged by the F.L.N., and now finally extinguished by the O.A.S., the battered ideal of the "third force" died at a time when Algeria had never been more in need of men of goodwill, and enemies of excess and violence. As is so often the tragic path of revolution, it was the Montagne that triumphed over the Gironde.

Back to Evian

When the second Evian Conference opened on 7 March the atmosphere was quite different from that established within the close confines of the "Yéti". Much had happened during the few weeks' interval. Between 22 and 28 February a Fifth C.N.R.A. was swiftly convened in Tripoli to ratify the agreements reached between Krim and Joxe. Against the sombre background of Salan's offensive in Algeria, Krim immediately came under hot fire from Boumedienne and the General Staff representatives. He had been "had" by the French, claimed Boumedienne; they had been granted loopholes through which they could wriggle out of honouring their side of the bargain, thus maintaining a "neo-colonial" grip on Algeria; through petroleum concessions made to the French Algeria's birthright had been sold out so that she would realise only one-twentieth of the royalties that should be her due. Backed by Ben Bella, the General Staff lobby also challenged the agreement whereby the Europeans would be entitled to representation in the future Algerian Assembly. Krim is said to have riposted acidly to Boumedienne: "And you who are at the head of the army, explain to us how you will expel the French? By arms?" In mistrusting the validity of the French undertakings, Boumedienne was supported by Krim's once inseparable deputy, Colonel Ouamrane, and another veteran fighter, Colonel Mohamedi Said. But, with the bulk of the military engaged in countering the O.A.S. and making dispositions for the future inside Algeria, Krim and the "politicians" had a majority in excess of the two-thirds required by the G.P.R.A. for ratifying a peace treaty. Accordingly, the Fifth C.N.R.A. "mandated" the G.P.R.A. delegates to "pursue the negotiations in course". An important rider was attached, however, pressing Krim that "clarifications" and further concessions should still be sought on the points criticised at the conference – notably, those concerning the future of the Europeans.

Unaware of the arguments at Tripoli, Joxe and his team were taken aback by the new rigidity their opposite numbers promptly displayed at Evian. Buron was soon noting that the Algerians seemed to be "even more frightened of their colleagues in Tunis" than of the O.A.S. But over the past few weeks the O.A.S. had left so great a mark that the French recognised that they were in a considerably worse position to negotiate than the previous month. Then, with neither Krim nor Dahlab actively seeking the departure of the Europeans, both sides had taken gambles on the future; now the ground had shifted perceptibly, and Joxe's hard-fought efforts on behalf of guarantees for the *pieds noirs* already seemed largely academic. In the words of Yves Courrière:

Backed by the Europeans, the O.A.S. had done so much that it was no longer a question of the majority of the *pieds noirs* remaining. Perhaps a tiny minority would cling on. And meanwhile the repeated crimes were burning each day a few more of the bridges between the two communities. Hatred was building up.

"What", asked Buron, "was the point of proclaiming a cease-fire if, as soon as fighting ceased in the *djebel*, civil war then broke out in the cities? "

By 11 March, under the barrage of "clarifications" and further concessions demanded by the Algerians, the second Evian looked like following in the footsteps of the first. "I am anxious," recorded Buron. "Louis Joxe seemed to be very tired, that is if not actually ill, all day. The morale of the delegation is not very high." Joxe tried to force the pace, threatening the Algerians to break off if no progress were made over the next two days. A "nervous and irritated" de Gaulle was constantly on the telephone telling his delegation to threaten the Algerians that – if the worst came to the worst – France would go ahead with unilateral solutions, invoking the short-lived spectre of partition. 16 March was a day of intense cold, with the wind blowing like a tempest across the gloomy lake; on hearing of the murder of Feraoun and his associates, Buron says that the *Götterdämmerung* instincts of the O.A.S. made him think of "the Hitler bunker". And meanwhile there was still but little progress towards a peace settlement.

Then, suddenly, on 18 March it was all over: "*Et voilà!* We have finished; we have attached our three signatures opposite that of Belkacem Krim at the bottom of ninety-three pages, the fruit of the work of these twelve days," wrote Robert Buron. After seven and a half years of war, the cease-fire was due to operate with effect from midday on the 19th, both parties hoping that its announcement would at last bring about an end to the O.A.S. outrages.

The Agreement

How, from all the complexity of their ninety-three pages, preambles, chapters, headings and articles, can one distil the salient points of the Evian Agreements? First of all, they dealt with details of the cease-fire, including arrangements for the release forthwith of all prisoners. Next came a *déclaration générale*, recognising the full sovereignty of Algeria, in its territorial integrity, in accordance with the principles of "self-determination" as bestowed by the referendum of 8 January 1961. Early in this *déclaration* were recognised the rights of "French citizens" to share in equality the protection and privileges accorded to all Algerians over a transitory period of three years. At the end of this period they could either opt for Algerian citizenship or retain their French nationality, in which case they would become "foreigners" in Algeria. They could not have it both ways; thus had the French negotiators been forced to concede yet another major bargaining point, that of "dual nationality". The rights to which the "French citizens" would be entitled during the transitory three years were spelled out to include: respect for private property – no "dispossession" without fair compensation; a "fair and authentic" participation in public affairs; guarantees of non-discrimination in language, cultural and religious matters. All citizens of Algeria would also be equally protected against discrimination, or sanctions relating to any acts committed during the war and prior to the cease-fire.

Thus was the Number One question of the *pieds noirs* regulated – on paper.

A chapter on the "settlement of the military questions" gave France twelve months in which to reduce her armed forces to 80,000, and a further twenty-four months to repatriate them altogether; the lease of Mers-el-Kébir was fixed at fifteen years, renewable by agreement after that; leases on other military installations as were deemed "necessary" to France were granted, but for unspecified periods. Under "Economic and Financial Co-operation", France was committed to continue for three years, renewable, to provide aid "at a level equivalent to that of current programmes"; i.e. the multi-million franc Constantine Plan. Algeria would remain part of the franc zone, and Algerian workers would be free to remain in France. Under the all-important item of petroleum rights, a complex agreement permitted the French oil companies concessions on the bases of past enterprises, and preferential treatment for new exploration and development over a period of six years. To preside over the "transitory period", a Provisional Executive would be appointed – comprised of equal numbers of Algerians and French – and one of its first acts would entail the fixing of a referendum to ratify the Evian Agreements within three to six months of the cease-fire; not, as originally envisaged by de Gaulle at the time of his "self-determination" statement in 1959, after an elapse of four years. The Agreements ended with a pious "Declaration of Principles", to the effect that: "France and Algeria will resolve the differences that may arise between them by pacific means of settlement." (I.e. French forces still *in situ* would be precluded from intervening in the event of any infringement of the Algerian side.)

Thus, layer by layer, had the onion of French demands been peeled in the face of Algerian refusal to compromise: first, the French insistence on a prior cease-fire; then her refusal to recognise the G.P.R.A. as the sole *interlocuteur valable*; then de Gaulle's requirement of a four years' hiatus between a cease-fire and "self-determination"; then the Sahara, and then the safeguard of dual nationality for the *pieds noirs*. And so on.

In fact, almost every one of the above provisions was to remain a dead letter, overtaken by events for one reason or another.

Algerian jubilation: French misgivings

On the night of 18 March, over the transmitters of all North Africa, President Ben Khedda proclaimed triumphantly "a great victory of the Algerian people". It could indeed be said that, through its extraordinary consistency, the F.L.N. at Evian had fulfilled virtually all of its original war objectives as framed at the Soummam Conference back in 1956. In France *Le Canard Enchaîné*, abandoning its satirical style, blazoned in a bold headline: "To de Gaulle, from his grateful country: once and for all, *merci!*" The feeling of Frenchmen in general was one of relief but no rejoicing, accompanied by a great deal of criticism from all quarters. "We felt not the slightest surge of joy," wrote Simone de Beauvoir: "The Algerians' victory didn't just wipe out the seven years of French atrocities, suddenly brought out into the light of day ... the prevailing sentiment – 'Yes, the poor Germans; one realises now it wasn't their fault.'" There were others on the Left who attacked the amnesty clause in the Agreements for letting the "torturers" go unpunished. There were those like General Massu who condemned them for "betraying" the Muslim administrators and *harkis* who had remained loyal to France, while Lacoste castigated de Gaulle for "letting the petroleum go within forty-eight hours". Many felt that the main weakness of the Agreements was the lack of watertight guarantees for the *pieds noirs*; that de Gaulle in his haste had sold them down the river. "Our legitimate war aim", the liberal Germaine Tillion had written in 1960 "is the safeguarding of the lives and interests of a significant population which has its claims on France." Had this been achieved at Evian?

There were those who felt that *only* France was bound by the Agreements: with herself fettered to resolving future differences by "pacific means", with her army withdrawing, what possible sanctions could be applied against the G.P.R.A. if it failed to respect the Agreements? Other critics pointed to a small matter of validity; the Agreements had been signed with representatives of a body that was not even a legitimately constituted government – therefore, France would be bound, while a future Algerian regime could repudiate. (Indeed, within a month Chanderli at the United Nations would be claiming that the Evian Agreements were purely provisional, and capable of renunciation as soon as this would be in the interests of Algeria.) In France the Conseil d'État was to challenge the validity of the Agreements by pronouncing as "unconstitutional" the referendum endorsing them. "This government has required four years of war to impose on its adversary the solution which was precisely his final objective," was the caustic comment of Professor Maurice Allais, and many criticised de Gaulle for going too slowly over the four years from 1958, but too fast in the final weeks and days. Some of those, too, most intimately involved in bringing the Agreements to fruition were far from being entirely happy with the results. Tricot, the brain behind the scenes, held reservations that dealings for a cease-fire and for the future organisation of Algeria had to be compressed into one stage: "It was extremely bad to have to make arrangements for the future in an atmosphere of war and terror," he says in retrospect. For Robert Buron, it was "a very strange document" at the bottom of which his signature figured; he felt "conscious of having done my duty in the full sense of the word, but I do not experience any genuine satisfaction". In Paris, Premier Debré composed his letter of resignation, incensed in particular by the surrender of the Sahara. De Gaulle once again dissuaded him; then let him go the following month, once the dust had settled, replacing him quietly by banker Pompidou.

De Gaulle himself greeted the Agreements with characteristically cynical realism. To his cabinet the following day he remarked: "It's an honourable exit. It's not necessary to write an epilogue on what has just been done, or not done.... That the application of the Agreements will be capricious [aléatoire] is certain.... As for France, it will be necessary for her now to interest herself in something else." In his mind the subject of Algeria was now dismissed.

Cease-fire: but no peace

On the day of the cease-fire, Monday, 19 March, contemporary news films show tough, scruffily dressed men of Boumedienne's A.L.N. standing in one minute's solemn silence to commemorate the claimed one million Muslim dead of the seven-and-a-half-year war. Then followed scenes of wild emotion as the moudjadhiddine danced, hugged and embraced each other. In the pied noir strongholds of Algeria the news of the peace signed at Evian was greeted with dumb and glum disbelief. On a day of sparkling spring sunshine the streets of Algiers emptied, except for the constantly patrolling vehicles of the police and army. The O.A.S.'s first reaction was to go round ripping down the posters that had suddenly appeared, showing a Muslim and a European child smiling at each other above the caption, "For our children, Peace in Algeria." A general strike was called by Salan, and an O.A.S. order went out declaring that – in addition to the civil law-enforcers, the C.R.S. and the gendarmerie – the French army was now considered an enemy. Far from leading to an end to O.A.S. violence as the delegations at Evian had hoped in hastening signature, the week after the cease-fire brought the bloodiest interlude that Algiers had yet seen as the O.A.S. strained every muscle to nullify the Agreements.

The O.A.S. first extended its promiscuous attacks against Muslims of all walks of life, and both sexes, with the Deltas issuing a total ban on Muslim employees entering the European quarters of Algiers.* On the 20th, the

* This ban, and the tragedies which it led to, were explained by one of the O.A.S. leaders responsible for the decision on the ground that the F.L.N. had ordered all Muslim workers to supply information on their European employers. "In Algiers there were a mass of O.A.S. command posts, so for our own security we had to persuade the Muslims not to come into the European areas to protect our organisation against espionage. It was hard, and horrible, but it was essential; it was more than a strategic effort for apartheid, it was a tactical means of survival."

day after the cease-fire, an O.A.S. deserter lieutenant sighted a 60 mm. mortar from a Bab-el-Oued balcony at the Place du Gouvernement, which, at midday, was thronged with happy Muslims. Six bombs fell into the packed crowd, killing twenty-four and wounding fifty-nine, and creating a murderous urge for revenge which – for the first time – the French army and F.L.N. officials at hand collaborated to control. Two days later twenty men of the O.A.S. "Z Commandos", equipped with machine-guns and bazookas, trapped a gendarmerie patrol emerging from the Tunnel des Facultés. They knocked out three of the half-tracks, killing eighteen gendarmes and wounding twenty-five. Three events now marked the climax of pure civil war, of Frenchmen killing Frenchmen. On the 23rd two army trucks loaded with young conscripts were surrounded by hostile *pieds noirs* in Bab-el-Oued. A new addition to Degueldre's Deltas, called an "A-Commando" after its leader Jacques Achard, arrived on the scene and attempted to disarm the soldiers. Apparently a Muslim private nervously cocked his sub-machine-gun; Achard's squad ruthlessly opened fire, killing outright seven of the conscripts and wounding another eleven. "It was", admits Pérez, "a very grave action." Salan's instructions had been obeyed, but the massacre of the young conscripts totally transformed the attitude of the army – hitherto almost passively neutral – towards the O.A.S. A determination to avenge fallen comrades took over.

In a towering rage, the French Commander-in-Chief, General Ailleret, now ordered a full-scale assault on the O.A.S. stronghold of Bab-el-Oued. At first gendarmerie armoured cars raked the façades of apartment buildings with heavy .50 calibre machine-guns. But the O.A.S. marksmen fired back. Then, in the afternoon, 20,000 French troops – led by Ailleret himself – moved in and sealed off Bab-el-Oued with its some 60,000 inhabitants. Tanks fired their cannon at point-blank range into suspected O.A.S. snipers' nests. In the evening a flight of T.6 planes flew in to strafe the still rebellious quarter with rockets and machine-guns. It was a scene more familiar to an army coup in Bolivia than anything ever experienced on French territory. For three days the "reduction" of Bab-el-Oued continued, and at the end of it the bullet-riddled walls, shattered windows, gutted cars in the streets and dangling trolley-bus cables resembled scenes from Budapest of 1956 – which, right from the beginning, Roger Degueldre had told Captain Sergent was what he wanted to create in Algiers. The fighting cost the French forces fifteen dead and seventy-seven wounded, while the Bab-el-Oued casualties were estimated at twenty killed and sixty wounded; 3,309 arrests were made and 1,110 weapons of various kinds seized, together with 100 kilos of *plastique*. During those days of siege, and afterwards, the uncommitted residents of Bab-el-Oued found themselves caught in a grim no-man's-land between the O.A.S. and the F.L.N. "We didn't dare go into the Casbah for fear of being kidnapped or killed by the F.L.N.," recalled a

Jewish school-teacher, Madame Lorette Ankaoua: "nor did we dare go into the European shops behind our house for fear of the O.A.S. So small Arab children in my class smuggled us bread secretly in their dirty haversacks. It was all we had to eat."

Crushed as Bab-el-Oued might seem, there was more to come. On the 26th the O.A.S. mounted a mass demonstration to sweep along the whole *pied noir* population to the *monument aux morts* in protest against the treatment of Bab-el-Oued. Reckoning that anything up to 500,000 people might turn out, the new Algiers prefect of police, Vitalis Cros, declared all demonstrations banned and called up troop reinforcements to stiffen his twenty-five squadrons of *gendarmes mobiles*. The key role fell upon the 4th Regiment of Tirailleurs, one of the last regular units still containing a majority of "loyal" Algerian troops, which had just arrived – exhausted and tense – from operations in the *bled*. A few days previously their commanding officer, Colonel Goubard, had reported to the Commander-in-Chief, General Ailleret, that his Tirailleurs – averaging twenty years of age and with only eighteen months' training – had proved themselves in the *djebel* but were in no way conditioned or trained for police activities in the city. Ailleret promised that the Tirailleurs would not be used in Algiers; but somehow, incredibly, the order was never passed down. Thus, at a time when nerves were at breaking-point in Algiers, these totally unsuited Algerian troops found themselves holding a road block in the centre of Algiers, across the Rue d'Isly by the Grande Poste, close to where Ortiz had erected his barricades in January 1960.

Despite the ban on demonstrations, shortly after 2 p.m. a wave of *pieds noirs* surged up the Rue d'Isly. They began jostling the Tirailleurs, who were obviously panicked by having to deal with a mob at such close quarters. Suddenly shots were fired by an unknown hand from a rooftop on the Rue d'Isly. The young Tirailleurs began spontaneously to shoot back, as they would have done out in the *djebel*. They shot, and shot – wildly, and at point-blank range – into the crowd. Among the journalists to witness it, Yves Courrière recalls that the horror of the scene was something he would never forget all his life. It was a repeat of the deadly fusillade which had prefaced "Barricades Week" in 1960 – only worse, with women and old men caught up in the murderous cross-fire. The crowd stampeded, and were fired after as they ran; men and women flattened themselves to the ground, then tried to crawl for safety to the Grande Poste or into nearby shops, with a hail of bullets following them. In the shattered window of one elegant boutique two corpses were found grotesquely sprawled among bullet-ridden dummies. Agonised shouts of "*Arrête ton feu, arrête ton feu, arrête . . . !*" went unheeded. When the shooting was finally stopped, forty-six dead and 200 wounded were picked up, more than a score of whom died subsequently. Afterwards some 2,000 cartridge cases were counted. Lengthy enquiries were held but, although the identity of the sniper on the roof was never clarified, it was generally assumed that he had belonged to the O.A.S., aiming deliberately to provoke a massacre that would speed the breakdown of order in Algiers. Whatever the truth, it was criminal negligence to place the Tirailleurs in such a predicament.

The O.A.S. decapitated

During the siege of Bab-el-Oued de Gaulle issued a curt instruction to Debré: "Immediate action must be taken to smash the criminal action of terrorist bands in Algiers and Oran." But, disastrous as it had been, the week following the cease-fire in fact marked the peak in the fortunes of the O.A.S. and a turning-point in the struggle against it. In Algiers, guarded day and night by eight C.R.S. gunmen, the new tough prefect of police, Vitalis Cros, had taken over; meanwhile, the underground work of "Professor Ermelin", alias Michel Hacq, and his "Force C" was at last beginning to bear fruit. In Oran a new army commander, an ex-trooper called General Katz, had assumed personal control of the battle. After the killing of his Deuxième Bureau chief, Katz installed himself in the prefecture, where the windows had been shot out, put his mattress on the floor to be out of the field of snipers' fire, and read Saint-Simon by night to distract himself from the incessant shooting and bombing outside.

It was in Oran that on 25 March, between the assault of Bab-el-Oued and the Rue d'Isly massacre in Algiers – the first arrest came of an O.A.S. leader. With its preponderance of *pieds noirs*, with the wind in its dusty streets that seemed if anything to exacerbate violent tempers, Oran had given itself over perhaps even more completely to the O.A.S. than Algiers. March had begun with a particularly odious F.L.N. atrocity at Mers-el-Kébir: Muslims had broken into the house of a *pied noir* night-watchman during his absence, disembowelled his wife and smashed the skulls of his five- and four-year-old children against a wall. The predictable *ratonnade* had followed, with black-jacketed youths setting fire to Muslim shops in Oran and killing four Muslims "while attempting to evade arrest". A few days later Oran's civil prison was conflagrated by a crude butane and petrol bomb, creating a panic and killing two Muslims. On the 22nd the O.A.S. – with total impunity, and apparently aided by the bank clerks – pulled off the biggest bank raid in history to date, getting away with 2,200 million francs (about $4,700,000 or nearly £1,000,000) from the Banque d'Algérie in the centre of Oran.

Meanwhile, the O.A.S. boss in Oran, General Edmond Jouhaud – "Soleil bis" – was often to be seen promenading quite openly along the front under his alias of "M. Louis Gerbert, school-teacher", with shaved head and bushy moustache. On 25 March General Katz got a "break" when an

O.A.S. suspect under interrogation admitted that he had met Jouhaud in "a particularly high building on Oran's Front-de-Mer". The one building fitting this description was Le Panoramique skyscraper. As units despatched by Katz closed in on it, radio intercepts picked up an obvious warning in code – "The flowers are going to be watered" – which confirmed his suspicions. Inside Le Panoramique Jouhaud, holding a staff briefing, looked out of the window when a helicopter flew close and was horrified to see that the whole area below was filled with helmeted troops watching his windows through binoculars. In a few minutes there was a knock on the door. Jouhaud insisted on his identity as "Louis Gerbert", but soon became confused on details of pedagogy; one million francs in brand new notes were found in the apartment; and Salan's deputy finally condemned himself by signing a form to certify the removal of personal effects "E. Jouhaud" instead of "L. Gerbert". By the following night Jouhaud was in the Santé prison, along with Challe and Zeller.

On hearing of Jouhaud's arrest, Salan's reaction was, "De Gaulle will have him shot ... unless he catches me first." He ordered General Gardy to take over in Oran, but the days of the O.A.S. ascendancy there were numbered. Salan, too, had become even more ineffectual as Commander-in-Chief of the O.A.S.; increasingly isolated, increasingly inscrutable, in dispute with his subordinates, and all the time with Hacq's net closing invisibly in on him. On 7 April information from a captured German deserter from the Legion led the police to the hideout of the O.A.S.'s most effective and deadly operator, Roger Degueldre. With him at the time were five other O.A.S. leaders, including Pérez and Achard. "Degueldre simply refused to hide," Pérez told the author, "the five of us went to ground, hidden in the lavatory behind a false wall. The police came in, took Degueldre and went away." A myth of invulnerability had come to surround the Delta leader, in which he had evidently begun to trust himself, believing that his *baraka* and his false papers would get him by. Fearless to the end, knowing that he faced the firing-squad for his deeds, Degueldre never talked. Nevertheless, less than a fortnight after his arrest came Salan's turn – within a day or two of the "Mandarin"'s planning his withdrawal to Spain.

For weeks Hacq and the Sûreté Nationale had been painstakingly grooming an undercover agent called Jean-Marie Lavanceau, a former sergeant-major of Massu's 10th Para Division, now become a police officer. Helped by such impeccable credentials from his army service, Lavanceau – with considerable courage – ferreted his way through various O.A.S. cut-outs to obtain access to "Soleil" himself. With the pretext of being an intermediary from Messali's M.N.A., wishing to bring its former members into the O.A.S., he was passed from Achard to Captain Ferrandi, who promised him an interview with Salan for the next day – 20 April. Lavanceau was

tracked to his rendezvous by a black Peugeot, similar to those used by the
Deltas. Three men on motor scooters, with sub-machine-guns concealed in
beach-bags, cruised innocently in the street, while 250 gendarmes were
waiting in the background to seal off the neighbourhood. Entering the
apartment where his O.A.S. contact led him, Lavanceau was astonished to
find an almost unrecognisable Salan, his black dyed hair and moustache
giving the elegant "Mandarin" an almost coarse look. For some time
Lavanceau managed to stall about his mission; then Ferrandi rushed in,
shouting that there were police outside. Lavanceau threw open the door
and called in the waiting men. Fearing a possible O.A.S. riposte, they
hustled Salan into a car, then into a helicopter to the army headquarters at
Reghaia, still protesting that he was not Salan. At Reghaia he was met by
an ice-cold General Ailleret, occupying the post that he had once held,
who told him curtly: "You have had enough people killed; now you are
going to pay for it." In civilian clothes and looking more like a worried
petit commerçant than the man who, back in 1958, had once held the fate
of Algeria and France in his hand, the "Mandarin" was then bundled into
a Dakota bound for Paris and the Santé.

On hearing the news of Salan's capture, de Gaulle's laconic comment
was: "Eh bien, not a minute too soon!" Then, when told that Georges
Bidault had been designated Salan's successor, he added caustically: "At
last, some good news!" Meanwhile, even before the capture of Degueldre
and Salan, the O.A.S.'s one and only attempt to raise the standard of
revolt outside the cities in the *bled* had collapsed in pieces. Under the
idealistic Colonel Gardes, a detachment had tried to establish itself in the
Ouarsenis near Orléansville, hoping for support from dissident army units;
and the *harkis* of the Bachaga Boualem. But neither had materialised;
Gardes's expedition had been dispersed by a "whiff of grapeshot" from
French aircraft; the Bachaga, France's most loyal ally, realising which
way the wind was now blowing, withdrew to the south of France with his
remaining *harkis*. Then, on 4 May, André Canal – "Le Monocle" – was
picked up by the French police. The O.A.S. was all but decapitated but still
the killing continued.

The scorched earth

On 7 April the composite Provisional Executive established by Evian
began its work of preparing Algeria's transition to independence, under
the presidency of the former speaker of the Algiers Assembly, Abderrahmane Farès. Symbolically, it was also the day that saw the capture of
Roger Degueldre. In the former office of the Government-Delegate, Farès
pronounced words that summed up sadly so much of what had passed:
"The relations between Algeria and France are a graveyard of missed
opportunities." On 8 April de Gaulle's referendum for the French people

to declare their opinion on the Evian Agreements returned a massive vote of ninety per cent of *ouis* among those who polled. It was a vote of sheer lassitude. As a last viceroy to help guide the Provisional Executive and preside over the French withdrawal, de Gaulle had sent Christian Fouchet to be High Commissioner as replacement for Jean Morin, the exhausted Government-Delegate. Supported by de Gaulle's own *éminence grise*, Bernard Tricot, Fouchet was a tall, fifty-year-old Parisian with iron-grey hair who, in 1955, had been Minister for Moroccan and Tunisian affairs when these countries were given their independence by Mendès-France. His brother had died at the side of General Leclerc in his wartime march. A serious but intensely humane personality, Fouchet found the role of "receiver" a thankless one. The first task allotted him by de Gaulle was to restore calm; but it was, he admits with understatement, "extremely difficult to impose *sagesse* upon a country which knew only passion". On his arrival, Fouchet appeared on television to warn the *pieds noirs* in direct terms that "The whole world will range itself against you if you attempt to go back on what has been decided and concluded. . . . You would be the principal and earliest victims." He condemned the O.A.S. as "madmen and criminals", and urged the *pieds noirs* to "chase them out, because nothing is lost. . . ." But now the majority of the *pieds noirs*, whether disgusted by horrors perpetrated by the O.A.S. or terrified for their own futures, had but one thought – to get out as quickly as possible themselves.

Fouchet's pleas for sanity went unheeded by the O.A.S., which – like the headless monster it now was – threshed about in its protracted death throes, inflicting the most terrible and senseless wounds of its whole existence. In the madness of these last days, contemporary news films show disconnected shots of young O.A.S. thugs returning from the beach, then donning para tunics over bare shoulders and calmly getting into cars with their sub-machine-guns to set off on the evening's killings; *pied noir* women repeating frenetically to the newsmen, "*Jusqu'à la mort, Monsieur, jusqu'à la mort!*"; an elderly lady tapping out "*Al-gé-rie fran-çaise*"; Muslim women riposting with their eerie, triumphal *you-you-you-you* ululations. April and May were, says ex-prefect Vitalis Cros, "horrible months, because terrorism had become completely blind".

On 20 April, by way of revenge for the capture of Salan, the Deltas murdered twenty-four Muslims in Algiers alone. On 2 May there was an appalling massacre in the port of Algiers, when a powerfully booby-trapped car exploded amid a crowd of unemployed dockers looking for work. In this one incident alone sixty-two dockers were killed and 150 horribly injured. The following day what might have been the most infamous outrage of the whole war was only narrowly averted. To the heights above the Casbah the O.A.S. had driven a petrol tanker containing over 3,000 gallons of fuel and were planning to roll it down into the crowded Muslim quarter, where it would almost certainly have caused a satanic conflagration. Only the presence of mind of a local fire brigade (including *pieds noirs*) forestalled the disaster. A week which cost the lives of 230 Muslims ended with the calculated and separate killing of seven *fatmas*, elderly charwomen employed by Europeans, on their way to work. This cruel and pointless act particularly shocked French opinion; in the O.A.S. itself it was deplored by Gardes, and women operatives like Anne Loesch testified to a deep sense of shame.

Up to this point the F.L.N. in Algiers – secure in the knowledge that it was about to inherit the earth – had shown remarkable discipline and restraint. Now pressure from beneath forced the leaders to execute a reprisal. Seventeen bars known to be frequented by the O.A.S. in various parts of the city were hit by carefully co-ordinated grenade and machine-gun attacks; the result – seventeen European dead and thirty-five wounded. The next day, 15 May, came the inevitable O.A.S. reprisal: the result – fifty-six Muslim dead, thirty-five wounded. But, not for the first time, the O.A.S. was proved to be defeating its own ends; principally because of the atmosphere of terror created by the O.A.S., and despite its threats of "sanctions", since the beginning of April no less than *one hundred thousand pieds noirs* had already left the country – or one in ten of the total European population. Now, in its despair at realising that all was lost, the O.A.S. adopted a "scorched earth policy".* If the French cannot, or will not, remain, the O.A.S. argued, then we shall leave Algeria as it was when they arrived in 1830. After a brief respite, on 7 June the University of Algiers library was burned; then followed the destruction of schools, laboratories and hospital facilities – the finest benefits that French civilisation had bestowed on Algeria. In the biggest explosion to date, Algiers's fine new Hôtel de Ville was blown up; finally, in June, Oran's vast B.P. oil storage tanks went up in a great pillar of smoke.

Finally a truce – and exodus

From their prison cells both Salan and Jouhaud had interceded with the O.A.S., calling upon it to halt the fruitless carnage and destruction. Then, on 17 June, there was announced one of the more extraordinary events of this extraordinary war: the O.A.S. and F.L.N. had concluded a truce. Already, in April, Major Azedine, formerly the redoubtable and much-wounded veteran of Wilaya 4, had been sent by the G.P.R.A. to Algiers to

* The explanation given by one of the O.A.S. leaders for the "scorched earth policy" is as follows: "You have to remember Arab mentality – to impress the Arabs, you've got to make a solemn performance of killing a man. Don't just shoot him, but put him up against a wall with a firing squad. In revolutionary war the riposte must be, if possible, both rapid and spectacular. So it was with the 'scorched earth policy'. We had to do something that would really make them understand the significance of what was happening...."

reorganise the Z.A.A. structure and prepare the takeover of the city for the time of the French withdrawal. After a particularly nauseating outrage, when Deltas had destroyed a clinic they considered to be an F.L.N. "hospital", gunning to death nine Muslim patients in their beds, Vitalis Cros had taken the unprecedented initiative of seeking out Azedine in a desperate attempt to collaborate in combating terrorism. Next, the shadowy political brain of the O.A.S. who had assumed leadership since the capture of Salan, Jean-Jacques Susini, the first to realise that the battle was lost, made contact in mid-May with Farès, the president of the Provisional Executive. Nothing came of these talks, but a bridge was created between Susini and the F.L.N. representatives. Under the mediation of Dr Mostefai of the Provisional Executive and Jacques Chevallier, the former liberal mayor of Algiers, a truce was finally concluded on Sunday, 17 June. In a piece of mad, irrelevant arrogance that typified the whole movement, Susini posed one final condition: the O.A.S. must be specifically mentioned in Dr Mostefai's broadcast statement. Three days later the curfew that had cloaked Algiers for so long was finally lifted. Bar a few isolated, free-lance incidents, the Algerian war was at last over. In less than a year the O.A.S. had killed 2,360 people in Algeria, and wounded another 5,418; according to the calculations of Vitalis Cros, in the Algiers zone alone their activities over the last six months of the war had claimed *three times as many civilian victims* as had the F.L.N. from the beginning of 1956 onwards; i.e. including the Battle of Algiers. On 1 July Algeria held its own referendum on the Evian Agreements; 5,993,754 voted *oui* against 16,478 *nons*; ten per cent, representing chiefly the *pieds noirs*, abstained. Two days later President de Gaulle recognised Algerian independence.

Following the conclusion of the O.A.S.–F.L.N. truce on 17 June, Bernard Tricot noted an immediate and almost miraculous détente in Algiers: "It was beautiful weather; one perceived that during this sad spring the flowers had burst into bloom in the gardens; under the sunshine the city was plunged into a Sunday silence not broken by the noise of any explosion, any shooting; never had the women seemed so charming." But it was all very deceptive; masked by the summer sunshine the final act of the Algerian tragedy – and one of its saddest – was taking place. Only a few days later Tricot visited Bab-el-Oued and was shocked to find the quarter, once seething with colour and animation, all but deserted; its streets that still bore O.A.S. slogans on every corner, as well as signs of the recent siege, were now apparently tenanted only by a few old crones. One of the greatest mass-migrations of the twentieth century was under way. "The whole coast is ready for departure; a shiver of adventure ripples through it," Camus had written in a strange prophecy in 1939. "Tomorrow, perhaps, we shall leave together." During that month of June alone, no less than 350,000 of the million *pieds noirs* left Algeria, compared to the

100,000 which the French government had calculated might depart over the first year of Algerian independence. No words of assurance by High Commissioner Fouchet or Farès could stem the panic-ridden exodus. Cars were put up for sale at £10 apiece, or simply abandoned in the street; parking lots looked like scenes from the British evacuation of Dunkirk. The smart shops in the Rue Michelet offered their entire stocks for sale at knock-down prices; bar-keepers simply closed the shutters and left. "Let's face it," a senior French official told British journalists, "the whole of Algeria's up for sale." Business came to a halt. In Bab-el-Oued great pyres were lit in the street as the *pieds noirs* burned sofas and chairs as well as the souvenirs from happier times – aquatints of the Conquest, framed photos of *grand'maman*, of family picnics to celebrate the "breaking of the *mouna*" – rather than let "them" take possession. From Oran, all the European doctors left; in the filthy streets, as yet another echo from *La Peste*, rats scurried about in open daylight.

At the airports and down at the harbours of Algiers and Oran there were the most heart-rending scenes. Permitted only two suitcases per person, the *pieds noirs* queued day and night for passages out of the country they had been born in: uncomprehending children clutching a precious doll; old people weeping silently in equal incomprehension. With their papier-mâché suitcases, Europeans as poor as many of the Muslims who were replacing them stretched awnings of bedspreads between crates on the quay to protect themselves against the midday sun during the long wait. Then the boats came. Like Boabdil, the last Moorish King of Andalusia, sighing for his lost paradise, but with the roles reversed, many a European wept inconsolably as the last sight of waves breaking on the Algerian coast slipped slowly out of view.

Among them the last of the O.A.S. leaders also made their exits. Pérez, hoping to the end – like Hitler in the Berlin bunker – for a lethal split to occur between his enemies, and for a possible "Palestinisation" of Algeria, sailed away to Alicante. Colonel Godard left for Greece, Dufour and Gardes for Spain. Only Susini lingered on, a haunted figure, possessed by some crazy curiosity to visit the Casbah, where – in all his life as a born *pied noir* – he had never once set foot. Then he too slipped away, landing in Italy on 30 July, his twenty-ninth birthday. As an additional instalment of the final tragedy, on the evacuation boats was also almost the whole of the Algerian Jewish community. To many who had sympathised, actively or passively, with the F.L.N. throughout the war, their expulsion at the hands of the Muslims came as a cruel shock. "Why are you making us leave, because after all we are your friends?" the Ankaoua family asked their Muslim neighbours. "Then we locked the door, taking the key with us. We thought we might be able to return. We still had hope . . . until we reached the airport at Maison-Blanche. Then we knew it was the end."

Over a hundred thousand Algerian Jews, many of them impoverished, backward and disease-ridden, poured into metropolitan France.

But they were more fortunate than the *harkis* and the other loyal Muslims who fought for France, and who were now abandoned to their fate to be massacred in their thousands by their vengeful brethren.

The last victory

By the beginning of August, of the 250,000 European inhabitants of Oran only 40,000 were left. When the exodus was all over it was estimated that 50,000 *pieds noirs* had gone to Spain; 12,000 to Canada; 10,000 to Israel; and 1,550 to Argentina. But the huge mass, 1,380,000 strong (which included the luckier Muslim refugees) – equivalent then to the combined population of the two biggest French cities after Paris – had flooded into France. Only 30,000 stayed bravely, or hopelessly, behind. To fill the empty farms and tenements, Muslim strangers from the hills and the *bidonvilles* swiftly arrived, armed with F.L.N. orders to requisition and occupy. On the days succeeding Algeria's formal acquisition of independence the streets of Oran and Algiers became a sea of white, green and red flags, filled with wildly cheering and chanting Muslims. Despite the total anarchy threatened by the sudden departure of the Europeans, the take-over was effected with almost miraculous smoothness. Disciplined troops arrived to assume point duty from French gendarmes; from somewhere technicians appeared who could maintain the essential services of gas, electricity, water and sewage that had been deserted by the Europeans; in the hospitals A.L.N. doctors and nurses from the field arrived to help the few Europeans who had remained. Tense as were the last days, they were marred by only one major incident against the *pieds noirs* in Oran, at the beginning of July. As seven *katibas* moved triumphantly into the city, some Europeans opened a suicidal fusillade. Out of all control, a wave of Muslims swept into the half-empty European quarters, indiscriminately cutting the throats of men, women and children; some of them within sight of French troops strictly obeying the edict of non-intervention now imposed on them by the Evian Agreements.

If the Oran massacre represented the final flickering out of any hope of reconciliation between the two races that still may have existed, it was also the final violence – at least between Algerians and Frenchmen. On 4 July the tricolour was lowered in Algiers for the first time in 132 years as High Commissioner Fouchet, the last of France's all-powerful pro-consuls, left for home. Consulting de Gaulle whether he should be present at the flag-lowering ceremony or not, Fouchet after a pause of several seconds had been told simply: "*Je crois que ça serait inutile....*" But as he left the massed bands played *Le Marche Consulaire* composed for Napoleon after Marengo – something Fouchet would never forget. "It was a victory march," he explains. "That may seem curious, but really it was symbolic because in these last days it represented a great victory over ourselves.... And, after all, wasn't de Gaulle's decision on Algeria in effect a great victory over himself?"

CHAPTER TWENTY-FIVE

The Page is Turned

1962 onwards

Come then, comrades, the European game has finally ended; we must find
something different. We today can do everything, so long as we do not imitate
Europe, so long as we are not obsessed by the desire to catch up with Europe.
Europe now lives at such a mad, reckless pace that she has shaken off all
guidance and all reason. . . .

Frantz Fanon, 1965

The dangers of liberty

"LIBERTY is dangerous, as hard to live with as it is exciting," declared
Albert Camus on receiving the Nobel Prize in 1957. The hard truth of this
was to be brought home to the jubilant Algerians even before the French
flag had been lowered in July 1962. After seven and a half years of war
and grim hardship there would still be neither peace nor order for tragic
Algeria. A period of turbulence lay ahead, comparable in miniature to that
which Shakespeare depicts as following upon the removal of the established
order of King Richard II. Moving into the vacuum left at all levels by the
departing *pieds noirs*, the infant nation at once found itself enmeshed in
the most acute administrative problems. Through their objective of wiping
out the rebel Organisation Politico-Administrative, General Challe and his
predecessors had also effectively killed off many of the best-educated and
politically most sophisticated Algerians: the country's potential leaders. At
the same time the corps of native administrators which France – laboriously
and always too slowly – had been expanding since 1954 was still far from
numerous enough to fulfil the roles so suddenly imposed upon it; added to
which, in the first passions of independence many were regarded by the
victorious F.L.N. as "quislings" and were promptly sacked – or worse.
Whereas, in the 1950s, Tunisia and Morocco were endowed with established systems of government and administration, when Algerian independence came her government had existed only in exile. Thus she was
afflicted by a lack of cadres and a lack of experience; but, worst of all, the
many latent rifts within the leadership now burst through the thin papering with which the exigencies of war had covered them heretofore. Frantz
Fanon had predicted that war would achieve unity among the Algerian
élite; peace produced quite the opposite.

The explosion had begun at the end of June. The C.N.R.A. was meeting once again in Tripoli, this time to forge a programme for the future that would be the most important statement of F.L.N. principles and aims since the Soummam Conference of 1956. A new ingredient of dissent had immediately been injected into the proceedings by the arrival of Ben Bella and his comrades, at last liberated from their years of incarceration. The Ben Bella faction, backed by Boumedienne and the General Staff and, more improbably, by Ferhat Abbas and his ex-U.D.M.A. faithfuls, launched a vigorous attack on the G.P.R.A. on its "surrender" to the French at Evian specifically, and its conduct of affairs in general. Ben Bella called for the substitution of the G.P.R.A. by a "Political Bureau", consisting chiefly of the five ex-prisoners. Mohamed Khider had already resigned from his post as a Minister of State to the G.P.R.A. Even among the five, however, personal relations were far from rosy:

> Boudiaf and Ben Bella, after spending five years in jail together, couldn't stand each other. They would argue over anything – whether the tea should be served hot or cold, how much sugar should be in it. It was just like a scene out of Sartre's No Exit. The crisis was simply a scramble for power. Abbas backed Ben Bella because he was bitter over having been replaced by Ben Khedda [said Mabrouk Belhocine, who had attempted to act as mediator].

Meanwhile, in its turn the General Staff came under fierce fire from the representatives of Wilayas 2, 3 and 4, i.e. the "heartland" Wilayas farthest removed from the Moroccan and Tunisian frontiers and the tentacles of the General Staff. In asking the G.P.R.A. to restrain the General Staff from interfering with them, these Wilayas reflected wartime resentments at the failure of Boumedienne's Army of the Exterior to assist them, as well as throwing a last beam of light of blazing relevance on the whole affair of Si Salah and the Wilaya 4 "separate peace" initiative of 1960.

On 30 June, the day before Algeria held its referendum, the G.P.R.A. took the unprecedented step of dissolving the General Staff and dismissing Boumedienne, amid scenes that were the most tumultuous ever witnessed within the leadership of the F.L.N. Writing of this period in *Le Monde* one pro-F.L.N. French journalist, Jean Daniel, was "shocked by the intensity and vindictiveness of the rivalry, and astonished to find that mutual recrimination among Muslim leaders was much worse than it had been between the rebels and the French". The essentially uncombative Ben Khedda withdrew from this bear-garden to Tunis before the end of the Tripoli congress, a tactical error thereby leaving the way open to Ben Bella. Boumedienne refused to recognise the G.P.R.A.'s sanctions against him, and began moving his powerful A.L.N. into the interior. Over the next two months Algeria had, in effect, three governments: the G.P.R.A., under President Ben Khedda; Ben Bella's Political Bureau (backed by

Boumedienne and the army); and, squeezed like an insignificant and brittle nut between these two powerful opposites, President Farès's Provisional Executive as set up under Evian. There were further hostile groupings within the country as each Wilaya took up its own position, with Wilaya 4 capriciously moving in to take control of Algiers. Kabylia began to show signs of returning to its traditional separatist animosities vis-à-vis the Arabs, with Krim returning to his homeland to set up Wilaya 3 as an anti-Ben Bella stronghold. For the rest of this bitter summer warring cliques and bands marched and counter-marched across the prostrate body of the so-recently jubilant country, in scenes reminiscent of Brecht's *Mother Courage*. There were rival killings in the cities and the country-side; dissident groups took, once again, to the mountains where, as guerrillas, they would have to be wiped out in actions as savage as any-thing against the French. One Wilaya leader challenged another to a duel with machine-guns, and total civil war loomed close, with the distraught population crying to the warring factions: "*Sba'a snine, barakat!* [Seven years, that's enough!]"

The massacre of the harkis: overall war casualties

According to Ait Ahmed, these convulsions of the summer of 1962 cost the lives of a further 15,000 Algerians. But the worst fratricidal horrors were reserved for those Muslims who, like the *harkis*, had continued to fight for France. De Gaulle had never shown much sympathy for them; to a Muslim deputy, ten of whose family had already been killed by the F.L.N. and who had protested that on "self-determination" "we shall suffer", de Gaulle had replied coldly, "*Eh bien! vous suffrirez.*" As General Challe had feared (and it was one of the prime factors in his revolt), the peace agreements contained no guarantee sufficient to save these Algerians now from the wrath of their countrymen, in whose eyes they were nothing but traitors. Out of the quarter of a million who had worked for the French less than 15,000 had managed to escape from Algeria – many of them with Bachaga Boualem. In France they were, for the most part, to live lives of poverty, unappreciated and unassimilated. Of the fate of those that remained, however, harrowing stories came out of Algeria. Hundreds died when put to work clearing the minefields along the Morice Line, or were shot out of hand. Others were tortured atrociously; army veterans were made to dig their own tombs, then swallow their decorations before being killed; they were burned alive, or castrated, or dragged behind trucks, or cut to pieces and their flesh fed to dogs. Many were put to death with their entire families, including young children. Compelled by the terms of the Evian Agreements to stand by and witness this massacre of their former allies, the agony of the French army was extreme. In some cases, acting under orders, units had been forced to disarm the wretched *harkis* on the promise of replacing them with better weapons – then sneaked away in the middle of the night, abandoning them to their fate. It was a tragedy even more odious than that of the Russian prisoners-of-war handed back by the Western allies in 1945. Estimates of the numbers of Algerians thus killed vary wildly between 30,000 and 150,000.

These aftermath killings also help make the total Muslim casualty lists of the seven and a half years of war all the more difficult to compute accurately. According to French figures, their forces lost 17,456 dead (including no less than 5,966 killed "accidentally", and 892 officers killed in action); 64,985 wounded and injured, and 1,000 missing (including deserters). Far less severe than American casualties in Vietnam, the French casualty rate during most of the war ran at lower than that claimed by road accidents in France. European civilian casualties, caused by 42,090 listed acts of terrorism, are put at over 10,000, among them 2,788 killed (including the O.A.S. victims in the final year of the war) plus 500 "disappeared". French estimates put the Muslim dead as follows: 141,000 male combatants killed by the security forces; 12,000 members of the F.L.N. killed in internal purges; 16,000 Muslim civilians killed by the F.L.N.; 50,000 Muslim civilians abducted, and presumed killed, by the F.L.N. On top of this has to be added the killing of *harkis* and other Algerians in the settlement of accounts during the summer of 1962, as well as a further 4,300 Algerians from both the F.L.N. and M.N.A. killed in metropolitan France in the course of the war. The number of overall Muslim wounded can only be guessed at. To General Jacquin, Challe's former Deuxième Bureau chief, Belkacem Krim claimed after the war that it had cost the Algerians a total of 300,000 in dead. Today, however, Algeria adopts the round figure of *one million* as representing her war dead. When one takes into account additionally the numbers of Muslim wounded who must have succumbed, civilians who were killed accidentally during French *ratissages*, those who disappeared mysteriously in such operations as the Battle of Algiers, and those who died from starvation and exposure (recalling that no less than 1.8 million Muslims were uprooted from their homes during the war), then, even if figures do not justify the total of one million, they must stand well in excess of the computations of either the French army or Krim.

Finally, what, in purely material terms, did the war and the resultant severance of Algeria cost France? Computations are complex and confused by the division between what was purely military and what was economic expenditure, as well as by the problem of just how much of France's defence budget was spent exclusively on Algeria. One reasonable set of figures puts the military cost of the war *per annum* as rising from 2,800 million (new) francs in 1955 to 10,000 million by 1960, showing a total of between fifty to fifty-five milliard for the seven and a half years of war.

Substantial as were France's contributions to Algerian economic reforms, even at the peak of the Constantine Plan expenditure here barely exceeded a quarter of the military outlay. This latter accounted for between fifty to sixty per cent of France's defence budget, and is set by Hartmut Elsenhans in *Frankreichs Algerienkrieg* as representing ten to fifteen per cent of the total French budget. The burden of this is more readily apparent when one recalls that, until the end of the Fourth Republic and the early years of Gaullism, France already lived with a heavy deficit. One additional, hidden cost of considerable significance came as a consequence of a labour shortage in France caused by the absence in Algeria, from 1956 onwards, of half a million men with the colours. It was a shortage that coincided with a time when both the French population graph was suffering from the "hollow classes" (the children not born during the Second World War) and resurgent West Germany was making her first bid for world export markets. The result was serious inflation and loss of productivity; the latter estimated conservatively even by economists of the "hawk" faction to have run at three to four milliard (new) francs per year, representing an almost greater strain to the French economy than the actual military costs.

To meet this shortage of industrial manpower, which way did France turn? She increased the intake of Algerian immigrant workers so that their numbers actually rose by over thirty per cent in the course of the war, bringing a curious paradox in its wake. By 1960 the Algerian workers in France were sending home wages equivalent to about one-third of the earnings of the whole agricultural labour force in Algeria, which thus helped France by helping the Algerian economy. But at the same time those higher earnings also enabled the F.L.N. fund-raisers in France to purchase more weapons with which to shoot at the French conscripts whose places they were filling at home. Both before and during the war (and a similar picture prevails today), for all their benefit to the French economy, the Algerian migrant workers' franc earnings almost certainly contributed more to the stability of the Algerian economy. With regard to the overall colonial profit-and-loss account, Algerian wine exports to the mother country constituted a perpetual embarrassment, while her raw materials (in which she was the least rich country of all the Maghreb) contributed relatively little. When the war began in 1954 French commerce with Algeria was comparable in value to that with the tiny Saar territory; in 1958–9, it accounted for only seventeen per cent of France's export trade, while eighty per cent of Algeria's exportable products were bought by France, and her trade deficit (which then ran at 3.8 milliard (new) francs) was largely financed by France. If one excludes the imponderable factor of the loss of the oil resources developed by French knowhow and capital, the ending of the war and the severance of Algeria must be reckoned a net gain to France's economy. Certainly it was from the date of

Algerian independence in 1962 that France's own economic "miracle" stems – even though after that moment she continued still to bolster Algeria to the extent of approximately £700,000 a day.

From Ben Bella to Boumedienne

By the end of that first turbulent summer of 1962 Ben Bella had established his ascendancy, and in late September he pushed out Ben Khedda to become independent Algeria's first president. The problems – economic, cultural, administrative and political – that he inherited seemed never-ending. The economy was still totally tied to that of France, and – with 4½ million Algerians deemed to be in a state of total poverty – it was only American surplus wheat that kept the population alive over the first months of independence. Almost immediately, Ben Bella demanded a revision of the Evian Agreements (with which, of course, de Gaulle had never permitted him to be formally associated), declaring his government not bound by them, and holding them to be incompatible with the Tripoli Programme of June in its far-reaching schemes of socialisation. Laws were passed to nationalise all "vacant properties" and take over *pied noir* farms, turning them into collectives run by self-appointed *comités de gestion*. Though these actions were strictly in breach of the Evian Agreements, in 1963 France – under her part of the articles of "co-operation" – nevertheless handed Algeria generous sums of financial aid to cover her mountainous deficits.* But despite foreign aid and the respite granted by living off the "fat" of the *pied noir* holdings, Ben Bella's grandiose schemes of socialisation caused the infant state to totter from crisis to economic crisis.

Out of touch with external reality after his long incarceration, Ben Bella veered more and more towards measures of abstract socialism, more and more towards left-wing orientations; in his personal rule, more and more towards authoritarianism and the "cult of the personality" so primordially repugnant to the F.L.N. Observing his triumphal entry into Tunis, the Braces remarked: "In a crowd Ben Bella moves as though he were alone. He is intent on his own vision and seems scarcely aware of what people about him are doing." Speaking to William Quandt, an old schoolmate of Ben Bella's recalled how he had been "a good soccer player, but he never forgot the galleries. He wanted to be number one. Ben Bella always wanted his team-mates to pass him the ball so that he could score. He was the same way in politics."

One by one his former colleagues fell away, or were purged. Ferhat Abbas, the old-school liberal who had helped him to power, was soon at odds with his anti-Western policies and was expelled from the F.L.N. in 1963. In April 1963 the influential Khider resigned once again – this time

* In 1963 Algeria received from France loans of 1,300,000,000 francs – compared with only 500,000,000 and 250,000,000 from the U.S.S.R. and China respectively.

from the post of Secretary-General of the F.L.N. At almost the same time Ben Bella's Foreign Secretary, Mohamed Khemisti, was mysteriously assassinated outside the National Assembly. In June Boudiaf, one of the *neuf historiques* of 1954, was arrested on Ben Bella's orders, and the following month the third of Ben Bella's prison stablemates, Ait Ahmed, announced that he was going into opposition to "fight" Ben Bella. ("Are we in the country of Duvalier," he asked, "or are we in Algeria?") He then took to the maquis, together with another war veteran, the Kabyle leader Colonel Mohand Ou el Hadj. By the end of the year Ben Bella was at war with the King of Morocco (whom he described as a *roi fantoche, un criminel*) over territorial rights. Scandals and corruption became rife, and two million Algerians were unemployed. In 1964 Ben Bella's residence came under fire, and armed revolt broke out round Biskra led by Colonel Chaabani. Ait Ahmed and Khider supported the revolt, with the latter declaring that the regime was "slipping dangerously towards fascism and totalitarianism". With the aid of Boumedienne's troops, Chaabani was rounded up and executed and Ait Ahmed imprisoned. Khider fled to Switzerland, together with the F.L.N. "treasury" so painstakingly collected from Algerians in France and at home during the war. He was followed into exile by Abbas and Bitat, among many others of the old guard.

In all this period Ben Bella had come to depend increasingly on the support of Boumedienne and the army. With most of his rivals dead, in prison or in exile, by the eve of the Afro-Asian Conference of June 1965 Ben Bella looked at last secure. Then Boumedienne moved with the army which, ironically, had put Ben Bella in power and kept him there, and the tanks supplied by Ben Bella's Soviet allies (who had but recently awarded him the Lenin Peace Prize). Though himself under sentence of death from Ben Bella, Ait Ahmed warned him "There's going to be a coup against you." Ben Bella was arrested, and Boumedienne took over the Government. The reasons given for Ben Bella's removal were his excessive addiction to the "cult of the personality", his "liquidation of revolutionary cadres", his ideological confusion, his proneness to foreign (i.e. Eastern bloc) influences, and his improvidence with Algeria's vital resources. Boumedienne had at last arrived, and the arrival of this taciturn and unknown colonel took the world as much by surprise as it did Ben Bella, who was returned to prison or house-arrest for another fourteen years.

France – the settling of accounts

Though her predicament was in no way so grim as Algeria's in 1962, after the long war France too had her house to put in order, accounts to settle. The first was the bringing to justice of the captured O.A.S. leaders. On 11 April 1962 General Edmond Jouhaud faced his judges. Now clean-shaven, the *pied noir* air force general declared that he had but one regret:

"not to be able to die on Algerian soil". Among the defence witnesses was the widow of Albert Camus, who made a plea for clemency tragically eloquent of the *pied noir* dilemma. "I feel divided," she told the court, "half-French and half-Algerian, and, in truth, dispossessed in both countries which I no longer recognise, since I never imagined them separated." Jouhaud was also helped by a letter from Salan, still at large, in which he assumed full responsibility for all Jouhaud's acts in the O.A.S. Nevertheless, after three days, the death sentence was read out. Women fainted in court but Jouhaud accepted the verdict impassively. For six weeks execution hovered over him. His coffin had, allegedly, already been measured, and de Gaulle in his memoirs admits that "my first reaction was to allow Jouhaud's case to take its course". In *L'Express* Servan-Schreiber clamoured for immediate execution as a "signal of hope" for France, but a flood of appeals for mercy poured in to the Élysée, supported strongly by Premier Pompidou. Although it was not until November that Jouhaud heard that his sentence had been finally commuted to life imprisonment, what really saved him was the fate of his leader, now also captured and in the dock.

Amid powerful emotions, Salan's trial opened on 15 May in the same court where once Marshal Pétain had been sentenced to death. To Janet Flanner's unsympathetic eyes, the defendant resembled "an elderly, pessimistic silver fox", looking as if the anticipated death sentence had already been carried out; his recently dyed hair, growing out white over his ears but still a mawkish henna colour on top, imparted a "clownlike" appearance. In fact, Salan was the one person at his trial never to lose his dignity, always the imperturbable "Mandarin". In a calm voice he read out his particulars: "ex-general of the Colonial Army, Grand Cross of the Legion of Honour, Military Medal, Cross of the Liberation, wounded in action . . ." etc., etc., then, announcing that he would answer no questions, Salan read out a long statement. "When one has known the France of courage," he declared, "one can never accept the France of capitulation." Recalling May 1958, he claimed he had been "duped" by "the one I gave power to". He insisted that his responsibility for the O.A.S. had been total, and that henceforth he would remain silent. Over a hundred witnesses, among them the highest personages in the republic, filed in and out of the stand. For Salan there appeared ex-President Coty, the Maréchale de Lattre de Tassigny (who – still in her widow's weeds – made a powerful impression), and General Valluy, who questioned sorrowfully, "I wonder how we ever reached this point?" François Mitterrand rekindled the bizarre episode of the "bazooka" attempt on Salan in 1957, pointing an accusatory finger at Michel Debré. The ex-premier rose to refute the accusations. Salan was brilliantly defended by Tixier-Vignancour, and on the eighth day of the trial a verdict of guilty, but "with extenuating circumstances", was read out to a packed court; the sentence was life imprisonment, but Salan's life was saved. His supporters broke into an ecstatic *Marseillaise* in the court-room; at the Élysée de Gaulle erupted in rage at the judges' leniency, and four days later had the tribunal suppressed.

With Salan's life spared, it would hardly have been consistent to execute his deputy; thus Jouhaud too escaped the firing-squad. But, as a junior officer unsupported by the galaxy that had come forth to testify for Salan, Lieutenant Roger Degueldre was to bear the full brunt of the law. On 28 June, at the sinister Château de Vincennes, where Napoleon had the Duc d'Enghien executed, the leader of the Delta killer commandos was sentenced to death. His mistress (who bore him a son shortly before the trial) and a team of O.A.S. faithfuls attempted to "spring" Degueldre from the Santé; when this failed they examined no less than fifteen alternative schemes for assassinating de Gaulle in vengeance. Nevertheless, little more than a week after his sentencing, Degueldre was marched before a firing-squad inside the Fort d'Ivry. Wearing his para's uniform, he sang the *Marseillaise* and declared himself proud to have kept his oath not to abandon Algeria to the F.L.N. It appears that the execution was appallingly botched, lasting an interminable quarter of an hour, with the squad firing wide and no less than five *coups de grâce* having to be administered before the agonised victim was finally despatched.

France "free to look at France"

With Algeria lost and its leaders removed, the O.A.S. and its affiliates still writhed on in France like a headless snake under the nominal leadership of Georges Bidault, Colonel Argoud and Captain Sergent. The *plastiques* continued to explode aimlessly in France, and over a dozen further attempts were made to assassinate de Gaulle. The most spectacular, and failing by a mere hair's-breadth, took place at Petit-Clamart in August 1962, the month after the lowering of the flag in Algiers, when the car carrying the President and Madame de Gaulle was shot up by a band led by Lieutenant-Colonel Jean-Marie Bastien-Thiry. Outraged by the threat to his wife, de Gaulle saw to it that Bastien-Thiry followed the fate of Degueldre, the first senior French officer to pass before the firing squad in many years. An all-out, ruthless campaign followed to smash the O.A.S.* once and for all. From Bavaria, where he and Bidault were in refuge, Colonel Argoud had entered into correspondence with the distinguished British military historian, Captain Liddell-Hart, desiring to explain to him why, "for the past three years, I have led the fight of my life against the imposture of a man, supported, alas, by the cowardice of a whole people". Liddell-Hart had replied that he found it "difficult to understand the course pursued and methods practised by such sincere and thoughtful people as yourself", but that he was interested to learn more. At the beginning of

* Renamed, under Bidault, the Conseil National de la Résistance (C.N.R.).

February 1963 a final letter arrived from Argoud, announcing his intention to visit Liddell-Hart in London in a few weeks' time. Argoud never arrived; instead he was found, trussed like a turkey, in a van outside the Paris Prefecture of Police, where the staff had been tipped off to come and collect him. It appears that a new outfit of *barbouzes* had been despatched from France to "snatch" Bidault, but had got hold of Argoud instead in the centre of Munich during the *Rosenmontag* festivities. The kidnapping, not unlike Napoleon's spiriting away from Baden of the Duc d'Enghien, provoked the worst breach in Franco-German relations of the post-war era. Nevertheless, it fulfilled de Gaulle's aim; in April Bidault fled to Brazil, via Lisbon; the O.A.S./C.N.R. broke up; the last *plastique* exploded in Paris in July 1963.

"In the year of grace 1962," wrote de Gaulle in his memoirs, "France's revival was in full flower. She had been threatened by civil war; bankruptcy had stared her in the face; the world had forgotten her voice. Now she was out of danger." Though it was not true of his own life, as the O.A.S. assassins still lurked and skulked, France herself was indeed "out of danger" with the ending of the Algerian war. Life began to resume its course with customary celerity. The Brittany farmers were embarked upon an "artichoke war"; Academicians began to fret about the incursions of *franglais*; in the Assembly, what de Gaulle dubbed the "snarlers and grousers" were already raising their voices in anticipation of the end of the Fifth Republic and an electoral replacement of de Gaulle. He had served his purpose. But otherwise the title of the new Vadim–Bardot film, *Le Repos du Guerrier*, seemed to set the tone. Already in 1962 France's gross national product was rising by 6.8 per cent in the year. Shed of the load of Algeria, her economy was to begin to show a miraculous blossoming from planting done in the latter years of the Fourth Republic and four years of Gaullism. France was, as de Gaulle had promised in 1960, beginning "to marry her time". De Gaulle began to travel ever more widely, to remind the outside world of the sound of France's "voice". It was a sound not always harmonious to the ears of her friends as she broke completely with N.A.T.O., embarked upon her own go-it-alone *force de frappe*, and closed the door on Britain's entry to the E.E.C.

As one distinguished American correspondent, C. L. Sulzberger, re-marked, Salan had "become a symbol of the defeated past". Once he and his comrades had been disposed of, the French army could finally put behind it the harrowing memories of so many tragic defeats, from 1940 onwards. It could purge itself of all the "bad dreams" of brutality and torture and self-division inflicted by the Algerian war, and – though the process would take a painfully long time – look toward the future, equipped with all the atomic panoply of modern warfare to distract it from the past. On 15 June 1964 the last French troops pulled out of Algeria, but already the technical modernisation dreamed of by de Gaulle was well under way.

In every aspect France was now, in the words of Dorothy Pickles, "free to look at France".

A different ending?

Could it all have been otherwise? Could the Algerian war have ended any differently? The historian can record for the benefit of the leaders what went wrong, but – in his feckless and unhelpful way – he is not necessarily there to tell them how they could have got it right; nor is it the purpose of this book to enter into a lengthy dissection and critique of French and Algerian errors. Various points of no return in the war perhaps deserve to be recapitulated, and certain general observations made. To begin at the beginning, in November 1954 France was caught at a major disadvantage because, in contrast to Britain over India, no French politician, not even Mendès-France or Mitterrand, let alone the Communists, could contemplate any kind of French withdrawal from Algeria. Mollet the Socialist echoed Mendès-France the Radical: "France without Algeria would be no longer France." Throughout those critical first years, when a compromise peace might have been conceivable, France was hobbled by the ball-and-chain of Algeria forming an integral part of French territory. From then on she was hobbled by what the army wanted, or would not permit. As Yves Courrière remarks at the beginning of his remarkable four-volume study of the Algerian war,

> Nobody ever wanted to look the problem in the face. The metropolis was only interested in Algeria when European blood flowed. No one wanted to believe in the conflict. No one wanted to consider the conflict as a war. No one wanted to consider the Muslims as men. When they did, it was much too late.

When, in the early days, the priority was to institute the reforms claimed by moderate Muslims – and so badly needed – it was almost invariably a case of "too little, too late".

In the second place, France was constantly and repeatedly hampered in her Algerian policy by the intervention (generally immoderate) of the hyper-articulate *pied noir* lobby. The *pieds noirs* were never strictly honest, even to themselves, as to what they *really* wanted. Despite all the brouhaha, it was not *Algérie française*; what the majority wanted was a *pied noir* Algeria, ranging between South Africa at its best and its worst, but under the umbrella of French protection. At various times in this book the author may seem to have been unduly censorious of the passionate and blinkered community that the *pieds noirs*, taken as a whole, represented. But it is essential to remember in the end that for every opulent *grand colon*, for every reactionary opponent of all reform, for every noisy "ultra", for every violent counter-terrorist (and, later, Delta killer), there were perhaps a dozen hard-working and impoverished simple fishermen, small farmers, carpenters and *gardes-champêtres*, only relatively better off than their Muslim neighbours, and with but one desire: to be allowed to continue to live, and make a living, on the soil where they and their fathers had been born. The *grands colons* could (and did) afford to get out, write off their stake in Algeria, and start up somewhere else before the debacle of 1962. But not the *petits blancs*. Thus (not unlike the artisan class Rhodesians who backed Ian Smith), fear at losing all drove them progressively into hard-line reaction – finally, in desperation, into the arms of the O.A.S., which, in tragic paradox, was to make it impossible for any of them to remain at all in the native land. The other tragedy of the *pieds noirs* was that they were never able to produce a leader of stature – let alone anyone who could have treated in a statesmanlike manner both with the French government and the Muslim "moderates" while carrying his own community with him. Thus, by default, they were to become represented – and indeed symbolised – by the *bistrotier*, Jo Ortiz.

From the French army's point of view, their tragedy was that at various points they could see with agonising clarity (and not without reason) that they were winning the war militarily. But (not unlike the American commanders in Vietnam) it was not given them to perceive that, at the same time, their chances of winning the war politically and on the wider world stage were growing ever slimmer. The army felt (again, not without reason) that it had been lied to, betrayed and abandoned by the man it brought to power; but the case may be put that, had their vision perhaps been less focused upon the immediate front, the deception could have been avoided – or at least avoided earlier – before the catastrophe of April 1961. As it was, until the army had been bent to his will – or broken, as tragically happened in April 1961 – de Gaulle could not risk proceeding with an acceptable policy of "self-determination".

Though it is always dangerous to become enmeshed in the "might-have-beens" of history, a number of turning-points in the war may be suggested. First, there was the fall of Mendès-France in 1955, after which the best hope of reforms and a gentle slope towards an Algerian solution that might have been acceptable to the majority of Muslim moderates diminished, if not vanished. Then there was the wasted opportunity of that period of hope and euphoria on all sides which followed the advent of de Gaulle during the summer of 1958. Finally, for France, there was the slim hope of a *paix des braves* as represented by the Si Salah episode of 1960. Seen from the F.L.N. point of view, the red-letter dates from November 1954 onward might begin with the Bandung Conference of 1955, internationalising the "Algerian problem"; followed by the Soummam Conference of 1956 and the self-defeating error by France, which shortly succeeded it, of sequestrating Ben Bella and his colleagues; then came de Gaulle's admission of the principle of "self-determination", a real watershed in the war. In January 1960 "Barricades Week" ended with de Gaulle triumphant, but the cause of *Algérie française* ruined. December of the same year saw de Gaulle's policy of "association" ruined by the Muslim demonstrations in Algiers and victory at the United Nations, while the generals' putsch of April 1961 – the most dangerous moment both for de Gaulle and the Western world – marked the inevitability of de Gaulle being forced to negotiate bilaterally with the F.L.N. Finally, the O.A.S. campaign opening in the summer of 1961 was to signify the collapse of any hope of a *pied noir* future in independent Algeria.

On the other hand, even if the O.A.S. had never raised its ugly head, the extraordinarily rigid consistency of the F.L.N.'s demands ever since the earliest days leads one to question whether, once the last hope of a compromise with the "third force" Muslim moderates had been peeled away, any solution could have been reached that would have guaranteed the survival of the *pied noir* minority in Algeria indefinitely. Taking into account the huge discrepancy in wealth, property and land between the two communities – nine-tenths belonging to one-tenth – the excruciating land hunger of the Algerians coupled to their soaring birthrate, racial stresses and *pied noir* intolerance, and – perhaps above all – the accumulated hatreds of seven and a half years of war, could the Europeans realistically have remained more than a few additional years at best?*
Without the O.A.S. the departure of the *pieds noirs* could probably have been "phased out" more gently, less tragically, over a period of years and months rather than days. But, just conceivably, the verdict of history may be that the enactment of so brutally sharp and absolute an exodus was more realistic – possibly even more merciful – in the long run. Was Boumedienne's, rather than Krim's more tolerant, line the right one after all in 1962?

Then there is the role of the Communist world in the Algerian war. At many points in the war it has been seen how cautious was the moral support given the F.L.N. by the French Communist Party, when not actively hostile, and how limited and tardy were the arms shipments it received from the Soviet Union. The poor Soviet performance was to set up resentments that would continue to influence Algerian policies three decades after the war. On the other hand, the Eastern bloc did furnish throughout a lever, without which the F.L.N. would probably have been unable to manoeuvre de Gaulle into negotiating, finally, on their terms.

One is left with the controversial role of de Gaulle, criticised both for

* To the author Christian Fouchet, de Gaulle's last High Commissioner, admitted that even at the time of Evian he never foresaw that the *pieds noirs* would all be able to stay forever: "It would certainly have been impossible for them to have continued to hold land – there would, at best, have been a transitional period of, say, fifteen years – then they would have had to give up."

going too slow and too fast. As far as the latter reproach goes, in the last stages of negotiations he suffered from the lesson not learned by Kissinger in Vietnam, or perhaps by the Israelis *vis-à-vis* the Arab world, or by the South Africans; namely, that peoples who have been waiting for their independence for a century, fighting for it for a generation, can afford to sit out a presidential term, or a year or two in the life of an old man in a hurry; that he who lasts the longest wins; that, sadly, with the impatience of democracies and their volatile voters committed to electoral contortions every four or five years, the extremist generally triumphs over the moderate. Just keep on being obdurate, don't deviate from your maximum terms, was the lesson handed down by the F.L.N. and remains as grimly valid today – whether for Northern Ireland or the Middle East or southern Africa. One after another de Gaulle saw his principles for peace eroded in the face of the F.L.N.'s refusal to compromise. As his disillusion grew, so did his resolve to liquidate the war with all speed. In this final haste injustices were perpetrated, such as the exclusion from the peace talks of any representative Algerian faction (e.g. the M.N.A.) other than the F.L.N. Yet de Gaulle did liquidate that savage war.

When all is said and done, de Gaulle's achievement was immense, and the gratitude owed him by France as well as the Western world no less. As ex-Premier Debré remarked to the author, "It was a miracle that we didn't collapse into civil war after Algeria; and this we owed to de Gaulle." The prosperous stability of post-1962 France stems to an important extent from the consequences of de Gaulle's coolness and sense of timing in May 1958, and his steadfast refusal then to come back as the army's man. If he had been strictly "straight" with the Massus, Challes and Salans all along, could the disastrous putsch of 1961 have been avoided? On the other hand, recalling the dangerously delicate balances of May 1958, might not such blinding honesty simply have brought about de Gaulle's overthrow and replacement by a military junta in 1959 or 1960, or even late 1958 – leading possibly to civil war in France itself? Had de Gaulle lost his deadly game with the army, France might well have undergone an experience similar to Portugal's – a right-wing military dictatorship, followed by collapse and left-wing ascendance, when it was at last realised that the "colonial" war in Algeria could never be won. His sibylline secrecy and ambiguities, his dubious promises and his cautious timing, may have prolonged the war and increased the uncertainty of the *pieds noirs*, and the way he extricated France from Algeria may not have been done well – but certainly no one else could have done it better. Perhaps the best summing up came from the aged leader of those other dark days of 1940, Paul Reynaud: "The war did not end in favourable conditions, but in the only conditions that were possible."

For the rest of the modern world (and not least Southern Africa), the French experience in the Algerian War – a prototype of its kind – continued to offer its compelling lessons, most of them painful, for anyone prepared to heed them. There was the failure of a materially mighty Western power to combat a civil insurrection equipped with little more than ideology, without resort to the means one condemns in one's enemy; in Algeria, the instrument of torture, as well as being fundamentally wicked in itself, was proved to be a boomerang weapon. There was the failure of the West to comprehend Third World aspirations; and the failure of the moderates everywhere to prevail against the extremist minority on either side; the *Gironde* is sent packing by the *Montagne*.

France, ten years on: the "pieds noirs" assimilated

Ten years after the liquidation of the Algerian war, the face that France showed to the world was, once again, that of a truly great power, more self-confident than she had been at any time since before 1914, and certainly more prosperous in material terms. The economic revival of France under the stewardship of de Gaulle has been one of the miracles of the Western world, second only to Federal Germany's recovery after 1945. No more remarkable yard-stick of it exists than the way in which France assimilated the over one million *pieds noirs* who flooded to her shores.* The adaptation of the uprooted *pieds noirs* to their new homes has been no easy process. Of the thirty thousand who went to hot and dusty Alicante on account of its resemblance to Oran, many – like an eminent ophthalmologist who started a night club rather than practise his profession, because that involved taking out Spanish papers – never felt at home there, despite their Spanish origins. "The *pieds noirs* of Alicante, when they stroll along the sea-shore," wrote *Le Monde*, "invariably gaze to the other side of the Mediterranean. In Alicante they are still in exile." Viticulturists of Alsatian stock who went to found vineyards in Corsica found themselves *plastiqué* once again – this time by jealous and less industrious Corsicans. Of the *pieds noirs* who headed for northern France, their "souls died", says Anne Loesch with sad nostalgia. Of herself, exiled in a grey Paris, she wrote, "I yearn to run across the beach and look at the sun dying in the sea."

So most of them stuck where the sun was, in the Midi, generally close to Marseilles. Some built colonies of white houses with flat roofs and patios and bougainvillaea over the door, to remind them of their lost homes. But if they sought climatic warmth, they did not necessarily find it in the hearts of their neighbours. Too often the *provençaux* regarded them as an alien race, as threatening competition, calling them *sales pieds noirs* much as they in turn had once scorned the *melons* and *ratons* of Algeria, and barring their homes to them. Sometimes the local village grocer would make a point of short-changing his ingenuous *pied noir* customers. When

---

* What would have happened had the exodus taken place during a time of economic recession, instead of boom, daunts the imagination.

the farmers went shooting, memories of nightmares from years past would reassert themselves, causing children to shout in terror, "The Arabs are attacking!" Adults, when describing their new lives in France, would still look instinctively over their shoulders, in case the O.A.S. might be listening: "You never know; it's all still so close...." If they missed the cheap domestic help of the *fatmas*, the exiles also claimed to miss the companionship of the "good Arab" and the whole ambience of the Muslim world in which they had grown up. The first state aid they received from France – subsistence allowance of 450 (new) francs per couple per month, *déménagement* loans of 20,000 francs – was far from generous. Many who had lived in modest comfort in Algeria found themselves reduced to the fringe of poverty; some took up with former members of the O.A.S., smuggling heroin and running protection rackets in Marseilles, extorting money from other *pieds noirs*. Nevertheless, by the end of the 1960s, such was the absorptive power of France's booming economy, it could be claimed that, by and large, there was no "*pied noir* problem".

The same could not be said about the other side of the coin, the Algerian immigrant workers in France. Granted certain preferential treatment by Evian, driven from home by persistent unemployment to prosperous, labour-hungry Europe, their numbers had mounted steadily ever since the war ended, until by 1973 they were close on 800,000. For the most part these Algerians lived like third-class citizens, their plight concealed from the eyes of other Frenchmen. Existing in rat-infested *bidonvilles*, or six to a tenement room, without women and on the poor food that their rock-bottom wages would provide, over eighty per cent of the Algerian workers performed the *travaux pénibles*; generally the heavy, dangerous or distasteful labour eschewed by Frenchmen. Nearly three-quarters of them were illiterate, and therefore unlikely ever to better themselves. But every year they were able to send home an impressive total of one milliard francs (then £100m.), vital to the Algerian economy. With relations seldom brilliant between the French proletariat and the sweated-labour Algerians, in the summer of 1973 there was a major explosion after a white bus-driver had his throat slit in the centre of Marseilles by an apparently unhinged Algerian. Suddenly it seemed as if the war was starting again: whites machine-gunned Algerian cafés in the city and threw Molotov cocktails into their lodgings; a sixteen-year-old boy was shot down by men in a moving car. In Toulouse fifty paras rampaged through the streets on a *ratonnade*, beating up any North African they encountered. "We have had enough," shrilled a right-wing Marseilles newspaper, *Le Méridional*: "Enough of Algerian thieves. Enough of Algerian vandals. Enough of Algerian loudmouths. Enough of Algerian troublemakers. Enough of Algerian syphilitics. Enough of Algerian rapists...." In Algiers a furious Boumedienne halted all further emigration and declared that – regardless of the cost – he would bring all his compatriots home from France if they could not be properly protected. But, such were mutual needs of interdependence in what the Algerians call "the damned inheritance", the breach was swiftly healed. Ten years later the Algerian work force in France still numbered approximately three-quarters of a million.

And so, imported across the Mediterranean, the prickly relationship between Algerian and Frenchman, Algerian and *pied noir*, French and *pied noir*, continued with but little reprieve.

What happened to them? The "Centurions"

In the fullness of time, de Gaulle's modernisation of the post-Algerian army resulted in the most sweeping metamorphosis. Many famous regiments, some of them the toughest fighting units in the West since 1945, and whose names had held the limelight for so many years, so many campaigns, disappeared or were totally transformed. For a time even the legendary Foreign Legion seemed doomed. The great bronze globe from its *Beau Geste* parade ground at Sidi-Bel-Abbès was uprooted, then reinstated at a new headquarters in Aubagne, outside Marseilles. Once masters over infinite miles of desert, mountain and rice paddy, within the limits of France's shrunken empire the Legion found its sphere of operations confined to small islands like Corsica, Tahiti and Martinique. Most of those who had led it through Vietnam and the Algerian war disappeared rapidly. In the army as a whole, senior officers – the men of forty in Algeria – weighed down by all the burden of bad dreams and stresses that the past had imposed on their beloved army, left prematurely, settled down to writing their memoirs, or withdrew entirely. General André Beaufre, France's greatest military thinker, who resigned rather than take command over a still bitterly divided army, died early. General Gambiez, the ill-starred Commander-in-Chief at the time of the 1961 generals' putsch, retired in 1967 and took up writing history. Colonel Trinquier, the tough para leader during the Battle of Algiers, went to Katanga as a mercenary before the end of the Algerian war, then retired to devote himself to viticulture. The ace of all the paras, and prototype of Lartéguy's *Centurion* colonel, Marcel Bigeard, was one of the few to remain in the service and attain the ultimate heights. A four-star general in 1975, Bigeard was appointed State Secretary in the Ministry of Defence by President Giscard to "remoralise" the army and purge it of the revolutionary and "permissive" elements sapping it from within.

Finally, the controversial and forceful General Massu was to perform one further role of greatest moment. Reprimanded in 1962 for publicly demanding the release of his fellow generals imprisoned after the 1961 putsch, then appointed, nevertheless, to command French forces in Germany, in the critical month of May 1968 the ever-loyal Massu received a secret visit from de Gaulle, who wanted to be reassured of Massu's and the army's support in the event of deepening internal trouble in France. Massu gave him the required assurance, apparently on the condition of de Gaulle granting an act of grace for the imprisoned officers. Later that year, de Gaulle proclaimed an amnesty for all those under sentence for acts committed during the war. Massu then went into semi-retirement with a small office in the Invalides, writing two fearlessly outspoken books on the Battle of Algiers. At the time of President Giscard's conciliatory state visit of 1975, Massu declared that he too would be happy to return to Algeria and "shake M. Boumedienne's hand" – if invited.

The "fallen angels"

Of the army's "fallen angels", some of those who managed to escape the long arm of French justice had adventurous careers. Broizat, the monastic para colonel of "Barricades Week", was one of the last O.A.S. leaders to leave Algeria; he fled to Spain, then migrated to New Caledonia to dedicate himself to religion. Pierre Sergent, leader of the O.A.S. in France, and sentenced to death *in absentia*, went into hiding in Belgium, Holland and Germany under various pseudonyms until the 1968 amnesty, when he returned to France. Colonel Jean Gardes, after dodging arrest in Spain, made his way to Argentina, where – remembering some of his mother's recipes from the Restaurant des Ministères – he established an unmilitary but extremely successful business making pâtés. On the amnesty he too returned to Paris. Averse to reading the many books about the Algerian war, he is fed "digests" by his wife and is distressed when not enough is made of his lasting attachment to the Muslims of Algeria. Godard, the expert on counter-revolutionary war, eventually took refuge in Belgium after the collapse of the O.A.S. in 1962, but – unlike most of his colleagues – he did not return home after the 1968 amnesty. Running a small factory near Mons and tending his aviary, he became increasingly embittered and died at an early age in 1975. Of those who spent time in French gaols, Argoud – sentenced to life imprisonment after his humiliating kidnap by the *barbouzes* – was also released in 1968. Since then, with a mystic belief that he could determine character from handwriting, he set himself up as a graphologist in the Vosges, remarried, spending his leisure time playing the piano and preparing his memoirs, grandiloquently called *Decadence, Imposture and Tragedy*.

Of the *quarteron* of generals imprisoned after the 1961 putsch, only Zeller did not write his memoirs, and none of them continued to see each other. Salan energetically produced books at the rate of a volume a year, well into his seventies. Always the elegant "Mandarin", with silver hair lightly tinted mauve or saffron, according to his mood, he lived in a comfortable Paris apartment surrounded by gilded buddhas, carved elephant tusks, opium pipes and all the artefacts of the Far East which he so loved. His pension was restored, and his many decorations for valour – but not his campaign ribbons, nor his rank. Nevertheless, "though I am just plain Monsieur Raoul Salan, everybody calls me *mon général* and they often salute me in the street!" he would claim. He spoke unashamedly and without reservation of all that was past, and visitors would often be taken aback to hear a full general, who once reigned over commands comparable to those of an Eisenhower or a Montgomery, describing his prison life with the relish of an old lag: "It was difficult getting used to obeying whistles, you know . . . The Santé was bad; the *gardes mobiles* were really not at all nice . . . Tulle was better . . . But the worst was being locked up at 11 p.m. and the doors not opened until 7 a.m.; I can assure you, we were not spoilt!" In 1984 Salan died, not quite surviving to see the thirtieth anniversary of the war in which he played so equivocal a role.

Challe, of all the rebel officers perhaps the one most commanding sympathy, was released in 1966 after serving five years of his fifteen years' sentence, amnestied in 1968 with the rest, and stricken with cancer of the throat.* Against all odds he survived, and ran a freight company from a small office near the Gare St Lazare, surrounded by devoted and caring secretaries. Behind his desk hung an ancient map of the Barbary Coast. He would still speak passionately of France's betrayal of the "loyal" Algerians, believed that the war could have been won, and that Europe lost her great opportunity to create a "bridge" to Africa through Algeria. Deeply pessimistic, he felt that "Europe now is finished". In a hoarse voice that obviously pained him, and with emotion, he would declare: "*Je ne regrette rien*; except for having failed." He died in 1979.

Of the non-military contingent who put themselves on the wrong side of the law, Pierre Lagaillarde remained in Spain until the amnesty, and then returned to be a small-town lawyer in the French provinces, abandoning any grandiose political pretension. For a time Jo Ortiz ran a night-club in Majorca, but – finding the language of his forebears difficult to master – also returned to the south of France after 1968 to pursue his vocation. Dr Jean-Claude Pérez, the O.A.S. chief of operations and Degueldre's superior, made his way from Spain to South America and then to Paris, where he created a thriving medical practice. He talked volubly and uninhibitedly about the O.A.S. and its *opérations ponctuelles*, stating that he would be prepared to "act" again if it were necessary. Georges Bidault, the former Resistance leader who was once de Gaulle's Foreign Minister and who inherited Salan's mantle, spent four and a half years in exile in Brazil after being refused entry to the United States, and then returned to retire in Paris, a sick, lonely, and embittered man. Some of the former O.A.S.

* During his first weeks in prison he wrote his account of the 1961 putsch, *Notre Révolte*, at top speed on the assumption that de Gaulle was certain to have him shot.

leaders continued to remain at odds with the law, organising bank raids in France's Mediterranean cities, to culminate with the famous "sewer coup" of 1976 in Nice. In 1977 the "Delta" squads raised their ugly heads again, claiming the random killing of an Algerian night-watchman in Paris. Other murders have been laid at the door of the O.A.S., such as that of Prince Jean de Broglie, one of de Gaulle's negotiating team at Evian; and, in 1978, of Henri Curiel, a mysterious international agent of part Jewish and Egyptian blood, allegedly with K.G.B. connections, who aided F.L.N. networks abroad during the war. Both murders remain unsolved.

French leaders and "grands colons"

The only one among the "fallen angels" to be again prominently active in politics was Jacques Soustelle, de Gaulle's wartime intelligence chief and the governor-general most beloved of the *pieds noirs*. In exile from 1962 onwards (when, he claims, at least two attempts – once in Brussels, once in Lisbon – were made to kidnap him *à la* Argoud), Soustelle characteristically refused to accept the amnesty of 1968 – on the grounds that he had committed no crime. Eventually he won his point and returned once more to being – briefly – Deputy for Lyon, still brimming over with ebullient passion, intellect and wit, whizzing back and forth from the Assembly, his bulky frame crammed into a Mini-Minor.

Soustelle's successor in Algiers, Robert Lacoste, retired to tend his roses in the Dordogne, which he represented as Socialist Senator, discussed vigorously the Algerian War, but refused to write his memoirs. His successor, Paul Delouvrier, maintained a modest reticence about his time in Algiers, having returned to the world where he was happier – that of economics and high finance, appointed by de Gaulle to run France's Electricity Board. Of the numerous French politicians to preside over the years of Algerian turmoil, Guy Mollet, the veteran Socialist, man of Suez and (next to de Gaulle) the longest to remain at the helm, was also one of the first to die, in 1975, at the age of sixty-nine. Among the *pied noir* leaders the all-powerful Senator Borgeaud withdrew much of his wealth from Algeria before the final crash, then died in France. His feudal domain at La Trappe was turned into a "Museum of Colonialism" in the first flush of Algerian independence; then, when the joke wore off, it became an agronomic institute. Schiaffino, the shipping magnate, somehow managed to maintain both the family fortunes and his shipping lines after independence. Comte Alain de Sérigny, banished from Algeria, his *Echo d'Alger* closed down in its fiftieth year after the 1961 putsch, ran a brewery from Paris. His office contained all the bound copies of the *Echo* and proudly displayed on a wall a family tree of his colonial ancestry. But, showing no signs of impoverishment, Sérigny claimed he had little time to keep up with his old *pied noir* friends and associates. Almost alone among the *grands colons* to remain in Algeria after independence, Jacques Chevallier, the liberal ex-mayor of Algiers, became vice-president of the Algiers Chamber of Commerce from 1963 to 1966, greatly respected by the Algerians and a token that, had they been genuinely prepared to co-operate and share responsibility with the Muslims, some future for the Europeans could have existed. He died in 1971, aged only fifty-nine. Of the "loyal" Muslim notables, most of whom withdrew to France after 1962, perhaps the best-known was the *harki* leader, the Bachaga Boualem; once overlord of 33,000 hectares and twenty-four tribes, he escaped to own forty hectares of rice-fields in the Camargue tended by his family and the surviving *harkis*, observing that the *mistral* blows across his property "as furiously as the wind of history".

The Algerians

For many of the numerous Algerian principal actors in the war, independence brought no happy ending. As of 1973, the sole member of the *neuf historiques* to hold senior government office was Rabah Bitat, Boumedienne's Minister of Public Works. His story provides a romantic epitaph to the war: released with Ben Bella in 1962, he then married Zohra Drif, one of Yacef's "heroines" from the Battle of Algiers. She herself had spent five years in French prisons, then returned to complete her law studies and become secretary-general of the Algerian École Nationale d'Administration. Zohra Drif's fellow bomb-carrier from the Battle of Algiers, Djamila Bouhired, married her defending lawyer, then divorced him and returned to run the Algerian branch of Max Factor – with Zohra Drif, one of a small minority of today's truly emancipated Algerian women. Another girl terrorist, Yasmina Belkacem, who lost both her legs at the age of 15 when her own bomb exploded, was to be seen at the thirtieth anniversary war celebrations, still an attractive, courageous and uncomplaining young woman, a living memorial to the horrors of urban terrorism. Their former boss, Yacef – having escaped the death sentence three times – took to making films after his release in 1962, co-producing one of the most remarkable of all time, *La Battaglia di Algeri* (1965), and acting his own part in it. Most of the revolutionary "old guard" withdrew – or were forcibly withdrawn – from politics. Of the veteran nationalists, the oft-imprisoned M.N.A. leader Messali Hadj, lived in retirement (at last unrestricted) outside Paris; Ferhat Abbas in the suburbs of Algiers, on a pension from his pharmacy. Ben Khedda, Abbas's successor as president of the G.P.R.A., still young but equally retired when I met him in 1973, then lived in a charming house in a garden suburb of Algiers, apparently subsidised by the state – in that it seems out of proportion to the modest pharmacy he still ran nearby.* Boussouf, Ben Tobbal, Major Azedine and

* In March 1976 Ben Khedda and Abbas entered the political lists again, briefly,

Colonel Ouamrane devoted themselves to business, with Ouamrane granted the fiefdom of Algiers's principal service station. Boudiaf, Ait Ahmed and Lebjaoui, already in exile under Ben Bella, remained abroad running various splinter groups in opposition to President Boumedienne.

Standing for a regime of social democracy combined with private enter-prise, Lebjaoui lived in Geneva under protection of a powerful watch-dog – "just in case". Certainly, in the past some of his fellow opponents of the regime have met with disquietingly violent ends. Mohamed Khider, one of the *neuf historiques* and Ben Bella's fellow internee, had – as already noted – gone into exile during Ben Bella's reign. He had taken with him the F.L.N.'s wartime "treasury", totalling some £6 million, which he controlled in his capacity as secretary-general of the party, declaring that the funds would be banked to finance the opposition against Ben Bella. When Boumedienne ousted Ben Bella, Khider stayed abroad in opposition; and the money remained in a Swiss bank. Then, one day in January 1967, Khider was shot down by unknown assailants in a Madrid street. Some-thing similar seems to have happened to Gorel, the O.A.S. "treasurer" who later disappeared in suspicious circumstances and has never been seen since.*
The fate of Khider was also shared by the most senior maquisard of them all, Belkacem Krim, former Foreign Minister of the G.P.R.A. and the man who led the Evian negotiations for Algeria. Disillusioned by politics and the revolution, after 1962 Krim turned to making a livelihood from selling jewellery. When Boumedienne, Krim's enemy from the earliest days, had come to power, Krim too went into exile and formed an opposition group. Declaring in 1969 that "seven years of independence were worse than seven years of war", Krim was sentenced to death (*in absentia*) on charges of treason and conspiring with foreign powers. He took to travelling heavily armed, but his undoing was indirectly caused by the sudden coming to notoriety of Leila Khaled and the Palestinian hijackers in the autumn of 1970; in an airport check his automatic was found and removed from him. A few days later he was discovered weaponless and murdered in a Frankfurt hotel. The means of his death seems, ironically, to have been the same as that which he had tacitly approved for Ramdane Abane in 1957 – strangling.

With the death of Krim, only four of the *neuf historiques* of 1954 remained alive. Of these, Ben Bella continued to be held under close arrest

in signing a manifesto to President Boumedienne demanding democratic freedoms and an end to the conflict with Morocco over the Polisario. Both were placed under house arrest; Ben Khedda died a short time later.

* After six years of legal wrangling, the Swiss Supreme Court finally ruled against the Algerian government's claim to the money, on the grounds that Khider had paid it into a personal account, and that he was the real owner – not the F.L.N. "which at the time had no legal existence". Thus the money remains, apparently, still in limbo and presumably frozen indefinitely. Following Gorel's presumed death, the identity of the ultimate beneficiaries of the missing O.A.S. funds remains a mystery.

in a house inside an Algerian army camp, vicinity unknown. From time to time there were grim rumours that this last of the old Algerian revolutionaries had been murdered, or his tongue cut out. In fact, though no other outsider had access to him, he was permitted to marry and raise a young family. With the coming of President Bendjedid, Ben Bella was then allowed to leave the country, to take up a voluntary exile in Switzerland. In 1985, he and his one-time fellow internee in France, Ait Ahmed, set up a "United Front" in opposition to Bendjedid's government in Algiers. It was ironic that Ait Ahmed, brother-in-law to the murdered Khider, had also once been under sentence of death under Ben Bella's own brief regime. Both claimed they still had to live in fear of assassination in Switzerland. Unable ever to see him previously, when the author was at last able to track Ben Bella down at his secret hideout in exile, though sixty-nine and despite having spent so much of his life in prisons, French and Algerian, Ben Bella still presented a vigorous-looking figure. Reputedly being financed by Ghadafi to destabilise Bendjedid, he insisted that his much more moderate regime was "just a continuation of Boumedienne"; but, with him and Ait Ahmed disagreeing on many fundamental issues, politically Ben Bella seemed a spent force. A sad man, he spoke of his nostalgic longing to be back at his home in Marnia; in Europe "one is cut off from everything that is dear – it is horrible!"

Following his takeover in 1965, Boumedienne remained firmly in power, challenged once only by an abortive uprising led by Colonel Zbiri in 1967. Then, on December 27th, 1978, he died prematurely of a rare disease, and was succeeded by Chadli Bendjedid. The coming of Bendjedid in itself marked a break with the past; instead of succeeding a forcibly deposed incumbent, this relatively unknown wartime colonel was elected peaceably by the Council of the F.L.N. The fourteen post-war years of Boumedienne, however, left a deep imprint which needs to be recorded in any study of the Algerian war; for modern Algeria is inseparably the child of wartime Algeria. The tone of Boumedienne's Algeria was predominantly austere, and Islamic, and one of Cromwellian honesty. He ran it as a single-party military dictatorship, but restored nerves left ragged by the eight-year-long war, while laying the foundations both for the political stability and relatively high economic prosperity that endured into the 1980s. The adjectives that applied in 1954–62 continued to describe her under Boumedienne: tough and uncompromising, admirable and big-thinking, dour and undemonstrative, untrusting and secretive. The high walls that protect the villas of Algiers remained symbolic of the national passion for reticence. Boumedienne (and Bendjedid after him) was the very antonym of the "cult of the personality," in sharp contrast to his neighbour Bourguiba. Seldom seen except when opening an industrial project or a housing estate, or addressing the Third World, when Boumedienne made his voice heard from behind those high walls, though often not helpful to the West, it was predictably consistent, never frivolous and seldom near-sighted. Western businessmen dealing with Algerian heads of industry discovered them to be just as indefatigably hard bargainers as did the French at Evian. Often a Western concern and one from the Communist world would find themselves coupled in the same project by the untrusting Algerians, the one checking and balancing out the other. But once a deal was made with the bright young men (many of them United States-trained) who run the Algerian economy, it generally stuck and was stuck to.

"In the space of only a few years, Algeria has transformed itself into a vast building site," claimed Boumedienne on the tenth anniversary of independence, in 1972. The odds were almost as immense as those facing the F.L.N. in November 1954; a backward economy, an impoverished soil, high illiteracy, twenty-five per cent unemployment (in 1972) and heavy under-employment, and an exploding population of already fifteen to sixteen million with one of the highest growth rates (3.5 per cent per annum) in the world. Always in the background there were the nagging problems of Algeria's excessive dependence economically on France – which the Algerians do not consider to have been balanced out by the vast sums of aid finance that they have received from across the Mediterranean. In solving this problem, and at the risk of further serious friction with France, Boumedienne pursued roughly the same tough policy as his pre-decessor. After expropriating French farm holdings, Ben Bella went on to make a first step (just before he was deposed in 1965) towards nationalising the oil and gas properties, by demanding that fifty per cent of their revenues be repatriated to Algeria. In 1971 Boumedienne completed the process by taking over a majority holding in all the companies. France retaliated by boycotting Algerian oil, ceasing imports of Algerian wine (long an apple of discord with French viticulturists), and withdrawing technicians. The dinar broke away from the franc, relations between the two countries tottered, and the Algerian economy looked stricken.

In the years that intervened, however, much changed. Algeria went to every country in the world, regardless of political hue, for aid and technical knowhow; American oil and gas men, Russian steel men, Japanese chemical engineers, Chinese military advisers, Spaniards, Britons and Romanians, West Germans and East Germans swarm about the country. Economic relations with France stabilised, if not harmonised, with the seal set upon them by President Giscard's state visit of April 1975. French technicians returned, so that the French colony in Algeria now already numbered some 65,000, including 7,000 teachers sent under the "cultural co-operation" clauses of Evian (one of the few provisions to survive). Algeria's efforts to pull herself up by her own bootstraps were truly remarkable. Largely based on her natural gas reserves, reckoned to be among the biggest in the world, her heavy industry showed an astonishing growth rate. Boumedienne's Algeria did not think in terms of four-year plans but in terms of a generation ahead. Everywhere one found evidence corroborating his tenth anniversary claim; vast housing complexes under construction; new industrial plants set in huge compounds that show extraordinarily ambitious forward thinking. The errors, when they occurred, were on the same grandiose scale as the achievements. But certainly no developing country (and few developed countries) visited by the author revealed a more impressive effort in material self-improvement. As far as the Arab world is concerned, in terms of economic efficiency and accomplishment, Boumedienne made Algeria its undisputed leader.

Pace-setter of the Third World

Post-war Algeria had its failings, and its critics. Sartre and the other left-wing French supporters of the wartime F.L.N. deplored that it had not gone further towards Marxism, that it failed to "export the revolution" to France. (An extreme revolutionary like Frantz Fanon would have found himself a prophet without honour in Boumedienne's Algeria.) The emancipation of women lagged behind the promises of the war years, with the equality they had come to enjoy then forgotten in peace: "The woman is treated according to the racist principle of apartheid; she is still 'colonised'," complained Fadela M'Rabet in La Femme Algérienne. Efforts to control the bursting birth-rate were inadequate. Agriculture was a black spot; some of the farms taken from the pieds noirs were maintained at least as immaculately as by their past owners, but others were choked with weeds and incompetently managed; agrarian reform (as in so many emerging countries) remained an elusive chimera. To the West, Algeria's belligerent noises towards Israel, on the demands of the Third World, on commodity prices, seldom offered comfort.

Yet no one could deny the distinctive place that Boumedienne's Algeria, an under-developed nation fifteen million strong, had carved for itself in the world. Politically it stood – and still stands – apart; Socialist but not Marxist, it was as wary in its relations with Soviet Russia as with the U.S.A. Externally it zealously preserved its image as a revolutionary state, friendly to almost all other revolutionary movements; yet internally its own society, where Islam remains very much the binding cement, was highly conservative. If there is one country to which Boumedienne's Algeria might most profitably be compared, it was perhaps Tito's Yugoslavia, just as the F.L.N. at war bore a certain affinity with the Yugoslav partisans of the Second World War. Apart from Algeria's proud independence of East and West, it was in her role of eminence in the Third World where the parallel is most relevant. More even than Tito at his zenith, Boumedienne was himself leader of the Third World. It was his taciturn authority that has welded it together, that set its tone. It was in Algiers that the mammoth Non-Aligned Conference took place in September 1973, probably the most significant congress of the Third World since the Bandung Conference of 1955 which gave the F.L.N. its first recognition in the outer world. It was also in Algiers in September of 1973 that, under Boumedienne's guiding influence, the diplomatic and political dispositions against Israel, as well as the oil weapon, were co-ordinated, providing the essential prelude to the "Ramadan War" of the following month. Following the triumph of Arab unity which ensued, and the undreamed-of power which the accompanying "oil war" revealed, Boumedienne's stature emerged hugely enhanced. When he spoke of the demands for equal shares for the world's poorer nations – "We are ready to fight to get it, just as, not long ago, most of us had to fight for our political independence . . . we have come to understand that it is only by a show of strength on our part that they (the rich countries) will understand that we mean business" – his reputation, both as an uncompromising fighter in war and leader in peace, ensured that his (and Algeria's) voice were taken seriously.

From Boumedienne to Bendjedid

When Chadli Bendjedid succeeded Boumedienne, from the beginning of 1979 onwards subtle changes slowly took place, almost surreptitiously. Photographs of the two men seemed symbolic; the gaunt, austere and unsmiling features of the wartime leader contrasted with the comfortable bourgeois face that you might almost expect to meet in an English golf club, perhaps a retired colonel. Algeria tended to slip from the world headlines. Under Bendjedid, Algeria ceased adopting extreme postures in the outside world (and particularly in Middle East politics) in favour of concentrating on domestic matters. The grandiose (and sometimes disastrous) industrial projects launched under Boumedienne gave way to consumer goods. In 1984, Algiers itself throbbed with vast and apparently insoluble traffic jams, that Western index of prosperity. The young were well clothed, and there were no signs of the terrible malnutrition rampant south of the Sahara. But, in a nation with bursting population explosion where the average age was 19, economic problems remained menacing. High price structures made it difficult to sell Algerian natural gas on glutted world markets; as in so many emerging countries, a rich agriculture had been nearly ruined by early collectivisation and was only gradually being rectified by opening to private enterprise. But, whether Algeria continues along the road of moderation charted by Bendjedid – so it seemed at the time – or regresses to a Boumedienne-style of authoritarianism, must to an important extent depend on its success in mastering its economic problems.

Algeria's new mood of benevolent moderation was exposed to the world when – to mark the 1984 celebrations – Bendjedid granted some fifty post-humous amnesties. The men thus rehabilitated included not only leaders who had been liquidated during the war, but also fallen angels who had revolted against either Ben Bella or Boumedienne during the post-war years. Among the wartime leaders forgiven were Si Salah, and the two tracked down and murdered abroad: Krim and Khider. Explicitly absent were the *harkis* who had served France. So, too, was Ramdane Abane; for obvious reasons, so long as any of those implicated in his death remained alive, the legend of the hero "killed in action" had to be allowed to persist. But, in Chadli Bendjedid's Algeria of 1984, veterans were much less inhibited in discussing what really happened to men like Abane and Si Salah, in a manner that would have been inconceivable under the shadow of Boumedienne ten years previously.

Algiers itself seemed a much more open society, more smiling and less dour, as the war years receded further in human memory. With many young Algerians trained in France or the U.S., the country looked increasingly northward and westward and away from the East. The successful role of Algerian diplomacy over the Teheran hostages in 1980 brought her into closer proximity with the United States – which she welcomed. In the saga of the hijacked airliner in 1985, Algeria was reckoned by Washington to have acted as honourably as circumstances permitted. Though Algeria continued to back Polisario against America's ally, King Hassan of Morocco, their support was limited by balanced fears that the fall of Hassan might lead to a Khomeini-style revolution and Islamic fundamentalist anarchy on Algeria's western flank. Only to a lesser degree was Algeria concerned about the succession to the ageing Bourguiba on her Tunisian flank.

"Don't look on us as an *Arab* people," remarked Bendjedid's Foreign Minister, Taleb Ibrahim, to a foreign diplomat; "We are Mediterranean people in an Arab context." It revealed just how complex is the Algerian identity. Yet, even though Algeria *is* an Arab nation, the legacy of the past is such that no amount of calculated "arabisation" will erase completely the 130 years of links with France. As of 1978, a large proportion of Algerians still remained francophone; to many it was still a *lingua franca*, often used with pride as a sign of education. As the correspondent of *The Times* wrote after President Giscard's simple but moving welcome by Boumedienne in 1975, the first time the *Marseillaise* had been played at an official Algerian ceremony in thirteen years: "France and Algeria are like an old couple who have been married many years, had a tremendous bust up, divorce, and then decide to make up. Emotion will never be altogether absent from their relationship; it will never be completely straightforward."

The fading ghosts

From that mortified relationship of the past the ghosts, though fading, have lingered most pervasively in Algeria. As I wandered around the *bled* in 1973, for the first time, I recorded for the last pages of my account how the tokens of destruction of those seven terrible years had not even then been effaced.

Along the main roads, like rows of neatly felled trees, the power pylons lie where they were blasted by the F.L.N., and frequently you have to bounce your way across rocky fords where destroyed bridges have not yet been replaced. High up on Kabylia's Col de Tametz cows saunter in and out of the gutted remains of what was once a luxury hotel for Algeria's wealthier *colons*. Everywhere there are the empty shells of farmhouses, barns and homesteads, sometimes whole villages. Memories have blurred as to who was responsible for each separate tragedy: was it an isolated *pied noir* farm destroyed by the *fellagha*, or a Muslim *douar* razed by the French army in reprisals? On their broken walls, superimposed upon each other like the strata of archaeological diggings, the rival war slogans remain clearly legible:

ALGÉRIE FRANCAISE!

DE GAULLE – VOTEZ OUI

O.A.S. – SALAN

And finally, more emphatic than all the rest:

F.L.N.

Every few kilometres along the railway that runs through the savage Aurès mountains, the cradle of the revolt in 1954, stand the gaunt skeletons of French watch-towers. But their purpose seems hardly less remote than the marvellously preserved arches and columns of the nearby Roman garrison of Timgad. Here – in the same breath – Chaouia women try to sell you a Roman oil lamp, a Second Empire cock (minus its works), or a fifty-year-old French flat-iron. All seem to belong to an equally vanished past. In the French villages of the Mitidja the parish churches are boarded up and gently dying. Overlooking Oran stands a vast votive sanctuary, built in thanksgiving after a past plague, surmounted by a Virgin with hands outstretched as if imploring for the compassion that *Algérie française* so tragically lacked. In its deserted cloisters visitors may find a half-starved cur eating a dead pigeon, the chapel altars defaced by Arabic graffiti. Above

Algiers, Notre Dame d'Afrique has an air of even greater abandonment. The shutters of the small boutique which once sold candles and religious bric-à–brac are rusted firmly shut, the eucalyptus trees dying unwatered. In comparison, the Catholic Cathedral in Algiers seems to have had a happier fate, by reverting once more to being a mosque, busy and alive. Along the lovely beaches around Algiers, what were once the weekend villas of the *pieds noirs* stand abandoned, stucco flaking, curtainless windows staring blankly out across the Mediterranean. Half a generation ago they would have comprised a cheerful, thriving and typically French bourgeois resort such as one might find in Brittany or Arcachon; now, though a few prosperous Algerians are refurbishing the deserted homes, the remainder seem haunted by resentful ghosts. These seaside hamlets are deader and colder places than ancient Roman Tipasa, whose glowing ruins nearby seem somehow younger than the similar relics of French bricks and mortar scattered all over contemporary Algeria, testifying glumly to the perishability of Western civilisation.

At Sidi-Bel-Abbès, a town plonked down in the middle of dusty nowhere that was once the home of the Foreign Legion, it is hard to find any trace of *Beau Geste*. In answer to discreet enquiries, while *Parlez-moi d'amour* oozes nostalgically from the radio, a local restaurateur affects never to have heard of *La Légion*: "Yes, there was a *campe de triage* [vetting centre] up here, and a torture camp (you know what torture is, *m'sieur?*) over there. There were foreigners there, of course, who did the torturing – lots of Germans. But, as for a Foreign Legion, *j'en sais rien.*" At Zéralda the barracks from which the 1st R.E.P. marched out forever in 1961, singing Piaf's *Je ne regrette rien*, have been bulldozed to make way for a vast new tourist complex. At Sidi Ferruch, the beach where the French landed in 1830, an even more ambitious complex and marina have been built. "We thought this was the most appropriate kind of monument," Algerian officials explain; "so the French can land here again – but this time with their travellers' cheques!"

At Toudja in Kabylia, the wartime devastation of which so shocked Jules Roy, new fig trees have been planted and a new clinic built next to the former French barracks, part of which is now used as a school. A mountain stream rushes through the village; it is a green and peaceful demi-paradise. But the lack of men in their thirties and forties is conspicuous. A youth with a flute will proudly take you round the village, pointing out the lovely *"Arbres de France"* (acacias, "one of the good things left behind by France!"), but he cannot recall exactly where the fighting took place, or just what it was about. The Algerian attitude towards history seems, to Europeans, a curious one. "The page is turned," they tell you. Even in the Algiers Casbah there is not a single plaque or inscription to remind one of the house where Ali la Pointe was blown up, where Yacef hid, or where some of the more legendary of the F.L.N. freedom-fighters fought so tenaciously against Massu's paras.

In Algiers, too, most of the streets were renamed soon after independence. (It was said, apocryphally, that, in the early days of xenophobia, Constantine's Boulevard Anatole France had been rechristened Anatole Algérie.) Rue des Colons, with some poetic justice, is now Rue des Libérés; Place du Gouvernement, Place des Martyrs. The Forum, scene of the wild moments of crowd hysteria when the para colonels tumbled the Fourth Republic, is now the Esplanade de l'Afrique. The elegant Rue d'Isly bears the name of Ben M'hidi, the F.L.N. leader who died mysteriously in French hands during the Battle of Algiers. The prancing equestrian statue to the rebel chief, Abd-el-Kader, has replaced that of his vanquisher, Marshal Bugeaud. In the same square the office of General Salan – once the target of the "ultra" bazooka – is now F.L.N. party headquarters. The "Otomatic", haunt of the *pied noir* "ultras" which was bombed during the Battle of Algiers, has become the "Cercle des Étudiants", now catering to an almost all-male Muslim clientèle. The "Casino" night-club, so brutally bombed during Yacef's second offensive in the Battle of Algiers, has become a dour club for Algerian officers. With the going of the *méditerranéen-et-demi pieds noirs*, certainly Algiers has lost its erstwhile gaiety. The sun beams down on Algiers – but the inhabitants do not smile back. It is a surly city, harrowed by the stresses of over-population and under-employment; with the architecture of Cannes, but the atmosphere of Aberdeen. During the day the cafés are thronged with all-male, typically Arab society. At night the city, responsive to President Boumedienne's own personal brand of puritanism, closes down like wartime Toronto on a Sunday. The once exclusively *pied noir* areas of Algeria have become so totally Arab in atmosphere that one wonders how the French dreams of "integration" or "association", or the liberal hopes of a Camus for a multi-racial society of the 1950s, could ever have come true. Despite the Timgad-like bricks and stones left by the *pieds noirs*, were they ever really here at all?

"Everything fades," says Camus, quoting a cemetery ex-volto, "save memory." But the nostalgia can be overdone. Today's Algerian is a thoroughly pragmatic individual. Near Skikda (ex-Philippeville) there is a paradigm of the Algeria of the present and future. The Plage Jeanne d'Arc once housed a rest and rehabilitation centre for Bigeard's paras returning from operations in the *bled*. Now bulldozers constructing an immense new oil refinery have crunched through the road to the beach settlement, leaving it isolated from the outside world. Shutters hanging crazily askew, the bistros and "discos" and "dancings", where once Massu's centurions chatted up the local girls, are sliding aimlessly into the sea, leaving a spaghetti-like tangle of reinforcing rods protruding from the ephemeral prefabs. By some miracle, here and there geraniums still flower out of untended window-boxes. But perhaps even by now Plage Jeanne d'Arc has disappeared forever beneath the pounding surf – more immemorably than either Roman Timgad or Tipasa.

Certainly by the thirtieth anniversary of the war in 1984 the Plage Jeanne d'Arc had gone without a trace, and a few more relics of the *présence française* had expired with it. On the way to Camus's ravishing Tipasa then I noted how the typically France bandstands that once dominated the main square of small provincial towns were no longer there. In the heart of Algiers itself (a much less dour, perhaps more self-assured city, than I remembered it from 1973), on the Plateau des Glières which had provided the focus for the events of 1958, the hideous Monument aux Morts still stood. But – instead of removing it in its entirety – the Algerians had simply rendered over with cement its excessive bas-reliefs to colonial feats of arms. Meanwhile, superbly sited above the city and visible from every part of it, stands the vast new monument to Algieria's war dead. Representing three vast palm fronds ingeniously cantilevered against each other and over three hundred feet high, designed by Polish architects and constructed with Canadian knowhow – it is in itself almost a symbol of post-1962 Algeria's balancing act between East and West. Beneath, a museum contains a vivid record of suffering and resistance under the 130 years of French rule. At its heart one descends into a crypt in polished black granite; in the centre is a simple patch of desert sand embracing a rock from the Aurès mountains where that savage war began on November 1st, 1954. It is an imposing and solemn place – about a thousand light years removed from that memorial on its sea-girt promontory at Tipasa, where a carefree Albert Camus once rejoiced in that other Algeria.

Tragically, it was very soon evident that the bright hopes of 1984 were – once again – to be dashed. Under worsening economic conditions, Fundamentalism led by the F.I.S. [Islamic Salvation Front], came to acquire a growing ascendancy throughout the country. Alarmed at their power, the F.L.N.-based regime under Liamine Zeroual in 1992 cancelled the second round of the National Elections. From then on escalated a new civil war, which by the time of the next elections three years later, had killed perhaps as many as 50,000 people – over twice as many as all the French fatalities, civilian as well as military, during the eight years of the War of National Liberation. The targets of the slaughter, as well as the techniques, seemed rooted in those horrendous years of conflict. One of the first, eminent victims of terrorism that June was the President himself, Mohamed Boudiaf. Almost sole survivor of the greatly respected *"neuf historiques"*, he had been brought back at seventy-three to head a government of reconciliation. As an echo of the 1950s, two weeks alone of January 1994 saw 116 Algerian policemen assassinated, in a deliberate attempt to sow the kind of fear that had gripped the populace during the struggle against the French. Magistrates, *evoluées* women who refused to wear the veil (and to whom the Revolution had brought such high hopes of emancipation), novelists, journalists and intellectuals all appeared high on the Fundamentalist hit-list.

Also targeted, in a determined effort by the F.I.S. to ruin the country's economy by scaring off badly needed external investment, were foreign journalists and technicians. Distinguished political leaders, like Ait Ahmed, were driven – once more – into exile, for fear of their lives. The Government met terror with counter-terror. There leaked out accounts of torture, executions without trial, and "disappearances" that recalled the worst moments of the French Occupation. As in the '60s, during the reign of the O.A.S., terrorist bombings now struck at Metropolitan France again.

In 1995, two rays of hope appeared. Oil exploration in Algeria made the world's biggest oil discoveries for the past year. But would these now be put to the salvation of the country's desperate economic problems, and to countering the demands of overpopulation – that fertile field on which Fundamentalism breeds so readily – or would they be, once again, profligately wasted, as under Boumedienne?

Then, in November of 1995, Zeroual held the long-promised national elections. Closely watched by international observers, they seemed properly conducted and, despite threats of "days of blood", resulted in a 61 per cent landslide vote for the Government. It was heralded as a triumph for moderation and hopes rose high for the beginning of a new era of reconciliation for the strife-weary Algerians.

Yet, within days – and only eight hours after Zeroual took the oath of office – the most senior Algerian general to be killed so far was felled by terrorists in a smart suburb of Algiers.

How much longer, Algerians ask themselves, is hope to go on being deferred, as the clock moves closer to the fiftieth anniversary since the War of Liberation began on that historic day of 1 November 1954?

Afterword

HE knew what those jubilant crowds did not know but could have learned from books: that the plague bacillus never dies or disappears for good; that it can lie dormant for years and years in furniture and linen-chests; that it bides its time in bedrooms, cellars, trunks and bookshelves; and that perhaps the day would come when, for the bane and the enlightening of men, it roused up its rats again and sent them forth to die in a happy city.

Albert Camus, *La Peste, 1947*

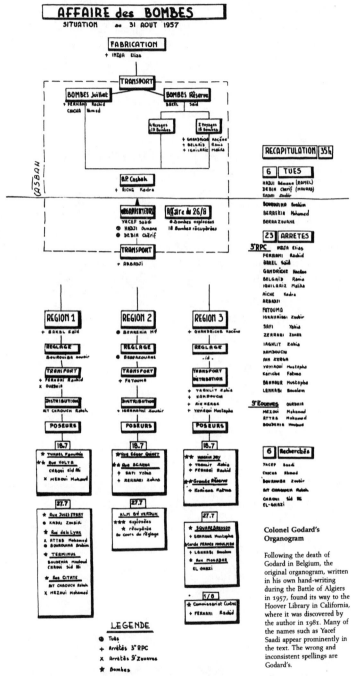

Colonel Godard's Organogram

Following the death of Godard in Belgium, the original organogram, written in his own hand-writing during the Battle of Algiers in 1957, found its way to the Hoover Library in California, where it was discovered by the author in 1981. Many of the names such as Yacef Saadi appear prominently in the text. The wrong and inconsistent spellings are Godard's.

Political and Military Abbreviations

A.L.N.	Armée de Libération Nationale
A.M.L.	Amis du Manifeste et de la Liberté
B.E.L.	Bureau d'Études et de Liaisons
B.P.C.	Bataillon de Parachutistes de Choc
C.C.E.	Comité de Coordination et d'Exécution
C.N.R.	Conseil National de la Résistance
C.N.R.A.	Conseil National de la Révolution Algérienne
C.R.S.	Compagnies Républicaines de Sécurité
C.R.U.A.	Comité Révolutionnaire d'Unité et d'Action
D.O.P.	Détachement Opérationnel de Protection
D.P.U.	Dispositif de Protection Urbaine
D.S.T.	Direction de la Surveillance du Territoire
F.A.F.	Front de l'Algérie Française
F.L.N.	Front de Libération Nationale
F.N.F.	Front National Français
G.-G.	Gouvernement-Général
G.P.R.A.	Gouvernement Provisoire de la République Algérienne
G.R.E.	Groupement de Renseignement et d'Exploitation
M.N.A.	Mouvement Nationaliste Algérienne
M.P.C.	Mouvement pour la Communauté
M.R.P.	Mouvement Républicain Populaire
M.T.L.D.	Mouvement pour le Triomphe des Libertés Démocratiques
O.A.S.	Organisation Armée Secrète
O.P.A.	Organisation Politico-Administrative
O.S.	Organisation Spéciale
P.C.A.	Parti Communiste Algérien
P.C.F.	Parti Communiste Français
P.P.A.	Parti du Peuple Algérien
P.S.U.	Parti Socialiste Unifié
R.C.P.	Régiment de Chasseurs Parachutistes
R.E.P.	Régiment Étranger Parachutistes
R.P.C.	Régiment Parachutiste Coloniale
R.P.F.	Rassemblement du Peuple Français
S.A.S.	Section Administrative Spécialisé
S.D.E.C.E.	Service de Documentation Extérieure et de Contre-Espionage
S.F.I.O	Section Française de l'Internationale Ouvrière
U.D.M.A.	Union Démocratique pour le Manifeste Algérien
U.F.N.A.	Union Française Nord-Africaine

U.G.T.A.	Union Générale des Travailleurs Algériens
U.T.	Unités Territoriales
Z.A.A.	Zone Autonome d'Alger

Chronology

<table>
<tr><td>1830</td><td colspan="2">France occupies Algiers</td></tr>
<tr><td>1847</td><td colspan="2">Abd-el-Kader surrenders</td></tr>
<tr><td>1871</td><td colspan="2">French loss of Alsace-Lorraine steps up colonisation of Algeria</td></tr>
<tr><td>1936</td><td colspan="2">Blum–Viollette reforms for Algeria: not implemented</td></tr>
<tr><td>1940</td><td colspan="2">Fall of France</td></tr>
<tr><td>1942</td><td>8</td><td>November: Allied landings in Algeria and Morocco</td></tr>
<tr><td>1945</td><td>8</td><td>May: V.E. Day: Algerian revolt in Sétif followed by severe reprisals</td></tr>
<tr><td>1954</td><td>7</td><td>May: Fall of Dien Bien Phu in Indo-China</td></tr>
<tr><td></td><td>18</td><td>June: Mendès-France comes to power</td></tr>
<tr><td></td><td>1</td><td>November: All Saints' Day: the Algerian war begins</td></tr>
<tr><td>1955</td><td>25</td><td>January: Soustelle appointed governor-general</td></tr>
<tr><td></td><td>6</td><td>February: Mendès-France falls</td></tr>
<tr><td></td><td>18–24</td><td>April: F.L.N. attend Bandung Conference of "Third World"</td></tr>
<tr><td></td><td>20</td><td>August: F.L.N. massacre pieds noirs at Philippeville</td></tr>
<tr><td>1956</td><td>26</td><td>January: Mollet succeeds Faure as prime minister</td></tr>
<tr><td></td><td>2</td><td>February: Soustelle goes, replaced by Lacoste</td></tr>
<tr><td></td><td>18</td><td>May: Palestro Massacre of French conscripts</td></tr>
<tr><td></td><td>20</td><td>August: Soummam Conference established F.L.N. policy</td></tr>
<tr><td></td><td>30</td><td>September: Yacef's girls bomb Milk-Bar and Cafétéria: Battle of Algiers begins</td></tr>
<tr><td></td><td>16</td><td>October: Interception of Athos loaded with arms from Egypt for F.L.N.</td></tr>
<tr><td></td><td>22</td><td>October: Ben Bella hijacked and imprisoned by French</td></tr>
<tr><td></td><td>5</td><td>November: Anglo-French landings at Suez</td></tr>
<tr><td></td><td>14</td><td>December: Salan appointed Commander-in-Chief in Algeria</td></tr>
<tr><td>1957</td><td>7</td><td>January: Massu's paras take over Algiers</td></tr>
<tr><td></td><td>16</td><td>January: Bazooka attempt to kill Salan</td></tr>
<tr><td></td><td>28</td><td>January: General strike begins in Algiers – broken by paras</td></tr>
<tr><td></td><td>21</td><td>May: Mollet falls: France is 22 days with no government</td></tr>
<tr><td></td><td>31</td><td>May: Massacre of peasants by F.L.N. at Mélouza</td></tr>
<tr><td></td><td>2</td><td>July: J. F. Kennedy's speech supporting Algerian independence</td></tr>
<tr><td></td><td>24</td><td>September: Yacef captured: Battle of Algiers won by Massu</td></tr>
<tr><td></td><td>5</td><td>November: Gaillard succeeds Bourgès-Maunoury as prime minister</td></tr>
<tr><td></td><td>26</td><td>December: Liquidation of Ramdane Abane</td></tr>
<tr><td>1958</td><td>7</td><td>January: Saharan oil begins to flow</td></tr>
<tr><td></td><td>8</td><td>February: French bomb Sakiet in Tunisia</td></tr>
</table>

15 April: Gaillard falls; France 37 days with no government

13 May: Algiers mob seizes government buildings and demands de Gaulle

1 June: de Gaulle becomes prime minister

4 June: de Gaulle makes triumphant visit to Algeria (*"Je vous ai compris"*)

19 September: G.P.R.A. (Provisional Government of the Algerian Revolution) formed

3 October: de Gaulle offers *paix des braves* to the rebels

12 December: Challe and Delouvrier replace Salan

21 December: de Gaulle is elected president of France

1959 22 July: Operation "Binoculars"; climax of Challe offensive

16 September: de Gaulle offers Algeria "self-determination"

1960 19 January: Massu sacked for attacking de Gaulle's policy

24 January: "Barricades Week"; "ultras" shoot gendarmes

29 January: de Gaulle speaks, revolt collapses

23 April: Challe "promoted" away from Algeria

10 June: Si Salah makes abortive peace approach to de Gaulle

25–29 June: French peace talks with F.L.N. at Melun: failure

6 September: "Manifesto of the 121" inciting conscripts to desert

28–29 September: Ferhat Abbas goes to Moscow and Peking

23 November: Joxe and Morin replace Delouvrier

9–13 December: Muslim backlash as de Gaulle visits Algeria

20 December: United Nations recognises Algeria's right to self-determination

1961 25 January: O.A.S. emerges: assassination of Maitre Popie

20–26 April: "Generals' putsch" in Algiers: de Gaulle triumphs

25 April: France explodes atomic bomb at Reggane in Sahara

19 May: 19 O.A.S. explosions in Algiers

20 May–28 July: First peace talks at Evian: failure

19–23 July: Fighting between France and Tunisia at Bizerta

8 September: Assassination attempt on de Gaulle at Pont-sur-Seine

1962 7 February: Bomb intended for Malraux in Paris blinds girl of 4

February: O.A.S. kill 553 people

7–18 March: Second Evian peace talks: agreement signed

19 March: Cease-fire between French and F.L.N.

20 April: Salan captured

17 June: Truce between O.A.S. and F.L.N.: exodus of *pieds noirs*

1 July: Referendum on independence

15 September: Ben Bella becomes president

1965 19 June: Boumedienne overthrows Ben Bella

1978 27 December: Death of Boumedienne; Bendjedid becomes president

1984 Signs of some liberalisation of one-party F.L.N. regime
1992 Government under Liamine Zeroual cancels second round of national elections. F.I.S. banned and civil war begins.
June: Mohamed Boudiaf assassinated
1994 Vast new oil deposits found in Algeria
1995 New national elections return Zeroual by landslide 61 per cent majority

Bibliography

Abbas, Ferhat, (1) *Guerre et Révolution d'Algérie* (Paris, 1962)
——, (2) *Autopsie d'une guerre; l'aurore* (Paris, 1980)
Abun-Nasr, J. M., *A History of the Maghreb* (Cambridge, 1971)
Ageron, Charles-Robert, (1) *Les Algériens musulmans et la France* (1871–1919) (Paris, 1968)
——, (2) *Histoire de l'Algérie contemporaine, 1830–1960* (Paris, 1970)
Ait Ahmed, Hocine, *La Guerre et l'après-guerre* (Paris, 1964)
Allais, Maurice, *L'Algérie d'Evian. Le réferendum et la Résistance algérienne* (Paris, 1962)
Alleg, Henri, *La Question* (Paris, 1958); tr. *The Question* (London, 1958)
Alleg, H., with Jacques de Bonis, Henri J. Douzon, Jean Freire, Pierre Haudiquet, *La Guerre d'Algérie*, 3 vols (Paris, 1981)
Amrani, Djamal, *Le Témoin* (Paris, 1960)
Amrouche, Fadhma, *Histoire de ma vie* (Paris, 1968)
Aron, Raymond, (1) *La Tragédie algérienne* (Paris, 1957)
——, (2) *L'Algérie et la République* (Paris, 1958)
Aron, Robert, et al., *Les Origines de la guerre d'Algérie* (Paris, 1962)
Azedine, Commandant, (1), *On Nous Appelait Fellaghas* (Paris, 1976)
——, (2) *Et Alger ne brûla pas* (Paris, 1980)
Bacri, Roland, *Et alors? et voila!* (Paris, 1971)
Bauer, Hans E., *Verkäufte Jahre* (Gütersloh, 1958)
Beaufre, André, *La Guerre révolutionnaire* (Paris, 1972)
Beauvoir, Simone de, *La Force des choses* (Paris, 1963)
Beauvoir, Simone de, and Halami, Gisèle, *Djamila Bupacha* (Paris, 1962); tr. (London, 1962)
Bedjaoui, Mohammed, *La Révolution algérienne et le droit* (Brussels, 1961); tr. *The Law and the Algerian Revolution* (Brussels, 1961)
Behr, Edward, *The Algerian Problem* (London, 1961)
Belloula, Tayeb, *Les Algériens en France* (Algiers, 1965)
Bencherif, Ahmed, *L'Aurore des mechtas* (Algiers, 1969)
Bennabi, Malek, *Mémoires d'un témoin du siècle* (Algiers, 1965)
Bidault, Georges, *D'une Résistance à l'autre* (Paris, 1965); tr. *Resistance: The political autobiography* (New York, 1967)
Bigeard, Marcel, *Contre guérilla* (Algiers, 1957)
Bollardière, Jacques de, *Bataille d'Algiers, bataille de l'homme* (Paris, 1972)
Boualem, Bachaga, *Les Harkis au service de la France* (Paris, 1963)
Brace, Richard and Joan, (1) *Ordeal in Algeria* (New York, 1960)
——, (2) *Algerian Voices* (Princeton, 1965)

Bromberger, Merry and Serge, *Les 13 Complots du 13 mai* (Paris, 1959)

Bromberger, Merry and Serge, Elgey, Georgette and Chauvel, Jean-François, *Barricades et colonels, 24 janvier 1960* (Paris, 1960)

Bromberger, Serge, *Les Rebelles algériens* (Paris, 1958)

Buchard, Robert, *Organisation Armée Secrète* (Paris, 1963)

Buis, Georges, *La Grotte* (Paris, 1961)

Buron, Robert, *Carnets politiques de la guerre d'Algérie* (Paris, 1965)

Callot, C., and Henry, J.-R., *Le Mouvement national Algérien. Textes 1912–1954* (Paris, 1978; Algiers, 1981)

Camus, Albert, (1) *Noces* (Paris, 1938)

——, (2) *L'Étranger* (Paris, 1942); tr. *The Outsider* (London, 1946)

——, (3) *La Peste* (Paris, 1947); tr. *The Plague* (London, 1948)

——, (4) *Le Mythe de Sisyphe*; tr. *The Myth of Sisyphus* (New York, 1954)

——, (5) *Actuelles III Chroniques algériennes 1939–1958* (Paris, 1958)

——, (6) *Resistance, Rebellion and Death* (London, 1961)

Challe, Maurice, *Notre révolte* (Paris, 1968)

Cahrby, Jacques, *L'Algérie en prison* (Paris, 1961)

Chevallier, Jacques, *Nous, Algériens . . .* (Paris, 1958)

Chikh, S., *L'Algérie en Armes ou le temps des certitudes* (Paris, 1981)

Chouraqui, André N., *Between East and West – A History of the Jews of North Africa* (Philadelphia, 1968)

Clark, M. K., *Algeria in Turmoil* (New York, 1959; London, 1960)

Coulet, François, *Vertu des temps difficiles* (Paris, 1967)

Courrière, Yves, *La Guerre d'Algérie*, 4 vols:

  (i) *Les Fils de la Toussaint* (Paris, 1968)

  (ii) *Les Temps des léopards* (Paris, 1969)

  (iii) *L'Heure des colonels* (Paris, 1970)

  (iv) *Les Feux du désespoir. La fin d'un empire* (Paris, 1971)

Cros, Vitalis, *Le Temps de la violence* (Paris, 1971)

Crozier, Brian, (1) *The Rebels* (London, 1960)

——, (2) *The Morning After* (London, 1963)

——, (3) *De Gaulle*: (ii) *The Statesman* (London, 1973)

Debré, Michel, *Ces Princes qui nous gouvernent* (Paris, 1957)

Delarne, J., *L'O.A.S. contre de Gaulle* (Paris, 1981)

Déon, Michel, *L'Armée d'Algérie et la pacification* (Paris, 1959)

Drif, Zohra, *La Mort de mes frères* (Paris, 1960)

Droz, B., and Lever, E., *Histore de la guerre d'Algérie, 1954–1962* (Paris, 1982)

Duchemin, Jacques, C., *Histoire du F.L.N.* (Paris, 1962)

Elsenhans, Harmut, *Frankreichs Algierienkrieg, 1954–1962; Entkolonisierungsversuch einer Kapitalistischen Metropole um Zusammenbruch der Kolonialreiche* (Munich, 1974)

Ely, Paul, *Mémoires: (ii) Suez – Le 13 mai* (Paris, 1969)

Fabre-Luce, Alfred, *Gaulle deux* (Paris, 1958)

Fanon, Frantz, (1) *L'An Y de la révolution algérienne* (Paris, 1959)

——, (2) *Les Damnés de la Terre* (Paris, 1961); tr. *The Wretched of the Earth* (London, 1965)

Fauvet, Jacques, and Planchais, Jean, *La Fronde des généraux* (Paris, 1961)

Favrod, Charles-Henri, *Le F.L.N. et l'Algérie* (Paris, 1962)

Feraoun, Mouloud, (1) *La Terre et le Sang* (Paris, 1953)

——, (2) *Journal, 1955–1962* (Paris, 1962)

——, (3) *Textes sur l'Algérie* (Paris, 1962)

Ferniot, Jean, *Les Ides de mai* (Paris, 1958)

Ferrandi, Jean, *600 jours avec Salan et l'O.A.S.* (Paris, 1969)

Flanner, Janet, *Paris Journal, 1944–1965* (New York, 1965; London 1966)

Flaubert, Gustave, *Salammbô* (Paris, 1863)

Fouchet, Christian, *Mémoires d'hier et de demain*: (i) *Au service du général de Gaulle* (Paris, 1971)

Gale, John, *Clean Young Englishman* (London, 1965)

Gaulle, Charles de, (1) *Mémoires d'espoir: (i) Le Renouveau, 1958–1962* (Paris, 1970)

——, (2) *Discours et messages (avec Le Renouveau* (Paris, 1970)

Gide, André, *Journal* (Rio de Janeiro and Paris, 1943–1949]l tr. (New York, 1947–9)

Godard, Yves, *Les Paras dans la ville* (Paris, 1972)

Gordon, David C., (1) *North Africa's French Legacy, 1954–1962* (Cambridge, Mass., 1962)

——, (2) *The Passing of French Algeria* (London, 1966)

——, (3) *Women of Algeria, an Essay on Change* (Cambridge, Mass., 1968)

Greer, Herb, *A Scattering of Dust* (London, 1962)

Hamon, H., and Rotman, P., *Les Porteurs de Valises* (Paris, 1979)

Hammoutene, A., *Réflexions sur la guerre d'Algérie* (Paris and Algiers, 1982)

Heilbrunn, Otto, *Warfare in the Enemy's Rear* (London, 1963)

Henissart, Paul, *Les Combattants du crépuscule*; tr. *Wolves in the City: The Death of French Algeria* (London, 1971)

Holt, P. M., et al. (eds.), *Cambridge History of Islam*, ii (Cambridge, 1970)

Hutchinson, M. C., *Revolutionary Terrorism; The FLN in Algeria 1954–1962* Stanford, 1978)

Jeanson, Colette and Francis, *L'Algérie hors la Loi* (Paris, 1955)

Jeanson, Francis, (1) *Notre guerre* (Paris, 1960)

——, (2) *La Révolution algérienne. Problèmes et perspectives* (Paris, 1962)

Jenkins, Roy, "Political Leadership in Britain and the United States", *Sunday Times Magazine*, 2 September 1973

Joesten, Joachim, *The Red Hand* (London, 1962)

Jouhaud, Edmond, *O mon pays perdu! De Bou-Sfer à Tulle* (Paris, 1969)

Julien, Charles-André, *L'Afrique du Nord en marche* (Paris, 1952)

Jureidini, P. A., *Casebook on Insurgency and Revolutionary Warfare, Algeria, 1954–1962* (Washington, 1963)

Kessel, Patrick and Pirelli, Giovanni, *Le peuple algérien et la guerre* (Paris, 1963)

Lacheraf, Mostefa, *L'Algérie: nation et société* (Paris, 1965)

Lacouture, Jean, *De Gaulle* (Paris, 1965); tr. (New York, 1966)

Laffont, Pierre, *L'Expiation* (Paris, 1968)

Lagaillarde, Pierre, *On a triché avec l'honneur* (Paris, 1961)

La Gorce, Paul-Marie de, (1) *La République et son armée* (Paris, 1963)

——, (2) *De Gaulle entre deux mondes* (Paris, 1964)

Lartéguy, Jean, (1) *Les Centurions* (Paris, 1960); tr. *The Centurions* (London, 1961)

——, (2), *Les Prétoriens* (Paris, 1961); tr. *The Praetorians* (London, 1963)

Lebjaoui, Mohamed, (1) *Verités sur la révolution algérienne* (Paris, 1970)

——, (2) *Bataille d'Alger, ou bataille d'Algérie?* (Paris, 1972)

Lentin, Albert-Paul, (1) *L'Algérie des colonels* (Paris, 1958)

——, (2) *Algérie entre deux mondes*: (i) *Le Dernier quart d'heure* (Paris, 1963)

Leulliette, Pierre, *St Michel et le Dragon* (Paris, 1961); tr. *St Michael and the Dragon* (London, 1964)

Loesch, Anne, *La Valise et le cercueil* (Paris, 1963)

Luethy, Herbert, (1) *France Against Herself* (New York, 1955)

——, (2) *The State of France* (New York, 1957)

Lyautey, Louis Hubert Gonzalve, *Paroles d'action . . . 1900–1926* (Paris, 1927)

Macmillan, Harold, [Memoirs]:

(ii) *The Blast of War, 1939–1945* (London, 1967)

(iv) *Riding the Storm, 1956–1959* (London, 1971)

(v) *Pointing the Way, 1959–1961* (London, 1972)

Mandouze, André (ed.), *La Révolution algérienne par les textes* (Paris, 1962)

Manévy, Alain, *L'Algérie à vingt ans* (Paris, 1960)

Mansell, Gerard, *Tragedy in Algeria* (London, 1961)

Mao Tse-tung, *Mao Tse-tung on Guerilla Warfare* ed. Samuel B. Griffith (New York, 1961)

Marighela, Carlos, *For the Liberation of Brazil* (Harmondsworth, 1971)

Maschino, T. M., and M'Rabet, Fadéla, *L'Algérie des illusions* (Paris, 1972)

Maspéro, François (introducer), *Droit à l'insoumission, le "dossier des 121"* (Paris, 1961)

[Maspétiol Report], *Groupe d'études des relations financières entre la métropole et l'Algérie, rapport général* (Paris, 1955)

Massu, Jacques, (1) *La Vrai Bataille d'Alger* (Paris, 1971)

——, (2), *Le Torrent et la digue* (Paris, 1972)

Matthews, Ronald, *The Death of the Fourth Republic* (London, 1954)

Merle, Robert, *Ahmed Ben Bella* (Paris, 1965)

Mitterrand, François, *Présence française et abandon* (Paris, 1957)

Monteil, Vincent, *Soldat de fortune* (Paris, 1966)

Morland, Barange, and Martinez (pseud.), *Histoire de l'Organisation de l'Armée Secrète* (Paris, 1964)

Moss, Robert, *Urban Guerillas* (London, 1972)

Motley, Mary, *Home to Numidia* (London, 1964)

Moureau, Maurice, *Des Algériens accusent . . .* (Paris, 1959)

M'Rabet, Fadéla, *La Femme Algérienne* (Paris, 1964)

Nicol, Alex, *La Bataille de l'O.A.S.* (Paris, 1963)

Nora, Pierre, *Les Français d'Algérie* (Paris, 1961)

Noureddine, Meziane, *Un Algérien raconte* (Paris, 1960)

O'Ballance, Edgar, *The Algerian Insurrection, 1954–1962* (London, 1967)

Ortiz, Joseph Fernand, *Mes combats* (Paris, 1964)

Ouzegane, Amar, *Le Meilleur combat* (Paris, 1962)

Paillet, Claude, (1) *Dossier secret de l'Algérie* (Paris, 1961)

——, (2) *Deuxième Dossier secret de l'Algérie* (Paris, 1962)

Passeron, A., *De Gaulle parle* (Paris, 1962)

Pickles, Dorothy, *Algeria and France* (London, 1963)

Plume, Christian, and Demaret, Pierre (pseud.), *Target de Gaulle* (London, 1974)

Quandt, William B., *Revolution and Political Leadership: Algeria, 1954–1968* (Cambridge, Mass., 1969)

Roy, Jules, *The War in Algeria* (New York, 1961)

Salan, Raoul, *Mémoires: Fin d'un Empire*
    (iii) *Algérie française* (Paris, 1972)
    (iv) *Algérie, de Gaulle et moi* (Paris, 1974)

Sergent, Pierre, (i) *Ma peau au bout de mes idées* (Paris, 1967)
    (ii) *La Bataille* (Paris, 1968)

Sérigny, Alain de, (1) *La Révolution du 13 mai* (Paris, 1958)

——, (2) *Échos d'Alger*: (ii) *L'Abandon, 1946–1962* (Paris, 1974)

Servan-Schreiber, Jean-Jacques, *Lieutenant en Algérie* (Paris, 1957)

Servier, Jean (1) *Dans l'Aurès sur les pas des rebelles* (Paris, 1955)

——, (2) *Adieu Djebel* (Paris, 1958)

——, (3) *Demain en Algérie* (Paris, 1959)

——, (4) *Les Portes de l'année* (Paris, 1962)

Simon, Pierre-Henri, *Contre la Torture* (Paris, 1957)

Smith, T., *The French Stake in Algeria, 1945–1962* (London, 1978)

Soustelle, Jacques, (1) *Aimée et Souffrante Algérie* (Paris, 1956)

——, (2) *L'Espérance trahi, 1958–1961* (Paris, 1962)

——, (3) *La Page n'est pas tournée* (Paris, 1965)

Sulzberger, C. L., *The Test: de Gaulle and Algeria* (London, 1962)

Susini, Jean-Jacques, *Histoire de l'O.A.S.* (i) (Paris, 1963)

Talbott, J., *The War without a Name: France in Algeria, 1954–1962* (London, 1981)

Taleb, Ahmed, *Lettres de prison* (Algiers, 1966)

Terrenoire, Louis, *De Gaulle et l'Algérie. Témoignage pour l'histoire* (Paris, 1964)

Thayer, George, *The War Business* (New York, 1969)

Thomas, Hugh, *The Suez Affair* (London, 1967)

Thorez, Maurice, *Textes choisis sur l'Algérie* (Paris, 1962)

Tillion, Germaine, (1) *L'Algérie en 1957* (Paris, 1957)

——, (2) *Les Ennemis complémentaires* (Paris, 1960)

——, (3) *L'Afrique bascule vers l'avenir* (Paris, 1961)

——, (4) *Le Harem et les cousins* (Paris, 1966)

Tournoux, Jean-Raymond, (1) *Secrets d'état* (Paris, 1960)

——, (2) *L'Histoire secrète* (Paris, 1962)

——, (3) *Jamais dit* (Paris, 1971)

Tricot, Bernard, *Les Sentiers de la paix, Algérie 1958–1962* (Paris, 1972)

Trinquier, Roger, (1) *La Guerre moderne* (Paris, 1961)

——, (2) *Guerre, subversion, révolution* (Paris, 1968)

Tripier, Philippe, *Autopsie de la guerre d'Algérie* (Paris, 1972)

Vallet, Eugène, *Un Drame algérien: la verité sur les émeutes de mai 1945* (Paris, 1948)

Vidal-Naquet, P., (1) *La Raison d'état* (Paris, 1962)

——, (2) *Torture, Cancer of Democracy* (Harmondsworth, 1963)

Viratelle, Gérard, *L'Algérie algérienne* (Paris, 1970)

Williams, Philip M., (1) *Politics in Post-War France* (London, 1954)

——, (2) *Wars, Plots and Scandals in Post-War France* (Cambridge, 1970)

Yacef, Saadi, *Souvenirs de la bataille d'Alger* (Paris, 1962)

Ysquierdo, Antoine, *Une Guerre pour rien* (Paris, 1966)

FILMS

La Battaglia di Algeri, Pontecorvo, 1965

La Guerre d'Algérie, Yves Courrière and Philippe Monnier (Reggane Films)

SELECTED BIBLIOGRAPHY OF WORKS PUBLISHED SINCE 1975

Ahmed, Hocine Ait, *Mémoires d'un Combattant: L'Esprit d'Indépendance 1942–1952* (Paris, 1983)

Albes, Wolf Dietrich, *Albert Camus und der Algerienkrieg, Die Auseinandersetzung der algerienfranzösischen Schriftsteller mit dem "Directeure de Conscience" im Algerienkrieg, 1954–62,* (Tübingen, 1990)

Aubert, Pierre, *Le Secret des Rousses* (Paris, 1985)

Benyahia, Mohammed, *La Conjuration au Pouvoir* (Paris, 1988)

Bergot, Erwan, *Le Dossier Rouge: Services Secrets contre FLN* (Paris, 1976)

Dahlab, Saad, *Mission Accompli* (Algiers, 1990)

Doré-Audibert, André, *Des Françaises dans la Guerre de Libération* (Paris, 1995)

Faivre, Maurice, *Un Village de Harkis: des Babors au Drouais* (Paris, 1994)

François and J. P. Séréni, *Un Algérien nommé Boumedienne* (Paris, 1976)

Haroun, Ali, *La 7e Wilaya: La Guerre du FLN en France 1954–1962* (Paris, 1986)

Hidouci, Ghazi, *Algérie: la Libération Inachevée* (Paris, 1995)

Jacquin, Henri, *La Guerre Secrète en Algérie* (Paris, 1977)

Kettle, Michael, *De Gaulle and Algeria 1940–1960* (London, 1993)

Khedda, Benyoucef Ben, *Les Accords d'Evian* (Algiers, 1986)

Les Origines du 1er Novembre 1954 (Algiers, 1989)

Lahouari, Addi, *L'Algérie et la Democratie* (Paris, 1994)

Maillarde, Etienne, *L'Algérie Depuis* (Paris, 1975)

Mammeri, Khalfa, *Abane Ramdane, Héros de la Guerre d'Algérie* (Paris, 1988)

Minces, Juliette, *L'Algérie de la Révolution (1963–64)* (Paris, 1988)

Minne, Danièle, and Amrane, Djamila, *Femmes Au Combat* (Algiers, 1993)

Montagnon, Pierre, *L'Affaire Si Salah* (Paris, 1987)

Murray, Simon, *Legionnaire; The Real Life Story of an Englishman in the French Foreign Legion* (London, 1978)

Stora, Benjamin, *La Gangrène et l'Oubli: la mémoire de la guerre d'Algérie* (Paris, 1992)

Talbot, John, *The War Without a Name* (London, 1980)

Teguia, Mohammed, *L'Algérie en Guerre* (Algiers, 1988)

Brett, Michael, "Anglo-Saxon attitudes: The Algerian war of Independence in Retrospect" (article in Journal of African History, vol. 34, 1995, pp. 217–235)

Reference Notes

As noted in the Preface, since 1954 a mountain of published material has appeared on the Algerian war, the vast majority in France, a discouragingly small proportion in Algeria itself. The foregoing bibliography alone contains 300 book titles; yet they represent only the author's own selection out of a far larger total. Among periodicals, since there was not one of significance in Europe, the United States, or the Third World which, during those seven and a half years, did *not* devote long columns to the Algerian war, I make no attempt to list them here, except where a specific reference has been made in the text. I may equally be accused of neglect in having meted out the same cavalier treatment (in the interests of space) to the pyramids of contemporary tracts and pamphlets. As it is, many of the published works that are listed here bear, inevitably, the marks of self-justification or of propaganda, and suffer all the limitations of contemporary chronicles. But, provided these limitations are discounted, they have their value nonetheless. France has not yet released official papers relating to the war; on the other hand, so much has already been divulged in the writings and personal reminiscences of participants that it is to be doubted whether the overall picture of the war will be greatly changed when the secrecy barrier is lifted. The same may be conjectured about the unreleased Algerian source material, though for a different set of reasons.

There exists no single-volume history of the war that is satisfactory in itself (hence the temerity of the present book, undertaken in an attempt to fill at least a corner of the void). Books so far published tend to be partial, either in their sympathies or because dealing with only a portion of the overall picture. Of those authors to whom I have referred generally almost throughout, the following should be mentioned. The best-selling, four-volume work by Yves Courrière, running to over 1000 pages, provides the most detailed day-by-day account of the war itself. The primary source material used by Courrière – particularly in his interviews with such F.L.N. leaders as the late Belkacem Krim – is irreplaceable. On the other hand, he is sharply criticised in contemporary Algeria for relying excessively on the version of events given by Krim and other latterday opponents of the Boumedienne regime, and has been accused by *pieds noirs* of undue hardness to their cause. His books are also, by definition, journalism (but good journalism) with its limitation of occasionally falling short on historical perspective, and they deliberately make no effort to relate the coeval march of events in metropolitan France. One of the most objective, and sensible, concise general accounts remains that of Edward Behr, an Anglo-American journalist frequently on the Algerian scene, even though it was published before the war ended, and is therefore incomplete. Another foreign journalist's book similarly incomplete is Michael Clark's, terminating shortly after the advent of de Gaulle. More than most, Clark generally supports the *pied noir* case; nonethless, his book contains much useful documentation. More up-to-date, but equally critical of the "policy of abandon" and also well documented, is Philippe Tripier. A valuable and trustworthy neutral witness close to the F.L.N. leadership is the Swiss journalist, Charles-Henri Favrod. Also good on the F.L.N. cadres are Gordon and Quandt. Although I have derived much material from individual Algerian works relating to specific aspects, there remains, alas, no source on the war as a whole by an Algerian writer.

In the interests of space such "general" books as the above are only mentioned below specifically where I am particularly indebted. For the same reasons, I have not mentioned each time the mass of periodicals consulted throughout. I must, however, single out the *Historia* series (published by Tallandier from 1971 onwards, and totalling over three thousand pages) entitled *La Guerre d'Algérie*. I have found this series, and its illustrations, useful for background consultation throughout (though, occasionally, it tends to be imprecise on dates and similar points of detail), and also for the signed articles by (chiefly French) participants. I have also consulted the official F.L.N. periodical, *El Moudjahid* (abbreviated where specifically mentioned below as *EM*), throughout; though with obvious caution on account of its overt propaganda content.

As much of the material used comes either from information supplied by participants (notably Algerian) who requested to remain strictly anonymous, as well as from other secret or sensitive sources privately communicated, I have been compelled to designate these references simply as "AH notes", which also embraces my own personal diaries and notes.

Where information, or comment, derives from personal interviews I have set down the name of the principal in small capitals. Works to be found in the bibliography bear the author's name only; where there are more than one by the same author, the appropriate number (e.g. Camus (2)) is given; a particular volume in the same work (e.g. Courrière iv) is designated in roman figures.

1. *"A Town of no Great Interest"*

Sétif: Macmillan(ii), Robert Aron, Julien, BOURGUIBA, TEITGEN, SÉRIGNY, Tillion(2), *The conquest and early French administration*: Quandt, Robert Aron, Abun-Nasr, Ageron(1), (2), Abbas, Holt, Gordon(3), Nora, Pickles, Mitterrand, Julien. *Attempts at reform*: Servier(1), Julien, Robert Aron, Pickles, Gordon(3), Camus(5), Tillion(2), Motley. *The Growth of nationalism to end of the Second World War* : Quandt, Julien, Gordon(3), HALIQ, BEN KHEDDA, BOURGUIBA, TILLION, Favrod, Robert Aron, Abbas, AH notes, Camus(5), Macmillan(ii), Crozier(3), Bacri, *L'Entente*, 23 Feb 1936, for Abbas statement.

2. *"Ici, c'est la France"*
The country: Camus in general, especially on description of *pied noir* life and character, Beauvoir, Gide, AH notes, Roy. *The people: Muslims*: Quandt, Gordon(3), Roy, Fanon(2), Julien, AH notes. *The pieds noirs*: Robert Aron, Lartéguy(1), (2), Camus(1), (2), (4), (5), Lentin(2), Nora, Bacri, Roy, Tillion(2). *The Jews*: ANKAOUA, Chouraqui, Clark, Nora, Fanon(1), Julien, Favrod.

3. *In the Middle of the Ford*
French *"gifts" to Algeria*: Robert Aron, Tillion(3), Quandt, Camus(5). *Land hunger and population explosion*: Favrod, Robert Aron, Gordon(2), Behr, Tillion(3), Nora, Camus(5), Raymond Aron(1), (2). *France distracted*: Matthews, Williams(1), de Gaulle(1), Flanner, Behr, Mitterrand, AH notes. *Electoral swindles in Algeria*: Robert Aron, Julien, Soustelle(1), Behr, Nora, Mitterrand, Tillion(2), Pickles, Clark, Favrod. *Nationalism after Sétif*: Quandt, Robert Aron, Merle, Gordon(2), Favrod, Julien, S. Bromberger, BOURGUIBA. *The neuf historiques*: Courrière(i), Favrod, Gordon(2), Soustelle(1), S. Bromberger, Behr, AH notes.

4. *All Saints' Day, 1954*
The C.R.U.A. finalises its plans: EM, Courrière(i), S. Bromberger, Soustelle(1), Flanner. *The first day of war*: S. Bromberger, Merle, Clark, Servier(1), Courrière(i), Tripier, EM. *The first French reactions*: Tournoux(1), TILLION, MITTERRAND, AH notes, Flanner. *French military riposte; the first winter*: Leulliette, SErvier(1), (2), Lartéguy(1), TILLION, S. Bromberger.

5. *The Sorcerer's Cauldron*
Soustelle: AH notes, Soustelle(1), SOUSTELLE, MENDÉS-FRANCE, TILLION, de Gaulle(1), Greer, Williams, Tillion(2), (3), Maspétiol Report. *Collective responsibility*: Soustelle(1), Tripier, Servan-Schreiber, Simon, Nora, Lentin(2), Lartéguy(1), Vidal-Naquet(2). *The Philippeville massacres and conversion of Soustelle*: Marighela, Clark, Soustelle(1), Courrière(ii), Massu(1), Tripier, Leulliette, MITTERRAND. *Camus and civil truce*: AH notes, Camus(4), (5), (6), Raymond Aron, Beauvoir, Fanon(1), Nora, Soustelle(1), Flanner.

6. *The F.L.N.: From Bandung to Soummam*
F.L.N. policy and leadership: CHANDERLI, BOURGUIBA, MOLLET, AH notes, Merle, Mitterrand, Quandt. *Abane*: Quandt, Lebjaoui(1), BOURGUIBA, S. Bromberger, Greer. *The F.L.N. consolidates: first rifts*: Servier(1), Soustelle(1), Greer, Fanon(1), (2), Tripier, Favrod, S. Bromberger, Gordon(2), Tillion(2), (3), CHAULET. *Soummam*: Quandt, Gordon(2), Tripier, AH notes, Tillion(2), Merle.

7. *The Second Fronts of Guy Mollet*
Mollet sends conscripts: Tournoux(1), Servan-Schreiber, Clark, Fanon(1), MOLLET, BEAUFRE, Lebjaoui(2). *Lacoste and reforms*: Gale, Tournoux(1), Flanner, Seriver(2), LACOSTE, MOLLET, Salan(iii), Tripier. *Suez and the Ben Bella hijacking*: Thomas, LACOSTE, MOLLET, MENDÈS-FRANCE, Macmillan(iv), Jenkins, AH notes, Merle, Tournoux(1), Tricot, Leulliette, Massu(1), Lartéguy(1).

8. *"Why We Must Win"*
France's "New Revolutionary Army": Trinquier(1), (2), *Die Zeit*, March 1975, Tournoux(1), Servier(1), Beaufre, BEAUFRE, MASSU, COULET. *Pacification*: Manévy, Greer, Leulliette, TEITGEN, COULET, Gale, Servan-Schreiber. *Motivations for winning*: Raymond Aron(1), Mitterrand, de Gaulle(1), Bollardière, Coulet, Servan-Schreiber, Lartéguy(1), *Salan and the "bazooka" conspiracy*: SALAN, TEITGEN, DEBRÉ, Salan(iii), AH notes, Fauvet, Henissart, Tournoux(1), M. and S. Bromberger, Massu(1).

9. The Battle of Algiers
Preliminaries – first bombs: Tripier, AH notes, Pontecorvo film (and throughout Battle of Algiers), Drif, Courrière(ii), Lebjaoui(2), Massu(1), Tillion(1), Fanon(2), S. Bromberger. *Massu called in*: Massu(1), (2), MASSU, Godard, S. Bromberger. *Torture, and protest against it*: out of an immense literature consulted, principal sources as follows: Reggane film, Godard, Vidal-Naquet(2), MITTERRAND, TEITGEN, MASSU, TILLION, LACOSTE, JOXE, AH notes, Servan-Schreiber, Massu(1), Trinquier(1), (2), Salan(iii), Lebjaoui(2), Leulliette, Alleg, Bollardière, Camus(2), Simon, Fanon(2), Behr.

10. Lost Round for the F.L.N.
Yacef's second offensive: Yacef, S. Bromberger, Salan(iii), Gale, Massu(1), Tillion(2), (3), TILLION. *Hunting down of Yacef and Ali la Pointe*: Salan(iii), Massu(1), MASSU, Tripier, AH notes. *Black moments for the F.L.N.*: Tripier, Gordon(2), Fanon(1), Tillion(3), S. Bromberger. *Liquidation of Abane*: EM, Lebjaoui(1), (2), LEBJAOUI, Courrière(iii), COURRIÈRE, Historia, Behr, S. Bromberger, AH notes, BOURGUIBA, Tripier, Favrod.

11. The World Takes Notice
France discovers the war and the growth of anti-war feeling: on the mood and atmosphere in France, here and elsewhere, generally: Flanner, Beauvoir, Pickles; specifically here: TEITGEN, Vidal-Naquet(2), Simon, Historia, Camus(5), (6), Nora. *The F.L.N. and the Jeanson network*: Beauvoir, Lebjaoui(1), LEBJAOUI, F. Jeanson(1), (2), Taleb. *The fall of Mollet and French government stresses*: Pickles, Soustelle(1), Macmillan(iv) de Gaulle(1), AH notes, Raymond Aron(2). *Strained relations with the Anglo-Saxons*: Tripier, Brace(2), AH notes, Greer, *EM*; CHANDERLI. *Sakiet*: BOURGUIBA, Historia, Clark, Tripier, S. Bromberger.

12. Le Dernier Quart d'Heure
The harkis: Quandt, Servier(2), Boualem, Bollardière, Servan-Schreiber. *French "special operations"*: here and generally Courrière is well informed, AH notes, Historia, Servan-Schreiber. *Secret war outside Algeria*: Der Spiegel files, AH notes, S. Bromberger, Thayer, Joesten, Courrière(iii). *France and the Morice Line*: Sakiet: Historia, Manévy, Behr, Greer, S. Bromberger, Tripier, LACOSTE, Pickles, EM, Clark.

13. A Kind of Resurrection
The "thirteen conspiracies" and the coming of de Gaulle: M. and S. Bromberger remains one of the best blow-by-blow accounts of the events of May 1958; otherwise, Fauvet, Debré, Tournoux(1), Lagaillarde, Sérigny(1), (2), de Gaulle(1), Flanner, Crozier(ii), Behr, LACOSTE, GARDES, Historia, Salan(iii), Clark, Sergent(i), O'Ballance, Challe, Tripier, Macmillan(iv).

14. "Je Vous Ai Compris"
De Gaulle's first visit to Algeria: here and henceforth, de Gaulle(i), is obviously referred to throughout for his account of events; otherwise, Tripier, Favrod, Tournoux(1), Raymond Aron(2), Macmillan(iv), MACMILLAN, Reggane film, Sergent(i), Lartéguy(2), M. and S. Bromberger, Pickles. *The slow quest for a policy*: Tripier, Favrod, Tricot, Raymond Aron(2), F. Jeanson(2), Behr, Fabre-Luce. *De Gaulle purges the army and Salan*: Fauvet, O'Ballance, Behr, Historia, Tournoux(1). *Preoccupation in France*: Macmillan(iv), Flanner, Historia, Tripier, Raymond Aron(2).

15. The F.L.N. Holds its Breath
The impact of de Gaulle on the F.L.N.; the G.P.R.A. is formed: AH notes, Boualem; BRAHIMI, Tripier, EM, Courrière(iii), Quandt, Belloula. *The G.P.R.A. rebuffs de Gaulle*: Clark, Tripier, Historia, Favrod, Gordon(2), AH notes. *The A.L.N. under extreme pressure, Boumedienne*: AH notes, Tripier, O'Ballance, Feraoun(2), Historia, Courrière(iii), EM, New York Times Magazine, 13 Feb 1966, Quandt, BOURGUIBA, HALIQ, Gordon(2).

REFERENCE NOTES

16. Neither the Djebel nor the Night
The Challe plan: Roy, Challe, CHALLE, Fauvet, Boualem, O'Ballance, AH notes, Vidal-Naquet(2). *Political and economic initiatives; self-detemination*: Tricot, Challe, Tripier, Behr, Lentin, Sergent(i), SOUSTELLE, Roy.

17. "Aux Barricades!"
The "ultras" in revolt against de Gaulle: Henissart, *Historia*, PÉREZ, COURRIÈRE, BEAUFRE, GARDES, Courrière(iii), O'Ballance, Sérigny(2), M. and S. Bromberger *et al.* Paillat(i), Fauvet, Liddell-Hart archives. *The "bombe Massu"*: Paillat(1), M. and S. Bromberger *et al.*, Sérigny (2), Challe, Behr, Lagaillarde. *Barricades Week*: some of the best contemporary reports appeared in the *Daily Telegraph*, under the name of John Wallis, the Paris Correspondent who happened to be in Algiers; otherwise, M. and S. Bromberger *et al.*, Behr, Paillat(1), Sergent(i), *Historia*, Challe, Sérigny(2), Ortiz.

18. "This Prince of Ambiguity"
The morning after: O'Ballance, SÉRIGNY, MOLLET, Sergent(i), *Historia*, Behr, Macmillan(v), Challe. *Prince of ambiguity*: JOXE, TRICOT, MACMILLAN, TILLION, MENDÈS-FRANCE, MASSU, BEAUFRE, FOUCHET, Tournoux(1), Tripier, AH notes, Bidault, Pickles, Crozier(ii), Fauvet, Tricot. *The road to negotiations*: Courrière(iv), Passeron, Macmillan(v), SÉRIGNY, PINAY, BRAHIMI, *EM, World Today* (March 1960). *Si Salah and Melun*: Tricot, CHANDERLI, TRICOT, AH notes, *Historia*, Courrière(iv), Tripier, Ahmet, Pickles, Flanner.

19. Revolution in the Revolution
Conditions in the A.L.N.: Brace(2), Fanon(1), Gordon(3). *Algerian women at war*: Feraoun(3), Fanon(1), (2), Gordon(3), Tillion(4), Amrouche. *Ideology of the F.L.N.*: Gordon(2), Beauvoir, F. Jeanson(2), Brace(2), Fanon(1), (2), *EM*, Lacheraf, Behr, Favrod, AH notes, Quandt, Ouzegane, Tillion(2), (3), Taleb, Charby. *Jewish dilemmas*: Clark, F.L.N. bulletins, *EM, Historia*, Chouraqui, F. Jeanson(2). *Boumedienne consolidates*: Tripier, Quandt, *EM*, AH notes, O'Ballance.

20. De Gaulle Caught in the Draught
Anti-war sentiments in France: Flanner, Lentin(2), Vidal-Naquet(2), Pickles, Beauvoir, Bidault, Soustelle(2), Gordon(3), *Historia*, F. Jeanson(2). *Salan returns to Algiers*: Courriére(iv), SALAN, Salan(iv), Bidault, Paillat(i), Jouhaud, Ferrandi. *Delouvrier replaced*: de Gaulle(1), F. Jeanson(2), *Historia*, Tricot, Paillat(1). *December 1960 riots*: Behr, AH notes, *Daily Express* 10 Dec 1960, *Historia*, Courrière(iv), Lentin, Fauvet, Plume, Terrenoire, Jouhaud, Henissart, Passeron, Tricot, Tripier, Chouraqui, Flanner.

21. The Generals' Putsch
Rebels search for a leader; Challe: Fauvet, Pickles, GARDES, SERGENT, MASSU, CHALLE, SALAN, Henissart, Sergent(i), Lentin(2), Jouhaud, Massu(1), (2), Ferrandi, Challe. *The putsch and the C.I.A.*: AH notes, GAVIN, C.I.A. hearings, Brace(2), Fauvet, O'Ballance, Plume, SALAN, CHALLE. *The course of the putsch*: principally Fauvet, otherwise Challe, Sergent(ii), SERGENT, CHALLE, AH notes, Jouhaud, Ferrandi, Henissart, Buron, O'Ballance, Courrière(iv), M. and S. Bromberger *et al. The collapse of the putsch*: Fauvet, Jouhaud, Ferrandi, Challe, JOXE, TRICOT, CHALLE, GARDES, SALAN, PÉREZ, COULET, Behr, Pickles, Flanner, La Gorce(1), Henissart, Lentin(2), Reggane film.

22. Overtures for Peace
Strong negotiating hand of the F.L.N.: Fauvet, Challe, Tricot, Sergent(i), Tripier, Behr. *Evian, round one*: AH notes, Tripier, Behr, Tricot, Ait Ahmed, Bedjaoui. *The Sahara, and breakdown*: Pickles, Tricot, Behr, Quandt, Buron, Macmillan(v), Crozier(ii), SOUSTELLE, FOUCHET. *Bizerta*: BOURGUIBA, AH notes, Tripier. *Abbas replaced by Ben Khedda*: Quandt, Favrod, BEN KHEDDA, Tripier, AH notes, *EM*, Courrière(iv), F.L.N. material, Pickles.

23. *The Suitcase or the Coffin*

The O.A.S. takes over: Sergent(i), (ii), Courrière(iv), Ferrandi, Henissart, SALAN, PÉREZ, GARDES, Jouhaud, Susini, Buchard, Morland. *Degueldre's "Deltas"*: Courrière(iv), Sergent(ii), SERGENT, PÉREZ, GARDES, SALAN, Henissart, Lentin(2), Jouhaud. *The Barbouzes*: Historia, Henissart, Susini, Cros, Courrière(iv), Buron, PÉREZ. *Muslim riposte*: Sunday Times, 7 and 14 Jan 1962, Reggane film, F.L.N. material, ANKOUA, PÉREZ, Pickles. *The O.A.S. and the C.I.A.*: SALAN, GAVIN, C.I.A. hearings, AH notes, Plume. *The O.A.S. in France*: Soustelle(2), SOUSTELLE, SALAN, BIDAULT, SERGENT, Bidault, Henissart, Sergent(ii), Vidal-Naquet(2), *Historia*, Flanner, Beauvoir.

24. *Exodus*

Peace preliminaries: MACMILLAN, BEN KHEDDA, SOUSTELLE, Macmillan(v), Pickles, Tricot, Feraoun(3), Passeron, AH notes. *"Yeti" meetings*: Buron, JOXE, LEBJAOUI, DEBRÉ, Tricot, Historia, F. Jeanson(2), F.L.N. material, Tripier. *Salan declares total war*: Henissart, Feraoun(3), Ferrandi, F. Jeanson(2), Camus(5), Courrière(iv), Susini. *Second Evian*: Buron, JOXE, BEDJAOUI, TRICOT, DEBRÉ, LACOSTE, SALAN, Tricot, Pickles, Tripier, Allais, AH notes. *Cease-fire, but no peace*: Reggane film, PÉREZ, ANKOUA, Courrière(iv), Pickles, Henissart, Tillion(2), Tricot, Sulzberger, Jouhaud. *Scorched earth and exodus*: Henissart, Fouchet, PÉREZ, FOUCHET, GARDES, ANKAOUA, JOXE, Tricot, *Historia*, Loesch, Susini, Reggane film, Gordon(2), AH notes, Chouraqui.

25. *The Page is Turned*

The dangers of liberty: Quandt, Gordon(2), Pickles, Boualem, AH notes. *Casualties*: Historia, AH notes, Tripier, O'Ballance. *Ben Bella takes over*: Brace(2), Pickles, Ageron(2), Merle, Gordon(2), F. Jeanson(2), Fanon(2), Quandt, Lebjaoui(1). *France – settling of accounts*: Jouhaud, Henissart, Flanner, Sergent(ii), Bidault, Liddell-Hart archives, Pickles, de Gaulle(i), Crozier(ii), AH notes. *Ten years on*: Historia, New Yorker, Nov 1972, BEHR, TRICOT, FOUCHET, ANKAOUA, Chouraqui, Pickles, Gordon(2). *The dramatis personae*: Simon, various interviews, Historia, Sergent(ii), Paris-Match files, The Times files, AH notes, Henissart, Quandt. *Algeria today*: AH notes, Gordon(3), Viratelle, Maschino, BRAHIMI, Gordon(2). *The Times* and *Guardian* files, I.M.F. material, Observer files, Historia. Camus(3), (4).

Glossary

ancien combattant: veteran, ex-serviceman
bachaga: ("pasha") title given to an Arab governor
baraka: special grace or good fortune accorded from on high
barbouze: ("false beard"), underground government agent
Beni-Oui-Oui: abusive name for Arab *caid* collaborating with the French
bicot: abusive name for Arab
bidonville: shanty town
bled: French army name for the outback
bleu: double agent
bleuite: infection from double agent
bordj: fort
cachabia: heavy winter cloak
cadi: Arab judge
caid: Arab local governor
Chergui: a hot wind from the Sahara
colon: European settler
comité de gestion: management committee
commune mixte: commune in Muslin area, governed by European adminis-
    trator through Muslim *caids*
commune de plein exercise: commune on the French model with a Euro-
    pean mayor and elected municipal council (three-fifths European)
djebel: mountain
djemaa: Berber council of elders
djoundi (pl. *djounoud*): F.L.N. soldier
douar: hill village
évolué: educated Algerian (under French rule)
failek: F.L.N. battalion
faoudj: F.L.N. section (of soldiers)
fatma: domestic servant
fellagha: Arab guerrilla
fellah: Arab peasant
fidayine: F.L.N. guerrillas
figuier: ("fig-tree") abusive name for an Arab
garde-champètre: village constable
gégène: magneto used for torture
Hadj: title given to Muslims who have made the pilgrimage to Mecca
haik: veil covering woman's face
harki: Algerian soldier fighting for France

interlocuteurs valables: acceptable representatives (of the Algerian people as a whole)

jihad: holy war

katiba: F.L.N. company

képis bleus: ("blue caps") members of the S.A.S.

Maghreb: ("land of the setting sun") Tunisia, Algeria and Morocco

marabout: holy man, leader of a mystic order

mechta: neighbourhood of a village

melon: ("simpleton") abusive name for an Arab

mintaka: F.L.N. region within a Wilaya

moudjahid (pl. *moudjahiddine*): F.L.N. soldier

moussebiline: F.L.N. guerrillas

opération ponctuelle: O.A.S. execution

oued: dry river bed

pied noir: ("black foot") European settler in Algeria

ratissage: ("raking over") repressive "pacification" operation

ratonnade: ("rat-hunt") Arab-killing

"ultras": diehard *pied noir* conservatives, resisting all change

Wilaya: one of the six F.L.N. commands in Algeria

Index

The main biographical entry is put first and printed in bold figures. Bodies (such as the F.L.N. and O.A.S.) are indexed under their initials, not under their full titles, which are alphabetised as if they were single words.

INDEX

Grosser, Alfred, 239
Group of Seven, The, 277–8, 281, 283–4, 289, 349
Grout de Beaufort, Guy, 358
Guardian, The, 182
Guelma, 26, 71, 327
Guentis, 112, 117
Guenzet, 136
Guiana, French, 375
Guillaumat, Pierre, 358, 366
Guinée, 304–5, 345

Hacq, Michel, 493–5, 526–7
Hadj Ali, Bachir, 138
Halim, 388–9, 392
Hamoud, Nefissa, 399
Haouès, Si, 322–4, 326, 334
Hassan II, King of Morocco, 509, 541, 561
Hassi-Messaoud, 241, 341
Hassi-R'Mel, 341
Hejaz, 89
Henissart, Paul, 485, 517
Hentic, Captain, 256–7
Historia, 17, 228n
Hitler, Adolf, 115, 131, 185, 449n, 532
Ho Chi Minh, 78, 99, 131, 409
Hocine, Baya, 193
Hodna Mountains, 324, 335, 342
Holroyd, Michael, 19
Houphouët-Boigny, Félix, 277
Hourani, Albert, 16
Humanité, l', 27, 98, 297, 504
Hungary (1956 revolt in), 161, 163, 351, 363, 368, 430, 483, 524
Husaini, Hajj Amin, 131
Hussein, Dey of Algiers, 28–9

Ibn Khaldoun, 460
Ibn Saud, King of Saudi Arabia, 38
Ibrahim, Taleb, 561
Ichmoul, 89, 91, 102
Igbal, 143
Ighil-Ilef, 117
illiteracy, *see* literacy
India, 34, 275, 545
Indo-China: French war in, 66–9, 96, 164–5, 169, 175–9, 188–9, 222, 256, 259, 274, 354, 407, 409, 424, 437–8, 511; veterans from, 102–3, 113, 124, 138, 166–168, 419
industrial growth, 559
infant mortality, 63
inflation, 66
In-Salah, 455, 457, 459, 461
"integration", 108, 116–17, 123, 307, 345
interlocuteurs valables, 37, 99, 116, 135–6, 206, 239, 313, 321, 346, 397, 466, 486, 498, 518, 547, 583
I.R.A. (Irish Republican Army), 192n, 236, 318, 341, 410, 503
Islam, 35–8, 69, 116, 559; *see also* Muslims
Israel, 69, 157–8, 161–3, 246, 267, 445, 485, 533, 548, 559–60
Israeli Intelligence Service, 428
Italy, 32, 51, 58, 446, 532

Ivory Coast, 277
Izvestia, 446n

Jacomet, André, 423
Jacquin, General, 389–93, 538
Jean Bart (battleship), 318
Jeanpierre, Pierre, 167, 217, 264, 314
Jeanson, Francis, 237–8, 261, 307, 416–17, 419, 519
Jenkins, Roy, 163, 245
Jerusalem, 131
Jews, 35, 56, 58–9, 140, 145, 173, 410–11, 432, 532–3
Jordan, 129, 247, 327
Joubert, René, 491–2
Jouhaud, Edmond: **419–20**, 282; quoted, 53; retires to Algiers, 418; and revolt against de Gaulle, 426–7, 429–33; and putsch, 441–5, 448, 450–1, 459; sentenced, 462, 503n, 542–3; and O.A.S., 481, 484, 489, 530; captured, 526–7; trial of, 541
Journal d'Alger, 57
Joxe, Louis, 16, 206, 281, 377, 423, 447, 453–4, 467–8, 470–3, 487, 510–12, 514–15, 519–20
Juin, Alphonse, 74, 175, 322, 353, 366, 417, 423
Julien, Charles-André, 72

Kabyles/Kabylia: land ownership in, 31, 62; Arab judicial system imposed on, 35; described, 48–50; infant mortality, 63; Krim and, 77–8, 100, 103–4, 208; reinforces Mitidja, 93; on All Saints' Day, 94; "Kabyle smile", 112; tortured, 117; and Wilaya 3, 119, 131, 225, 322; "terrible silence" in, 134; internecine struggle in, 136; and Soummam Conference, 144; *djemaa* in, 165; Mélouza massacre, 221–2; conflict with Arabs, 256, 537; *bleus* in, 260; as loyal "redoubt", 289; and purges, 323; and Challe, 335–6 de Gaulle visits, 342, 431–432; Faure in, 360; and Si Salah, 390, 392; treatment of women in, 402; army propaganda in, 403n; General Simon and, 448, 451; condition today, 562
Kairouan (steamship), 419
Katz, General, 526–7
Kemal, Mustafa, 61
Kempski, Hans Ulrich, 357
Kennedy, John F., 151, 245, 247, 417, 446, 473, 498
Kerrata, 26
KGB, 554
Khaled, Leila, 556
Khemisti, Mohamed, 541
Khenchela, 89–91, 101
Khider, Mohamed, **76**, 75, 85, 130, 157, 319, 404, 466, 468–70, 509, 536, 540–1, 546, 556, 561
Khodja, Ali, 152–3, 252
Khrushchev, Nikita, 161, 316, 374–5, 383, 405, 464, 473

INDEX

frees, 341; and "self-determination", 347; hard-liners and, 408; influence in Paris, 459; later career, 555

Messmer, Pierre, 419, 449

Metz, 318, 358, 365, 438

Mexico, 169

Meyer, Albert, 167

M'hamed, Si, 251–2, 257, 323–5, 388n

Michelet, Edmond, 140, 281

Mihailovič, 135

Miliana, 137

Minne, Danièle, 192

Minvielle, Gérard, 17

Miguel, General, 294

Mitidja, 32, 45–6, 93, 191, 251, 277, 284, 360, 403, 474, 480, 561

Mitterrand, François, 17, 68–9, 86, 98–100, 106, 108–9, 113–14, 123, 126, 175, 181, 196, 233, 297, 441, 542, 545

M.N.A. (Mouvement Nationaliste Algérien), 128, 133, 135–6, 138, 221–2, 236, 257–8, 318, 404, 406, 409, 467, 527, 537, 548, 555

Moch, Jules, 292, 295–6

Mohamed, Hani, 259–60

Mohamed, Si, 388, 391–3

Mohammed V, King of Morocco, 159–61, 228, 248–9

Mollet, Guy: thanked, 16; supports Mendès-France, 99; becomes premier, 126; Communist support for, 137; visits Algiers, 147–52, 277; appoints Lacoste, 151; recalls reservists, 151, 170, 231, 268; Lorillot and, 152; and Socialists, 154; Alberian policies, 155; promises elections, 156; and negotiations with F.L.N., 157, 159, 161; and hijacking of Ben Bella, 159–61, 469; and Suez, 161–4; and Faure conspiracy, 181; and Tillion, 213; government falls, 214, 238–41; army view of, 219; Meany and, 244; Biaggi and, 275; fails for form government, 283; as Pflimlin's deputy, 290; backs de Gaulle, 292, 297, 341; as intermediary, 295; Lagaillarde and, 209; as de Gaulle's deputy, 300; Challe and, 311, 442; Salan and, 489; and *Algérie français*, 545; later career, 554

Monde, Le, 72, 98, 123, 148, 165, 233–4, 291, 297, 306, 333, 346, 500n, 505, 536, 549

Monnerot, Guy, 88, 91–2, 103

Monnerot, Madame, 91–2

Monnerville, Gaston, 298

Monnet Plan, 67

Monteil, Vincent, 110–1, 109, 115, 117–118, 142n

Montgomery, Bernard, 553

Montreux, 319

Moore, Barbara, 365

Morice, André, 230, 240, 498

Morice, Line, 230, 249, 261, 263–7, 314, 321, 323, 326, 328, 334, 342, 347, 399–400, 408, 412–13, 426, 537

Morin, Jean, 423–6, 428–9, 431, 433, 447–450, 452–3, 455, 486–7, 490, 492–4, 529

Moris, Roger, 394

Morocco: and independence, 67–8, 99, 106, 148, 176, 378, 529, 535; weapons promised from, 94; Monteil and, 110; aid to F.L.N., 130; unites serving with French, 152; Ben Bella and, 158–9; refugees in, 221, 325; Boumedienne's control in, 225; Abane in, 228; importance to F.L.N., 248; A.L.N. in, 412; G.P.R.A. conference in, 509

Moscow, 317, 328, 394, 404–5, 446n, 463

Mostaganem, 302, 320

Mostefai, Dr Chouki, 511, 531

Motley, Mary, 36

Moudjahid, El, 133, 139n, 227, 270, 317, 326n, 407, 477

Moulins du Chélif, 56

M.P.C. (Mouvement pour la Communauté), 434–5, 447, 492, 494

M'Rabet, Fadela, 559

M.R.P. (Mouvement Républicain Populaire), 66, 511, 515

M.T.L.D. (Mouvement pour le Triomphe des Libertés Démocratiques), 39, 70–7, 97, 111, 128, 130–1, 316, 477; *see also* M.N.A.

muezzins, 120

Munich, 544

Murphy, Robert, 42, 250

Muslims: French legislation regarding, 31, 33; discrimination against, 34–6, 61, 77, 116; political aspirations, 42–3, 69, 156; offered equal rights, 43; ancestry, 49; attitude to Jews, 59; education, 61, 155; land-hunger, 62–3, 155; unemployment, 63; earnings, 63; 154–5; enfranchisement of women, 69; reforms, 108, 155; and Camus, 125; F.L.N. terrorise, 134–5, 144; *ratonnades* against, 172–3, 210; army paternalism towards, 178; intellectuals and atrocities, 205; and Lauriol plan, 235; Muslim Legion, 262; fraternisation on 16 May, 290–1, 301; confidence in de Gaulle, 302; vote for de Gaulle, 304–5; and "integration", 307; and "self-determination", 347; absent from barricades, 364, 375; and transistor radios, 400; effect of war on women, 401–3; and on Muslim life, 401; moderates disappear, 421; begin to proclaim *"Algérie algérienne"*, 428–9; backlash in Algiers, 430–2, 434, 463–4, 508, 547; and second referendum, 435; and O.A.S., 472, 485–6, 513, 516; and partition, 473–4; G.P.R.A. fears for, 507; fate of loyal, 533, 537; occupy European areas, 533; casualty figures, 538

"Muslim Congress", 41

Muslim Students' Association, 40

Musmeaux, Deputy, 70

602

INDEX

Invalides, 294, 551; Kossuth, Place, 502; Lipp, Brasserie, 318; Ministères, Restaurant des, 354, 552; Orly Airport, 292, 394, 511; Orsay, Palais d', 292; Orsay, Quai d', 284, 503; Père Lachaise cemetery, 504; Prefecture of Police, 544; République, Place de la, 297; Rivoli, Rue de, 318; Saint-Lazare, Gare, 553; Saint-Martin, Canal, 409; Seine, River, 303, 409, 500; Sorbonne, 374; University, 233

Paris Journal, 231

Parlange, Gaston, 113, 115

"partition", 473, 520

P.C.A. (Parti Communiste Algérien), 26–27, 39, 43, 56, 59, 125, 128, 133, 136–8, 145, 405, 502

P.C.F. (Parti Communiste Français), 23–4, 27, 39, 66, 126, 136–7, 239, 294–5, 297–8, 304, 313, 318, 405, 416, 434, 459, 502, 547

peace negotiations: at Evian, 57, 136, 442, 466–8, 470–2, 486, 506, 510; Soummam terms for, 145; at Melun, 394–7, 466; Château de Lugrin, 473, 507; O.A.S. aim to frustrate, 485; G.P.R.A. attitude to, 508–9; at Châlet du Yéti, 510–15; second Evian, 518–20

Peintre, Claude, 440

Peking, 317, 394, 404–5, 463

Pérez, Jean-Claude, **350**, 19, 182, 351, 354, 373, 418, 450, 458, 462–5, 492, 495, 524, 527, 532, 553

Périgotville, 26

Perrin, Maurice, 487

Pétain, Philippe, 41–2, 59, 86, 353, 542

Petit-Clamart, 543

Pflimlin, Pierre, 277, 281, 283–5, 288–90, 292–3, 295–7

Philippeville, 53, 111, 171, 339, 562; massacres at, 119–23, 133, 140, 170

Piaf, Edith, 436, 460

Picasso, Pablo, 416

Pickles, Dorothy, 221, 234, 545

pieds noirs: origin of name, 30n; ancestry, 51; character of, 51–4, 279, 288; attitude to Arabs, 54–5, 64, 122, 290–1; politics and social status, 56; oblivious to F.L.N., 104; attitude to Salan, 180; reject *loi-cadre*, 240; Pétainist inclinations, 278; on 13 May, 284–8; and de Gaulle, 303, 341; and "integration", 307; reaction to "self-determination", 347; capacity for violence, 351; effect of "Barricades Week" on, 375–6; their "secondary importance", 381; riot in Algiers, 429–30; and end of putsch, 458, 460, 463; guarantees for, 466, 470–2, 479, 508, 514, 518–22, 547; O.A.S. pressure on, 484; morale rises, 487–8; exodus mooted, 506; reaction to peace agreements, 523; exodus begins, 531–3; disposition of emigrants, 533; Mme Camus on, 542; their lack of leadership, 545–6; life in exile, 549–51

Pinay, Antoine, 16, 241, 283, 384–5, 393

Pineau, Christian, 157, 162, 233, 246

Pleven, René, 66, 241, 283

Poland, 161

Polisario, 561

Pompidou, Georges, 279, 295, 319, 435, 466, 523, 542

Pons, Martial, 91

Pontecorvo, Gillo: *La Battaglia di Algeri*, 15, 167, 185n, 555

Pont-sur-Seine, 489, 500, 505

Popie, Pierre, 440, 480, 501, 517

Port-Gueydon, 72

Port Said, 163

Portugal, 175, 273, 445, 548

Pouilly, General, 444, 451–2, 454, 457

Poujade, Pierre, 107, 126, 148

P.P.A. (Parti du Peuple Algérien), 24, 39, 43, 245

Prague, 430

P.S.U. (Partie Socialiste Unifié), 505

Puchert, Georges, 263

Qatar, Emir of, 467

Quandt, William, 540

Querville, Admiral, 445, 449, 451

Queuille, Henri, 66

Quilici, François, 98

Rabat, 159, 316

racial prejudice, 54–5, 58–9, 74, 411

Racine, Jean, 453, 455

railways, 60, 67

Rains, Claude, 96n

"Ramadan War", 16, 560

Ramadier, Paul, 69

Ramdane, Abdelmalek, 94

Rassemblement de l'Algérie française, 351

Reggane, 366, 374, 459

Reggane Films, 17

Reghaia, 368, 429, 488, 528

Renard, Delphine, 503–4

reprisals, 114–15, 121–2, 124, 171–3, 183, 187, 192, 208–11, 269–70, 291, 411, 413, 430–2, 488–9, 495–7, 526, 530, 550

Réserve Générale, 332, 334–5

reservists, 151–3, 168, 170, 231, 268

Retz, Cardinal de, 128

Revolution, French, 61, 196

Reynaud, Paul, 548

Rhodesia, 53–4, 56, 148, 279, 485, 497

roads, 60, 114

Roche, Pierre, 17

Rocher-Noir, 424, 488, 494

Romain-Desfosses, Colonel, 167

Romans, 88, 91

Rome, 208, 224

Ronda, Marcel, 434

Roosevelt, Franklin Delano, 42, 151n

Rosenberg, Artur, 281, 317, 320

Rouen, 152

Roy, Jules, 50, 55, 330, 336, 338, 340, 347

Royal Navy, 47

R.P.F (Rassemblement du Peuple Français), 279

INDEX

INDEX

Vicky, 377
Vidal-Naquet, Pierre, 182, 201, 203, 233–234, 416, 500
Vie Catholique, La, 233
Viet-Minh, 67, 78, 83, 102, 166–7, 177, 179, 407
Vietnam, 67–8, 130n, 221, 244, 321, 396, 398, 405, 419, 507, 538, 546, 548, 551
Vincennes, 459, 543
Vincennes, Comité de, 417–18, 434, 498–9
Viollette, Maurice, 36–7, 41, 53, 70, 108, 299, 346
Viratelle, Gérard, 17
"Voice of the Arabs", 85
Voix de l'Algérie, 133
voting rights, 33

Warnier Act, 31
Washington, 247, 385
Wedgwood Benn, Anthony, 244
White, Sam, 17
Wilayas, 83, 222–3, 254, 264, 321–3, 325, 337, 352, 390, 392, 400, 469–70, 478, 537; Wilaya 1, 119, 141–2, 225, 322, 326; Wilaya 2, 118–19, 144, 225, 266, 323, 326, 337, 412, 426, 536: Wilaya 3, 119, 131, 222, 225, 259–60, 266, 322–3, 335–6, 387, 392, 536–7; Wilaya 4, 119, 225–6, 251–2, 257, 260, 322–5, 334, 387–94, 396n, 412–13, 443, 530, 536–7; Wilaya 5, 119, 144, 225–6, 323, 327–8, 333, 390n, 412; Wilaya 6, 223, 258, 322, 324
Wilde, Oscar, 46
wine industry, 32, 46, 51, 56, 62, 539

women: dress of Kabyle and Chaouia, 49; toughness of Algerian, 50; veiled and recluse Muslim, 50–1; and racial prejudice, 54–5; enfranchisement of Muslim, 69; in Battle of Algiers, 185–6; Tillion and Fanon on Muslim, 401; in guerrilla war, 402; in peace, 403; emancipation, 559
Wu, Robin, 17
Wuillaume Report, 197

Yacef, Saadi, **184**, 167, 183–7, 191–4, 208–9, 211–18, 222, 251, 259–60, 264, 270, 306, 314, 390, 401–2, 413, 490, 555, 563
Yacine, Kateb, 27
Yazid, M'hamed, **245**, 61, 71, 130–1, 219, 246–7, 250, 316–17, 321, 425, 464–5, 470, 496, 511
Yéti, Châlet du, 510–15, 519
Yugoslavia, 129, 175, 262, 406, 513, 559
Yugoslav partisans, 14, 135
Yveton, Fernand, 137–8, 204

Z.A.A. (Zone Autonome d'Alger), 184, 194, 260, 413, 531
Zabane, Ahmed, 153, 183, 185
Zavatta, Achille, 366
Zeller, Marie-André, 152, 426, 441, 444, 448–52, 456, 458–9, 462, 527, 552
Zéralda, 201, 371, 426–7, 448–9, 458–9, 481, 563
Zerrari, Rabah, see Azedine
Zibri, Colonel, 557
Zighout, Youssef, **118–19**, 144, 225
zones, interdites, d'opérations, de pacification, 166, 186.

OTHER NEW YORK REVIEW BOOKS CLASSICS[*]

*For a complete list of titles, visit www.nyrb.com or write to:
Catalog Requests, NYRB, 1755 Broadway, New York, NY 10009-3780

ABOUT THE AUTHOR

ALISTAIR HORNE was educated in Switzerland, at Millbrook School, New York, and at Jesus College, Cambridge, where he played international ice hockey. In World War II, initially a volunteer in the RAF, he served with the Coldstream Guards between 1944 and 1947, ending as a captain attached to MI5 in the Middle East. In the 1950s he was a foreign correspondent for the *Daily Telegraph* until taking up a full-time writing career in 1955.

Horne's trilogy of Franco-German conflict comprises *The Fall of Paris: The Siege and the Commune, 1870–71*, *The Price of Glory: Verdun 1916*, and *To Lose a Battle: France 1940*. In 1963, *The Price of Glory* was awarded the prestigious Hawthornden Prize; when first published in 1977, *A Savage War of Peace* won both the *Yorkshire Post* Book of the Year Prize and the Wolfson Literary Award. Other books include *The Lonely Leader*, a biography of Field Marshal Montgomery; *Small Earthquake in Chile*; and, most recently, *Seven Ages of Paris*, *La Belle France: A Short History*, and *The Age of Napoleon*.

In 1969 Horne founded the Alistair Horne Research Fellowship for young historians at St. Antony's College, Oxford. In 1993 he was made a Chevalier of the French Legion of Honor, and in 2003 he was knighted for his work in French history.

Alistair Horne is a specialist on Anglo-American relations, to which his autobiographic *A Bundle from Britain* belongs. He is currently working on an authorized biography of Henry Kissinger in 1973 and a second volume of memoirs.